CONTOUR IN TIME

CONTOUR IN

NEW YORK

TRAVIS BOGARD

TIME
The Plays of Eugene O'Neill

Revised Edition

OXFORD UNIVERSITY PRESS 1988

Oxford University Press

Oxford   New York   Toronto
Delhi   Bombay   Calcutta   Madras   Karachi
Petaling Jaya   Singapore   Hong Kong   Tokyo
Nairobi   Dar es Salaam   Cape Town
Melbourne   Auckland
and associated companies in
Beirut   Berlin   Ibadan   Nicosia

Library of Congress Catalogue Card Number: 74-186499

Library of Congress Cataloging-in-Publication Data
Bogard, Travis.
Contour in time.
Bibliography: p.   Includes index.
1. O'Neill, Eugene, 1888–1953—Criticism and interpretation.
I. O'Neill, Eugene, 1888–1953.   II. Title.
PS3529.N5Z568 1987   812'.52   87-34860
ISBN 0-19-505341-9 (cloth)
ISBN 0-19-504548-3 (paper)

First published in 1972 by Oxford University Press, Inc.,
200 Madison Avenue, New York, New York 10016

Revised edition published in 1988
by Oxford University Press, Inc.,
New York

First published as an Oxford University Press paperback 1988

Grateful acknowledgment is made to the following persons and publishers for permis-
sion to quote from the listed works:
From Hamilton Basso, "The Tragic Sense," *The New Yorker,* March 6, 1948: The
New Yorker.
From the correspondence of Richard Bennett and Felton Elkins: Miss Joan Bennett.
From Agnes Boulton, *Part of a Long Story,* copyright © 1958 by Agnes Boulton Kauf-
man: Doubleday and Company, Inc.

9 8 7 6 5 4 3 2 1
Printed in the United States of America
on acid-free paper

From Sheldon Cheney, *The Art Theatre*: Mr. Sheldon Cheney.

From Croswell Bowen, *The Curse of the Misbegotten*: Mrs. W. R. Elton.

From Arthur and Barbara Gelb, *O'Neill*: Harper and Row, Publishers, Inc.

From Susan Glaspell, *The Road to the Temple*, copyright © 1927, 1953 by Susan Glaspell: Curtis Brown, Ltd.

From Theresa Helburn, *A Wayward Quest*: Mrs. Eric Kocher.

From the correspondence of Sidney Howard: The Bancroft Library, University of California, Berkeley.

From Kenneth Macgowan and Robert Edmond Jones, *Continental Stagecraft*: Harcourt Brace Jovanovich, Inc.

From Kenneth Macgowan, *The Theatre of Tomorrow*: The Estate of Kenneth Macgowan.

From Eugene O'Neill

Hughie, copyright © 1959 by Carlotta Monterey O'Neill; *Long Day's Journey into Night*, copyright © 1955 by Carlotta Monterey O'Neill; *More Stately Mansions*, copyright © 1964 by Carlotta Monterey O'Neill; *A Touch of the Poet*, copyright © 1957 by Carlotta Monterey O'Neill: Yale University Press; *A Moon for the Misbegotten* and *The Plays of Eugene O'Neill*: Random House, Inc.; unpublished plays and non-dramatic writings, published and unpublished: The Estate of Eugene O'Neill.

From Otto Rank, *The Double*: University of North Carolina Press.

From Louis Sheaffer, *O'Neill, Son and Playwright* and *O'Neill, Son and Artist*; copyright © 1968, 1973 by Little, Brown and Company.

From Edward Sheldon, *The High Road*: Mrs. Theodore Sheldon.

From Lee Simonson, *The Stage Is Set*; copyright © 1963 by Theatre Art Books: Theatre Art Books.

From "Professor G. P. Baker," *The New York Times*, January 13, 1935, copyright 1935 by The New York Times Company; Alexander Woollcott, *The New York Times*, February 4, 1920, copyright 1920 by The New York Times Company; Louis Kalonyme, "O'Neill Lifts Curtain on His Earlier Days," *The New York Times*, December 21, 1924, copyright 1924 by The New York Times Company; "A Letter from Eugene O'Neill," *The New York Times*, April 11, 1920, copyright 1920 by The New York Times Company; Seymour Peck, "A Talk with Mrs. O'Neill," *The New York Times*, November 4, 1956, copyright © 1956 by The New York Times Company: The New York Times Company.

For Jane
with thanks for the compliments, kisses and gin.

CONTENTS

INTRODUCTION

You were born with ghosts in your eyes and you were brave enough to go looking into your own dark. . . .

. . . man's light, not God's—man's feeble striving to understand himself, to exist for himself in the darkness! It's a symbol of his life—a lamp burning out in a room of waiting shadows!

Tragic is the plight of the tragedian whose only audience is himself! Life is for each man a solitary cell whose walls are mirrors.

An autobiographer is an over-reacher. Much as wind and water leave traces of their passage on the surface of the land, an autobiographer seeks to shape a contour in time. He denies that his is like the lives of most men—a random sequence, jumbling instinctual action and chance into a drift of days. Disregarding the self-cancelling interplay of mastery and infirmity, he asserts that the course of his life is rational, and that, like the action of a drama, it moves toward a fulfillment in the complete understanding of its author-subject.

Eugene O'Neill's work as a playwright was such an effort at self-understanding. In the thirty years of his creative life, he completed drafts of sixty-two plays. Eleven were destroyed, and of those remaining, over half contain discernible autobiographical elements. No play written by O'Neill after 1922, except for his fugitive adaptation of Coleridge's *The Rime of the Ancient Mariner,* was free of them. The extent, variety and quality of the work signals a rare creative energy, but the energy's source lay in his need to find a pattern of explanation by which his life could be understood.

His was, in part, a quest for identity. Louis Sheaffer in his biography, *O'Neill, Son and Playwright,* records a conversation between O'Neill and his friend, George Cram Cook, who once remarked on O'Neill's habit of continually looking at himself in mirrors:

"You're the most conceited man I've ever known, you're always looking at yourself."

O'Neill replied, "No, I just want to be sure I'm here."[1]

The mocking half-truth reveals a deeper substance: O'Neill used the stage as his mirror, and the sum of his work comprises an autobiography. In many of his plays, with a bold directness of approach, he drew a figure whose face resembled his own, and whose exterior life barely concealed a passionate, questing inner existence. Around this figure, he grouped other characters who served as thin masks for members of his close family and for his friends and significant acquaintances. On the stage, their grouping forms a structure of relationships through which O'Neill moved to discover what in his life gave him identity.

As elements of works of art, the characters live for the most part independent of their creator; they stand in the round at an appropriate aesthetic distance. Yet the shape of the drama is formed by private matters. O'Neill's experiments with masks, asides, soliloquies and long monologues evolve from his necessity to make his personal quest a theatrical reality. The intense subjectivity of the plays, conflicting at times with the need theatre has for relatively objective delineations, accounts in part for the lyricism that emerges unexpectedly in many of his earlier works and toward the end of his life comes to dominate his stage. In such late plays as *Hughie*, *Long Day's Journey into Night* and *A Moon for the Misbegotten*, the dialogue repeatedly assumes a lyric, rather than a dramatic mode; narrative is suspended, and voices borne out of silence and darkness speak a threnody of pain and loss. The lyricism is a token of the fact that no other dramatist in the world's history, not even excepting Strindberg with whom O'Neill felt particularly allied, continually turned the theatre to such personal purposes.

The result forms a partial paradox. Using the stage with such intimate intention, O'Neill yet managed to produce the greatest plays of American dramatic literature, and, in the world theatre of the first half of the twentieth century, can be compared only to Chekhov, Shaw, Pirandello, and Brecht, all of whom wrote with more intricacy, wit and style than O'Neill, but never with more deep-rooted involvement.

O'Neill shaped the course of American drama in its most significant developmental period, from 1915 to about 1930. His theatrical innovations were admired, but their initial enthusiastic reception proved in time detrimental to his reputation. No dramatist has followed him directly in his use of such startling devices as the masks in *The Great God Brown* or the drums in *The Emperor Jones*. In other ways, however, he has been followed. For example, his innovative use of an exterior-interior setting for *Desire Under the Elms*, a scheme for achieving an uninterrupted flow of action, is now routinely called for by playwrights. A similar claim can be made for his pioneering use of sound and light as integral parts of his plays. Yet, to return to such devices as the drums or to similar massive assaults on an audience's sensibilities as the choral ensemble of *Lazarus Laughed* or the humming of the electrical plant in *Dynamo* or the foghorn in *Long Day's Journey into Night*: these theatrical effects were devised to shake his audiences from the spectator's habitual, lethargic "suspended disbelief" and to cause them to *believe*, to involve themselves directly, fully, committedly with the action, just as today the practitioners of "The Living Theatre" or "The Theatre of Ceremony" call on their audiences to become more participants than spectators. The direction signalled by O'Neill's theatre aesthetic in this regard has been taken by others.

O'Neill's influence as a man of the theatre can best be measured in general, rather than in specific terms. As he began to write, the theatre was dominated by a superficial realism which barely concealed a tawdry artifice. In 1918, efforts to move the American theatre toward the province of art were spasmodic attempts, lacking as visible proof plays that would attest to the truth of theory. In cooperation, first, with the Provincetown Players, then with an experimental theatre in association with Kenneth Macgowan and Robert Edmond Jones and finally with the Theatre Guild, O'Neill demonstrated decisively that drama could be an art. In very literal terms, his work between 1920 and 1928 proved the theories of "Theatre Art" to be valid. Admittedly, he was not alone in this. As the decade passed, serious theatre-goers in the United States increasingly were able to see important demonstrations of the new theatre aesthetics from sources both European and American. Among innovative dramatists in this country, however, O'Neill was clearly the leader, insisting in both his successes and his failures that his work be considered as an art.

In small ways and in large he pushed at the practical and theoretical limitations of the American stage, and, in doing so, he taught others to do the same. *Lazarus Laughed* is subtitled "A Play for an Imaginative Theatre." O'Neill, struggling to find someone capable of producing the play, said sourly that by the phrase he did not mean an "Imaginary Theatre." A theatre to produce not only that play but all of his works had to be forced into being. By his imagination and boldness and by his uncompromising sense of the value of his writing, he played a major role in bringing that theatre into existence. Much of what he did is now contemporary routine; many of the new theories he championed have become commonplace in the course of time. By the same token, the wheel, once it was invented, became obvious.

O'Neill worked alone. Then, as now, the theatrical world car-

rouselled around the serious playwright. The critical arbiters of his
first mature works were pranksters, men and women who pretended
that to take oneself seriously was to commit a grievous faux pas.
Speaking of the self-styled "Algonquin Wits," one commentator
has written, "The comic interpretation whether invoking simple
laughter, pathos, or moral disapproval, seemed always to stand as
their final statement on whatever issue stirred their fancy."[2] Judged
by the standards of many of his contemporaries, O'Neill lacked
"wit" and was deaf to the niceties of literary style. Yet he did not
lack humor, and his style, developed entirely for the stage, could be
measured only in the theatre—a fact that did not prevent several
of his published plays from becoming best sellers. Nevertheless, he
studiously avoided any form of communal living with the easy
writers and critics of his time. With a few exceptions—chiefly that
of George Jean Nathan—he relied on nobody's evaluation of his
work, any more than he relied on star actors to sell his dramas to
the public. Such established stars as Alice Brady, Alla Nazimova
and George M. Cohan, when they appeared in his plays, found their
"star quality" obscured by O'Neill's own presence. He needed such
actors no more than he relied on critical acclaim. His was a solitary,
dedicated, even obsessive life in art.

Setting aside all theatrical considerations, the content of his plays
would still have marked him as a leader. During the 1920's, his experiments with contemporary psychological theory proved challeng-
ing to his audiences, although in more sophisticated retrospect, they
seem obvious and oversimplified. Yet his studies of the Negro American remain vital, and stand as archetypes for playwrights seeking
to develop a "black drama." He became one of the best historical
dramatists since Shakespeare. His outspoken studies of women's
sexual drives, his use of myth as a basis for drama, his domestication
of Strindberg's expressionistic manner and statement have caused
many of his plays to retain their power. As an artist, he was always
a political non-partisan, and except for his Negro plays, he wrote
without real political awareness. Yet, to quote Kenneth Tynan, reviewing *The Iceman Cometh*, "O'Neill is one of the few writers
who can enter, without condescension or contempt, the world of
those whom the world has neglected."[3] In 1934, as the American
left-wing developed a theatre of its own, O'Neill entered into a
retreat from which he was not to emerge until 1946. So far as one

could then see, he had turned his back on the great period of social change that the Depression and the beginning of the Second World War occasioned. Yet in that solitary period, he began to shape the long cycle of plays on American historical subjects, attempting to discover in his own way, and without commitment to any special political cause, wherein the United States had faltered. The cycle, unproduced and largely destroyed, set no precedent, yet the directly autobiographical plays written at the end of his life reflect similar issues and have emerged as precursors of the American existential drama, remaining, perhaps, the only substantial American dramatic achievement with existential themes.

When *The Iceman Cometh* was originally produced in 1946, it was little understood, despite its *succès d'estime*. Its revival in the spring of 1956, when its run overlapped that of the first professional New York production of Samuel Beckett's *Waiting for Godot*, was a triumph and started an O'Neill renaissance. In the decade between the two productions, the philosophical shape of mid-century intellectual life in the United States had taken form, and in the perspective of what American theatre-goers had learned of Sartre, Camus, and Genet, among others, *The Iceman Cometh*, which O'Neill had written in 1939, made complete philosophic sense, as did *Hughie* and *Long Day's Journey into Night* when those plays were finally seen. Alone, and well ahead of the American pack, O'Neill had come to a vision compatible with the philosophy that was to govern a large part of the thought and action of this present world. He had only to wait for his audiences to catch up with him.

The dramaturgy of many of his plays embraces a realism that is at present somewhat out of fashion. Yet the theme and structure of *Hughie, The Iceman Cometh, Long Day's Journey into Night* and *A Moon for the Misbegotten* remain astonishingly contemporary. To read works by Arthur Kopit, Sam Shepherd or other followers of Edward Albee—to read Albee himself—is to enter where O'Neill walked nearly three decades ago. How many plays today are laid in an isolated, bizarre wasteland in which a few characters wander, lost and desolate, seeking someone to whom they can tell a story of a crime they have committed, and in making such confession find purgation? How many of these plays, *Who's Afraid of Virginia Woolf?*, *The Tiger*, can match the last four plays of O'Neill, each based on the telling of a confessional tale in a wasteland? Even the nature of the confession, so often a crime involving murder and centering on Oedipal incest, is anticipated in *A Moon for the Misbegotten*. Notably, too in *A Touch of the Poet, More Stately Mansions* and *Hughie*, O'Neill does more than hint at the contemporary predilection for dramas in which role playing or "games" are central elements.

In his isolation from the theatre and the world of affairs, O'Neill remained prophetically contemporary. By way of corollary, it should be said that in revival, O'Neill's plays sometimes seem to their audiences melodramatic and a little old-fashioned. There is reason for this. O'Neill began writing at the end of a period when a flamboyant, semi-presentational style of acting, one which placed a heavy emphasis on rhetoric and the stances of formal delivery, had held the stage for nearly a century. His father, James O'Neill, was almost the last of a long line of actors of romantic drama. Of necessity, O'Neill's heritage bound him to that theatre and its playing style. Late in his life, discussing the casting of a proposed production of *A Touch of the Poet,* O'Neill said,

> What [the role of Cornelius Melody] needs is an actor like Maurice Barrymore or my old man. . . . One of those big-chested, chiseled-mug, romantic old boys who could walk onto a stage with all the aplomb and regal splendor with which they walked into the old Hoffmann House bar, drunk or sober. Most actors in these times lack an air. If a playwright doesn't work up entrances fifteen minutes long for them and have all the other characters describe them in advance as something pretty elegant, noble, chivalrous and handsome, the audiences won't be able to accept them for much more than third assistant barkeeps, if that.[4]

O'Neill's own dramaturgy did much to end the demand for such actors, but it did little to aid the development which took its place. With the advent of the Depression, a new style of acting, relying heavily on adaptations of the teaching of Stanislavsky, emerged from such producing organizations as the Group Theatre, and became normative for American actors. In this period O'Neill did not work in the theatre. His active days of theatrical practice fell between the death of the old and the discovery of the new, and at a time when American acting was moving in transition between the two. During the 1930's, the style was characterized by a little of both the old and new manner, more representational and subtle than the old, but still involving some of the presentational aspects derived from the nineteenth century. The Lunts, John Barrymore, Judith Anderson, to name a few among many, developed the "transitional style" which, while it created a convincing illusion of human beings in action, at the same time made histrionic "points," not fearing to play to an audience's appreciation of an actor's virtuosity *as an actor,* knowing that a demonstration of a purely theatrical presence was a valid part of certain dramatic experiences.

From his first attempt as a playwright with a vaudeville sketch entitled *A Wife for a Life,* O'Neill always wrote for this kind of actor. That the last plays do not appear to be written in this vein is something of an illusion. In fact, O'Neill has incorporated into his cast characters who are concerned with role playing and who thus present themselves *as actors.* A large part of the characterization of both Cornelius Melody and James Tyrone rests in their being actors performing in the old, romantic tradition of O'Neill's father's theatre. Thus "performance" becomes in the late plays an element of characterization and theme, totally incorporated into the context of the play, and contemporary actors can play the role. Yet where this has not been done, as in *Mourning Becomes Electra,* the newer style of acting will not entirely suffice. The latter play, if it is not to seem an overwritten melodrama, must be approached in what has become essentially a period style.

Such a matter marks the inevitable inroads of time on the work of a major dramatist. They are the small erosions of the contour he left behind him. The study that follows attempts to trace the contour from its origin to its end, by discussing each of his works in the approximate chronological order of composition. The book is thus a form of biography, although it pays no heed to those events of O'Neill's life that did not have direct bearing on his professional career.

By virtue of O'Neill's central position in the drama of the modern world, this study also has become, within the limits its subject sets for it, a form of theatrical history. An appendix contains a complete factual record of important productions of O'Neill's plays.

The skein of indebtedness that binds my book is not easily unraveled. Initial research was made possible by a Guggenheim Foundation Fellowship and was carried on for the most part in the theatre collections of the libraries of Harvard University, Princeton University, The University of California at Berkeley, Stanford

University, the New York Public Library, the Museum of the City of New York, and Yale University. I have relied heavily on the assistance of the librarians and their staffs. I feel a particular debt of gratitude to Dr. Donald Gallup, formerly Curator of the American Literature Collection in the Beinecke Rare Book and Manuscript Library at Yale University. To help me, Dr. Gallup has repeatedly gone far beyond the routines of his normal duties—even so far as to read a portion of my draft manuscript to aid its accuracy. For his invaluable counsel, I have no adequate thanks. Dr. Gallup's successor, Dr. David Schoonover, has answered my many requests and inquiries with courteous promptness and has laid open the riches of the O'Neill collection to my research.

O'Neill's biographers have provided much of the basic information on which this work is framed. My reliance on the work of Arthur and Barbara Gelb is detailed in the footnotes, but such notes do not satisfactorily acknowledge the over-view of O'Neill's life that their important biographical study, *O'Neill*, initially provided for me. To Louis Sheaffer, upon whose *O'Neill, Son and Playwright* and *O'Neill, Son and Artist* I have drawn extensively for crucial information about O'Neill's career, I feel a major obligation. Mr. Sheaffer has allowed me access to his files of information, provided me with his copies of O'Neill's correspondence, given me photographs, answered my questions, and shared with me his own enthusiasm for our common subject. I count his friendship among the most valuable consequences of this book.

No one writing on O'Neill and his plays can do so in a state of original innocence. I have preferred in preparing the initial drafts of this work to restrict my research to the plays and primary source materials, since what I was seeking to detail in the first instance was a form of biography—the course of his life in art. Only secondarily has my purpose been to write a work of criticism. I am aware, however, that what I have set down in both general and specific ways is indebted to or overlaps books of criticism about O'Neill. Specific indebtedness is acknowledged in the notes, but more generally, I must acknowledge my obligation to Edwin Engel's *The Haunted Heroes of Eugene O'Neill* (Cambridge, Mass., 1953), in particular for the perceptions concerning O'Neill's reliance on the theories of Kenneth Macgowan. I have found the studies of Doris Falk and Doris Alexander helpful in many areas, and have profited by the perceptions of my colleagues, John Henry Raleigh in his study, *The Plays of Eugene O'Neill* (Carbondale, Illinois, 1965), and Frederic Ives Carpenter in *Eugene O'Neill* (New York, 1964). I have also been aided in revisions of the completed manuscript from recent studies by Egil Törnqvist, *A Drama of Souls* (Uppsala, 1968), and Timo Tiusanen, *O'Neill's Scenic Images* (Princeton, N.J., 1968).

At various stages in my work, my colleagues at the University of California and my friends in Berkeley have given me helpful information and criticism. In particular, emeritus professors Benjamin H. Lehman and Fred Orin Harris, and the late Mr. Everett Glass have shared their personal recollections of productions of O'Neill's plays. Dr. Pat M. Ryan and Miss Inez Ghirardelli have been friendly and solicitous informants. To Professors Charles Lyons, Henry May and Mark Schorer, I feel a particular and personal debt for their aid and encouragement and for their faith in this book.

Mr. Sheldon Meyer, my editor at Oxford University Press, has demonstrated supernal patience in waiting out the long preparation of this study. Mr. Sheldon Cheney, pioneer of the Art Theatre Movement in America, has generously helped me in all ways I asked. Information about Swedish productions of O'Neill's dramas was supplied to me by Dr. Karl Ragnar Gierow, then director of the Swedish Theatre Royal; by Dr. Gustav Hilleström, and by Mr. Bengt Eklund, who created the role of "Erie" Smith in the Stockholm première of *Hughie*. Miss Jessie L. Rowley, librarian of the Atlantic City Free Library, and Mr. Ronald Scofield, assistant editor of the *Santa Barbara News-Press* have answered queries fully. Mr. Paine Knickerbocker of the *San Francisco Chronicle* and Mr. Stanley Eichelbaum of the San Francisco *Examiner* have opened their files to help my research.

Who or what more? This book was really written with my students in English and Dramatic Art in classroom sessions in the University of California at Berkeley. Together we shared the results of our research and tried to evaluate the work and to understand its author. They are my collaborators. In this time, when naïve political voices cry that teaching and research are somehow antithetical, I can only offer this book and this acknowledgement as minor evidence to the contrary.

University of California, Berkeley   tb
June 1972, June 1986

CONTOUR IN TIME

I
THE TYRO
1913-1914

PLAYS WRITTEN IN 1913 ARE
A Wife for a Life
The Web
Thirst
Warnings
Recklessness

PLAYS WRITTEN IN 1914 ARE
Fog
Abortion
The Movie Man
Bread and Butter
Servitude
Bound East for Cardiff

1913—Eugene O'Neill was twenty-five,
living in New London, Connecticut, and setting up shop
as a reporter, a poet and a tyro playwright.
The face in the snapshot is the one he would describe
as Edmund Tyrone's in *Long Day's Journey into Night*.
In the photograph, as in the play, a young man's grace
masks a life of hardship and a waste of body and spirit
that had led him, a year earlier, to the edge of death.
In 1912, he attempted suicide in a New York flop-house.
He had just been released from a tuberculosis sanatorium.
He was divorced and father to a son he had never seen.
He had journeyed as a gold-prospector to Honduras
and as a sailor to Buenos Aires and England.
By choice, in New York and Argentina, he had sought companions
among the human debris of the world's waterfronts.
In the circle of his family, he had lived with—
or perhaps fled from—the knowledge that his mother
was a morphine addict and that his father,
the actor, James O'Neill, and his brother Jamie
were both failures in their art and lives.
Yet that summer, as he began to write,
he faced the sun and the long journey before him.

I N 1913 in a Connecticut tuberculosis sanatorium, Eugene O'Neill came to the end of a protracted adolescence. His illness was never disastrously severe, yet his encounter with tuberculosis was sufficiently fearful to cause him to fight for the first time against the drift of his life. The period at the sanatorium was one of self-assessment, of spiritual restoration, and of crucial decision. His recovery of health brought with it the idea of a destiny to which, during the forty years before him, he remained entirely faithful.

It was to become a tragic destiny. To fulfill it he manufactured solitude, and cut himself away from friends and family. His seeming indifference became a source of pain to those about him. Suffering hardened him and drove inward the gentleness and sensitivity that were the graces of his nature. Illness isolated him further, and the tremor in his hand reduced him to silence. Unable to bring it to completion, he destroyed the great cycle of plays whose writing had occupied almost half the span of his creative life. Then, when he could no longer write, he died, having lived in that spirit of total obsessive dedication which, because it renounces so much of the world's good, men see as both heroic and unjustifiable.

Eugene O'Neill's life in art was more than a dedication to playwriting. Like all such consuming quests, his became an attempt to find God and to know man. It began, however, more simply. At the sanatorium, he read Strindberg, Yeats, Lady Gregory, Brieux, Hauptmann.[1] Then, slowly, unskillfully and with great dependence on his reading, he began to write. In the beginning he showed little of that facility which in a tyro can be called "promise." The critic, Clayton Hamilton, who as a friend of his father viewed O'Neill's efforts with tolerance, at first tempered his encouragement of the young man.

Judging from the writers who influenced him most strongly at the outset, it was not clear that O'Neill would become a playwright. Aside from Strindberg, whom he specifically mentioned as having revealed to him what the drama could become, he read Ibsen and Shaw and their philosophical progenitors Nietzsche and Schopenhauer. Equally important, however, are the traces of non-dramatic authors, of the novels of Joseph Conrad and Jack London, and of the kind of ironic fable written by Guy de Maupassant and O. Henry. The early plays reveal characteristic tastes and foreshadow the development of techniques that were to become essentials of his dramaturgy, but most of them suffer from a narrative design suggestive of a short story, rather than a play, and, indeed, for a time in his early career, O'Neill experimented with short stories. Had it been a question of simple predilection, O'Neill might well have moved toward the writing of fiction. Yet, as his creative impulses strengthened and became less dependent on the work of others, his direction centered obsessively on the theatre. It was not entirely a matter of choice.

In his past, controlling choice, there lay the theatre of James O'Neill. For better or worse, the stage, if not the written drama, was his inheritance. Yet it was not a simple legacy. At one point, he spoke of "the hateful theatre of my father."[2] The phrase suggests more than distaste for the romantic theatricality of his father's star melodrama, *Monte Cristo*. Eugene O'Neill, like a vaudevillian's child, was in effect cradled in the trunk, carted like a property from stagedoor to stagedoor, or alternatively left in boarding schools while theatrical tours claimed his parents' presence. In American theatrical legend and in films, such a child is supposed to triumph, happily singing and dancing his way to the hearts of multitudes. "The theatre is in his blood," is the explanation: "He is of the dynasty." In a peculiarly perverse way, O'Neill lived the legend through, and the claim may be made that he could no more put away the theatre than he could put away his father, for they possessed him equally. He felt of the commercial theatre that it was a cheap-jack enterprise, soul-destroying, a kind of dope, hollow, false, demanding a wasteful expenditure of spirit. His father, as he later was to present him in *Long Day's Journey into Night*, had something of the same cheapness and pain-struck emptiness of soul. O'Neill's resentment of the one extended to the other.

Men in hate are bound as deeply as men in love, for hate has in it the same positive power to compel men to its center. In the midst of hate, as for his father, O'Neill felt for the theatre a heavy dedication. He was never stage-struck, yet his feeling was sufficiently strong to bind him closely to the theatre as an institution, even to the melodramatic theatre of his father, from which he never entirely emancipated himself. The theatre was a natural atmosphere for him. He learned its language early, and thought habitually in its terms. Although he is reputed never to have seen his later plays after their final dress rehearsals, and indeed, even so early as *Beyond the Horizon* showed signs of reluctance to attend performances, he assiduously worked through the rehearsal period of all his plays, bringing to bear on their final crucial shaping for the stage his full knowledge of theatrical practice. He did not let others do this job for him. *A Moon for the Misbegotten* was withdrawn during its pre-Broadway run because O'Neill was too ill to attend to essential revisions.* His cooperation with actor, designer, and director was always great, and although he stopped abruptly short of make-peace compromise, his assertion of his integrity as a dramatist was never merely dictatorial. He understood the theatre's necessities and came to terms with them as, in the end, he came to terms with the man his father was. Bound to them both in a profound psychological way, he had to face them, rather than to reject them and follow other creative paths.

O'Neill's first work for the stage was a piece for the theatre of his father. *A Wife for a Life* was written in 1913 and is not so much a play as a sketch designed to exhibit the virtuosity of a star actor, when, "at liberty," he took to the vaudeville stage on a personal appearance tour.** James O'Neill could readily have played the central

---

* The only play whose staging he did not personally oversee was the Theatre Guild's production of *Dynamo*, produced while he was living in Europe. He blamed its failure in part on his absence.

** In a letter to Mark Van Doren, dated May 12, 1944, now in the Princeton University Library, O'Neill claimed *The Web* as his first play. He acknowledges the existence of the earlier sketch, saying, "To be scrupulously exact, for the record, 'The Web' is *not* the first thing I wrote *for the stage*. I had some time before dashed off in one night a ten minute vaudeville skit, afterwards destroyed. But this was not a play. In fact, my friends in vaudeville crudely insisted it was not a vaudeville skit, either! It was nothing. And 'The Web' *is* the first *play* I ever wrote." O'Neill's distinction between a *skit* and a *play* is not one that can be followed out in close critical detail. The difference seems to lie in the concentration of the skit on the role for the star and in the purely anecdotal nature of the story.

role of the "Older Man," who believing that his wife had been unfaithful, has searched the world over to find and murder her suspected lover, John Sloan. When his life has been saved by young
Jack Sloan, he has not understood that his benefactor is the man he
has sought. The two have become partners in a prospecting expedition and, at the edge of the Arizona desert, have uncovered a rich
gold mine. At this juncture, word comes to Sloan that his beloved's
husband has been declared legally dead and that she is therefore
free to marry him. The Older Man then realizes Sloan's identity,
but he understands as well that his wife has turned to Sloan because
of his own drunkenness and brutality, and that the two have been
innocent of adultery. A moment of tension as the Older Man reaches
for his gun gives way to a burst of sentimental nobility. He continues to hide his identity, and Jack is sped East to his slightly biga-
mous marriage, leaving his friend to a soliloquy:

> Oh what a fool I have been. She was true to me in spite of what I
> was. God bless him for telling me so. God grant that they may both
> be happy—the only two beings I ever loved. And I—must keep
> wandering on. I cannot be the ghost at their feast. . . . "Greater
> love hath no man than this that he giveth his wife for his friend."
> [222]

O'Neill's debut is turn-of-the-century theatre at its worst, its
punch line salvaged, one suspects, from a witticism uttered during
a backstage gossip session.* Yet the sketch contains many of the elements which O'Neill was later to infuse with theatrical power. It is,
in fact, so characteristic of his practice that it can be used as an introduction to his dramaturgy. In so trivial a work, there yet emerges
a pattern of interrelated theatrical techniques that marks the beginnings of a style.

O'Neill conceived the play in 1912 when he accompanied his
father on a vaudeville tour which followed the Orpheum Circuit as
far west as Utah.[3] He was at pains to set his impressions of the
desert on the stage:

> The edge of the Arizona desert; a plain dotted in the foreground
> with clumps of sagebrush. On the horizon a lonely butte is out-
> lined, black and sinister against the lighter darkness of a sky with
> stars. [211]

---

* O'Neill played again with the verse (John, XV:13) at the end of his life in *Long
Day's Journey into Night* in Jamie's line "Greater love hath no man than this, that he
saveth his brother from himself." [167]

Complete with campfire and lone prospector, it is the customary stage setting for a desert scene, but O'Neill was alive to its quality as well as its appearance. Its mood caught his attention, and he attempted to relate it to the central action, giving it a more than decorative effect. The elementary symbolism of the black and sinister butte against the starry sky is obvious. It was an easy setting for the display of romanticized passion, not unlike the décor of most nineteenth-century melodrama, the Château d'If, for example. Yet there is a closer relation between the Older Man and his arid world than between Edmund Dantes and his stormy rock. The Older Man is intended to be a wandering ghost in a desert of spent passion. The wasted world is all he can inherit, and the setting reflects the substance of his grief as it suggests the course of his destiny. The imagery is obvious; today it is within the range of any amateur. Yet even such minor sensitivity to place was not axiomatic in the English-speaking drama of 1913. Ibsen and Chekhov had made notable use of setting to reveal inner substance of character, but in England, the most profound use of stage setting was primarily sociological, rather than psychological. In America, the realism of Belasco and his imitators, when it went beyond providing a merely decorative spectacle, again tended toward the creation of a world in which the social and economic circumstances would be sufficiently clear to explain aspects of the characters' behavior and to set certain problems for them to overcome. In producing Edward Sheldon's *Salvation Nell,* for instance, Mrs. Fiske had purchased a bar from a Bowery saloon in order to lend authenticity to the first act setting. Such realism provided environmental information, but did not reveal as O'Neill's settings at their best were to do the inner nature of the characters. In the English language at that time, only the productions of the Abbey Theatre in Dublin used setting for more than occasional psychological revelation. Ordinarily the stage provided no more than a world across which the action could convincingly move.

In *A Wife for a Life* evidently there is no need for the creation of an elaborate sociological background. The anecdote requires nothing. His own experience as a gold miner in Honduras, together with his western trip, enabled him to call for appropriate properties to detail the occupation of his characters and to define the economic and social framework of their world. It is a superficial inspection, but, generally speaking, O'Neill was never deeply interested in such background, preferring instead to concentrate on the life created by his characters in their private rooms, sketching only lightly the shape of the world outside.

To increase the concentration on the private worlds of his character, as the play progresses O'Neill cuts away even so much of this public scene as he has detailed in his initial description. At the play's end, the stage is reduced to an area illuminated by the campfire, and the Older Man is isolated in a dimly lighted micro-world wherein he enacts his passion. In *Long Day's Journey into Night*, where O'Neill takes pains to realize the sociological milieu of the Tyrone family, the same progression is made. At the end, the entire world of the play is reduced to a small circle of light in the fogbound house. In that circle, at last, father and son come to understanding, as if only in extraordinary isolation could one human spirit find its way to communion with another. Just so, however imperfectly, *A Wife for a Life* suggests a resolution of a relationship based on both love and hate when darkness comes and when the men are alone in the desert night. Throughout his career, O'Neill repeated the same effect, narrowing the focus in order to increase the intensity of revelation of his characters' inner existence. To discover it at the outset of his career is to mark it as an innate habit of his theatrical style.

Intimately connected with his use of place in a special and characteristic manner is his use of the soliloquy and aside. Again, the common practice of the theatre of his father caused him to adopt these conventions of dialogue without thinking, but the characters in *A Wife for a Life* live in a strange psychological isolation from one another. Communication between the two friends on ordinary matters is largely irrelevant, and frank speaking of their thoughts is made difficult by the circumstances of the plot, if nothing else. Of course, O'Neill had the problem of cramming enormous amounts of purely narrative exposition into a short scene. In a short story or novel, the careers of the two men could easily have been displayed at length. O'Neill, forced to compress his anecdote to a ten minutes' compass, causes the two to exchange copious amounts of gratuitous information, thinly disguised as fond reminiscence, for the audience's sake. There are, in addition, several moments when Jack expresses manly views about the desert, their luck, and the pure nature of women—opinions with which the Older Man briefly agrees or disagrees. These moments aside, the characters cannot really be said to speak to one another. Sloan, lost in ecstatic contemplation of his beloved, pays little attention to his friend, while the Older Man displays his emotion in a series of grimaces, ultimately explained in the final soliloquy. Although the Older Man reacts to the news that is told him, he rarely replies directly to what Jack says. There is no substantial interaction of character. Each man plays in isolation, and expresses his news and his emotions in semi-soliloquy.

In part, such practice stems from O'Neill's use of a setting for psychological purposes. In a setting whose chief service is to establish a sociological world, all characters may be said to face the details of place on an identical plane. Drinks are passed, doors are opened and closed, couches are used to bring characters into intimate dialogue. Details of such a setting are, really, a means of communication, an unspoken form of dialogue, used as all men may use the furniture of their world, to relate to one another. In a play whose setting is designed to permit direct symbolic revelation of psychological truth the contrary is true. All characters will not approach it equally. The setting has importance only for the central figure whose consciousness its symbols reveal, and who plays deeply into it. In an expressionistic play, at times, minor characters may appear to be little else than extensions of the setting, serving to sharpen the focus on the inner character of the protagonist. Psychological setting, in other words, controls point of view toward the one character it is designed to reveal. He alone has the rights of that world, and he may well appear to *be* alone in it, playing his action in isolation and expressing his deepest emotions directly to the audience, rather than revealing implicitly what he is through action and response to the world and other characters. So it was that, as O'Neill developed the crude psychology of the Older Man, the character became isolated by the very manner of his portrayal. Sloan is a foil to him, and moves outside the center of emotion that is the play's substance. At the most, he is a supporting actor, in vaudeville terms, a "feeder," almost a part of the setting rather than a character. The Older Man plays alone.

To list the plays of O'Neill in which the same effect is more skilfully achieved would be to list virtually the entire canon. *The Emperor Jones* and *The Hairy Ape* are, for entire scenes, monologues. *Strange Interlude* and *Hughie* are sophisticated extrapolations of the tendency revealed in his first work. It was a habit O'Neill never lost.

In the sketch, O'Neill was of course unconscious of his later purposes. The use of soliloquy and aside can be attributed more to inept imitation of nineteenth-century theatrical styles, to the needs of the vaudeville stage, and to difficulties with his narrative than it can to any embryonic expressionistic tendencies. Yet in his handling of other conventions he reached a little beyond the theatre of his father. He avoided, for example, a stereotyped confrontation scene between the two men. Sloan never learns the identity of his partner, and the revelation of the true state of affairs between them bears no resemblance whatever to the revelation of the identity of Edmund Dantes in the last act of *Monte Cristo*. Despite its patent absurdity, the star's role is underwritten, as O'Neill veers away from the full flood tide of passion that could so easily have swept over the stage. O'Neill in the beginning looked for tragedy in understatement rather than in heroic rant, in silent irony rather than in blustering confrontation.

O'Neill's leaning toward ironic rather than heroic tragedy can perhaps be taken as a sign of his modernity. What was offered as tragedy toward the beginning of the twentieth century throughout Europe centered more often in ironic defeat than in heroic achievement. Usually defeat was brought about by social circumstances, more than by character, thus enabling the dramatist to indict society at the same time as he raised pity for his hapless hero. In his narrative, O'Neill was evidently taken with ironies of circumstance, chance meetings, fortuitous discoveries and all the trappings of adventure stories. By no stretch of meaning can what happens be called tragic. Inherently improbable, the anecdote has the same sort of intricate weaving of accident that passed for irony in the stories of O. Henry and Guy de Maupassant. O'Neill's story falls far short of either. He has neither the adroit control of event nor the tendency to allegory of O. Henry, and he is unable to suggest any of the cynical quality of Maupassant's world view. The spectacle of men caught in a web of ironic circumstance becomes tragic only when it is viewed from a philosophical position enabling a writer to suggest that such events are caused by forces working in the world to determine the destinies of men. In the novels of Thomas Hardy, in Maupassant, in the naturalistic novels and dramas of Germany and

France, such perspective gave substance to the ironic crushing of mortal endeavor. Lacking even the perspective that his devotion to the novels of Jack London might have given him, O'Neill fell back on a far-too-involved narrative of incredible circumstances and on such superficial ironies as his curtain line summarizes.

It is a conspicuous lack. Without a world view whose origin is a philosophical, social or theological position, such drama as O'Neill seemed to be reaching toward would remain trivial and melodramatic. Yet, as if he instinctively knew that such a view was essential as a means of attaining a significant drama, he began immediately to move toward such a position, and emerged, once he had achieved it, as a writer ready to take his place on the public stage.

A Wife for a Life is trivial. It can be maintained that the effects and characteristics here noted are merely the results of ineptitude; that without taste or knowledge, O'Neill in imitation of his father's theatre, wrote a commercial work whose narrative could not be adequately set forth within the play's compass; that because of this he was forced to fall back on the soliloquy and aside; that therefore something of the characters' inner quality was forced to the surface; that, when it was, the setting inevitably appeared to have some symbolic value, but no more so than if it had been a barroom, an office, a public street. Whether the results be attributed thus to ineptitude or to the first gropings toward a new kind of theatre is perhaps not of real importance. Yet it is curious that these elements remain as essentials of his style. What is most important about them is that they are centrally connected with one another, and in the pattern of related phenomena, something of the nature of the man as an artist is to be seen from the outset. These are habits of his mind; from this way of devising, all else must develop.

A Wife for a Life was O'Neill's only contribution to the star-turns of his father's theatre. Made perhaps as an almost involuntary gesture, O'Neill copyrighted it, tried unsuccessfully to market it, and then forgot it. More potentially significant enterprises were in view.

O'Neill had returned from the vaudeville tour with his father to New London, Connecticut, in May, 1912, and had begun work as a reporter and columnist for the New London *Telegraph*. He supplemented his journalistic efforts by writing poetry imitative of much of his current reading: Wilde, Edward Fitzgerald, Kipling, Robert W. Service and Masefield. Behind him lay a life of incredible hardship and depravity of spirit. Early that year, he had attempted suicide. He was twenty-four; he had a two-year-old son he had never seen, and in October, he was to divorce the boy's mother. On December 24, he entered the sanatorium.

To him, 1912 was a crucial year. Until the end of his life, he worked to understand what lay behind him at that juncture. Yet in the beginning, the impulse which was to dominate his creative life appeared to be without psychological complexity. The writing in the columns of the *Telegraph* had set desire in motion; his reading in the sanatorium gave it shape; and when he returned to his home in May, 1913, he began to write in earnest. He turned out a few "photo-plays" for the infant film industry,[4] but in the main, he worked steadily at his own last on a variety of one-act and two full-length plays.* He wrote without real discrimination or control, struggling to learn the disciplines of his craft. In January, 1914, he approached Clayton Hamilton to ask him how a one-act play should be written. Hamilton replied that he should not worry about the craft of playmaking but should write about his life at sea.

"This has been done in the novel," Hamilton said. "It has been done in the short-story; it has not been done in the drama. Keep your eye on life—on life as you have seen it; and to hell with the rest."[5]

The advice, in fact, was not very helpful. For a young writer, the gulf between art and life is wide, and O'Neill, although he may have tried to follow Hamilton's advice, kept his eye much more firmly on the example of other writers than on the realities of his experience. Like other tyros, he was seeking masters in the hope of achieving mastery, and the plays of 1913-14, even *Bound East for Cardiff*, are heavily indebted to others.

At this stage, no one writer served him as a favorite model. Rather, he tried on a variety of styles, changing his mentor even

* The chronology of the composition of the early plays by Egil Törnqvist in *A Drama of Souls* (Uppsala, Sweden, 1968) places the composition of *A Wife for a Life* at the sanatorium in the spring of 1913. That fall, O'Neill wrote *The Web, Thirst, Recklessness* and *Warnings*. In the winter of 1914, he wrote *Fog*, and in the spring, *Bread and Butter, Bound East for Cardiff, Abortion* and *The Movie Man. Servitude* followed in the summer. (Cf. *A Drama of Souls*, 258.) *Thirst, Fog, Warnings, The Web* and *Recklessness* were collected in a volume entitled *Thirst and Other One Act Plays*, privately printed in 1914.

within the confines of a single play. The influence of Ibsen and Shaw are clear in *Servitude,* and there is a Shavian element in *Fog.* Strindberg comes to the fore in *Bread and Butter,* and then is apparently dropped as a guide. There are traces of Hauptmann in *The Web.* In other one-act plays, he appears to have been guided by O. Henry and Maupassant and by the novels of Jack London and Joseph Conrad. The result is hodgepodge. With the exception of *Bound East for Cardiff,* no one of the plays of the period is worth consideration in its own right. Most of them were unproduced. *Bound East for Cardiff,* of course, entered the world's repertory as part of the *S.S. Glencairn* cycle. *Thirst* received a single production by the Provincetown Players in Massachusetts during the summer of 1916, and *Fog* was staged by the Provincetown in New York in January, 1917. Neither has been revived in a recorded production, and there is not reason to quarrel with this neglect.

Inevitably, of course, despite their imitation and amateur excess, the plays reveal marks of later power. Yet what is interesting lies less in their spasmodic merits than in the pattern that can be traced through the group as a whole. Building on the technical elements suggested by *A Wife for a Life,* the plays, despite their variety of subject matter, form a unified group whose design sets forth the initial terms of the playwright's artistry and thought. They range in subject from scenes of well-bred suburban life to studies of prostitutes and pimps. They consider marital difficulties, questions of free love, the poverty of sailors, the need for artistic freedom, the insensitivity of commercial America, the problems of college students. In technique they range from semi-abstract, quasi-allegorical fables, through glossy domestic triangles, to squalid realistic studies of lower-class and slum life. Their narratives are sometimes intricate and in the worst sense "clever," and at other times they approximate a simple, plotless revelation that is a form of stage poetry. Their social awareness spreads from strenuous anti-capitalistic diatribe to an affection for the idle rich that characterizes the most slickly commercial Broadway fare. In genre and tone, they reach from outrageous melodrama and near tragedy to something like Shavian comedy. Yet, for all their diversity, when viewed as a group, they reveal a unity of effort and consistency of direction. Together, they converge on the significant initial definition of O'Neill's characteristic style achieved in *Bound East for Cardiff.* With this play he strikes once, firmly, in the center of his target. That it should have been written amidst so many errors of taste and judgment suggests that as he worked the goal was becoming clearer, and the dramatist's disciplines were being learned. Yet of this play, once it is viewed in the context of his other efforts, there is more to say than that O'Neill "kept his eye on life" and wrote of what he knew.

The first impression made by the 1913-14 plays is that they are a brace of brief melodramas. Setting *Bound East for Cardiff* apart from discussion for the moment, the others move inevitably toward a climax in mayhem. *Fog* provides a lifeboat and an ocean liner endangered by an iceberg; in each of the others, the climactic activity is graced by the spectacle of a character wandering around with a weapon in hand. *Thirst* offers a knife; in the others a revolver is drawn and the consequences are usually mortal. Murder occurs in *The Web, Recklessness* and *Thirst,* where it is coupled with death from exposure and an accidental tumble into shark-infested waters. In *Warnings, Recklessness, Abortion* and *Bread and Butter* the climax brings suicide. Only in *Servitude* is the gun unfired, the conclusion less than fatal.

Taken singly, each play approaches the limits of youthful self-indulgence. Yet, considered together, the plays reveal a kind of power arising in part from such steady, dominating violence. By its continual presence, as it arises from a wide variety of circumstances, the violence manages to convey that there is operative in the lives of all the characters something like a power of fate, leading them to the explosions with which their mortal existence ends. To suggest, at this stage in his development, that O'Neill was attempting to dramatize a view of the world and that the violence thus had philosophical implications is to lend too much dignity to the fact. Yet, *Servitude* aside, each attempts to create a tragedy out of what O'Neill came to call "ironic fate."

By "ironic fate," O'Neill meant that the lives of the characters are controlled, in despite of their wills, by a power of destiny that is inexorable, malevolent insofar as it can be said to have purpose, but in essence meaningless. In his early conception, man's fate is ironic in direct proportion to its incomprehensibility. Although men seek happiness and try to alter the miserable condition of their lives, their struggles only weave the strands of their webs more tightly about them. Will, therefore, leads to a kind of suicide, and hope is self-delusion. Such shallow and unformed pessimism does not approximate a world view, for O'Neill has neither philosophy nor theology to support his intuitions. In consequence, at the beginning, there is nothing to lend explanation to the destruction. There are only victims in a spiderless web.

To call such melodramatic destiny "fate" is to do little but to excuse youthful dramatic excess and the circumstantial trickery of the narratives. This granted, however, there remains something impressive in the way each of the characters is crushed by his environment. In spite of the nonsense of the individual stories, a pattern emerges dimly that was at least the beginning of a philosophical position. Man is caught by something—a force of an as yet unidentifiable nature whose power is absolute. O'Neill does not thus early claim that men belong to the force, or even that its power of dealing death is somehow to be associated with its power to give life. Yet these assertions will come, and from such perception, O'Neill will make his start toward tragedy.

His attempt to discover a world view in irony born of melodrama points toward a second characteristic of the group of plays. These efforts are not only without a clear philosophical conception, but they are often anti-intellectual. *Fog* and *Servitude* take the most explicit intellectual positions, yet neither is especially impressive for the quality of its thought. *Fog* strings together socialistic clichés borrowed perhaps from Shaw, while *Servitude* seeks to argue against the favorite heroine of Shaw and Ibsen, the so-called "New Woman." In neither play does O'Neill display a vestige of the power of the European playwrights to argue and attack. Despite his superficial indebtedness to them, he does not follow them as a propagandist for a new society. His social awareness was to develop slowly and was never to become a major focus of his statement. As in *A Wife for a Life,* he moved away from a broad social view, preferring to present an action that was essentially private.

Private emotion forms the basis of such positive elements as the plays offer. In none of them except *Servitude* does O'Neill permit his characters genuine hope. Man does not have the possibility of circumventing the fatal control. Yet once or twice, the characters are given insight into one another and are permitted to find in the resultant communion a momentary release from their problems. Full insight, such as comes to great tragic heroes, is impossible for these small creatures. They see no more of themselves or their circumstances than mortals ordinarily do. In trouble, men find one another more readily than they find God, and it is so here. The discovery of another human being who can serve as priest and friend is the nearest approach to an idea of good that O'Neill could at first achieve. It is not much—an accidental, impotent, transitory thing, that in the end remains as it began, a purely personal recoil from pain. Yet it is the only positive note discoverable in the plays.

Failing to discover ultimate patterns of meaning, the characters are left alone with their destinies. They are soiled and silent, unable to do more than face what must come. Never fully heroic, often acting on hysterical impulse, the lonely ones turn toward death as the only exit. To some of them death is a cessation of pain; to others, dying is a way of warding off life; to yet a third group, death is a way of expiation, a way of facing the dead. Needless to say, in the first plays, neither the positive personal communion nor the negative descent into death is evolved completely as drama or concept. Taken alone, each is a paltry thing. Yet a partial pattern of meaning evolves from the melodrama and from it greater plays are to be shaped. To mention *Titus Andronicus* is to suggest that such a course of development is not without precedent.

The play that most completely realizes the characteristics implicit in the group as a whole, and whose title may provide a metaphor for the central concept of each of the others, is the earliest, *The Web*. It is a naturalistic tragedy in the manner of Hauptmann. For such plays, the culminating emotions are pathos and horror generated from the shock of irony. O'Neill tries to serve a full measure of both in the story of the attempt of a hunted criminal to save a prostitute and her infant child from the villainy of her pimp. The course of action is predictable, as the revengeful pimp shoots the criminal, leaving the heroine to be arrested for his murder.* Misery is accumulated upon misery's head. The pimp forces the girl, Rose, to walk the streets in the rain, demands that she get rid of the child whose

---

* The play is not stageworthy, but it should be noted that the dialogue is phrased in slang nearly identical with that which O'Neill was later to write so effectively for Rocky, Margie and Pearl in *The Iceman Cometh*. So much of *The Web* at least would prove itself on a stage.

hungry crying disturbs him, threatens her with imprisonment should she disobey him, and beats her pitilessly. To compound her difficulties, O'Neill provides her with a desperate case of tuberculosis for which she can get no aid. The play was originally entitled *The Cough,* and O'Neill intended that her disease should be taken as symbolic of all the social evil for which there is no possible cure.

As a protest against such evil, the play is probably no worse than many more pretentious imitations of German naturalism. Like many of them, it fails because it is incapable of seeing the harrowing circumstances as more than a means of eliciting pity. With some small skill, it apes a manner, but finds none of the political and social substance that alone will justify the pathos by offering an explanation for the causes of such misery.

The fullest explanation of Rose's suffering is in effect no explanation at all, since it occurs in a stage direction and is not pointed by action. In the final moments of the play, O'Neill brings Rose to an awareness of the fate that has controlled her life. She makes no protest against it, but accepts what has come in silence:

> *She realizes the futility of all protest, the maddening hopelessness of it all. . . . All are looking at her in silence with a trace of compassionate pity on their faces.* ROSE *seems in a trance. Her eyes are like the eyes of a blind woman. She seems to be aware of something in the room which none of the others can see—perhaps the personification of the ironic life force that has crushed her.* [53]

Nothing more is said of fate or of an "ironic life force." Rose is shortly led away to be charged with murder as a clumsy policeman tries to comfort her child. Whatever form the "personification" took, what understanding she achieved in this blind moment is unclarified. Circumstances have closed in, and "a trace of compassionate pity," mixed with a sense of unjustified irony, is the extent of understanding.

The limited comprehension in the ending is partly the result of a self-imposed technical limitation. In this play, as in *A Wife for a Life,* the significant action lies less in external events than in the psyche of the central character. The soliloquy and aside in the earlier work served clumsily to present such an action. In *The Web,* however, O'Neill has accepted the completely realistic mode, and is barred from non-realistic devices. At this stage, he is not sufficiently accomplished to figure forth Rose's insight, yet in the light of the technical experiments to come—each evolved to present in action the inner substance of his characters—the phrase that comes to him to describe Rose's vision has significance. He thinks in terms of "personification," of a visual symbol for the unseen forces controlling her. He can not yet break open the forms of reality and move, in a phrase he was later to coin, "behind life." Yet the necessity of doing so is as clear as is his impulse toward the development of a symbolic technique. God is to be found in personification; *The Web*, for all its realism, hangs on the edge of expressionism.

The ending of the play is designed to shatter sensibilities. Yet it is not the play's most effective moment. Rose's silent acceptance of fate is in no way so telling as an earlier scene in which she and the gangster, Tim, united in loneliness, tell one another the stories of their lives. Their biographical accounts, intended to display the social evils that have warped their lives, are orthodox clichés of social protest. What is not trite is the communion established between them as they speak. They meet in haste, yet O'Neill allows their moment of contact to eddy out in time, so that, although they do not speak directly of their relationship, they talk with the intimacy of lovers. In defiance of probability, O'Neill manages to project a sense of their mutual understanding, evolving a relationship that is like love. The moment is more convincing than any other in the play.

Its small power arises from its evanescence. Theirs is the love of the misbegotten, and from it springs a semblance of hope. Tim gives Rose his money so that she with the child may escape from the crushing city environment. Inevitably, the money, when Tim has been killed, is taken as the motive for his murder and the proof of Rose's guilt. Love and hope turn upon their begetters with force and thus lend some validity to the play's irony. Yet the importance of these emotions lies less in their use in the plot than in their very presence in the play: something of value has been given birth, and the play is not merely negative. The confessional moment initiates a pattern that is later to achieve splendid effect in the last act of *Long Day's Journey into Night*, where confession, born of suffering, leads ultimately to mutual sympathy and understanding, and, in its moments of most devastating candor, to a partial justification of human worth. In *The Web* the suggestion is a poor thing, lost in a weak dramatization of the operation of an "ironic life force." Yet it is important that O'Neill, at the outset of his career, reached toward a pattern of action that, when fully developed, would assert itself as the major source of positive ethical value in his plays.

Lacking significant complexity in design and leading to no important insights into man's nature, *The Web* has at least the virtue of containing the elements with which O'Neill will work to create his tragic patterns. However crudely, the design is shaped. In the other minor works of 1914, the pattern is sketched less completely.

Recklessness and *Abortion,* both set on a higher social level than *The Web,* are in all ways less effective. *Recklessness,* together with *The Web,* was sent to the producer Holbrook Blinn, who at the Princess Theatre in New York was offering bills of one-act plays, including some Grand-Guignol, to what he hoped would be an elite audience. The sophisticates failed to support the venture and it disappeared before O'Neill's efforts could be considered for production.[6] *Recklessness,* however, brought a minor dividend later in O'Neill's career. The script was sold to Hollywood where in 1933 it served as the basis for a film entitled *The Constant Woman* with Leila Hyams and Conrad Nagle.*

Viewed without reference to O'Neill's other work, *Recklessness* is an outrageous marital melodrama in which a sneering husband, having discovered that his wife loves his chauffeur, first arranges that the chauffeur shall be killed in an automobile accident, and then comfortably accepts as inevitable the suicide of his wife. In the context of the companion works, O'Neill can be seen to be weaving another web of ironic fate in which circumstances defeat the thrust for happiness. It was not worth the effort. In spite of a suggestion that the wife and chauffeur are trying to find greater freedom and dignity through love, the mechanics of the plot defeat them without providing them love with a vestige of significance.

Abortion is more ambitious. O'Neill worked over the theme in several versions,[7] and created a play worthy at least of rudimentary concern. The scene is an unnamed eastern university, resembling

---

* According to the *New York Times,* February 12, 1933, *Recklessness* was the basis of a film first titled *Auction in Souls.* In a letter to Robert Sisk, dated July 4, 1932, O'Neill reported that he received $5000 for the rights to the play. To Sisk in March, 1933, he refers to *The Constant Woman,* noting that this title is not so senseless as the other. The film was produced by World Wide and released in May, 1933.

Princeton which O'Neill had briefly attended in 1906, and the play possibly reflects some of his concern over the pregnancy of Kathleen Jenkins, whom he had married in 1909. It is not, however, an auto-biographical play. Jack Townsend, the star baseball player, has seduced a poor girl from the "wrong" side of town. Her pregnancy has necessitated an abortion, and she has died following the operation. This news is conveyed to Jack on the evening of his greatest triumph on the baseball field. Faced by the tubercular brother of the dead girl, Jack admits his guilt. While the undergraduates chant his praises beneath his dormitory window, he expiates his guilt by suicide.

Jack's explanation of his role as seducer is rudimentary, yet with it, O'Neill appears to attribute the operation of fate to something more than such social circumstances as crushed Tim and Rose. Drawing a distinction between his love for his fiancée and for the dead girl, Jack exclaims,

> Do you suppose it was the same man who loves Evelyn who did this other thing? No, a thousand times no, such an idea is abhorrent. It was the male beast who ran gibbering through the forest after its female thousands of years ago. [154]

Jack's primitive chromosomes have left him powerless to guide his destiny, much as the diseased condition of society in *The Web* leads to Rose's downfall. Jack's fate, however, is determined in his blood, in the primitive inheritance that has soiled his essentially noble nature.

The conception of male beasts on the Princeton campus, having no foundation in visible reality, is probably to be attributed to the reverence for the primitive that O'Neill had found in Jack London's writings on the atavistic nature of men and dogs in such novels as *The Call of the Wild* and *Before Adam*. Yet London's Buck heeded the call of the wild for more convincing reasons than did Jack Townsend, and, as if he were bolstering a not very convincing ethnological thesis, O'Neill attempts to view his action in a frame of social reference similar to that which he could have found in Dreiser's *Sister Carrie*. O'Neill, however, is unable to approximate Dreiser's massive analysis of social problems and their effect on his characters' conduct and fate. His effort is confined to a contrast between Jack and the dead girl's brother, Joe Murray, who comes menacingly

from the slums to confront Jack with his guilt. The brother is whining and weak; that he has tuberculosis indicates that he is doomed.
His contrast with the golden boy is sharp, but O'Neill intended to
show that both are bound for the same depressing destiny. The comparison made, however, O'Neill drops it. He does not approach social protest, nor does he suggest any remedy for the inequities of
class. In the end, withdrawing from any large view of the social
opposition he has sketched, O'Neill makes Jack's suicide a matter of
merely private expiation.

The inward turn of the final moments is reminiscent of *The Web*.
Jack's death, like Rose's blind silence, is an acquiescence to fate. It
differs only in that it is not preceded by the confessional moment of
understanding. Lacking a partner to serve as priest, Jack's confession
becomes a mere acknowledgement of wrongdoing, and his pain, such
as it is, is unalleviated by understanding. With a certain courage
that lifts the play slightly from the merely pathetic, Jack goes alone
to his death. Much later, Lavinia in *Mourning Becomes Electra* will
move into the Mannon house to face her dead. Jack takes the first
tentative step in that lonely direction.

Solitary expiation of guilt, divorced from those questions of social
evils raised in the course of the action, is the concluding event of
two of the three sea plays in the *Thirst* volume: *Warnings* and *Fog*.
Warnings is the less effective. It tells of a ship's wireless operator,
Knapp, who is driven by poverty to continue in his work after he
has learned that he may become totally deaf. The moment inevitably comes when the ship is foundering. Having failed in his duty,
he refuses rescue when it comes and kills himself on the sinking
ship. The play's central situation was quite possibly suggested to
O'Neill by Joseph Conrad's *The End of the Tether*. Captain Whal-
ley in Conrad's story is driven by financial need to continue in command of his ship after he has become totally blind. When the ship
sinks, he, like Knapp, refuses rescue and dies. The resemblances,
however, lie only in narrative circumstance. O'Neill appears to have
distilled the melodrama from Conrad's tale with none of its sense
of heroism or moral point.*

---

* O'Neill, however, was fascinated by his story and returned to it again in 1918, re-
casting the plot as a patriotic short story. See below, p. 98.

Warnings is sharply divided between the sensational shipboard action and a long expository introduction laid in Knapp's home. In the first scene, Knapp's poverty is set forth in detail. Interminable scenes in which Knapp's wife and children complain of their poverty are brought to focus when Knapp determines to leave the sea because of his incipient deafness. At this point, in a long scene that perhaps owes something to Strindberg's portraits of nagging wives, Mrs. Knapp draws the utilitarian moral of the episodes already enacted: that Knapp cannot find other work at his age, that without his support, the family must face starvation, and that he is not economically in a position to do what is morally right.*

At the time he was writing the play, O'Neill was acting to a limited extent the role of the young radical. He had met Jack Reed on a foray into Greenwich Village, and it is said that he at one time intended to accompany Reed into Mexico to cover the Mexican revolution for a New York magazine.[8] Nothing came of the venture, but on May 17, 1914, the New York *Call* published his poem *Fratricide,* protesting vehemently against the incipient war between Mexico and the United States. The workers of the world are to be called to shed blood for Standard Oil and Guggenheim. They must not do so. The grandiloquent conclusion exhorts them:

> Comrades, awaken to new birth!
> New values on the tables write!
> What is your vaunted courage worth
> Unless you rise up in your might
> And cry: "All workers on the earth
> Are brothers and WE WILL NOT FIGHT!"**

Mrs. Knapp's reaction to her poverty reflects something of the same conventional radical ideology expressed here through the representations of her desperate condition.

* The play is O'Neill's first depicting family life. The embittered mother and the father viewed as a failure bear no resemblance to the two older Tyrones. Their names, however, are those of the Tyrones, James and Mary.

** Quoted in Ralph Sanborn and Barrett H. Clark, *A Bibliography of the Works of Eugene O'Neill* (Random House, New York, 1931), 117. For all O'Neill's sympathy for his Mexican brothers, he saw them only in the abstract. When he dealt with them in drama, in a one-act farce called *The Movie Man,* written in 1914, he saw them in terms only of stereotypes. The play posits that two representatives of "The Earth Motion Picture Company" go to Mexico and suborn a comic Mexican general to stage real battles for their cameras in return for ammunition and liquor. The play has understandably been forgotten.

> God knows your salary is small enough but without it we'd starve
> to death. Can't you think of others beside yourself? How about me
> and the children? What's goin' to buy them clothes and food? I
> can't earn enough, and what Charlie gets wouldn't keep *him* alive
> for a week. . . . We owe the grocer and butcher now. If they
> found out you wasn't workin' they wouldn't give us any more
> credit. And the landlord? How long would he let us stay here?
> You'll get other work? Remember the last time you tried. We had
> to pawn everything we had then and we was half-starved when
> you did land this job. . . . [72]

The chronicle of misery is nearly endless, the implication clear: the
workers are oppressed beyond their capacity to endure. Anchored
in character, the social views seem somewhat less superficial in their
presentation than in *Fratricide*'s outcry against a capitalist war, yet
essentially they lead nowhere. In the play his wife's complaint lends
substance to Knapp's dereliction of duty. His choice made, there remains only to show the catastrophe. The second scene, however, remains a purely theatrical anecdote having little to do with the play's
earlier economic and social perceptions. While it might be argued
that Knapp's fate has been brought about by economic pressures,
O'Neill does not draw such a moral. In his final moments, Knapp
makes no mention of his wife and children. His guilt overwhelms
him, and, like Jack Townsend, he becomes his own judge and exe-
cutioner. As in *Abortion* the latent social conflict is forgotten, obliterated by private guilt.

In *Warnings* and *Abortion*, O'Neill hangs indecisively between
two conceptions of fate, the one a consequence of social determin-
ism, the other the product of psychological forces moving within
the individual. The same tension is apparent in *Fog*, but in this
play an explanation for the disjuncture is that *Fog* is the first "autobiographical" play. Here, for the first time, O'Neill gives way to his
impulse to use the stage for self-portraiture, turning away from the
explanation of human misery in the world to seek it in melancholy
personal introspection.

Fog, like *Warnings*, is a sea tale, presented this time not realistically, but in a manner reminiscent of Strindberg's symbolical plays.
It tells of a Poet, a Business Man and a Peasant Woman drifting
in a lifeboat on a fog-shrouded sea. The woman, who does not speak
during the play, clutches her dead child. An ocean liner is on the

way to rescue them, but as they hear its whistle, the lifeboat scrapes against the side of an iceberg. Fearing that the rescuers will themselves collide with the ice, the Poet prevents the Business Man from crying out for help. Ultimately the rescuers are guided safely through the fog by the miraculous crying of the dead child. As the castaways move toward the rescuers, they discover that the child's mother, too, has died. At this point, the Poet turns back, and as the play ends, sits silently watching the dead with "eyes full of a great longing."

Evidently conditioned by the uproar following the sinking of the *Titanic* a year before its writing, the play manages to project some of the reality of the situation. Its most notable achievement, however, is in the creation of an atmosphere appropriate to the supernatural conclusion. At curtain, the boat with its passengers looms darkly through the fog, "A menacing silence, like the genius of the fog, broods over everything," [85] and, as the action progresses, a pale dawn accentuates the solitude of the figures. The iceberg, when it appears, is like "some horrible phantom of the sea." [99] With such scenic effects, O'Neill's imagination reaches beyond the capacities of any stage that might have been available to him, yet he is clearly justified in doing so by the use he makes of the setting. As he did in *A Wife for a Life,* he here tries to make it an integral part of his theme. The entire success of the play depends on the establishment of the mood of the sea, the fog and the ice. That mood, in turn, appears to have been sensed from a reading of Samuel Taylor Coleridge's *The Ancient Mariner.*

In 1924, O'Neill was to adapt Coleridge's poem for the Provincetown stage. It was an unsuccessful, belated reflection of his youthful admiration for the work. *Fog,* borrowing Coleridge's images of mist and snow and "ice, mast-high," is perhaps more responsive than the later play to the Coleridgean mood. Coleridge's re-creation of the sea's mystery enables O'Neill to project something of the inner quality of the experience he is narrating, and to create an appropriate setting for his death-ridden Poet.

Against the haunted background and in the midst of the miraculous action,* however, the dialogue of the two men sounds out-

---

* The rescuers who are guided to their destination by the crying of a dead child are also to be found in Chaucer's *Prioresse's Tale.* That O'Neill had read Chaucer is doubtful; nevertheless a source tale may be suspected for his story.

of-key. It is oddly Shavian in its subject if not its tone. The Poet takes the view that the death of the child is for the best:

> Could you conscientiously drag him away from that fine sleep of his to face what he would have to face? . . . The child was diseased at birth, stricken with a hereditary ill that only the most vital men are able to shake off. . . . I mean poverty—the most deadly and prevalent of all diseases. [88]

He suggests that all men are responsible for the miserable condition of humanity, a position which the Business Man quickly rejects. The Business Man is no more than a cartoon, and the Poet's arguments annoy him without touching him. At the end, after he has displayed his craven nature by attempting to hail the approaching steamer, he is allowed to pass from the action, puzzled by the mystery of the child's cry, but essentially unshaken in his position. His arguments for capitalism have had no substance, his character no force in the play.

The Poet's arguments, clichés that they are, gain little from the lack of significant opposition, yet it is not the quality of the argument that matters. Burdened with a sense of the futility of human life and the ineffectiveness of social remedy, he turns to the dead, longing for death like Larry Slade in *The Iceman Cometh*, because of his discouragement with social causes. The Poet's death wish, however, is not really explicable on the basis of the discussion which has preceded its appearance. It is a private emotion, the result of complexities of personality rather than a result of social despair. Even as he speaks his stock radical phrases, he reveals a personal revulsion against life. The play would have it otherwise, but the Poet seeks death because of what he, not the world, is.

The poet who first emerges here is to reappear frequently in O'Neill's dramas, and it is well to look at his face. It is an oval face, "with big dark eyes and a black mustache and black hair pushed back from his high forehead." [90] Photographs from this period make clear that these features, especially the dark eyes, the mustache and high forehead were the notable attributes of O'Neill's own face. The temperament and the views similarly reflect the mixture of radicalism and romanticism that O'Neill possessed and recapitulated in the self-caricaturing portrait of Richard Miller in *Ah, Wilderness!*

Such identification in so slight an instance is difficult to substantiate, and, were it not for O'Neill's known habits of self-portraiture in central roles in his later dramas, the suggestion would be untenable. In *Fog*, there are no biographical details of the Poet's life provided that may be compared with the facts of O'Neill's life. Yet the poet who dreams on death appears so regularly in the O'Neill canon, and in the end is drawn in such complete and identifiable detail, that this early anticipation of the later self-images may be taken as the first of the many dramatic projections of O'Neill's self.

Gratification of an autobiographical impulse perhaps explains why a tension exists between the social criticism and the mysterious, quasi-poetical exploration of death. The first is simply something to talk about until the significant action develops with the coming of the rescue ship. The second, to whose reality the details of scenery, the mood and the personality of the one vital character contribute, is more eloquent. Melancholy, unmotivated longing for easeful death is the heart of the play. Originally generated in his reading of the poems of Dowson and Swinburne, the poets dearest to O'Neill's most unambiguous self-portraits, Edmund Tyrone and Richard Miller, and colored by the dark response to life which many adolescents hold as they come alive to the world about them, the desire for death was yet to O'Neill more than a mawkish pose.

By drawing himself as the Poet in *Fog*, O'Neill attempted to give form to an impulse within himself, but the dark substance of the character, all that he could at first discover, was insufficient for understanding. Twice he had been thrown to the edge of death; in his writing now, what he was doing was in part finding his way back to life. Death for him was much more than a darkness of thought. There were few external aids to his attempt to understand himself. The fashion for Freud was not yet at the full in the United States. O'Neill's analysts were fin de siècle poets, to whom he responded gratefully for more reasons, perhaps, than most young men of his time. They alone gave voice to his sentiments, and following them, he to an extent rejected the intellectual possibilities of both life and art, seeking instinctively for meaning in the recesses of personality where inexplicable, unverbalized feeling concentrates.

To be sure, a superficial connection may be made between the condition of society as the Poet images it and his desire to lose himself in the limbo of fog and ice. Yet it is not to the end of social criticism that the symbolic details of the setting are finally devoted. They serve as did the details in *The Ancient Mariner*, and as similar developments of setting in *The Emperor Jones* were to do, to project the inner substance of the central character, and, doing so, they move the play away from its realistic moorings toward expressionism. The play does not quite cast free from realism. The characters move in a comprehensible context of space and time which necessitates their behaving in a realistic manner, but the impulse to move behind appearance is present in the play and arises from O'Neill's effort to place his own emotion directly on stage.

Thirst, although strikingly similar in design to *Fog*, is much more frankly experimental in its use of the stage. Three people from widely separate social levels—a Mulatto sailor, a Dancer and a Gentleman—are cast away on a raft. Now instead of the Ancient Mariner's fog, there is a Coleridgean sun, glaring down. Heat waves writhe upward from the deck of the raft, and circling the castaways are sharks whose fins can be seen cutting the water. As in *Fog*, what O'Neill asks for is a scrupulously realistic décor, but the setting is intended to suggest something of the essential horror of thirst as well. The play, although it is not marked by such tension as *Fog* revealed between social criticism and private emotion, is both realistic and abstract. Curiously, when the play was produced by the Provincetown Players in 1916, William Zorach, the group's designer, attempted to treat it in a stylized manner. Feeling that stage designs should be less realistic, more "like art," he proposed setting the play against a background of formalized waves. His attempt to lead O'Neill into the young world of the Art Theatre was ended by the director George Cram Cook and by John Reed, who insisted that O'Neill was a realist and demanded that the waves be made of "realistic" painted canvas, animated in the Monte Cristo tradition by a stagehand wriggling about underneath.[9]

The stylistic quarrel could not easily be resolved within the context this play offered; indeed, its resolution was to wait until almost the end of O'Neill's life. In *Thirst*, however, it was not an aesthetic dilemma. The play is neither realism nor symbolism but a somewhat dismaying mixture of both. Its story of the efforts of its three characters to survive in a hopeless situation is one more tragedy of "ironic fate," in which all perish. The characters are intended as representatives of three of the world's estates, but no general meaning finally evolves. Instead their minimal psychological realism involves them in an intricate tangle of relationships that proves finally to be merely anecdotal. They mean nothing as symbols, and as individuals, their passion, like the sea on which they float, is crumpled canvas. They follow an entirely predictable course from elegance to shark bait, with side orders of madness, miscegenation and cannibalism.

Yet again, there are hints of something further. *Thirst* reveals more clearly than its companions that O'Neill is moving toward an understanding of what he meant by "an ironic life force." In *Thirst,* it is clear, the sea somehow controls the destinies of the castaways. The sun that parches them is likened to "the great angry eye of God," [3] a symbol of destiny. The tendency to personify the sea's force revealed in *Fog* is made even clearer in *Thirst.* The image of the eye of God, owing something, perhaps, to Stephen Crane's red sun pasted in the sky like a wafer, to Conrad, and certainly to Coleridge, suggests that O'Neill seeks theological explanation of man's destiny in the personification of natural forces. It is a step beyond the "personification of the ironic life force" whose secret Rose alone knew—at once more specific and more adequate in concept. The generalized sense of the fog as being in some way a visualization of the limbo the Poet sought is now made less passive and atmospheric. It becomes more directly controlling. The sea's heat drives the Dancer mad; the Gentleman, the most civilized of the trio, fights the elements that seek to control him; the Mulatto sailor (a role played by O'Neill in the play's only recorded production) accepts his lot and is content to drift with the sea, taking what comes. He dies because the Gentleman attacks him and both fall overboard. Yet, O'Neill suggests, without the accident, he might have survived through simple acquiescence to the power personified in sea and sun. It is a rudimentary statement at best, yet the conception that there is a power like a God's in the forces of the sea initiates O'Neill's theological explorations.

In the two longer plays of the period, *Servitude* and *Bread and Butter,* O'Neill makes more ambitious efforts at argument, but he does not materially advance the bill of particulars already set forth. Of the two, *Servitude* is the more sustained intellectual effort. It is strongly influenced by Ibsen and Shaw and represents work in a genre that O'Neill did not frequently elect: the domestic drama.

Servitude is what Shaw would have called a "disquisitory" drama debating the role of women in marriage. David Roylston, a playwright, has written eloquently of the need for women to assert their individuality so that they may become something more than married chattel. Strongly influenced by Roylston's Ibsenesque morality, Ethel Frazer has left her husband and sought the playwright, asking for further guidance. She tells him,

> I was in love with an ideal—the ideal of self-realization, of the duty of the individual to assert its supremacy and demand the freedom necessary for its development. You had taught me the ideal and it was that which came into conflict with my marriage. I saw I could never hope to grow in the stifling environment of married life— so I broke away. [237]

Nora, slamming the door on Torvald Helmer, has run straight to Ibsen, who, as *Servitude* has it, is no more emancipated than Pastor Manders. To teach him to have the courage of his morality, Mrs. Frazer tries to make him see that his own wife has been forced to serve him as a kind of bondswoman. Mrs. Roylston, Patience's monument, will have none of such teaching. She is content to sit in her husband's shadow, type his plays, and lend substance to his mask. What began as an account of the "New Woman" of Ibsen and Shaw is, by the final curtain, converted to a sentimental version of *Candida*, arguing that marital happiness lies in the placid acceptance of bondage.

Roylston is brought to see his indebtedness to his wife:

> I've lived with her all these years and forgotten how much I owed to her. She has protected and shielded me from everything—made my opportunities for me, you might say—and I took it all for granted—the finest thing in my life! Took it all for granted without a thought of gratitude, as my due. Lord, what a cad I've been! What a rotten cad! [293]

"Happiness," Mrs. Frazer tells him, "is servitude."

"Of course it is!" he replies enthusiastically. "Servitude in love, love in servitude! Logos in Pan, Pan in Logos! That is the great secret—and I never knew!" [294]

The insight is very nearly unavailing, since Mrs. Frazer's husband arrives with gun in hand, prepared to kill Roylston, his wife's suspected lover. Quickly won over to the prevailing acceptance of things as they are, he and his wife go happily off, leaving the Roylstons united anew in firm understanding.

"Don't you know it was your duty to claim your right as an individual," David asks her, "to shake off the shackles my insufferable egotism had forced upon you? Don't you understand that you have stifled your own longings, given up your own happiness that I might feel self-satisfied?"

Mrs. Roylston is given the curtain line: "That was my happiness," she says primly. [303]

O'Neill's view of marriage as happy bondage anticipates the matrimonial concepts set forth in *The First Man, Welded* and *Strange Interlude.* In none of the later plays, however, is he so satisfied with the idea of Pan in wedlock's Logos as he here appears to be. In the next five or six years, Strindberg, whose influence in 1914 is with one exception lightly felt, would take firm hold of him and cause him to assert emphatically that marriage is made in hell. At this stage in his career, however, he is ready to see marriage not as a web, but as a relationship that promises an all-embracing good.

The condition of being described as "Pan in Logos" means, presumably, that within the frame of marriage men and women can learn to achieve a Dionysian ecstasy. The phrase comes from the second part of Ibsen's *Emperor and Galilean,* at the end of Act III where it refers to the relationships between the Dionysian commitments of Emperor Julian and the Christian view of life.* O'Neill's use of the phrase has little bearing on Ibsen's meaning. His understanding of Pan comes perhaps as much from Nietzsche as from Ibsen or Shaw, for in his domestication of the concept, he appears to mean that in marriage, the Roylstons must submerge their individualities by an ultimate act of will which is in itself a denial of will. Happiness is to be found in an unthinking acceptance of one another that destroys all separateness and leads to a "Dionysian" ecstasy of belonging.

The concept is tentative and interesting less for what it initially is than for what it rejects of Ibsen and of Nietzsche. Shaw found

* In an article entitled "Ibsen and O'Neill, a Study in Influence" (*Scandinavian Studies,* August, 1965, Vol. 37, No. 3) Egil Törnqvist argues what is probable that O'Neill took the phrase from Ibsen via Shaw's *Quintessence of Ibsenism.* Shaw quotes the passage and explicates its meaning at length.

in Nietzsche a vocabulary and to a degree a philosophical position to aid him in his quest for ways to remedy society's problems. The controlled, conscious, self-liberated "New Woman" that Shaw devised, following Ibsen, became Doña Ana searching for the father for the Superman. The power of mind to seize and guide the power of unconscious life caused Shaw to develop aspects of the Apollonian mode of being as set forth by Nietzsche. Yet O'Neill, rejecting Shaw and Ibsen, also rejected the Apollonian aspects of Nietzsche, finding greater good in the subjugation of consciousness, in forgetting, in participating in the Dionysian rhapsody he felt might be discovered in suburban marriages. Pan, not Apollo, in Logos is what O'Neill seeks in this cursory anticipation of later full-scale treatments of the unknowable life force.

O'Neill's choice contains the elements of a paradox. For a young radical to reject the positive social recommendations of Ibsen and Shaw in the interest of justifying on philosophical grounds the routine of nineteenth-century marriage has two possible explanations. The first is that such a justification was a staple commodity of turn-of-the-century theatre in England and America. Yet the play has a more ambitious intellectual argument than most pretending to debate the subject, and the conservatism of O'Neill's solution has perhaps a more significant explanation than that of theatrical tradition.

In the majority of the plays already examined, O'Neill has set forth certain social evils as an integral part of his theme, yet he has concluded his examination by turning away from attempted solutions, leaving his characters immersed in themselves, heedless of the world about them. The plays have a contracting action, moving from a reasonably wide perspective on the affairs of men to a private world where a final, individual action must be played out, often without an antagonist. At the end of each play, the sense is conveyed that the central character is gripped by a force whose presence he dimly feels and to which he belongs. Except for the Poet in *Fog*, the characters do not seek to identify themselves with the force or to immerse themselves completely in it. Yet its power underlies their action, as his primitive bestial impulses drove Jack Townsend to sin. Its presence puzzles the will and serves to vitiate any social protest the plays might have made. Will, however, is antithetical to happiness. The only value in will is to cause a man to subject himself to the power that owns him, as the Roylstons appear to do at the end of *Servitude*. As yet, the idea is incompletely seen, unlocated and for the most part unnamed—although O'Neill's use of Dionysian vocabulary suggests that a name is not far to seek. The tracings are prophetic of the themes of O'Neill's first mature dramas.

In *Bread and Butter* O'Neill takes a very different view of marriage. Modeled after Strindberg's denunciation of the marital state, the play expands its focus to include a depressing picture of its hero's attempts to live a creative life in a middle-class American society.

John Brown is the youngest of three sons of a Connecticut hardware merchant. At thirty, the oldest brother, Edward, is a conventional adherent to the ways of the town's best people. He is an alderman, on his way to becoming mayor, and has hopes of holding yet higher office. The second son, Harry, is a rounder who frequents taverns and brothels, living a life of good-humored dissipation. There are two sisters, Mary at twenty-eight already confirmed as an old maid, and Bessie, a vivacious youngster, a year older than John.

> [John] is an altogether different type from the other members of the family; a finer, more sensitive organization. In appearance he is of medium height, wiry looking and graceful in his flannel clothes of unmistakable college cut. His naturally dark complexion has been burnt to a gold bronze by the sun. His hair, worn long and brushed straight back from his forehead, is black, as are his abnormally large dreamer's eyes, deep-set and far apart in the oval of his face. His mouth is full lipped and small, almost weak in its general character; his nose straight and thin with the nostrils of the enthusiast. When he experiences any emotion his whole face lights up with it. In the bosom of his own family and in the atmosphere of their typical New England fireside he seems woefully out of place. [9]

John has been destined by his father to study law, but he rebels at entering college. He wishes above all things to paint. His fiancée, Maud Steele, persuades Brown's family that he should be permitted to follow his own bent, but it is soon apparent that her sympathy for his artistic leanings rests in the hope that John will become a successful commercial artist.

In Greenwich Village, John, living with three other painters, comes into inevitable conflict with both his family and the Steeles, who wish him to return to Connecticut, marry and settle down. The conflict is defined by his teacher, Eugene Grammont:

> Mon Dieu, but our friend John seems to have a hard fight before him. It is too bad. Never in my long experience as a teacher have I met a young man who gave finer promise of becoming a great artist—and I have taught many who are on the heights today. He has the soul, he has everything. . . . And behold these worshipers of the golden calf, these muddy souls, will exert all their power to hold him to their own level. . . . And I am afraid they may succeed if, as you say, he loves one of them. He is not one of the strong ones who can fight against discouragement and lack of appreciation through long years of struggle. He is all-too-sensitive and finely-keyed. I have noticed of late how his work has fallen off. It is as if the life and vigour had departed from it. His mind has not been able to joyfully concentrate on the Art he loves. [22]

Later, one of John's roommates apostrophizes:

> It would be God's blessing for John if the Old Master [Grammont] were his father instead of the present incumbent. Why is it fine things like that never happen? . . . Even his name—John Brown! Isn't that the hell of a name for an artist? Look better at the top of a grocery store than on the bottom of a painting. The only thing recorded in the Book of Fame about a John Brown is that his body lies moldering in the grave—nice thought, that! [24]

The worshipers of the golden calf go strenuously to work. They brush aside his protests that children are not the possessions of their parents and return him to his home and to Maud's arms and a job in her father's store.

The fourth act describes the results of his weakness. John makes the rounds with Harry, and Maud takes consolation in the company of Edward, who has loved her over the years. Unable to stand John's moral decline, she nags him incessantly. In reply, he tells her that they are "two corpses chained together" and begs for a divorce. She refuses and continues to berate him until in a frenzy he leaps at her and begins to strangle her. Stopping just short of murder, he rushes upstairs and puts a bullet through his head. At curtain, Maud runs screaming into the street.

In several ways, *Bread and Butter* is the most uncharacteristic play of the group. There are resemblances, of course, to the other works: the emphasis on the need for individual freedom to pursue a creative life recalls certain of the early arguments in *Servitude,* and the animosity displayed toward the materialists has a parallel in the view taken of the husband in *Recklessness* and the Business Man in *Fog*. The play, however, contains none of the concept of ironic fate, nor the sense that a blind spirit controls the affairs of men. There is no expression of the Dionysian immersion of the will,* and, for once, O'Neill does not permit the social context of the play to give way to private exploration.

Nevertheless, the play holds in it much that formed O'Neill's sense of himself. John Brown is O'Neill's second attempt at self-portraiture. His face corresponds in most details to the face of the Poet in *Fog* and to O'Neill's own appearance. John's association with his brother Harry parallels Eugene's own relationship with his easy-living brother, Jamie, and the initials of one of his loves, Mai-belle Scott, are perpetuated in the name of his heroine. Accounts of that early romance suggest that O'Neill, as a young, "artistic," non-conformist, frequently stepped on the toes of proper New London society in his pursuit of the girl.[10] The specific biographical reflections are less of concern, however, than are the qualities with which O'Neill invested his theatrical alter ego.

However mawkishly, John Brown anticipates the later heroes who waste away in spirit because they cannot obtain adequate nourishment for their desires in their world. Robert Mayo of *Beyond the Horizon* and Dion Anthony of *The Great God Brown* are cut to the same pattern as John Brown. Although the later conflicts are more complex, the similarity among the characters is strong. Each of the three is married to a woman who has a little beauty but who is incapable of understanding her husband's deepest need. Ruth Mayo and Margaret Anthony both fail the test of sensitivity to which their husbands bring them, as Maud fails John.

Thus isolated at home, the heroes of the later plays when they move in the world are brought into conflict with another man who

---

* The only hint of any of these concepts passes without comment in the fourth act. On the walls of his home, John has hung two of his canvases, *"in the Impressionist style, a landscape and a seascape."* The paintings are emblems of what John has lost, Samson's locks hung as trophies in the Philistine tents. They represent the dream unfulfilled, a power unused, an ungratifiable longing, but their subject has a potential significance beyond the frame of the play. Shortly, in *Beyond the Horizon*, O'Neill will find the sea and the land to be the poles of man's being, epitomizing the forces to which he belongs. The beginning of this concept is here mutely set forth in the images that dominate the room where John is destroyed.

epitomizes social values hostile to the protagonist. As a foil to John stands his brother Edward, complacent, self-centered, destructive. In similar relationship to the later heroes stand Andrew Mayo, Robert's brother, and William Brown, Dion's partner. In *Bread and Butter*, the hero's opponent is scarcely a serious antagonist. His function is generally to define at close range the world to which John Brown has committed himself and in which he must move as an alien. By the light of this figure, the consequences of John's choice are fully revealed. He stands condemned as a man who has failed to follow his destined course and who thus has deserted his sole good. In such action, delineated sketchily here in the antagonism between the sensitive and insensitive denizens of a commonplace world, O'Neill was later to find the central tragic pattern of his early successes.

Against the background sketched here, O'Neill wrote *Bound East for Cardiff*, the play he was to offer two years later to the Provincetown Players, during their second season on Cape Cod. The other plays of the crew of the *S.S. Glencairn* were not to be written until the Playwrights' Theatre had provided him with his first stage, but *Bound East for Cardiff*, as a part of the cycle, ranks with O'Neill's established work, rather than with his juvenilia. Its seeming maturity, however, does not mean that it is substantially different from the other work of 1914. What it manages to do is to draw into focus most of the tendencies revealed in the others, to capitalize on the technical devices developed in them and to discover a center of meaning which was not merely the result of post-adolescent attitudinizing. That it attains such concentration, economy of means, and significance generally is attributed to the fact that O'Neill was for once following Hamilton's advice and writing of the life he knew. Certainly some of the sailors on the *Glencairn* are drawn from life and the details of shipboard existence seem authentic. Yet there is in this play a quality of verisimilitude that none of the other sea plays of this year even partially possesses. It is not enough to know how a thing looks; to project it on stage, to convince an audience of its reality, a writer must understand its nature. What makes the play convincing is not so much what O'Neill knew from his experience as a sailor, but rather what he learned about that experience from reading the novels of Joseph Conrad.

Bound East for Cardiff takes its reality from Conrad's *The Nigger of the Narcissus*, a work O'Neill had read in 1911, shortly before he set to sea.[11] O'Neill's experience at sea enabled him to confirm the truth of Conrad's account of the sailor's life, but the rendering of that truth, the way of giving it dramatic reality was learned not at sea but through Conrad's artistry. At least through 1920, with the writing of *"Anna Christie"* in its final form, the impact of Conrad on O'Neill's work was deeper than that of any other writer. In Conrad, O'Neill first discovered a mature articulation of his instinctual sense of man's destiny—the concept of men moving in the pattern established by an elemental force to which they belong and by which they are controlled in spite of the pressure of their individual wills. To Conrad also is to be attributed O'Neill's first attempts to write dramas that depend less on intricate narrative and clever characterization than on that quality Conrad sought to achieve in *The Heart of Darkness*: "It was no longer a matter of sincere colouring. It was like another art altogether. That sombre theme had to be given a sinister resonance, a tonality of its own, a continued vibration that, I hoped, would hang in the air and dwell on the ear after the last note had been struck."[12]

To enter the forecastle of the steamer *Glencairn* is to meet the brothers of the crew of the *Narcissus*. O'Neill, perhaps more conscientiously than Conrad, has provided a variety of racial types, a liberal sprinkling of Scandinavian and British seamen as the core of the watch, together with a sufficiency of other nationalities to suggest a microcosm on shipboard. Lacking the irony and the romance with which Conrad illumines his characters and setting, the occupants of the forecastle are nevertheless the same toiling, unthinking group as are to be found aboard the *Narcissus*. Like Conrad's Belfast, O'Neill's Cocky tells his tall story as the action opens; complaints are registered against the officers and the food; and the major action is counterpointed against the discordant commentary of the Cockney sailor.

Both works turn on the death of a crew member suffering from damaged lungs. James Wait and Yank are not by any measure the same man, nor are the issues raised by their deaths similar except in the unifying sense of awe their deaths evoke in their companions. Yet O'Neill has felt the force of Wait's long journey to death and has caught some of its quality in his charting of Yank's drifting course along the boundaries of consciousness. Both men recoil from the thought of being buried at sea, and both in the end mistake death for physical darkness, Wait in his request that the cabin lamp be lighted, Yank in complaining that the fog has entered the fore-castle. Where Wait dies in the midst of a calm that breaks as his body is given to the sea, Yank's last moments are spent during a fog that lifts when he has died. Yank complains of the "rotten" night, of the steamer's fog warning sounding incessantly: "I wish the stars was out," he tells his friend, Driscoll, "and the moon, too; I c'd lie out on deck and look at them, and it'd be easier to go—somehow." [489] His hatred of the oppressive enclosure of the forecastle seems to reflect the constant contrast drawn in the novel between the stifling interior life of the crew's quarters and the wider, more open life on deck.

Such parallels as these are inexact and might be merely fortuitous were it not for the relation of the sailors to the sea—a relationship that holds the largest meaning of both works. To Conrad, the mem-bers of the crew are "the everlasting children of the mysterious sea," a phrase which gave the title *Children of the Sea* to the first Ameri-can edition of the book. The men are ignorant and insignificant, and the sea is unfaithful to them. Their difficulties cannot be de-fined: "The problems of life seemed too voluminous for the narrow limits of human speech, and by common consent it was abandoned to the great sea that had from the beginning enfolded it in its im-mense grip; to the sea that knew all, and would infallibly unveil to each the wisdom hidden in all errors, the certitude that lurks in doubts, the realm of safety and peace beyond the frontiers of sorrow and fear."[13]

Later, in *"Anna Christie,"* O'Neill was to write more explicitly of the governance of the sea, but implicitly in the dialogue between Yank and Driscoll the same emphasis is made as in Conrad. What the two men have in common is the life the sea has shaped for them. They have followed a derelict course: "one ship after another, hard work, small pay, and bum grub; and when we git into port, just a drunk endin' up in a fight, and all your money gone, and then ship away again. Never meetin' no nice people; never gittin' outa sailor-town, hardly, in any port; travelin' all over the world and never seein' none of it; without no one to care whether you're alive or dead." [486] As Yank says, "There ain't much in all that that'd make yuh sorry to lose it." The farthest reaches of their thought is to consider finding a small farm where they may forget the sea. Yet the expression of this rebellious wish is followed by a passage of reminiscence in which both men take a kind of toughly sentimental satisfaction as they remember the stag films in Barracas, the brawls in barrooms, the smells and the swindles, the drunks, the arrests that have provided the substance of their lives. However sordid their lives have been, the two men have achieved a kind of satisfaction in it.

Remembrance ends with Yank's death. From the center of his fear emerges his wish to die on deck under the stars and moon. Were the sea clear, Yank could find death easier and agree more readily to the destiny which has been his. At the end there is kindness for him. As he dies he sees standing before him the figure of "a pretty lady dressed in black." In *The Web* the form of the personification of the life force Rose saw was unspecified. Yank's hallucination is of the same nature as Rose's, but the image is clearer and is stated in the action. In *Bound East for Cardiff*, the life force lies in the sea. None of the crew has life other than that which the sea has provided. The life it has given it also controls and can end at will. As the sea crushed out Yank's life, so it will claim the lives of all those who sail on it. The sailor's desire to leave the sea is willless hope, a sentimental illusion that can never be brought to reality. To personify such a force as a pretty, mourning woman is startling, yet not inappropriate. Its sentimental suggestions can be credited to the same desire for gentility that causes Yank to regret not meeting "nice people." It is a vision in accord with his character. As symbol, however, it further suggests that the sea is ultimately kind, that it receives its own gently and that it mourns for them. Moreover, it mourns as a mother mourns, for in O'Neill, as in Conrad, the sailors are its children. *Bound East for Cardiff* was first copyrighted under Conrad's title, *Children of the Sea*.

In drawing a picture of men bound in life and death to the sea, O'Neill relies on Conrad for one further suggestion: that men caught in a common destiny find in their relationship with one another a bond that gives value to their existence. In the play, under the compression of the single act, the discussion between Yank and Driscoll, in large part a monologue by the dying man, must serve to establish the sense of communion. Yank's memories, to which Driscoll assents both in monosyllabic words and in the silent strength of his grief, cause them both to realize the force of the bond holding them to one another. The mute, rough guards down, the world reduced by the fog to a lighted circle, the two men at last express understanding and a common good. Dramatic compression causes the scene to fringe on the sentimental as Conrad's account never does. Slowly, around the death of Wait, Conrad builds the sense of men drawn together in ignorant understanding of a mutual problem and is saved from sentimentality by the deliberately paced, implicit development of his narrative and by the irony that the character of the Nigger casts over the common purposes of the men. Yet it is the same point, developed by O'Neill in terms of the isolated confessional moment that is characteristic of many of the earlier plays.

O'Neill is unable, of course, to project so vividly as Conrad the sense of the ship moving across an immense and mysterious entity. Yet with the fog, the chiaroscuro effect of his lighting, and with the ironic pattern of sound created by the warning whistle, an accordion player, the crew's laughter and the cry of "All's Well" from the watch, O'Neill has attempted to establish in dramatic terms something of the reality of a ship and its environment.

To read *Bound East for Cardiff* together with its companion plays is to view it as something of a lucky strike. Yet it is not essentially different from the other plays and could easily have lost itself in their excesses. Like the others, it starts out to be a tragedy of "ironic fate," and it too centers on a duologue spoken in isolation, the voices emerging from a small area of light in a world otherwise dark. Hardly heard, half-understood, the voices speak in semi-soliloquy and in monologue, but the speakers are led to a partial comprehension of their circumstances and to some acknowledgment of their worth. Only in this last particular does *Bound East for Cardiff* differ from the others. That difference, which centers in the discovery that the men belong to the sea, is attributable to Conrad's perception about the relation of men to sea in his novel.

O'Neill was probably not entirely conscious of the implications of his play. The conception that men are or can be controlled by a powerful natural force underlies *Thirst* and *Fog*, but in neither play is it so marked as to approach an aware perception. Certainly it is not there clear that man's acquiescence to the force creates a sense of "belonging" from which arises a positive good, bringing order and meaning to life.

Yet the positive assertion—that men are not alone because they belong to the sea—is what rescues the first *Glencairn* play from the excesses of the other one-acts. Although it is imperiled by sentimentality, as the other plays are wrecked by melodrama, it is saved from disaster by the finer perception of both particular and general truth. O'Neill's observation of sailors' ways led him to depict them faithfully. The recollected experiences of Yank and Driscoll are in large measure O'Neill's own and are as convincing as faithful recording of fact can be, but these are wrought into a true line of dramatic action by the need both the characters have to grope toward a discovery of an underlying truth in their lives. O'Neill had tried before to present such truth, but hitherto, he had managed only a negative statement: Ironic fate crushes men. In the other plays, the characters have been victims whose circumstantial defeat has made them objects of so little concern that melodrama has been repeatedly used to evoke even the most superficial pity. Yank and Driscoll do not need such transfusion, and they surmount pity to call forth a true sympathy both for their particular circumstances and for the general view of man that Conrad helped O'Neill to understand.

Bound East for Cardiff can thus be seen to draw to partial fulfillment those elements of his craft with which O'Neill was natively endowed and for which he found reinforcement in the writing of others. By temperament he was a realist with a strong feeling for the influence of place on men's lives, something of a pessimist with a young man's readiness to explain tragedy too easily as "ironic fate." He had an ear for the vagaries of human speech, especially in marked forms of dialect, and he followed a poetic impulse that revealed itself not so fully in words as in stage images created by lighting and patterns of sound. Finally, he was a dramatist less concerned with sociological, more with psychological truths. This is the portrait which the plays of 1914 draw, and it is one of considerable quality. It is, indeed, a portrait of an artist.

In view of the achievement of *Bound East for Cardiff*, its sureness of effect, its nearly professional artistry, it is curious that almost two years lapsed before O'Neill moved ahead along the lines the sea play projected. The explanation, if explanation is possible, is that shortly after he wrote it he went to Harvard to study in George Pierce Baker's playwriting classes, "The 47 Workshop." He submitted *Bound East for Cardiff* with his letter of application for admission. Although Baker accepted him, he told O'Neill that the work was not a play at all. O'Neill, as he later told Barrett Clark, "respected his judgement."[14]

II

THE STUDENT
1915-1916

PLAYS WRITTEN IN 1915 ARE
The Dear Doctor (destroyed)
A Knock at the Door (destroyed)
Belshazzar with Colin Ford (destroyed)
The Sniper
The Personal Equation

PLAYS WRITTEN BEFORE THE SUMMER OF 1916 ARE
Atrocity (destroyed)
The G.A.M. (destroyed)
Now I Ask You

1914—That fall, O'Neill, following a high aesthetic line, entered the haven for all would-be playwrights, George Pierce Baker's "47 Workshop" at Harvard, "determined," he said, "to be an artist or nothing." His earlier formal education was limited but adequate: Catholic boarding schools and academies, followed by a semester at Princeton University from which he was suspended for academic malingering. Thereafter he began his nomadic adolescence, but in or out of school he read and educated himself with Jack London, Stephen Crane, Frank Norris, Nietzsche, Ibsen, Strindberg, Dostoevsky, Conrad, and, as his narcissistic fin-de-siècle pose suggests, Dowson, Wilde, Edward Fitzgerald, Francis Thompson, Baudelaire. He stayed at Harvard only a semester and then moved to Greenwich Village, where his friends included a gang of criminals, "The Hudson Dusters," and a collection of Village intellectuals: Jack Reed, his mistress, Louise Bryant, Mary Heaton Vorse, Maxwell Bodenheim and the anarchist Terry Carlin. With them, O'Neill espoused political and social causes and deserted for a brief time the posture of a poet.

To O'Neill, who had so long lived outside the frame of any establishment, entering a directed course of study undoubtedly seemed a more decisive commitment than it in fact proved to be. With the sponsorship of Clayton Hamilton and financed, however grudgingly, by his father, O'Neill enrolled in George Pierce Baker's class in playwriting in the fall of 1914. By attending Harvard, he was in effect asking again what he had earlier asked of Hamilton: "How do you write a play?" His work in Baker's classes showed him that he already knew, or was close to knowing, the only answer he could accept to that question.

He reacted to the Harvard atmosphere by playing the heller from New London, Connecticut, rubbing against the grain of the school's respectability. His comment on the work of a fellow student, "Cut it to twenty minutes, give it a couple of tunes and it's sure-fire burly-cue,"[1] suggests a tendency on his part to dazzle the dutiful. Yet in his own way, in class, he too was dutiful. His letter of application for admission is a model of grammatical respectability ("My father is James O'Neill, the actor, of whom you may perhaps have heard . . ."), and it displays a fearful sincerity ("With my present training I might hope to become a mediocre journey-man playwright. It is just because I do not wish to be one, because I want to be an artist or nothing, that I am writing you."[2] Once admitted, he followed Baker's teaching scrupulously with one clear result: Whatever talent he had shown was all but wiped out as he worked to achieve what Baker called "dramatic technique."

In his maturity, O'Neill was never very specific about his reaction to Baker's work. Writing a memorial statement at the time of Baker's death, he spoke gracefully of the teacher's sympathetic response to his students, but his words do not suggest any deep-seated obligation:

> It is difficult in these days, when the native playwright can function in comparative freedom, to realize that in that benighted period a play of any imagination, originality or integrity by an American was almost automatically barred from a hearing in our theatre. . . .
>
> In the face of this blank wall, the biggest need of the young playwright was for intelligent encouragement, to be helped to believe in the dawn of a new era in our theatre where he would have a chance, at least, to be heard. And of the rare few who had the unselfish faith and vision and love of the theatre to devote their life to this encouragement, Professor Baker's work stands preeminent. . . .
>
> Not that the technical points, the analysis of the practice of playmaking taught in his class, were not of inestimable value to us in learning our trade. But the most vital thing for us, as possible future artists and creators, to learn at that time (Good God! For anyone to learn anywhere at any time!) was to believe in our work and to keep on believing. And to hope. He helped us to hope—and for that we owe him all the finest we have in memory of gratitude and friendship.[3]

Around Baker's name there clings an aura of academic martyrdom. His struggle with the Harvard authorities to persuade them to accept a course in playwriting as valuable to the disciplines of a university led him finally to leave his position and to go to Yale University, where he became instrumental in founding the Yale School of Drama. He was a man who believed in what he did, fought for it and communicated a belief in its worth to his students. No doubt a sense of rebellious purpose burned in them all, and from that fire came the hope of which O'Neill spoke.

In Baker's classes, therefore, O'Neill was no heller. He was attentive, cooperative—a dark, aloof, silent, absorbed listener. He participated fully, and he conscientiously attempted to put into practice Baker's recommendations. They were, after all, supposed to turn him into an artist of the theatre, as Baker's star pupil, Edward Sheldon, author of *Salvation Nell* and other successes, had been metamorphosed from student to professional a few years earlier. So he followed the rules and wrote, and what has survived is dreadful—without question the worst writing he ever did. Its interest, even in the light of plays to come, is negligible. All that can be seen in the scripts is the struggle of a not apparently talented man, possessed of a shockingly immature view of human nature, to fabricate a narrative that might operate on the stage. Ironically, for the only time in his life, O'Neill became what he went to Harvard to avoid becoming, "a mediocre, journey-man playwright."

Baker's theories of playwrighting are contained in his book *Dramatic Technique,* published in 1919. The book is a reworking of class notes and lecture material delivered in 1913. In his introduction, Baker acknowledges that his book is more apparently dogmatic than his classes were in practice. He notes that the principles he annunciates must be adapted to individual needs, and that it is not intended "to replace wise classroom instruction."[4] His sense of academic cause is expressed at the outset, as he notes that the dramatist, who is popularly held to be born, not made, is denied "the instruction in art granted the architect, the painter, the sculptor, and the musician." In the same paragraph, in a phrase presumably designed to impress his academic colleagues, he speaks of "the science of drama-making."[5] What follows, with extensive illustrations of good and bad procedure, is a detailed discussion of the problems of writing a realistic play in the manner of Arthur Wing Pinero. To a student who felt that Pinero had achieved the summit of dramatic art, the book was undoubtedly useful, even liberal, for Baker is at pains to point out that after a dramatist is experienced in the practices he describes, he may break from them, "at times," to achieve his ends.

To Baker, the drama is an impersonal art and should be entirely self-contained, without novelistic intrusions by the author. The essential purpose is "to create an emotional response in the audience," and dramatic action, which he calls "illustrative action," must be devised so as to convey emotion accurately.[6] To develop these concepts, he sets forth what appear to him to be examples of good and bad dramatic practice. Characterization must be created from convincing motivation and adequately developed transitions, and "A play which aims to be real in depicting life must illustrate character by characterization which is in character."[7] Narrative arrangement must be interesting and clear. Dialogue, whose three essentials are "clearness, helping the onward movement of the story, and doing all this in character," should possess "charm, grace, wit, irony or beauty of its own."[8] A dramatic narrative involves the development of confrontations or discoveries—which Baker calls "situations"—and he illustrates the process in a long analysis of the nineteen "situations" in the second act of Pinero's *The Magistrate*, concluding that "Certainly Sir Arthur knows how to 'hold a situation.' "[9] He advocates a method for preparing a script that O'Neill followed all his life, suggesting a draft of a scenario for "clearness," and to ascertain that the play has "good construction and correct emphasis." The scenario is followed by a series of drafts which in each revision improve characterization and make dialogue attractive, and with which the dramatist "shapes his material more and more in relation to the public he wishes to address."[10] At the stage door, Baker abandons his pupils. What goes on thereafter is not to his interest, nor, perhaps, within the range of his knowledge.

To be fair to Baker, it must be remembered that his chief interest was in the efforts of his students in the classroom. His flattering attention allowed even the dilettantes among them to be taken seriously. However, except for mechanical suggestions, it is not clear that he led them to any vision. His book is limited to a laborer's craftsmanship and is notable for being entirely uncritical, entirely unaware of the major currents that moved both in the world at large and on the turn-of-the-century stages. By 1919, any man alert to the theatre who was not bound by the heaviest commercial fetters should have been aware of the turn the American theatre was taking toward the provinces of art. More importantly, a man assuming Baker's responsibilities should have seen the forces defined in the theatres of Europe since before the beginning of the century. There were numbers of texts to evoke awareness. Sheldon Cheney's *The New Movement in Theatre* had been published in 1914, and was followed, three years later by his *The Art Theatre*. In 1913, Huntly Carter's *The New Spirit in Drama and Art* offered a detailed and copiously illustrated analysis of European stagecraft. In 1914, Hiram Moderwell's *The Theatre of Today* discussed at length the artistic and intellectual roots of the contemporary drama, not only with reference to theatrical and scenic innovations, with which the other writers had been largely concerned, but also to such playwrights as Tolstoy, Chekhov, Gorky, Strindberg, Bjørnson, Molnar, Wedekind and many lesser writers. All of these men are unmentioned by Baker, who with a kind of lazy eclecticism, illustrates his principles of technique with examples drawn from Pinero, Edward

Knobloch, Bulwer-Lytton, Shakespeare and Tennyson's *Becket*. Shaw and Ibsen are perfunctorily treated, but Baker shows no awareness of their difference even as craftsmen from the other dramatists he mentions. Whether the art of the drama—as opposed to a mechanically perfect script—was discussed in the classroom cannot be ascertained; the presumption is that it was not. The point at this remove is unimportant, except that one of his students found no light while he sat in Baker's classroom. O'Neill, before he came to Baker, had read Nietzsche, Schopenhauer and Strindberg, and, with a generous assist from Conrad, had written a play whose essential nature Baker was not equipped to understand. Within a decade he was to write dramas that would demonstrate decisively the jejune nature of Baker's idea of technique. Yet for a semester, O'Neill obediently followed Baker's precepts.

At Harvard, O'Neill completed three plays and collaborated on a fourth. Of these, *The Sniper*, in one act, and *The Personal Equation,* in four, survive. The others were *The Dear Doctor,* a one-act comedy based on a short story O'Neill later discovered to have been pirated from a vaudeville sketch, and *Balshazzar,* a Biblical drama in six scenes which he wrote with a fellow student named Colin Ford. Immediately after leaving Harvard, and still under Baker's influence, he wrote a pantomime, *Atrocity,* and two one-act comedies, *The G.A.M.,* whose subject was the I.W.W., *A Knock at the Door,* and the sole surviving work from this period, a four-act satire, *Now I Ask You.* Also showing signs of Baker's teaching is a scenario probably completed in the spring of 1917, entitled *The Reckoning.*

Each of the extant plays has a strong narrative line, is scrupulously plotted, establishes strong "situations," based on sudden disclosures, theatrical confrontations and surprising turns of plot. The dialogue is developed with care and with some attention to its "beauty." O'Neill has been at pains to provide each work with exciting "curtains," and has striven toward situational ironies that, however, lie at a far remove from the ironic world view he had tried to formulate in *The Web*.

The Sniper is perhaps closest to his beginning work. It tells of a Belgian peasant, Rougon, whose family has been killed by invading German armies. In sorrow and rage he becomes a sniper, but is caught and executed. The story of the small man struggling in a web of circumstance is reminiscent of that of *The Web,* but the play rides heavily on its combination of gunfire and lamentation and seeks to develop a strong coup de théâtre from Rougon's discovery that his wife and his son's fiancée, whom he had thought safe, have been caught in a German cross fire. The work is little more than an anecdote, illustrative of the atrocity of war, intended to appeal to an audience's horror at the Prussian "rape" of Belgium. The Province-town Players produced *The Sniper* once, in February, 1917; thereafter, like O'Neill's other "war" plays, *The Movie Man* and *Shell-Shock,* it was advisedly forgotten.

The Personal Equation, although more elaborate, is at heart no better. It tells the story of Perkins, a mild-mannered second engineer on a trans-Atlantic liner, his son, Tom, and Tom's mistress, Olga Tarnoff, a beautiful anarchist. In order to strike the spark that will set off a worldwide strike of the workers, Tom agrees to dynamite the engines of his father's ship when it docks at Liverpool. The explosion will be the signal for the "International Workers of the Earth" to seize power from the labor unions and lead the world from slavery. Tom in disguise ships on the voyage, but as the liner docks, war breaks out in Europe. The working men refuse to back the I.W.E., but Tom agrees, with the help of his more radical ship-mates, to wreck the engines. Olga, disguised as a man, arrives on the ship, and it is revealed to the audience that she is to bear Tom's child. The play's climactic "situation" is the confrontation of Tom and his father in the engine room when Perkins is forced to shoot his son to save the engines. The last act presents Tom, reduced to idiocy by the bullet, in a hospital bed across which Olga and Perkins effect a reconciliation, agreeing to devote their lives to caring for the invalid:

PERKINS   Look! He's awake again. He's looking at us. (*They both go to the side of the bed*)

OLGA   (*Tenderly*) Poor little child! (TOM *reaches up and takes one of her hands*) See! He's taken my hand. (TOM *holds his other hand out toward his father*) He wants to take yours. (PERKINS *puts his hand in* TOM'S. *He and* OLGA *look at each other in wonder across the bed.*)

PERKINS   (*In stifled tones*) Tom! (*To* OLGA) Do you suppose—he understands?

OLGA   Yes, I feel sure he does.

PERKINS   Then—he has forgiven me.

OLGA   He has forgiven *us*. (TOM *lets both of their hands go and turns his eyes again to the ceiling*) [IV, 16]

A final scene attempts to cap this moment of hope and heartbreak with a passionate anti-war speech from Olga that ends with her crying "Long live the Revolution." Tom hears her words and mimics them with a *"low, chuckling laugh."* His vacant eyes turn from side to side and *"a stupid smile plays about his loose lips. . . . Olga stares at the figure in the bed with fascinated horror—then covers her face with her hands as the curtain falls."* [IV, 20]

O'Neill's attempt to duplicate the ending of *Ghosts* leaves everything to be desired, yet the drawn-out reconciliation scene is precisely the sort of "situation" Baker advocated. Attempts are made to follow such pieces of Baker's advice as to work in exposition naturally, e.g., "Tell me about [your father]. I'm interested. We've been together for nearly half a year now and you hardly ever mentioned him except to say he was second-engineer on the San Francisco." [I, 10] O'Neill has tried to make his dialogue clear, in character and beautiful:

OLGA   . . . To me the birth of a child is a horrible tragedy. To bring a helpless little one into a world of drudgery and unhappiness, to force upon it a mouldy crust of life—what heartlessness and needless cruelty! There are much too many of us here already. No; I will wait until life becomes a gift and not a punishment before I bestow it upon a child of mine. I will offer no children to Moloch as sacrifices. (TOM *stares at the floor but does not answer— a pause*) Make me a better world, O Husband-Man, and I'll be proud and not ashamed to bear children.

That O'Neill was not always able to sustain such a level of eloquence is suggested by Tom's reply:

TOM   (*Frowning*) I was only asking you to consider the possibility. [I, 8]

Dialect was another of Baker's ways of beautifying dialogue. Aside from several forms of American English, O'Neill writes for people speaking in dialects reflecting their backgrounds in Germany, Scotland, Ireland, Holland and Great Britain, including Cockney. Although he handles the talk of the crew with a sense of authority, the effect is not always felicitous, as in this speech of an I.W.E. chief:

HARTMANN   Nein. [The next war will not be fought in] Mexico, or this coun-
           try—yet. That, in truth, would be horrible enough, but this, that
           is more terrible a thousand times. It will all the nations involve.
           (*Nodding his head*) Over there—in Europe. Too long have the
           jealous dogs growled over their bones. This time, I fear, they will
           fight. If they do—(*He makes a hopeless gesture*) it will be the
           smash-up, le debacle. And our cause will most of all suffer. The
           revolution will be fifty years put back. [I, 12]

So far as the rules permitted, O'Neill tossed into the play much
that appears to have been of momentary concern to him, but very
little that was to become of serious interest.* The ideas of Shaw and
Nietzsche, together with a wide variety of hazily understood anarchist pronouncements, can be traced in the pages. For example, at
one moment, Olga relies on *Thus Spake Zarathustra* to express her
hope for her child: "I'll bring up our child with a soul freed from
all adorations of Gods and governments if I have to live alone on a
mountain top to do it." [III, 8] Or again, a version of Shaw is put
into an anarchist's mouth: "At the end of my supposititious war of
manly extermination there will be ten or twenty womanly women
for every unmanly man who has refused to die on the field of honor.
Yet breeding must go on. The women, above all, will demand it.
The new race must be created to enjoy the new freedom." [I, 18]
Such talk vies with melodrama to capture the audience's interest.

In retrospect, it is possible to see that some elements of the play—
involuntary gestures, really—will prove serviceable when couched in
sharply different forms. The line "The soul of man is an uninhab-
ited house. . . ." [I, 13] foreshadows faintly the Mannon mansion
in *Mourning Becomes Electra,* just as Tom's comment about "the
contrast between us grimy stokers and the first class cabin people
lolling in their deck-chairs" [I, 20] anticipates *The Hairy Ape.* In a
comedy scene between Perkins and his housekeeper, there is a suggestion of the relationship between Chris and Marty Owen in *"Anna
Christie,"* and Perkins's love for his engines hints at Reuben Light's
love of the dynamo: "I was lonely—after [my wife] died. That's why
I came to love the engines so." [II, 13] His seeking out the engines
as a love object may even suggest in the dimmest outline Ephraim

---

* At one point, a Nihilist speaks of the possibility of creating "a new art, a new
ideal—perhaps even a new theatre." [I, 18] The last five words are deleted in the typescript, presumably as out of character.

Cabot's groping movement toward the barn in *Desire Under the Elms* after he tells his wife of his loneliness.

The most important thematic anticipation is the conception of the "hopeless hope," which O'Neill was to develop three years after writing *The Personal Equation* in *The Straw*. At the end of the play, the Doctor has told Olga and Perkins that there can be no hope for Tom to regain his sanity, but he admits that in cases of the sort no sure prediction can be made. Thus, although he refuses to give them hope he does not finally deny the possibility of Tom's recovery. After their reconciliation, Olga tells Perkins, "We'll take good care of him together, you and I, and we'll fight for that one hope the doctor held out. Who knows? It may be a real hope, after all." [IV, 16] The concept embodies the seed of not only *The Straw* but such later works as *Hughie* and *The Iceman Cometh,* but its first appearance is only a mitigating moment of optimism in O'Neill's dubious tableau.*

The Personal Equation is a work of rich complexity compared to *Now I Ask You,* although the latter is in a conventional sense a better made play than its predecessor and has a certain interest in that, along with *The Movie Man,* it is the only surviving comedy from O'Neill's early years. It opens with a prologue that offers a startling coup de théâtre. A young girl is alone in a darkened room. In the hallway offstage, a man and woman call to her and leave the house. She takes out a revolver and presses it against her body. As the curtain descends sufficiently to obscure the stage, a shot rings out. The action that follows is antecedent to the prologue:

Lucy Ashleigh is engaged to Tom Drayton, a "clean, wholesome young American." Unfortunately, Lucy is foolishly given to pursuit of the latest intellectual fads. In the present instance, following Nietzsche, whom she has read avidly, she believes that marriage is slavery and that free love offers the only possibility of a right relationship between a man and a woman. Tom, who has been warned

---

* Louis Sheaffer indicates possible autobiographical elements in the relation between Tom and his father. Sheaffer points out that Tom's contempt for his father's thirty-year servitude as second engineer parallels O'Neill's contempt for his father who had appeared as the Count of Monte Cristo for the same period. As Sheaffer sees it, the relationship in the play reflects O'Neill's opinion that his father should have been a first-rate, rather than second-rate actor. (Cf. Sheaffer, 307)

by Lucy's mother to pretend to take Lucy seriously, accepts Lucy's suggestion that they bypass the wedding ceremony. Lucy's bourgeois origins, however, make her mistrustful of unlicensed sex, and she decides to marry Tom, provided he will sign certain articles of agreement, such as "For sociological reasons I shall have no children," or "I may have lovers without causing jealousy or in any way breaking our compact." [I, 27]

Three months later, when Lucy and Tom are married, they are visited by Leonora Barnes, a "synchromist" painter,* and Gabriel Adams, a poet. Whereas in the first act, Lucy dressed herself and behaved as if she were the excessively melancholy heroine of a Russian novel and quoted Strindberg to the effect that the "daughter of Indra discovered the truth. Life is horrible, is it not?", [I, 17] in the second she is playing Candida—in her relations with Gabriel—and Hedda Gabler—in her relations with Tom. She admits to a fascination for "General Gabler's pistols" and longs for someone to come with vine leaves in his hair. That person, for her, is Gabriel, a spoiled, conceited, pompous sponger, apparently living in sin with Leonora in a Greenwich Village studio, but in fact married to her.

Gabriel, a wolf in Marchbank's clothing, makes love to Lucy: "Can't you read the secret in my heart? Don't you hear the song my soul has been singing ever since I first looked into your eyes?" [II, 18] Inevitably Tom interrupts the love scene, quarrels with Lucy, but then, guided by Mrs. Ashleigh, pretends to develop an affair with Leonora, who has been attracted to Tom because he is like Nietzsche's "Big Blonde Beast."

By the third act, Lucy has become bored with Gabriel and unhappy about Tom's betrayal of her. As Tom and Leonora leave for the theatre, she takes out the pistol as if to shoot herself. Again the curtain drops as at the end of the prologue and the shot is heard. When the curtain rises again, Lucy is lying on the floor. The cast quickly assembles, discovers that Lucy is not injured and that the pistol was not loaded. The shot, it is quickly explained, was really a tire blowing out. The chauffeur, who within the space of perhaps

---

* Baker, in discussing techniques of characterization suggested that "lifelikeness" of a character must be achieved by supplying detailed bits of activity illustrating his characteristics. Leonora, at her entrance into Mrs. Ashleigh's elegant drawing room, rolls her own cigarette, smokes it in an ivory holder and illustratively crushes out the stub on the carpet.

ninety seconds has set a pit-stop record brings the repaired tire into the living room so that O'Neill can have his curtain line:

LEONORA   (*Turning to* LUCY *and pointing dramatically to the tire*) General Gabler's pistol! Fancy that, Hedda! [*Epilogue,* 3]

If it be asked why Lucy should be humored, rather than spanked, O'Neill's answer is ready to hand. As Mrs. Ashleigh explains matters to Tom, the "young, wild spirit of youth . . . tramples rudely on the grave-mound of the Past to see more clearly to the future dream." She admits that in most the spirit fails as they grow older, but in some "it becomes tempered to a fine, sane, progressive ideal which is of infinite help to the race. I think Lucy will develop into one of those rare ones." [I, 13]*

Leaving Harvard did not clear the Baker virus from his system. A scenario of 1917 called *The Reckoning* shows him once again attempting to write a play in the manner of "The 47 Workshop." The script was to consider the rise of a young ruffian to an important Senatorial position. The hero has made a girl pregnant, and in a quarrel with her stepfather, fells him with a hammer. His sweetheart causes him to believe he has murdered the older man, arranges his escape and then forces him to marry her. His guilt causes him to reform his way of life and his exemplary conduct ultimately leads him to Congress. At the play's end, as the Senator prepares to make a decisive speech urging the entry of the United States into the War, his son discovers the truth. A long reconciliation scene follows, bringing a promise of happiness all around. In the general development of its rags-to-Congress narrative, the story is reminiscent of two works by O'Neill's most successful predecessor in Baker's classes. Edward Sheldon's *The High Road* details a girl's climb from a low position to one of extraordinary prominence in political circles, and his *The Nigger* presents a politician faced with a sudden, personal dilemma that threatens to interfere with his career on the eve of an important political occasion. In the scenario, however, O'Neill re-

---

* Agnes O'Neill took up *Now I Ask You* after O'Neill had laid it aside. The play was copyrighted in 1917, but in 1920 and 1921, two letters from Agnes O'Neill to her husband indicate that she is working on the script. The first, an undated letter written probably in 1920, during the time that *Beyond the Horizon* was in rehearsal, promises Eugene that he will like the last act. The second, written January 10, 1921, states that she has welcomed his suggestion that she get to work on the script as a "great stimulus." The correspondence is in the Harvard University Library.

vealed nothing of major moral or social concern. It promised nothing, and the play was, wisely, left unwritten.*

Taken as a group, the Harvard plays are remarkable in two ways. The first is that they reveal the author's continuing susceptibility to outside influence, both from other dramatists and from theorists of the theatre. O'Neill's willingness to follow the lead of another had been anticipated by his imitations of Jack London and Conrad in his first works. Yet his surrender to Baker's teaching to the point where it completely eradicated his own impulses was of another order of magnitude than his borrowing of congenial themes or story ideas. Nietzsche, Strindberg and Ibsen were already his intellectual mainstays. To treat them as materials for mockery, as he did in *Now I Ask You,* was in effect to make of them little more than George Cram Cook and Susan Glaspell made of Freud in their farce, *Suppressed Desires.* The act was a kind of self-betrayal which could have silenced him before he started. He was insecure—especially as he turned from his early picaresque career to a life of the mind. Yet to accept without qualifications not only the ideas of craftmanship but the literary and dramatic tastes that Baker offered was excessively naïve. He was not a child; he was twenty-eight years old, theoretically an experienced man. Yet he entered Harvard as if it were wonderland and did as he was told. Later he appears to have seen what had happened. Toward the end of 1916, he undertook to pay a somewhat slavish tribute to one of the gods who had suffered because of his iconoclasm. In imitation of Strindberg's *The Stronger,* he set to work on *Before Breakfast,* a play that like *Now I Ask You* is concerned with Village Bohemian life, but one which is opposite to it in tone, emphasis and notably in technique. It was a deliberate form of atonement, an attempt to free himself of the effect of such counsels as Baker gave him, and it succeeded in redirecting his creative work toward less alien country. In the end, the flirtation with Baker did not matter. He threw the influence off easily, but his acceptance of Baker's ideas and methods pointed to a danger. Later, the influence of Kenneth Macgowan was to have the same conse-

---

* Agnes O'Neill developed the play and in 1924 copyrighted it as "The Guilty One" under the pen-name Eleanor Rand. Optioned by William A. Brady, it was never produced.

quences of nearly ruining him as a playwright, for he accepted Macgowan as readily, as naïvely, as he accepted Baker.

To speak of warped intentions and diminished powers is to imply
further that the Harvard plays form a negative example of the
important fact suggested by the plays of the *Thirst* volume, that
O'Neill's style and statement are inextricably interwoven. Neither
in essence nor in appearance do the Baker plays have any quality
that can be called "O'Neillian." Except when drawing the crew of
the liner in *The Personal Equation*, O'Neill wrote as a stranger to
himself. However imitative, his earliest works were clearly his own
in manner and substance. Although they did not succeed, they
sought to illuminate an inner world wherein, for O'Neill, drama lay.
Perhaps the most readily apparent difference in the Harvard works
is the way that O'Neill creates an external world for the action. In
none of them is there a use of psychological space—that effect of a
world contracting around the characters, of a world that has meaning only in relation to what they are. Instead, O'Neill painted a realistic canvas and set his characters in front of it, giving it a literal,
temporal and sociological realism that has no hint of the lyric use
of setting, ultimately to become one of his greatest attributes as a
dramatist. Gone too are the patterns of sound and light that emerged
poetically in *Bound East for Cardiff,* and the monologue, with which
O'Neill was to achieve his most satisfactory moments in the theatre,
is unused.

With the basic elements of his theatrical style eliminated, the
characters that they had been designed to project also disappeared.
The meditative seekers do not appear, nor do the self-portraits that
obligated O'Neill to attempt to portray some true human feeling.
Baker had said that drama was "impersonal," and in these plays the
cardboard impersonality of all the characters is deadly. O'Neill even
betrays his most typical hero, the poet, turning him, in the figure of
Gabriel Adams, to a contemptible charlatan, viewed much as the
philistine businessmen in *Bread and Butter* viewed John Brown.
While it might be said that O'Neill was satirizing bad art in his depiction of the affected Bohemians of *Now I Ask You,* he is at no
pains to suggest that art can be anything but absurd. Without some
standard of measurement, the condemnation of Adams condemns
all art as pretense, all artists as spongers on society.

Under such pressures, his themes shifted. Instead of an exploration of man's inner life, O'Neill attempted to write plays that contain a "political" message, notably in the tentative espousal of anarchist causes in *The Personal Equation*. Here, however, O'Neill revealed himself to be a muddled radical at best. Olga and Tom are shown in the beginning to be dyed in red wool, but as the play progresses, Olga's militancy is softened by her love for Tom and by her pregnancy. She turns to a position which if it is not conservative, is at least much less radical than that which she had earlier held. Tom, she states, was lured into the movement by his love for her and was not really a radical at heart. Thus O'Neill might be said to have upheld the anti-radical nationalism reflected in old Perkins's behavior. Yet, although Olga is "redeemed" in this view, she closes the play with a speech on the value of world revolution and the defeat of nationalism. Let them eat cake and have it, too: the play viewed in terms of its social doctrine makes no sense. It may therefore be questioned whether O'Neill was sure of his own social position, indeed, whether he was clear as to what the anarchist doctrine really involved, beyond what he had picked up in conversations with his friends.*

With little understanding and no firm convictions, O'Neill wrote of material far from his centers of concern. Interestingly, none of the characters in any of these plays reveals a sign of the need to belong to something greater than the world in which he moves. In these plays, there beats no pulse of the life force that has the power of a God; they are spiritually, thematically lifeless. The readiest evidence is provided by a comparison of Olga's speech concerning bearing children** with the words of the Poet in *Fog* on the same subject. The Poet says,

> What chance had that poor child? Naturally sick and weak from underfeeding, transplanted to the stinking room of a tenement or the filthy hovel of a mining village, what glowing opportunities did life hold out that death should not be regarded as a blessing for him! . . . If you could bring him back to life would you do so? Could you conscientiously drag him away from that fine sleep

---

* In Act I, p. 18, after a speech by one of the characters on the value of war as a purgative to old orders, Tom says "with a puzzled look": "That's rank Nihilism." Then he adds uncertainly: "Isn't it?" The lines were deleted in the manuscript, perhaps because the uncertainty was originally O'Neill's.
** Quoted above p. 54.

> of his to face what he would have to face? Leaving the joy you
> would give his mother out of the question, would you do it for
> him individually? [88]

Both speakers protest too much and make their points with excessive emphasis, yet Olga's words are simply false rhetoric, while the
words of the Poet, however mawkish, maintain some control and
suggest a sincerity of feeling that renders them not quite empty.

Setting aside, at Baker's behest, the rudimentary techniques, characters and themes he had begun to explore, O'Neill wrote of nothing
in an imitative style. Baker led him away from all that he believed
and from all human necessities—self-exploration above all—that had
caused him initially to write. Those with talent who followed
Baker's lead found a facile success with Broadway producers, but
such a road could offer nothing to a discoverer like O'Neill. It
was a thoroughly shopped street, offering no possibility of either
poetic or psychological truth. It led away from the sea, as it led from
the self, and O'Neill could not walk down it. At the end of the spring
term in 1915, although he at first intended to return, O'Neill turned
his back on Harvard and disappeared into the Greenwich Village
scene, from whence, a year later, he went to Provincetown, Massachusetts, and from there set out on another road entirely.

III

THE AMATEUR
1916-1917

PLAYS WRITTEN DURING THE LATTER PART OF 1916
AND THE BEGINNING OF 1917 ARE
Before Breakfast
In the Zone
The Long Voyage Home
The Moon of the Caribbees
Ile

DURING THIS TIME, O'NEILL ALSO WROTE
Tomorrow, a short story
The Hairy Ape, an uncompleted short story, now
    destroyed
The Reckoning, a scenario (see Chapter II)

1916—In the summer, O'Neill with Terry Carlin
went to Provincetown on Cape Cod for what became a fateful meeting
with George Cram Cook and his wife, Susan Glaspell.
It was a summer of freedom and excitement. Cook and his friends
seized on O'Neill's youthful plays as part of the bills
amateur actors were staging in a shed on Mary Vorse's wharf.
The venture prospered and the actors, formally organized,
continued as The Provincetown Players in New York.
Success was good, even amateur success,
and O'Neill sensed his power and moved forward with authority.
He fell in love with Louise Bryant, but she ended
the affair and followed Jack Reed to Moscow.
O'Neill turned to a woman who resembled her, a young writer,
Agnes Boulton, who thought him melancholy, strange,
but admired him for the dangers he had passed
as, for example, an able-bodied seaman on the American Line.
His history of tuberculosis kept him from the war,
and, through 1917, he lived alternately in New York
and Provincetown, writing short plays and stories,
two of which were published that year in magazines of quality.
A reputation was clearly in the making, and
professional success lay not so far beyond the horizon.

THE story of the stagestruck amateurs who in 1915 produced two plays on a front porch in Provincetown, Massachusetts, has become part of the folklore of the American theatre. The visitor to modern Provincetown looks reluctantly on quaint gift shops, summer "cottages" and unattractive sand dunes. Nothing there, unless it be the untouched center of the sea itself, remains of the world which, it is now claimed, gave birth to the modern American drama. The activities of the Provincetown Players in their early days are wrapped in a sentimental mist, and memory is tender with them.

There is no reason not to view the Players affectionately, just as any group of theatrical amateurs may claim the charitable sympathy of their audiences. Their story is, in fact, no different from that of hundreds of others throughout the country, whose activities in some measure seem to compensate for a lack of rural folk games. Such groups are summer insects, rippling lightly the surfaces in which they drown. Their conception is in the heat of talk, and they are born amid a drumming of hammers and a frenzied splashing of sizing and stipple. Success is to them as unexpected as failure. Neither profits them substantially, for they are prey to warring temperaments, to disaffection, to economic pressures, to fatigue and, if they find strength enough to survive all these, to professionalism.

Inevitably in such a group, if the energy of idealistic enthusiasm develops into the motivation of conscious purpose, there arises the professional. His appearance spells the end of the fun, even if normal general attrition has not yet set in. The few groups that survive do so because they move rapidly toward the firm grounds of a professional organization.

In the Provincetown Players, the professional was Eugene O'Neill.

Without him, they would have been long forgotten; it is doubtful that they would have survived even one season in New York City. He quickly became their most marketable commodity; his presence defined their aims for them; he was proof of their worth as an organization. Yet he was also their destroyer, for he alone moved in the course of the significant life of the group from amateur to professional.

The Players were determined amateurs. Their early criticism of the Washington Square Players, who had set them an organizational model, was that they had turned too quickly toward professionalism by hiring a director. Later, when both were operating in New York, the Provincetown tended to look down on its rival because the "professionals" kept a press book and invited critics to first nights—actions which revealed something of the business motives of Broadway itself. The attitude of the Provincetown group changed somewhat when they discovered that the Washington Square Players were being credited with the discovery of Eugene O'Neill. Then the press book was kept and the critics invited, and other minor signs of creeping professionalism became apparent.

Yet by 1916, when they moved into Macdougal Street in Greenwich Village, it was probably too late, if ever there had been hope, for them to turn professional as the Washington Square Players were to achieve metamorphosis into the Theatre Guild. A line had been sharply drawn through the center of the organization, and on either side of it stood the two men chiefly responsible for the Provincetown's survival. The extent of the quarrel between the group's leader, George Cram Cook, and Eugene O'Neill is now impossible to determine, but "Jig" Cook's summation of the Provincetown's achievement suggests strongly that he felt O'Neill's success had destroyed the Players. Although O'Neill was what Cook claimed he was seeking, an American playwright of genius, and although he cooperated with him to the full, he was temperamentally unable to come to terms with what O'Neill released in the organization. Cook's was a life of dedication to an ideal that was never fully formulated, a seeker after a shrouded goal, a man for whom the search was more important than the good being sought. Susan Glaspell rightly titled her memoir of her husband, *The Road to the Temple*: it was the road and not the temple that mattered. Speaking of Cook's particular power "to riddle, to defend, to invite," she added: "Sometimes I wish the Provincetown Players had been a magazine."[1] The magazine, she seems to have felt, would have permitted him to experiment in endless amateurism, to live as if he had tasted Ponce de Leon's fountain and was thereafter free to seek perpetually and not to find. It was O'Neill's discovery of his own power, his increasing mastery of the drama, bringing with it new needs and giving to the group new goals, that in the end sent Cook to a self-imposed exile in Greece, from where, whenever he looked back, he viewed the course of the Players with resignation and a touch of bitterness.

What moved Cook in the beginning was probably not the quest for a native playwright or for a native drama. One suspects that this idea—stated as the Players' raison d'être—was formulated to mark a difference from the predilection of the Washington Square Players for foreign plays. In the absence of interesting American playwrights, such a goal was born of necessity, but it continued as a hallmark of their activity as the Theatre Guild. The Provincetown, searching out a cause, joined the hunt for native playwrights, a quest that reaches far back into the history of this country and from time to time has assumed something of the comic proportions of the quest for the Great American Novelist. Before O'Neill, there was no reputable candidate for the dramatic honors, and his existence gave the group's devotion to native drama some validity. Later, Cook was to say that the failure of the Players was evidenced by its inability to uncover other American dramatists of a stature comparable to O'Neill's. As the group came together, however, the stated aim sufficed, and when it moved to New York, O'Neill's suggestion was followed: that the group be called "The Playwrights' Theatre." So far as Cook himself was concerned, however, the purposes of the theatre closest to his heart were less literary.

Cook's interest was caught by idea of theatre as a community. "One man," he wrote, "cannot produce drama. True drama is born only of one feeling animating all the members of a clan—a spirit shared by all and expressed by the few for the all. If there is nothing to take the place of the common religious purpose and passion of the primitive group out of which the Dionysian dance was born, no new vital drama can arise in any people."[2]

His animating idea clearly was not the quest for American drama or even for a theatre. His words, which were accepted as the credo of the Players, center firmly on the idea of the communal spirit.

Unlike the later Group Theatre, Cook fixed no political point of rallying, nor did he advocate such localized aesthetics as gave rise to the rural drama in regional theatres a few years later. What was important was the clan, united in festal ceremony in honor of Dionysius, late sprung up in America. Cook looked upon the theatre as an inevitable ritualistic outcropping of a group so oriented, but for him the group came first, the theatre second. The theatre, he said, was "Work done in the spirit of play," a way of working that had "the only true seriousness."[3] He remained an amateur of theatre and, in the word's French sense, of life. Throughout his active association with them, he sought to maintain the Players as an oasis of spirit in a dusty world.*

Behind his amateurism lay an abiding admiration for Athenian Greece. His was not an antiquary's interest in the past, nor did professional scholarship inhibit his idealistic, visionary attempt to summon to the present, for the spiritual resuscitation of himself and others for whom he cared, something of the qualities he sensed in the Greek Idea. His associate on the board of the Provincetown Players, Edna Kenton, described his enthusiastic purpose: "Back to Greece!—that was Jig's solution for every modern ill. Back, rather, to the spirit of Greece for its lesson, and then a return to re-evoke the group spirit from modern life."[5] In the end, his desire led him away from America, back physically to Greece, where before he died he convinced himself that he had indeed found among the shepherds of Mount Parnassus the community of feeling and endeavor that he called "Greek" and that provided the serenity of his dreams.

The concept of Grecian "group spirit" was supplemented by the writing of Friedrich Nietzsche whom Cook had read with awareness and whose doctrine he preached with enthusiasm. Nietzsche's description of the Dionysian way seems especially to have appealed to him. The worship of Dionysius that underlies the manifesto of the Provincetown Players is as Nietzschean as it is Greek. Nietzsche's popularity in America was high in the second decade of the twen-

---

* Susan Glaspell wrote that "because of his integrity of idea, [the Players'] conspicuous success never made him see as less important the work of those who had not yet succeeded, who might never, in the usual sense of the word, succeed. If certain things we did reached the larger public, then perhaps our intensity should more and more go into the work which also had meaning, but which might be harder to project. The things that others would do were not so particularly our individual job. To *cause* better American plays to be written—that is what he kept saying."[4]

tieth century as English translations of his work began to appear. After 1910, he became required reading for any young intellectual, but Cook had read him in German as early as 1899 and wrote of him,

> Nietzsche brings not only new ethical feeling but new ethical ideas. Not every one has the courage, and ability, to admit these new ideas with no fear or favor, and let them win if they can. But those who do so admit the ideas of Nietzsche find in the fight they wage against old ideas, more drama, more story, more poetry, than is generally found in drama, story, or poetry. . . . The spiritual passion of Nietzsche's writing is too keen, too intense, to be readily endured in those times when life keys one's own nerves high. It is precisely to our times of dulness that Nietzsche offers the sting of his perpetual pain and joy. He is a creator of the creative mood.[6]

Importantly for O'Neill, as well as for the other members of the Provincetown Players, Cook served as Nietzsche's prophet, selecting and teaching those elements of Nietzschean doctrine that best combined with his romanticized view of ancient Greek ideals. By these lights, his theatre was to become a Dionysian outgrowth of classic culture, a theatre truly of the group, amateur in the best sense, and far removed in its ceremonial spirit, in its methods and in its products from the commercial theatres of New York.

Cook gave the group the best he had, both of his dreams and his physical energies. His best was good. He dreamed of a theatre to be built in New York, and, as he planned it, perhaps an analogy with the development of the Greek theatre from ritual dancing places occurred to him, for his theatre was conceived as a sophisticated metamorphosis of the wharf shed at Provincetown on which the Players had first formally convened. He wrote,

> The first stage of the Players on the wharf at Provincetown was in four sections which could be picked up by hand and set at various angles and levels. These reappear in the new stage—four transverse sections lifted or lowered or tilted by obedient hydraulic jacks into a zig-zag ascent, any hillside slope or tower or terrace. The new dome, so planned as not to interfere with a well-equipped fly-gallery (counter weights permitting operation from the stage level), is used in connection with the new structural invention which makes it possible to raise the curtain and play your play in pure space. Nothing is there but infinity and the stage broken into big plastic elements with which you may compose. Also the pro-

scenium. You push a button to make it higher, lower, wider, narrower, shallower, deeper. The four elements combine into one deep stage; they separate into three stages—fore stage, main stage, inner stage, to be used in swift succession of changing scenes—and so restoring to the drama its Elizabethan power of story telling.

Behind, around, above this trinity of stages there is nothing to mask—nothing to conceal—a pleasant symbol of artistic sincerity.

Permitting the swift handling of bulky scenery—as massive as any play may need—this playing space does not compel the use of a single inch of scenery. With flats and drops, flies and borders out, with no surfaces put there to hide other surfaces, the artist of the theatre shall at last be free to let his human figures and chosen objects receive mystically deep significance from their background of infinity.[7]

Cook's projected theatre anticipated, although it may have reflected some of their early talk in this vein, the efforts of such designers as Robert Edmond Jones to build a temple for "the artist of the theatre." Evidently, Cook had heard of the developments of the European theatre which were shortly to revolutionize stage production in the United States. It is an entirely workable idea for a stage. Yet in its "pleasant" symbolism, in its careful practicality concerning pushbuttons, counterweights and obedient jacks, it is a little naïve, the work of a visionary seeking to pass as a master of his craft.

Cook's practical work in the theatre was equally clearheaded, equally amateur. To cite a crucial, but typical example, in 1920 O'Neill showed him the script of *The Emperor Jones,* then titled *The Silver Bullet.* In Cook's view, the play could be staged only against a "background of infinity." Nothing, evidently, was more finite than the tiny stage of the Provincetown Playhouse. Their scenic stock-in-trade had been to that time small interiors giving vistas of too-colorful skies wrinkling above painted ground rows. From Germany, however, had come word of a scenic innovation, a plaster dome, curving to provide an unequaled sense of space, even on a small stage. Against its concavity, light could be played in flexible, infinitely variable combinations, the texture of the plaster providing a reflecting surface for light that no flat cyclorama could equal in depth or subtlety. The dome, Cook realized, was the only means to give O'Neill's play significant scenic realization. Moreover, no American theatre possessed such a device. The temptation to innovation was as great as the artistic purpose, yet the Province-town treasury amounted to $360. Over Cook's instant insistence that the dome be built, the guiding committee of the theatre fell out. Such as it was, the group spirit was severely shaken by simple economics.

Characteristically, Cook walked over the opposition. When Dionysian group spirit became a simple matter of majority rule, Cook turned dictator. Spending such funds as he had for plaster, wire and steel, he built the dome himself. As Edna Kenton tells the story, she went to the theatre to discover Cook at work:

> Jig was there alone, at the back of the stage, in a cluster of steel netting, iron bars, and bags of cement. He was making plaster, in workmen's clothes. I thought of *A Half Hour in Heaven* [a play rejected for the Provincetown theatre because it could not be adequately staged], of God and his angels working in space. Jig was working alone, creating space itself. It was a nice enough little comparison, and I did not miss the irony of it—a dictatorial god . . . "animating the group spirit." In spite of all the dome was going in, Jig's "must" had found its only way.
>
> He looked up as I came down the aisle, then turned his back on me and finished throwing in his batch of mixed plaster. I stepped on the stage and sat down, waiting. He worked slowly until he had finished the work. Then he turned.
>
> "There's to be no argument about this," he said suddenly. "I've had enough from everybody. The Emperor has *got* to have a dome to play against. You see, Edna, it begins . . . thick forest at first . . . steadily thinned out . . . scene after scene . . . to pure space . . ." He was telling me the story and the action and the scene of *The Emperor Jones*, standing against the plaster ellipse that was "space." And as he went on, it began to happen—one of his hours of creative talk of the rarest and finest. . . .
>
> Jig directed the first production of *The Emperor Jones*. I know this because I was there and watched him do it. We were all there, all over the place. The group spirit was rampant, and to play with the lights on the dome was the best game of all.[8]

It is an account revealing in its ironies. The force of Cook's vitality speaks through it, and it shows clearly the reverence he could command. Yet it also betrays something of the amateurism that relies on happy inspiration and the rushing in of fools. Miss Kenton is alive to the irony of the dictatorial God "animating the group spirit," but a still deeper irony lies in the fact that Cook's dedicated efforts to serve O'Neill's play, efforts that brought the Provincetown Players their finest moments, destroyed the theatre for which Cook was both God and day-laborer.

The Emperor Jones was an amateur production of a professional's play. Miss Kenton's assertion that Cook directed the first production reflects a rumor that Arthur Hopkins had taken over the directorial position in the final stages of rehearsals. Whether true or not, many members of the group appear to have felt a need for a professional director. A similar situation developed with the settings against the dome. Having built it, the group was uncertain how to use it most effectively. Cumbersome settings in the usual manner proved so unsatisfactory that a few days before the opening, Cleon Throckmorton was called in to save the situation. His solution was to start over and to use simple cutouts, which, in silhouette against the dome, served to frame the play in space. Thus even in rehearsal, the production requirements of *The Emperor Jones* made clear that Cook's ideal for the Players had never been a substantial, central motive for the group. Evidently, a professional playwright brought with him obligations that amateurs were unable to fulfill, however willing they were to give of their substance for his play's eventual triumph.

After the production had brought world fame to the Players, Cook, for a moment, felt professional longings and so far deserted his ideal as to urge his own play, *The Spring*, for uptown production. Its failure and his own integrity of spirit caused his idealism to reassert itself. He left the United States to live in Greece, from where, in 1923, he wrote the obituary for the group as he had envisioned it:

> Three years ago, writing for the Provincetown Players, anticipating the forlornness of our hope to bring to birth in our commercial-minded country a theater whose motive was spiritual, I made this promise: "We promise to let this theater die rather than let it become another voice of mediocrity."
>
> I am now forced to confess that our attempt to build up, by our own life and death, in this alien sea, a coral island of our own, has failed. The failure seems to be more our own than America's. Lacking the instinct of the coral-builders, in which we could have found the happiness of continuing ourselves toward perfection, we

have developed little willingness to die for the thing we are building.

Our individual gifts and talents have sought their private perfection. We have not, as we hoped, created the beloved community of life-givers. Our richest, like our poorest, have desired most not to give life, but to have it given to them. We have valued creative energy less than its rewards—our sin against our Holy Ghost.

As a group we are not more but less than the great chaotic, unhappy community in whose dry heart I have vainly tried to create an oasis of living beauty.

Since we have failed spiritually in the elemental things—failed to pull together—failed to do what any good football or baseball team or crew do as a matter of course with no word said—and since the result of this is mediocrity, we keep our promise: We give this theater we love good death; the Provincetown Players end their story here.

Some happier gateway must let in the spirit which seems to be seeking to create a soul under the ribs of death in the American theater.[9]

The "richest" member of the group was Eugene O'Neill, and there can be little question that he was desirous of a fuller professional life and greater recognition as an artist than any pseudo-Grecian attempt to realize the Dionysian spirit in Greenwich Village could offer him. Not that fame, as Broadway offered it, was his spur, nor even that Cook's Nietzschean concepts were alien to him. Rather, he reached out for something more than the Provincetown could ever offer, because, as he worked, he began to learn that fine theatre, like any art, involves the total mastery of all relevant disciplines and that, in the end, all serious artists are in the best sense professional.

Without doubt, the Provincetown Players provided him with a convenient standing place. By the time of the opening of *The Emperor Jones* on November 1, 1920, they had staged the original production of twelve of his one-act plays.* In his formative years in

---

* These were, in order of production, *Bound East for Cardiff* (July 28, 1916), *Thirst* (Aug., 1916), *Before Breakfast* (Dec. 1, 1916), *Fog* (Jan. 5, 1917), *The Sniper* (Feb. 16, 1917), *The Long Voyage Home* (Nov. 2, 1917), *Ile* (Nov. 30, 1917), *The Rope* (Apr. 26, 1918), *Where the Cross is Made* (Nov. 22, 1918), *The Moon of the Caribbees* (Dec. 20, 1918), *The Dreamy Kid* (Oct. 31, 1919), *Exorcism* (Mar. 26, 1920).

their theatre, O'Neill evidently had ample opportunity to learn and to experiment. Yet he had other footings. During the same four-year period, the Washington Square Players staged the first production of *In the Zone* on October 31, 1917,* J. D. Williams staged *Beyond the Horizon* early in 1920 with a professional cast, George C. Tyler opened *Chris Christopherson* in an out-of-town tryout the same spring and had also agreed to produce *The Straw,* well in advance of the triumph of *The Emperor Jones.* With the exception of the *Glencairn* plays and *The Emperor Jones,* O'Neill's most ambitious work depended for its hearings on the professional managers, Tyler and Williams. Nevertheless, the Provincetown was his first *atelier,* and in considering O'Neill's development as a playwright, it is important to look at what he was before he met Cook at Provincetown in the summer of 1916, and at what, with his aid, he shortly became. For both the man and the Players, it was a decisive meeting.

In Greenwich Village after O'Neill had left Harvard, his greatest necessity was to unlearn the lessons Baker had taught him. He was far from his mark, the simplicity and directness of *Bound East for Cardiff* forgotten. At first, he worked diligently, writing on the average seven hours a day, but nothing came of it beyond slick trash. Gradually, as his work came to a standstill, his energies flagged, and he fell from his disciplined life into debauchery. He saw much of his brother, Jamie, and found a kind of comfort in the limbo of life that such saloons as The Hell Hole offered him. There, his friends were rough men, truck drivers, gangsters, and down-and-outs who asked nothing of him and in whose company he could neglect his flagging literary career without apology. Elsewhere in the Village, he met Maxwell Bodenheim, Mary Heaton Vorse and the loqua-

---

* The production of *In the Zone* brought the Provincetown Players into sharp rivalry with the Washington Square Players. The latter group courted the critics as the Provincetown, guided by its idealism, did not. *In the Zone* brought O'Neill substantial publicity, such as he had never received from the Provincetown productions of five of his plays. Many members of the Provincetown group felt that they should come into the open, especially when the *New York Times* credited the Washington Square Players with the discovery of Susan Glaspell's *Trifles,* Cook and Glaspell's *Suppressed Desires, Bound East for Cardiff* and *Ile.* Cook protested, but was told in print that "the performances in Macdougal Street are private. To the general public the primary means of making the acquaintance of the work of Miss Glaspell or Mr. O'Neill lay in the production of the Washington Square Players." [Quoted in Kenton, 94]

cious anarchist, Terry Carlin, whom he later portrayed as Larry Slade in *The Iceman Cometh*. Such intellectual pretentions as he voiced were in behalf of anarchist causes, but the mask of anarchy fit him poorly, and he soon laid it aside. His association with Carlin, however, brought him to Provincetown, and through Carlin he was put in touch with the Players.

In the summer of 1915, the group that became the Provincetown Players had begun to experiment with the drama. On the Cape, at first at the home of one of their members, later in the shed on Mary Heaton Vorse's wharf, they had produced four one-act plays, *Constancy* by Neith Boyce Hapgood, *Suppressed Desires* by Cook and Glaspell, *Change Your Style* by Cook and *Contemporaries* by Wilbur Daniel Steele. They had also in a manifesto written by Cook and Hapgood defined their Dionysian concept of drama.

In 1916 the heat of the New York summer became increasingly oppressive, and O'Neill and Carlin came to Provincetown. Returning to the sea shook O'Neill from the creative doldrums into which he had drifted. He began to write more purposively and perhaps purgatively in an effort to rid himself of the Baker virus. The play on which he worked was *Before Breakfast,* a short monodrama, closely imitative of Strindberg's *The Stronger*. It is the first play in two years in which something of O'Neill's authentic voice can be heard. No other, among the plays of this period, so clearly anticipates the next major phase of his career.

O'Neill, before he met Baker, had read and admired Strindberg's work. Years later, in a letter accepting the Nobel Prize, O'Neill mentioned that in 1913 it was his reading of the Swedish dramatist that "first gave me the vision of what modern drama could be, and first inspired me with the urge to write for the theatre myself."[10] In the Harvard year, the inspiration was not strongly felt; Strindberg was not a favorite of Baker. Thus, in returning to an original impulse, and following the pattern of Strindbergian drama so closely, O'Neill appears to have been retracing his steps in search of inspiration he had lost.

What Strindberg's dramas would have meant to a young American writer in the early years of this century is not difficult to imagine. In the naturalistic plays, the extraordinary sharpness of focus, the strength of the major lines of action, the shocking sexuality and the psychological force of the characterization would have combined to make the work of every other contemporary dramatist pallid by comparison. To one like O'Neill, whose taste was for a subject matter much stronger than the routines of sin and redemption that had passed for an image of life in much American theatre, Strindberg must have seemed like Truth's original. In the hidden life of O'Neill's own family, the complex interpenetration of love and hatred, similar to that which he found in *The Father* or *The Dance of Death,* may have lent verification to the Swedish dramatist's view of life. Something of that view he had earlier tried to make his own in the final scene between John Brown and his wife in *Bread and Butter.* That he felt an instinctive, personal sympathy for what he found in Strindberg's work is suggested by the fact that he there portrayed himself as a character caught in a Strindbergian pattern. In *Before Breakfast,* he drew even closer to his model, and again around a self-portrait wrote a deliberate imitation of *The Stronger.*

Compared to its original, *Before Breakfast* is a paltry affair. Like *The Stronger* it is a monologue spoken to a silent listener by a woman who seeks to triumph in a sexual battle. Mrs. Rowland is a slatternly, shrewish alcoholic, whose long uninterrupted tirade inveighs against her husband for his attempts to write, his drinking and his failure to get a job and provide something better for her than the squalid coldwater flat in which they live. She opens his mail and discovers that he loves another woman, maligns her character and continues at length about her unwillingness to give him a divorce. Her husband, Alfred, mute and unseen except for the moment that his hand—"*a sensitive hand with slender fingers*" [629]—reaches tremblingly on stage from the bathroom for some hot water with which to shave, crumbles under the pressure of her words and cuts his throat. The play's ending is identical with that of *Bread and Butter.* When Mrs. Rowland discovers her husband's body, she runs screaming from the room.

O'Neill was far from his model. In effect, he aped the technical manner and the superficies of Strindberg's subject matter but caught none of its sophistication. He missed entirely the essence of Strindberg's dramaturgy—the sharply focused conflict. In this short work, there is no contest. Mrs. Rowland's monologue is only expository, lifeless and static, and, while it manages to depict something of her character, it involves her in no significant action. Such action, such conflict as the play has is left offstage in the bathroom, where Alfred must make the choice between life and despairing death.

Alfred, the poet, is O'Neill's most typical protagonist, and, in miniature, is a self-portrait placed as was John Brown in a chamber of pseudo-Strindbergian horrors. He was well educated at Harvard, but now he passes his days loafing around barrooms, wasting time "with that good-for-nothing lot of artists from the Square" [627] or mooning around "writing silly poetry and stories that no one will buy." [628] His life as it is sketched is close, if not identical, to that which O'Neill lived in the Village, and, in the Provincetown production, the sensitive hand was played by O'Neill in his last performance on the stage.

No doubt at first O'Neill felt that he had caught something of Strindberg's power, and, moreover, that he had stated a truth of his own experience. Yet the neurasthenic self-portrait romanticizes the play, turning it into a routine picture of the artist and the philistine, in a manner totally foreign to Strindberg's unsentimental attitude toward his characters. To a degree, the situation was to continue throughout O'Neill's career. He remained a devotee and champion of Strindberg, and in several plays sought to imitate his subject matter and style. Invariably in these plays he introduced a portrait of himself, as if by placing himself in such a context he could explain something of his own realities. The juxtaposition, however, produces no clarity. The plays move in their emotional content and the general tenor of their sympathies far from their original. For all his admiration, he could not respond to Strindberg with such instinctive understanding as he responded to Conrad. The difference is perhaps that Conrad's work related to a less complex, freer, more exterior phase of his life. Strindberg led him into an area of his personality which until the end of his life he did not understand.

Certainly, by the time of its production O'Neill had lost interest in *Before Breakfast* except as a technical experiment with monologue. In the last analysis, the monologue is an accompaniment to Alfred's unseen crisis. Its weight, rather than its words, drives him to suicide. The weight was what mattered. Edna Kenton quotes O'Neill as wondering "how long an audience will stand for a monologue. . . . How much are they going to stand before they begin to break?" In her words, "He didn't care about the success of the play—he cared only about the reaction of the audience to monologue, trick shocks, trick relief. It was a deliberate experiment for a definite result—the endurance of the audience."[11] *Before Breakfast* is thus the first of O'Neill's experimental plays, his first gesture toward the growing cult of the Art Theatre. Following it were other experiments with monologue in *The Emperor Jones, The Hairy Ape, Strange Interlude* and, at the end, *Hughie* and the final scene of *The Iceman Cometh*. By reason of its technical experimentation alone, it must be considered as of more importance than its content justifies.

Whether O'Neill knew it or not, the experiment with monologue was not totally conceived in imitation of Strindberg. In many of his earliest plays, he had used monologues to depict his characters in the isolation of their own feeling. In *Before Breakfast,* oriented around Strindberg, and carried to extreme, the monologue was redefined, and it was sufficient to give him at least the glimmering of direction. Whether the step he took was a wise one may be debated, but for better or worse it was decisive. In the rush of plays that followed in 1917, other preoccupations concerned him, but by 1920, it was clear that he had chosen to move in the direction of theatrical experiment and the Art Theatre, a course he did not finally desert until 1933, when he completed *Days Without End*.

Before Breakfast was not finished when Carlin met the Cooks by accident in a Provincetown street. The Players had reassembled and made plans to continue. Cook was searching everywhere for plays for his group. Carlin had nothing, but he mentioned O'Neill. The encounter of O'Neill and the group has been movingly recorded by Susan Glaspell. The shy, tough, silent young man, reputed to have a "trunkful" of plays, was asked to bring one of his works and read it to a group assembled at Cook's home that evening. In something like agony, O'Neill waited in the dining room while the play was read aloud. When the reading was finished, the Players had gained a new purpose and direction. "Then," Miss Glaspell wrote, "we knew what we were for."[12] The purpose was to prove not quite what they thought at the time. O'Neill's rise to fame was in a different rhythm from the Dionysian dance improvised the summer before, and in committing themselves to him, the Players profaned the heart of their mystery. For the moment, however, they had found a point of assembly.

The play O'Neill brought them was *Bound East for Cardiff*. It was a sensitive choice. With the sea as an integral element in the lives of the summer people, with the diminutive, sea-surrounded stage at their disposal, no better play could have been found. It was ready-made for the talents and facilities of the amateur actors. Most importantly, however, in offering it for production, O'Neill was tacitly asserting his own truth. Reaching back beyond the academic efforts of his student days, he selected the one play that was really characteristic of his genius, just as he had pulled back from the discontent of the winter and returned to the sea and to himself. In a small way, life in Provincetown that summer must have seemed like a resurrection. Swimming far out from the land, tanning himself on the silent dunes, he came again into his right element and to his own métier.

When the summer was over, the Players enthusiastically departed for New York to set up their theatre. O'Neill did not join them. He stayed in Provincetown to write until October, when he went to New York for rehearsals of *Bound East for Cardiff* in which he was to play the Second Mate as he had in the Wharf Theatre production. He remained in New York until February, while the Players produced the finally completed *Before Breakfast*. Then he returned to Provincetown, where by April he had completed *Ile* and the other *Glencairn* plays.

The deliberate attempt in writing *Before Breakfast* to find a right orientation for his work was continued in the three plays about the crew of the *S. S. Glencairn*. Setting aside Strindbergian novelties, he returned in technique and theme to the point he had left two years earlier. That the plays form in small compass a cycle, and so anticipate O'Neill's later complex cyclic formations, is accidental. Their first performance as a cycle was that by a group called the Barnstormers in Provincetown on August 14, 1924. Neither O'Neill nor Cook ever appears to have considered the four as a unit, and no definitive order of the plays was ever established.* In their first productions, they were treated as separately conceived one-act plays, and in this light, setting aside the continuity of characters and scene, they each reveal certain of the necessary further steps toward the

* O'Neill co-produced the set of four in New York in November, 1924. The order they there received was *The Moon of the Caribbees, The Long Voyage Home, In the Zone* and *Bound East for Cardiff.*

disciplines of stagecraft and the clarification of the major theme that he had found in *Bound East for Cardiff*.

The first play was *In the Zone*,[13] and, while in O'Neill's opinion it was the least successful of the three, it had the greatest success. The wartime story made it popular. It was sold to *The Seven Arts*, although the magazine failed prior to the play's publication. Its production by the Washington Square Players received favorable commendation, and, as a result, it was purchased by Martin Beck for a vaudeville tour.

O'Neill, who by the time of its production in October, 1917, had absorbed some of the Provincetown Players' idealism, mistrusted its success. He later told Barrett Clark that it seemed the "least significant" of all his plays:

> It is too facile in its conventional technique, too full of clever theatrical tricks, and its long run as a successful headliner in vaudeville proves conclusively to my mind that there must be "something rotten in Denmark." At any rate, this play in no way represents the true me or what I desire to express. It is a situation drama lacking in all spiritual import—there is no big feeling for life inspiring it. Given the plot and a moderate ability to characterize, any industrious playwright could have reeled it off. . . . I consider *In the Zone* a conventional construction of the theater as it is.[14]

Thus O'Neill in 1919, two years after writing the play.

Whether his mistrust was more than a prideful convolution of spirit can be debated. Clark notes accurately that the play gains a greater "feeling for life" when it is played in conjunction with the other *Glencairn* plays, than when it is staged as an isolated work. Alone, its sentimental central situation dominates, and its wartime scene becomes the source of the merest melodrama. Its story is slight, but intricate. Smitty, the focal character, does not belong with the crew, but has sought the sea as refuge from his troubles on the land. As the *Glencairn* sails through waters controlled by German U-Boats, the frightened crew come to think of Smitty as a spy. A black box, in which he carries love letters from a girl who has rejected him, is taken to be a bomb. Smitty's humiliation as the crew open and read the letters is the climax of the action. As it stands, the narrative is anecdotal and leads to quasi-ironic "discoveries" and to a "situation" of which Baker might well have approved. Sensing the theatricality of the final moment, O'Neill rejected the work. Nevertheless, the play contains elements that were important to explore.

Like many of the *Glencairn* crew, Smitty was modeled after a person O'Neill had known, a young Englishman he had met in Buenos Aires. He had spun a romantic and sentimental yarn about his past, much in the manner of those who were later to occupy Harry Hope's saloon in *The Iceman Cometh*.[15] O'Neill's attraction to him as the protagonist for a play was perhaps because he resembled the poet-hero already sketched in *Fog, Bread and Butter* and *Before Breakfast*. The character, a sentimental and neurotic dreamer, manifests an unusually sensitive response to those elements in his environment that are hostile to him. He is desperately aware that he does not "belong" in the world where he exists. For O'Neill, who had sought to depict the crushing power of an "ironic life force," such a character was not only congenial; a greater awareness than that offered in the final vision of Rose or of the dying Yank was a dramatic essential. As a contrast to the unthinking, muscular ape-like members of the crew, to whom thought is strange and whose only happiness is to function smoothly in their environment, O'Neill came naturally enough to a man like Smitty, a restless alien moving in an unending quest for belonging. What is absent in the play, as O'Neill realized, is a context for the action that has power to generalize the incident.

He brought to the play a considerable technical skill, particularly in suggesting through sound and light patterns the tension of men under wartime conditions at sea. In the play, the full moonlight becomes at once a romantic symbol for Smitty, and, since it makes the *Glencairn* visible to the enemy, a source of terror to the men. Much of their fear is conveyed in passages such as these:

DAVIS   . . . You won't be calling him [Smitty] all right when you hears what I seen with my own eyes. (*He adds with an air of satisfaction*) An' you won't be feelin' no safer, neither. (*They all look at him with puzzled glances full of a vague apprehension.*)

DRISCOLL   God blarst ut! (*He fills his pipe and lights it. The others, with an air of remembering something they had forgotten, do the same.* SCOTTY *enters.*)

SCOTTY   (*in awed tones*) Mon, but it's clear outside the nicht! Like day.

DAVIS   (*in low tones*) Where's Smitty, Scotty?

SCOTTY   Out on the hatch starin' at the moon like a mon half-daft. [518]

What is here more eloquent than speech is silence. The stage direction following Driscoll's expletive reveals an awareness of psychological tension and a power to express it in stage business that is not easily attained. Phrases like *"with the air of remembering something they had forgotten"* provide the actors with the means to fulfill the silence. The pause before Scotty's entrance is a long one, yet O'Neill has seen the uses of the silence and employed it to convey more fully than dialogue would ever do the tension of men on a submarine-haunted sea. Against the tension, Smitty's "half-daft" behavior, his silent yearning toward the betraying moonlight, strikes another key, at odds with the dominant fear of the ship's crew. To cap the effect, there is pouring through the forecastle alleyway the bright light of the moon itself. Technically it is a work of quality.

Yet what is achieved here is no more than the narrative permits. In *Bound East for Cardiff* the same techniques had revealed the relation between the men and the sea and caused them to be viewed as the sea's children. Here, a less elemental relationship is suggested, and the sea remains a background for personal relationships bred of the special wartime circumstances.

In *The Long Voyage Home*, the scope widens, although the essential thematic consideration—that the crew of the *Glencairn* are tied to the sea—is not yet explicit. *Bound East for Cardiff* implied that the sea could punish thoughts of rebellion—potential acts of will such as Yank's desire to find a home on land. There, however, the stronger conception was that the sea was kind to those who, without thought, live along the lines of force her strength laid down. In *The Long Voyage Home*, the conception of the sea as avenger is primary, but in describing the sea's punishment of rebellion, O'Neill fell back on the somewhat mechanical plotting that had characterized his plays of "ironic fate."

Like Yank, Olson, the protagonist, acts in accord with a half-understood need to leave the sea and to return to his family's farm. He has tried before:

> But I come ashore, I take one drink, I take many drinks, I get drunk, I spend all money, I have to ship away for other voyage. So dis time I say to myself: Don't drink one drink, Ollie, or, sure, you don't get home. And I want go home dis time. I feel homesick for farm and to see my people again. . . . Yust like little boy, I

> feel homesick. . . . You know, Miss Freda, my mother get very old, and I want to see her. . . . [506]

To his enforced temperance, signaling as it does an unaccustomed act of will, his shipmates react with a certain awe. Driscoll, roaring drunk, cries in his praise:

> 'Tis a foine sight to see a man wid some sense in his head instead av a damn fool the loike av us. I only wisht I'd a mother alive to call me own. I'd not be dhrunk in this divil's hole this minute, maybe. [498]

Thus they celebrate and protect his intention, but their efforts are futile. Olson is cut out of the herd, doped, robbed, and shanghaied on a jinxed ship. What matters is not the activity of the plotters. They are only agents, performing the sea's will without animosity or responsibility. O'Neill even allows a moment of sympathetic communion like that between Rose and Tim to occur between Olson and Freda, his betrayer. But a more important force than she sends him on his fatal voyage. When he hears that the jinxed ship is in port and is bound around Cape Horn, he says "I pity poor fallers make dat trip around Cape Stiff dis time year. I bet you some of dem never see port once again." [507] The implication is strong that the sea will not let Olson live.

On the narrative level, a trick is played, hope is cheated and Olson's action is ironically frustrated. Thematically, the play states that the land for all the sailors is an alien world and they are unable to deal with its intricate duplicity. On land, as not at sea, where their fellowship binds them in a crude purity of heart, they meet evil. Yet, as the sea's men, they are not touched by it. Only Olson, in a state of apostasy, becomes a victim to it. He is doomed because he is bound to the sea, which, like a God, has power to bless or to curse.

That the suggestion is made only by implication is perhaps a sign of O'Neill's increasing ability to make his points with subtlety. Here there are no personifications of ironic life forces, nor visions of pretty ladies in black. Yet it is also true that lacking the touch of awareness that Rose and Yank were given, Olson goes to his fate as a mere animal with no sense of what has brought him down. O'Neill's judgment of *In the Zone*—that it did not convey a "big feeling for life" and that it lacked "spiritual import"—might also be the judgment of *The Long Voyage Home*. In neither has O'Neill created unequivocally the sense of an operative fate guiding the lives of the sailors. Both hold their focus on individual acts of will and their consequences. Yet when the four *Glencairn* plays are staged as a cycle, this effect is diminished. In the whole, what men will is rendered unimportant in relation to their predestined course of life at sea. To commit an act of will is in fact to act hostilely toward the sea in whose grip they move. In the larger context, the sentimentality and the melodrama are minimized, and a pattern of "spiritual import" emerges.

That this is so is largely due to the fourth play, *The Moon of the Caribbees,* in which, of all the *Glencairn* plays, O'Neill took the greatest pride. "No one else in the world," he said, "could have written that one."[16] His estimation of the worth of his dramas was often at considerable variance from the critical estimate of others, but in this instance, at least, his judgment must be respected. *The Moon of the Caribbees* is the first signal O'Neill gave of the achievement of his final plays. Far more than any other play of this year, it marks a turning point. Where *The Long Voyage Home* and *In the Zone* in a variety of ways repeat the effects of his pre-Baker work, *The Moon of the Caribbees* moves forward and must be accounted a considerable step. What he gained in this play he did not entirely retain, yet he was able to return to its manner at the end of his life and to rediscover its early secret as one of the sources of his late tragedies.

The Moon of the Caribbees is a nearly flawless dramatic poem. To realize its qualities from a printed text is impossible, for it is so completely a drama that its power cannot be captured from its dialogue alone. To describe the play as a "mood piece," heavily dependent on "atmosphere," is to excuse, without understanding, the fact that it has no conspicuous narrative as do *In the Zone* and *The Long Voyage Home.* The totality of the drama lies in the mood, for, as O'Neill said, "the spirit of the sea . . . is . . . the hero."[17] In this, it reverses the proportion of the other *Glencairn* plays where the qualities and power of the sea were left a little vague. Now, as if deliberately, O'Neill rids himself of narrative in the conventional sense, of attempts at subtle character revelation and of character conflict insofar as these shape the action. Instead, he sets himself to dramatize such a fragmentary episode as those that filtered through the memory of the dying Yank. It is a play which Baker would have found formless, without beginning, middle or end. Yet it contains the fullest sense of life that O'Neill had put on his stage, and years were to pass before he would again equal it.

O'Neill was aware of its seminal importance to his career. To Clark, he wrote that it was his "first real break with theatrical traditions. Once I had taken this initial step, other plays followed logically."[18] It was not, perhaps, so simple as this. The essence of *The Moon of the Caribbees* is its extraordinary simplicity, its firm refusal to turn aside from its purposes for any obvious theatrical effect.

The significant failure of his earliest works had been failures of narrative. The tawdry stories, demanding so small an act of imaginative conception and requiring heroic efforts of taste and style to prevent their lapsing into melodramatic nonsense, had in large measure prevented his achieving work in which he could take secure pride. His distaste for the heavy plotting and the "theatrical" revelations of *In the Zone* shows that in writing *The Moon of the Caribbees* he deliberately tried to create a work that would not be betrayed by its story.

What the play depends on are the maturing qualities of O'Neill's emerging theatrical style. As the curtain rises and the main deck of the *Glencairn* is revealed, *"A melancholy Negro chant, faint and far off, drifts, crooning, over the water."* The chant continues through the play, its significance made clear in the final stage direction, where it is described as *"the mood of the moonlight made audible."* Moon and chant are properties of the sea; through them, a spell is cast over the men binding them to the sea and to one another as if they had been hypnotized.

The men sit on deck in small groups, waiting for native women to come aboard and bring them rum, and holding inaudible conversations. Gradually the chant penetrates their talk and reduces them to silence. Driscoll, whose attention is toward the shore, alert for the coming of the women, reacts to the song with irritation. Smitty, whose mood matches the melancholy of the music, agrees that the song is depressing. The men try to describe the song—a keening song, a funeral song, something, at least, with the qualities of a religious chant. Later, the old Donkeyman makes a similar comment, comparing it to a hymn heard outside a church on Sunday. The funerary suggestion of the music gives rise to ribald discussion of the habits of cannibals, and then, in the expectation of revelry, they fall silent. In the quiet, the chant is heard again. Three bells strike and the play—whose running time is almost exactly a half hour, ending with the striking of four bells—begins.

The first action is one of rebellion against the chant. In the sailors' daily lives, the routines of the sea and the ship obscure any ultimate questioning. Now, in the calm, the chant disturbs them, as if it had aroused in them a dim awareness that the sea's power over their lives is absolute. In the music, the sea's spell is made audible, and Smitty, whose reaction is the most conscious, articulates the group's sentiment: "I wish they'd stop the song. It makes you think of—well —things you ought to forget." Then rousing himself from unaccustomed depression, Big Frank calls to Driscoll to sing something to drown out the song.

Driscoll's chanty leads to the coming of the women. The noise level grows as rum is passed, fights begin and end and the crew moves from the deck into the forecastle. As the door is shut, the brief turbulence of sound ends, and the chant reasserts itself as an accompaniment to Smitty's reflections on his past, memories conjured up by the pull of the music.

The revelry in the forecastle grows, the men burst out onto the deck and a dance tune is introduced, again drowning the chant. A fight begins, Paddy is knifed, yet, when the brawling subsides, the chant is heard again, placid as the moon and as unresponsive as the sea that has cradled the sorrow, brutality and revelry on the ship.

The chant is the central agent of the conflict in the play, the protagonist against whom the men react. The other elements are transient appearances. Smitty's reminiscences, the Donkeyman's quasi-philosophical commentary, the brawl, the dance, the drunkenness lie outside the play's core. The men are defined by their relationship to the offstage song. To Smitty, who, as the Donkeyman points out, is not made for the sea, the song is a source of conscious sorrow. All that he has tried to escape floods back to his mind as he hears the music. To the Donkeyman, whose acceptance of his destiny is unresentful the song is no problem, melding with the surroundings in which he has found peace. To the others, in whom life burns more fiercely, the song is disturbing but never to the point that it brings them full awareness. With their minds on the revelry to come, it strikes a discordant note, and they throw their vitality against it without seeking to understand their reaction.

The revelry of the crew in reaction to the song has been total, thoughtless, Dionysian and paradoxically at its fullest measure an act of complete surrender to what the song has hinted. They have been absorbed in a life process. Will has been vanquished, individuality submerged, and personality, freed of longing, regret and hope, has expressed itself merely in energy. The men's absorption into the controlling element that the song makes manifest is viewed without moral perspective. Drunkenness, mass fornication, near-murder are not seen as good or evil, for they are not reached by conscious or subconscious choice. The acts committed have in them the amorality of innocence and something of half-comprehended ritual observances to a God whose meanings and identity are mysterious.

In the play, thought and its ensuing conscious actions are the sources of unhappiness. Smitty's memories bring him to despair and separate him from the physical revelry of the crew. As he drinks to drown thought, he yearns toward the moon, as if he is seeking to will himself to belong to the world of the sea. It is an impossible attempt. In no way can he join the crew in their unthinking outpouring of energies. He rejects the advances of the native girl, Pearl, and as he does so, his alien nature arouses in her a viciousness akin to hatred. She slaps him, rejecting the attitude that has bred in her a flicker of awareness of what she is. Hers is a blow struck at an object that has caused thought and disrupted for a moment her identification with her world. In all instances, except in the perspective of the old Donkeyman, thought is the goad, the instigator of unhappiness. Only when the conscious mind is subdued, when the men are able to enter completely into the occasions the sea sets for them, do they find the kind of adjustment that brings momentary peace. Then, they no longer hear, or if they hear do not resent, the call over the water that is the sound of their fate.

In *Long Day's Journey into Night*, Edmund Tyrone speaks of his identification with the sea as a mystical vision:

> I dissolved in the sea, became white sails and flying spray, became beauty and rhythm, became moonlight and the ship and the high dim-starred sky! . . . And several other times in my life, when I was swimming far out, or lying alone on a beach, I have had the same experience. Became the sun, the hot sand, green seaweed anchored to a rock, swaying in the tide. Like a saint's vision of beatitude. [153]

Edmund's words are O'Neill's last and most positive description of a current that ran deep in his life. His second wife, Agnes Boulton, recorded his swimming far out for long hours and playing with a seal that cavorted beside him.[19] When his life permitted, he lived close to the sea. In California, at Tao House, well inland from the Pacific Ocean, the interior décor recalled that of Peaked Hill Bars, his home on Cape Cod, and in his study there were detailed models of sailing vessels mounted on the walls above the fireplace, which brought memories of the sea where from the window he could see only brown hills.* In 1928, while he was living in France at a far remove from the sea, he began a play which he said was "the grand opus of my life." It was an autobiographical work called *Sea-Mother's Son* and was subtitled *The Story of the Birth of a Soul.*[20] The title was an apt description of O'Neill, who felt for the sea something of the relation of son to mother, and, in nearly synonymous terms, of man to God. The conscious articulation of the concept emerged during the writing of the *Glencairn* plays, and gave them the thematic unity appropriate to a cycle.

At first the theme's quasi-religious implications remained latent in the suggestions of the sea's power to be either kind or vengeful, while more explicitly, O'Neill presented the sea in terms similar to those developed by naturalistic novelists to explain the indifferent powers that control men's fates and place their lives in ironic perspective. Yet there is a difference. As examples of American naturalism, the *Glencairn* plays are strongly personalized and devoid of the scientific attitudes of many of the American novelists. To be sure, the reversed evolutionary process upon which Frank Norris based his portrait of Vandover and which gave Jack London his Buck are suggested by O'Neill. The crew is made up of brutish men, and occasionally O'Neill toys with the idea of man's reversion to the animal. For example, in *The Moon of the Caribbees,* during a quarrel Cocky calls Paddy "A 'airy ape," [461] and the phrase was perhaps the genesis of a short story of 1917, now destroyed, called *The Hairy Ape,* the progenitor of the play he would write in 1921. Yet in the story of the anthropoid stoker, as with the *Glencairn* sailors, O'Neill does not follow the lines set by the greatest naturalistic novelists. His own response to the sea, affected perhaps by Conrad's romanticism,

* Carlotta Monterey O'Neill once said that O'Neill disliked the swimming pool at Tao House because it was closed in by a small depression in the hills, and he was unable to look out.

led him toward a less pessimistic view of man than that found in Crane or Dreiser or Norris. Indeed, O'Neill's view of man's relation to nature owes as much to Emerson and his followers as it does to the naturalists.

O'Neill's early insight told him that nature was benevolent, and that the most a man can hope for is to come into such a condition of being that he feels "dissolved" into her elements, harmoniously united in an ecstasy of belonging. Should man pull away from such harmony, assert the power of his will, seek after goals set by material-istic, ego-satisfying drives, he is filled thereafter with a sense of loss that makes him prey to neurosis and that condemns him for the rest of his life to seek re-identification with the God-force. The best life is that which operates below the level of conscious, self-determined action. More conscious apprehension dooms men to an endless quest. Thus, for all the somber cast of his thought, O'Neill was not in the beginning deeply pessimistic. Even when man was lost, the hope of belonging remained. Even should hope turn hopeless, the dream persisted to haunt life like a dark and yet sustaining force.

In *The Moon of the Caribbees,* O'Neill perfected in one-act form what he had earlier called a "tragedy of fate." No longer was fate loosely labeled "ironic," nor did he there revel in the spectacle of man's being crushed by his social environment. Irony was now local-ized in Smitty's rueful self-appraisal, and no man was made a victim of circumstance alone. The view was broadened, and men were seen as creatures of profound forces in their world. Being Sea-Mother's sons, their harmonious participation in the sea's process was perhaps the nearest they could come to happiness. Thus the theme, devel-oped in the last play, lends depth to the others, even to *In the Zone,* and it points ahead to other, more impressive works to come.

The Moon of the Caribbees was the end of the first phase of O'Neill's career, a small work of high perfection, free of dependence on other authors, and one that, as O'Neill rightly said, only he could have written. Where the achievement was to lead him was not clear, and such satisfactions as it provided were necessarily short-lived. The opportunity to experiment on the Provincetown stage was ir-resistible, and in the suddenly stirring currents of the post-war American theatre, O'Neill made tentative moves to test his powers in other directions than the realism of the *Glencairn* plays per-mitted. There was much to be learned, much to accomplish. He had not, as yet, written a presentable full-length play, but his reputation was growing, and several long plays were emerging in scenario form. Equally important, as he found his subject matter, the themes raised questions he was required to answer. What for instance of less passive men than the Paddys and the Driscolls? What of men who sought to fulfill destinies of which they were totally aware? And what of their contraries, the aware men like Smitty whose will was powerless and who could only live in hope? The first he wrote of in the short play about Captain Keeney and his wife, *Ile;* the second he treated as a short story, entitled *Tomorrow.*

Like *Before Breakfast, Ile* is the account of a marriage in which one of the partners is destroyed by the other. In *Ile,* however, the marriage is not viewed as a Strindbergian shackling of hateful opposites but almost with sympathy. Basing his play on a true story of a wife who had sailed with her husband and had lost her mind after enduring a long and hard voyage,[21] O'Neill's play presents Annie Keeney as a fragile woman who has gone with her husband to sea despite his protest that a whaling ship is no place for a woman to live. She has dreamed of her husband as a Viking but has learned the truth of her romantic illusion when she is locked in an icebound sea for an interminable winter, surrounded by mutinous sailors and isolated from her kind and her comforts. Captain Keeney's harshness is bred in him by the qualities of the ship which he must master. He can do no less than what he came for: to fill his ship with oil. Her plea that they return moves him—he is no monster—but his acquiescence is momentary, for at the moment he gives in, the ice to the north breaks, whales appear and he goes forward after the oil. Mrs. Keeney escapes into madness.

Ile is unlike the *Glencairn* plays in that the sea is not intended to be the center. That the ice opens when it does is a matter of circumstantial convenience at best. What is new in this play is the driving action of Keeney, who superficially resembles a lesser and domesticated Captain Ahab. In Keeney, for the first time, O'Neill draws the character of a man who commits a decisive act of will. Except perhaps for Olson's abortive effort to leave the sea in *The Long Voyage Home,* all of O'Neill's important characters had been bound, willless, incapable of decision, acquiescent to their fate. Keeney is a change.

He is not presented as the villain of melodrama. The portrait is carefully sympathetic, and the strongest possible case is made for his pursuit of the oil. His pride, his manhood are bound up in the drive; without the oil he is nothing, and, although she becomes an object of pity, Mrs. Keeney can be blamed for her failure to understand this essential characteristic of her husband.* Even so, his will verges on the compulsive and irrational. Like his wife, Keeney is not far from madness.

O'Neill's treatment of the theme is somewhat overstated, yet the direction of his exploration was essential. The question the play asks in the context of his other work is whether man's only happiness lies in acquiescing to the forces of his environment, or whether he has in himself the power to control or to defeat his fate. By thrusting Captain Keeney to the edge of megalomania, O'Neill answered his question negatively. All Keeney can accomplish is destruction, but in *Ile*, the answer is not yet complete. Will, here, is not set in a convincing pattern of destiny such as he wove in *The Moon of the Caribbees*. However, he was shortly to bring the two concerns together, and when this was done, the design of his early tragedy would be complete.

The last work of the period to be considered offers a second alternative to the mindless destiny of the *Glencairn* crew. If will leads to disaster, what of hope, which may or may not lead beyond awareness to action? In his story *Tomorrow*, O'Neill makes a tentative, further exploration of what he had touched on in the ending of *The Personal Equation* and of what will prove in *The Iceman Cometh* to be a major tragic theme.

James Anderson, the story's central figure, is identical to James Cameron, the "Jimmy Tomorrow" of *The Iceman Cometh*. Like Cameron, Anderson lives in expectation of a return to respectability —always to happen tomorrow. He has been a newspaper correspondent in South Africa, and hopes through the assistance of a friend to return to his job as a reporter. The job becomes available, he spruces himself for the effort, finds he cannot write and returning to "Tommy the Priest's," the saloon in which he lives, he throws himself from the window of his room.

* Sheaffer [385] suggests that Mrs. Keeney is the earliest image of O'Neill's mother in the plays.

Many of the elements distributed among the characters of *The Iceman Cometh* are to be seen in Anderson's background and character, and the story also contains a number of autobiographical elements. The central figure is based on James Byth, once a press agent of O'Neill's father's, who had roomed next to O'Neill at Jimmy the Priest's. Byth, a former Boer war correspondent, killed himself as the fictional Jimmy did.[22] In the story, a seaman named Lyons, reminiscent of Driscoll in the *Glencairn* plays, provides a strong-minded contrast to the ineffectual hero. The narrator, Art, is evidently modeled on O'Neill himself. A canceled passage from the manuscript of the story reads in part, "I don't expect you to believe it. You know that I write plays and you'll lay it to my innate sense of the dramatic. But it is true—as true as I'm sitting here boring you with my yarns." In the body of the story, the narrator mentions ironically that he has written a play about Belshazzar's Feast and the Fall of Babylon in seven acts and blank verse—evidently a reference to O'Neill's work on the same subject at Harvard. The manuscript also contains a canceled introduction describing life at "Tommy the Priest's" and makes reference to the narrator's days as a sailor.

Although the story and characters are autobiographical, the theme of *Tomorrow* may well have been suggested by the writer whose work had already proved a fruitful source to O'Neill, Joseph Conrad. In 1903, Conrad had published a story called by the same title as O'Neill's, and, in 1905, had dramatized it as *One Day More*. The play was not published until 1926, but it is probable that O'Neill knew the story, which appeared in the volume *Typhoon and Other Stories*.

Conrad's tale is of old Captain Hagberd, a former coastal skipper, who waits in hope that Harry, his son who has run away to sea as a boy, will return and live again with him on the land. The Captain's desire to see his son again has reached the point of obsession: he has contracted, in Conrad's phrase, "the disease of hope," which forces him never to think of the future in any other terms but tomorrow, when the son will surely come. Living for "tomorrow" distorts the future and obliterates the present: "It's always tomorrow . . . without any sort of today."[23] Inevitably, when the son appears, the father rejects the fact that tomorrow has come and refuses to acknowledge him. The son leaves, and the old man is left in an "everlasting tomorrow."

Here, in a different narrative, is the essence of O'Neill's short story and of much more that he wrote when he turned his attention to those who seek to live by trusting to "hopeless hope." His imitation of Conrad's story was not circumstantially so close as was his imitation of *The Nigger of the Narcissus* in *Bound East for Cardiff,* but again O'Neill appears to have found in Conrad the essential definition of a problem that his own experience could verify in other terms. Conrad enabled O'Neill to see Anderson, as he had enabled him to see the *Glencairn* crew, in a wider perspective that gave the characters more than anecdotal significance.

O'Neill's story is an interesting and able work in its own right. Its point of view toward its destitute protagonist is kindly, but it is saved by the narrator's irony from sentimentality or trickery in its narrative style. In the manuscript version, immediately after Jimmy's suicide, a message arrives stating that Jimmy has just inherited £20,000. The episode, wisely, was deleted in the published version, in favor of an ending in which the drunks, having heard the sound of the fall, enter the courtyard and discover Jimmy's body. O'Neill ended his story simply: "The sky was pale with the light of dawn. Tomorrow had come."*

In later elaborations of the theme, O'Neill would continue to be concerned with the plight of will-less men, living in listless inaction, suspended in time. As if they were at the bottom of the sea, their days are spent in a crepuscular eternity. Sometimes, memory stirs, and when it does, a semblance of consciousness returns. Man is roused from death-in-life and he regains for a moment the sense of human identity, if only in his awareness of his pain. Then, hope for tomorrow offers some small remedy for the pain, even though hope is delusion, never to be brought to the test of reality. In the destinate scheme of life in which O'Neill's characters move, hope without action is in some measure the opposite of such acts of will as that of Captain Keeney. Yet when hope is coupled with action, like will it becomes a destroyer. At this stage in his thought, O'Neill can say only that if man is to survive he must accept without thinking the endless inevitable drift. Any attempt to escape brings death on the verge of tomorrow.

* Sheaffer [382] notes that in accepting the story, Waldo Frank, an editor for the *Seven Arts,* which published the story in June, 1917, asked for the correction of "a few minor imperfections." The trick ending, presumably, was one of them.

IV
PAUSE
1918-1919

PLAYS WRITTEN IN 1918 ARE
Beyond the Horizon
Till We Meet (destroyed)
Shell-Shock
The Rope
The Dreamy Kid
Where the Cross Is Made
The Straw
S.O.S. (short story)

PLAYS WRITTEN IN 1919 ARE
Chris Christopherson
Honor Among the Bradleys (destroyed)
The Trumpet (destroyed)
Exorcism (destroyed)

1918—O'Neill married Agnes Boulton in Provincetown. The marriage began well, but Jamie arrived, bringing trouble. Together, the brothers drank heavily, constantly, and at times Agnes became little more than a resentful caretaker. Eugene fell ill; she took him away from Jamie to her family home, where, as Eugene recovered, the marriage became more stable. In 1917, O'Neill's reputation had grown rapidly, but in 1918, only three short plays were staged, and in 1919, only one. He had completed *Beyond the Horizon;* it was optioned for Broadway production perhaps with the Barrymore brothers. The project died. Eugene worked at two other long dramas and pecked carelessly at one-act plays and at fiction aimed at that most common of markets, the *Saturday Evening Post.* James O'Neill was injured by an automobile, and the accident brought father and son closer together than they had ever been. As testimony of his love, James, in 1919, bought for his son the abandoned Coast Guard station at Peaked Hill Bars on Cape Cod. The summer there was rewarding, if lonely; and as the year ended, Agnes and Eugene came in to Provincetown, where on October 30, O'Neill's second son, Shane, was born. But the career that a year earlier had seemed fair was at a standstill. Creative energy flagged, and alcohol again became a problem.

Louis Sheaffer Collection

> Gene woke up and read for awhile, and then said he'd like the soup, but another drink first. He finished one *Saturday Evening Post* and began another, and about four o'clock he had another drink and read again. . . . The doctor had told me to give him a sleeping pill but Gene said wryly that the *Saturday Evening Post* was his narcotic.[1]

THE picture of O'Neill fogged in with a hangover and the *Saturday Evening Post* recurs with depressing frequency in the account his second wife has provided of their years together in 1918 and 1919. Agnes Boulton says little about her husband's writing, aside from noting that when he was sober he locked himself away and wrote for long hours, but her memoir implies that at this time he wrote not so much because he was impelled by a strong creative urge as because he found in writing an excuse for solitude. Certainly what he wrote suggests that after the considerable achievement of the *Glencairn* plays his career had lost its stability and its power of progression and had come instead to a doldrums from which he could not free himself.

Early in 1918, carried forward by the creative momentum of the previous year's work, he completed *Beyond the Horizon,* but thereafter pecked at a group of relatively unimportant one-act plays and at drafts of *The Straw* and *Chris Christopherson.* Perhaps led by his wife's small success as a writer of pulp fiction, he also turned his hand to two straight commercial ventures.

One of the latter, a short story entitled *S.O.S.,* was evidently suggested by his reading of the wartime fiction of the *Saturday Evening Post,* and in quality is about equal to what the magazine was then publishing. The tale is an adaptation of his *Warnings,* and tells of

John Lathrop whose marriage is endangered when he loses his job as a telegrapher. He takes a position as a wireless operator on a freighter traveling between New York and Buenos Aires. As in the play, John becomes deaf and fails to hear the warnings radioed to the ship—in this instance of a German raider engaged in unrestricted submarine warfare* off the South American coast. His ship is captured and sunk after the freighter's crew has been transferred to the raider. John's hearing is unexpectedly restored when the raider's guns fire at another ship. Still pretending to be deaf, he stabs the German wireless operator and radios the ship's position to shore. The raider is captured, but not before the Germans discover what John has done and execute him. John is hailed a hero and his wife is granted a government pension.

The story, written late in 1918, would have been of little interest to the post-war magazine market,** nor would the dramatic sketch, *Shell-Shock*, which O'Neill appears to have written for the same audiences that turned *In The Zone* into a commercial success in vaudeville. *Shell-Shock* tells of a returning hero, decorated for having crawled out into "No Man's Land" to rescue a wounded friend. The friend died as Jack brought him in, and now, sometime after the event, Jack has convinced himself that he went to the rescue only to get some cigarettes he knew his friend to be carrying. Cigarettes are his fetish, he smokes incessantly, buys packs he does not use, borrows from his friends and hoards butts. His problem is resolved when he is convinced that the fixation is only his way of burying the memory of the horror of his friend's death. After what is possibly the shortest course of psychoanalysis on record, Jack returns to normal.

That O'Neill, who the year before had written so fine a play as *The Moon of the Caribbees,* would produce two efforts so lacking in creative force, so imaginatively shallow, is shocking. That he felt some despair at the emptiness of his work is perhaps betokened by the fact that he destroyed four of the eight one-act plays written in

---

* Submarine raiders fascinated *Post* readers throughout the war, as did the heroic solo venture that resulted in the raider's capture or sinking.

** His interest in magazine fiction was perhaps increased by his success in 1917-18 when *The Long Voyage Home, Ile* and *The Moon of the Caribbees* were accepted by George Jean Nathan for publication in the *Smart Set.*

these two years.* To be sure, those that he saved and published were not without consequences. *Where the Cross Is Made* was shortly to be revised as the full-length *Gold; The Rope* anticipates some of the elements of *Desire Under the Elms;* and *The Dreamy Kid,* O'Neill's first black drama, opened the way to *The Emperor Jones* and *All God's Chillun Got Wings*. In these and in the longer plays, O'Neill underwent some limited development, but nothing that he did in these two years after *Beyond the Horizon* was of first importance, nor can the time be understood as a period of growth. The years 1918-19 are nearly empty, significant only by their contrast with the two years that followed.

By 1921, O'Neill had achieved a solid national reputation and was on the way to international fame. By that time, six of his full-length plays had received professional productions. Three had failed,** but two were Pulitzer prizewinners, and one, *The Emperor Jones,* had made theatrical history. Release from the doldrums, when it came, was complete.

Agnes Boulton's narrative stops in the fall of 1919, with the birth of their son, Shane. The time was a little short of the moment of change. O'Neill's listlessness gave way to the new creativity early in 1920, when *Beyond the Horizon* was at last readied for its Broadway opening. Upon its completion in April, 1918, O'Neill had sent the script to the producer, John D. Williams, who accepted it, but then did nothing with it. More than anything else, O'Neill needed that production. The small successes, the critical favor that the Provincetown productions offered him were insufficiently gratifying to offset the aura of amateurism that hung about them. To be the fair-haired boy of a village coterie was not enough, nor was it sufficient to see a work half-realized by middling actors in impoverished productions. A future that meant writing one-act plays to satisfy the limited needs of a small playhouse repertory was tantamount to slavery. The production of *Beyond the Horizon* in a large theatre

* Titles of the destroyed works are *Till We Meet, The Trumpet, Exorcism* and *Honor Among the Bradleys. Exorcism* was produced by the Provincetown Players in March, 1920. (See below p. 108.) *Honor Among the Bradleys* may be the play referred to by Agnes Boulton [254] that O'Neill wrote after meeting a family of squatters. The family consisted of father and mother and seven blonde, beautiful, unmarried and pregnant daughters. Of the other plays, nothing is known.
** The three failures *The Straw, Gold* and *Chris Christopherson* were all drafted in the years 1918-19, although *Gold* did not go beyond scenario form in those years.

and with a cast of actors who could realize his vision of his script meant a way forward. Yet for two years production did not come. During the period of waiting, O'Neill wrote without real incentive or energy in that condition he called "hopeless hope." Even the Provincetown's production of *The Moon of the Caribbees* in 1918 was of small interest to him as he literally waited for the postman to bring him word from Williams.[2]

He had every reason to live in expectation. The most optimistic theatrical rumor fed his hopes. Williams assured him that production waited only until both John and Lionel Barrymore could free themselves of other commitments so that they might play Robert and Andrew Mayo.[3] It was a fair promise, but when John Barrymore signed for Arthur Hopkins's production of Tolstoy's *Redemption*, its fulfillment was impossible. Williams suggested waiting until that production had failed, as it surely would. O'Neill grimly wished it the worst luck, but against all likelihood, Barrymore made the work a hit. Williams fell silent about O'Neill's future. Other major plays, *The Straw* and *Chris Christopherson,* were drafted and then set aside, because as he told Agnes, "I don't want to start on *Chris* or *The Straw* and then have to leave it for rehearsals. . . ."[4] At the Provincetown's request he wrote *The Dreamy Kid* for their new season, and then when that was found unsuitable, he worked up the last act of his scenario for *Gold* under the title *Where the Cross Is Made*. Little by little, however, the energies that had carried him steadily through 1917 and the writing of *Beyond the Horizon* in 1918 flagged. The banked fire threatened to die.

The diffidence bred by waiting is revealed in the generally slipshod writing in the surviving one-act plays. Technically they are uninteresting. O'Neill did little with his characteristic patterns of light and sound, except once, in *Where the Cross Is Made*, where he called for an effect that is elaborately grotesque. Previously, his settings had both interest and truth. Now both were lacking. The setting of *The Rope* is perhaps mute testimony of an almost complete failure of imagination. It is a barn on a farm near the New England seacoast. Double doors open at the back and give a view of the sea, and the sound of the waves is heard throughout the action. In fact, the stage plan duplicates the stage of the wharf shed theatre the Provincetown Players used on the Cape, which also had large double doors at the back opening to the sea. O'Neill turned it to a barn by adding a hayloft, and then to a grotesque by adding a noose hanging from the hayloft.

In *The Road to the Temple,* Susan Glaspell describes a time when she was under pressure for a play but had no conception of a subject. She went into the wharf shed and sat for the morning before the empty stage, summoning inspiration. Gradually, as she stared at it, the stage took on the contours of a kitchen, became peopled with characters and, once the process was ended, she had in hand one of her most successful one-act plays, *Trifles.*[5]

One suspects that the story was repeated in Provincetown circles, perhaps by Cook, voracious to find plays, with the suggestion that this was a short step toward successful playwriting. Whether or not O'Neill in fact entered the theatre and followed Miss Glaspell's procedure in order to get an idea for a play is immaterial. He wrote *The Rope* in Provincetown, and it clearly has something of the forced plotting—plotting that is essentially arranged to explain the noose in the setting—that such a procedure might bring to pass.*

In technical execution, the plays are deeply flawed. All of them have clumsy exposition. When she was producing *The Rope* at the Provincetown, Nina Moise complained of the amount of narrative with which the play opens. O'Neill replied loftily in words that smacked of Baker's precepts, "It's dramatic exposition if I ever wrote any, and characterized, I flatter myself. . . . If the thing is acted naturally all the exposition will come right out of the characters themselves."[6] He would presumably have made the same defense of a number of curiously motivated exits and entrances, as for example his arrangement of the stage for a duo scene in *The Rope* by writing for the unwanted third character the following exit line: "I'll step outside a second and give you two a chance to git all the dirty things you're thinkin' about me off your chest." [589] Any defense would have been specious, for technically the play is inexpert and its companion pieces little better.

None of the short plays is invested with the high degree of imaginative visualization that characterized the *Glencairn* cycle. O'Neill at times appears to have seen his characters only dimly. For example, Luke, the son in *The Rope,* is described upon his return home as being twenty-five, but he has left home at sixteen and has been gone

* The plan of the wharf shed is used again in the second act of *Gold* whose scenario was written at about the same time.

for five years. In the original acting script of *Where the Cross Is Made,* a stage direction called for a one-armed man to place both elbows on the table, "in a gesture of despair."[7]

Such trivial errors are only a token of the slackness that manifests itself in all these works. They are all conventional pieces, incapable of mustering enough energy for experiment and rarely passing beyond the melodramatic.

The only genuine experiment was ludicrous in execution, if not intent. In *Where the Cross Is Made,* he tried as he had in *Before Breakfast* to apply a more than normal pressure on the spectators' sensibilities so as to discover how much an audience could bear. At the climax of the play, the ghosts of three sailors enter, bearing a treasure chest. As they appear, all sound stops and the light turns green, flooding the room in "rhythmic waves":

> *Water drips from their soaked and rotten clothes. Their hair is matted, intertwined with slimy strands of seaweed. Their eyes, as they glide silently into the room, stare frightfully wide at nothing. Their flesh in the green light has the suggestion of decomposition. Their bodies sway limply, nervelessly, rhythmically as if to the pulse of long swells of the deep sea.* [571]

O'Neill, in creating such a Guignol effect, was attempting to suggest the reality of an illusion that had come to a mad sea captain and his son, but his insistence on using "live" ghosts caused an uproar at the Playhouse. To everyone but O'Neill, it was clear that the ghosts could not "glide silently" on the creaking boards of the Provincetown stage. O'Neill was asked to make the ghosts imaginary. He refused, saying: "No . . . they're rotten, but they won't be so bad tomorrow night, beyond the first twenty rows anyway. This play presumes that everybody is mad but the girl. . . . I want to see whether it's possible to make an audience go mad too. Perhaps the first rows will snicker—perhaps they won't. We'll see."[8] The results of the experiment were clear. In *Gold,* the full-length version of the play, the ghosts remain in the imagination.

The experiment is of interest chiefly because it suggests that O'Neill, however idly, was turning toward expressionism. In fact, of course, the intent of the scene is quite the opposite of expressionism. O'Neill's desire was to achieve a super-realism with all barriers to full commitment on the part of the audience broken down. They were to believe in the total reality of the ghosts. Yet his means to this end was to cause the audience to accept a point of view other than that which would be normal. The action is to be filtered through the consciousness of one of the characters, a technique which is essential to expressionism as O'Neill knew it in Strindberg's practice, where audiences are forced to assume the presence of an overriding consciousness, a Dreamer or a Wanderer, through whose mind the action is to be viewed not as a "real" experience, having precise *loci* in time and space, but as incoherent, fragmented experiences arranged in non-logical concatenations.

The experiment had consequences both positive and negative. As a move toward a heightened realism, it led him directly toward the visions and the drumbeats of *The Emperor Jones,* but it also suggested a danger that was to emerge ultimately as a genuine stylistic crisis. The matter had first come into doubt when Cook and Zorach argued over the production style for *Thirst* as to whether O'Neill was a realist or something more. The presence of an experiment that moves in two possible directions, toward realism and expressionism marks a stylistic danger to come.

Although the three one-acts are very different in setting and in tone, their central narratives are remarkably similar. Each centers on an aged, dying parent-figure and a child who is worthless. A homecoming is the central event in each of the plays, and upon that event, the older protagonist has developed a fixation that amounts to madness.

Thus, in *The Dreamy Kid,* the dying Negro grandmother waits desperately for her grandson, a gangster wanted by the police, to come to her. In *The Rope,* old Abraham, a New England farmer, waits for his son whom he has driven away with harsh treatment, to return to the farm and collect his inheritance, a rope with which to hang himself. In *Where the Cross Is Made,* Isaiah waits for his ship, the *Mary Allen,* to return with a treasure he and his crew had discovered and buried years before when they were cast away on a South Pacific island. Nightly, he stalks a poop deck built on the roof of his house, watching for the ship's riding lights. The play makes clear that the treasure is worthless and that the ship has been wrecked. Yet his obsessed conviction that it will return is so great that it infects his son Nat with unwilling belief. Both father and son are caught by meaningless hope that drives both mad.

Perhaps reflecting O'Neill's own frustrations in the matter of *Be-*

yond the Horizon, each of the three plays centers on defeated hope. In *The Dreamy Kid,* the gangster must come to his grandmother to avoid a curse that will fall on him if he does not see her before she dies. Yet his expectation of luck fails, and at the play's end, he is about to be gunned down by the police.

In *The Rope,* when his son, Luke, returns to Abraham, he proves to be a worthless, loud-mouthed braggart. Abraham receives him with joy, but is so overcome with emotion that he loses the power of rational speech. He can only indicate that he wants the boy to hang himself in the noose. The boy turns violently on his father and plots with his brother-in-law to torture the old man in order to force him to reveal the whereabouts of a thousand dollars in gold. They leave the barn, and as the play ends, Mary, Abraham's feeble-minded granddaughter, swings on the noose. It pulls away from the beam, and the bag of money falls to the floor. The child takes the coins and, playing "Skip-Rock" with the gold, throws them into the sea.

In Isaiah's case, mad hope spreads like an infection. The old man has mortgaged his home to outfit the treasure ship. To save what is left of his inheritance, his son plans to commit his father to an asylum. An early scene between Nat and his sister reveals the extent to which Nat has been consumed by his father's madness. He shows the girl the treasure map with the traditional cross indicating where the chest has been buried, and, although he admits that it is worthless, he tells her that the map has dominated his life:

> It's stood between me and life—driving me mad! *He* taught me to wait and hope with him—wait and hope—day after day. He made me doubt my brain and give the lie to my eyes—when hope was dead—when I knew it was all a dream—I couldn't kill it! . . . God forgive me, I still believe! And that's mad—mad, do you hear? [566]

Nat, aware of the danger of being possessed by dreams, burns the map, but his rebellion against the dream's power is useless. At the climax, the ghosts of the drowned sailors enter the room, and both father and son are convinced that the *Mary Allen* has come home. Isaiah dies of a heart attack, and Nat takes his place on the captain's walk, watching the sea.

The plays, despite their lurid narratives and their melodramatic maniacs, have at least this small importance: they are early developments of a theme that will lead O'Neill to the creation of some of

his finest theatre, for each contains the germinal idea of the hope
that holds men to life, of the lie of the pipe dream that, however,
meaningless, nurtures the dispossessed. The matter is made most
explicit in *Where the Cross Is Made,* when Nat, hung between
"facts" and dreams, between sanity and madness, acknowledges that
his father knows the truth as he does himself. But he adds:

> Oh he *knows* right enough. . . . He *knows,* Doctor, he *knows*—but
> he won't *believe.* He can't—and keep living. [558]*

The Rope and *Where the Cross Is Made* can claim attention for
two further developments: the use of myth and legend to broaden
the base of the narrative and the emergence of autobiographical
strands in the narrative action.

The title, *Where the Cross Is Made,* perhaps implies that the cross
marking the location of the treasure is intended as a Christian symbol and that Isaiah bears in his prophetic hope a resemblance to the
Biblical prophet.** Yet the Robert Louis Stevenson tale of treasure,
together with the macabre conclusion, makes such a parallel at best
connotative and, in the theatre, without dramatic substance.

The Rope, on the other hand, is consciously built on the parable
of the prodigal son in Luke XV, a portion of which is quoted during
the action.*** Part of the play's force, together with some of its pathos, is generated in the scene in which Abraham asks Luke to hang
himself. As he speechlessly tries to indicate his joy at his son's return
by pointing to the rope which hides the inheritance, he seems to be
asking that the boy, like the Biblical prodigal, acknowledge his guilt
and seek forgiveness that he may be received again into his father's

* The view that hope, however futile, can keep a man alive was one that O'Neill had
explored a year earlier in his short story, *Tomorrow. The Rope,* like the short story,
borrows from Conrad's tale, *Tomorrow.* Both the play and Conrad's narrative are
based on the parable of the prodigal son, and each centers on an obsessed, nearly
insane father who longs for his son to return from the sea so that he may receive his
inheritance. In both, father and son are finally estranged, and both endings stress the
tricks that hope can generate in the mind. Interestingly, all three of O'Neill's plays
convey something of Conrad's image of a prodigal ironically disinherited.
** An undated clipping in the Provincetown Players' scrapbook notes that "Muriel
Hope will read *The Sign of the Cross* by Eugene O'Neill with plays by Lady Gregory
and Strindberg." Whether O'Neill once considered using the title of the Biblical epic
for his play or whether it is Miss Hope's error, the alternate title is suggestive. The
scrapbooks are in the Theatre Collection of the New York Public Library.
*** In addition there is perhaps reference to the story of Abraham and Isaac in the
episode where O'Neill's Abraham brings his son to the point of a sacrifice that would,
if it had been executed, have turned to a scene of forgiveness and reunion.

house. In the last analysis, O'Neill does not substantially illuminate either the play or the parable by duplicating the action in this way. At best, he achieves an ironic reversal of the parable's recognition scene, but no more. Yet it is at least a start toward the extensive parallelism that widens the scope of such plays as *Desire Under the Elms, Mourning Becomes Electra* and *The Iceman Cometh.* Unexpectedly, too, it appears to have led O'Neill close to direct autobiography.

What is most interesting in the one-act plays is the emergence of autobiography in the midst of the mélange of realism, melodrama and romance. In earlier works, some autobiographical elements had been evident. The clearest examples, however, were confined to a relatively static self-portrait and, except tentatively in *Bread and Butter,* O'Neill did not develop the character in narrative patterns that reflected the significant relationships of his own life. Now, the situation begins to change.

Several biographers have suggested that the relationship between Abraham and Luke resembles that between O'Neill and his father.[9] As he pictured his father in *Long Day's Journey into Night,* O'Neill stressed the man's miserliness and depicted the complex intermingling of love and hate he felt for his younger son, who, like Luke, was a returned sailor. Luke's face corresponds to the physical type of the Poet in *Fog* and of John Brown, having dark hair, large brown eyes and a weak mouth. In action, however, he shows none of the sensitivity of the earlier self-portraits. There, he is depicted as a swaggering ne'er-do-well, a man "wised up" in the ways of the world. In this respect, he is not unlike some details of the portrait O'Neill was ultimately to draw of his brother Jamie in the Tyrone plays and *Hughie.* It is as if, in creating Luke, O'Neill had subconsciously compressed the figures of both himself and his brother into a single "prodigal," asking for but not finding a reconciliation with the father.*

The possibility that these suggestions are of some substance is affirmed by Louis Sheaffer's suggestion that one of the determining influences on the play was David Belasco's lavish production in 1917

---

* See further below, Chapter X. The play also lays stress on a mother who has deserted her family and whose absence has contributed to the crisis between father and son. Jamie was in Provincetown with his brother during the time of the play's composition.

of *The Wanderer,* based on the prodigal son parable, in which
James O'Neill starred as the father.[10] It is not difficult to imagine
that to Eugene and Jamie, the spectacle of James enacting the lav-
ishly forgiving father occasioned extensive cynical commentary.
That some of that attitude was released in the ironic turns on the
Biblical account contained in *The Rope* seems probable. By no
stretch can the play be called directly autobiographical, yet it is a
step toward a fuller account of important personal relationships
than the earlier self-portraits had permitted. Surprisingly, if wise-
cracks about "Old Gaspard, the miser" playing the prodigal father
came easily to James O'Neill's sons, the father in the play is treated
with sympathy, while the son remains a callow, unaffecting villain.
O'Neill possibly saw more than he at first expected to see.

Autobiography in *Where the Cross Is Made* is less clear. The fact
that the old man is to be sent to a hospital by his son conceivably
reverses the situation O'Neill faced when his father sent him to the
sanatorium. Louis Sheaffer has suggested that the *Mary Allan,* the
lost ship Isaiah has named after his dead wife, is a reference to the
mother O'Neill felt he had lost. O'Neill's mother's full name was
Mary Ellen Quinlan.[11] The points are small ones, yet it appears that
in writing the two plays, O'Neill moved closer to significant self-
depiction than he had done before.

Certainly *Exorcism,* which he destroyed after its production by
the Provincetown on March 26, 1920, was direct autobiography.
Judging from the reviews and from accounts of those who saw it,
the short play was a dramatization of O'Neill's suicide attempt in
1912. So far as its narrative can be reconstructed, *Exorcism* concerned a young man, Ned Malloy, who lives, as O'Neill had, in a
waterfront saloon. Alexander Woollcott's review in the *New York
Times* describes Ned as feeling a revulsion against his life among
the city's refuse, yet as being unwilling to surrender to his family's
demands and make what the reviewer called a "prodigal-son return"
to them.[12] Even the prospect of going to the west to farm does not
please him. To resolve his problems, he takes morphine. He is saved
by two of the bums at the flophouse, one a drunk named Jimmy who
suggests the hero of O'Neill's *Tomorrow.* When he returns to consciousness, he finds his two saviors tediously telling one another the
same dreary stories of their lives and futile hopes. Nothing has

changed, yet, in the process of death and rebirth, Ned's relationship with the world around him has subtly altered. O'Neill's Lazarus, later, will discover in not dissimilar circumstances, that all that has held him to the world has been exorcised by his death and that he is no longer doomed to failure. Ned, the first Lazarus, is released from his bondage and finds strength and will to work in the west. As O'Neill later told the story of his own attempted suicide, the affair became something of a comedy of drunken error.[13] Nevertheless, the emotional implications of the play were probably close to those O'Neill felt after he had returned to life. It was not long after the attempted suicide that O'Neill entered the sanatorium and discovered at last the direction his life was to take. His personal experience can legitimately be called a "resurrection," and judging from accounts of his dramatic treatment of it, O'Neill thought of it in these terms.

Exorcism was O'Neill's second attempt in these years to deal with his past directly. The first he had written in the fall and winter of 1918-19, in the period of lull before *Beyond the Horizon* was produced. The play, whose title shifted from *Eileen Carmody* to *The Hope in this Twain* to *Mirages* became known finally as *The Straw,* an image intended to suggest the difference between life and death that even the most nebulous hope can make. The narrative, however, recounts in some detail O'Neill's experiences at the sanatorium, especially his abortive romance with a fellow patient, Kitty MacKay, who appears as the heroine, Eileen.

To shift from presenting persons he had known to depicting himself onstage was not, of course, a large step so long as the character of the autobiographical figure was not subjected to a detailed analysis. In *The Straw,* O'Neill treats himself much as he treated the friends of his sailor days, with a certain objectivity that sought no genuine revelation. The name he gave to his fictional self was Stephen Murray* of whom some years later he said, "I confess I believe there is a great deal of the 'me' of that period in 'Murray'—unintentionally."[14]

---

* "Murray" was the name of a nurse who was kind to him and who gave him a copy of Francis Thompson's *The Hound of Heaven,* which he had not read before. Louis Sheaffer suggests that the name "Stephen" was borrowed from that of Stephen Dedalus, and points to a possible influence on the play of Joyce's *A Portrait of the Artist as a Young Man* and *Dubliners.* [447]

To claim that Stephen Murray was an unintentional self-portrait is absurd. To be sure, in the published text, Murray's face departs at some particulars from the face of the earlier self-portrait. O'Neill mentions Stephen's high cheekbones, intelligent, large hazel eyes, and large mouth, but he stresses Stephen's habit of protecting himself with a *"concealment mechanism of mocking, careless humor whenever his inner privacy is threatened,"* and he refers to this habit as *"a process of protection."* [348] In the manuscript version, the face is less protected, much closer to the faces of John Brown and the Poet. O'Neill describes the face as *"long and thin. His high forehead, broad and rugged; his large thick-lipped mouth perversely self-indulgent, weak, and ironical. . . ."*[15] Nothing is said here of a "process of protection," a description in the revision that might be taken to mean that O'Neill was creating a mask for his own, too recognizable face.

Of related interest are some of the manuscript's canceled passages in which Murray describes his own life. His mother has been long dead. She was a woman with musical talent who had married a real estate agent. Stephen is the youngest of four children, and claims his mother did not want him at his birth. From high school, as his career is traced, he went to Yale where his drinking and his wild escapades caused him to be expelled at the end of his freshman year. He fell ill of what he calls "summer pneumonia" and during a long convalescence began to read poets, novelists, philosophers, the *Rubáiyát* of Omar Khayyám, Nietzsche and Tom Paine. His reading turned him into a radical, and for a time he had thought himself a born rebel. Recovering from his illness, he took a job as a reporter to escape having to work for his father. Late hours and dissipation caused him to contract tuberculosis and sent him finally to the sanatorium.

The parallels with O'Neill's own life as set forth in *Long Day's Journey into Night* and in his biographers' accounts are close. Stephen's absent mother, who has musical talent, and his father who buys and sells real estate are reflections of Mary and James Tyrone, she who desired to become a concert pianist, he who professed poverty because of a variety of real estate transactions. Through Edmund Tyrone, O'Neill expressed his feeling that he was an unwanted child, a detail which, together with the general conformity between Stephen's career and O'Neill's life up to the time of his suspension from Princeton, is sufficient to establish the biographical core of the character.

The reasons O'Neill altered the draft version are complex. Some, of course, was simply cutting for length, but beyond this, the quasi-parodistic presentation of his parents as a real estate salesman and wife was unworthy. Not that O'Neill was a model of filial piety. Nevertheless, there were limits of taste that made the near burlesque needlessly personal. Furthermore, the matter was irrelevant and distracting. The play is not about Stephen Murray. It centers on its tubercular heroine, Eileen Carmody. Throughout the play, she is an innocent victim of her father and family, of her fiancé, and of Stephen himself. To create sympathy for her, O'Neill opens his play with a scathing picture of her father. Bill Carmody is a dour, miserly Irish peasant, brutally selfish and too fond of liquor. After he is convinced that his daughter has contracted more than a cold and must be sent immediately to "Hill Farm Sanatorium," he complains at spending the weekly charge of seven dollars needed to save her life. The father of Eileen's prototype, Kitty MacKay, was as he is portrayed in the play, parsimonious and resentful of his daughter's illness. The character is therefore to be accounted an actual portrait. Nevertheless, the relationship between father and daughter incorporates some of the disgust with the miserly father that O'Neill later was to express as his own at the climactic moments of the first Tyrone play. Undeniably, some of O'Neill's experiences at the time he entered the sanatorium form part of the image. Carmody must be viewed not only as a picture of a man O'Neill had seen, but also as a cartoon of James Tyrone.

The possible parallel between MacKay and James O'Neill suggest a second reason why O'Neill may have suppressed the directly autobiographical details of Stephen's portrait. By 1918, he and his father were growing closer. James had purchased the abandoned Coast Guard station at Peaked Hill Bars on the Cape as a wedding present for his son. It was a loving gift that O'Neill received gratefully. He responded, too, to his father's genuine interest and pride in his developing career as a dramatist. At the end of James's life, understanding was developing to something like love, and O'Neill's memory of his adolescent indignation stopped short of potential libel of his father by drawing a close parallel between James and Bill Carmody or by the inclusion of trivial and needless detail about Stephen's background.

A final reason for blurring the image of himself as Stephen may have been his somewhat ambiguous relationship to Kitty MacKay. In the details of her life and in her physical appearance, Eileen Carmody is nearly identical with her actual counterpart. Photographs show Kitty to have had the mass of wavy dark hair, parted in the middle and combed over her ears that O'Neill describes, and in both Kitty and Eileen "the oval of her face is spoiled by a long, rather heavy, Irish jaw." [344]* Kitty was the oldest of ten children and assumed care of the family after the death of her mother. O'Neill cuts the family to four younger children, but, as Kitty did in life, Eileen worries continually about their welfare.[16] There is no doubt that O'Neill and Kitty broke one of the rules of the sanatorium by involving themselves in a flirtation. As the play suggests the balance of devotion was on the girl's side, rather than on O'Neill's and he, after he received his discharge, never saw her again. She died of her disease in 1915.

The play's account of the love affair is true in its general outlines. Kitty developed a strong interest in the iconoclastic young writer. Insofar as the regimen of the sanatorium permitted, the two had a chaste "affair," confined for the most part to literary matters, she encouraging him to write and reading dutifully the books he recommended. No doubt the love Kitty felt for O'Neill was out of proportion to its provocation. O'Neill responded to her warmth and interest, and when it was no longer needed, he let her go. He had made her no commitment, owed her nothing. Yet the play suggests that he felt a guilt about his ultimate neglect of her that conceivably led him to hide his own features under a mask—Stephen's "concealment mechanism."

Stephen Murray is drawn in unexpectedly negative terms. He is a shallow, mildly talented and cynical man. Although he has done some writing on a small town newspaper, in the sanatorium, he spends his time dreaming before the fire. He is bored and lazy, and although he admits that he has ideas for stories, he complains of never having had time to write them down. Eileen sensibly points

---

* The same features are to be seen in Sara Melody in *A Touch of the Poet* and Josie Hogan in *A Moon for the Misbegotten*.

out that now he has nothing but time, an idea that strikes Stephen as magnificent inspiration. He eagerly follows the suggestion, determined to write and sell stories of small-town life to the *Saturday Evening Post*. He adds, "But you must promise to help—play critic for me—read them and tell me where they're rotten." [361] His ambitions are greatly enlarged when his first story is sold. Then: "—wait till I turn loose with the real big ones, the kind I'm going to write. Then I'll make them sit up and take notice. They can't stop me now." [368]*

When his case is diagnosed as being arrested, Stephen leaves Eileen behind. His letters dwindle away and she pines and dies, much as Kitty MacKay died. O'Neill's image of himself at the time, although blurred, is far from complimentary. In the perspective that time permitted him, it reads more like a self-judgment, verging on condemnation.

A sense of guilt possibly led him to devise an ending that deviated far from the forlorn facts. In the last act, Eileen lies dying. As all terminal cases are, she is to be sent to another hospital so that healthier patients will not be reminded of the dying. Stephen returns for a checkup and is asked by a benevolent nurse to pretend that he loves Kitty so that her last weeks may not be passed in despair. He agrees, but as he lies to her, he discovers that what he speaks is truth, that he genuinely loves her. Passionately, he makes plans to marry her and take her to the West where she may yet recover. Love, he tells her, will work a miracle, and even the hope of a miracle will hold her to life. In a final scene with the nurse, he cries out exultantly: "You'll see! I'll make Eileen get well, I tell you! Happiness will cure! Love is stronger than—" He breaks off, despairing in the face of the certain fact of Eileen's approaching death. To the nurse he says, "O why did you give me a hopeless hope?"

The nurse, consolingly replies with what passes for a revelation: "Isn't all life just that—when you think of it? . . . But there must be something back of it—some promise of fulfillment—somehow—somewhere—in the spirit of hope itself." [415] The play ends with ambiguous optimism.

Caught as he was in a semi-autobiographical narrative, the conclusion was perhaps the best that circumstances permitted. For

---

* The words probably reflect O'Neill's own impatience to progress to works of greater scope than the Provincetown permitted.

Eileen to have made a miraculous recovery would have suited the films or the theatre of Jane Cowl, but it would have betrayed whatever loyalties O'Neill felt toward Kitty MacKay and been no more than a wishful expiation of his own feeling of neglect. To have permitted her to die in Stephen's arms in Camille-like spasms would have proven harrowing and, in all probability, meaningless. The ending moving midway between exultation and despair and striking a note of embittered romanticism that he was to sound again, notably in *Welded* and *All God's Chillun Got Wings,* was not a compromise. In the phrase "hopeless hope," O'Neill came to the central theme of all the plays he had worked on since *Beyond the Horizon,* and one which would provide a substantial element of O'Neill's truth.

It means—or it comes to mean—something more than the maniacal fixation on an anticipated event that he toyed with in *The Rope* and *Where the Cross Is Made.* Here, it begins to suggest that men must accept any kind of delusion, force themselves to believe any falsehood if they are to survive the frightening courses of their lives. Significantly, there is no suggestion that Eileen will live. Both know better, but even without the possibility of fulfillment she and Stephen must hope, for hopelessness cannot be borne. Elsewhere in the play, such hope is called a "pipe dream that keeps us all going," [350] and the words imply that the object of desire does not matter, so long as desire exists. The concept, in the phrase wrung from Stephen at the play's climax, crystallizes one of O'Neill's most important themes, even though it loses its full meaning in the romantic ambiguities which resulted from O'Neill's attempt to pay a debt to the ghost of Kitty MacKay.

Considering O'Neill's practical theatrical experience up to 1918, *The Straw* is a work of considerable merit. The play is ambitious, calling for a cast of approximately sixty persons, and was clearly one that the Provincetown Players could not mount. O'Neill's faith in it was great, but it had less than enthusiastic response from commercial managers. It was rejected by both J. D. Williams and the Theatre Guild, newly formed from the Washington Square Players. In September, 1919, he submitted it to George Tyler, who had agreed to produce *Chris Christopherson,* saying that the work was "far and away the best and truest thing I have done."[17] Tyler's production of it, in November, 1921, proved otherwise. The rehearsals were troubled, and at the last moment the opening was delayed while a substitute for an unsatisfactory actor playing Stephen was rehearsed. An opening in New London was not successful, and the New York run —off-Broadway in the Greenwich Village Theatre because of the "grim" subject matter—lasted twenty performances. The work was reasonably well received by its critics, but in comparison to the excitement that audiences had by then learned to expect from O'Neill on the basis of *Beyond the Horizon, The Emperor Jones,* and *"Anna Christie,"* *The Straw* by 1921 seemed a minor work.

Spasmodically during 1918 and 1919, O'Neill worked at the draft of another long play, *Chris Christopherson,* which George C. Tyler readied for production less than a month after *Beyond the Horizon* was finally scheduled. It failed lamentably, but at best it was an inept script, and one which can most satisfactorily be considered in relation to *"Anna Christie,"* the play it finally became, two years later. The important production was that of *Beyond the Horizon.* When it at last was staged, the fallow period came to an abrupt end, and O'Neill emerged as a full-fledged member of his profession. The Pulitzer Prize which it garnered the following year made his standing official.

Although it had a professional cast and was presented by a major commercial producer in an uptown Broadway theatre, *Beyond the Horizon* was at first approached tentatively. John D. Williams, once he could no longer look on the play as a vehicle for the Barrymore brothers, gave it little attention. He finally committed himself only to a series of three special matinees at the Morosco Theatre, where it was scheduled to play concurrently with the run of a successful Elmer Rice melodrama, *For the Defense.* Its cast, which included Richard Bennett, Helen MacKellar and Edward Arnold, was recruited from the Rice Company and from that of another melodrama, *The Storm.* Although hastily rehearsed and shoddily produced, it was nevertheless received with high praise from both critics and audiences. It opened February 3, 1920, and by February 23 it moved to the Criterion and thence, on March 9, to the Little Theatre for an extended run.

O'Neill had sent the script to Williams in April, 1918. It had languished in the producer's office until Richard Bennett discovered it and cajoled Williams into the trial production. Bennett's contribution to the play's success was, by his own estimate, extensive. In a letter to a friend, Felton B. Elkins, he suggests something of the scope of his labors. Elkins had sent Bennett a play hoping it would be brought to Williams's attention. Bennett replied that Williams had promised to read the play but had not done so thus far. He continued:

> Of course, I realize that the fate of your hope rests on the doing of this play. Personally, I believe in it. And if I were so capitalized to do the things I want to do, I should make it my next play instead of the O'Neil play, which I started to blue pencil day before yesterday, and God knows, it needs some blue penciling. As I read it now, it seems terribly stretched out, and a lot of words with little active material. But having done so much with a rotten subject, such as I have been getting, I myself think that with the acquiescence of the author, a great play can be made out of "Beyond the Horizon."[18]

Two months after the play opened, he wrote again to Elkins expressing satisfaction in his faith and his labors:

> Of course you have learned by this time that O'neil's play is one of the Season's sensations and strange as it may seem, we are playing to really splendid houses.—now we are in a regular theatre—The Little—I closed For the defense to big business in order to keep Beyond the Horizon in NY and we are growing every day in advance. I shouldn't be surprized if we stayed here until July—I am . . . sending you a review which I think—the best written of all the glorious tributes we received on the play—Its glorious to have done it Felton—very few beside Williams believed in it and even he got cold feet—I had to do it all cast it cut it and produce it—still I owe the finding of it to him. I've lost many pounds and am very tired. But what matters that.[19]

The extent of Bennett's textual revisions cannot now be determined, but his work and his faith made theatre history. Although the play was so somber in tone, so unrelieved by comedy or melodrama that many reviewers predicted that it could never achieve a Broadway run, they were all immediately impressed with its quality, which in the United States had no precedent. The only American drama with which it was readily to be compared was *The Great Divide,* William Vaughan Moody's melodrama of fourteen seasons earlier. In more contemporaneous theatre, St. John Ervine's *John Ferguson,* which the Theatre Guild had staged in the spring of 1919, alone was comparable, but *Beyond the Horizon* was preferred to the British play as being of "larger aspect and greater force."[20] Perhaps the play seemed more impressive than it is. In retrospect, it blends into the landscape of many later works written by O'Neill and others; but in its time, it was a signal, the first view of the serious American drama, and the history of its reception is important.

In general, the journalistic criticism was acutely responsive to the play's statement and sharply critical of its structure. O'Neill's play is the story of two brothers, Robert, a dreamer and poet who longs to go to sea and seek the promise that lies beyond the horizon, and Andrew, a more practical man, whose desire extends no farther than the family farm which he tends expertly. A love affair between Robert and Ruth, a girl both brothers love, drives Andrew to sea and keeps Robert on the farm. The play depicts the gradual decline of the marriage and concludes with Robert's death. One reviewer saw the play only as a depiction of "the misery which follows the union of a man and woman who are incompatible,"[21] but for the most part, the reviewers rightly understood the search of the dreamer, Robert Mayo, as the quest of a man for his proper element. Alexander Woollcott, in the *New York Times,* wrote that Robert is "chained to a task for which he is not fitted, withheld from a task for which he was born. . . . At the end he crawls out of the farmhouse to die in the open road, his last glance straining at the horizon beyond which he has never ventured, his last words pronouncing a message of warning from one who had not lived in harmony with what he was."[22] From Woollcott's analysis, it is clear that O'Neill's first major statement of his earliest tragic theme, one which he had evolved through the writing of the *Glencairn* plays, was understood without ambiguity.

Successful in understanding Robert Mayo, the reviewers were less able to comprehend Ruth and Andrew. Ruth was seen merely as a drag on Robert's aspiration, a creature of instinct, who turned into a whining slut. Andrew, although he was understood as a complement to Robert, was not viewed as a dispossessed man, who, like Robert, is forced to seek salvation far from his native element. Significantly, in commenting on these two roles, the reviewers turned to a consideration of the performers, rather than of the characters, finding Miss MacKellar vivid and able, Edward Arnold too melodramatic to do justice to the play's realistic style.

Satisfied with the play's central character, its theme, its realism and its dialogue, the reviewers to a man found fault with the play's structure. In effect, they sent O'Neill back to Baker's classroom, objecting to the exposition as clumsy, and in particular faulting what they called a "chronic looseness of construction," especially as it was evidenced in the division of each act into two scenes, one in the farmhouse, the other on an open road. The poor production perhaps occasioned their censure. In its original staging, the play ran close to four hours,[23] much of which was spent in interminable waiting while the scenes were being shifted. Especially in Act III, the change of scene was thought to dissipate the emotional force of Robert's death. Woollcott, who objected to the scenery as being painted "in the curiously inappropriate style of a German postcard," took the play severely to task on this score, and other reviewers were no less outspoken.*

Despite the critical carping at technical problems, *Beyond the Horizon* made O'Neill an important American dramatist. At the time of the Morosco opening, his second long play, *Chris Christopherson*, was being readied for a March tryout in Atlantic City, and *The Straw*, for which O'Neill had the highest hopes, had been taken

---

* From this distance, it is impossible to reconstruct the pre-production history of the play in detail, but such evidence as is available suggests that Bennett may have called upon O'Neill to make drastic revisions in the structure of Act III. At some point after the opening, it appears that the play was staged without the final scene, concluding with Robert's exit from the farmhouse and the quarrel between Andrew and Ruth. The program for the Morosco opening lists only one scene for Act III, the farmhouse, and in his précis of the play for *The Best Plays of 1919-1920*, Burns Mantle makes no reference to III,2. On the other hand, Woollcott and Kenneth Macgowan in their reviews of the opening matinee refer specifically to the difficulties in the division of Act III. It seems possible that after the opening, an attempt was made to telescope the two scenes, perhaps following a plan that had been accepted during rehearsals at a time when the original program was being printed. Later decision, after the program was printed, may have rejected the revision and the play was staged as written, while the program went unchanged. O'Neill's comment on the matter of the scene division is instructive: "One scene is out of doors, showing the horizon, suggesting man's desire and dream. The other is indoors, the horizon gone, suggesting what has become of his dream. In that way I tried to get the rhythm, the alternation of longing and loss. Probably very few people who saw the play knew that this was definitely planned to produce the effect. But I am sure they all unconsciously *get* the effect. It is often easier to express an idea through such means than through words or mere copies of real actions." [Gelb, 411] Of a revival in 1926, Gilbert Gabriel in the *New York American* wrote that O'Neill's stagecraft was better understood than at first: "We are used to his rondeau effects, we have accepted his reiterative chanties of fate as an artful and powerful dramatic means."

under option by George Tyler. In process also were *Gold* and a new work, *The Silver Bullet,* which was to become *The Emperor Jones.* The production, in short, was accompanied by a renewed sense of energy manifested not only in the number of plays O'Neill had in hand but also in an important development of his themes and techniques. The play seemed a work of a new and vital imagination, and its success was unquestionably valid. Certainly the play is the first major work of the O'Neill canon. It is fully characteristic. It is also a clearly "American" play, and thus an important "original." Yet, as with many of the one-act plays that had preceded it, O'Neill relied heavily on the work of others for important seminal inspiration and general direction. *Beyond the Horizon,* like *Bound East for Cardiff,* is at once original and deeply derivative.

In 1926 in a letter to Edward Sheldon, O'Neill acknowledged two important influences on his work:

> Dear Edward Sheldon:
> I was immensely grateful for your wire about [*The Great God*] *Brown.* Your continuous generous appreciation of my work during the past years has meant a great lot to me, has been one of the very few things that have gratified me and satisfied me deep down inside. I say this—and I want you to *know* I say it!—with the deepest sincerity. Your *Salvation Nell,* along with the work of the Irish Players on their first trip over here, was what first opened my eyes to the existence of a real theatre as opposed to the unreal—and to me then, hateful—theatre of my father, in whose atmosphere I had been brought up. So, you see, I owed you this additional debt of long standing.[24]

The debt to both Sheldon and the Irish Players is evident in *Beyond the Horizon.*

After a stormy run in Boston, where Synge's *The Playboy of the Western World* generated its customary riots, the players from the Abbey Theatre had come to New York in November, 1911, under the management of George Tyler. Riots were expected when the Synge work opened, and wisely the directors determined to hold back its production until audiences had had a taste of the Players' quality. They opened, therefore, with a bill of short plays, including *The Rising of the Moon* and *Spreading the News* by Lady Gregory and a two-act tragedy by T. C. Murray called *Birthright.* O'Neill saw all the Players' New York performances, and his general indebtedness to their quasi-poetic, yet realistic, style is important, if obvious. More particular is his debt to Murray's play. His borrowing from it was extensive and continuous throughout his life.[25]

Birthright is a Cain and Abel story set on a small Irish farm owned by Bat Morrissey and his wife, Maura. Hugh, the elder of their sons, is to inherit the farm, while the younger, Shane, leaves to make a new life for himself in America. Hugh, in his father's opinion, is less able to run the farm than Shane for he has other interests than farming. He is a poet, something of a dreamer, but also he is interested in sports and has become the village hero because of his skill at hurling. In sharp contrast to Shane, whose whole life is centered on the farm, Hugh likes dances and other forms of amusement. In Shane, Bat recognizes one of his own kind, but Hugh is alien to him. He feels that no one to whom the farm is not an entire way of life should inherit it, and, when Maura complains that he is hard on Hugh, he tells her what the farm means:

BAT   . . . Hard, is it? That's the quare saying from your mouth. I'd like to know who is hard. When I bought this place thirty years ago with the bit o' money I made in the States what kind was it? Tell that an' spake the truth! Tell it now!

MAURA   A cold place it was surely—a cold, poor place, with more o' the rock, an' the briar, an' the sour weed than the sweet grass.

BAT   Well, an' who blasted every rock that was in it?

MAURA   Sure, 'twas no one but yourself, Bat.

BAT   An' who rooted out the briars, and often tore 'em out with his own two living hands?

MAURA   (*conciliatingly*). 'Twas yourself I know. Alone you did it.

BAT   (*with rising anger*). An' maybe you'd tell me now again who drained the western field that was little better than a bog—an' who built the strong fences an' planted the thorn on them—an' who made the land kind where the grass was that dry and coarse you'd think 'twas the strings o' the lash on that whip beyond? Tell me that, will you? Tell me that now?

MAURA   Sure, I know, Bat, 'twas yourself—and the good God that gave you the great strength.

BAT   *I'm hard*, am I? I've been out in the darkness before the dawn, an' remained stuck in the trench an' the furrow all day, till the black darkness came on me again, and the moon came up, and the faintness on me that I couldn't walk into this house for staggering no better than a cripple or a man that would be drunk. An' for what, I ask you? For what Maura? For my brave Hugh, for an idler and a scamp and a-a-a worthless blackguard! I'm hard, Maura, am I?

MAURA   Wisht, sure, I didn't mean it. I didn't mean it at all. I didn't, indeed, Bat.

BAT   I'm hard, am I? 'Tis your son is hard, and you know it. The sweat o' my body an' my life is in every inch o' the land, and 'tis little he cares, with his hurling an' his fiddling an' his versifying and his confounded nonsense! . . . I tell you again—an' mind my words for it—'tis the black look out for this place when *he* gets it, an' only for your talk, an' your crying, 'tis that blackguard's name an' not his brother's would be on that trunk there this night!

MAURA   Wouldn't it be the queer thing entirely, Bat, to send the eldest son away, and he with your own father's name on him?

BAT   Would it, then? Would it? Tell me, had I ever to go away myself? What was good enough for me ought to be good enough for my brave Hugh—but of course *I'm* only a poor ignorant ploughman, and he's the scholar. The scholar! God bless us!

MAURA   Don't talk foolish, Bat. Sure no one thinks that way of you, and least of all the boy himself . . . (*half musingly*). 'Tis the strange thing surely, his own father to be the only one in the parish that's not proud of him; and everyone talking of him, and the priest himself praising him, and his picture in the paper for the great rhymes he made. . . .

BAT   That's more o' your foolish talk, an' 'tis you have helped to make him the kind he is. Your blood is in him. I see it in every twist and turn of his and every wild foolish thing coming from his mouth. . . . Good God, woman, will his grand rhymes an' his bits o' meddles an' his picture an' the people's talk pay the rent for us? . . . Well, surely, 'tis the foolish thing for a farmer to marry any but wan with the true farmer's blood in her. I should have guessed long ago what 'ud come of it when I married wan that had other blood in her veins. . . . But Shane isn't gone yet—and maybe he'd never go! . . .[26]

The difference in the brothers is somewhat crudely dramatized. Hugh's sensitive, poetic nature is suggested when he disgraces himself by fainting while shoveling a manure pile, and Shane's affection for the farm is shown by his concern for a mare who is the pride of Bat's eye. When the spectators at a hurley match bring Hugh home in triumph, they startle the mare who shies and breaks her leg, despite what Shane can do to calm her. The mare must be shot. Maura comments,

> 'Tis the terrible misfortune, surely. 'Tis the great loss entirely. . . . And Bat, sure, 'twill kill him, and he always so proud of the brown nearly mare. . . . The poor thing, and she always so good and willing, and the great worker for seven long years.

Shane reacts bitterly to the shooting:

> Do you know there was a kind of quare feeling come over me, an'
> I turning the gun at her?—a kind of shiver it was, an' a mist before
> my eyes. . . . 'Tis strange I'll be feeling going across in the big
> ship, an' thinking of the lonely look in her big eyes with the death
> coming down on them like a dark dream.[27]

Evidently, *Birthright* is a play that stirred O'Neill's imagination
deeply, and some aspects of his creative processes can be judged from
the use he made of the play. He saw the play in 1911, and it provided him with the germinal plot idea for *Beyond the Horizon,*
seven years later. O'Neill's story of two brothers, one a poet, the
other a true farmer, with the former due to possess the land while
the latter must go to sea, is too close to the structure of relationships
in *Birthright* to be put down as mere coincidence. *Beyond the Horizon* is a re-imagining of the elements of Murray's play which by
1918 might well have been only a general recollection of a good plot
idea.

The process, however, did not stop there. His imagination continued to feed on Murray's characters. Some residue of its initial
impact remained in 1924, when he wrote *Desire Under the Elms,*
retelling again the story of the struggle of a farmer's sons for the
land. The long dialogue between Bat and Maura, in which Bat attributes his "hardness" to the qualities of the land is seminal to
Ephraim Cabot's great monologue on the same theme in the second
act of *Desire Under the Elms,* and Ephraim, like Bat, feels that his
wives were unfit to bear him the right kind of sons.

Years later, in 1935, it appears that when he was writing *A Touch
of the Poet,* although by then he may have remembered nothing of
Murray's play, he found welling into his mind an image of an Irish
peasant woman, waiting while her husband's mare was being shot.
In creating the character of Nora Melody, he may also have recalled
how Maura waited for one of her family to return by keeping busy
about the house during a long vigil in the night.

The evidence suggests that O'Neill had been so deeply moved by
his first sight of the Irish Players in Murray's work that the play
embedded itself in his subconscious mind. A residuum of that emotion remained with him, letting half-forgotten images come to the

surface whenever the connotative conditions were right,* and especially whenever he wrote of the land. Such a process may be no more than one of the usual processes of creativity, and, at its best, with O'Neill as with other writers and their "sources," the germinal elements take radically different form and meaning when they are fully developed. Occasionally, O'Neill was trapped in slavish imitation, as when in *Before Breakfast* he imitated Strindberg and was caught less by a genuine commitment than by an intriguing concept, manner or style. More often, the process permitted O'Neill to respond emotionally and completely, and to re-see his source material in his own terms, as he did in his use of Conrad in *Bound East for Cardiff* and of Murray's play in three of his major works.

To say that he responded emotionally does not mean that he was incapable of formulating consciously the "influence" on his work. What is interesting is that he does not mention those works that, like *Birthright* or Conrad's tales, lay close to the center of his creative impulses. Instead, in discussing the sources of *Beyond the Horizon,* he casts back to an autobiographical experience.

> I think the real life experience from which the idea of *Beyond the Horizon* sprang was this: On the British tramp steamer on which I made a voyage as an ordinary seaman . . . there was a Norwegian A.B. and we became quite good friends. The great sorrow and mistake of his life, he used to grumble, was that as a boy he had left the small paternal farm to run away to sea. He had been at sea twenty years and had never gone home once in that time. I don't imagine he had written home or received a letter from there in years.

> He was a bred-in-the-bone child of the sea if there ever was one. With his feet on the plunging deck, he was planted like a natural growth in what was "good clean earth" to him. If ever man was in perfect harmony with his environment, a real part of it, this Norwegian was.

> Yet he cursed the sea and the life it had led him—affectionately. He loved to hold forth on what a fool he had been to leave the farm. There was the life for you, he used to tell the grumblers in the fo'c'stle. A man on his own farm was his own boss. He didn't have to eat rotten grub, and battle bedbugs, and risk his life in storms on a rotten old "Limejuice" tramp. He didn't have to wait for the end of a long voyage for a pay day and a good drunk.

---

* It is perhaps worth noting that when his second son was born in 1919, shortly after he completed *Beyond the Horizon,* he named him Shane.

> No, sir. A man on his own farm could get drunk every Saturday night and stay drunk all day Sunday if he wanted to! (At this point the fo'c'stle to a man became converted to agriculture.) Then too, a man on a farm could get married and have kids. . . .

The sailor O'Neill describes is doubtless the same man who inspired the figure of Olson in *The Long Voyage Home,* where O'Neill first began to articulate the sense of a man's relationship with elemental forces. The thematic concept provides the strongest link to Robert Mayo, whose connection with the Norwegian sailor is somewhat tenuous. As O'Neill explained it:

> I thought what if he had stayed on the farm with his instincts? What would have happened? But I realized at once he never would have stayed. . . . I started to think of a more intellectual, civilized type—a weaker type . . . a man who would have my Norwegian's inborn cravings for the sea's unrest, only in him it would be conscious, too conscious, intellectually diluted into a vague intangible romantic wanderlust. His powers of resistance, both moral and physical, would also probably be correspondingly watered. He would throw away his instinctive dream and accept the thralldom of the farm for—why, for almost any nice little poetical craving—the romance of sex, say.
>
> And so Robert Mayo was born. . . .[28]

The account of the genesis of the character is evidently aimed at public consumption. It shows O'Neill emerging as a public figure and capitalizing to an extent on his rough-and-tumble past. His ironic treatment of Robert Mayo as the victim of a "nice little poetic craving" is far from the way he is presented in the play. The uncharacteristic sophistication of the statement may well reflect the easy cynicism of such associates as George Jean Nathan with whom he had been corresponding.

In fact, Robert Mayo is one of the many early self-portraits, and in describing him O'Neill first uses the phrase that will become a significant key to the description of his tragic hero:

> He is a tall, slender young man of twenty-three. There is a touch of the poet about him expressed in his high forehead and wide dark eyes. His features are delicate and refined, leaning to weakness in the mouth and chin. [81]

In his lineaments, the faces of John Brown, the Poet in *Fog,* and something perhaps of Smitty, are to be seen clearly. Later heroes, all "touched" with poetry, will be cast in the same mold and will be similar in appearance. If O'Neill's account is in any degree true, to turn his staunch sailor friend inside out meant that what he found as an opposite was himself. The publicity is little more than a mask, for in Robert Mayo, O'Neill explored his own truth.

In the play, O'Neill plunges Robert into a Strindbergian matrimonial drama, much as he had done earlier with John Brown and Alfred Rowland, and as he later was to do with other self-portraits, Dion Anthony, Curtis Jayson in *The First Man,* and Michael Cape in *Welded.* Ruth and Robert Mayo are shackled to one another in soul-destroying bondage of the sort that O'Neill had discovered in *The Father* and *The Dance of Death.* The primary effects are the same in *Beyond the Horizon* as they are in Strindberg. After the death of spirit, the man plunges toward physical death and the woman moves toward infidelity. That the tone of the play is not especially like Strindberg's is partly the result of its merger with the Irish folk drama that supplied the basic narrative situation, and partly also because a third "source" somewhat diminished the Strindbergian overtones.

Legend has it that the title for the play came from a conversation O'Neill held with a small boy on the Provincetown shoreline. The boy wondered what lay "beyond the horizon," and the phrase provided O'Neill with his title.[29]

Whether the anecdote is true or not, any reader of the literature of the United States in the first quarter of the twentieth century will recognize in the title's imagery what might be called the "Horizon Syndrome," an affliction that manifested itself in countless inspirational poems, stories and short plays in precisely the way O'Neill used it—to suggest boundless aspiration for a somewhat vaguely defined freedom of spirit. To cite a single, potentially influential example: in November, 1912, Edward Sheldon's play, *The High Road,* was produced in New York. It is the story of a farm girl who is seduced by a traveling artist and leaves home. In the course of her life she becomes a woman of some political prominence.* Early in the play, Sheldon gives full development to the horizon imagery. The high road leads through apple country, "winding like a rib-

---

* In its general outlines, Sheldon's play bears some resemblance to O'Neill's scenario, *The Reckoning,* written in 1917. See above, 58.

bon,* until it is lost in the far distance of the violet hills."[30] The first act love scene between Mary Page and the artist, Alan Wilson, provides an example of the inspirational motif:

MARY   (*pointing*)—Do you see where the moonlight hits the rocks on the top of that hill? It makes it look like a house all built o' gold. . . .

ALAN   I've climbed those hills. . . . It's hard work, but I didn't care. I just pushed along and thought of the welcome waiting for me at the top.

MARY   An' what was it like when ye got there?

ALAN   There was nothing but the plain, bare rocks.

MARY   Wasn't ye awful disappointed?

ALAN   Perhaps—just at first—but then right off I saw the golden house again. . . . Across the valley—on the hills beyond! . . .

MARY   An' when ye'd climbed up the next hill, it was just the same? . . . An' no one's ever walked into the house an' sat close by a winder an' looked out over the world?

ALAN   Not one. Only each time that you climb a hill it seems a little bigger and a little brighter. . . .[31]

Although O'Neill was clearly writing in a recognizable vein, *Beyond the Horizon* was rightfully received as a compelling original. As his first major play, it properly builds on all his most significant earlier work. His sense of a special relationship between man and his environment had emerged at the outset of his career in his perceptions about the sun and the fog and especially about the power the sea has over men's lives. To this he added the relatively recent idea, derived in part from Conrad, of the power of hope to sustain men. Then, in depicting the details of Robert's marriage, he drew upon his understanding of husbands and wives derived from Strindberg. Finally, in Robert and Andrew, he sketched the poetical self-portrait and its materialistic counterpart with which he had been occupied since *Fog*. What emerged finally was the memorable figure of a man "touched" with poetry, O'Neill's true tragic protagonist. Robert was a man who was out of harmony with his environment, who could not "belong" and who therefore was condemned to live between hope's eternal optimism and the inevitability of despair. *Beyond the Horizon* is thus a summing-up of O'Neill's early years as a playwright; at the same time, the merging of his major thematic

---

* O'Neill's description of his first setting also calls for apple trees and for a road *"in the distance winding toward the horizon like a pale ribbon between the low, rolling hills."*

preoccupations produced a new structure which would serve as a base for further development. It is also true, as is often the case with the emergence of an important playwright, that the tragedy defined for its audiences certain formulations which they chose to accept as beliefs of their society.

In retrospect, the causes of the success of *Beyond the Horizon* are complex. To be sure, the play was a naturalistic tragedy in the modern mode by a young American playwright whose career had excited interest. Its production was a labor of love by important actors who had idealistically rejected wearisome commercial success as a testament of their faith in it. It appeared in a context of growing enthusiasm for the new theatre as an art form, and it was sufficiently well written to merit serious discussion. Yet, there have been equal successes under similar conditions. Jesse Lynch Williams's *Why Marry?*, which won the first Pulitzer Prize in 1918, Zona Gale's *Miss Lulu Bett* or Owen Davis's *Icebound*, which received the award in 1921 and 1923 respectively, were in their ways equally impressive. Yet these plays are forgotten and *Beyond the Horizon* survives. It does so because, with great clarity and with the simplicity of a fable, its theme established a major tragic motif of American drama.

Man's relationship with nature has, of course, been a constant theme in literature under a wide variety of formulations and interpretations. The concept of natural man as being an exemplar of the good, or of reversion to nature as indicating the brute in man, of man's soul as being in or out of tune with nature, or of man turning endlessly in space as the victim of uncomprehending forces of his environment—none of these has novelty. Yet O'Neill's use of man's desire to belong to nature as the source of a tragic action was an important new variant on an old theme. It was one that was to appeal to a great number of American dramatists, following O'Neill's lead, in the 1930's and 1940's, and it was to form a major motif of his own cycle on American history, *A Tale of Possessors, Self-dispossessed.*

As developed by O'Neill tragic disharmony with nature is depicted most often in terms of private, personal loss in such figures as the Hairy Ape, Eben Cabot or Dion Anthony. Many of those who came after him broadened the scope beyond a purely personal focus to include social disorders and to picture man as a victim of suffocating societal pressures. Even here, however, from American authors, the explanation of the malady of both the individual and his society is the fundamental dislocation between man and nature.

For example, in Robert Sherwood's *The Petrified Forest,* the nomadic Alan Squier, after citing Eliot's "The Hollow Men," explains that the poem refers to the intellectuals who have attempted to package nature. Nature, however, is hitting back, not through floods and holocausts, but through neuroses, and is "proving that she can't be beaten. . . . She's taking the world away from the intellectuals and giving it back to the apes."[32] Sherwood's view of a blindly vengeful nature as the cause of the modern distemper prevails over all other indictments of society in the play. In Maxwell Anderson's *High Tor,* the American is viewed as a stranger to his own land, a pessimistic base for a sweet-sour comedy. The action of Sidney Howard's *They Knew What They Wanted* is interpreted by the commentary of a rationalist doctor and a simple country priest, but neither reason nor faith resolves the potentially tragic situation of the comedy. Instead, the grape farmer, Tony, whose capacity for simple charity and power of forgiveness are derived from his long-harmonious association with the earth, brings peace to the troubled relationships. As a final example, Arthur Miller's *Death of a Salesman* finds everyman's problem to be caused by his divorce from the land. Willy remembers the grassy plains of the west, the music of the flute, the shadowy patterns of leaves, and his last action is the frantic, symbolic gesture of planting seeds in the sterile earth.

In the light of later developments, *Beyond the Horizon* proved a seminal play, establishing a theatrical pattern which endured for at least two decades. Inexpert as it was in many of its elements, in the whole it showed O'Neill to be a dramatist who could speak significantly to his audiences, by presenting them with a meaning which was accepted as an important truth, and in effect an aspect of national belief: that man will only be complete when he lives in a right relationship with the earth.

The cosmos of the play is equally divided between land and sea. If Andrew had stayed on the farm, if Robert had gone to sea, each would have held true to his essential nature and been able to live in harmony with the elements around him. The implication, therefore, is that Robert belongs to the sea and Andrew to the land. It is not enough to say that Robert's longing for the sea is "too conscious, intellectually diluted into a vague, romantic wanderlust." The phrase might have held true for Smitty, yearning toward the moon on the deck of the *Glencairn*, but Robert, in the cup of the hills, cut off from the horizon, is imprisoned, forcibly held back from joining the element to which he rightly belongs. His weakness and his romanticism are irrelevant; until he can unite himself with the sea, he can be no stronger. On land, the unyielding furrows are sterile, and, by the same token, Andrew finds no nurture at sea but travels unmoved to romantic shores, seeing only abused land. Andrew's corruption is epitomized by his perverting the farmer's instinct and gambling in wheat. Robert makes the point specifically: "You used to be a creator when you loved the farm. You and life were in harmonious partnership. And now—." [161]

Andrew and Robert stand sharply opposed, the poet and the materialist in the same relationship as the figures had been set in *Fog*. The fact that the two, now, are brothers is suggestive. O'Neill sees them—perhaps because he sensed in his relationship with his own brother a similar radical opposition—positive and negative images of what he called "longing and loss." Despite the gulf between them they are chained together, and, later, in more complex plays he will repeat the same strange fraternal conflict—for example between Dion Anthony and Billy Brown in *The Great God Brown* and between the two halves of John Loving's personality in *Days Without End*.

In the action of *Beyond the Horizon*, there is no solace. Like the sailors of the *Glencairn*, Andrew's wants are easily satisfied, but the source of his discontent remains unlocated. Robert, however, is different, for he is touched with a poet's power of vision and is able to bring unspoken needs to a level of consciousness. He is able to articulate hope, to sense what lies beyond the farthest range of vision.

To be sure, in the play he does not frame matters in such terms. Admitting he is a failure, he says that he can justly lay some of the blame for his stumbling "on God." [161] Yet it is hard to understand how God is to be blamed for Robert's ruin. "God" in such a scheme can mean little more than such a hostile, "ironic life force" as destroyed the heroine of *The Web*. O'Neill, emerging as a poet, is no longer concerned with what is totally negative, as such derivative deterministic conceptions essentially were. To him, now, the real forces in the play are the powers in the sea and the land that, while they reject alien children, hold out promise of peace and harmony to those who truly belong. The promise is important. Robert claims it at the end of the play, mistakenly asserting that he has won it through "sacrifice":

> And this time I'm going! It isn't the end. It's a free beginning—the start of my voyage! I've won to my trip—the right of release—beyond the horizon! . . . Ruth has suffered—remember, Andy—only through sacrifice—the secret beyond there— . . . the sun! . . . Remember! [168]

With these words he dies, leaving Andrew and Ruth spiritually exhausted, *"in that spent calm beyond the further troubling of any hope."*

What Robert means by "sacrifice" is not clear. So that he can marry Ruth he drives Andrew from the farm, denies the power of the sea and proceeds then in a stumbling and incompetent course in a service, the land's, for which he is not fitted. Ruth turns against him, their child dies and the farm fails. But Robert, who has made no choice beyond the initial determination, has not sacrificed, nor is there any indication that his death is a sacrificial atonement for his initial error. On the contrary, although his original action has caused suffering, his death is close to a blessing, both a release from pain and a reunification with the element that is rightfully his. Yank's death in *Bound East for Cardiff* hinted at something of the kind. Now, it is clear, Robert's death ends what Georges Bataille would call the "discontinuity" of his being.[33] Discarding through death his individuating consciousness, ridding himself of the poet's awareness of the need for belonging, he moves through death into the mainstream of continuous life energy. In Edmund Tyrone's word, he has "dissolved" into the secret.

Even if hope is not fulfilled in life, Robert's destiny would be unlike that of the *Glencairn* sailors, restless denizens of a world they do not understand. Awareness breeds hope and its accompanying suffering. Yet for the poet such pain defines his end: in seeking to belong to the life force, he will yearn for entire forgetfulness, the relaxation of the tensions of desire and for the trustful loss of consciousness. Having been born, he is doomed to "discontinuity," and, except in such transitory moments as Edmund Tyrone describes, when "the veil is drawn back," he must live without belonging. Seeking to belong, however, suffering the lack of harmony, he will come to know, if not to achieve, his God, his home, his proper good.

V
AMATEUR'S END
1920

PLAYS WRITTEN IN 1920 ARE
The Ole Davil (completed in 1921 as "*Anna Christie*")
The Emperor Jones
Gold
Diff'rent
The First Man (completed in 1921)

1920—a year of promises fulfilled and benefits reaped.
Beyond the Horizon, finally produced on Broadway in February,
received the Pulitzer Prize, and the Provincetown production of
The Emperor Jones had a success equaled by few American plays.
A second long play, *Chris,* had failed, but its revision,
"*Annie Christie,*" was waiting in the wings, and Eugene's imagination
was alive with projects stimulating to contemplate.
There was tragedy: late that summer his father died of cancer,
but James had lived long enough to understand something of
his son's genius and to take pride in his achievement.
James's death broke a spell that had held the family captive:
Ella, with the Church's help, cured herself
of her addiction; and, in response, once she had proven her strength,
Jamie stopped drinking and followed her back along the road to health.
Reunited, mother and son turned to the problems of James's estate.
Now, increasingly, Eugene was called a "leading dramatist,"
and his picaresque early life proved good copy for interviews.
Young, serious and responsible, he sat for formal photographs
that were published with captions of praise in such journals
as the new voice of the theatre renaissance, *Theatre Arts Magazine.*
The days of the amateur were clearly behind him.
He even approached financial solvency.

ON the night of November 1, 1920, *The Emperor Jones* took O'Neill and the Provincetown Players beyond any horizon they had envisioned. Against Cook's plaster dome, moving in chiaroscuro through Cleon Throckmorton's silhouetted setting, and energized by the performances of Charles Gilpin and Jasper Deeter, the play amply repaid the faith that had been lavished upon it. It was proof that the Players had fostered a truly American playwright; it was proof that O'Neill's dedication to his art was in fact a true vocation; and it demonstrated conclusively that there was an untouched world of theatre yet to be explored in America. What *Beyond the Horizon* had suggested—that an ordinary American could become a subject of pathetic concern and on occasion could rise to the height of a tragic figure—was abundantly demonstrated in the account of the rise and fall of Brutus Jones. Moreover, the technical excitements of the play, with its drums, its sustained monologue, its rapidly shifting settings framed into a single desperate action were almost blinding in their virtuosity and in their assurance of important theatrical things to come. Not only the literate American drama, but the American theatre came of age with this play.

The play was an overnight success. The Provincetown had had no experience with a run-away hit and coped bewilderedly with the long lines waiting to buy tickets the morning after the opening. Operating on a subscription system, the box office sold a thousand subscriptions during the first week of the run, and extra performances were scheduled to accommodate the demand. By late December, the little playhouse was overwhelmed, and under the management of Adolph Klauber, the play moved to an uptown engagement, somewhat hesitantly offered at a series of special matinees like those with which *Beyond the Horizon* had been launched. The matinees were scheduled for December 27, 28, 30 and 31, and again the play triumphed. The special engagement was extended for five weeks, until on January 29, it began a regular run, that climaxed with a two-year road tour.[1]

The success was the rock on which the Players foundered, yet their demise was inevitable from the very nature of their idealism. More important in considering the development of O'Neill's work is that *The Emperor Jones*, while it confirmed O'Neill's direction and justified his dedication, set him on a path that at its farthest end was to prove artistically perilous. For with the play, O'Neill accepted the dicta of the American Art Theatre movement and began to write plays that moved far from his realistic style. He became a writer from whom "experiment" was expected, and one who would sometimes put the dictates of style over the development of theme and character.

The Emperor Jones charts a difficult course between expressionism and realism. In its inception, it was little different from the realistic plays of the past. The figure of Brutus Jones was suggested, O'Neill said, by the character of a bartender he had known, but other acquaintances and the figures of Henri Christophe and Haiti's President Sam, who, like Jones, had a silver bullet, contributed elements to the portrait. A prospecting expedition to Honduras in 1909 gave O'Neill a sense of the reality of a jungle, and he claimed that the pulse of blood in his eardrums during a bout with malaria on that trip gave him the idea of the drum beat used throughout the play.[2] Another important influence was a book of photographs of primitive African sculpture by Charles Sheeler.[3]

Two of O'Neill's favorite authors may have contributed something to the formation of *The Emperor Jones*. The recollection of Buck, Jack London's dog-turned-wolf in *The Call of the Wild*, may have suggested the racial atavism of the last moments of Jones's life. In Joseph Conrad's *The Heart of Darkness* the graphic depiction of man's capitulation to the primordial darkness of the jungle may also have helped to create the picture of Jones, clad in the burlesque uniform of exploitation, but reduced in the end to primitive nakedness, to rags that in Conrad's words "would fly off at the first good shake."

Yet in its dramatic form and in many aspects of its theme, the primary source of O'Neill's play is, unexpectedly, Ibsen.*

The parallels between *The Emperor Jones* and *Peer Gynt* are many and specific. Both plays are about fugitives, running in desperation through the shards of their lives toward a dimly seen salvation whose discovery depends on their learning their essential identities. Much compressed and less oriented toward allegory, O'Neill's play is no more intense than Ibsen's, particularly in those scenes where Peer is alone and in flight—at first from the Trolls, then in the Arabian desert, and finally from the Button-Moulder and his sentence of damnation. The actions of both plays focus on terror and self-discovery, and the crucial moment in both are acted in brief scenes by the protagonists alone onstage, speaking in monologue.

Not only in their dramatic rhythm, emotional pattern and general shape of the action, but in specific episodes, similarities occur. The most notable is Jones's meeting with the Little Formless Fears at the beginning of his flight. As O'Neill describes them,

> *They are black, shapeless, only their glittering little eyes can be seen. If they have any describable form at all it is that of a grub-worm about the size of a creeping child. They move noiselessly, but with deliberate, painful effort, striving to raise themselves on end, failing and sinking prone again. . . . From [them] comes a a tiny gale of low mocking laughter like a rustling of leaves.* [189]

When they are dispersed by his revolver shot, Jones reassures himself that "Dey was only little animals—little wild pigs, I reckon."

The Fears are a compound of many of the mysteries Peer meets on his forest run: the formless Boyg, the leaves that talk in the voices of children and the trolls themselves, who, when truly seen, are pigs.

The first title of *The Emperor Jones* was *The Silver Bullet,* an indication of the importance of the bullet in the play's design. Jones's bullet is his emperorhood epitomized in a single destructive symbol; it is his talisman, his rabbit's foot, his fate. When it is gone, he must go to his death. In *Peer Gynt,* the bullet is paralleled by the silver button, Peer's legacy from his father, his squandered inheritance, his wasted soul. Peer, like the silver button, must be melted down again into the mass.[4]

---

* The relationship is mentioned without detailed elaboration in an interesting short study by Egil Törnqvist, "Ibsen and O'Neill, A Study in Influence." *Scandinavian Studies* (August, 1965, Vol. 37, No. 3), 221.

Both button and bullet symbolize the essence of the self of the protagonists, and in both, that self is called an "Emperor." Peer is the Emperor of the Gyntian Self, dreaming of ruling Peeropolis in the kingdom of Gyntiana, but he is crowned in a Cairo madhouse and his government, founded on "wishes, appetites and desires," controls a kingdom of lies, dreams and cheating illusions. The Emperor of Self is an Emperor of self-deception, whose life-lie forms the trumpery substance of his existence. At the end of his life, he realizes that he is empty, an onion stripped of exterior covering to reveal nothing at the center. Down on all fours in the forest, he compares himself to an animal and writes his own mock-epitaph, "Here lies Peer Gynt, a decent chap, who was Emperor of all the beasts."[5] At the play's end, Peer will discover where his Empire lay, but although Ibsen's ending in tone and meaning is very different from O'Neill's, both playwrights reduce their Emperor-heroes to the condition of groveling animals.

The conformity of the two works in shape and theme is close, although it is difficult to estimate whether O'Neill was aware of the parallels. Ibsen's stage images seem to have formed part of the storaged material on which he drew just as he used his memory of life on the waterfront and at sea. In the end, whatever its indebtedness, The Emperor Jones is authentically O'Neill's in form and statement, an outgrowth of many of the experiments he had undertaken in the years before. The long monologue, developed to a self-conscious point in Before Breakfast, is now used superbly to its fullest extent. The concentration of light in surrounding darkness to suggest the spiritual isolation of his characters becomes now a significant stage image. The Negro dialect, with which he had experimented crudely in The Dreamy Kid, is made an authentic language. Finally, the attempt with the ghosts in Where the Cross Is Made to catch an audience up into madness is repeated in the form of the visions Jones sees and in the drum beat directed as much toward the audience as toward Jones.

O'Neill's success with all of his stage devices, his conscious skill at controlling the effects he needs, mark the play, despite its reliance on Ibsen, as an original work. It was the first major drama of the new American theatre, and it has remained vital, although, in retrospect, it is not so easy to say why as it is to assess the historical and permanent values of other works of literature that appeared in 1920, such as Lewis's *Main Street*, Fitzgerald's *This Side of Paradise* or T. S. Eliot's *Poems*. In comparison with these, *The Emperor Jones* lies a little outside its time, showing small interest in the war-ruined world of the early twenties nor in man's attempt at new social formulations. Such relevance as it has to its period lies in its production history, rather than its qualities as a work of art. The excited praise of the performance of the black actor, Charles Gilpin, whose performance as Brutus Jones brought him immediate stardom, led to a series of serio-comic encounters as the Drama League of New York City awarded him an accolade for being one of those who had contributed significantly to the drama during the year but then refused to invite him to the testimonial dinner. The League's president was quoted as saying that "Mr. Gilpin would not wish to sit down at table with the other prizewinners," and he added that this was especially true since his performance, although distinguished, had shown his race to bad advantage. The fact that the play's author was among the invited prizewinners capped the illogic of the argument. The immediate response was a boycott of the dinner loudly announced by most of the prizewinners. Miss Mary Garden stated flatly, "I would be willing to sit with Mr. Gilpin. I would like to know who in New York would not sit with him." Not to be outdone, Miss Gilda Varesi, star of *Enter Madame,* announced her willingness as well. Gilpin remained cool, the nonsense was resolved with the appearance of amicability and the awards dinner was a success.

That dinner was perhaps the climactic moments of the actor's career, for Gilpin ran afoul of O'Neill's temper by altering lines and permitting himself careless performances. O'Neill refused to hire him for the London production and cast instead a young actor, Paul Robeson. Robeson's star rose as Gilpin's fell. Moss Hart's account of Gilpin's agonizing drunken performances in a 1926 revival of the play tells the tragic end of the story.[6] Whatever talent burned in Gilpin was consumed inwardly by the inevitable frustration that followed upon such success as he had had. He was a somber-spirited, restrained man, who damped his fires with rueful humor and with silence. That he was the first black to achieve a major success in the legitimate theatre in the United States did not become for him a matter for public comment. Contemporary interviews suggest only his personal satisfaction in receiving his just due as an actor, not as a representative of his race. His comment on the Provincetown's

1924 revival with Paul Robeson carries no sense of social crusade: "I created the role of the Emperor. That role belongs to me. That Irishman, he just wrote the play."[7]

O'Neill later praised Gilpin as being one of the few actors who had fully realized his own vision of the role, but Gilpin did not make the play. The central social and artistic point lay in the role itself. Taken as an ethnic study displaying the racial characteristics of the American Negro, the part by present-day perspectives is an unacceptable stereotype of the Negro in terms of a crap-shooting, razor-cutting Pullman porter. Its sympathetic point of view toward Jones, and the extension of his personal history into a broader perspective so that Jones becomes a crude personification of black history, does not significantly alter matters. Like Vachel Lindsay in *The Congo,* O'Neill attempted to depict the forces that come "creeping through the black," and he suggests that the Negro is, like London's Buck, only a step removed from the brute. Although he has evidently read Conrad's *The Heart of Darkness,* O'Neill makes no generalization such as Conrad does that there is a savagery in the hearts of all men. Instead, it is the Negro who is essentially uncivilized, wearing contemporary sophistications as a loosely fitting mask over an incorrigibly savage countenance. In its own time, the point of view was possible, and, when disguised by theatrical excitements, acceptable, but today, the ethnic and social implications of the play can no longer command respectful attention.

Yet what held attention, and to a degree disguised the essential racism, was the fact that Brutus Jones was the first important role written for a Negro actor that was more than a walk-on part, a comic turn, a vaudeville sketch. Such a play as James Forbes's *The Travelling Salesman,* in which O'Neill's brother appeared, is typical. In the second act of the comedy, a black waiter—played by a white actor in minstrel-show blackface—appears for a pair of scenes intended to provide comic embellishment. A single example suffices:

> (*A knock at the door*)
> BLAKE   Come in. (*Enter* JULIUS . . .) I don't want the porter, I want the bell-boy.
> JULIUS   I'se the bell-boy.
> BLAKE   Then send up a waiter.
> JULIUS   I'se dat, too.
> BLAKE   I guess you're the whole works?

JULIUS   I'se the staff of the Elite.
BLAKE   Drinks for a large party!
JULIUS   Can't serve no drinks, boss.
          (KIMBALL, WATTS *and* COBB *look at* JULIUS)
BLAKE   What kind of a stall are you giving me?
JULIUS   'Tain't no stall, it's a solemn fac': Clerk downstairs won't allow it.
          . . . The bar done shut down last night.
COBB   Julius, haven't you a private stock?
JULIUS   No, sir, I never drinks durin' office hours.
BLAKE   (*Taking a half dollar*) Julius, what could you do for that?
JULIUS   (*Grinning*) Most anything, sir.
WATTS   Think—(*Holding up half dollar*) . . .
KIMBALL   (*Holding up half a dollar*) Think hard! . . .
COBB   (*Holding up half dollar*) Think quickly (*Shaking coins, etc.*) . . .
JULIUS   Well, gentlemen, you're all mighty persuasive. (BLAKE *gives* JULIUS
          money; COBB *does same*) I might get you something.
ALL   Ah!
JULIUS   I might get you some tea. . . . (WATTS *jumping forward* . . .
          BLAKE *holds him.* JULIUS *frightened runs up-stage*)
JULIUS   (*Coming down*) I think you might all be partial to this brand of
          tea. Guess you never drunk none a my Scotch breakfast tea. (*They
          all laugh*)
KIMBALL   Now, you're shouting!
BLAKE   Vamp! . . .
WATTS   And vamp quick.
COBB   Bring me a double portion. (JULIUS *exits* . . .)[8]

By contrast with such vile stuff as this, one of many such scenes
that held the stage beyond the time of *The Emperor Jones,* O'Neill
provides for the black actor a true action: a movement both psychological and physical toward a goal whose achievement is fulfilling
and complete. Like all valid dramatic action, it forms the core of the
play's meaning and its unity. Gilpin's success came in part from the
fact that he was the first black to play a role instead of a routine.
His despair arose fundamentally because no other play offered him
a similar opportunity.

What the action of Brutus Jones means, set apart from its stereotypical embellishments, is not entirely obvious. As with the outer
covering of many of O'Neill's major works—the overly simple Freudianism of *Strange Interlude,* for example, or the Nietzschean exultation of *Lazarus Laughed*—the explicit thematic content is not the
real source of the play's energy nor is it a determinant of the play's

final meaning. Like *Beyond the Horizon*, *The Emperor Jones* is a play about man's relationship with a possessive God, and in pursuit of this theme, O'Neill turns the play away from its more obvious symbols, toward a highly personal statement.

The heart of the matter, as O'Neill felt it, lay in the book of photographs of African Negro sculpture by Charles Sheeler. Sheeler's photographs are handsome, and do full justice to the shadows and mysteries which the masks and wooden effigies configure. The heart of darkness resides in these images. Even today, when African folk art is much more widely to be seen than in 1920, the photographs stir the imagination, make a darkness visible. Here Lem has sat for his portrait and the mask of the witch doctor holds terror.

Looking at them for the first time, one might well feel that the African Negro is a simple and relatively unsophisticated being, only a few generations removed from the jungle. It would not be difficult to call his sophistications "primitive" and to assume that the heirs of such artists had some powerful and distinctive affiliation with the Gods who look out from the pages of Sheeler's book. In the pulse of the contemporary black, one might maintain, jungle drums beat and recall the service his ancestors paid to these Gods. Yet, the argument might run, the Negro no longer serves these Gods. In white civilization, he has become a new entity, an individual, not one of a horde, howling in communal self-abandonment. He has acquired a white man's name, an occupation, and has assumed the responsibilities of law, judgment, punishment. Evolving from the primitive, he has become something other than his anonymous native essence and has superimposed a new self on his truth.

In doing this, he has denied the primordial God, just as Robert Mayo, in a quite different context, denies the sea. The action of *The Emperor Jones* lies as does that of Thompson's *The Hound of Heaven* in flight, but it is flight toward something, an action responsive to the movement of the primitive God to reach forth and claim its own. Jones's acts of will, his pride, his conscious individuality as Emperor are the false masks of a white savage. At the end, the black must cast himself upon the God and return home.

The climactic moments in scene seven suggest that Jones's homecoming is a form of salvation. As the scene begins, and as he meets the Witch Doctor, he moves slowly and in puzzled fashion. *"As if in obedience to some obscure impulse, he sinks into a kneeling, devotional posture before the altar."* He withdraws from his devotions, but then, stirred by the incantations of the Witch Doctor, he turns again to the altar, completely hypnotized: *"His voice joins in the incantation, in the cries, he beats time with his hands and sways his body to and fro from the waist. The whole spirit and meaning of the dance has entered into him, has become his spirit. Finally the theme of the pantomime halts on a howl of despair, and is taken up again in a note of savage hope. There is a salvation. The forces of evil demand sacrifice."* [201] At once, Jones realizes he must become the sacrifice. He crawls toward the Crocodile God, close to an acceptance of his end. In the last moment, however, he draws back, refuses to be possessed by the God and fires the silver bullet. The God disappears, and Jones, the last vestige of his emperorhood expended, lies whimpering in the deserted circle, *"as the throb of the tom-tom fills the silence about him with somber pulsation, a baffled but revengeful power."* [202]

In firing the shot, Jones has sought to be Emperor to the end, but, as O'Neill's description of the dance makes clear, by insisting on his sense of conscious self, he has denied finally the God whose creature he rightfully is, has refused to enter where he belongs. In one view, perhaps, Jones's refusal to surrender is heroic for the force is called "evil." In another it is folly, for whatever salvation, whatever true identity he seeks will not come until he loses his emperorhood, the false and fugitive self. Now, however, although he has fled toward his home, he has cut himself from the source of his being. The dark God turns punitive and brutal, and Jones must die without benison or the hope of return.

Divorced of its theatricality and its superficial social concerns, *The Emperor Jones* reads as a theological melodrama rather than as a play about the racial heritage of the American Negro. The attempt to belong to the God and the failure of the attempt is the same action that O'Neill had traced in *Beyond the Horizon* and that he was evolving at the same moment in the draft versions of *"Anna Christie."* Only in its exotic decor, in its use of the black actor, and in its seemingly novel theatrical style did the play do more than O'Neill had accomplished earlier.

The play's style, of course, seemed highly experimental and can still be looked upon as the first major American drama in the expressionist mode.* Clearly, when Jones's visionary encounters are projected beyond the range of his own memory, O'Neill moves past the limits of the realistic stage, opening surfaces to reveal the forces underlying his action, detailing the racial origins of his protagonist's fear. As he does so, the visions become less specific, more emblematic, and the spectator, at once roused and hypnotized by the drumbeats, is asked to enter into the irrational experience, to feel the panic, to lose his own sense of orientation. To the degree that he is able to divorce his action and his spectators from their own spatial and temporal reality, O'Neill turns his play successfully toward expressionism.

The difficulty, however, is that, after the action has ended, much in the manner of a Gothic novelist whose whole purpose is to scare his readers with seemingly supernatural horrors, O'Neill provides an explanation for the visions that Jones has seen and brings the entire play safely to harbor in "reality." The explanation lies in the voodoo magic of the native chief, Lem. Lem's magic has sent the devils and ghosts hounding after Jones. Lem's tribe has cast the spell with the drums, and they have spent the night melting coins to make another silver bullet. Lem weaves the web that captures Jones, and states flatly: "We cotch him." Expressionism or realism? It cannot go both ways. Either the visions come from Jones as part of his racial heritage, or they come from Lem and the magic of the vengeful natives. Once the fact of magic is accepted, the play becomes explicable in realistic terms throughout and its theological meanings are lessened if not vitiated.

As the play moves in theatre, the ambiguity of its mode is not really important. O'Neill's drums worked as he hoped they would to involve the audience. The devices seemed modern and suggested that dramatic point of view could be shifted as Strindberg had done in *The Dream Play* or *The Spook Sonata*, but in the end they led to what was really an old-fashioned theatre. James O'Neill would never have understood a performance that did not seek to make the audience weep, cringe, cry out or cheer. O'Neill in this was his father's inheritor, asking his audiences to commit themselves totally,

---

* It antedates Elmer Rice's *The Adding Machine* by three years and e. e. cummings's *him* by eight.

but with the aim of accepting his action as entirely real. The stylistic ambiguity of *The Emperor Jones* is the first important sign of a problem of mode that had arisen earlier, of a crisis of dramaturgy occasioned by the use of the techniques of expressionism to effect the ends of the realistic theatre.

The success of *The Emperor Jones* was not readily repeated, and for the rest of the year, and for part of 1921, O'Neill pulled back toward a curiously domestic kind of play. He completed *Gold,* the full-length version of *Where the Cross Is Made,* and, in the fall, his play of the life of a New England spinster, *Diff'rent.* By March, 1921, he had finished the first draft of his autobiographical play, *The First Man. The Ole Davil,* the revision of 1918's *Chris Christopherson,* was completed in the fall of 1920 and was finally readied for production as *"Anna Christie"* in 1921. No one of these has the range and excitement of *The Emperor Jones,* and only one, *"Anna Christie,"* was successfully produced.

Gold, which J. D. Williams produced on June 1, 1921, is a play of very little interest, elaborating without significant incrementation of meaning the narrative of its one-act predecessor. The first act, pure Robert Louis Stevenson, details the finding of the treasure and adds to the adventure the murder of two members of the crew who refuse to believe that the treasure is other than Malayan junk jewelry. The second act is concerned with the Captain's sense of guilt and the beginnings of the retributive madness that will overtake him and his family. In the final acts, retribution comes in the death of the Captain's wife, the loss of the treasure ship and, at the end, Bartlett's own admission, shortly before he dies, that the treasure is junk.

In the longer version, O'Neill loses sight of what was most powerful in the shorter—the sustaining lie of the pipe dream. Although an almost maniacal belief in the gold causes Captain Bartlett to put the treasure hunt above all other obligations, he resembles more the whale hunter of *Ile,* a seeker after a purely materialistic goal, than the ghost-ridden dreamer of the one-act play. As he appears in the longer play, he is involved chiefly in a struggle with his wife and with his conscience. She has learned of his complicity in the murder of the crewmen, and his guilt causes an estrangement between them, so that in the end she sickens and dies. The concentration on family problems and matters of conscience diffuses whatever power the short play had, and loses the theme of the dream and madness.

In the fall of 1920, at approximately the same time as *The Emperor Jones* was being readied for production, O'Neill wrote the second of the period's domestic dramas, the two-act study of a repressed New England spinster, *Diff'rent*. The Provincetown Players produced it in December, 1920, on the bill that followed *The Emperor Jones*. The play, first called *Thirty Years*, but evolving its final title from the continual, almost choric repetition of the word "diff'rent" in the first act, is O'Neill's first real venture into Freudian psychology. It is not entirely satisfactory. Emma Crosby's insistence that her fiancé, Caleb, shall come to her marriage bed sexually "pure" is given no explanation in terms of her family or her circumstances. Neither is a clarifying psychological explanation provided for her unexpected switch in Act II, when, thirty years after sending her lover away, she suddenly throws herself at his twenty-three-year-old nephew. Equally mystifying is Caleb's fidelity. His attempt to maintain his "purity" in defiance of all the laws of nature when a native girl slips into his bed, his suicide after thirty years of dog-like devotion to Emma, measured by any standard of reasonable human conduct are substantial improbabilities.

Yet the play, which had some small success, riding tandem with *The Emperor Jones* in its Broadway production, is not to be lightly dismissed. For one thing, there is an intensity about the writing, a quality not quite to be defined that keeps it from the ludicrous. For all the carefully prepared details of the historical New England scene, and the studied dialect, the play takes a sharp inner turn, and focuses as only a few of his earlier plays had on the emotional action of its central character. O'Neill was perhaps less interested in offering plausible psychological motivation for Emma's destiny in the world than in projecting the intensity of her feeling. In truth, the play is betrayed by its narrative, for its concerns, at heart, seem to be something other than a study of repressed sexual instincts.

Emma's desire is that her marriage with Caleb shall be a different kind of relationship from that which is usual. Caleb describes for her the romantic charm of the tropical islands where he lost his virginity. Although she refuses his explanation and rejects him as a suitor, it is not entirely clear that she opposes the sensuality of his description. In trying to describe herself as different from other girls, she says,

> Oh, I don't mean I'm any better. I mean I just look at things diff'rent from what they do—getting married, for example, and other things, too. And so I've got it fixed in my head that you and me ought to make a married couple—diff'rent from the rest—not that they ain't all right in their way. [496]

It can of course be taken that Emma here is suggesting that sexual purity shall be maintained even in marriage. Yet as O'Neill has presented her in the first act, Emma is a girl of considerable charm, and aside from her fatal sense of difference, not unattractive. Her face *"gives an impression of prettiness, due to her large, soft blue eyes which have an incongruous quality of absent-minded romantic dreaminess about them."* [494]

Her romanticism is parallel to, not different from the image of the warm and romantic tropical islands Caleb describes. She is not cold, but her romantic dreaminess suggests that she wants from Caleb something more than sexual innocence. Her idealism demands from him a condition of perfection, a surrender to a goal romantically conceived but stubbornly sought, a dream that is essential to happiness. Caleb has sensed the difference of the islands, and responded to their strangeness. Emma's dream of difference has something of the same quality, a search for something less mundane, true, more absorbing. O'Neill called the play "A tale of the eternal, romantic idealist who is in all of us—the eternally defeated one," adding, perhaps in an attempt to universalize his heroine, "In our innermost hearts, we all wish ourselves and others to be 'diff'rent.' We are all more or less "Emmas'—the more or less depending on our talent for compromise. Either we try in desperation to clutch our dream at the last by deluding ourselves with some tawdry substitute; or, having waited the best part of our lives, we find the substitute that time mocks us with too shabby to accept. In either case we are tragic figures, and also fit subjects for the highest comedy, were one sufficiently detached to write it."⁹ Emma's dream of difference, in other words, must be viewed as similar to Robert Mayo's dream of going beyond the horizon.

To define the dream of difference is not an entirely easy matter. Clearly, when Emma appears in the second act, her freshness withered, and her face covered with a mask-like make-up, she has become the tragi-comic figure who has tried to find a shabby substitute for the dream's reality. Her suicide is the despairing end to a life mocked by time. Yet this is the aftermath of the dream denied, and what the dream is remains obscured, hidden beneath the sexual allegory of the narrative.

Difference insofar as it can be understood within the play's context appears to be the complete subjugation of two individuals in marriage in such a way that they will form a new entity, "a married couple—diff'rent from the rest." Attempting to explain her rejection of him, Emma acknowledges that she is unconcerned about his small slip with the native girl. "What you done is just what any other man would have done—and being like them is exactly what'll keep you from ever seeing my meaning." [516] She continues to tell him of her belief that as they grew up together their relationship had a special quality, that it was, in some indefinable way, rare and uncommon. For Emma, at least, the relationship with Caleb was to be the dream to which she sought to surrender, the resting place that provided perfect fulfillment, where the drive to possess and the desire to be possessed were reduced to an essential condition of harmony. That Caleb cannot understand this is her reason for renouncing the dream, and the play in its final moments, as both Caleb and Emma commit suicide, becomes an early statement of what will be one of O'Neill's major themes: the horror that comes to those who deny their dreams.

Diff'rent fails because it is unable clearly to define the nature of the dream, and because Emma's tawdry substitute for the dream has pathos without real substance. Once she has been brought to her senses and has seen herself as a grotesque scarecrow, she takes the trappings of the house she has redecorated in order to entice the younger man—the new curtains, rugs, furniture—and piles them in the middle of the floor. It is a pathetic gesture, but insufficient to give her even such stature as O'Neill provided for Robert Mayo. The play, in part at least, refuses to develop its largest, quasi-allegorical possibilities, but remains anchored in a domestic world, blurred as a result.

Similar problems beset the third of the "domestic" tragedies of the years 1920-21. *The First Man* is an attempt to write a modern, sophisticated play that would yet incorporate some of the concepts that had emerged in the romantic studies of the sea. The manner is that of the realistic Strindberg, but the play also includes certain elements of social satire and appears to have an autobiographical basis. It opened at the Neighborhood Playhouse on March 4, 1922, with Augustin Duncan as Curtis Jayson. Reviews of the production and of the play ranged from the negative to the violently condemnatory. There was general agreement among the critics that the play was miscast, that Duncan was too old and that a vital idea had been lost in murky writing. It was noted, however (and the comments may well reflect concerns of the playwright), that O'Neill was essaying comedy scenes with some success and that he was now proving he could handle group scenes on his stage. The reviewers were evidently becoming aware of his habit of reducing his action to monologues.

In *The First Man,* O'Neill returns to the scene of *Bread and Butter*—Bridgetown, Connecticut—and again vents his hostility against the philistine middle class. As the reviewers of the 1922 production noted, the play divides itself into two major themes, first, the personal story of the anthropological explorer Curtis Jayson and his wife Martha and, second, the conflict between Martha and Curt's relatives. The latter theme is designed to satirize the small-minded gossips who condemn Martha for her friendship with Curt's best friend, Edward Bigelow. These scenes, in which a forthright woman defies the town's scandalous gossip, are well below the level, but reminiscent of Carol Kennicott's defiance of the denizens of Gopher Prairie. It should be noted that *Main Street* appeared in 1920, just before O'Neill wrote *The First Man.*

The uncharacteristic social satire set aside, the domestic story follows a pattern which, by this time, O'Neill has worked over in *Ile, Gold* and *Diff'rent.* In each, a somewhat fanatical central character sets his dream and consequently his will over the good of those immediately about him. As the labored exposition makes clear, Jayson is a romantic, a rough-and-tumble dreamer, who has essayed many occupations, guided by his quest for romantic adventure.

"Why," Bigelow asks him, "did you elect to take up mining engineering at Cornell instead of a classical degree at the Yale of your fathers and brothers? Because you had been reading Bret Harte in prep school and mistaken him for a modern realist. You devoted four years to grooming yourself for another outcast of Poker Flat."

A try at mining engineering in Nevada has been followed by a time spent prospecting, but there, as Bigelow points out, Jayson found nothing but different varieties of pebbles:

> But it is necessary to your nature to project romance into these stones, so you go in for geology. As a geologist, you become a slave to the Romance of the Rocks. It is but a step from that to anthropology—the last romance of all. There you find yourself—because there is no further to go. You win fame as the most proficient of young skull-hunters—and wander over the face of the globe, digging up bones like an old dog. [555]

In his hero's career-sketch, with its variety of activities, its stress on wandering the earth, even in the prospecting detail, O'Neill is recalling some of the contours of his own life, but as his notes on the manuscript draft of the play suggest, he conceived of Curt as a "fanatic"[10] and thus, presumably, as something other than a self-portrait. Curt is portrayed as a quester, seeking for what was popularly known in the 1920's as "the Missing Link," and hoping to find the secret of man's origins. His search for the source ranks him with both Robert Mayo and Brutus Jones: with Robert because his idealistic drives were bred in part by dreams and hope, and with Jones because his action leads him backward toward a point of origin in the primitive past that in some measure explains his present.

As Caleb in *Diff'rent* was called upon to share Emma's dream, Martha is forced to accept her husband's hope as her own. She appears successful in subjugating herself to him, willing herself to accept his dream, but her acceptance is not complete. She describes a time in Tibet when, having tried to be all that he asked, she found herself tired with the venture and, out of harmony not only with her husband, but, unexpectedly, with the earth itself.

> I became horribly despondent—like an outcast who suddenly realized the whole world is alien. And all the wandering about the world, and all the romance and excitement I'd enjoyed in it, appeared an aimless, futile business, chasing around in a circle in an effort to avoid touching reality. [585]

To save herself, it becomes clear to her that she must separate herself from her husband's dream, to find the origins of life not in physical questing, but in bearing a child and thus, as she puts it, "completing" herself. To Jayson, her pregnancy is treachery, the destruction of his dream and the essential center of their marriage. The play attempts to motivate his violent antipathy toward having a child by positing that two children born early in their marriage had died, yet his opposition to Martha's pregnancy clearly goes beyond rational explanation. O'Neill appears to see it in a Strindbergian light as the natural hostility of male and female principles. Martha implies this when she cries,

> Oh, Curt, I wish I could tell you what I feel, make you feel with me the longing for a child. If you had just the tiniest bit of feminine in you—! . . . But you're so utterly masculine, dear! That's what made me love you, I suppose—so I've no right to complain of it. [584]

She implores him, as he has loved his dream, to love the "creator" in her. He cannot. O'Neill, faithful to his Strindberg, makes compromise in the war of men and women impossible. Only a momentary armistice can be found in passion, but as Jayson tells her that he loves her, he adds, "You are me and I am you." His words cause Martha to draw away and to reply "Yes, you love me. But who am I? You don't know." On the note of estrangement, the scene ends, leaving Martha alienated and alone.

What she has rejected is a view of marriage that demands such complete mutual involvement of husband and wife that both lose their individuation in the formation of a new entity. What Emma thought of as marriage with a difference is somewhat clarified by Jayson's petition to his wife. Shortly, in *Welded,* O'Neill will again try to spell out the concept which he first expressed hesitantly in *Servitude* as "Pan in Logos," and which, if autobiographical accounts be true, he sought in his own marriages.

"You are me and I am you" is not, however, a concept that comes to be realized in *The First Man*. O'Neill's conclusion to the story of the Jaysons is harrowing. Martha is in painful labor. She will die when the child is born, but in the interim, throughout the third act, her offstage screams form a painful punctuation to the action. The scene is one of extraordinary technical difficulty, and one which would need the maximum theatrical resourcefulness to bring off. It is a bold experiment, paralleling O'Neill's impulse earlier displayed with ghosts and drums to make an audience bear as much direct assault as possible.

When Martha dies, Jayson comes near to madness. He refuses to see the child and prepares to depart for Tibet without acknowledging the child in any way.* There is even the threat that he may murder the child who has destroyed his marriage. In the end, however, a resolution is effected as the baby is left with an aged aunt who is relatively free of the corruption of his other relatives.

The First Man remains an unsatisfactory, mis-stressed play, but one which in O'Neill's development was crucial. It announces unambiguously the theme centering on the paradox of true marriage and human individuality from which he will evolve several later studies, including Welded and Strange Interlude.

The three domestic dramas of 1920-21 are curiously similar to one another in that in each, one of the partners is a dominating, neurotic fanatic whose demands result in the death of the beloved. It is tempting to read into the repeated central situation autobiographical detail relevant to O'Neill's own marriage, just as the sense of total commitment to the marriage relationship expressed in Diff'rent and The First Man appears to reflect something of O'Neill's personal concerns. On the other hand, O'Neill's imagination in each of the three plays does not seem to have been deeply fired by the narratives or their significance. The three plays are flaccid performances, and it may be that each comes to a partially tragic conclusion for very little reason except the need to do something to save the script. He doubtless knew that he was far removed from what he had accomplished in The Emperor Jones and from what he was slowly working toward in "Anna Christie," a play that stubbornly refused to evolve as a tragedy and which became in fact one of O'Neill's two comedies, almost in despite of its author's wishes.

In November, 1921, "plainly showing all the outward evidences of belonging to the world's oldest profession," Anna Christie, in the person of Miss Pauline Lord, entered Johnny-the-Priest's saloon and spoke one of the memorable lines of the American drama: "Gimme a whiskey—ginger ale on the side. . . . And don't be stingy baby." [14] Only the year before she had first appeared on the stage in the person of Miss Lynn Fontanne as a respectable British typist, whose

* It should be mentioned that O'Neill's first child was born in 1910, while O'Neill was gold prospecting in Honduras. He did not see him until 1921. Possibly, too, in Jayson's resentment of the child, there is a reflection of O'Neill's personal resentment at Agnes's pregnancy in 1919.

greatest oath was "By jimminy," and who eagerly refreshed herself after the fatigues of an Atlantic crossing with a cup of her father's scalding tea. Anna's decline and fall was as rapid as it was remarkable.

The date was March 8, 1920, the place Atlantic City, and the play, then titled *Chris Christophersen** was heralded by the *Atlantic City Press*. An advertising flyer puffed the première by stressing O'Neill's achieved reputation, based on the success of *Beyond the Horizon* and on the recently published Boni and Liverwright edition of the one-act sea plays:

> A new play by Eugene O'Neill, a young playwright who is already proclaimed by the leading critics of New York as not only one of the foremost of living dramatists writing the English tongue but as one of the most striking individual literary figures that America has produced in the present generation is announced by George C. Tyler.

Despite its publicity, the play was in trouble from the first. Personal problems prevented O'Neill from giving it the attention it urgently needed. During rehearsals, he had been ill with flu. In February, his father had had a stroke, and it was learned that he was dying of intestinal cancer. Shortly before the opening, word reached him that his wife was seriously ill in Provincetown and required his presence. Among the many medical demands, that of being a play doctor was not one he could readily fulfill.

In the author's absence, Tyler did what he could with the script, cutting its sprawling length so sharply that the curtain rang down before 10:30. Nothing sufficed, and the play closed in Philadelphia. Plans to publish it were forgotten, presumably because within the year O'Neill was at work turning Anna from typist to trollop and in the process altering both structure and theme in the light of the perceptions that his work on *Beyond the Horizon* and *The Straw* helped to mature.

He produced three versions of the work, *Chris, The Ole Davil* and *"Anna Christie." The Ole Davil,* when severely edited and provided with a new ending became substantially the final version of

---

* The short title, *Chris,* is used in the early reviews and by O'Neill in most of his references to the play. The spelling of the family name was changed to the Swedish form, "Christopherson" in the second version, *The Ole Davil.* The play was originally called *Tides.*

the play. Curiously, although *"Anna Christie"* was a success from the first, O'Neill reacted to it much as he had to *In the Zone,* mistrusting his achievement so that at one time he debated excluding it from a collection of his best plays. In letters to editors and critics, he fought a long defense of the play attempting in arguments by which he himself appears to have been only half convinced to make it something other than it is: one of the few comedies in the naturalistic mode.[11] *Chris,* on the other hand, was a play he liked in spite of its faults. He reluctantly gave up the old man as the central figure, and to the end, attempted to force Chris's view of the sea as a malevolent force, an "ole davil," onto the play as a whole. Chris was a character he understood, but Anna, when she emerged as a woman uninvolved in a Strindbergian matrimonial web was strange to his stage, and Mat Burke, whose power and confidence made him anything but a neurotic dreamer, was a figure altogether new. Writing as truly as he could, O'Neill let Anna and Mat find their way to happiness, then loudly announced he mistrusted their future. Remembering, perhaps, some of Baker's enthusiasms, he fought his own sense that their marriage was a "Henry Arthur Jones compromise," and he maintained that what appeared to be happiness was only another trick of the sea controlling the destinies of its children. He even tried to make evidence of tragic fate what is in the context of *"Anna Christie"* an inevitably comic point, the marriage of Catholic Mat to Lutheran Anna.* In short, he did all he could, in the final revisions, to make the play what *Beyond the Horizon* was, a tragedy of frustrated destiny, when, in fact, *"Anna Christie"* as it finally evolved reached a conclusion in the happiness and fulfillment essential to comedy.

Back of his dissatisfaction lie four matters which perhaps serve to explain why he never quite came to terms with the play. First is the memory of a play, Chris's play, that he never managed to write. Second are certain conflicts of meaning in the play's theme that came from his source material. Third are the defects in structure of *Chris Christopherson.* Fourth, his own ambitions—his correct, but perhaps too self-conscious sense of his importance to the American theatre that led him and his critics to consider facile and unworthy all but the most hope-undermining spectacles.

* In *The Ole Davil,* Anna is converted to Catholicism.

In his one-act sea plays, with a minimum of narrative, he had been able to reveal his sailors at a crucial moment when the sea's control of their lives is felt strongly. His technique enabled him to portray men he had known with unusual verisimilitude. For such a play, Chris was excellent material. In his days on the waterfront, O'Neill had roomed with a man who was the original of Chris, a deepwater sailor who hated the sea, and who finally undertook to leave it. Yet knowing no other life, he was forced to accept a job as a barge captain, sailing the coastal waterways at the edge of the ocean. He spent his time ashore at Jimmy-the-Priest's saloon, drinking nickel whiskey and razzing the sea. One night, in October, 1917, he fell overboard and drowned in New York Harbor.*

What O'Neill would have made of Chris's death is clear from the *Glencairn* plays. Yank, Driscoll and Olson all hate the sea, try to leave it and are prevented from doing so. The story of the old deepwater sailor who became a barge captain, like the others, offered evidence of the sea's way with those who seek to betray it. It was material ready-made for another one-act play.

In the first scenes of *Chris*, O'Neill wrote what was substantially that play. The setting, "Johnny-the-Priest's" saloon, is filled with longshoremen, sailors and derelicts. If Chris differs from the others, he does so because of his energy, which appears now as drunken humor, now as an obsessive hatred of the "dirty ole davil," the sea. Like Robert Mayo, Olson, and Yank, he hopes to live on the land, but, finding there no life, he has made for himself a crustacean existence, moving between land and water, clinging to his barge as to an intertidal rock.

Neither Anna nor Marthy Owen appear in the first version of this scene. Instead, there come two sailors, Mickey and Devlin,

---

* Cf. Sheaffer, 202. O'Neill told a more theatrical story describing how Chris stumbled home from the saloon on Christmas Eve, fell to the ice as he tried to board his barge and froze to death. While Chris undoubtedly had a counterpart among O'Neill acquaintances, he also has a literary progenitor in Captain Harry Hagberd in Conrad's *Tomorrow*. Hagberd was a retired coasting skipper who had never taken to the sea and pursued his calling within sight of the land. Describing him, Conrad wrote "Many sailors feel and profess a rational dislike for the sea, but his was a profound and emotional animosity—as if the love of the stabler element the land had been bred into him through many generations." When it became possible, he left the sea and did what he could to prevent his son from becoming a sailor. Of his son's hoped for return from the sea, he says " '. . . the sea can't keep him. He does not belong to it. None of us Hagberds ever did belong to it.' " Cf. Conrad, *Tomorrow*, 249, 251.

whom Chris had known when he was bosun on the windjammer, *Neptune*. They are dismayed to learn that Chris has fallen so low as to captain a coal barge. Had he deserted the sea entirely, they would not have blamed him so much as they do when they learn that he has chosen such a contemptible limbo. They tell him bluntly that he must go with them to find a "tall, smart daisy of a full-rigged ship with skys'ls—a beautiful, swift hooker that'll take us flyin' south through the Trades." [18] Chris refuses their offer violently, and goes drunkenly home to his barge as the scene ends.

Here, in outline, is a one-act play about Chris, an adequate companion piece to the stories of the *Glencairn* crew. Add to what he wrote the news of Chris's death, and the demonstration of the sea's power to reclaim its flotsam is complete.

Although it was ready to hand, O'Neill rejected this play, probably because of his weariness with one-acts and his ambitions to master longer forms. In the beginning, this may have been the entire conscious motive for giving Chris a daughter and a different destiny. Certainly, neither Anna nor Mat formed part of the original conception. Chris and whatever he was to mean stood firmly at the center. Yet as he had worked through his theme in the short sea plays and in *Beyond the Horizon,* he perhaps saw implications of his concepts that needed testing.

The problem arose from Chris's view of the sea as a malevolent force whose sole aim was to destroy those who came within its reach. To a degree, Chris's view was like that which O'Neill had earlier expressed in the *Glencairn* plays. The sea was fate and a sailor could not escape its power, but that the fate was inevitably destruction, as Chris maintained, was less certain. O'Neill had said it was when in *Thirst* he described the sun as "the great angry eye of God," and he had showed Olson's end as a trick of the "ole davil sea." Yet, in yearning toward the sea, Robert Mayo had found in it the source of his hope for salvation. Even though it was an unrealizable dream, was it a lure toward destruction? O'Neill's own experience, as the words of Edmund Tyrone express it, had shown him that there were moments when being possessed by the sea was the supreme good for some men. Was the ecstatic identification of man and sea only an instance of man's being possessed by a devil who cheats will by calling to impulses a man cannot control. Is it witchcraft or is it blessing? In *Chris* and the revision that followed its failure, O'Neill questioned Chris's view and developed his own conviction that human beings could find happiness by living simply in the sea's drift, empowered by its surge.

In *Chris,* the exploration of the question confounds itself in ambiguity. Anna comes to her father's barge, cool, poised, ambitious. Night school, shorthand, college courses, a career are what she contemplates. Her father persuades her to take one trip on the barge, and she finds in the quiet, foggy journey a kind of peace, and senses in the sea a power which to her is strange but not wholly alien. Nothing disturbs her calm of spirit. Even when the barge breaks loose from its tow and drifts into the steamer lanes, she cannot think that the sea that has proved so unexpectedly welcoming will lead to her destruction.

Her belief is justified, for although the barge is rammed and sunk by the freighter *Londonderry,* Anna and Chris are rescued. Almost at once, Anna finds herself attracted by the handsome second mate, Paul Andersen. Chris, in a rage that Anna has fallen in love with a sailor, attempts to murder Andersen. He fails, and the play ends with Chris returning to the sea as bosun on the *Londonderry,* and with Paul, fired by Anna's ambition, determined to study for promotion so that, exercising a captain's privilege, he may sail the sea with his Viking bride.

The story was evidently inspired by O'Neill's reading of such romances of the sea as Peter B. Kyne's "Cappy Ricks" stories in the *Saturday Evening Post.* The excess of narrative alone destroyed any hope for a mood-piece about Chris. Indeed, after Anna appears, strong in her direction toward self-fulfillment, Chris can no longer hold stage center. His is a character defined by its lack of will, and if it is to be truly limned, he must take no action. Like the drunks in *The Iceman Cometh,* he must sit passively, complaining and doing nothing. His antagonism to Anna's betrothal is part of his chronic hatred of the sea, but the attempted murder falsifies the portrait of the man O'Neill had known. Notably, Chris is so incapable of action that he must be goaded to attack Paul by a malicious steward—one of O'Neill's few "villains." Chris's acceptance of the marriage comes as he crouches, strangely passive despite the knife in his hand, and overhears a long love scene. In the melodramatic climax, he is reduced to much less than the obsessed, brooding man O'Neill had known—the man who was ripe only for death. To force him as O'Neill did to violent self-determining action for the sake of his narrative is to betray his character.

Not only is Chris made less impressive than he should have been, but Paul is caught up in an insoluble dilemma. Paul, like Chris, is a refugee from his destiny. Both men had, in the seaman's phrase, "swallowed the anchor." Paul defines the term as meaning "to loose your grip, to whine and blame something outside yourself for your misfortune, to quit and refuse to fight back any more, to be afraid to take any more chances because you're sure you're no longer strong enough to make things come out right, to shrink from any more effort and be content to anchor fast in the thing you are." [III, ii, p. 6]

Paul's contentment with his berth as second mate is his weakness. His job, like Chris's barge, is an ethical tideflat. It lies between the responsibility of the officers and the physical labors of the crew. It is a peaceful world, where a man, freed of ambition, can follow the course of his life without pressure as a "citizen of the sea." Anna's love, however, fires him, as their impending marriage moves Chris, into a less phlegmatic pattern of action, and the play ends rosily.

Andersen's phrase "citizen of the sea" points toward the conflicting element of the theme. Anna, like her later, fallen counterpart, has known nothing of the sea. Yet in the fog, drifting on the barge, she talks as the sailors talked in the first scene, urging Chris to return to deepwater sailing and to his right element. She, unlike her father, has neither fear nor hatred of the sea. If something happens, she feels it will be God's will. To this Chris cries out in protest: The sea is not God! But as he speaks, the foghorn of the *Londonderry* is heard for the first time, and shortly thereafter, both she and her father are adrift, and Anna has met Paul Andersen. Clearly, although O'Neill has tied a heavy weight to an orthodox love story, his implication is that the sea *is* God, that its ways are not to be resisted and, considering the ending, that its ways are benevolent.

Anna and Paul share an identification with the sea, responding to its power as if that response were an inheritance of their blood. They, like all who are her citizens, belong to the sea and permit her to transmute her energy into will through them. Such citizens are necessarily will-less, but their drift is at the sea's direction, and their reward is the special, elemental belonging that the worship of a nameless God makes possible.

Chris fails because its two central thematic conceptions refuse to merge. Is Andersen, as a "citizen of the sea," to be condemned because he has "swallowed the anchor"? Is it not enough to belong in total identification with the God, or must one take arms against the sea as Andersen decides to do and struggle to shape an individual destiny? Andersen's resolution is evidently makeshift. In the perspective of *Beyond the Horizon* and the desire of Robert Mayo to belong to a large elemental force, Andersen's "citizenship" is not to be denied its value. Yet O'Neill causes him to renounce it, and substitutes instead—the year is 1919—a "go-getter," dismissing his earlier considerations of the sea as a force of destiny with the easiest of compromises—the happy ending based on self-reform to gain the affection of a pretty girl.

Unsuccessful in formulation, the importance of *Chris* is its demonstration that O'Neill was attempting to think his way through the ethical and theological problems that his conception of the sea raised. Again, perhaps, he had been led into the thematic trap by Conrad. Both the belief in the controlling power of the sea and certain of the details of Chris's portrait had been developed with assistance from Conrad's stories. Paul's dilemma is also Conradian in character. In *The Shadow Line, The Secret Sharer, The Heart of Darkness,* to name only a few, Conrad's heroes are faced with a problem similar to Andersen's, the necessity of making a moral choice, even of creating that choice should circumstances not readily present one. The simple life for them is to go with the sea, to succumb to the pull of the Congo jungle, to ride in the direction the element moves them. Repeatedly Conrad's heroes pull back from this, sensing that without some firm, conscious moral commitment, they are less than they should be. External passivity is countered by internal moral action as a man seeks a decisive issue to prove his manhood and to resist the sea. Paul's decision reflects a similar concern to take charge of his life and to reap reward. In O'Neill's context, however, there is nothing of Conrad's finely honed ethical tension, in part because Andersen is incapable of any but the palest moral perception, but more importantly, because O'Neill's view of the sea had by the time he wrote *Chris* shifted away from Conrad's.

In the beginning, he could accept Conrad's metaphor of the sea as a mother, but at least by the time he wrote *The Moon of the Caribbees*, to belong to the sea had become an almost religious devotion. Although he could experiment with Chris's view that the sea was a devil, in truth he felt that its force was God-like, or at least that by committing themselves to it, men came as close to God as life permitted. Conrad never went so far as O'Neill. The sea was the context of moral struggles to him, one which isolated, clarified and made them heroic. O'Neill, seeking the total commitment to life Edmund Tyrone describes, felt in the sea a continuity of being that in time came to form the basis for a theology of belonging.

Through 1920 and into 1921, O'Neill worked on the revisions of *Chris Christophersen*, and in the process brought the play into line with the concepts that had been set forth most coherently in *Beyond the Horizon*. In revising, seeking the simplicity of narrative of *The Moon of the Caribbees* and *Beyond the Horizon*, he eliminated most of the picaresque story elements—the ramming of the barge and all that followed. Then, to strengthen the mood, he darkened the play, and in an effort to bring the question of the sea's power into focus, he put the sea into the title role: the play became *The Ole Davil*.

Certain hints for the new plan were perhaps derived from Edward Sheldon's *Salvation Nell*, which O'Neill had seen about 1908 and to which he acknowledged an indebtedness.* The first scene of *Chris* is a simple box set showing only the bar. For *The Ole Davil*, he needed also to show the back room where the ladies could enter. To accomplish this, he moved the barroom to one side and presented a divided scene, bar and backroom separated by a partition. This setting was substantially like that of Act I of *Salvation Nell*, also divided between bar and the "Ladies' Buffet." In its time, Sheldon's setting was something of a sensation. Aided by his star and mentor, Minnie Maddern Fiske, Sheldon turned his barroom into a realistic triumph, offering an authentic Bowery bar on stage. The total effect was one of complete realism, and became a nine days' wonder. O'Neill's memory of it may well have guided him in solving a technical difficulty—that of bringing Anna on in the first act.

---

* In his review of *"Anna Christie,"* Kenneth Macgowan compared Pauline Lord's performance to that of Mrs. Fiske as Nell. Cf. the *New York Globe,* Nov. 3, 1921.

He may also have been caught by Sheldon's sentimental tale of Nell's rise from near-prostitute to the captaincy of a Salvation Army unit, which, while it is not at all the story of *"Anna Christie,"* still has points of contacts in the main line of action leading to a happy ending following reform of character.

Whatever the debt to Sheldon, the real influence on the development of *The Ole Davil* and *"Anna Christie"* was O'Neill's own work in *Beyond the Horizon,* particularly the clarification he there made of his themes. In *Beyond the Horizon,* he had studied the effects of the land on a citizen of the sea. The frustration of Robert Mayo, his failure in both his life and his work, his death by consumption are all roughly parallel to the exposition of Anna's career before she comes to the sea. The rootless, bitter woman of the first act is what the land has made of one who is the sea's creature. Although she is unable to bespeak her needs, an inarticulate longing has pulled her toward the sea and the redemption it offers. With Chris, in the first version, O'Neill discovered that when a derelict, essentially will-less, was given motivation that caused him to take part in a narrative action, he must move up from the bottom on which he lies. He could fall no further. So with the second Anna. Conceivably she could have been brought lower. She could have lost Mat or, because she displays signs of tuberculosis, she could have died of consumption. However, such an end, in her case, would have offered one more dreary image of the wages of sin, and, since O'Neill did not think of her as a sinner, the point was not worth making. The real morality lay in her discovery of the sea, her purgation and her rise to cleanness and hope. Whatever the sea was to do to her was better than what the land had done, because she belonged to the sea, not the land. Redemptive and gentle, the sea is good and Chris's view is wrong.

Chris is also refuted by the presence of Mat Burke, the Irish stoker devised to replace the Conradian weakling, Paul Andersen. For Mat, as for Chris, there was a living original. O'Neill depicted him as the powerful Driscoll in the *Glencairn* plays and, under somewhat different guise, as Yank in *The Hairy Ape.* "He was a giant of a man," as O'Neill described him: "He thought a whole lot of himself, was a determined individualist. He was very proud of his strength, his capacity for gruelling work. It seemed to give him mental poise to be able to dominate the stokehole, do more than any of his mates. . . . He wasn't the type [to] just give up, and he loved life."[12]

Although O'Neill did not verify the identification, in his friend's character lies the source for Mat Burke, more poetically visualized in his powerful love of life in *"Anna Christie"* than in the other plays* Mat is a true "citizen of the sea." In his energy, the thematic ambiguity that confused the portrait of Andersen is eliminated. Mat is like a personification of the sea, and he brings to crucial test Chris's conception that the sea is evil. It is his voice, hailing the barge from the storm-swept open boat, that in the second and third versions answers Chris's frightened protest, "Dat ole davil sea, she ain't God!" His strength is comparable to that of waves and tides, and he glories in the power that enabled him to bring his ship-wrecked comrades to safety by his sheer strength. His nature is defined by his instinctive belief in the power and vitality he shares with the sea. To his force, as to the sea, Anna responds, and he, in turn, goes to her with an instant recognition that she possesses the same cleanness and, in her way, the same strength.

So long, therefore, as he and Anna maintain the simple directness of mutual recognition and response, they find happiness. On the land, where alien forces have influence, they lose themselves and one another, until they are able by an act of groping but aware self-renunciation, to assert their love and come again into a right relationship with the sea's force. Their quarrel and separation is land-induced, and only by a deliberate acquiescence to what the sea has wrought in bringing them together are they able to shape their destinies. By accepting one another, they go with the sea, per-haps to the quick, clean death by drowning Mat speaks of, but surely to happiness.

The ending of *The Ole Davil*, reducing Chris to a subordinate role, makes the point clearly:

> CHRIS (*who has been staring at his beer absentmindedly, moodily with a sort of somber premonition*) It's funny—you and me shipping on same boat dat vay. It's queer. It ain't right. Ay don't know—it's dat funny vay ole davil, sea, do her vorst dirty tricks, yes. It's so.

* Captain Hagberd's son in Conrad's *Tomorrow* displays some of the restless energy and powerful self-assurance of Mat Burke. He says at one point that he should have been born "in the open, upon a beach, on a windy night," and sings the "Song of the Gambucinos. . . . The song of restless men. Nothing could hold them in one place—not even a woman."

BURKE   (*with a hearty laugh of scorn*) Yerra! Don't be talking! The sea means good to us only, and let you lave her alone. She'll be welcoming you back like a long-lost child, I'm thinking.

CHRIS   (*shaking his head: implacably*) Dirty ole davil!

BURKE   (*shouting to* ANNA) Will you listen to the old bucko, Anna? He's after putting up his fists to the sea again.

ANNA   (. . . *laughing*) Oh, for gawd's sake! [119]

The Ole Davil ends in laughter, and Chris's brooding is seen not as prophecy, but as the personal idiosyncrasy it really is.* In this ending, too, the belief is asserted that one should not "put up his fists" against fate, but rather trust that the sea means no harm, especially to its lost children like Anna and Chris. This is the belief that makes happiness possible, but, oddly, it is the one that O'Neill repeatedly sought to deny, both in his final version of the ending, which gave Chris the last brooding word, and also in his subsequent published comment on the play, where he maintained that the play is only the gawdy introduction of an unwritten tragedy.

The final version of the ending returns the focus to Chris, after the lovers are united. Then, discovering that he and Burke are to ship out together, Chris says that "it ain't right. Ay don't know—it's dat funny vay ole davil sea do her vorst dirty tricks, yes. It's so."

Burke agrees with him, "I'm fearing maybe you have the right of it for once, divil take you." The two men lapse into gloom and stare out into the foggy night.

Anna protests, pouring out a round of beer and crying "Cut out the gloom . . . Come on! Here's to the sea, no matter what! Be a game sport and drink to that! Come on!

She and Burke drink the toast to the sea, but Chris remains looking into the night, *"lost in his somber preoccupations"* and muttering the curtain line: "Fog, fog, fog, all bloody time. You can't see vhere you vas going, no. Only dat ole davil, sea—she knows!" O'Neill adds a stage direction: *"The two stare at him. From the harbor cames the muffled, mournful wail of steamers' whistles."* [78]

This ending is a compromise between the two possibilities explored in *Chris* and *The Ole Davil*. Chris's dark mood colors the happiness of Anna and Mat and raises their own apprehension.

---

* There is perhaps some doubt which ending was used in the original production, that of *The Ole Davil* or of the script as printed. Reviewers speak of the action ending in laughter, which is the ending of *The Ole Davil*, not *"Anna Christie."*

Characteristically, Anna readily accepts the sea and its potential dangers, but the men are less courageous, more fearful of the future. Yet nothing here says that Chris's premonition of trouble is real. At the core lies another truth: "You can't see vhere you vas going," a phrase whose meaning negates the possibility of prediction of any destiny and makes trust in the sea the only possible human course. It is by no means inevitable that the sea will betray trust or that the ending will be tragic.

O'Neill was pushed to his defense of the final version as a tragedy not only by his own uncertainty, but by many critics who found the play depressing, felt its narrative forced, but agreed with the comment of one reviewer that "It is to be suspected . . . that a story which so logically travels the path of tragedy has been tampered with in order to give it at least a hopeful if not quite happy ending."[13] The consensus was repeated in magazine articles in the ensuing months, and the ending was continually called "contrived" or "the worst anticlimax I have ever seen in the theatre."[14]

In defense of his ending, O'Neill wrote at length to the *New York Times*, saying, "In the last few minutes of 'Anna Christie,' I tried to show the dramatic gathering of new forces out of the old. I wanted to have the audience leave with a deep feeling of life flowing on, of the past which is never the past—but always the birth of the future—of a problem solved for the moment but by the very nature of its solution involving a new problem. . . . It would have been so obvious and easy—in the case of this play, conventional even—to have made my last act a tragic one. It could have been done in ten different ways, any one of them superficially right. But looking deep into the hearts of my people, I saw it couldn't be done. It would not have been true. They were not that kind. They would act in just the silly, immature compromising way that I have made them act; and I thought that they would appear to others as they do to me, a bit tragically humorous in their vacillating weakness."[15] To George Jean Nathan, he wrote: "The happy ending is merely the comma at the end of a gaudy introductory clause, with the body of the sentence still unwritten. (In fact, I once thought of calling the play *Comma*.)"[16]

Neither his justifying commentary nor his attempt in the play's final version to give the three characters a sense of foreboding "that although they have had their moment, the decision still rests

with the sea which has achieved the conquest of Anna,"[17] was sufficient to turn the play toward tragedy. *"Anna Christie"* remains a
story of love finding its way over parental and societal opposition,
a fact which, in this context, testifies to the benevolence of the sea.

To say why O'Neill so mistrusted what he had done is not entirely possible. In his mind there remained the death of the Chris
he had known—a death similar to that he had devised for Robert
Mayo, in flight from the sea. Nagging, too, was the fate of the original of his Mat Burke. Driscoll, so full of the strength of life, had
inexplicably killed himself, leaping overboard in mid-ocean. The
mystery of his suicide was, by O'Neill's admission, part of the genesis of *The Hairy Ape*. The death of the two men may well have
caused him to feel that he had somehow betrayed their characters
in devising different destinies, and that, since the play's finished
theatrical form did not coincide with the facts of his experience,
the play's philosophical pattern was, somehow, a lie.

Then too, at the time of the revisions, he was seeking guidance
from George Jean Nathan, guidance he was attempting to follow
both in general and specific matters. Nathan and his associates in
the critical smart set looked with mistrust on anything that smacked
of the popular theatre. Under his tutelage, O'Neill was ambitious
for tragedy, impatient with anything that suggested a routine popular success. Conceivably this desire to turn the plays toward darkness led him to be wary of his conviction that men somehow iden-
tified themselves with natural forces, sometimes to the point of
entire commitment. At this point in his development, the dissolution Edmund Tyrone seeks was only a matter of sensibility, lacking
any firm basis in philosophical or theological doctrine. As a formulated philosophy, when he came to accept the idea of a Dionysian
immersion in life as Nietzsche extolled it, the belonging he sought
to describe in both *"Anna Christie"* and *Beyond the Horizon* became something more philosophically trustworthy than a "vague
romantic wanderlust" or the ephemeral response to the sea felt by
a lost girl on a fogbound barge.

Yet what O'Neill did in the final version of his comedy-in-spite-
of-itself was to set forth positively what *Beyond the Horizon* had
stated by negative implication: that men are by a quality in their
blood united with a vital force that is their origin and end. Taking
many forms, called by many names, the force gives men their iden-

tity and integrity, and it is the source of their power. To belong to it completely is to know fully happiness and peace, and once man has sensed the possibility of such unity, belonging becomes the end of his questing. Sometime, tragically, men refuse their destinies, and fight against being possessed. They seek identity in separation, in nay-saying, in flight from their source, and they make their lives disastrous because they attempt to live against the lines that the impulses in their blood have charted. Among the characters in O'Neill's early plays, only Mat and Anna trust the divinity to which they belong and willingly live out the full course of their fate without rebellion. For them it is enough to trust. To belong to one another is to belong to the sea, and in that, although he fought the conclusion through three versions, O'Neill could not finally deny there is happiness.

VI

THE
TRIUMVIRATE (1)

Welded (1922)
All God's Chillun Got Wings (1923)
Desire Under the Elms (1924)

1921—the year of the production of *"Anna Christie,"*
for which O'Neill received his second Pulitzer Prize.
The play's popularity disturbed him and he listened carefully
as his associates George Jean Nathan, Arthur Hopkins,
and the designer, Robert Edmond Jones, spoke of theatrical art,
and of new directions the American theatre could take.
He met the critic Kenneth Macgowan and formed with him and Jones
a producing "Triumvirate" that took over
The Provincetown Playhouse and set out to domesticate
European methods of stagecraft in a series of plays
startlingly revolutionary in their production styles.
The playwright who best exemplified Macgowan's prediction
of the shape of theatrical things to come was Strindberg,
whom O'Neill called "the precursor of all modernity in our theatre."
In imitation of Strindberg's major styles, O'Neill wrote
quasi-expressionist plays he called "Behind Life" drama,
and plays characterized by an intensified realism
he called "Supernaturalism." His new image
reflected the tastes of the proponents of the Art Theatre
as he expounded his theories of theatre to the press
and posed for photographs whose carefully arranged backgrounds
might have been designed by Jones himself.

Nickolas Muray photograph

BETWEEN the Provincetown's production of *Diff'rent* in December, 1920, and of *The Hairy Ape* on March 9, 1922, *Gold,* *"Anna Christie"* and *The First Man* received professional productions. *The Hairy Ape* from the beginning had interested Arthur Hopkins, the producer of *"Anna Christie,"* who used the Provincetown production as a testing ground for the script. He collaborated with James Light on the direction, paid the costs of the Provincetown production and, by April 17 had moved the play to Broadway. George Cram Cook's organization produced one more play, Susan Glaspell's *Chains of Dew,* and then disbanded for its so-called "holiday," never to be reformed as Cook had envisioned it.

Diff'rent was, thus, the last of O'Neill's apprentice works. He was approaching the place where he could demand the best that America's fully professional theatres could provide him, and his ambitions rode high. Nevertheless, there were obstacles. *Gold,* *"Anna Christie"* and *The First Man* had each to wait a year before production, and in that period he had completed his play about Ponce de Leon, *The Fountain,* which no producer would touch, and which was to wait three years before it went onstage. O'Neill, as always, did not wait well. New projects absorbed him, and scripts in which he had great faith grew cold as they made the rounds seeking an interested buyer. Moreover, both *Gold* and *The First Man* were box-office and critical failures. *Gold,* as staged by J. D. Williams, was marred by inadequate sets and a deplorable cast whose star, Willard Mack, failed to learn his lines and improvised much of his dialogue. It ran for ten nights. *The First Man,* almost universally rejected, ran for twenty-seven performances. A similar fate awaited *The Straw,* which was not produced until November 1921 and which ran for only twenty performances.

It seems inevitable that O'Neill would seek a more satisfactory way of bringing his plays to the stage—some means over which he would have control and that would permit him to experiment as he had done with the Provincetown Players under Cook. Clearly, however, the organization, whatever form it took, had to be both professional and at the same time dedicated to the highest theatrical ideals. Except for rare producers like Arthur Hopkins, Broadway was notoriously short on such idealism.

In the years immediately surrounding the First World War, Broadway's deaf ear was turned against the devotees of the Art Theatre who, in a number of short-lived but successful ventures around the country, were attempting to bring to the theatre new methods of play production, conceived in the light of aesthetic standards derived from European sources. Some evidence of what the new standards were had been seen. The tour of the Irish Players in 1911 had opened many eyes to a new kind of drama and a new style of acting. In 1912 and 1913, the Manchester Repertory Company toured with plays by Galsworthy, Masefield, Arnold Bennett and Shaw, and in 1912, Max Reinhardt's elaborate Arabian Nights "mimo-drama," *Sumurun,* was brought to New York by Winthrop Ames. In 1916 and 1917, Diaghilev's *Ballet Russe* appeared in this country. The importations were only confirmation of the rightness of many American endeavors in the same line. As early as 1907, the productions of Greek tragedy by Margaret Anglin had offered exciting possibilities. So, later, had the Chicago Little Theatre, under the direction of Maurice Browne, and Livingstone Platt's Toy Theatre in Boston. When they came into being, the Provincetown Players and the Washington Square Players formed a significant part of the new movement, but throughout the country groups with similar force and purpose were attempting to define the nature of the new spirit in theatre; from Los Angeles to Detroit, throughout the Midwest and South, the energy displayed in working with nothing and for nothing but spiritual reward was outstripped only by the corporate idealism which they all showed.

The ideals were markedly similar from group to group, spokesman to spokesman. The significant voice of the new movement was finally heard when the magazine *Theatre Arts*—its title a manifesto of sorts—began publication in 1916 under the editorship of

Sheldon Cheney, who in 1914 had published a pioneering work, *The New Movement in the Theatre*. Cheney's book defined the limits and aims of the movement, and the definitions are important to the direction that O'Neill's playwriting career took after 1922, indeed had begun to follow before the end of the first phase of the Provincetown Players.

Cheney felt that in Europe in the first decade of the twentieth century, there had been a renaissance of dramatic activity which bid fair to rival the theatrical renaissance during Elizabethan England. The forerunners, Ibsen, Hauptmann, Wedekind and others, by 1914 had given way to a new generation of important playwrights, among whom he listed with approval Galsworthy, Shaw, Barrie, Maeterlinck, Schnitzler, Rostand and Brieux. Using their work as a basis for examination, he defined three forms of drama with which the Art Theatre must be concerned.

The first is the "aesthetic" drama, which he defined as "a typical theatric art that is as far as possible removed from the emotional and intellectual elements, tending to become purely sensuous."[1] The second type, which he called "psychologic," is the contrary of the first, a drama of thought and emotion "divorced as far as possible from visual and sensuous appeals, affording deep emotional experience and intellectual stimulus."[2] The third, called a "re-theatralizing" of the drama, is "an attempt to bring all the arts of the theatre into more perfect relation with the limitations of the playhouse; and to invent a stagecraft that will serve to mount beautifully the plays of either the aesthetic or psychologic type."[3]

There is implicit in Cheney's aesthetic the suggestion that the Art Theatre would find least congenial the "psychologic" theatre, whose chief exponent in English was John Galsworthy. Nevertheless, he and his fellow playwrights were men of deep sincerity. "They strive above all to be true to themselves. But as they are men who live deeply and study and write passionately, they are at the same time true to life and to art. Their plays are truly dramatic, rather than theatric; they are natural, but not slavishly photographic: they incorporate only detail that is organic to the dramatic design; they interpret rather than imitate; they deal with inner spiritual forces, rather than with outward melodramatic happenings; they affect the emotions, and indirectly the mind, by a quiet development of character, rather than pleasing the outward sense and surface feelings by sensationalism. Their work is usually *social* drama in the best sense. It is humanitarian, because they reflect contemporary life, and the spirit of the age is humanitarian."[4]

What mattered to Cheney, as it did to all followers of the new theatrical art, was the inner spirit, and if the psychologic drama possessed this, there was no reason to think that it could not be staged in a vital and progressive manner. It was a matter of faith to Cheney: "In the theatre and in the church, the deeper chords of spirituality are touched as nowhere else in life,"[5] and this alone was worth seeking. The artist interprets life, whether he is "idealist" or "realist." "Both show forth not the outward semblances of nature but the essences of life," although the realist keeps closer to man's actual experience, while the idealist "strays into higher flights of imaginative experience. One tends to the particular, the other to the general," but both "seek more precise knowledge of the facts of life and . . . employ an ennobling idealism in interpreting that knowledge."[6]

The enemy was evident. It was what Cheney called "naturalism," and by which he meant the "servile imitation of nature." To his mind, almost any commercial production sought to reproduce the surfaces of life in the shallowest manner—with drops exhibiting crude painted perspective of exterior or interior scenes, with harsh unmodeled lighting, with, in the case of David Belasco, a clutter of objects on stage all of which were irrelevant to the action, and many extraneous special effects which excited an audience in their own right, however inappropriate they were to the play's meaning.*

For Cheney, this was the crux of the matter. "The new stagecraft," he wrote, "exists in the attempt to fit the method of presentation perfectly to the play."[7] He mentioned other designers, George Fuchs and Jacques Rouché, but it was evident that to

---

* Belasco, whose "aesthetic" was commercially successful, was the *bête-noire* of all preachers of the Art Theatre. Nevertheless, he was clearly seen as one who in stagecraft at least was a part of the movement. Cheney, for example, noted that his position of command over all aspects of his productions was essential to the achievement of art in the theatre. He praised the unhurried care with which Belasco prepared a play for the stage and noted that in its lighting his work was more advanced than that of any other American producer. Cheney also credited him with ridding the American stage of the painted, flat set, replacing it with a true box set whose details were three dimensional, as in life.

Cheney, Gordon Craig was the one god and Max Reinhardt was his prophet. Craig's work in the area of "aesthetic drama" was deeply impressive to Cheney. He wrote at length of the pure aesthetic spectacle of Craig's über-marionettes, of mimo-drama, as evidenced by Reinhardt's *Sumurun* and *The Miracle,* but especially he praised the simplicity and beauty of Craig's screen settings. Craig had shown a new conception of theatre as being something decorative, relying on beautiful movement and design—a work "visually effective rather than emotionally stirring or intellectually interesting."[8] Craig also had producers aware of the need for a single artist in total control of all aspects of the production so that the drama could achieve an aesthetic unity and atmospheric harmony appropriate to the mood and inner truth of the play. In conclusion, Cheney, turned from Craig to discuss the work of Reinhardt and others and to talk of new developments in theatre crafts, and theatre architecture, mentioning especially the plaster dome, a sample of which Cook was to construct six years later at the Provincetown.*

The definition of theatre art that Cheney provided in his first two books was taken up by many voices thereafter. A surging awareness of possibility came over the country. All inveighed against the theatrical syndicates, against the personality actor, against outmoded methods of stagecraft. Some pinned their faiths in the regional theatres arising in smaller cities than New York, but Cheney had prophetically warned that "the great American dramatists will be distinctly of the city,"[9] and he meant New York. Evidence that the New York theatres were dedicated to "art" was in Cheney's time minimal—to be found for the most part in the work of Arthur Hopkins and Winthrop Ames, in the Washington Square

---

* In a subsequent work, *The Art Theatre,* published by Knopf in 1916, Cheney assessed the Art Theatre movement throughout the United States. He paid particular attention to the work of Maurice Browne and the Chicago Little Theatre and of Sam Hume at the Detroit Arts and Crafts Theatre. Both men had begun to achieve in practice what Cheney had praised in theory two years earlier. Hume, whom Cheney had known for his work at the Greek Theatre at the University of California at Berkeley, had studied with Gordon Craig and had developed a Craig-like setting of screens which could be variously placed to suit the needs of most productions. Browne's work is noteworthy for its integrity and its truth to spiritual and aesthetic ideals. Many of the same allegiances were revealed in the first issues of *Theatre Arts Magazine* which Cheney edited, beginning in 1916.

Players, who by 1918 had declared themselves to be professional*
and established themselves as the Theatre Guild, and in the work
of the Provincetown Players and Neighborhood Playhouse.** Hopkins, of course, had produced *"Anna Christie"* and the professional
production of *The Hairy Ape,* but O'Neill was turning out plays
far more rapidly than Hopkins could mount them, even had he
wished to do so. At one point, O'Neill had tried to interest the
Theatre Guild in *"Anna Christie,"* but the project, which involved
the Guild's co-producing with George Tyler, was dropped, and the
Guild turned down the script of *The First Man.* Idealistic or not,
the established Art Theatres were a limited market. O'Neill's problem was to find a theatre which could serve him as the Provincetown Players had served him at first, but which would be both
professional and idealistic, adhering to the new sense of theatre art
as Cheney and others had defined them. As the need grew, the answer came. Eugene O'Neill met Kenneth Macgowan.

Macgowan was O'Neill's age and had been a drama critic in Boston, Philadelphia and New York. In 1919, he became an associate
editor of *Theatre Arts Magazine* and was quickly accepted as a
prophet of the new movement in theatre. His first two books, *The
Theatre of Tomorrow* (1921) and *Continental Stagecraft* (1922), on
which he collaborated with Robert Edmond Jones, were, like
Cheney's book, seminal investigations. Macgowan set himself
against the theatre which was only "realistic" and preached the
quest for a new realism which would be revelatory of spiritual values. The new theatre, he said, will create drama which moves, with
the help of the new scenic and lighting methods, toward spiritual
abstractions. Some present-day realistic plays, such as *Rosmersholm*
and *Beyond the Horizon,* not only imitate life but illumine it.
Such a play "goes so much deeper [than the ephemeral exterior] for
the substance of its art that it has values which are . . . eternal."
Nevertheless, "we are turning away . . . from their higher realism
because we are seeking an intense inner vision of spiritual reality

---

* Cheney notes that the Washington Square Players thought of themselves as profes-
sionals, but mixed both amateur and professional actors with unsatisfactory results.
Cf. *The Art Theatre,* 97 and 115.
** Other "revolutionaries" working on Broadway were Brock Pemberton and J. D.
Williams whose somewhat reluctant production of *Beyond the Horizon* must be
viewed as a straw in the winds of change.

which will push the selective process so far that to call the result realism will be an absurdity."[10] The new drama "will attempt to transfer to dramatic art the illumination of those deep and vigorous and eternal processes of the human soul which the psychology of Freud and Jung has given us through study of the unconscious, striking to the heart of emotion and linking our commonest life today with the emanations of the primitive racial mind."[11] Elsewhere he defined spiritual qualities as being those which give us a "subliminal sense of mysterious age-old processes alive in us today."[12] Although he spoke in the main of new developments in stagecraft and lighting which would make possible the new, abstract and symbolic art, he felt certain that once the new stagecraft had evolved into a totally efficient instrument, it would "attract the playwright and cause him to write in a style suited to [its] exigencies."[13] The future of this kind of playwriting he felt lay in America, as a young country with a youthful literature, and as one of many outlets for the nation's burgeoning spirit.[14]

Continental Stagecraft, his collaboration with Robert Edmond Jones, was dedicated "to the Playwrights of America," and implicit in its theme is the belief that playwrights, designers and directors must work closely together in evolving theatrical works of distinction. Macgowan began by speaking of realism and its opposite: Realism, which has been in vogue for perhaps fifty years, sees truth in terms of its literal representation of men in action. Resemblance and plausibility are the tests, and "It is the business of the realistic playwright to draw as much as possible of inner truth to the surface without distorting the resemblance to actuality."[15] The opposite of realism dispenses with the need for resemblance. It has the free techniques of romanticism, coupled with the modern insights provided by psychological research. "The question is both of technique and materials, for an inner truth is to be found in a study of the unconscious mind which will not brook the obstructions of actuality and resemblance. Inner truth is so much more important than actuality that the new type of drama will not bother itself to achieve both, and if one must infringe on the other—which must happen in almost every case—then it chooses quickly and fearlessly the inner truth."[16] Such a dramatic style he called anti-realistic, presentational or expressionistic. What was to be sought was an inner shape, a "significant form," whether the mode be realistic or its opposite. Seeking examples of both modes, he described in detail the Moscow Art Theatre production of *The Cherry Orchard* as an example of superb realism which found its "significant form"; his favorite example of the expressionist play was *The Hairy Ape,* "a play that grows greater in the perspective of Europe."[17]

The stage artists, he noted, have an easier time with expressionism than have the playwrights. Working only in color and design, they are released from the questions of morality and the "pull of actual life." Designers with the example of recent French painting to guide them can move toward the abstract freely, indulging in pure vision to find, as if the stage were music, "beauty and ecstasy."[18] Macgowan's review of the theatrical machines of the German theatre appears somewhat disenchanted. Reinhardt, for him, turned out to have feet of clay. He felt that stage machinery could be eliminated from the theatre, if the playwright worked with the régisseur and the artist to make machinery unnecessary. Together they could "seek the subjective instead of the physical . . . thrill us with the mysteries and clarities of the unconscious, instead of cozening us with photographic detail or romantic color. For all this they need imagination in setting, not actuality. Form carries the spirit up and out. Indications speak to it louder than actualities. Design, which is of the spirit, drives out mechanism, which is of the brain."[19]

Macgowan acknowledged that plays of the expressionist theatre might be written without the aid of a régisseur or artist, but he doubted that they could be produced without close and detailed collaboration. Certainly acting appropriate to expressionism would never come without a "presentational ensemble" to banish representational acting. The need clearly was for a theatre, essentially simple in its means, dedicated to the principles of the highest theatrical vision and evolved and energized through the collaboration of great dramatic artists.

Kenneth Macgowan was a man who had the courage of his vision. Through his association with Jones, it was inevitable that he would be drawn into O'Neill's orbit. Together, the three men provided the talent essential to the creation of just such a theatre as he had envisioned. From O'Neill's point of view, the alliance would fill the need that his problems of production made painfully evident. For Jones, who, except for his work on *The Hairy Ape,* had long ago left the Provincetown Players Macgowan's vision undoubtedly seemed attractive in that it provided a place where he could work both as a stage artist and as a director. The formation of the "triumvirate," as the press called it, was not long in coming. The theatre that was ready to hand was the now dark Provincetown Playhouse. There, the first season of "The Experimental Theatre," opened on January 3, 1924, with the American première of Strindberg's *The Spook Sonata,* followed by a revival of Anna Cora Mowatt's comedy, *Fashion.** The third bill included Molière's *Georges Dandin* and O'Neill's arrangement of Coleridge's *The Ancient Mariner.* A revival of *The Emperor Jones,* with Paul Robeson in Charles Gilpin's role, followed. The final bill of the season was O'Neill's *All God's Chillun Got Wings,* again with Robeson.

O'Neill's working association with Macgowan had begun in the spring of 1921. At that time, as he set to work on *The Fountain,* he asked both Macgowan and Jones to suggest background reading. Macgowan did some research for him and sent O'Neill in Provincetown lists of books about the conquest of the Americas. O'Neill was grateful, expressed his admiration of the critic and told him that he felt they were "fated for a real friendship." The tone of his letters quickly became intimate and affectionate, and with some candor he discussed details of his work in progress, as well as his personal problems.

In July, 1921, Macgowan and his wife visited the O'Neills in Provincetown, and their friendship was confirmed. In August, when they had returned to the city, O'Neill wrote "I felt from the first that Eddie [Mrs. Edna Macgowan] and you were old friends— and, rarer than that—pals—and that I was free to do as I liked with every confidence that you would do the same and enjoy yourselves doing it. All of which is great stuff! So come again! Come often, stay late! You will always be as welcome as the waves." He adds a note concerning *The Fountain:* "So far this act has devel-

---

* The revival of *Fashion,* one of the Experimental Theatre's greatest successes, and one which led to a number of revivals of nineteenth-century American plays, appears to have been selected with a certain ironic intention. A cardinal principle of the Art Theatre movement was that nineteenth-century stagecraft—painted drops, wing pieces and the like—was all wrong. Jones, who staged the play, designed impeccable period sets of great charm, containing all the elements that adherents of the new stagecraft hated in theory.

oped very well, I believe, with many added touches creeping in since I discussed it with you."[20]

The discussions between the two men evidently revealed to both their common idealism concerning the theatre. Macgowan expressed his distrust of most professional theatre men, and O'Neill replied that he understood his friend's suspicions. He was concerned, however, that Macgowan not include him among the rank and file of Broadway theatrical hacks:

> Usually, I have no doubt,—knowing theatrical folk as well as I do —you have just grounds for suspicion. But with me you ain't got —even if you did have in spite of yourself. Because I don't think of you as a critic but as a fellow-worker for the best that we can fight for in the theatre in all directions. Both members of that same club, that's what I mean. Most critics are too tired to be that. Most playwrights, too. The rest of us ought to stick together—not by the usual mutual back-patting of "little groups of serious thinkers"—but by sincere mutual criticism. In that way we'll all be helped, and the theatre in the bargain.[21]

The statement is just short of an appeal for the development of some form of collaborative work.

From April to June, 1922, Macgowan and Jones made the European tour which resulted in *Continental Stagecraft*. In these same months, the Provincetown Players declared their holiday. By the spring of 1923, Macgowan's scheme for a reorganization of the Provincetown Players had taken form. At the outset he mentioned to O'Neill many names for possible collaborators; Irving Pichel was apparently at one time considered as a co-director. O'Neill, however, insisted that Macgowan be the absolute head, and proposed a "Senate" of nine members, including four actors—Pichel, Clare Eames, Roland Young, Jacob Ben-Ami, two playwrights—himself and someone who understood comedy—and designers Robert Edmond Jones and Norman Bel Geddes. Of his own function on the board, he wrote, somewhat incoherently,

> My greatest interest in this venture, as I guess you know from what I've said, would be as a person with ideas about the how & what of production rather than original writing—I mean there are so many things outside of my own stuff that I have a creative theatre hunch about as being possibilities for experiment, development, growth for all concerned in working them out. Perhaps I'm mis-

taken about myself in this capacity. At any rate, I'm willing to work these out with whoever is interested & pass them on to whoever is interested—to work as one part of an imaginative producing scheme, if you "get" me from this jumble. You see, all these ideas of mine are being incorporated into my own plays bit by bit as they fit in but I can't write plays fast enough to keep up with the production-imagination section of my "bean!" It would be suicidal to attempt it. . . . If I wish my work to grow steadily more comprehensive & deeper in quality, I've got to give it more & more of my possible sum-total.[22]

As evidence of his seriousness, he suggests projects for the theatre: his adaptation of *The Ancient Mariner* and his Marco Polo play— now in scenario form—an adaptation of a Norse Saga and a new play by Djuna Barnes.

In September, O'Neill wrote advocating strongly that the name of the Provincetown Players be dropped from the new theatre's title, and he objected in significant emphasis to the new directors' being *"actively* associated" with the old group of bickering partisans. A complete reorganization of policy was essential. Macgowan was to rule as artistic dictator, but at the same time, in a letter of unusual length, he took Macgowan to task for his proposed manifesto for the theatre. His statement indicates how thoroughly he has accepted the principles of the Art Theatre as evolved by Cheney and Macgowan himself:

Your manifesto is too meekly explicit, the plays you list too much what might be found on the repertoire of a dramatic club. I think you ought to inject a lot of the Kamerny spirit into your statement with the emphasis on imaginative new interpretations, experimentation in production. That's what that theatre ought to mean in New York today, Kenneth! That's what N.Y. lacks right now! That's the gap we ought to fill. And that idea is the idea we've been interested in, it seems to me. But where is it in your manifesto? Nowhere! And do you know why? Because that old man of the sea, P.P. [Provincetown Players] is on your neck. You're trying to collect subscriptions in the name of a dead issue, in the spirit of straddling compromise.

Don't get sore at the above. I'm raving because this isn't developing as you, Bobby [Robert Edmond Jones] & I dream—as Bel Geddes & others dream—and unless it's going to be that dream, or at least, approximate it in spirit, then what's the use? If this is going to be just another repertory Guild on a smaller scale, what's the use? If it's going to be anything of anything that is or has been in N.Y., again what's the use? The opportunity is for the unique or nothing.[23]

The cry was for manifest difference, and to a degree the Experimental Theatre at the Provincetown Playhouse provided it. The success of *Fashion* in the first season forced the company to find another stage at the Greenwich Village Theatre, but by the summer of 1925, the triumvirate was operating only the latter, leaving the Provincetown Playhouse to be run by James Light and a few members of the first Provincetown organization. By 1926, O'Neill had severed connections with both organizations and from that time forth worked with the Theatre Guild.

Between 1921 and 1926, however, and with Macgowan's principles and the Experimental Theatre in mind, O'Neill conceived and wrote much of *The Fountain, The Hairy Ape, Welded, All God's Chillun Got Wings, Desire Under the Elms, The Ancient Mariner, Dynamo,* a dramatization of the Book of Revelations, entitled *The Revelation of John the Divine, The Great God Brown, Marco Millions, Strange Interlude* and *Lazarus Laughed.** In contrast to the plays written between 1917 and 1920, which, with the single exception of *The Emperor Jones,* do not attempt astonishing departures in theatrical style from what was normal for the period, the works undertaken in the subsequent five-year period are all conceived in the spirit of the Art Theatre experiment. Indeed the plays fall readily into Cheney's categories: As "psychologic drama," there are *Welded, All God's Chillun Got Wings, Desire Under the Elms* and *Strange Interlude*; as "aesthetic drama," O'Neill offered *The Fountain, The Ancient Mariner* and *The Revelation of John the Divine*; and as the third "re-theatralized" drama, that which seeks to invent new stagecraft in order to incorporate all the arts of the theatre equally, there are *Dynamo, The Hairy Ape, The Great God Brown, Marco Millions* and *Lazarus Laughed,* each of which pushed beyond the bounds of routine stagecraft and which in the case of *Lazarus Laughed* required for its full realization a new form of playhouse such as Macgowan and Jones had envisioned in their

---

* *Dynamo* was not completed until 1928. *The Revelation of John the Divine* was never completed. The thirty-five-page typescript, is little more than a copy of sections of the King James version.

project for the conversion of the Cirque Medrano to theatrical purposes.*

That O'Neill consciously followed Cheney is of course not at issue. Yet he was writing in a time when the life of the theatre revolved around such categories and for a theatre whose purpose was defined by one of the movement's principal theorists. In Robert Edmond Jones, who during the time of the Experimental Theatre emerged as a director as well as designer, he found a régisseur capable of thinking of the total design of a production. Both his collaborators opened doors for him, and he entered willingly, for the sake of experiment.

Experiment and something more. The theorists had spoken of the need of idealism in all dramatic enterprise. There must be, they had insisted, an element of spirit evolving from even the most "naturalistic" plays. Cheney had called for American dramatists with the souls of poets to create an imaginative drama capable of making the theatre's function comparable to that of the church. Macgowan too cried out for men of sensitivity and vision to work in the theatre. The theatre, he said, is the art "nearest to life; its material is almost life itself. This physical identity which it has with our very existence is the thing that can enable the artist to visualize with amazing intensity a religious spirit of which he has sensed only the faintest indications in life. He can create a world which shines with exaltation and which seems—as it indeed is—a world of reality. He can give the spirit a pervading presence in the theater which it once had in the life of the Greeks and of the people of the Middle Ages. And when men and women see eternal spirit in such a form, who can say that they will not take it to them?"[24]

Whatever O'Neill derived from such inspirational prose could only conform to his own impulses. The most significant of the plays written before 1921 had instinctively worked toward a similar statement—that behind life there lay a spiritual force to which men belonged, but whose nature could be intuited only through a sense of belonging. The light of diurnal existence obscured the light of the spirit: life was a mask on the face of God. O'Neill, a renegade

---

* *Continental Stagecraft* concluded with the description of the authors' project for transforming the Cirque Medrano in Montmartre to a theatre in the round, perhaps the first mention of a stage completely encircled by an audience in modern times.

Catholic, was yet intent on seeing that face. Interpreting literally the idealism of the proponents of the Art Theatre, he sought to go further than his early studies of men seeking to belong had taken him. The new stagecraft appeared to offer him the opportunity to penetrate deeply into man's psychological and spiritual reality, and perhaps even to image God on the stage. Far more significant than the fact that the plays written between 1921 and 1926 coincide with the categories established as appropriate to the new movement in the theatre is the fact that they are all religious dramas.

Of the three plays of the period that conform to Cheney's "psychologic" category, *Welded* is the least satisfactory. A failure in its own time, it has not had a recorded revival in this country, although it has a relatively successful production history in Sweden and Denmark. O'Neill began the play in 1922, and completed it the following February. It was produced by the Experimental Theatre in cooperation with Edgar Selwyn on March 17, 1924, in a trouble-ridden production that was universally damned. Neither the director, Stark Young, nor the stars, Doris Keane and Jacob Ben-Ami, had faith in the play, and, although O'Neill complained that in certain respects the actors had failed to realize the work in their performances, he was finally inclined to shrug it off as not worthy.

While he wrote it, however, it seemed to him unusually significant. The play is a development of the exploration of marriage begun in *Diff'rent* and *The First Man*, cast this time in what appears to be a fictional representation of his own marriage with Agnes O'Neill. The protagonists are a playwright, Michael Cape, and his actress wife, Eleanor. The rivalry of their careers, the demands made by the playwright on his wife, the sense conveyed of marriage as a special kind of mutual commitment all suggest that the work contains autobiographical elements. Yet whatever the reflection of his life story, it is relegated to the background by his effort to write a play that will be entirely "real." O'Neill's comment on the play shows how completely he has accepted the tenets of the Art Theatre with reference to the new realism:

> I want to write a play that is truly realistic. That term is used loosely on the stage, where most of the so-called realistic plays deal only with the appearance of things, while a truly realistic play

deals with what might be called the soul of the character. It deals with a thing which makes the character that person and no other. Strindberg's *Dance of Death* is an example of that real realism. In the last two plays—*The Fountain* and the one I am working on now [*Welded*]—I feel that I'm getting back as far as it is possible in modern times to get back, to the religious in the theatre. The only way we can get religion back is through an exultance over the truth, through an exultant acceptance of life.[25]

The reference to *The Dance of Death* makes clear that in *Welded*, O'Neill continued to write about modern marriage in Strindberg's vein.* Yet there is an important change from such earlier studies as *Bread and Butter, Before Breakfast, Beyond the Horizon* and *The First Man*. Indeed, there are changes from Strindberg himself, as if O'Neill were seeking a truth different from Strindberg's. Although Michael is presented as a creative artist trapped by marriage as the earlier heroes had been, he and his wife are more than "two corpses chained together." The difference is in the presentation of the woman, who now is more—and is felt by her husband to be more—than either a destroyer of her husband's genius or a victim of his selfishness as Ruth Mayo and Martha Jayson were. Eleanor is neither victim nor villain. She is now given the status of full partner in the marriage, and as such she has an identity in her own right and is a real participant in the struggle to establish the right grounds for their relationship.

The new concern for women does not mean that the play is free of Strindbergian touches. At one point the play's hero is driven to attempt to strangle his wife, and at another he inveighs against women with Strindbergian misogyny: "You're all the tortures man inflicts on woman—and you're the revenge of women! You're love revenging itself upon itself! You're the suicide of love—of my love—of all love since the world began!" [475] Yet, despite such passages, Eleanor is more sympathetically envisioned and more fully developed than any earlier heroine except Anna Christie. It is at least possible that O'Neill realized the fact, for at one point he has his

---

* On January 23, 1922, Sidney Howard wrote to his sister that his wife, the actress Clare Eames, "has been playing special performances of that dreary moron, Maeterlinck, and is going on, now, to do a Eugene O'Neill play—very powerful and fine and an extraordinary comedy of modern marriage for two people in seven acts—called "Made in Heaven." I read it last night. It's horrid but downright thrilling." The play became *Welded*. Miss Eames did not, however, play the role.

playwright hero comment on the qualities of the women characters in his plays before he had met Eleanor: "Why, my women used to be death masks. But now they're alive as you are." [445]

Eleanor Cape is not more "alive" than Anna Christie. Nevertheless, her character is much more complex and demanding than that of any of his earlier figures. To this point in his career, O'Neill's characters have been presented vividly, but without significant inner conflict. Even Robert Mayo, in whom something like an inner struggle emerges, is really caught in a tension between the land and sea. His is a conflict that has a physical, not psychological cause. Alone among the earlier characters, Emma Crosby seems impelled to her strange choices by some division of elements that emerge deeply from within her personality. Yet she, like the others, is seen for the most part from the outside, and the truth of her nature remains unclear.

O'Neill's dramaturgy, especially his use of the monologue, had suggested much earlier that psychological probing was to be a major element of his theatre, and in *Welded,* he attempts for the first time to present the inner struggle of his characters more directly than by detailing their response to external physical conflict. Now imagery and a variety of technical devices are brought into play to illuminate their psyches.

One of the clearest signs of the new view of character is O'Neill's insistence that Michael and Eleanor are psychologically masked, and that their persons are therefore divided between an exterior and an interior being. Repeatedly he speaks of them as wearing "masks," and of Eleanor's face in particular as "mask-like."* It is an image confined for the most part to the stage directions and not, therefore, entirely viable in theatre, but other technical devices aid the suggestion that they are divided souls.

In his lighting plan, for example, O'Neill attempts to dramatize the intense reality of the private lives beneath the mask. He has always used small patches of area lighting to express the isolation and loneliness of his characters. Now, however, he very deliberately calls for a radically innovative lighting plan that is aimed at inner illumination. With one unimportant exception, O'Neill does not permit any conventional light sources on his stage—no lamps, fire-

---

* Cf. 462: "her face growing mask-like and determined"; 463: "her face like a mask"; 465: "her face again becomes mask-like. . . ."

places, windows.* To dramatize the isolated inner condition of his characters, O'Neill uses only two pieces of lighting equipment, two follow-spots, one centered on Michael, the other on Eleanor. The other characters are seen only in the light that spills from these, and have, in consequence, importance only to the protagonists. Michael and Eleanor move, each alone in his egocentric circle, speaking across a void of darkness which their love must somehow bridge.** If it does nothing else, the lighting scheme, like the imagery of the masks, would underscore the impression of the double life that is the source of the characters' mutual antagonism.

The impression of life-in-isolation is conveyed through other physical means. For example, early in the play when, after a quarrel, Eleanor and Michael are estranged to the breaking point, O'Neill calls for them to sit in two chairs, stage center, each speaking words that the other hears, yet does not hear:

> *Their chairs are side by side, each facing front, so near that by a slight movement each could touch the other, but during the following scene they stare straight ahead and remain motionless. They speak, ostensibly to the other, but showing by their tone it is a thinking aloud to oneself, and neither appears to hear what the other has said.* [452]

The effect is repeated at the beginning of Act III, as the process of their reunion begins.

O'Neill's earlier concern for sound in his plays is now evident not in an extensive use of offstage sound effects or in choric patterns of dialogue. In this play, he uses silence. Commenting on the production, he said that the actors did not understand the use of the pauses indicated in the script, especially in the third act, where

---

* The exception is in Act II, scene ii, in the prostitute's room. As Michael and the girl enter, a glow from a streetlight on the window shade and a light from the hallway silhouettes the entrance.

** The New York production was not lighted in so unconventional a manner (cf. Törnqvist, *A Drama of Souls*, 107), but the experiment might prove interesting. While follow-spots, muted by general stage lighting, are used to increase the radiance on star performers, such unrelieved illumination in the theatre would be very difficult, even painful to watch. Nevertheless, the harshness and the physical pressure are not irrelevant to the qualities of the play. Stark black and white comprise the essence of the work; there is no color, no softening of the effect. The raw follow-spots would stress this and might work to excellent theatrical purpose. Among other things, when Michael and Eleanor come together, as at the play's end, the increased brilliance of the overlapping spotlights would have an important emotional effect.

"What was actually spoken should have served to a great extent just to punctuate the meaningful pauses."[26] The pauses are extensive in number and in length. For example, in two pages, [484-5] twelve long pauses are called for. They are not in any ordinary sense pauses for rhetorical effect, nor are they to be filled with stage business. To the contrary, they slow the action to a halt and cause the characters to appear as if they are in some strange trance. Words float up through silence tentatively and with the greatest hesitation as the man and the woman grope toward one another. Silence is a vital part of the play's emotional substance suggesting an inexpressible yearning born of isolation.

Each of these technical inventions is designed to destroy the play's realism and move its style toward what O'Neill called "supernaturalism." In 1924, for the opening production of the Experimental Theatre, *The Spook Sonata*, O'Neill wrote a program note praising Strindberg as "the precursor of all modernity in our present theatre." Strindberg carried naturalism to such a peak of perfection that a play like *The Dance of Death* must be called "supernaturalism" to indicate something of its rare quality. The old naturalism represents "our Fathers' daring aspirations toward self-recognition by holding the family kodak up to ill-nature." Today, such playwriting is banal: "We are ashamed of having peeked through so many keyholes, squinting always at heavy, uninspired bodies—the fat facts—with not a nude spirit among them; we have been sick with appearances and are convalescing; we 'wipe out and pass on' to some as yet unrealized region where our souls, maddened by loneliness and the ignoble inarticulateness of flesh, are slowly evolving their new language of kinship." And he coins a phrase to define the qualities of Strindberg's further move to expressionism, calling *The Spook Sonata* a "behind-life" play.[27]

O'Neill's praise of Strindberg for his ability to penetrate surfaces by the intensification of "naturalism" is parallel to Macgowan's praise of Chekhov and to Cheney's sense that the "psychologic" theatre of the new movement should deal with "inner spiritual forces rather than with outward melodramatic happenings."*

Clearly the intention of O'Neill's stage devices is to prevent *Welded* from being viewed as a merely "naturalistic" play. Played

---

* O'Neill's "supernaturalistic" techniques are studied at length in Törnqvist, *A Drama of Souls.*

with conventional lighting and blocking, the pauses overridden by actors who are enacting the feeble narrative rather than the characters, *Welded* is a sorry spectacle—the story of two hopelessly egoistic artists who have difficulty in their marriage, who separate with the wife seeking a love affair with a family friend and the husband going to a prostitute, but who come at last together in an incomprehensibly ecstatic reunion. Under such circumstances, the play is meaningless, its dialogue absurd, its theme vacuous.

Welded in final estimate may be all these things, but in its attempt it is very different from the conventional judgments it has received. O'Neill's plot is less a narrative than a design. Its movement in time and space is unimportant. What O'Neill has tried to achieve is a movement in depth, below surfaces, in order to image as directly as possible "the lonely life of one's own which suffers in solitude." [477] Such suffering is out of time, and the Capes are cut off from any significant outside reality. Away from one another they have no life. What hope exists for them lies in their being able to reach one another. The action of the play is almost entirely a spiritual action, developed in isolation and silence.

Although it leaves the inanities of his first long play, *Servitude*, far behind, *Welded* develops its theme in part from that juvenile work which was also concerned with the marriage of a playwright and which centered on the theme of "Pan in Logos," the discovery of a God in marriage. Its relation to the sense of "difference" that Emma Crosby wished to find in her marriage to Caleb is also marked. Indeed the treatment in *Welded* of such questions as mutual possession and the total commitment to another human being defines the issues murkily set forth in *Diff'rent*.

As a playwright, Michael Cape is one in the line of O'Neill's poet figures. His artistry, compared to Eleanor's acting, is primary in its creativity, hers secondary, and O'Neill stresses his belief that he has created her as an artist by providing her with the roles she plays. To a degree, the state of the marriage reflects these assumptions concerning their professional lives. Michael is the primary, the moving energy that shapes the relationship, while Eleanor is forced into a role he devises for her and which threatens her sense of selfhood.

The poet in Michael drives him to search for a true spiritual reality, a creative source that has the power of a God. Michael, however, is not a poetical farmhand mooning toward the horizon. He cannot unite, as do less sophisticated characters O'Neill has drawn, with some powerful element in nature that will be a God for him. To find his truth, he must create it by evolving it through marriage. In a conception somewhat allied to the Nietzschean view of marriage's possibilities expressed in *Thus Spake Zarathustra,* he speaks of the sacrament they have sworn:

> We swore to have a true sacrament—or nothing! Our marriage must be a consummation demanding and combining the best in each of us! Hard, difficult, guarded from the commonplace, kept sacred as the outward form of our inner harmony! [448]

He describes his quest in terms that might have been used by Curtis Jayson, of primitive cellular creation:

> . . . let's be proud of our fight! It began with the splitting of a cell a hundred million years ago into you and me, leaving an eternal yearning to become one life again. . . . You and I—year after year—together—forms of our bodies merging into one form; rhythm of our lives beating against each other, forming slowly the one rhythm—the life of Us—created by us!—beyond us, above us! [448]

Toward the end, Michael exclaims that "Life guides me back through the hundred million years to you. It reveals a beginning in unity that I may have faith in the unity of the end." [488]

Michael's conception of life as having a total unity and of love as being a manifestation of faith in that unity lies at the core of *Welded.* Michael asks Eleanor to turn inward, into love, to help him cut them both away from the world outside and to lose her individuality with him in complete union. She cannot do so. She is not endowed with her husband's vision, and for her to possess him completely does not involve a loss of the sense of self. Yet she too is searching. She speaks of her need for love, for something she has been unable to find until her marriage. In its early days, the marriage was the end of her quest. She cries: "I lost myself. I began living in you. I wanted to die and become you!" [447] As she says, it was a difficult ideal: "Sometimes I think we've demanded too much. Now there's nothing left but that something which can't give itself. And I blame you for this because I can neither take more nor give more—and you blame me! . . . And then we fight!" [448]

There comes a point when a commitment as total as dying must be made. At this brink Eleanor draws back and when she does, Michael's action becomes for her an intolerable burden. In the love scene which opens the first act, it is as if Michael were hypnotizing her. She is drawn into his passion, fired with his fire. An interruption occurs, and she breaks from the spell, her body reacting "as if she were throwing off a load." [449] She explains it as rebellion:

> It's so beautiful—and then—suddenly I'm being crushed. I feel a cruel presence in you paralyzing me, creeping over my body, possessing it so it's no longer my body—the grasping at some last inmost thing which makes me—my soul—demanding to have that, too! I have to rebel with all my strength—seize any pretext! Just now at the foot of the stairs—the knock on the door was—liberation. . . . And yet I love you! It's because I love you! If I'm destroyed, what is left to love you, what is left for you to love? [453]

In the woman's terms, awareness is essential to love. It is more like possession than commitment. She tells him, "I desire to take all of you into my heart," which means, in effect, to possess him completely. "My love for him," she cries at one point, "is my own, not his!" [469]

Her resistance is destructive. When he cannot bring her to a point of surrender, he breaks away and goes to a prostitute, trying to use sex as a means of revenge. She in turn seeks an affair with a friend. Neither, however, can bring such sterile drives to their goals. The will to deny life is powerless and the quest for unity continues.

At the time of its New York production *Welded* was dubbed the "I love you-I hate you play" but it is not an account of an off-again, on-again romance, nor is it the story of the attempt of a man and wife to possess one another. The play's central conflict emerges from Eleanor's desire to remain aware so that she may possess his love and Michael's insistence that they both renounce the sense of self entirely, so that they may possess and be possessed, mutually, equally, with only the sense of union, the source of life itself to give their relationship meaning. At the end, while both realize that any unity they may achieve is transitory and that vision is ephemeral, both make a deliberate attempt to renounce self to attain Michael's goal. The vision failing, they will be cast again into torment, but this burden must be accepted:

Our life is to bear together our burden which is our goal—on and
up! Above the world, beyond its vision—our meaning! [488]

At the last moment of the play, arms outstretched, Michael and
Eleanor moving in a semi-hypnotic, trance-like state find their way
to one another. Their united bodies form a cross, symbolic of both
the burden and the exaltation, and suggesting that the vision
"above the world," the sense of God in marriage, can be achieved
only by a wholehearted willingness to accept both the torment and
the joy of total communion.

In many of its aspects—much of its dialogue, the entire second
act—*Welded* is totally unsatisfactory. Yet there is a difference between a bad work of art and something that is merely bad. *Welded,*
however inadequate its execution, is not a shoddy piece of commercial theatre, and it is conceived within the scope of theatre art as
the best practitioners defined it in 1922. The problem of breaking
through the realistic aspects of the play to the "super-naturalism"
O'Neill admired in Strindberg is not here successfully solved. Yet
the play clarifies much with which O'Neill had been concerned since
his tyro days, and it points ahead in a variety of ways, thematically
and technically, toward the final achievement in the group of marriage studies, *Strange Interlude.* Certainly it is a far and remarkable
step beyond the simple problem play, *The First Man,* to the complexities of characterization and technique revealed in *Welded.*
O'Neill's next venture in this line, his next "super-natural" play
was to prove even more difficult and was, in some ways, less
successful.

At the beginning of Act III of *Welded,* describing an aspect of
the relationship between Michael and Eleanor, O'Neill writes,
*"They act for the moment like two persons of different races,
deeply in love, but separated by a barrier of language."* The image
was germinal to the concept he evolved in his next play, completed
in the fall of 1923 and entitled *All God's Chillun Got Wings.*

A thematic sequel to *Welded,* the new play continued to study
the problems of a marriage in which the husband and wife are
deeply committed to one another and yet are divided by a profound
sense of alienation which prevents their happiness. The question in
Welded was explored in a context that was, effectively, placed out
of time and out of society. Now, however, O'Neill recast the ma-

terials of the earlier play in a broader social context and focused on the marriage between a Negro and a white girl.

Inevitably, at its first performance in 1924, it produced an uproar of major proportion in New York City. The casting of Paul Robeson opposite a white actress, Mary Blair, drew forth poison pen letters, bomb threats and an unusual amount of villification in the press. One writer suggested that outraged morality would be assuaged if an octoroon actress were to replace Miss Blair as the heroine. In the end, the threat of violence died away, although the city's mayor refused to grant work permits for the children in the first scene. On opening night, the director, James Light, read the scene aloud and the rest of the play was performed without incident. O'Neill, commenting on the furor, said enigmatically that "the suggestion that miscegenation would be treated in the theatre obscured the real intention of the play."[28]

O'Neill's comment could imply that miscegenation is not the central matter of the play, and that underlying the social problems of the narrative there is a more private theme. It is perhaps relevant that the play is arranged in two acts, the first ending with the marriage and with the departure of the couple to live in France, the second beginning with their return after a two-year residence abroad. O'Neill reduces the material that might have evolved as a full second act to a short narrative exposition. Yet to a play concentrating on the social problems of the marriage, the European experience is crucial, for it details how, despite their having found friends abroad and moved freely, they could by no means achieve peace of mind without having faced the issues their marriage created in their native land. By not dramatizing this material, O'Neill might be said to be veering away from the social considerations raised by his narrative to concentrate on other matters.

Similarly, his ending cuts the two off entirely from the outside world, catching them up in an ecstasy of personal communion not unlike that which resolves the problems of Michael and Eleanor Cape, but it is not a conclusion that resolves or even sums up the considerations of race that O'Neill had earlier introduced. Again, O'Neill's suggestion that miscegenation is not the "real intention" must be considered.

That the story of miscegenation overlays a more personal theme is signaled, perhaps, by the names O'Neill gave his hero and heroine—the names of his own parents, Jim and Ella.[29] As in *Welded,* an element of autobiography threads through the imagined story. Read in the perspective of *Long Day's Journey into Night,* Ella's insanity, which reduces her at the end of the play to the condition of a young and fragile girl, can be seen as reflecting the trance-like condition that dope induces in Mary Tyrone. Ella's madness prevents Jim from fulfilling himself as a lawyer, and, in this, O'Neill possibly suggested that his mother's continued dope-taking was a weapon she used to prevent his father's fulfilling himself as an actor. Yet such possibilities are without real artistic consequence, for nothing in the drama casts significant light on O'Neill or his family. At best, O'Neill can be said to be using private knowledge to test the truth of the relationships among his characters. For once, the autobiographical impulse led outward.

Whatever O'Neill meant by the play's "real intention," what he has accomplished is, for 1924, a bold treatment of the social and personal problems that emerge from an interracial marriage. In its time it could be seriously compared only to Boucicault's *The Octoroon* (1859) and Edward Sheldon's *The Nigger* (1909), but neither older play explored its subject so directly nor so truthfully. For example, it is startling that the major voice of criticism of the marriage comes not from the whites but from the hero's sister, Hattie. Her black militancy, truculent in its hatred both of the whites and of her brother's Jim-Crowism, together with her sense of the beauty of her racial heritage, yet rings with immediacy a half-century after she was conceived.

O'Neill's comment was directed at the vituperation the play's advance publicity aroused which misleadingly suggested that he had written a sensational, realistic treatment of miscegenation. In his view, he had attempted to do more than this. Certainly he was alive to the social problems, but important to his scheme were the personal lives of his hero and heroine. He saw, rightly, that the social and personal problems were deeply interwoven, and that to project the complexity of his subject he needed more than reportage. He set himself to develop a story and characters that would be both real and more than real, in short, "super-natural." In the end the play is not expressionistic, yet a number of technical devices are clearly introduced to permit a more-than-realistic perspective on his action.

For example, the first act is laid at the intersection of two streets, one occupied by whites, the other by blacks. The difference between the two races is at first projected by an elaborate sound pattern; choric laughter—constrained and without natural emotion from the white street—and natural and committed laughter from the black. Supplementing the laughter, music distinctive of white and black culture is sung antiphonally between the groups. The sound scheme dramatizes the fact that the races meet, converge, but do not really mingle. O'Neill creates a small point of irony out of the difference between the reaction of white and black to the sense of fertility in the spring.* Only the blacks can respond to the stirring in the earth. The whites are soulless, and the city has stunted the growth of all the children who play on these streets and become gangsters, pimps and whores when they grow up.

The devices aim at presenting essences rather more than literal truth, and they enable O'Neill to sketch the background of his history in a series of short vignettes that trace the growth of the friendship of Jim and Ella. As children, they are close, but then as racial awareness comes to them, their relationship becomes strained and though for a time they attempt desperately to save their friendship by switching racial identity, he by drinking chalk, she by blackening her face, in the end they separate. Jim incurs the hatred of the blacks because of his ambition and Ella becomes a whore. The act ends as they meet again and marry. When they do, the long sociological exposition is completed, and the play's proper action—the private story—can begin.

In Act II, the technical innovations serve a fuller purpose than the devices which permitted O'Neill to encompass the childhood and adolescent lives of Jim and Ella in Act I. When they return from France to Jim's mother's apartment, the play turns to a private scene as the two work out the personal consequences of their marriage. Ella's increasingly irrational behavior conflicts with Jim's drive to study law and pass his bar examinations. The two are locked together in a Strindbergian marriage, destructive to both. To dramatize the trap closing, O'Neill required that the room in which they live should shrink as the action progresses, the ceiling lowering, the walls closing in so that all the objects in the room, and in particular a Congo mask which Hattie has given them as a

* All scenes except II, ii, are set in late spring.

wedding present, become larger, more dominant and threatening. The device is related to O'Neill's reduction of the space of his action to a narrow focus of light, but the effect is different. In *Long Day's Journey into Night*, a sense of release comes as the fog surrounds the house, cutting off the intrusions of the world. Peace comes to James Tyrone and Josie Hogan in *A Moon for the Misbegotten* when the moonlight softens and in part hides the ugly realities of the day. Here, however, there is no peace. The room is a cage, a cell to which the two are condemned.

Awareness of the trap comes gradually to Jim and Ella. At first she views her marriage as a personal redemption. In the world outside, she had fallen, but Jim has helped her to find spiritual health, and his protection has given her a sense of well-being. Their acceptance by the people of France has enabled them to live for two years in peace, yet they have each felt the peace to be illusory, based on an evasion both of the social and personal issue between them, much as their childish efforts to change their colors had failed to admit the reality of their circumstances. As their awareness of living in a false world grows, Ella begins to withdraw, isolating herself and Jim by a wall of fear bred of shame. Only when the withdrawal is complete, when no eye can look in upon them, does their marriage achieve sexual completion. During the first year of their marriage when they lived in an exterior world, they have lived "like friends—like a brother and sister," [325] but in their isolation, they become "as close to each other as could be . . . all there was in the world to each other." [326] Although Ella is satisfied to live so, to Jim such isolation becomes unbearable. He convinces Ella that they must "be really free inside and able then to go anywhere and live in peace and equality with ourselves and the world without any guilty, uncomfortable feeling coming up to rile us." [326] Thus at Jim's urging, they return to America, where Ella's fear redoubles to the point where she becomes a madwoman. Only when she is isolated by madness from all external awareness can she love him or accept his tenderness. Jim, feeling that her suffering is born of her love for him, accepts his bondage to her and cherishes her in her madness.

Jim is a fated man. In Act I, Mickey, the white gangster, tells him to "stay where he belongs," but the word "belongs" is used differently here than in other of O'Neill's plays. It does not mean as with other of O'Neill's protagonists that Jim belongs to some elemental force. Jim belongs to his people, and has the duty of working, as a lawyer, to ameliorate them. Although at one point he says gloomily, "We're never free—except to do what we have to do," he feels the necessity to help overcome the handicaps society has placed on him. Like his father, who had progressed from semi-slavery to a respectably prosperous condition, Jim too must rise. He cries to Ella that he needs to become a lawyer, "more than anyone ever needed anything. I need it to live." [317]

Ella tells him that she wants him to be the best lawyer in the country, thereby showing the world that he is the "whitest of the white." [329] In justifying his desire to Hattie, he echoes her phrase:

> I can do anything for her! I'm all she's got in the world! I've got to prove I can be all to her! I've got to prove worthy! I've got to prove that she can be proud of me! I've got to prove I'm the whitest of the white! [335]

Because of Ella's fear, Jim's motivation changes. Hattie rightly calls such an ambition traitorous to his race. Passing the bar examinations becomes for Jim a way of "passing" racially. The premise is as false as drinking chalk to change his color had been, and in the end neither Jim nor Ella can accept it. The goal is right, but the motivation is wrong and Jim fails. In school, despite his knowledge of the law, as he stands on the threshold of the white world, he becomes tongue-tied with fear bred of the tension that Ella's shame and her madness have created in him.

The sense of shame of being black, shame born bitterly of his love for Ella, brings him into conflict with the play's principle racial symbol, the Congo mask presented to them by Hattie who is the interpreter of its symbolism. Ella's first sight of it causes her to recoil as she recognizes in it all the elements of blackness which have terrified her. Hattie forces it upon her as if it were a truth long hidden:

> It's a mask which used to be worn in religious ceremonies by my people in Africa. But, aside from that, it's beautifully made, a work of Art by a real artist—as real in his way as your Michael Angelo. (*Forces* ELLA *to take it*) Here. Just notice the workmanship. [328]

Defiantly, Ella begins by mocking her fear of the mask, but it is clear from the first, that she recognizes in the mask the source of her shame—Jim's black heritage. She replies to Hattie,

> I'm not scared of it if you're not. . . . Beautiful? Well, some people certainly have queer notions! It looks ugly to me and stupid—like a kid's game—making faces. (*She slaps it contemptuously*) Pooh! You needn't look hard at me. I'll give you the laugh. (*She goes to put it back on the stand. . . . Then turns suddenly on* HATTIE *with aggressive determination*) Jim's not going to take any more examinations! I won't let him! [328]

Her attempt to deny the power of the mask by preventing Jim's achievement of his ambitions turns the mask to a sinister force in their lives. Yet it is the symbol of a rich culture, rooted in religion and expressed in works of art. Hattie's life is a demonstration of the value of the culture in defining racial goals. She has no need to "buy white"; her need is to be black with dignity. She is not content with her mother's attempt to do her duty as God mapped it out along a road where black and white cannot mix. Prejudice must be conquered by strength, and she tries to imbue Jim with comparable power, hating Ella because she is white, but more because she has severed Jim from his heritage.

In contrast to the cheap, gaudy furnishings of the room, the mask by virtue of its workmanship and its religious spirit achieves a power that is revengeful, even diabolical. The diabolism arises, however, from Jim's attempt to "buy white." From its stand it urges Jim toward his goal, but at the same time, because Jim follows his goal with a sense of shame, it dooms him to fail, casts him out of his race. Jim, the mask insists, must succeed as a black, not as a white. To Ella, therefore, the mask is all she fears. It is the blackness in Jim to which she cannot belong and which has caused her shame. In a demented frenzy at the end of the play, she stabs it and cries "The devil's dead. See! It couldn't live—unless you passed. If you'd passed it would have lived in you." [340] Thereafter, her triumphant escape into madness forces Jim to give up his goal and to live with her in the diminishing cell.

Ella's murder of the mask is symbolic genocide, just as her insanity is symbolic of all white prejudice that demands of the Negro that he become Jim Crow. In her fear, her shamed sense of uncleanness, her paranoid hostility, she fully exemplifies the hatred of one race for another. When Hattie objects to Ella's prejudice, Jim replies that the prejudice lies "Deep down in her people—not deep in her." Hattie replies, "I can't make such distinctions. The race in me, deep in me, can't stand it." [334] By such action and comment, O'Neill causes his audience to see in the symbolism of the story the wider ethnic concerns of the play. Ella's madness can, indeed must, be taken as a symbolic condition, rather than merely as an interesting, somewhat clinical quirk of character. Her pathological problems are those of the entire white race, and the drama of miscegenation by means of the quasi-expressionist devices goes beyond the sensational subject matter and the somewhat superficial sociology of the first act to a significant, complex and despairful statement on important aspects of race relations.

Yet, O'Neill, with the "theology" of *Welded* in his mind, has an additional turn to make in the play's action. Jim belongs to the race whose pride is imaged in the workmanship of the mask. Like Robert Mayo who left the sea for the sake of a girl, Jim Harris deserts his right goal for Ella. Yet Jim's love of Ella is more passionate, more like worship than was Mayo's for Ruth. It contains some of the force of Michael's love for Eleanor. In Act I, scene iii, he kneels in the street before her and begs to be allowed to serve her:

> —to lie at your feet like a dog that loves you—to kneel by your bed like a nurse that watches over you sleeping—to preserve and protect and shield you from evil and sorrow—to give my life blood and all the strength that's in me to give you peace and joy—to become your slave!—yes, be your slave—your black slave that adores you as sacred! [318]

As he speaks the final words, he beats his head on the pavement in a *"frenzy of self-abnegation."*

Jim's need to serve Ella as someone sacred supplants his need to serve his race and his gods. In this, he is not unlike Michael Cape whose desire is to set aside all things that relate to his individual self in order to serve, through love, the divinity that resides in love. Ella is not asked, as Michael asks Eleanor, to make the same sacrifice of self, but as she withdraws into the privacy of madness where she lives only for Jim, she comes to a point that is almost the same as that to which Eleanor comes at the end of *Welded.*

In Act II, scene ii, Jim tells Hattie,

> I have no own good. I only got a good together with her. I'm all she's got in the world! Let her call me nigger! Let her call me the

> whitest of the white! I'm all she's got in the world, ain't I? She's all
> I've got! You with your fool talk of the black race and the white
> race! Where does the human race get a chance to come in? [336]

The passage prefigures the play's ending, when after crying that he
does not understand how God can forgive Himself for what He has
done to them, Jim willingly accepts his role as black slave, playing
both the self-abnegating boy of the first act and the kind, protecting
old "Uncle Jim" whose protection Ella in her madness implores.
He prays fervently to be made capable of suffering:

> Let this fire of burning suffering purify me of selfishness and make
> me worthy of the child You send me for the woman You take away.
> [342]

In the ethnic context of the play, Jim's surrender spells a defeat for
the blacks, yet the tone of the play's conclusion is not one of defeat.
Rather, Jim is transfigured, and he weeps *"in an ecstasy of religious
humility,"* crying in his final words, "Honey, Honey, I'll play right
up to the gates of Heaven with you!" His exultation parallels that
expressed at the ending of *Welded:* "*Our* life is to bear together
our burden which is our goal—on and up! Above the world, beyond
its vision—our meaning!" [488] Jim's vision, like Michael's lies
beyond the world and can be found only in the deep recesses of the
personal relationship with Ella. There, beyond desire and struggle,
transfigured with the simplicity of God's children, perhaps, O'Neill
suggests, they can beat fate and find God.

The third of the realistic plays completed during the period of
his association with the Triumvirate was *Desire Under the Elms,*
which O'Neill said he wrote at Ridgefield, Connecticut, "in the
winter and spring of 1924" and finished in June.[30] Like *Welded*
and *All God's Chillun Got Wings,* the new play accepted the recommendations of the prophets of the Art Theatre movement that a
realistic play, to have value, must move toward a more profound
realism, revealing the psychological essences and primitive mythic
forces working in modern lives and attempting to reach a state of
"spiritual abstraction." O'Neill's earliest plays in this vein were, on
the whole, tortured, ambiguous and forced. In *Welded* and *All
God's Chillun Got Wings,* as in the earlier *Diff'rent,* the requirements of a scrupulous imitation of the appearances of life often ob-

scured what O'Neill felt to be the spiritual essence behind life. Each of the earlier works is as much a case history of persons with vivid neuroses as it is the super-natural revelation of profound human and spiritual truth. In *All God's Chillun Got Wings*, O'Neill manages to suggest not only that the characters of Jim and Ella are convincing human beings, realistically apprehended, but also that they epitomize general marital and racial problems. Yet their story is hurried in statement, and its resolution is as much melodrama as it is an action eliciting the "religious exultation over the truth" that O'Neill valued. The tension between the demands of the surface narrative and the symbolic underpinnings is dangerously strong.

In *Desire Under the Elms*, however, all strains are eased; surface and interior actions are brought into perfect conjunction. Technical experimentation is no longer self-assertively symbolic as were the shrinking rooms and follow-spots of the earlier plays. Now experiment serves realism and also, unobtrusively, opens the play to fuller perspectives. The characteristic *dramatis personae*—poetic hero, Strindbergian woman, materialistic brother, aloof and difficult father—are present, but they are drawn without the self-consciousness that derives from excessive autobiographical concern.* The typical themes—the yearning for a lost mother, for a home, for identification with a life force to be found in nature, and for the discovery of a god in marriage—are rooted, at last, in a credible fiction and characterizations. In all respects, *Desire Under the Elms* fulfills the promise of O'Neill's early career and is the first important tragedy to be written in America.

O'Neill's own response to the play was guarded. He wrote it rapidly and talked little about it while it was being written.** After it opened, O'Neill told Walter Huston, who played Ephraim Cabot, that he had dreamed the play in its entirety, a claim he also made for *Ah, Wilderness!*[31] A note in his Work Diary indicates a more conscious process, saying that the "idea" for the play occurred to him in the fall of 1923.[32] It is not possible to trace the elements of

---

* The elements of autobiography are traced in Gelb, 538 ff., and by Philip Weissman, "Conscious and Unconscious Autobiographical Dramas of Eugene O'Neill," *Journal of the American Psychoanalytic Association*, V, July, 1957, 432-60.

** In contrast to his usual practice, there is scarcely a mention of the play as a work-in-progress in his letters to Macgowan.

the dream, if dream there was, as scholars have traced the antecedents of Coleridge's dream of Xanadu. O'Neill's own play, *The Rope*, anticipated his use of the New England locale and the character of Ephraim. T. C. Murray's *Birthright*, with its monologue describing the hardness of the farmer's life, was centrally formative. The legends of Oedipus, Phaedra and Medea, along with Nietzsche's *The Birth of Tragedy*, are nearly co-equal in importance. But there also exists the possibility of another, closer "source" than any of these—one whose proximity is so close as to raise a question of plagiarism. That work is Sidney Howard's *They Knew What They Wanted*, produced by the Theatre Guild with Pauline Lord on November 24, 1924, twelve days after O'Neill's play opened.

Although the plays differ sharply in texture and tone, the structure of their narratives is close. Each situation centers on the coming of a woman with dubious antecedents to a farm where she becomes the wife of an aging farmer. In each, she is seduced by a young, restless farm worker and becomes pregnant. In O'Neill's play, the relationship is explicitly incestuous; in Howard's, where such a theme would have wiped out the comedy, incest is remotely suggested in Joe's remorse at having betrayed old Tony's affection, which is like that of a father for a son. Finally, although each playwright seeks a different direction in resolving his situation, both dispose of their characters in accordance with forces that appear to emanate from the land. To an extent, of course, the similarities can be explained by the fact that in selecting their subjects, both authors were influenced by the generic elements of the American folk play. Such a reason accounts for the similarity between *"Anna Christie"* and *They Knew What They Wanted.** Nevertheless the close approximation of the central stories, coupled with O'Neill's demonstrable habit of building his plays on the works of others, makes it a possibility to investigate that he created *Desire Under the Elms* after having seen the manuscript of Sidney Howard's comedy.

Interestingly, in 1925, Howard and the Theatre Guild were involved in a plagiarism suit by an author who claimed that Howard had stolen from him the central situation of a husband's being incapacitated on his wedding night, leaving his bride to be seduced by another. In defense, searching for analogues to his comedy,

* See above p. 128 and below p. 205.

Howard pointed out that *They Knew What They Wanted* was similar to the narratives of *Candida, Pelléas and Mélisande* and *Paolo and Francesca,* and he made much of the fact that it was intentionally patterned after the legend of Tristan and Isolde. So far as Howard was concerned, the incapacitation of the husband was the point at issue and he made no use of the parallels O'Neill's play offered.

Howard's attitude toward O'Neill's work was warm and his praise unstinting. In December, 1924, he wrote to Barrett Clark expressing outrage for both himself and O'Neill after Robert Benchley had reviewed their plays as "French triangles." He added that he was delighted with Clark's review of *Desire Under the Elms,* and commented *"There's* a fine play!"[33] In an article in the *New York Times,* he was lavish with commendation,[34] and in the preface to the original publication of his play he commented on the similarity between the two works, saying that he and O'Neill could agree "that no two plays could possibly bear less resemblance to each other than this simple comedy of mine and his glorious tragedy. . . ."

At the plagiarism trial, which Howard easily won, the judge accepted his testimony that the plot had been noted down in the summer of 1922 and that two acts of the scenario were in type by March, 1923. Howard's correspondence bears this out: in June, 1923, he wrote to his sister that he had in hand two scenarios, a California comedy and a fantastic comedy about pirates. He wrote part of the California comedy in Europe in August, and, with the play unfinished, started his return trip in September, going directly to Hollywood, where his wife, Clare Eames, was to make a film with Mary Pickford. The play was finished in Hollywood by November 21, 1923, when he wrote to his agent, Harold Freedman, "I have today finished 'They Knew What They Wanted' which is the comedy I summarized to you last summer and which I wrote out in Venice. It is a good play, very human and funny and simple and clear—I think. It is my contribution to the Macgowan, O'Neill, Jones venture. I hope they will consider it a contribution." There follows a letter of 1923, dated simply "Sunday," discussing with Macgowan the casting of his play and suggesting that his wife, Clare Eames, who had played the lead in the Experimental Theatre production of *Fashion,* be considered as the heroine.

The evidence, therefore, places the script of *They Knew What They Wanted* in the hands of the Triumvirate several months before O'Neill began work on his scenario, at about the time he stated he got the "idea" for the tragedy. Curiously, at this point, the correspondence between Howard and the Triumvirate breaks off. No reply from Macgowan has been preserved in the Howard papers, and there is no further mention that the play was a contribution to the Triumvirate's venture, except that in a deposition made at the time of the trial, Howard stated that the Theatre Guild was not the organization for whom the play was written.

In the end, proof fails, yet the possibility remains suggestive, and the dubious story of the dream, together with O'Neill's uncharacteristic silence about the play as he wrote it, breeds the suspicion that O'Neill was aware that his planet and Howard's were momentarily in uncomfortably close conjunction. If so, it was not a matter of which either playwright expressed cognizance, for neither work was diminished. Perhaps all that needs to be said of the possibility is this: that if O'Neill took anything of real importance from Howard, it was the humanity, simplicity and clarity that Howard rightly found his comedy to contain upon its completion. Howard's major service was to make the way smooth for O'Neill as Conrad's *The Nigger of the Narcissus,* Murray's *Birthright* and Ibsen's *Peer Gynt* had earlier done.

For whatever reason, O'Neill worked with unusual freedom in writing his tragedy. The lack of tension is revealed in many ways, perhaps chiefly in the play's economy of means and its avoidance of startling stage effects and grotesque characterization. In *All God's Chillun Got Wings,* the Congo mask is introduced into the play somewhat arbitrarily, accompanied by a lecture from Hattie as to its meaning and merits. The action associated with it, particularly Ella's "murder" of the mask, forces a symbolic interpretation on the play that may well result in an effect of contrivance and unintegrated artifice. The symbolism arising from the setting of *Desire Under the Elms,* however, is of another order of merit. To be sure, as O'Neill describes the scene in a preliminary note, the meaning of his setting is explicit and forced. The elm trees brood over the house with "a sinister maternity . . . a crushing, jealous absorption. . . . They are like exhausted women resting their sagging breasts and hands and hair on its roof, and when it rains their tears trickle down monotonously and rot on the shingles." [202] Fortunately the novelistic rhetoric that links the elms with Eben's dead mother and with an exhausted life force holds no meaning beyond the printed page. In the context of the play's realistic action, the elms are not symbols in any discrete or absolute sense. Their meaning is reached only as the characters become aware of their presence, and as the elms, in consequence become part of the action. When, for example, Ephraim Cabot associates the evil he feels in the house with something dropping from the trees, their significance is made clear and psychologically plausible, their symbolism an element of the play's core. They do not, as the Congo mask did, warp the drama's action in order to justify their presence.

The design of the setting was O'Neill's own, as the crude sketches he made to guide Robert Edmond Jones attest. The plan which permitted the simultaneous revelation of the interior and exterior of the house was created to solve the problems of the lengthy scene shifts that had destroyed the rhythm of *Beyond the Horizon.* O'Neill, who aimed again at the effect he had sought in the earlier play—a contrast of cramped and dark interior with radiant exterior—developed a simultaneous setting whose exterior walls were removed to reveal the rooms within. Settings using such devices are routine on today's stages, but they were not in 1924. Whether the technique was O'Neill's invention or not, the setting of *Desire Under the Elms* makes the first important use of the device on the modern stage and must rank as one of O'Neill's most influential innovations.

Within the setting, O'Neill moves the action easily, establishing in the swing from interior to exterior a loosely defined rhythm that is amplified by the cyclic pattern of time. The story is concentrated into three days, one in summer, one in fall and one in spring. Each act follows the course of its day from late afternoon or early evening until the following dawn. The fluid unity of the setting and the cyclic control on the action that his time-scheme exerts cause the play to approximate classical unities of action, place and time and enable O'Neill to avoid the picaresque narrative style of such a work as *Chris Christopherson.*

The use of time and place are successful in part because O'Neill has set the play firmly in a historical context. *Desire Under the*

Elms was not his first venture into historical drama. *The Fountain* of 1921 marked his debut as a historian, but its romanticized view of history is unlike the realistic imagery he created of New England in 1850. O'Neill is entirely convincing that the Cabots sprang from that world. Unlike much that passes for history in theatre, the Cabots are not moderns in costume. To envision them as contemporary beings is not really possible, despite the Freudian overtones in their portraiture; neither can they be conceived of as coming from an earlier period in American history. They are only of their time and place. Notably the play contains no elaborate devices to suggest the period. A few specific references, such as those to the Gold Rush or the songs that are sung, establish the calendar time, but the reality of historical period like the symbolism emerges from the characters themselves. They could not exist in a time different from their own because their problems and their way of reacting to them arise from the world that O'Neill, now emerging as a major historical dramatist, has created for them. The setting, as it is in all great plays, is finally the creation not of the designer, but of the playwright, who evolves its reality through his action.

Such mastery of technical and stylistic means marks the work of a great dramatist of any period. The manifest technical ease eradicates the absurd distinction between the "commercial" and the "art" theatres. Certainly, when O'Neill's tragedy was first produced it was a product of the avant-garde activities of the Triumvirate, staged in what was to become known as an off-Broadway theatre. Yet its standards were professional in the actors it employed, the critics it courted and the publicity on which it capitalized.* Significant too is the fact that it was created within the limits set by an acknowledged and essentially commercial theatrical genre, the genre indeed of *"Anna Christie"* which O'Neill had mistrusted as too easy, too like routine Broadway fare.

Desire Under the Elms follows in its general pattern that of the American folk drama as it was developed in the 1920's for popular commercial consumption. In these works, produced both on Broad-

---

* In February, 1925, the District Attorney of New York City tried to close the play, by demanding that it be completely rewritten. A "Citizen's Play Jury" ultimately cleared the play of charges of obscenity. Similar accusations were to follow it on tour in many cities. Characteristically, O'Neill felt that the publicity hurt the play, saying "We got a large audience, but of the wrong kind of people." [Cf. Gelb, 577]

way and in the regional theatres springing up throughout the country after the war, there evolved conventionalized patterns of action, character and belief that became for O'Neill among many others one form of theatrical language. The folk play centered thematically on the response of the characters to the land on which they lived. Close to the soil, their identities and destinies were shaped by a force they sensed moving in the earth. The influence of the land was shown in many ways, in the depiction of the hardship that comes when the land turns sterile or in the joy that the land in springtime brings to its people. Most frequently, the significance of the land was made clear by means of a character whose responsiveness to the earth served to bring into the range of consciousness the nature of the environmental forces that shape men's destinies. Old Chris, responding to the sea rather than to the land, is such an interpreter, and, in the work of other dramatists, there are, for example, Tony in *They Knew What They Wanted,* Jeeter Lester in *Tobacco Road* and, to a lesser extent, Aunt Eller in *Green Grow the Lilacs.* This character, forming as he does an important link with the earth, is rooted where he belongs. In contrast, there is introduced into the action a nomad, usually a young man, who moves restlessly from place to place because he has not yet learned where he belongs. Joe in *They Knew What They Wanted* is a migrant worker, only dimly responsive to the beneficent influence from Tony's grapevines. Matt Burke, although he is aware of the sea's power within him, reveals something of the restlessness of the type, and Curly in *Green Grow the Lilacs* is another such character. The woman with whom these men come into contact is frequently an alien, often a city-dweller who comes to the land by accident, as Amy in *They Knew What They Wanted* came, or as Anna came to the sea—suspicious and a little afraid but discovering ultimately that she has come home.

Dialect and rural coloration necessarily form a feature of the style of these plays, and the narratives dramatize the lives of people whose horizons are limited and whose emotions are to a degree repressed, but who normally should be able to obtain a kind of blessing through the simplicity of the routines of their lives. It is of course possible for the dramatist to deny the possibility of blessing from the land. *Tobacco Road,* for instance, depicts rural existence as intolerable, ingrown, incestuous, damned. Yet even in this play,

Jeeter's only desire is to die as he lived on the land, and there is a moment at the end when he runs the soil through his fingers that suggests at least the possibility of benison in the earth.

Into this conventionalized pattern of dramatic narrative, *Desire Under the Elms* fits precisely. Ephraim's sense of the earth as the source of his salvation, Eben's feeling of dislocation on the farm, Abbie's alien strangeness and her desire to come home are entirely in the tradition. The elements of incest and adultery, the violence, the crudity are all potentials of the pattern, and, in its thematic exploration of the nature of a "hard" and an "easy" God, the play sees the land both as fertile and as sterile, as giving blessing and as demanding cruel service.

When a dramatist works within a tried theatrical convention, he has two ways to proceed. He may either vary the essential pattern, as Somerset Maugham varies the late-Victorian triangle story in *The Circle* for the sake of a trick and a surprise ending, or he may fulfill it completely as Shaw uses the same pattern in *Candida*. The latter is the more difficult, but more rewarding course, and it is the one O'Neill followed in his folk tragedy. In doing so, he achieved a freedom and a security by the very fact that, through its knowledge of the conventions, his audiences could anticipate the movement of the narrative and understand it without the interference of surprise. Surprise blinds perception; suspense is movement toward the known; tension emerges from foreknowledge and expectation of consequence; satisfaction comes in the fulfillment of prediction. In *Desire Under the Elms,* there is conveyed a sense of operative destiny. The characters are fated men and women moving in predictable courses to known ends, an impression that is achieved partly by the dramatist's acceptance of the elements of the genre.* The result, for O'Neill is that within the pattern he is released from the necessity of devising fictions to embody his meaning. The fiction is there, and he can explore to the full the philosophical and theological implications of his action. The freedom he achieves is complete and the results are profound.

The multiplicity of views it is possible to take of the action of

* The one "surprise" is Abbie's murder of her child rather than her husband. She acknowledges this as an error. Yet in the play's context, the death of the life that has come to her is made a vital issue, and the variation on the pattern is not a melodramatic shock.

Desire Under the Elms is a result of O'Neill's freedom. His plays immediately preceding the tragedy are not complex. Their ambiguities appear to arise more from unwitting ambiguity of statement than from subtlety of thought. In this play, however, interpretation is free to move complexly on several levels that merge, finally, in a single action.

At its least complex, seen as a realistic narrative of life on a mid-nineteenth-century farm, the play presents a convincing account of its characters moving in time. It is a work written in the best tradition of American realism. It is full, but not cluttered with detail; it is credible; and it produces that sense of local and particular inevitability that, in realistic drama and fiction, detailed psychological portraiture can sometimes evolve. In this primary, frontal view of the play, each individual is responsible for his fate. Despite the play's grounding in psychological theory, O'Neill has not contrived destinies for his characters by forcing them into patterns prefabricated by Freud. Oedipal patterns of incest emerge both in Eben's love for Abbie, and in his seeking out the prostitute Min, with whom his father and his brothers have slept. Yet such patterns in the action do not need a Freudian gloss to be understood. By contrast, the sociological and political theories which governed Arthur Miller's determination of a fate for his Willy Loman, suggest that Willy's fate is less a truth of his character than a demonstration of a thesis. The Freudian patterns of *Desire Under the Elms,* however, appear to be characteristic modes of behavior for the individuals under such circumstances as the play defines. Freud is used less for his theories than for his truth, a truth that had preceded Freud by millennia.

Again, viewed as a realistic narrative, the play contains elements characteristic of the naturalistic tragedy of Zola and Hauptmann —those grim, depressing narratives of small men and women defeated by societal and evolutionary forces they cannot control. Yet, as with his use of Freud, O'Neill convinces his audiences that this story is in no way contrived to demonstrate a sociological point. Focusing less on the pressure of external circumstance, more on the response to circumstance by the central characters, he strikes a just balance between an exploration of the harshness of their rural world and the people themselves. Ephraim, Eben and Abbie command sympathy not because they are victims of forces they cannot control, but because they are capable of choice and responsibility. The choices they make are not forced upon them, but O'Neill, aware of the pressures of the farm on its people, is careful to show how the choices evolved, and permit audiences to draw conclusions about that world from the perspective of his characters' choices.

Although the play as a psychological and sociological work maintains an unforced and convincing quality of human truth, more impressive is the way in which it transcends naturalism and becomes a poetic tragedy, capable not only of presenting temporal, local and specific truths, but of achieving the more general perspective that important tragic drama holds on the human condition. Such perspective, after all, was what the drama of heightened realism was supposed to achieve.

The play's narrative and its characters are entirely typical of O'Neill's work. Eben is the hero touched with poetry, but unlike Robert Mayo, he is not a sentimental creation, taking out his frustration in moody longing for beauty. He has in him a "repressed vitality," an animal quality that gives him maturity and manliness foreign to the earlier dreamer. Yet, like Mayo, he reveals the same need to belong. He seeks the same identification with nature and moves listlessly in alien places, in the kitchen, the world of women where he can sink no roots. His desire brings him into inevitable conflict with more hardened souls whose needs are less because they are aware of less.

Eben's sensitivity is the core of the play's poetic extension beyond simple realism. His sensibility creates a perspective within the action that permits a view of all the characters *sub species aeternitatis,* as images of more than particular, external truths. Eben's need, which generates his habits of thought, enlarges the meaning of the life on the farm, giving the events the qualities of a symbolic action, and providing a context wherein may be understood general and universal meanings. Through Eben, for instance, the beauty of the farm is made real, and through his awareness, Abbie is linked with that beauty. He causes Ephraim to become aware of the natural forces that shape his life and enables him to define the nature of the hard and easy Gods, and to clarify the influences that are concentrated in the sinister elms. Through Eben's touch of poetry, the farm is transformed, and what transpires there is heightened as is the action of great poetic drama.

To reinforce the generalized poetic perspective, O'Neill has given his dialogue special properties that lift it above merely realistic speech. No doubt the dialect spoken on the farm is real in that it can be heard in the mouths of New Englanders even yet. Furthermore, at no point is the rhetoric aggrandized beyond the level appropriate to the station of the characters. The decorum of the realistic theatre is rigidly observed. Yet as the dialogue is spoken, semi-literate and monosyllabic though it is, it emerges under the pressures of the emotions generated in the action as a special and rich language supportive of the play's widest conceptions. It extends its meanings by overtone and implication to present both the multi-levels of the characters' consciousness and, at the same time, their symbolic significance, welding both particular and general into a tonal pattern that has appropriateness, broad meaning and beauty.

Like all poetic dialogue, O'Neill's is rhythmic, but in this play there is none of the overly crafted, highly conscious rhythmic effect found in other of his works. Where rhythmic repetition occurs, it does so naturally, as in Eben's quasi-illiterate use of the word "warm" and the ironic changes rung on the word "pretty" in his final soliloquy in the play's second scene:

> Waal—thar's a star, an' somewhar's they's him, an' here's me, an' thar's Min up the road—in the same night. What if I does kiss her? She's like t'night, she's soft 'n' wa'm, her eyes kin wink like a star, her mouth's wa'm, her arms're wa'm, she smells like a wa'm plowed field, she's purty . . . Ay-eh! By God A'mighty she's purty, an' I don't give a damn how many sins she's sinned afore mine or who she's sinned 'em with, my sin's as purty as any one on 'em!
> [211]

The rhythm is achieved through the repetition of words and broken phrases—in the continual, choric repetition of "Ay-eh," for example, or in such passages as the "stichomythic" duet between Eben's brothers, Simeon and Peter:

EBEN   . . . Why didn't ye never stand between him 'n' my Maw when he was slavin' her to her grave—t'pay her back fur the kindness she done t'yew?
(There is a long pause. They stare at him in surprise.)
SIMEON   Waal—the stock'd got t' be watered.
PETER   'R they was woodin' to do.
SIMEON   'R plowin'.

PETER   'R hayin'.
SIMEON   'R spreadin' manure.
PETER   'R weedin'.
SIMEON   'R prunin'.
PETER   'R milkin'.
EBEN   (*breaking in harshly*) An' makin' walls—stone atop o' stone—
           makin' walls till yer heart's a stone ye heft up out o' the way o'
           growth onto a stone wall t' wall in yer heart! [208]

To form imagery and rhythms that evolve naturally from character and setting, but which yet elicit from rural speech rhythms
something of the strangeness, the uniqueness of poetry is a device
O'Neill may have learned from the work of Synge and other dramatists of the Abbey Theatre. Whatever the source, the technique as displayed in the inarticulate self-justification of Simeon and Peter creates a vivid impression of the way in which diurnal realities obscure
moral perception. At the same time, the words that suggest the simple
rhythms of farm life provide a foil and balance to Eben's fuller perception of the heart as a stone.

Eben's imagery is drawn from the reality of the farm, indeed
helps to create that reality. It is neither decorative nor inappropri-
ately philosophical. Like all else in this play, verbal imagery comes
from character and action, as Ephraim's biblical cadences do, for
instance, or as Abbie's desire for Eben is expressed in terms of her
response to the land itself:

> Hain't the sun strong an' hot? Ye kin feel it burnin' into the
> earth—Nature—makin' thin's grow—bigger 'n' bigger—burnin' in-
> side ye—makin' ye want t' grow—into somethin' else—till ye're
> jined with it—an' it's your'n—but it owns ye, too—an' makes ye
> grow bigger—like a tree—like them elums. [229]

The partly ironic phallic imagery expresses Abbie's langorous
response to the sun's heat. Beyond the moment, however, her words
are to be heard as are the images of other more formal dramatic
poems, within the context of a chain of images. Imagery of the sun
forms a poetic motif threaded through the play. In the opening
dialogue, for example, Eben, Simeon and Peter all respond to the
setting sun:

          EBEN   (*gazing up at the sky*) Sun's downin' purty.
SIMEON *and* PETER (*together*) Ay-eh. They's gold in the West.
          EBEN   Ay-eh (*Pointing*) Yonder atop o' the hill pasture, ye mean?
SIMEON *and* PETER (*together*) In Californi-a! [205]

For Simeon and Peter, the sunset holds a vague promise of riches to be found in the golden west, and, a little earlier, it has called to Simeon's mind the memory of his dead wife, Jenn, who had hair "long's a hoss' tail—an' yaller like gold." It conveys a sense both of loss and promise and emblemizes the source of his restlessness and the end of his quest. For Eben, the sun is less and more: a manifestation of the beauty of the farm. It is the agent of the farm's fertility, but when it disappears he has no need to follow it beyond the hill pasture that borders the universe. Although Eben hates the walls of stones that bind in his heart, his desire is not to break out of bondage but to find in the house and in the earth the life he needs. The imagery of the sun thus arises in many contexts and develops meanings crucial to the play. It is, in fact, the last image, where all meanings that have accrued around it, those of nature, of love, of covetousness, are synthesized and restated:

> EBEN   I love ye, Abbie. . . . Sun's a-rizin'. Purty, hain't it!
>
> ABBIE   Ay-eh. (*They both stand for a moment looking up raptly in attitudes strangely aloof and devout.*)
>
> SHERIFF (*looking around at the farm enviously* . . .) It's a jim-dandy farm, no denyin'. Wished I owned it! [269]

Through such skeins of imagery, O'Neill suggests the nature of the desires and destinies of his character on a broad, even symbolic, scale. Yet the imagery remains "natural," its poetic structure concealed by the tight speech rhythms and the dialect that applies a styptic to its overly fecund flow.*

Desire Under the Elms, bearing all the characteristics of O'Neill's individual style and predilections, moving comfortably within the frame of popular dramatic tradition, extends its reach toward poetic tragedy in other ways than its dialogue. The narrative's stress on murder and incest is potentially lurid and melodramatic, yet it also moves the work toward the special concerns of all tragic drama. However one may finally judge the play, its subject matter is neither trivial nor arbitrary. In this play, O'Neill was first attempting what he later undertook more explicitly in *Mourning Becomes*

---

* In this connection it should be noted that Ephraim's monologue in Part II, scene ii is one of the great lyric passages in modern drama. The monologue is of course a characteristic of O'Neill's style, yet unlike many it gives no sense of being forced on the occasion. It arises from the moment, and it remains entirely appropriate to the semi-literate man who speaks it, even as it is patterned into poetic rhetoric.

Electra: to construct a tragedy-by-analogy, using ancient Greek tragedy in an American setting in order that something of the power of the earlier dramatic literature would emerge and strengthen his own concepts.

The play is reminiscent of the circumstances of the story of Phaedra and Hippolytus, and in Abbie's murder of the child, the dim outline of Euripides' *Medea* appears. Neither *Medea* nor *Hippolytus* is a precise source for O'Neill's story. He has used his "source material" much more freely than he did in *Bound East for Cardiff* or *The Emperor Jones* or than he was to do in *Mourning Becomes Electra.* The reminiscence is evoked by tone and texture more than by detailed imitation. What is important is the release of emotion the subject matter permits. One speaks hesitantly of a subject matter "proper" to tragedy. There can be no absolute prescriptions, yet the emotional range of this work is not readily paralleled in other plays of the period, even in O'Neill's own, and this manifestation is in part attributable to the classical analogues. Further, the subject matter justifies in part the lyric eloquence with which the characters speak of their destiny. With such passions as theirs, they speak with convincing propriety in a heightened manner, and in the stark, seemingly elemental confrontations, they appear to be responding to a force of destiny that is at once real and mythic.

If tragedy is in any way ritualistic or if its enactments are to be purgative in any sense, the narrative must be a matter of important public concern. Sociological or political theories wrought into tragic stories are insufficient to provide more than the show of ritual. Great tragedy bespeaks the most profound psychological needs of the culture which produces it. The mythic qualities of the *Oresteia* or of *Oedipus* reflect qualities of Greek life which analysis more profound than that of history must reveal. These dramas are responses to myth, assuming its qualities and its relation to the central needs of the culture which cherished them. In their characters, language and action they give articulate form to the submerged communal desires of a people, and thus bring it to a level of popular awareness, provocative of passion and purgation. In search of such awareness, O'Neill reached back in time to mythic circumstances derived from an earlier culture and reshaped them to the basic story of human desire and its aftermath he narrated for modern America. In this way, he formed a story in a typical tragic pattern: his characters follow a course of sin and find redemption in recognition of error and the assumption of responsibility. Yet he did not do so in an attempt to be "Greek." The pattern is re-formed and domesticated, ultimately assumed as O'Neill's own, and told for the sake of his own time.

That America between the two great wars was a mother-oriented society has been the subject of extensive recent comment. In the 1920's and 1930's, however, the truth was chiefly to be remarked in the drama which functioned as a reflector of a scarcely appre-hended truth. Since it relies on mass responses, and is irrevocably public, as opposed to novel and poem which evoke private re-sponses from individual readers, it necessarily speaks to and takes its life from those beliefs which many men hold in common. In a sense the drama tells everybody what everybody knows or at least chooses to believe. The stereotype and the cliché are elements of its life blood. The greatest dramatists see the human roots in these elements, and thereby speak to the truth that has evoked them, too easily, from popular belief.

In the films of the time, the mother's boy was occasionally the subject for comedy and the basis of the comedic personality of such actors as Harold Lloyd and Harry Langdon. For the most part, however, the films created the sense of the American hero as vigorous, competent, individualistic and self-reliant. This image, however, was denied in the drama, where the competence and inner strength of the American male was continually questioned. There, under many guises and with many changes of tone, he was shown to be a child questing through a hostile world in search of a lost mother. Sidney Howard's *The Silver Cord* is perhaps the most ob-vious and painful example of the phenomenon, yet it is surprising in how many other plays a version of the quest appears, and how often the heroine fulfills in some measure the role of mother to the lost hero. Mention may be made of Sidney Kingsley's *Dead End,* with its motherless slum children and its gangster-villain, Baby-Face Martin, who returns to the tenements of his boyhood to seek out a mother who rejects him. S. N. Behrman's typical heroine is sought partly as a mother by the heroes loosed in her sophisticated salons, notably in the scene which ends the second act of *Biography,* be-tween Marion Froude and Richard, the left-wing journalist. The quest is apparent in the comedies of Philip Barry, in, for instance,

Holiday, where the nursery is seen as a place of special value because it is reminiscent of the dead mother, and it can be found in such works as Odets's *Awake and Sing,* where Bessie Berger's attempt to hold her family together during the Depression has forced her to withdraw from her family those necessary qualities of tenderness and love which alone will redeem them.

The theme of the lost mother and the weak and questing son was important to O'Neill for many personal reasons. Yet as the work of other dramatists amply demonstrates, it was not only his private concern. It was a theme important to his society, as that society was represented in microcosm in his audiences and in the public that read his works with sufficient eagerness to make them best-selling books. His assumption of a position of leadership in his theatre may well be attributed in part to his sensitive treatment of what was an American "universal," a social truth, a cultural need.

Desire Under the Elms differs from other plays exploring this theme in that it does more than present a simplified, somewhat stereotypical response to the Oedipal drives in American society. Rather, centering on the theme as a basic pattern of American mores, it frames an action that attempts to understand the need by defining it in terms of large philosophical concepts that may be able to explain and thus partly to resolve the tensions the hopeless quest creates. Unlike most of his contemporaries who remained content with the observation of a social phenomenon, O'Neill provided a philosophical scheme that permitted a broad interpretation of his central concern. The scheme was Nietzsche's.

In the writing of Friedrich Nietzsche, O'Neill found a congenial philosophy. He had read *Thus Spake Zarathustra* as early as 1907, and no doubt the quasi-mystical experiences involving the loss of consciousness in visions and dreams which he described in the *persona* of Edmund Tyrone made him responsive to Nietzsche's description of the truth that could be revealed in Dionysian ecstasy. He was slow to find a use for Nietzsche in his drama, preferring the distillations to be found in Jack London, George Bernard Shaw or in George Cram Cook's conception of the theatre as a Dionysian dance. Yet the identification with the sea of which he wrote in *"Anna Christie"* and *Beyond the Horizon,* the quest for a God that forms the thematic core of *The Emperor Jones, The Fountain* and *The Hairy Ape,* the ecstatic loss of self in marriage extolled in *Welded,* all point to his ultimate acceptance of Nietz-sche's doctrine as the theological matrix of his drama.

In using Nietzsche's doctrine, O'Neill was necessarily highly selective. *Desire Under the Elms* does not dramatize the work of the philosopher but takes from his books, especially *The Birth of Tragedy,* the elements O'Neill felt to be compatible with his own sense of truth. With Nietzsche's conception of the Dionysian way of life, O'Neill felt entirely in accord. He understood well that consciousness can be subdued by a kind of rapturous apprehen-sion, analogous to drunkenness and to dreaming, and that through such intoxication, truths can be reached that are only dimly to be known through cognitive, structured perception.

Nietzsche equates the Dionysian apprehension with intoxication, a rapture that demolishes the defenses of the *principium individua-tionis.* He speaks of "the powerful approach of spring penetrating all nature with joy," and describes how, when Dionysian emotions awake, man, as if he were under the influence of a narcotic, relin-quishes self-awareness: "the subjective vanishes to complete self-forgetfulness."[35] Under the spell, "all the stubborn, hostile barriers, which necessity, caprice or 'shameless fashion' has set up between man and man are broken down. Now, at the evangel of cosmic har-mony, each one feels himself not only united, reconciled, blended with his neighbor, but as one with him, as if the veil of Mâyâ had been torn and were now merely fluttering in tatters before the mys-terious Primal Unity."[36] By the mystic rapture of Dionysus, "the spell of individuation is broken, and the way lies open to the Moth-ers of Being, to the innermost heart of things."[37]

Although he was later to make Nietzsche's vision of the "Univer-sal Oneness" a subject of more explicit concern, in its broadest meanings his action implies the centrality of that concept to his play. Abbie takes Eben's mother's place; she is his lover and mother; she becomes pregnant. In her presence the farm becomes warm and fertile, and she and the farm become as one. Through her, Eben achieves an intoxicant rapture, born of a desire that transcends the walls of stones and the confines of the narrow rooms of the house. Together, in love, they come into a profoundly right relationship with the energy that vitalizes the earth, a force that is in effect the power of nature itself. The love story of Abbie and

Eben is in effect a dramatization of the condition Nietzsche called "Dionysian."

In opposition to the Dionysian forces, Nietzsche placed powers he called "Apollonian." Apollo's art Nietzsche described as incessantly hostile to the Dionysian state:

> For I can only explain to myself the *Doric* state and Doric art as a permanent war-camp of the Apollonian: Only by incessant opposition to the titanic-barbaric nature of the Dionysian was it possible for an art so defiantly-prim, so encompassed with bulwarks, a training so warlike and rigorous, a constitution so cruel and relentless, to last for any length of time.[38]

As he develops the conception. Nietzsche maintains that the Apollonian could lead humanity by satisfying men's need for beauty, and that he could create a hierarchy of joy that would free the world from the Dionysian hierarchy of terror.

O'Neill had little interest in the joy of Apollonianism. He understood, however, the concept of the constant hostility between the two powers and agreed that "Wherever the Dionysian prevailed, the Apollonian was routed and annihilated."[39] In *Desire Under the Elms,* O'Neill made the anti-Dionysian force approximate to Puritan Christianity, and he tied it in with a fundamentalist, Old-Testament deity, and with the rigorous repression of the flesh and the subjugation of impulse to rock-hard will. Nietzsche spoke of the Dionysian's taking down Apollonian culture stone by stone, as if it had been built in the same way Ephraim erected the stone walls on his farm. Nietzsche's imagery was perhaps as important as his thought, and from it O'Neill framed actions fundamental to his play—especially the conflict between a man who sought to achieve a Dionysian rapture and another who was dedicated to a life of unflinching self-denial and hardship, to whom the service of Dionysus seemed immorally easy and was in effect anathema.

The suggestion of the tragedy's central conflict had been dormant in much of O'Neill's earlier drama. The poet-heroes of whom he had written were to a man "Dionysian" in essence, if not detail. The great change in the new tragedy lay in the antagonist, who in his earlier versions had been only a materialist who sought to control the elements of his world. As Andrew Mayo gambled in wheat, as Jones made himself a materialistic Emperor, so all of O'Neill's

anti-Dionysians sought power in what they could clutch, enslave
and manipulate. Ephraim Cabot marks a change in O'Neill's view
of the enemy. With Nietzsche's help, O'Neill was able to see this
opponent of the Dionysian as being in his turn a God-driven man,
one who, despite his materialism and his stubborn individualism,
also "belonged" to a power greater than himself. As O'Neill gained
this perspective, what followed in the play was almost inevitable:
the warfare of Eben and Ephraim became the embodiment of a
theological conflict based broadly on the antagonism of the Dionysian and the Apollonian forces Nietzsche had described, a conflict
fought in the "universe" of the farm, in the particular arena its
center, the house, created.

The theological conflict is presented explicitly in Ephraim
Cabot's monologue in Part II, scene ii, when, moved by his desire
for Abbie, he attempts to reach her by confessing something of his
nature and telling her of the hardships in his past. The essence of
his statement is that he has grown hard in the service of a hard
God. "God," he says, "hain't easy"; His presence is in the stones
that must be piled up in a cruel life of sacrificial service so that
the farm may be fertile. The service is justified by God's command-
ment to Peter to build his church on a rock. Ephraim says, "When
ye kin make corn sprout out o' stones, God's livin' in yew!" He
tells Abbie of a time when in despair at so many stones, he gave
up the farm and journeyed west and farmed a broad meadow
where there were no stones, where "Ye'd on'y to plow an' sow an'
then set an' smoke yer pipe an' watch thin's grow." But the easy
way had no salvation in it, and he returned to the stony farm and
re-entered the service of the hard God.

The loneliness of the life on the farm was part of Ephraim's devotion, but at times, when hefting the stones became overbearingly
difficult, when solitude made him "despairful," he sought out a
woman, the whore, Min, or he took a wife, the mother of Simeon
and Peter, and later, when she died, the mother of Eben. His first
wife stood beside him, working hard, but "she never knowed what
she was helpin'." With her, Ephraim was always lonesome. After
her death, it was not so lonesome: "The farm growed. It was all
mine! When I thought o' that I didn't feel lonesome." His second
wife, whom he married because her people contested his deeds to
the land, was pretty and soft. Ephraim acknowledges that she tried

to be hard but failed because "She never knowed me nor nothin'. It was lonesomer 'n hell with her."

Then, for a third time, he hears a call in the Spring, "the voice o' God cryin' in my wilderness, in my lonesomeness—t' go an' seek an' find!" The voice in the wilderness has led him to Abbie, but in her presence as in the presence of the other women, he feels divided from his God, more lonesome, for this reason, than before he had found her. It is as if he had been driven by an alien force, not his hard God, but by another, one that stimulates desire and breeds weariness with the stones.

At the end of his monologue, he realizes that Abbie has not understood him, perhaps has not even heard him as she yearns for Eben in the adjoining bedroom. He leaves her and stumbles through the night to the barn, "whar it's restful—whar it's warm," and as he rounds the corner of the house, he stretches up his arms into the night and cries out to a God he understands, "God A'-mighty, call from the dark!" The hard God he has served is no longer there to hear him, and, as always when women come to the farm, he is wretched in his loneliness. The women—certainly Eben's mother and Abbie—serve a different God, one who is soft, if not easy, fecund, closely allied with the generative powers of nature, and capable of desire. Later, in *Strange Interlude,* O'Neill will write of the two principles as God the Father and God the Mother. In *Desire Under the Elms,* the conflict between the hard and—in Ephraim's term—easy Gods, the former associated with Ephraim's ascetic Puritanism and essentially masculine strength, the latter associated with Abbie and the fertility of the farm, is the thematic center of the play.

The setting is larger than the stage can show. Conveyed in the dialogue is a picture of the farm, fertile but without the luxuriance associated with natural fertility, settled in a bowl of hills, a pale sky contrasting with the isolated, monumental elms in the farmyard. Rows of stone walls wander across it, marking its boundaries, and through them passes a road which leads vaguely "away." At the center stand the house and barn, in good condition, but still suggesting buildings on the edge of ruin. The exterior walls are "a sickly grayish, the green of the shutters faded." The shingles of the house are rotting from the water that drips off the elms. It is as if the house were deserted and had no life.

While ordinary enough, the house still contains a mystery, for its central room, Eben's mother's parlor, is dark and sealed away. It is not the ordinary closed parlor, reserved for company use only. It is a haunted room, inhabited by his mother's ghost. Eben thinks of it as a room devoted to her memory. Caring for the house, cooking and doing the woman's service, he moves as if he were an acolyte, tending a shrine from which the saint has gone.

The image of the house as a shrine or church is not entirely fanciful. The action of the play begins with the ringing of a bell from the porch as Eben calls his brothers to supper, much as a congregation is called to prayer by the tolling of a bell. His first word, spoken as he looks up to the sunset-colored sky, is "God!" followed by a word spoken with *"puzzled awe,"* the devotional "Purty!" The congregation that comes, the oxen-like brothers from the field, are in Eben's view aliens who do not know the proper forms of devotion, for the service he has undertaken is the service of a priestess, not a priest, and the absent deity is female. Perhaps for this reason, as they approach the house, the men remember dead women. Simeon is reminded of his lost wife, Jenn, and Eben speaks fiercely of his mother.

Such memory has no sustenance. Jenn's name evokes in Simeon and Peter a vague restlessness and is linked with the promise of California gold. Eben's memory of his mother causes him to attack the life around him, blaming his brothers for their failure to help her or take moral responsibility for what happened to her. By turning continually to thoughts of his mother, he finds a way to rebel against the life he is forced to live, retreating from the farm's hardness toward a warmer and more gratifying commitment.

Isolated on the land, the lonely men walk hopelessly through the tired routines of their lives, dreaming only of possessing something that might satisfy them. Simeon and Peter hold to their vision of the riches in the West; Eben dreams of possessing the farm. Both desires are loosely associated with women—Jenn, Eben's mother—but for none of the brothers does the desire to possess material wealth betoken a real need. Simeon's restlessness is merely a reaction to the loss of Jenn. His aim in going west is dimly comprehended, and, although it is clothed in the imagery of bright promise, its ill-success is suggested when he and Peter sell their rights to inherit the farm for the thirty pieces of gold Eben steals from Ephraim. Having sold their birthrights, they leave, quasi-biblical prodigals who will not return to their home.

Eben's need, more articulated by his awareness, is manifested first as a lust for the land that if gratified will dispossess his father from the farm, leaving him in sole charge. Like his brothers, he at first seeks satisfaction in a dream of material possession, yet as the play proceeds it becomes clear that his hatred of his father and his legalistic claims of ownership are only signals of a truer desire, to rediscover through an identification with the land the security love of his dead mother brought him. He has filled the void her death created with vicious hatred, but for all that, his quest is positive and at heart selfless. He desires not to possess, but to be possessed by the force he knew in her love and which he associates with the "purty" land. What this implies is a total renunciation of the self.

His quest for the source of the feminine power in the land sets him apart from his brothers and brings him into fatal opposition with Ephraim and his hard God. To Eben, the prostitute, Min, whom he visits in a kind of incestuous revenge on his father, is warm and soft like the summer night, "like a wa'm plowed field," and he acknowledges the birth of a force in him that is like the fertile power of nature itself, "growin' an' growin'—til it'll bust out—!" Simeon, mocking him, says "Lust—that's what's growin' in ye," but lust is only the manifestation of frustrated desire. For Eben, the true, the consummate condition of being is to belong to the land as an unborn child belongs to the womb. Curiously, moved by this desire, his view of the land changes, and it is no longer stony and unyielding, but warm and filled with life.

Dominant at the heart of the play are, then, the two powerful forces moving through the land and giving it its character: a power that lies in the stones and a power that resides in the soil. The former demands the self-denial and the control Ephraim gives it; the latter promises peace and fulfillment in return for complete surrender. The characters are aware of them. Simeon acknowledges the presence of such powers when, speaking of the death of Eben's mother, he says, "No one ever kills anybody. It's allus somethin'. That's the murderer." [207] Others in the play respond in varying degrees of awareness to the forces that control their lives, as Ephraim calls to the God of the Lonesome, as Eben pays devotion to his mother's ghost, and as Abbie speaks of the force of nature, say-

ing that nature "owns ye . . . an' makes ye grow bigger—like a tree—
like them elums." [229]

Essentially, it appears that the two forces are to be equated with
the Gods Dionysus and Apollo. Yet while Nietzsche's *The Birth of
Tragedy* provided the philosophical underpinning the drama
evolved from O'Neill's perception that men who are forced to serve
alien Gods are doomed to loneliness. This had been Eben's case
until Abbie came, but when they have loved, the feminine principle asserts itself, and Abbie, in the service of the Mother God, finds
contentment for herself and brings it to Eben. At the same time,
however, Ephraim suffers a sense of alienation and loss—and specifically of the power to serve the hard God who appears to have
been driven from the farm by the service Abbie and Eben pay to
God the Mother.

Ephraim's dispossession has been signaled by the desire that drove
him out to "learn God's message" in the spring. His language is
that of an Old Testament prophet, but the desire that moves in
him and that drives him to find Abbie is strange to him. He is
made aware that he is withered and dry, a branch fit only for the
burning, and to reassert his former devotion, he invokes the God
of the Old and Lonesome. Simeon has said his father's search for a
wife was "whoring," but it was more than this. In succumbing to
the desire for life and in deserting the God of the Stones, he has
whored not after a woman but a false God, God the Mother. Yet
he cannot live in the alien God's service. He says to Abbie, "It's
cold in this house. It's oneasy. They's thin's pokin' about in the
dark—in the corners." [238] In the end, he is driven from the house,
an apostate cast into darkness.

The Dionysian God demands surrender and the suppression of any
act of conscious will. Good lies in loss of consciousness, sexual rapture, drunkenness, and in an unthinking response to the life-giving
forces of the earth. When he is possessed by it, even Ephraim pays
halting tribute to its power by quoting Biblical images of sex and
fertility ("yer belly be like a heap o' wheat") and when he is moved
by desire, he tacitly acknowledges the presence of the Mother God,
saying to Abbie that "Sometimes ye air the farm an' sometimes
the farm be yew." [236] Such admission, however, is temporary and
in Ephraim a madness that indicates how much he has deserted the
limits of his proper devotion, limits that were defined by the stone

walls he built as he sought to possess and subdue the farm. Ephraim's is a God served by an unrelenting pressure of will, so single-minded as to amount almost to mania. Or so it seems to Ephraim's neighbors who ridicule his servitude.

The Dionysian power is released when Eben takes Abbie in the night on the sofa in his mother's parlor. Then the mother's ghost disappears, and despite their adultery and their incest, they love free from guilt. The victory of the force they honor comes to a climactic celebration in the dance that opens Part III, the revel celebrating the birth of Abbie's child by Eben. At the party, Ephraim, the supposed father, acts the role of the satyr, capering in the dance, drinking and bragging of his sexual prowess, while his neighbors mock him to his face. The revels mount in tempo and die at their height. Abbie leaves and joins Eben by their child's cradle, and Ephraim drunkenly staggers outside to stand beneath the elms. The music dies, and a noise *"as of dead leaves"*—the gossiping whispers of the guests—comes from the kitchen. Then, Ephraim feels most strongly the maternal power concentrated in the trees:

> Even the music can't drive it out—somethin'. Ye kin feel it droppin' off the elums, climbin' up the roof, sneakin' down the chimney, pokin' in the corners! They's no peace in houses, they's no rest livin' with folks. Somethin's always livin' with ye. . . . I'll go t' the barn an' rest a spell. [253]

At the Dionysian climacteric, Ephraim is alone.

Later, the guests gone, Ephraim convinces Eben that Abbie has tricked him into fathering the son who will finally possess the farm. Eben's failure to believe in Abbie's love marks the end of the Dionysian reign. He leaves her, crying that he is going to get drunk and dance, but after the betrayal, he is incapable of plunging into forgetful surrender to the God. Abbie clings to him and passionately asks whether he would forgive her if she could prove that she had not schemed against him: "If I could do it—ye'd love me agen, wouldn't ye? Ye'd kiss me agen? Ye wouldn't never leave me, would ye?" Eben replies sardonically, "I calc'late not. But ye hain't God, be ye" [258]

Abbie's murder of her child is her attempt to be God, but the act of self-denying will, the sin against love and the life of the Dionysians, is more proper to the service of Ephraim's God than to hers. Hearing of her action, Eben cries out, "Oh, God A'mighty! A'mighty God! Maw, whar was ye, why didn't ye stop her?" To this, Abbie replies, "She went back t' her grave that night we fust done it, remember? I hain't felt her about since." [261] Her words suggest that perhaps now the ghost will return and wander restlessly, since the God has left. Ephraim in his desolation threatens to set fire to the house and barn: "I'll leave yer Maw t' haunt the ashes." His words are akin to recognition of the force that has haunted him:

> If he was Eben's [baby], I be glad he air gone! An' mebbe I sus-picioned it all along. I felt they was somethin' onnateral—some-whars—the house got so lonesome—an' cold—drivin' me down t' the barn—t' the beasts o' the field. . . . Ay-eh. I must've suspicioned —somethin'. Ye didn't fool me—not altogether, leastways—I'm too old a bird—growin' ripe on the bough. [264]

Momentarily, he considers going west, but at the last, he realizes he cannot leave.

> I kin hear His voice warnin' me agen t' be hard an' stay on my farm. I kin see His hand usin' Eben t' steal t' keep me from weak-ness. I kin feel I be in the palm o' His hand, His fingers guidin' me. . . . It's a-goin' t' be lonesomer now than it ever war afore— an' I'm gittin' old, Lord—ripe on the bough. . . . Waal—what d'ye want? God's lonesome, hain't He? God's hard an' lonesome! [268]

At the end Ephraim's God has returned to the farm vanquishing the maternal force that Eben and Abbie had served and betrayed.

Yet what is left for them, displays a final, perhaps unexpected, turn, and with the conclusion to his tragedy, O'Neill introduces a new motif in his writing, centering on a concept of the power of will. When it is no longer possible for them to belong to their God, the lovers have one recourse—to belong to one another. Earlier, their love generated the rapture that permitted them to achieve the Dionysian immersion into the life force. It brought them in tune with the fertility of the land and its divinity. Now, however, the God has left the land, and they are ejected from the Garden. As Adam accepted Eve's sin, Eben must accept Abbie's, for what is left to them cannot lie beyond themselves. In turning back to Ab-bie, after his violent rejection of her strange act of faith, Eben re-establishes their love so that they need to rely on nothing outward.

Earlier, in *Welded,* O'Neill had written of two who attempted to find God in marriage, but in the final moments of *Desire Under the Elms,* there is only an assertion of responsibility and an acceptance of the destiny their love has brought. Without God, man has only himself to provide surcease from loneliness.

The play's ending awakens echoes of older tragic patterns that conclude with the protagonist's acknowledgement of his responsibility for a general guilt. Making such admission Eben becomes nearly heroic in the eyes of his father who speaks grudgingly of his admiration. Eben's act is perhaps one which Ephraim's God would exact from one of his servants, based as it is on a consciousness of guilt and a need for expiation. Yet in the reunion of the lovers, O'Neill is announcing strongly what will be a solution for those who cannot "belong." It was a concept which he touched crudely in so early a play as *The Web,* and which in his final plays he will develop into a major statement: that when all is lost, the only good is in finding another being, equally lonely and alienated, in whose presence comfort can be gained and loneliness forgotten for a time.

At the end, O'Neill's God-oriented tragedy comes to focus on man. The shift is made without a jar, and the play achieves a fullness of statement and form which no earlier work of his had attained. It is a major work of art prepared by a playwright who in mastering his craft and completely understanding the implications of his theme had finally come of age.

VII
THE
TRIUMVIRATE (2)

The Fountain (1921)
The Hairy Ape (1921)
Marco Millions (1923-25)
The Rime of the Ancient Mariner (1923)
The Revelation of John the Divine (1924)
The Great God Brown (1925)
Lazarus Laughed (1925-26)

1922—a year of turn and change, things dying, things new-born. For the first time, Eugene met his elder son, Eugene, Jr., and was introduced to the handsome actress, Carlotta Monterey. Suddenly, in Los Angeles, his mother died; Jamie, who was with her, despairing at her loss, began to drink again. The train bearing the bodies of the dead mother and drunken brother arrived in New York City the night The Hairy Ape opened. His plays prospered, but personal strains told: He drank, sometimes almost uncontrollably, and a nervous tremor manifested itself in his hands. His family gone, he began a restless search for a home, first in Ridgefield, Connecticut, then in Bermuda, where in 1925 his daughter, Oona, was born. Determined effort finally enabled him to stop drinking. Honors came to him: in 1925, a gold medal from The National Institute of Arts and Letters, in 1926, an honorary degree from Yale University. And the plays, in spite of personal tragedies and emotional difficulties, came rapidly— faster, in fact, than the "Triumvirate" could stage them. O'Neill, left with a backlog of unproduced scripts, began to seek a fully professional producing organization.

BOTH Sheldon Cheney and Kenneth Macgowan had visualized a collaborative effort of designer, director and playwright aimed at the creation of a theatre that would realize the aesthetic ideals of Gordon Craig. It was to be a dramatic experience that did not necessarily rely on dialogue or the routine skills of the playwright. It would minimize, if it did not eliminate, the actor. Reinhardt's mimo-drama *Sumurun* had suggested the possibilities of such a full theatrical spectacle, and, in the United States, experiments with color organs, masks and choreographic acting had stimulated further undertaking in such a vein. Although some elements of this theatrical aestheticism undoubtedly entered into the creation of *Lazarus Laughed,* O'Neill's efforts at pure spectacle were insignificant. Twice, in collaboration with Jones and Macgowan, he created scenarios for such a theatre. Both works were written in 1924 and were adaptations. The first, *The Rime of the Ancient Mariner,* was perhaps a silent acknowledgment of a debt he had owed Coleridge from the time of *Fog* and *Thirst;* the second, *The Revelation of John the Divine,* remained unfinished.

The latter script, which was to have formed half of a double bill with *The Rime of the Ancient Mariner,*[1] represents little more than a cutting of the King James version by perhaps one-third. O'Neill made a preliminary sorting-out of the solo voices, choric passages and "stage directions," and he indicated one or two elements of design and action. For example, as John the narrator recites Chapter 8, verses 3, 4 and 6, O'Neill called for special lighting and sound effects: "Trumpet—wailing and cries from back of dome and below—noise of hail—crimson fire from above descends down dome."[2] For the most part, however, the work is unformed, undramatized.

O'Neill's final stage direction gives perhaps some indication of the direction of the action. He wrote, "John slowly rises, shaken and weak, but exalted,—in a trembling note of ecstasy,"[3] but this is the only indication of a dramatic development. The rest is oratorio.

The Rime of the Ancient Mariner was produced in 1924 by the Experimental Theatre on a double bill with Molière's *Georges Dandin*. It was not a success. Coleridge's poem is slightly cut, with some of the lines being converted to stage directions, e.g., *"He holds him with his skinny hand."* O'Neill amplified the action, bringing onstage a chorus of six masked sailors who mime the tale as the Mariner narrates it. He called for screens to form such scenic elements as the house where the marriage is taking place and the icebergs. The lighting is elaborate, and a special-effects machine was required for projections of clouds and stars on the plaster dome. Music and choreography all filled their places. James Light, who with Robert Edmond Jones staged the work, commented that the "finished effects" were "reached primarily through an understanding of the meaning of the poem, through an understanding that we wished them to indicate a flow of emotion, not at all to represent action. Unconsciously they developed a sense of form, a sense of rhythm and because of this . . . what they do affects the audience much as music does."[4] In his review, Alexander Woollcott noted that "The production was singularly childish. In the effort of this generation to break suffocated out of the narrow confines of the traditional theater, they have tried to throw away everything which may, by some chance, have delighted their grandfathers. It is therefore not to be wondered at that, in thus beginning all over again, they achieve something of the accent of a nursery entertainment."[5] A similarly sour attitude toward experiment was apparent in George Jean Nathan's comment that *The Rime of the Ancient Mariner* was useful "chiefly as an occasion to experiment with masks and shadow lighting." He reminded all concerned that such experiments require a play to be of any value.[6] O'Neill, although he maintained an affection of sorts for *The Rime of the Ancient Mariner,* evidently shared their opinions. He had much more important projects in hand than such minor editorial work.

His major creative effort during the time he was directly associated with Macgowan and Jones was in the style of expressionism as it was generally understood in that period. Macgowan had called expressionism "anti-realistic" in its refusal merely to imitate the surfaces of experience, and he had noted that it used the free techniques of romanticism to penetrate toward psychological and spiritual truths. He had held also that in developing plays in this mode, the collaboration of playwright, designer and director was necessary since the playwright has to depend on color and form and a more presentational acting style than was customary.

O'Neill's first effort to write in the expressionistic mode was *The Emperor Jones.* Its success undoubtedly confirmed his belief that this was a direction an important modern playwright should take. In the year following, he wrote two new works in the style, *The Fountain* and *The Hairy Ape.* The latter was discussed in embryo with Macgowan, and as he began writing *The Fountain,* the possibility of a collaboration with Macgowan and Jones was clearly in his mind. On March 18, 1921, he wrote to Macgowan, "I have asked Bobby Jones also to suggest reading for me. I am hoping that he will be able to come up here either before or after his trip abroad. By that time my idea of the whole play ought to have more form and substance—and he could tell me just how the thing appeared to him from his angle—and we might combine. It would be an intensely interesting experiment, I believe, to work this thing out in harmony from our respective lines in the theatre—one not done before, as far as I know. For my part, a clearer understanding of what he is striving for would be of inestimable value. . . . Perhaps you could fix it so that you folks and Bobby could make it at the same time. That would be fine if you could. I want all your suggestions on this *The Fountain* opus that you can give, you know."

In two superficial ways, *The Fountain* fell into the expressionist camp. First, it was a romantic costume play. Macgowan in *The Theatre of Tomorrow* had listed the number of plays in America in recent seasons which had turned away from the slavish imitation of the present to move back in time. He felt that such a turn toward the exotic was indication of a desire to increase the imaginative range of the theatre in contemporary life. Romanticism was, in its way, "anti-realistic," and as a style resembled expressionism.[7] Second, in its structure, it moved away from the formulas that had chained the theatre to trivial realism. Macgowan inveighed against the "constructed" play, the three-act formula which imitators of Ibsen in his realistic period had made the norm of a theatre-goer's experience. He called for a much freer sense of form, one that would avoid artificial compression and illogical happenings so that a forced continuity in time could be maintained. An increase in the number of scenes seemed to him an inevitable consequence as the plays achieve a significant inner form. A technique comparable to that of the film might be envisioned, he felt, that would permit the play to move freely with the mind of the audience.[8] *The Fountain,* responsive to such doctrine, is not divided into acts but into "Parts" and contains, in all, eleven scenes. O'Neill's understanding of its shape is detailed in a letter he wrote on April 8, 1921, to Macgowan: "As for act or scene divisions, I have no rule either one way or the other. I always let the subject matter mould itself into its own particular form and I find it does this without my ever wasting thought upon it. I start out with the idea that there are no rules or precedent in the game except what the play chooses to make for itself—but not forgetting that it is to be played in a theatre—('theatre' meaning my notion of what a modern theatre should be capable of instead of merely what it is). I usually feel instinctively a sort of rhythm of acts or scenes and obey it hit or miss."

The romantic qualities of the play were not lost on the audiences. Burns Mantle commented that the play "is not for the 'Anna Christie' branch of the Eugene O'Neill alumni. It is rather for 'The Emperor Jones,'–'Where the Cross Is Made' group. It is such a poetic romance as any true dreamer might write for the pleasure of writing it, and with little thought of selling it to the theatre."[9]

O'Neill's program note for the play's production stresses the romanticism inherent in the story:

> The idea of writing *The Fountain* came originally from my interest in the recurrence in folk-lore of the beautiful legend of a healing spring of eternal youth. The play is only incidentally concerned with the Era of Discovery in America. It has sought merely to express the urging spirit of the period without pretending to any too-educational accuracy in the matter of dates and facts in general. The characters, with the exception of Columbus, are fictitious. Juan Ponce de Leon, in so far as I have been able to make him a human being, is wholly imaginary. I have simply filled in the bare outline of his career, as briefly reported in the Who's Who of the histories, with a conception of what could have been

the truth behind his "life-sketch" if he had been the man it was romantically—and religiously—moving to me to believe he might have been! Therefore, I wish to take solemn oath right here and now, that *The Fountain* is not morbid realism.*

Not only in its romantic re-telling of history and in its fluidity of form but also in its language, the play attempted to ally itself with the new theatrical movement. Both Magowan and Cheney had asked for a poetic drama. Macgowan, more specifically, had expressed his dislike of Shakespearean imitations in dead iambic pentameter, and he had felt it sufficient if a dramatist were to achieve the rhythmic prose of Synge or of O'Neill in *The Emperor Jones.*[11] Nevertheless, O'Neill in the early drafts of *The Fountain* framed the dialogue in language close to blank verse, a loosely cadenced iambic measure, which he later restructured as prose. His aim, as he stated it to George Jean Nathan, was "to gain a naturalistic effect of the quality of the people and speech of those times . . . with little care for original poetic beauty save in the few instances where that is called for."[12] The comment is a little defensive, for many viewers took the play sharply to task for its language.[13] O'Neill's statement that he was creating a "naturalistic" language, realistically appropriate to his historical figures is, in the face of his evident striving for poetic effect, unconvincing. Rather, it appears that he sought through the verse to move "behind life," releasing in the play the power of poetry to present inner reality by imagery and rhythm. To a limited extent, the original verse patterns can be reapproximated from the prose text.

---

* Perhaps an impulse that led to the writing of *The Fountain* came from a play by George Cram Cook entitled *The Spring.* It was produced by the Provincetown Players in January, 1921, the same season as *The Emperor Jones,* shortly before O'Neill began to write *The Fountain.* Cook's play was one in which he took pride, and its failure in the aftermath of the success of *The Emperor Jones* led him to leave his theatre in bitterness. *The Spring* is a story of modern and primitive times, dealing with an Indian legend of reincarnation and of a magical spring in which a vision of the unity of all souls, all nature can be seen. The vision leads its holder toward new horizons: "Do you know what this means? It means that you and I, before we die, may turn the thought of the world as sharply as Darwin did—but inward. This is a voyage greater than that of Columbus!—for what we seek is—the unknown hemisphere of the soul—You and I are going to set sail into ourselves; for there, in the ocean of the unconscious, is the shore of our new world."[10] The resemblance between O'Neill's and Cook's themes is marked and the use of American Indian subject matter suggests that O'Neill may have been led to the story of Ponce de Leon by Cook's work. In detail, however, there is little resemblance.

Pentameter ghosts haunt such speeches as Maria's:

> If you are still my friend you will not wish it.
> It was my final penance that you should know.
> And, having told you, I am free, for my heart is dead.
> There is only my soul left that knows the love of God.
> Which blesses and does not torture. Farewell once more, Juan.
>
> [381]

Without reliable evidence as to the extent of O'Neill's revisions of the verse when he printed it as prose, the fact is clear that had he left the dialogue in verse form, what he would have written would have been only a somewhat heightened poetic prose, similar to that of *Lazarus Laughed* which could serve him as the idiom of his questing central character.

The potential gain of such an idiom was the opportunity to speak of God and of man's quest for God directly in a way his realistic plays had not permitted. In *The Fountain,* O'Neill writes for the first time of the Catholic faith from which he had turned in early manhood. Yet it is probably not true to say as the Gelbs do that here "O'Neill tried, for the first time on a large scale, to dramatize his private and never-ending struggle with his Catholic conscience."[14] Catholic faith is treated in this play as a part of the historical background. Luis's final statement that the dead hero "lives in God" is appropriate to Luis's character, not to any generally held Catholic position. Juan's sense as he dies is that he will be "resolved into the thousand moods of beauty that make up happiness." In dying he has re-entered the Fountain of Eternity, which is the Fountain of eternal youth. God in this play is a force of eternal nature, not the Catholic deity. Together with the image of man as a seeker who desires to be possessed by the eternal life forces that move around and through him, this view of God has characterized all of O'Neill's religious thinking from his first plays forward. The importance of *The Fountain* and its poetry is that O'Neill can now deal explicitly with the thought that had been implicit in so many of his dramas up to 1921.

In his research for the play, among the books Macgowan had provided for him, he read Frazer's *The Golden Bough.* The anthropological concerns which had marked many of his earlier works, including *The Emperor Jones* and the recently completed *The*

First Man, and which were to reappear in *The Hairy Ape* written later in the same year, were perhaps confirmed and strengthened by Frazer's work, for Juan Ponce de Leon follows the route taken by many of O'Neill's earlier heroes, back to his origins in a natural, life-giving source.

In the beginning, however, Juan is not the questing poet. He bears a strong resemblance to Andrew Mayo, whose journey to foreign lands is characterized by a materialistic desire for possession, but who remains blind to the mystery of the exotic worlds about him. He is introduced as a man of war, speaking war-mongering slogans, and, bent on an expedition of plunder with Columbus, he lives with "disciplined ability and confident self-mastery." Only when his love for Beatriz leads him to seek the source of life in the eternal spring does he change. Then, predictably, he becomes O'Neill's poetic hero, questing God. The change has been slightly anticipated by a stage direction when Juan is introduced in the first scene. O'Neill calls him *"a romantic dreamer governed by the ambitious thinker in him."* O'Neill has combined in Juan the opposites that he first set forth as Robert and Andrew Mayo.

The story of *The Fountain* is characteristic. The hero, capable of sensitive and idealistic vision, is transformed by his materialism into an enfeebled monster, moving soullessly through a corrupt society, far from his natural world. In *The Fountain,* however, following his "romantic and religious" inclinations, O'Neill reverses the usual course of his narrative—which would normally end with the hero's destruction—and causes the dreamer to emerge from the man of iron, and, in death, to triumph. It is an important change, and it comes about because through the demands of the expressionist theatre he is empowered, if not forced, to be explicit about the nature of the God with which he had earlier dealt only by implication. Now, with the symbol of God on the stage in the vision of the Fountain of Youth, O'Neill must show God not as implacable, revengeful or, for that matter, even aware of man. God *is,* as Nature *is,* and man need only recognize his presence to be caught up in the force of life at its most profound. Once the force is known, once the vision is made real, man is in harmony with his world.

The harmony is expressed in the play at the outset by Don Luis's translation of a Moorish song:

> There is in some far country of the East—Cathay, Cipango, who knows—a spot that Nature has set apart from men and blessed with peace. It is a sacred grove where all things live in the old harmony they knew before men came. Beauty resides there and is articulate. Each sound is music, and every sight a vision. [386]

The image of the old harmony, born of sacred, primordial peace is a vision of Eden, of Paradise, even, in the context of this play, of America. Juan at the outset rejects the vision, crying "There is no profit in staking life for dreams"; yet out of his despair in failing to gain riches in the New World, there is born in him a dream of something other than golden cities, and he comes at last to a quest for the essence of the vision of the song.

As Juan moves into the forests to seek the fountain, O'Neill returns to the technical scenic devices of *The Emperor Jones*. The walls of the forest are close in around the spring, and Juan, wounded and alone, speaks as Brutus Jones had done, in soliloquy, calling for a vision of "what I am that I should have lived and died!" The vision comes, a masked figure of a woman who is Death, followed by a second vision of his beloved, Beatriz, who is "the personified spirit of the fountain" and who sings its song:

> Life is a fountain
> Forever leaping
> Upward to catch the golden sunlight
> Upward to reach the azure heaven
> Failing, falling,
> Ever returning,
> To kiss the earth that the flower may live.
>
> [439]

Other visions come: a Chinese poet and the Moorish minstrel who sang the tale of the sacred grove. Juan curses them because he feels they have damned him. Yet, as the phantoms disappear, he calls out to them, "Have you no vision for the graspers of the earth?" The vision he is granted is one of all the faiths of the earth passing into the fountain. Beatriz reappears, this time masked as an aged crone. He realizes that age and youth are the same "rhythm of eternal life," and that death is nothing. The figure of Death unmasks, and becomes Beatriz, soaring upward in the heart of the fountain which he now senses is "That from which all life springs and to which it must return—God! Are all dreams of you but one dream?" [441]

The final scene of the play, in which Juan discovers himself reborn in his nephew who loves the young Beatriz, daughter of Juan's former mistress, is a somewhat too literal proof of the capacity of life to renew itself, but it is enough to confirm the truth of his vision to Juan. He dies crying, "One must accept, absorb, give back, become oneself a symbol." As he dies, his reincarnated self sings the song of the fountain.

The ecstatic rush of feeling at the end of the play was unquestionably the kind of outpouring that those who wrote of the need for spirituality in the theatre cherished. Yet, although O'Neill was excited as he wrote, neither he nor his critics liked it much when it appeared on the stage* O'Neill classed *The Fountain* with *Gold* and *The First Man* as "too painfully bungled in their present form to be worth producing at all."[15]

Notably in each of the "bungled" plays, production was long deferred, and O'Neill was forced to accept compromises in casting and staging. While waiting, he wrote other plays that were more immediately important to him. In September, 1925, more than four years after he had written *The Fountain,* and after it had made the rounds of several producers, including Arthur Hopkins and the Theatre Guild, he complained to Macgowan that the work which the Experimental Theatre was putting in on the production of *The Fountain* was interfering with the production of *The Great God Brown.* "*Brown,*" he wrote, "needs much more careful casting, more time, and more careful preparation than 'The Fountain.' To me it is worth a dozen *Fountains.*" Clearly, by the time *The Fountain* appeared on stage, O'Neill had no further interest in it. The style was forced, the romantic theatricality of little interest, and the play's reliance on elaborate stage devices and expensive production created a mechanical core to the fervor that falsifies the lyric impulse. Moreover, the relatively explicit analysis of the nature of God may have seemed in the retrospect of four years less effective than the treatment of the theology of the "graspers of the earth" in

---

* The similarity between the expression of religious ecstasy at the end of *The Fountain* to passages at the end of *Welded* and *All God's Chillun Got Wings* is not coincidental. Each represents an attempt by O'Neill to shape the dramatic action so that it ends on a moment of significant religious experience.

Desire Under the Elms, which had been written and produced in 1924.

He may also have felt that in giving his tragic fable a new, positive ending, he had lost the essential drama of suffering that had marked such early successes as *Beyond the Horizon, The Emperor Jones* and certain of the *Glencairn* plays. Juan's story, so long as he persists in an essentially false pursuit for materialistic gain, is not dramatic. In the first scenes of the play, he is capricious, mercurial, antagonistic to most of his fellows, but all conflict in which he is involved is based on superficies of character, especially his "Spanish" hot-headedness. Although he occupies the center of attention, he does nothing.* All occasions when he seems to act, as in the scenes displaying his hostility to Columbus and, later, to the nobility and the natives of the New World, are contrived. This is not to say that there are not scenes of interest**; nevertheless, they do not dramatize Juan as a religious quester. Commenting on the failure of the play, O'Neill said that he thought the critics were right in saying that it had no action.[16] The judgment, at least of the first eight scenes of the play, is valid. Juan's true action begins only when the dreamer in him overthrows the "ambitious thinker," when, two-thirds through the play, Juan "stakes his life for a dream" and follows what has before seemed to him only a cursed life-lie. Then, the dream of golden cities becomes a vision of God, and, significantly, at this point, the lyric qualities of the dialogue begin to justify their presence and become more like poetry and less an awkward attempt to re-create the "naturalistic speech" of the people of times past.

In late November, 1921, while *The Fountain* was still incomplete in its first draft, O'Neill began another project that was to evolve as *The Hairy Ape.* In 1917, he had written a short story of that title concerning the "revolt" of a stoker who finally joins the I.W.W. He had submitted it for publication, but it was rejected

---

* At one point, Juan is so slightly involved that O'Neill writes a desperate stage direction: *"Juan paces back and forth, humming to himself,"* [378] apparently on the theory that the character has to look busy even if he is not.
** Scene ii on Columbus's flagship is the first indication of O'Neill's power as a historical dramatist. He has re-created the moodiness and the tensions of the voyage with sensitivity, and has caught in his sketch of Columbus something of the almost messianic quality of the man.

and he later destroyed it.[17] In the same year, he had come across his central image while writing *The Moon of the Caribbees:*

> COCKY   (*angrily*) . . . You ain't no bleedin' beauty prize yeself, me man. A 'airy ape, I calls yer.
> PADDY   (. . . *truculently*) Whot's thot? Say ut again if ye dare.
> COCKY   (. . . *snarling*) 'Airy ape! That's wot I says! [461]

It is possible also that his extensive reading of the *Saturday Evening Post* in the years 1918 and 1919 contributed some suggestions. Amidst the sea stories that the magazine regularly published there is one by Richard M. Hallet entitled *Ticklish Waters,* in which Slim Williams saves his ship by keeping the fires going under the boilers when all seems lost:

> The stiff yellow flame leaped to the crown sheet, fanning his face with a fierce glow, stinging the skin on his chest, warming him, and bringing his own resolution to this same white heat. He was invulnerable, surely! He felt as if he had got the ship on his back and had power to wade ashore with it. He felt a heroic necessity binding him to save the ship's life, even at the expense of his own. What was his own, indeed? Perhaps only a dream. . . .

As the fires gradually take hold and the ship regains power, his ecstasy mounts:

> In his exultation he hit an iron door back of him, a booming blow with his fist. . . .
> "Have you got all the coal out of there?"
> The grinning apes all about him nodded and gibbered. . . .[18]

Something of Yank's manner and his power may have been suggested by the valiant Williams.

When it was fully conceived, the play was written with great speed. A tentative commitment to cast Louis Wolheim as Yank was made in November before the script was written. The first draft was completed before Christmas, requiring about three weeks' writing, and the final revisions were made by the third week in January. On December 24, 1921, O'Neill wrote to Macgowan of his satisfaction with the work in words that indicate his attention as a playwright to Macgowan's theories of drama:

> Well, *The Hairy Ape*—first draft—was finished yesterday. I have been taken with a terrific splurge of intensive labor on it and was able to get it done in a little less than three weeks. It was one of those times when the numbers seemed to come. I was so full of it, it

just oozed out of every pore. And the result, I think, is at least astonishing, whether for good or evil. It has changed and developed immensely in the doing and you will find it much different from the bare outline as I sketched it to you. I don't think the play as a whole can be fitted into any of the current "isms." It seems to run the whole gamut from extreme naturalism to extreme expressionism—with more of the latter than the former. I have tried to dig deep in it, to probe in the shadows of the soul of man bewildered by the disharmony of his primitive pride and individualism at war with the mechanistic development of society. And the man in the case is not an Irishman, as I at first intended, but, more fittingly, an American—a New York tough of the toughs, a product of the waterfront turned stoker—a type of mind, if you could call it that, which I know extremely well. . . . Suffice it for me to add, the treatment of all the sets should be expressionistic, I think.*

Arthur Hopkins, whose production of *"Anna Christie"* in November, 1921, had proved a success, was interested in the new O'Neill work and offered to help James Light with the direction. Evidently with an eye to moving the play to Broadway should it prove itself in the Provincetown production, he arranged that Robert Edmond Jones should "assist" Cleon Throckmorton with the settings. *The Hairy Ape* opened at the Provincetown Playhouse on March 9, 1922, and on April 17, Hopkins took it uptown for a successful Broadway production and tour.**

Although in its external manner, it bears little resemblance to the other plays that O'Neill wrote in these years, it is not essentially different from their thematic explorations. Like *The First Man,****

* The reference to Yank's having been Irish in the original conception suggests that the question of the suicide of O'Neill's stoker friend, the Irishman, Driscoll, formed one of the roots of the play. O'Neill admitted as much in an article for the *American Magazine,* November, 1922: "It was the why of Driscoll's suicide that gave me the germ of the idea [for *The Hairy Ape*]."[19]
** *The Hairy Ape* was the last successful presentation of the first phase of the Provincetown Players. A comedy by Susan Glaspell, *Chains of Dew,* completed the season, at which point, the Cooks went to Greece and the Provincetown "holiday" began.
*** *The Hairy Ape* opened five days after Augustin Duncan's production of *The First Man.* This was the third time in O'Neill's short career that two of his major works had opened in close proximity. *Beyond the Horizon* had opened February 2, 1920, and *Chris Christopherson* on March 8. *"Anna Christie"* opened November 2, 1921, and *The Straw* on November 10. The phenomenon was to be repeated once more when the Theatre Guild opened *Marco Millions* on January 9, 1928, and *Strange Interlude* on January 30. The strain on a playwright during the rehearsals of his work is great. O'Neill's ability to fulfill heavy obligations to his theatrical enterprises is worthy of comment.

The Fountain and *All God's Chillun Got Wings, The Hairy Ape* deals with what may loosely be called "anthropological" subject matter, expressed in terms of a search for the origins of life and making reference to atavistic remnants of primitive man appearing in modern society. O'Neill's "ape" is a neanderthal stoker, controlling the furnace gang on his ship with animalistic power and the confidence that is born of total security in his place. Thought does not trouble him until he is made aware of the contempt held for his bestiality by members of another world of which he is only dimly aware. Then thought comes, and he is driven from his security to a frenzied run through New York City, seeking again the primitive sense of "belonging" that he has lost. His effort is disastrous, and he dies in the cage of the great ape in the Central Park Zoo.

Thus, *The Hairy Ape* studies man's attempt to come into harmony with his world, to find to whom, to what he can belong. In doing so, it dramatizes the same theological quest that had formed the basis for *Welded* and *The Fountain* but without question, it is a better play in the theatre than its predecessors. Its success paralleled that of *The Emperor Jones,* and O'Neill was to create no comparable theatrical excitement until the Theatre Guild produced *Strange Interlude* in 1928. The style of the play, which must have seemed exactly what the proponents of the Art Theatre ordered, placed O'Neill as an experimenter far to the front of the avant-garde in America, and doubtless confirmed his decision to experiment with new forms of theatre.

Yet the play, written at the beginning of O'Neill's commitment to the new movement, betrays a stylistic problem which was in the end to bring his career to a crucial dilemma, one that he summed unawarely in his gleeful phrase about the play's style: "It seems to run the whole gamut from extreme naturalism to extreme expressionism."

Among the plays of the 1920's, *The Hairy Ape,* for all its seeming originality of style and substance, is perhaps the most derivative. It is framed in eight short scenes as *The Emperor Jones* was, and like the earlier play, it concentrates on its hero's run through a kind of wilderness to his eventual destruction by a primitive force. The play owes something as well to O'Neill's earlier realistic plays of the sea. Paddy's praise of the days of the sailing ships, when "a ship was part of the sea, and a man was part of a ship, and the sea joined all together and made it one," is an explicit statement of the view of men as "children of the sea." The same attitude toward steam ships had been expressed in the first act of *Chris Christopherson* when Mickey and Devlin attempt to persuade Chris to sail with them:

MICKEY   We'll find a clean, smart ship for the three of us. . . . No lime juice tramp this time! I've my bellyful of steam. To hell with it!

DEVLIN   To hell with steam!

MICKEY   We'll find a tall, smart daisy of a full-rigged ship with skys'ls—a beautiful, swift hooker that'll take us both flyin' south through the Trades.

DEVLIN   (*sings*) Oh, away Rio!

MICKEY   A sweet slim clipper like the old ones, Chris. If there's one left on the seas, we'll find her! [18]

Stripped of its expressionistic scenic requirements, the first four scenes, up to the point where Yank leaves the ship, are not essentially different from the earlier sea plays.

Yet, by 1921, O'Neill had heard much from Macgowan and others of the German expressionist drama. A letter to Macgowan, dated July 1, 1921, asks Macgowan to bring to Provincetown some illustrated pamphlets on the German Theatre. *The Theatre of Tomorrow* describes in detail Georg Kaiser's *From Morn to Midnight,* in which a bank clerk runs from established security to destruction, commenting on its division into seven scenes, its use of soliloquies and its mixture of terror and humor, both of which "cut close to those strange psychic realities of life which come often with the effect of a hypnotic interlude in logical normal existence."[20] He concludes his praise of the play with the comment that "Kaiser has succeeded in getting past the surface of reality. He has penetrated the basic stratum of man's psyche. To do this, I take it, is the purpose of expressionism."[21] He continues to discuss romantic drama as a step in the right direction, adding that once audiences are accustomed to something other than realism, they will accept "an imaginative treatment" of lives in Main Street or Harlem.[22] He is concerned to note that "the grandeur of the play of the future must lie not in a superhuman figure, but in the vast and eternal forces of life which we are made to recognize as they play upon him. The expressionist puts it rather rhetorically when he writes: 'Let the characters be great in the sense that their existence, their lives, share the great existence of the heavens and the earth —that their hearts united to all that occurs, beat in time with the universe.' . . . The drama must seek to make us recognize the things that, since Greek days, we have forgotten—the eternal identity of you and me with the vast and unmanageable forces which have played through every atom of life since the beginning. Psychoanalysis, tracing back our thoughts and actions into fundamental impulses, has done more than any one factor to make us recover the sense of our unity with the dumb, mysterious processes of nature. We know now through science what the Greeks and all primitive peoples knew through instinct. The task is to apply it to art and, in our case, to the drama."*

Whether *The Hairy Ape* is directly indebted to *From Morn to Midnight* or not, it clearly owes much to Macgowan's enthusiasm for the German expressionist drama.** O'Neill's first plan for his narrative was to return Yank to the stokehole where his failure to "belong" would leave him alienated and alone. Such an ending would have thrown the play inevitably back into the realistic context of the first four scenes, bringing the same sense of return to normalcy after a strange psychic voyage that the final scene of *The Emperor Jones* achieves. The ending upon which O'Neill decided was one stylistically more appropriate to the expressionistic second half of the play, and one quite in line with Macgowan's dictum,

* Macgowan, 263. O'Neill had received a copy of Macgowan's book as a Christmas present in 1921. His letter to Macgowan wherein he stated that he had just finished *The Hairy Ape* in first draft was written December 24. He there mentioned that he will not "cheat by unveiling your Christmas gift before the due time," although he knew what it was. He wrote, "I am darned eager to see how it is gotten out and to be able to read it as a whole." Evidently he and Macgowan had discussed its contents and he had read some of it in draft.

** Cf. Clark, 83. Clark quotes O'Neill as stating that he had read *From Morn to Midnight* before he wrote *The Hairy Ape,* but not before the idea for it was in his mind. Characteristically, he denied any influence: "The point is that *The Hairy Ape* is a direct descendant of *Jones,* written long before I had ever heard of Expressionism [he had, of course, read Strindberg], and its form needs no explanation but this. As a matter of fact, I did not think much of *Morn to Midnight,* and still don't. It is too easy. It would not have influenced me." Clark adds that he does not know whether O'Neill had read Kaiser's *Gas* trilogy but he rightly points out similarities between that work and *Dynamo.* There are close similarities between *The Coral* and *The Hairy Ape,* notably in Act II of Kaiser's play, when the idle guests of the Billionaire, seated under an awning on the deck of a yacht, find their empty world invaded by a stoker who has been overcome by the heat. The contrast of the deck-side luxury and the stokehole is similar to that which O'Neill draws in scenes ii and iii of his play.

that the hero of the play of the future would be a kind of every-man caught up in a great issue that would stress his unity with the mysterious processes of the forces of nature.

The Hairy Ape, then, is a play prompted in its stylistic develop-ment by Macgowan's enthusiasm that splits the ticket sharply be-tween realism and the new expressionism. Stylistically, it lies at a half-way point in O'Neill's career.

In describing the first scene, the fireman's forecastle of a trans-Atlantic liner, O'Neill writes that the setting, with the lines of the bunks and upright supports made of white steel, should cross one another *"like the steel framework of a cage."* In the cramped space, the firemen who inhabit the cage should resemble *"those pictures in which the appearance of Neanderthal Man is guessed at."* The stokers, like the crew of the *Glencairn,* represent a wide variety of nationalities and types, but essentially they are to be alike. As to the visual elements of the scene, O'Neill is specific: *"The treatment of this scene or of any other scene in the play, should by no means be naturalistic."* [207] However, the action which takes place in this and the following settings is not anti-naturalistic. Onstage, the actors playing the stokers may indeed look like Neanderthal men, but they will also look like the popular conception of stokers, stooped, heavy-shouldered, somewhat brutish. Similarly, there is little need for a designer to distort the forecastle space. A fore-castle *is* a cramped space and the lines of the bunks do suggest a cage. The second scene is *"a section of the promenade deck"* which contains no significant visual distortions, but is intended to con-vey *"the beautiful, vivid life of the sea."* In scene iii, the stokehole is one in fact, depicted as O'Neill knew stokeholes to be from his own experiences crossing the Atlantic on the *S.S. New York.* No degree of visual distortion will change the fact that O'Neill's scenic requirements in the first half of his play are for purely realistic settings. The non-naturalistic treatment is chiefly decorative.*

The action, evolving as it does from O'Neill's knowledge of the sea, makes no demands on the setting except for purposes of real-ism. Nothing of Kaiser's use of expressionist symbol is called for by what happens. To be sure O'Neill attempts to create a certain stylization of the action. Remembering the effect of the drums in

---

* The stoking procedure is incorrect, altered so as to achieve a rhythmic effect. See *A Drama of Souls,* 159, n. 6.

The Emperor Jones, he calls for an extensive orchestration of sounds of violence: the *"tumult of sound"* made by the drunken sailors as the curtain rises, *"the brazen clang of the furnace doors as they are flung open or slammed shut, the grating, teeth-gritting grind of steel against steel, of crunching coal, . . . the roar of leaping flames, the monotonous throbbing of the engines."* [223] These sounds are built into a rhythm, *"a mechanically regulated recurrence, a tempo"* which is evidently intended to enhance the strangeness of the whole. Yet, in the context of a stokehole the sounds are to be expected and are all essentially naturalistic.

Twice, O'Neill turns to something more than realism. From the crew, he calls for a choric effect that will suggest they are mechanical elements, dehumanized. Their voices are to have *"a brazen metallic quality as if their throats were phonograph horns,"* and he attempts to evolve a stylized choric statement on the word "Think":

> voices   Don't be cracking your head with ut, Yank.
> You gat headache, py yingo!
> One thing about it—it rhymes with drink!
> Ha, ha, ha!
> Drink, don't think!
> Drink, don't think!
> Drink, don't think! (*a whole chorus of voices has taken up this refrain, stamping on the floor, pounding on the benches with fists.*) [210]

The chorus effect was intended to suggest that the men were no more than machines. It is an attempt to move "behind life"—a clearly expressionistic device. As such, however, it is defeated by the individual who discovers that "Think rhymes with drink." A realistic thought-process, by no means non-naturalistic, has been introduced, and the choric tumult follows it in what can be taken as a logical or "natural" concatenation.

Perhaps the only genuinely non-naturalistic element in the early scenes is the pose which Yank assumes when he is attempting to puzzle out the questions that have been raised. Then he sits in the attitude of Rodin's "The Thinker." The Rodin sculpture held for O'Neill an evolutionary significance appropriate to the play—brutish man attempting to puzzle out the truth of his existence and perhaps to better it, mind triumphing over brute force. Rodin's bronze, however, is far from pessimistic, and considering the course

Yank is to follow, question may be raised as to the appropriateness of its ironic use here. Under any circumstances, deletion of the pose would not materially damage the scenes. What is important is that Yank should think, not that he should quote Rodin.

In the first four scenes, although scenic distortion in the expressionist manner is possible, it is never essential. These scenes restate the themes that O'Neill has treated before in the *Glencairn* cycle and *"Anna Christie"*: that a sailor is a creature of the sea and can have no will beyond the sea's will. Many of the effects, brought here to new levels of theatrical excitement, are to be found in so realistic a play as *The Moon of the Caribbees*—the sound patterns, for example, or the use of songs or the seemingly ad lib lines of seamen's voices forming a choral accompaniment to the main action. O'Neill's attempt to move "behind life" by expressionist means is defeated for two reasons: As they are conceived, the characters are so primitive that they are in appearance what they are in essence. They are simple organisms, and no layers of sophistication mask them to be stripped away as Brutus Jones's "Emperorhood" is taken from him. The second reason is that O'Neill's technical skill in depicting Yank and his crew is superb realism. Motivations are clear, strength and weakness of character underlie and make plausible all patterns of thought, and even Yank's long monologues emerge convincingly from situation and character. Yank is more comprehensible as a man than as a symbol. If he becomes a symbol, he does so in the way Chekhov's characters attain more than individual, personal significance—by the very depth of his reality.

In the stokehole, Yank belongs. His credo—that he is the force at the bottom that makes the entire mechanized society move—is right. He *is* such a force until the meeting with Mildred causes him to doubt himself and sends him out in a frenzied effort to destroy the God of power he has served at his furnace-altar. When Yank moves uptown, briefly, the conditions change, and for one scene the non-naturalistic treatment has relevance. On Fifth Avenue, Yank moves amazed like a Neanderthal Alice in a hostile Wonderland. What an audience sees is a kind of reality but distorted as it might be when filtered through Yank's consciousness. Yet the beginning of the scene, judged by the dialogue alone, is naturalistic. Yank and Paddy, joking and bumbling, explore a world they have not seen before. As the scene develops, however, and as Yank's anger at the unseeing passersby mounts uncontrollably, the play becomes for a moment expressionistic. Yank's fury at the masked creatures* causes him to attack them brutally, but his blows have no effect. Instead it is he who recoils after each punch. Now it is the action and not the scenery which is being treated in a non-naturalistic way and for a moment, O'Neill writes completely in the expressionistic mode.

The ending of scene v is the only moment in the play which can be accurately called expressionistic. The prison scene that follows, although the cage symbolism is continued, is in fact realistic, its style determined by Yank's conversation with unseen prisoners in adjoining cells. The scene in the I.W.W. Hall again evolves no symbolic action. Through both scenes Yank is treated as he was in the first half of the play as a realistic figure who moves coherently in time and space, and as one whose psychological development is credible. He is shown as an individual, obsessed with the idea of proving his worth, put through a debilitating series of experiences, and brought in the end close to madness. The brutality of his treatment in the prison arises from his near dementia, and the rejection of his proposal to blow up the Steel Trust reduces him to incompetence. Under such circumstances, even his death in the gorilla cage has a minimal plausibility. Although it realizes in a stage image the symbol of ape-in-cage which has been developed from the first scene, it does not entirely break from the context which the play has established as "real."

The Hairy Ape is a play written by a dramatist to whom the realistic theatre was a proper element, but who had left that style and committed himself to a new and intriguing mode. But he was not a master of the style. Like his hero, O'Neill was lost in an alien territory which he could not quite make his own. A mixed style is not in itself a danger unless, as here, its elements work in diametrically opposed ways to achieve their end. O'Neill was successful theatrically in The Hairy Ape as in The Emperor Jones because he conceived realistically a character with enough power and a sufficient command of language to make credible the peripheral presentational expression of the themes. Yank's simplicity is the key. With more complex characters, as The Great God Brown and

---

* O'Neill did not call for masks to be used in the scene. The Provincetown's costumer, Blanche Hays, suggested their use. Cf. Gelb, 495.

Dynamo would shortly demonstrate, O'Neill's skill as a playwright was nearly confounded. For the moment, however, the duality of style was not damaging. O'Neill had written a play which appeared to be in a new mode, but which was not so startling as to alienate audiences trained in realistic theatre, and they responded to the play's thesis which, like the shape of the folk play, was to become an American dramatic "myth," the play of social protest.

The thesis which O'Neill develops is an easy one, characteristic of much American political thought in the 1920's and 1930's. As the theatrical myth has it, materialistic America distorts and deforms the individual's spirit, destroying man's creative potential by divorcing him from those qualities of humanity which give him dignity and the sense of manhood. The materialistic system is his enemy and the core conflict of the fable is his battle with the exponents of that system. A year after *The Hairy Ape* was produced, Elmer Rice developed the same fable in a more truly expressionistic mode in *The Adding Machine,* and the concept was shortly to become a staple commodity in the work of John Howard Lawson, Clifford Odets and Sidney Kingsley. Most recently the fable has served Arthur Miller to notable effect.

In general, it may be said that all versions of the fable narrating man's war with a capitalistic society can be resolved in one of two ways. If a playwright espouses a revolutionary political cause the resolution of the narrative is almost inevitably a call to revolution, as in the ending of *Waiting for Lefty.** If the playwright is less committed to a specific ideology, what he is likely to show is the crushing of the little man by the society, and he will draw from this parable certain truths concerning man's dignity and his innate capacity for human feeling, and will excoriate those evils in the world which crush out life and render men pathetic and a little ridiculous—the ending, in short, of *The Adding Machine* and *Death of a Salesman.*

Elements of the myth, hidden under romantic and historical nar-

---

* The call to revolution is sometimes stated more ambiguously, as in the endings of *Awake and Sing* or *The Little Foxes,* where the burden of social change is left to the young people in the plays. For example, Alexandra in *The Little Foxes* will leave her home to find some place where people do more than stand around and watch the foxes spoil the vines. Similarly in *Awake and Sing,* the final focus on the youth, Ralph, standing "full and strong," suggests in that context revolutionary potential without stressing an explicit message.

rative, were to be found in *The Fountain*, especially when O'Neill dwelt on Juan's materialism and showed it to be dominating his more humane qualities. In *The Hairy Ape*, the design emerges without ambiguity, and, considering the play's date, it may be held that here O'Neill created at least the outlines of the American drama of social protest. Thus, Yank, throughout the play, is linked with the evolutionary process—a thinking Ape. Yet, society, faced with the desire of the beast to become human, places him in cage after cage, condemning him without seeing him, mocking his power and life. So interpreted the narrative arouses emotions of protest against a world that victimizes any of its citizens this way.

Yet it is difficult to carry the condemnation beyond the sketchy indictment of the Fifth Avenue scene. It is there in outline, but not filled in with detail. By comparison, Arthur Miller's inspection of American society in *Death of a Salesman* is an almanac of facts. Willy Loman is crushed by Chevrolets and water heaters and silk stockings and economics that, in Clifford Odets's phrase, come down "like a ton of coal on the head." Yank meets his society only in symbolic contexts, and the indictment of society is imprecise because it is unspecific.

In his choice of endings, O'Neill veers away from either of the possibilities of the social problem play. On the one hand, there was the possibility for a positive, revolutionary ending—the one he appears to have provided for his short story in causing Yank to join the I.W.W. Yet O'Neill, in spite of having Jack Reed and Terry Carlin as drinking companions, was no convert to radical causes. The I.W.W. was not the answer any more than it had been when he wrote *The Personal Equation* at Harvard. His most specific indictment in the play is of the ineffective, bureaucratic anarchists. Revolution in such terms was impossible.

On the other hand, Yank is clearly not destroyed by the social system, even though at the end he exhibits symptoms of alienation leading to such madness as overcomes Willy Loman. Yank is destroyed, as is Brutus Jones, by a figure out of his own "racial" past, by a gorilla in the Zoo. It is impossible to make the equation, "Gorilla equals Society." The gorilla is caged because society is fascinated with but cannot find a way of relating to the essential brutality, the primitive nature in all men. As the gorilla must be caged, so Yank cannot be left free, but in meeting the gorilla, Yank meets not society but himself in another incarnation. Thus he may be said to have destroyed himself.

The ending of *The Hairy Ape* is at best ambiguous. As Yank dies, O'Neill writes a stage direction: ". . . *and, perhaps, the Hairy Ape at last belongs.*" "Perhaps" sounds a significant note of doubt. Writing of the play to Theresa Helburn well after the tragedy had become theatrical history, he said he found it "very timely. Because I think we are all a bit sick of answers that don't answer. *The Hairy Ape*, at least, faces the simple truth that, being what we are, and with any significant spiritual change for the better in us probably ten thousand years away, there just is no answer. . . ."* The comment, like the ending to the play, does not entirely clarify the implications of the action. In fact, in the opening scenes, Yank does belong —to the world of steam and steel in the stoke-hole—to the modern world. He looks like an ape, but he is not one. He thinks, and he acts with physical and moral courage. He is undeniably heroic, perhaps the most conventionally "heroic" figure O'Neill ever drew. Like other, more conventional tragic heroes, he is to fall in pride from his throne before the furnaces. He is even guilty of a form of hubris when he brags that he is himself the essential force of life: "I'm de ting in coal dat makes it boin; I'm steel and oil for de engines; I'm de ting in noise dat makes yuh hear it; I'm smoke and express trains and steamers and factory whistles; I'm de ting in gold dat makes it money! And I'm what makes iron into steel! Steel, dat stands for de whole ting!" [216]

The claim to be a God is hubristic but it is essentially creative. When he is dislocated from his furnaces and driven into the upper world whose energy he has helped create, he turns destructive and tries to wreck what he has built. What should follow is society's destruction of the revenger-hero, humbling him in his pride. What is not in view is a sudden tumble back down the evolutionary lad-

---

* Quoted in Theresa Helburn, *A Wayward Quest*, 271. O'Neill had become interested in the possibility of making operas on the order of Gershwin's *Porgy and Bess* from *The Fountain, The Hairy Ape* and *Marco Millions*. He noted that once Eric Coates had proposed creating a score for *The Hairy Ape*. The most active of the opera projects was in connection with *Marco Millions*. Kurt Weill and Richard Rodgers were mentioned as composers, Rodgers working with his librettist, Lorenz Hart. The project was dropped when it was learned that Jerome Kern and Oscar Hammerstein II were working on a Marco Polo musical, based on Donn Byrne's short novel, *Messer Marco Polo*.

der. The implication of the Rodin pose is one of upward evolution; it means that Yank's movement into society is leading him toward some self-knowledge and pulling him from brute force toward more thoughtful awareness.* O'Neill discards all this, and drops his hero back into darkness by suggesting that he can only belong to a force of simian brutality. The ending is reminiscent of that of *The Emperor Jones*, but the dark theology of the earlier play is inappropriate to the story of Yank, who has always "belonged" and who is very different from Brutus Jones.

To most adherents of the Art Theatre movement, the name of David Belasco was anathema. Some were willing to grant him a limited virtue. Cheney speaks approvingly of his thoroughness in preparing a play, of his technical improvements, particularly in the area of lighting, and of his having discarded canvas for solid, dimensional box settings. Macgowan links him with Reinhardt and Craig in turning away from cheap, ugly décor. In the main, however, Belasco's imitation of surface appearances was slavish and dull, a trivial naturalism whose product was without truth or delight. It is a matter of some amusement, therefore, to visualize the moment when O'Neill and Jones, the chief young Turks of the anti-Belasco theatre, with hat and the script of *Marco Millions* in hand, approached the enemy to interest him in producing O'Neill's new work. The proposal must have given even Belasco pause. As O'Neill wrote it, he told Macgowan, he let the sky be the limit and was putting "every fancy in."** The typescript of the first version was in fourteen scenes divided into eight acts and an epilogue. The acting script Belasco saw was a work which fell into two parts, each two and a half hours long. The producer was courteous, took an option on the play, and, it is said, offered to send Jones to China for two years to do research for the scenery. He dropped the option in April, 1926, and the play was also rejected by Arthur Hopkins and Gilbert Miller. It was not produced until 1928 when the Theatre Guild staged a much shortened version that O'Neill had prepared in 1927.

* In one scenario, Yank was to return to the stokehole.
** Unpublished correspondence, O'Neill to Macgowan. The letter is undated, but falls between April and July, 1924. In a postscript, O'Neill suggests that possibly Max Reinhardt might be interested in coming to the United States to direct *Marco Millions* in collaboration with the Triumvirate. At one time, O'Neill attempted to interest George M. Cohan, who later was to star in *Ah, Wilderness!*, in the role of Marco.

Like *The Fountain* and *Lazarus Laughed,* with which it is linked in its picaresque, romantic style, *Marco Millions* had to wait long for its production. Its charm, for a producer, lies in its comedy and in the opportunity it presents for stunning theatrical display. Yet any producer might pause upon discovering that thirty extras are called for in the Prologue to draw in the coffin of Princess Kukachin. Nor would the prospective cost of O'Neill's scenic "fancies" be in any way reassuring. Lee Simonson, who designed the Theatre Guild production, noted with something like despair that O'Neill "passes in review the architectural façades of five separate civilizations during thirty minutes of playing time,"[23] and he commented that the light plot for the production was very difficult.[24] The play was, he admitted, "a scene designer's holiday," and he wrote at some length about the way in which O'Neill's cuts, made for the sake of economy, injured the first act of the play in performance. Without the cut material, the scenes of the voyage of the Polos to China "seemed pointless and the play did not begin as a drama until the second act."* His comment is suggestive, in its implication that, although the play demands the fullest resources a theatre can muster,** the scenic requirements are more than decorative. It is costly, but not extravagant. O'Neill uses what he asks for.

The play, or something like it, had been in O'Neill's mind for many years. In 1917, to a friend named Slim Martin, he mentioned that he would some day write a play about Marco Polo.[25] In 1918, he conceived a play in "a multitude of scenes that would have appalled any producer. I wished to show a series of progressive episodes, illustrating—and I hope illuminating—the life story of a true Royal Tramp at his sordid but satisfying, and therefore mysterious, pursuit of a drab rainbow. . . ."[26] The play of the Tramp was never written. In its stead, O'Neill wrote the tragedy of Robert

* *The Stage is Set,* 117. Simonson is referring to the elimination of the silent groups of people, representing the ages of man from infancy to death whom Marco sees in Act I, scenes iii, iv, and v. His point is that the circle of figures place Marco not in a particular locality, but "in the presence of the patient pattern of Eastern civilization." Without these sequences, Marco's introduction to the East was without dramatic force or full meaning.
** Which it has never had. In an article in the *New York Times,* Jan. 22, 1928, Simonson complained about the inadequate machinery of the Guild's theatre, and many of the reviewers of that production objected to the long waits between scenes. The more recent production in 1964 was played on a thrust stage, without such full scenic realization as O'Neill envisioned.

Mayo who remained drably earthbound, incapable of pursuing his dream. What he did not dramatize fully in *Beyond the Horizon* was the story of Andrew Mayo, the brother who was denied even a dream, who went to sea and became "almost a millionaire" [156] and whose only reaction to the mysteries of the East was its smell:

> And as for the East you used to rave about—well, you ought to see it, and *smell* it! One walk down one of their filthy narrow streets with the tropic sun beating on it would sicken you for life with the "wonder and mystery" you used to dream of. [132]

Marco Millions can be viewed as the account of the voyages of Andrew Mayo.

There were other considerations which governed the shaping of the play. O'Neill stated that he became interested in the story of Marco Polo in 1921, while he was doing research on *The Fountain*. In that year, Donn Byrne had published *Messer Marco Polo*, a highly successful, somewhat precious novella, about a romance between Marco and the Kaan's daughter, Princess Golden Bells, as filtered through the lips of an aged, mysterious Irish story teller, whose language is a cross between that of the Abbey Theatre and Christopher Marlowe. His characterization of Marco is very much in the line of O'Neill's typical hero: Byrne's Marco is young, a poet, a dreamer. In Venice he hears of the beauty of the Princess and loving her, goes in quest of her. He is permitted to go with his father and uncle as a missionary, for the Kaan has asked the Pope to send him word of their religion. A strange, almost supernatural journey leads Marco to China where he is received with kindness by the Kaan and with love by the Princess. They marry, she dies, and, after he achieves a distinguished career as the servant of the Kaan, Marco returns disconsolate to Venice, having converted none but the Princess to Christianity. Had O'Neill ever set out to write a bitter-sweet exotic love story, *Messer Marco Polo*, devoid of its more fantastical excursions, might well have been the work. That it offered suggestions to him for the development of his play seems likely, since Marco Polo's own book contains no love story, nor is it especially concerned with Marco's Christian mission.*

Another tangential influence was at work in the novels of Sinclair

---

* In 1926, Manuel Komroff, O'Neill's editor at Boni and Liveright, published a selection of *The Travels of Marco Polo*. It is probable that O'Neill's interest in Marco prompted Komroff's edition.

Lewis, *Main Street*, published in 1920, and *Babbitt,* published in 1922, the year before O'Neill began to work on *Marco Millions.**
Lewis's image of a soulless, corrupt, mercantile America served to define the attitudes of many who to that time had been restless but not to the point of protest. More than the communism of Jack Reed or the anarchism of Terry Carlin, Lewis fed O'Neill's sense of what was wrong with America. Radical theory of protest is very well, but O'Neill found more imaginative stimulus in such satiric portraits as Lewis provided. Marco is Babbitt in Xanadu, yet O'Neill takes Marco farther than Lewis takes Babbitt. In Act II, scene i, when Marco tells the Kaan what his mayoralty of the city of Yang-Chau has achieved, he reveals himself to be the most outrageous fascist, a demagogue who has committed gross abuses of his powers:

> I even had a law passed that anyone caught interfering with culture would be subject to a fine! It was Section One of a blanket statute that every citizen must be happy or go to jail. I found it was the unhappy ones who were always making trouble and getting discontented. You see, here's the way I figure it; if a man's good, he's happy—and if he isn't happy, it's a sure sign he's no good to himself or anyone else and he better be put where he can't do harm.

To which the Kaan properly replies:

> [The citizens] complain that you have entirely prohibited all free expression of opinion.

Marco protests:

> Well, when they go to the extreme of circulating such treasonable opinions against me, isn't it time to protect your sovereignty by strong measures? [392]

In another incarnation, and for the clearest of possible motives, a complete absence of human feeling coupled with an intense cupidity, Marco would have been a willing adherent of Strength through Joy. Marco leaves China at this point, and the story centers

---

* George Jean Nathan in *The American Mercury*, in 1927 stated that *Marco Millions* was written in order to satirize the American business magnate, and in particular to irritate Otto Kahn who had disliked *The Great God Brown*. [Cf. Clark, 108] *Marco Millions* was completed in 1925, well before the production of *The Great God Brown*. Nathan's story may reflect a rationalization after the fact, based on the punning possibilities of Kublai Kaan and Otto Kahn, to whom O'Neill often referred ironically as "The Great Kahn."

thereafter on the love of Princess Kukachin. Marco reverts to mere Babbittry and the suggestion remains undeveloped. Nevertheless, brought to focus by Lewis's depiction of Babbitt, O'Neill's sense of the dangerous realities of materialistic America are presented in much more compelling and controlled terms than they had been in *The Hairy Ape* or in *All God's Chillun Got Wings*, and his sense of what thirst for material power does to an individual is more specific in this play than it was in *The Fountain*.

Marco's character is seen as the same combination of poet and materialistic thinker that O'Neill had last treated in the portrait of Juan Ponce de Leon. Now, somewhat clinically inspected, and with the element of the poet reduced to a minimal adolescent urge, the materialist emerges pure. Marco's pitiful soul is in his poem that a prostitute tears up early in the play. Thereafter, except for the moment when Kukachin's love awakens a brief response in him, Marco's soul is as the prostitute described it as she stamped the poem in the ground, "dead and buried." The problem Marco presents is therefore not so complex as that which O'Neill had undertaken in *The Fountain*. Marco need suffer no resurrection. He can move in his gilded effulgence, a dead man among the wonders of the world. The Kaan senses his deformity, comparing him to a humped jester. Marco's hump, however, is spiritual. As the Kaan says, "He has not even a *mortal soul*, he has only an acquisitive instinct," and he adds, in words that might have been spoken of Andrew Mayo, "He has looked at everything and seen nothing." [387] Marco, unlike Juan, has had no vision of golden cities. When he finds them, they are nothing to him. His creative imagination is devoted to the invention of paper money and gunpowder.

Not only in character and theme is *Marco Millions* like *The Fountain*. It resembles it in structure and in this particular it may also be compared with *The Emperor Jones, The Hairy Ape* and *Lazarus Laughed,* which he began in 1925. Each of them is a journey play, told in a number of scenes, and centering on the travels of its hero. The picaresque novel, of course, provides analogues in literary tradition, but there are fewer examples from drama to set beside O'Neill's account of the spiritual journey of his heroes in terms of a physical voyage. To an extent, *Peer Gynt* had provided suggestions that caused *The Emperor Jones* to assume the form of a physical and spiritual journey, but Ibsen, to the advocates of the

Art Theatre, was the master of an essentially outmoded naturalism. On the other hand, to Macgowan and to O'Neill, the preeminent theatrical artist was Strindberg, and in his work there were a number of notable examples of the so-called "Wander Play."[27]

Strindberg's "Wander Plays" include *Lucky Per's Journey, The Keys to Heaven,* the trilogy *To Damascus, A Dream Play* and *The Highway,* and they were written over the entire course of Strindberg's career as a playwright. They are, in many ways, his most directly autobiographical plays, and they are the ones in which he pushed beyond naturalism into the expressionist mode. Each of the plays centers on a quest for salvation by its hero. The structure, essentially picaresque, is evolved in a series of scenes, which like stations on a Via Crucis, lead to the hero's discovery of his soul and his coming to a right relation with God. The arrangement of the scenes is cyclic, and in some there is a conscious alternation of indoor-outdoor scenes, such as O'Neill devised for *Beyond the Horizon.* The symbolic content of the works is marked, and, as Strindberg developed the form in *To Damascus, A Dream Play* and *The Highway,* the reliance on picaresque realism gives way to the projection of an intense, evolving inner life. Strindberg described his technique in the prefatory note to *A Dream Play*:

> In this dream play, as in his former dream play *To Damascus,* the Author has sought to reproduce the disconnected but apparently logical form of a dream. Anything can happen; everything is possible and probable. Time and space do not exist; on a slight groundwork of reality, imagination spins and weaves new patterns made up of memories, experiences, unfettered fancies, absurdities and improvisations. . . . A single consciousness holds sway over them all—that of the dreamer. For him there are no secrets, no incongruities, no scruples and no law.

O'Neill's sympathy for the questing, poetic dreamer led him almost from the outset of his playwriting career to write "Wander Plays"-in-embryo. Elements of the genre are to be found in the *S.S. Glencairn* plays, and in *"Anna Christie." Beyond the Horizon,* presenting the voyager who does not travel, and *The Emperor Jones,* presenting the traveler who makes the voyage for other reasons than his spiritual salvation, can be viewed as sophisticated variations on the form. They are not, of course, but they suggest that O'Neill is looking in the same direction as Strindberg had gone. *The Foun-*

tain, *The Hairy Ape, Marco Millions* and *Lazarus Laughed* answer almost precisely to the requirements of the genre. The dream state in which the wounded Ponce de Leon views the apparitions at the fountain in Florida, the expressionistic manner of *The Hairy Ape*, which attempts to suggest a controlling point of view, the revelation in the Epilogue to *Marco Millions* that Marco has been seated in the audience viewing, and thus in a sense "controlling" the point of view the audience must take of the play, Lazarus's journey through the Mediterranean world to his crucifixion all suggest that O'Neill is now emulating Strindberg's depiction of wanderers questing God. Marco, evidently is not in search of his soul, or salvation, or love or anything of spiritual value. He is given no moment to show even a mild regret at losing what he finally saw in the eyes of Princess Kukachin. Instead, at the end of the play, he is engulfed in the fat world of Venice, barely visible behind mounds of food, unheard amidst the swilling sounds of his guests eating like hogs, and the repeated word "Millions." This Jonsonian scene is one of the darkest—and incidentally the most truly expressionistic—that O'Neill ever penned. Yet, despite this ending, Marco has made Lucky Per's journey. He has been to Damascus and beyond. The Kaan and his adviser, Chu-Yin, make amply clear that Marco can discover his soul; indeed, they urge the quest upon him. Marco's refusal, his inability to comprehend more in effect than "I breathe, therefore I have a soul," creates a sophisticated, ironic variation on the type, which despite its amusements and its beauty is a play with darkness at the center.

Some of the darkness came from a personal problem that the play in part reflected. In telling of Robert and Andrew Mayo, O'Neill had sketched, however lightly, something of the characteristics of himself and his brother, Jamie. Marco, like Andrew, has in him the spiritual emptiness of Jamie, who once wanted to write, but whose most significant creative achievement was to play in the farce called *The Travelling Salesman*. If it is there at all, the presence of Jamie in the character of Marco is deeply buried. Jamie died, hideously, in 1923, the year his brother began work on *Marco Millions*. Nothing of his manner, his cynicism, his self-abasement nor his humanity exists in Marco. Marco remains a cartoon, a dummy through whose mouth O'Neill voices anti-materialistic sentiments. Yet the ghost of Jamie in Marco may help to explain why, while on the surface *Marco Mil-*

lions is one of the simplest, most available and amusing plays of the canon, it is one of the most pessimistic. A traditional comment on the play is that it is the comedy of Marco, the tragedy of Kublai Kaan. Yet, in the context of *The Fountain, Lazarus Laughed* and even *The Hairy Ape,* and coming at a period in his life when O'Neill was seeking to bring to the theatre a sense of spiritual exaltation through the dramatization of man's quest for God, the play is also the tragedy of Marco Polo, whose unawareness of any life beyond what he can see makes him, despite his cock-sure step on the earth, a creature God cannot touch.

What finally may be said of *Marco Millions* lies less in its achievement as an individual work than in the concepts it released for the future.

O'Neill seems to have written easily as he let his "fancies" loose.* If *Desire Under the Elms* can be said to cap the efforts of his youth, *Marco Millions* opens ahead. As lines in *The Moon of the Caribbees* anticipated *The Hairy Ape,* so much in Marco points toward O'Neill's next four plays, *Dynamo, The Great God Brown, Lazarus Laughed* and *Strange Interlude.* For example, in calling Marco, who has not even a mortal soul, the "Image of God," [379] O'Neill is writing in the ironic vein that will ultimately produce Billy, the Great God Brown. Another view of him maintains that he is yet "unborn." This is said at the moment when Kukachin testifies that Marco indeed has a soul, to which Chu-Yin replies "A woman may feel life in the unborn." [397] For a passing moment, Kukachin takes on qualities that will be later developed in the portraits of Cybel and of Nina Leeds, an impression that is reaffirmed in the chorus sung as she finally meets her future husband, Ghazan Kaan. The women attendants sing of his coming:

> The lover comes,
> Who becomes a husband,

* The two-play version of the story would have provided better evidence of this point, and incidentally might give evidence that the play was once better constructed, in terms of its character development, than is the present script. There is a great gap between the ending of Act I and the beginning of Act II, where a space of fifteen years elapses. Marco is left as a child at the end of Act I; in Act II, he is the assured bureaucrat. Something more is needed to show his transition from adolescence to maturity. While one is willing to accept the child's being father to the man, what O'Neill shows is Marco's arrival in China and his departure. Marco's life under the rule of the Kaan could have been detailed with profit.

> Who becomes a son,
> Who becomes a father—
> In this contemplation lives the woman. [417]

Kukachin does not become such a personification of the maternal force as Cybel or Nina, but the implication is strong that in his future pictures of women, this conception will come to the fore, as it began to do in the portrait of Abbie Cabot in *Desire Under the Elms* written at the same time.

In other short passages, concepts which will receive full development in *Lazarus Laughed, Dynamo* and, to a lesser extent in *Strange Interlude* rise to the surface. In a moment of despair, the Kaan cries out,

> My hideous suspicion is that God is only an infinite, insane energy which creates and destroys without other purpose than to pass eternity in avoiding thought. Then the stupid man becomes the Perfect Incarnation of Omnipotence and the Polos are the true children of God! [426]

The view of God as a physical energy will characterize the Electrical God of *Dynamo* and provide imagery of God's power in both *Strange Interlude* and *Lazarus Laughed*. Nina, for example, speaks of life as being a "strange dark interlude in the electrical display of God the Father!" [199] and Lazarus describes men as being "quivering flecks of rhythm" beating down from the sun. [324]

The same plays rely on the sense of life as an interlude between two awakenings, and the motif is anticipated in the dialogue of the Kaan and Chu-Yin, who also speak of life as eternal in much the same terms as Lazarus will use. Finally, it may be noted that in the play's last scene, after the priests of Buddha, Confucius and Tao have failed to assert more in solace to the Kaan, sorrowing for the death of Kukachin, than that "Death is," O'Neill brings the Kaan to a kind of peace with the paradoxical truth that the living are dead, and the dead live, [438] a view he will restate with Lazarus's doctrine "Life is," in the pageant play to come.

Marco Millions was a play of its period, and it will remain so. Its ironic theme, like its Art Theatre aestheticism, is buried too deeply in time for it to emerge as a play of substance, important to later audiences. It was even partially buried by 1928 when it finally received its first production. Nevertheless, it was an important stop

on O'Neill's journey forward if for no other reason than in the releasing of images that were to prove germinal to plays yet to come.

Upon completing *Marco Millions* in 1925, four important projects occupied O'Neill's attention. One was *Dynamo,* for which he
had made some preliminary notes in 1924. Work on this play, however, was not to be undertaken in earnest until 1928. A second was
Lazarus Laughed, developed in scenario form in that year and completed in 1926. A third was his "woman play," as he referred to
Strange Interlude in its first inception.* Before any of these projects
were brought to fruition, however, O'Neill conceived and wrote a
second play about the man without a soul, treating him less ironically than he had in *Marco Millions,* bringing himself to a point of
compassion for the damned which he had not revealed before.

The Great God Brown was the last play by O'Neill to be produced by the Triumvirate. *Lazarus Laughed,* like *Marco Millions,*
was conceived for production by the group, but O'Neill's letters
written at the time of the production of *The Great God Brown*
show clearly his growing disenchantment with the circumstances
which had promised so fair a few years earlier. From March through
May 1925, he wrote enthusiastic notes to Macgowan regarding the
casting of the play, suggesting among others Clare Eames and John
Barrymore. By September, he was quarrelsome:

> Here's the way I feel about Brown—that it deserves as careful, or
> more careful, consideration than Belasco is giving Marco, and
> ought to get it. Otherwise it has no chance whatever, and might as
> well be withdrawn, at least for the coming season. At any rate I am
> emphatic in thinking that whatever plan you dope out, Brown
> should follow The Fountain. The reverse would be a great injury
> to me, I feel.[28]

Casting dilemmas arose. Eva LeGallienne and Florence Eldridge
were considered for the women's parts. Alfred Lunt might play both
Dion and Brown "as planned for Barrymore," and he suggested
Lynn Fontanne as a possible Margaret.[29] Discussion of the masks
began, but by the end of September, the play was not cast and
O'Neill, reflecting a disaffection similar to that of Robert Edmond

---

* O'Neill to Macgowan, September 28, 1925. "Lazarus is elaborately scenarioed—
wonderfully, I believe—also ditto my woman play, and I'm enormously excited over
both—will be able to start right in on either or both as soon as I'm unpacked. . . ."

Jones who was to leave the organization the following year, spoke bitterly of the course the Experimental Theatre had taken.

> What the hell are we, anyway? Why, compared to this, our first season at the P.P. [Provincetown Players] was ten years in advance of what we are now! It seems to me we're just nothing but another New York theatre. Candidly, Kenneth, I'm not interested in continuing with it next year. I'd rather go back to the P. P. The acting there might be more amateur—but so would the spirit be. We've become too professional. . . . The thing that galls me most is this—We've had "Brown" since June. "Brown" is important, we believe. Nevertheless "Brown" isn't cast yet and we don't know when it will be. Now no one can tell me that if we'd been paying half the attention to "Brown" we've been giving to all this other crap—I include in this road companies of "Desire" and recasting bickerings—we'd have had a cast for "Brown" long ago.[30]

The Great God Brown opened the following January, but by June all three of the directors of the new theatre had become fed up, and O'Neill had begun to look to the Theatre Guild as potential producers of both *Marco Millions* and *Lazarus Laughed*. After a sharp exchange of letters, verging so heavily on recriminations that each man took time to assure the other of his continuing friendship, O'Neill wrote:

> I'm sick and tired of old theatres under old conditions, of new theatres handcuffed by old conditions, of "art" theatres with fuzzy ideals and no money or efficiency—in fact, of *the* American Theatre as it exists.[31]

The pessimism was only to deepen as Macgowan's attempts to find a co-producer for *Lazarus Laughed* met repeated failures. With the production of *The Great God Brown*, O'Neill was through with the Art Theatre as a "movement."

The play, directed by Robert Edmond Jones, was well received,* but the reviews carried substantial warnings of future trouble. For example, one critic, after praising the play highly wrote, "Of course, everybody at the Greenwich Village Theatre being fearfully interested in the sublime processes of sceneshifting and mask-making, Mr. O'Neill has to build his plays for them around mechanical

---

* O'Neill complained to Macgowan that the masks did not work. "They only get across personal resemblance of a blurry meaninglessness," he wrote and objected that there should have been more time to study the theatrical problem and to light the masks properly. [O'Neill to Macgowan, August 23, 1926.]

novelties. Which may be why you get so much industrious putting
on and taking off of false faces and other rather rigid tricks of the
symbolistic trade in *The Great God Brown*."[32] Alexander Woollcott in the *Morning World* and "R. W. Jr.," in the *New York
Herald*[33] both objected to the vaudeville in the scene where Brown
is frantically attempting to play both himself and Dion. Many of the
reviewers mentioned Strindberg as being in some measure god-
father to the play, and "R. W. Jr." suggested that O'Neill had read
Strindberg "with more care than wisdom."

Yet praise exceeded carping, and most recorded impressions
stressed that O'Neill in this play penetrated more deeply into the
sources of man's thought (or, as Gilbert Gabriel put it in the *New
York Sun*: "Back to the secret springs of psychoanalysis . . .") than
he had done before. O'Neill, in short, had produced a combination of what Cheney would have called a "psychologic" drama and a
drama with a new, poetic form.

O'Neill had used masks in a number of his plays before *The
Great God Brown*. Some of the apparitions in *The Fountain*, the
mannequins the Hairy Ape meets on Fifth Avenue, a group of
mourners for Kukachin, and the drowned sailors in *The Ancient
Mariner* are masked, largely for decorative effect. Beyond these
minor uses, only the symbolic mask in *All God's Chillun Got Wings*
stands as fully functional in the drama. From any of these first uses
of masks, it is a far reach to that which O'Neill devised for the new
play.

Masks were, of course, a stock property of the Art Theatre aesthetics. Their theatrical possibilities had already been extolled by
Gordon Craig and William Butler Yeats, when in 1923 Macgowan
collaborated with the designer Herman Rosse in the publication of
a picture book with lengthy captions entitled *Masks and Demons*,
showing many styles of masks. Charles Sheeler's book of African
Negro sculpture, containing vivid photographs of African masks, no
doubt remained in O'Neill's mind. Considering the Nietzschean
elements of the play's theme, it is possible as well that *The Birth of
Tragedy* suggested a further use for the masks than O'Neill had
found before. Nietzsche had written,

> In the Dionysian dithyramb man is incited to the highest exalta-
> tion of all his symbolic faculties; something never before ex-
> perienced struggles for utterance—the annihilation of the veil of

> Mâyâ, Oneness as genius of the race, ay, of nature. The essence of
> nature is now to be expressed symbolically; a new world of symbols
> is required; for once the entire symbolism of the body, not only
> the symbolism of the lips, face, and speech, but the whole panto-
> mime of dancing which sets all the members into rhythmical mo-
> tion. Thereupon the other symbolic powers, those of music, in
> rhythmics, dynamics, and harmony, suddenly become impetuous.
> [32]

A little later, Nietzsche describes the Apollonian Consciousness as
"a thin veil hiding the Dionysian realm from man" [33] and in discussing the Dionysian origins of tragic character, Nietzsche maintains that "Dionysus *remains* the sole dramatic protagonist and . . .
all the famous characters of the Greek stage, Prometheus, Oedipus,
etc., are only masks of that original hero. In fact all the celebrated figures of the Greek stage . . . are but masks for this original hero,
Dionysus. [81]

Whatever the source, O'Neill, who began as early as *Bound East
for Cardiff* with Yank's vision of the pretty lady dressed in black to
develop symbolic configurations for the forces which he sensed as
man's true divinities, now comes with the mask to a new perspective on human experience. The perspective is not complex, although
the masks lead to a technical complexity. In fact, although they are
theatrically exciting, the view of man's condition which the masks
permit is not essentially different from that which he had already
taken of the repressed, passionate natures of the protagonists of his
New England plays, such as *Ile, Diff'rent* and *Desire Under the
Elms*. In *The Great God Brown*, O'Neill sees man as a prisoner in
his body. His only escape is in an inner direction toward the roots
of God he holds in himself. In all the world, there is no human being
he can comprehend or whose comprehension enables him to unmask
himself, and thus be freed of loneliness. In *Welded*, O'Neill had
offered the possibility that a man and a woman in a special and profound marriage relationship might achieve an ecstatic communion
in which both their isolated selves, in merging, would belong to a
greater unity that was the same as the Nietzschean "Oneness" with
all nature. Something of the same point was made in his depiction
of the relation between Abbie and Eben in *Desire Under the Elms*.
In *The Great God Brown*, however, such a union is seen to be impossible, and man is condemned to the cell of self until his death.

To the outer, hostile world, he must turn a face which will not startle by revealing the terrifying agony within him. It must be an expressionless face, bland and unchanging except as it is inevitably eroded by the ravages of his hidden struggle. Wearing the mask is not a matter of choice. Like the Mask Maker in Marceau's great pantomime, man is trapped in the mask, by circumstances, by his own fear and inhibitions, by his need to find some communion with the world beyond his cell. Edmond Dantes telegraphed by tapping on the rocks of his prison wall. In a prison that is not physical, the mask is man's only means of communication, its mouth the only means of crying across the void that separates him from all other human beings. Only by his mask may he be known.

In three "memoranda," published in the *American Spectator* in 1932 and 1933, after he had in fact ceased his experimentation with masks in his own drama, O'Neill wrote of his belief in their utility in solving certain problems of modern dramaturgy:[34]

> . . . I hold more and more surely to the conviction that the use of masks will be discovered eventually to be the freest solution to the modern dramatist's problem as to how—with the greatest possible dramatic clarity and economy of means—he can express those profound hidden conflicts of the mind which the probings of psychology continue to disclose to us. He must find some method to present this inner drama in his work, or confess himself incapable of portraying one of the most characteristic preoccupations and uniquely significant, spiritual impulses of his time. With his old—and more than a bit senile!—standby of realistic technique, he can do no more than, at best, obscurely hint at it through a realistically disguised surface symbolism, superficial and misleading. But that, while sufficiently beguiling to the sentimentally mystical, is hardly enough. A comprehensive expression is demanded here, a chance for eloquent presentation, a new form of drama projected from a fresh insight into the inner forces motivating the actions and reactions of men and women (a new and truer characterization, in other words), a drama of souls, and the adventures of "Free Wills," with the masks that govern them and constitute their fates.

His *"Dogma for the new masked drama"* is that "One's outer life passes in a solitude haunted by the masks of others; one's inner life passes in a solitude hounded by the masks of oneself," and in re-thinking his work, he suggests that *The Hairy Ape, All God's Chillun Got Wings, The Emperor Jones, Marco Millions, Mourning*

Becomes Electra and perhaps *Strange Interlude* should all have made a significant use of masks.

It was not true. During the writing of *Mourning Becomes Electra,* he had tried masks and found them unnecessary, and in his work diary for that play he had cautioned himself not to use such devices only because they were theatrically effective: to do so was to be no more than a member of the Broadway Show Shop he despised. Ironically, as he wrote his *Memoranda,* he was in the process of giving over all such grotesque experimentation. Yet it was almost inevitable that he should have experimented with the mask. Masked faces had been suggested in many of his early plays—in Rose's face at the end of *The Web,* expressionless and with eyes like those of a blind woman; in Emma's heavily made up face in the second act of *Diff'rent.* The experiment of *The Great God Brown,* however, taxed his power to its limits and opened the door to a blind passageway from which he would escape only with difficulty. The problem lay in his use of the mask in a new way, to do something that the drama, perhaps, can never do directly: in his own words, to "express those profound conflicts of the mind," and to write "a drama of souls," tracing "the adventures of 'Free Wills.' "

The "normal" use of the theatrical mask—setting aside its value for disguise in comedy—is to conventionalize the human individuality, to idealize man or to typify him. O'Neill recognized this use in speaking of a new type of play in which a masked mob might be "King, Hero, Villain or Fool . . . the main character,"[35] and he suggested that revivals of great plays might be played entirely in masks in order to prevent their becoming vehicles for star players. Then, he said, "We would even be able to hear the sublime poetry as the innate expression of the spirit of the drama itself, instead of listening to it as realistic recitation—or ranting—by familiar actors."[36] Such thoughts emerge from an ideal that may have come from O'Neill's association with George Cram Cook, whom he echoed when he spoke of the use of masks as an essential for the "imaginative" theatre, "a theatre that could dare to boast—without committing a farcical sacrilege—that it is a legitimate descendant of the first theatre that sprang, by virtue of man's imaginative interpretation of life, out of his worship of Dionysus. I mean a theatre returned to its highest and sole significant function as a Temple where the religion of a poetical interpretation and symbolical celebration of life is communicated to human beings, starved in spirit by their soul-stifling daily struggle to exist as masks among the masks of the living!"[37]

Lazarus Laughed, a play written for such an "Imaginative Theatre" as he describes, makes use of the masks in what may be called their normative theatrical way: to typify the members of the chorus, here grouped as the seven ages of man, from Boyhood to Old Age, into seven general character types: The Simple, Ignorant; the Happy, Eager; the Self-Tortured, Introspective; the Proud, Self-Reliant; the Servile, Hypocritical; the Revengeful, Cruel; and the Sorrowful, Resigned. Individuality is thus formalized and O'Neill's "mob" fulfills its choric function in a way similar to that developed in Greek drama.

In *The Great God Brown,* however, the mask is used to attain precisely the opposite value, to reveal the human individuality as directly and profoundly as possible. The mask being removed from Dion Anthony, what the spectator is supposed to see and what O'Neill astonishingly set himself to characterize is the human soul itself. This use of the mask is O'Neill's innovation, one which, as he suggested, follows necessarily from the development of psychological theories in the twentieth century, but one which was not characteristic of the theatre of his time.*

The consequences of experimentation in this direction were severe. The problem was not in the theatrically fascinating use of masks, but in the development of a language which could accompany such a direct look into the soul. What O'Neill means by a "drama of souls" is really not communicable directly by any verbal device. The "soul" is subverbal, and the great dramatist can do

---

* In a program note for the "Greenwich Village Playbill," Macgowan comments at some length on the atypical use of masks in *The Great God Brown,* saying that it is the first play in this century to use masks to any extent. "So far as I know, O'Neill's play is the first in which masks have ever been used to dramatize changes and conflicts in character. . . . O'Neill uses the naked face and the masked face to picture the conflict between inner character and the distortions which outer life thrusts upon it. With this established, he goes on to use the mask as a means of dramatizing a transfer of personality from one man to another. . . . The most interesting of all ideas surrounding the use of the mask among primitive peoples is that of Possession. . . . The skull or the mask of a dead man grips his soul, and whoever puts it on must be ready to have the soul enter into his body. Great shamans, mighty medicine men are made by this process. They walk in demoniac power. And sometimes, if they do not know how and when to take off that mask, they die possessed and tortured."

little else than to suggest it by the referential qualities of his poetry. Nietzsche's claim that the mask is a way of expressing the inexpressible essence of nature sheds significant light on O'Neill's use, where, once the mask is removed, the essence itself must be projected. O'Neill's mistrust of the superficial and misleading "surface symbolism" of realism is a sign that he wishes now to present directly on his stage *without symbolism* the naked essence of being. In *The Great God Brown* there are no important symbols, if a symbol is to be taken as a referential device for the expression of an inexpressible truth. Instead, the drama of souls is enacted before its audience as if it were a realistic drama, an impossible state of affairs since once the inexpressible is expressed, it is without meaning.

   The Great God Brown, despite its devices, is tied to the realistic theatre. It moves in space and time in a coherent and essentially realistic way, and its setting is sociological, rather than psychological, a space, complete with doors, windows, telephones and all the other accoutrements of daily living. O'Neill, indeed, reveals at several points a certain strain in handling his characters in the realistic context of the play. For instance, in III, i, Margaret must be brought to Brown's office for the crucial scene, in which Brown, unmasked, declares his love for her. As she enters the office, however, O'Neill is forced to have her develop a reason for her presence, a necessity only to a totally realistic drama: "I forgot to tell him something important this morning and our phone's out of order." [303] A similar problem develops in IV, i, when Brown switches frantically between his own mask and that of Dion's which he has usurped. Brown, as Brown, rushes from the room and returns wearing Dion's mask, but there has been no time for a costume change for the actor. As a realist, O'Neill worries about the matter and has Margaret note the fact that Brown and the supposed Dion are dressed alike: "Why, Dion, that isn't your suit. It's just like . . ." [316] Evidently, if its concern for the color of Brown's pants is an indication, *The Great God Brown* is something less than a "drama of souls." There is here a reminiscence of the quick change of disguise and the dashing in and out of doors of a bedroom farce or of such melodramas as *Dr. Jekyll and Mr. Hyde.* At best the play is a realistic, somewhat overwrought narrative complete with a police chase. Whatever they were intended to do, the masks play a not completely fulfilled part.

In his early play, *Bread and Butter*, O'Neill had treated the same subject matter, indeed had there written what might well be considered a first draft of *The Great God Brown*. The 1914 version considered the fate of the artist in a small Connecticut town. Its hero, John Brown, is a thinly disguised self-portrait, and the play's narrative is a conventional piece of autobiographical speculation that extrapolated certain domestic possibilities lying before the young O'Neill into a condemnation of marriage and of American philistinism that combined the most obvious aspects of Strindberg and Sinclair Lewis.

In *The Great God Brown*, O'Neill altered the story of *Bread and Butter*—it is no longer so directly autobiographical—but he kept most of its essentials. The play's statement is only superficially enlarged by the addition of the masks or of the Nietzschean material. In the earlier work, the hero's confidant was his teacher, the painter Eugene Grammont, a wise and sympathetic counselor. The role is retained in *The Great God Brown* but given to the prostitute Cybel, who makes explicit the sensitive hero's desire to reach the creative core of nature itself—a point implied in the early work by Brown's painting, particularly a seascape and a landscape, the sole vestiges of his artist's life that he retains in his marital bondage. The Faustian implications of *Bread and Butter*, suggested in the hero's willingness to sell his artistic soul for the sake of a woman, are developed more fully in the religious implications of Dion Anthony's name—a combination of Dionysus and St. Anthony—and in the name of Margaret, by which O'Neill wished to recall the Marguerite of *Faust*. The parallels with *Faust* are augmented by the gradual transformation of the Pan mask of Dion into the mocking face of Mephistopheles, at the same time as his true face becomes more saint-like and ascetic.[38]

The most important change in the later play was O'Neill's development of the character of the materialist, William Brown. In his earlier treatment of such figures, in Andrew Mayo or the cartooned Marco Polo, O'Neill had seen him chiefly as what might be called an "anti-poet," the adversary of the sensitive self-portraits. Now, O'Neill developed fully what the figure of Marco Polo had partly suggested to him: the anguish of the uncreative man, the despair of the man who cannot dream. As its title suggests, *The Great God Brown* holds the materialist up to crucial inspection and shows that like the poet, he has a capacity to suffer. Suffering comes to him, when, with the death of Dion, he moves into the play's focal position, attempting to live his life in Dion's mask. As O'Neill explained this turn in his drama:

> Brown has always envied the creative life force in Dion—what he himself lacks. When he steals Dion's mask of Mephistopheles he thinks he is gaining the power to live creatively, while in reality he is only stealing that creative power made self-destructive by complete frustration. This devil of mocking doubt makes short work of him. It enters him, rending him apart, torturing and transfiguring him until he is even forced to wear a mask of his Success, William A. Brown, before the world, as well as Dion's mask toward wife and children. Thus Billy Brown becomes not himself to anyone. And thus he partakes of Dion's anguish—more poignantly, for Dion has the Mother, Cybele—and in the end out of this anguish his soul is born, a tortured Christian soul such as the dying Dion's, begging for belief, and at the last finding it on the lips of Cybel.[39]

The explanation both of Dion and of Brown leaves something to be desired. O'Neill described Brown as "the visionless demi-god of our new materialistic myth—a Success—building his life of exterior things, inwardly empty and resourceless, an uncreative creature of superficial preordained social grooves, a by-product forced aside into slack waters by the deep main current of life-desire."[40] In conceiving of Brown as a "by-product" of the "life-desire," O'Neill has somewhat altered his view of the materialist. Both Andrew Mayo and John Brown became what they were because they denied their rightful heritage. Billy Brown, however, is created without a soul, and there is no explanation for this deformity. In truth, it appears, that O'Neill began by using Brown as a typical opposition for Dion, feeling no need to explain an epitome. Only when he began to concentrate on Brown as his protagonist in the latter half of the play did he ask the important questions about him, and then he did not always find the essential answers.

The Great God Brown begins and ends in a courtroom. In the prologue and epilogue set on a wharf, the benches form a rectangular space reminiscent of a court of law—an effect that is repeated by the arrangement of furniture in later scenes in the play.* To this bar of judgment, two men are brought for trial. They are like brothers, close enough in age to be thought of as twins. Cybel first notes this, saying, "You're brothers, I guess, somehow," [287] and later Brown, in a desperate moment, cries "We're getting to be like twins," [316] referring partly to Dion's suit that he is wearing, but with reference also to Dion's life that he has stolen.

The brothers are cast in the mold of Robert and Andrew Mayo, of Eben and his brothers, of Eugene and Jamie O'Neill** On the face of it, Dion is seeking after the source of life through the creation of works of art, while Brown, whose soul is dead, denies life, and even denies the necessity for the quest. In his explanation of the play, O'Neill stated that the frustration of the creative power made it a self-destructive force, a point he had already made in depicting the consumption of spirit in Robert Mayo. As the two men are brought to the bar, however, a somewhat different aspect of the dichotomy between poet and materialist is revealed, for it is Brown who most ardently seeks life, and it is Dion who, almost from the start, denies it.

Dion is first presented as a Pan. His mask is described as that of a "mocking, reckless, defiant, gayly scoffing and sensual Pan." The mask, however, is a "fixed forcing of his own face—dark, spiritual, poetic, passionately supersensitive, helplessly unprotected in its childlike, religious faith in life." [260] Masked, he speaks with a cynical, rebellious irony to his parents and to his friend. Alone and unmasked, he reveals his weakness:

> Why am I afraid to dance, I who love music and rhythm and grace and song and laughter? Why am I afraid to live, I who love life and the beauty of flesh and the living colors of earth and sky and sea? Why am I afraid of love, I who love love? Why am I afraid, I who am not afraid? . . . Why was I born without a skin, O God, that I must wear armor in order to touch or to be touched?

* Cf. "BILLY stands at the left corner, forward, his hand on the rail, like a prisoner at the bar, facing the judge," [258] and the reference in a later scene to "the same courtroom effect." [269]
** Dion is not described as a physical type, other than as "lean and wiry," but his character is entirely compatible with the earlier self-portraits. Moreover Dion's cynicism, fatigue and despair, as well as his debauchery, are all qualities biographers have associated with O'Neill. Dion speaks of having got paint on his paws in an effort to see God. So in The Great God Brown, O'Neill was making every effort to define the nature of his religious vision.

> . . . Or, rather, Old Graybeard, why the devil was I ever born at all? [264]

A lover of life Dion may be, but he cannot commit himself fully to the worship of Pan. He takes Margaret with language that suggests the Dionysian ecstasy:

> I love, you love, we love! Come! Rest! Relax! Let go your clutch on the world! Dim and dimmer! Fading out into the past behind! Gone! Death! Now! Be born! Awake! Live! Dissolve into dew—into silence—into night—into earth—into space—into peace—into meaning—into joy—into God—into the Great God Pan! [267]

It would seem to be a moment when Dion accepts life fully, without hesitation or restraint. O'Neill's stage directions say otherwise, for the lines are to be read *"with ironic mastery"*—a phrase which voids commitment and turns Dion to a mere seducer. The point is made clear a moment later. The moon passes behind a cloud, and blackness and silence hides their love-making. When the light returns, Dion's irony becomes explicit as he cries,

> Wake up! Time to get up! Time to exist! Time for school! Time to learn! Learn to pretend! Cover your nakedness! Learn to lie! Learn to keep step! Join the procession! Great Pan is dead! Be ashamed! [267]

On cue, Margaret cries, "Oh Dion, I am ashamed!"

Dion, who calls himself life's lover, ostensibly denies life because he understands that ecstatic communion cannot be sustained, and that man will be forced into his mask just as the Veil of Mâyâ must inevitably reshroud the dimly glimpsed truth. The world will frustrate ecstasy. Admitting that Margaret cannot face her lover without his mask on, it is still difficult to maintain that the world has at this moment so frustrated Dion that he denies life at the point of his orgasm. His cry "Great Pan is dead!" is almost one of revulsion at the sexual commitment itself, as if his rapturous penetration into life had somehow shamed him into ironic alienation from his desire.

Nietzsche in *The Birth of Tragedy* relates the anecdote from which O'Neill derived Dion's cry, the story of the "Greek sailors in the time of Tiberius who once heard on a lonely island the cry 'Great Pan is dead!' "[41] If O'Neill, who developed so much of the play from the writing of Nietzsche, had followed the Nietzchean scheme exactly, Dion would have appeared as a form of anti-Christ since, according to the philosopher, "Christianity was, essentially and thoroughly, the nausea and surfeit of Life for Life, which only disguised, concealed and decked itself out under the belief in 'another' or 'better' life. The hatred of the 'world,' the curse on the affections, the fear of beauty and sensuality, another world, invented for the purpose of slandering this world the more, at bottom a longing for Nothingness, for the end, for the rest, for the 'Sabbath of Sabbaths.' "[42] Under such a scheme, Brown in turn would have absorbed some of Ephraim Cabot's "Apollonianism." As an architect, a builder of cathedrals, he might well have assumed the role of the god of "plastic powers" that Nietzsche saw in Apollo. It is Apollo who held out "the Gorgon's head to . . . this grotesquely uncouth Dionysian"[43] and subdued him and brought him to reconciliation, thus enabling Greek culture to move from ritual to art, as well as to change the ritual itself, from animalistic orgies to those celebrating "universal redemption" and "glorious transfiguration."

O'Neill, however, does not follow Nietzsche. Instead, he sets in opposition *within Dion,* the Dionysiac anti-Christ and the Christian ascetic represented by the image of St. Anthony. It is really the emergence of the saint that causes Dion to deny life. His poetic supersensitivity, his "childlike, religious faith in life" is wrenched by an anti-Dionysian force to another direction. At the moment he first attempts to commit himself fully to life, he begins ironically to withdraw from it.

His withdrawal is marked by the changes in his mask and his face. The mask becomes increasingly Mephistophelian, Pan converted into Satan, and the face becomes "more selfless and ascetic, more fixed in its resolute withdrawal from life." [269] By the second act, the face is that of a martyr, "furrowed by pain and self-torture, yet lighted from within by a spiritual calm and human kindliness," [284] while the mask "has a terrible deathlike intensity, its mocking irony . . . so cruelly malignant as to give him the appearance of a real demon, tortured into torturing others." [294] When he prays, Dion resembles "a Saint in the desert, exorcising a demon." [273]

Dion's action, like that of John in the later *Days Without End,* is the exorcism of the demoniac self, the subduing of the Pan God by the ascetic forces of Christianity. The laws of the materialistic establishment to which one must awake from Dionysian rapture has little to do with the evolution of the Christian saint Dion becomes. His action and its opposition lie within him. Here of course, difficulty emerges, for Dion refuses to admit that he is the source of his revulsion from life. He has, he says, tried to find God through his painting: "I got paint on my paws in an endeavor to see God!" [282] Failing in this, he pretends to forswear his quest for God and ironically deifies materialism, the enemy, in the person of the Great God Brown. But has he in truth substituted Brown for Dionysus? He has failed as a painter: he says "It wasn't in me to be an artist—except in living— and not even in that." [271] More fully he boasts:

> I've loved, lusted, won and lost, sang and wept! I've been life's lover! I've fulfilled her will and if she's through with me now it's only because I was too weak to dominate her in turn. It isn't enough to be her creature, you've got to create her or she requests you to destroy yourself. [296]

His claim, as it is phrased here shortly before his death, requires analysis. Both Cybel and Margaret represent an aspect of the life force. Cybel, as the personification of the earth goddess, is the force of nature itself. Dion calls her "Mother Earth," and she is related to the image of seasonal change, particularly to spring and to autumn harvest. Dion loves her because she brings him a sense of quiet and calm that is almost prenatal. In Cybel's room, he speaks of the sweetness and purity of his mother and of his father whom he felt he knew only at the moment of his conception. Cybel becomes a mother, to whom he can turn as a child. Yet, if Cybel is life, it is difficult to see that Dion has been "life's lover." His worship of her power is not that of a lover.

Margaret also stands in relation to Dion as a mother. He says of her, "In due course of nature another girl called me her boy in the moon and married me and became three mothers in one person." [282] The three mothers, presumably, mean the reincarnation of his dead mother, the wife-mother of Dion's sons, and insofar as Margaret recalls Faust's Marguerite, the Virgin mother, to whom saints pray. Shortly before he dies, he turns on her with mockery, crying,

Behold your man—the sniveling, cringing, life-denying Christian slave you have so nobly ignored in the father of your sons! Look! (*He tears the mask from his face, which is radiant with a great pure love for her and a great sympathy and tenderness.*) O woman—my love—that I have sinned against in my sick pride and cruelty— forgive my sins—forgive my solitude—forgive my sickness—forgive me! (*He kneels and kisses the hem of her dress.*) [292]

Again, however, the worship by the life-denying Christian ascetic of the *Ewig Weibliche* is not to be construed as justifying Dion's claim to having "loved, lusted, won and lost." Nor, it may be said without elaboration, has his debauchery nor his drunkenness.

The simple fact is that Dion has not loved life, but has steadily denied it. Far from being the play's Dionysian, the anti-Christ, he is closer to its Christ, and his martyrdom is marked by appropriate quotation from Thomas à Kempis, the Sermon on the Mount and the Lord's Prayer. When the action of exorcism is complete, Dion blesses the satanic mask, saying, "Peace, poor tortured one, brave pitiful pride of man, the hour of our deliverance comes. Tomorrow we may be with Him in Paradise!" [291] Earlier, he has cried "Pride is dead! Blessed are the meek! Blessed are the poor in spirit!" [273] The lines suggest that it is the death of Pride, rather than the death of Pan, with which O'Neill in Dion is principally concerned.

Brown is Dion's brother. The two are bound together by the same ties of alienation and commitment which mark the relationship between Andrew and Robert Mayo and which will be the distinctive bond between Edmund and Jamie Tyrone. For Brown, the relationship is bondage. He is condemned to follow Dion's course, in a brutal parallel, suffering Dion's agony and sharing none of Dion's vision. Where Dion is Pan, Brown is a satyr; where Dion is Mephistopheles, Brown is Faust; and where Dion is a martyred Christ, Brown is a thief who must also be martyred.*

Brown is presented, through Dion's commentary on him, as the secure God of a materialistic society, an assured possessor of all he surveys, "piled in layers of protective fat." Cybel notes that he is "guilty," but her charge does not form a specific indictment. Dion is more detailed: "Vaguely, deeply, he feels at his heart the gnaw-

---

* Cf. 311 and 313, where Brown is compared to a goat; 294, where Dion explicitly plays the devil come to conclude a bargain; and 287 and 296, where Dion complains that Brown steals life from him.

ing of a doubt! And I'm interested in that germ which wriggles like a question mark of insecurity in his blood, because it's part of the creative life Brown's stolen from me!" [296] He cries "Brown loves me! He loves me because I have always possessed the power he needed for love, because I am love!" [298]

As he speaks, Dion is at the point of death, and his words move Brown to a jealous duplication of his martyrdom. When he assumes Dion's mask, he claims to be drinking Dion's strength: "strength to love in this world and die and sleep and become fertile earth, as you are becoming now in my garden—your weakness the strength of my flowers, your failure as an artist painting their petals with life!" It is a partial vision, the half-successful attempt of the Dionysian reveler to personate the god and thereby to assume his knowledge and his power. That it is insufficient is clear. Brown cannot create, for creation depends on vision, and Brown moves in the dark. What he cannot possess, he destroys, as in childhood he destroyed Dion's sand castle, and as he finally destroys himself. At the last moment, O'Neill gives him insight and allows him to speak in a burst of ecstasy, crying,

> Only he that has wept can laugh! The laughter of Heaven sows earth with a rain of tears, and out of earth's transfigured birth-pain the laughter of Man returns to bless and play again in innumerable dancing gales of flame upon the knees of God! [322]

The lyric thrust of his final words is perhaps less justifiable than the play's curtain line as the police captain confronts Cybel:

CAPTAIN   . . . Well, what's his name?
CYBEL   Man!
CAPTAIN   (Taking a grimy notebook and an inch-long pencil from his pocket) How d'yuh spell it?

Unexpectedly at the end not Dion, but Brown, the play's villain and villified victim, becomes an emblem of the human condition.

At crucial moments in their lives, both Dion and Brown enact their passion in the presence of Cybel, who directly and unambiguously represents that life force central to the play's meaning. O'Neill describes her as resembling an "idol of Mother Earth," and, in causing her to wear the mask of a prostitute, suggests that most men who seek a Dionysian forgetfulness find it in momentary sexual substitutes. Dion, however, sees her as life itself. He calls her

"Miss Earth," and his relationship with her is not sexual. With her he is a child. Although Brown knows her only as the prostitute, at the end she becomes his mother as well, comforting him as he dies, praying for him and pronouncing his partial vision real:

> Always spring comes again bearing life! Always again! Always, always forever again!—spring again—life again! summer and fall and death and peace again! . . . but always, always, love and conception and birth and pain again—spring bearing the intolerable chalice of life again . . . bearing the glorious, blazing crown of life again! [322]

Unfortunately, the doctrine of the Dionysian earth mother is not one which either of the men can accept. Until he dies, Brown never sees her without her mask or hears her message. Dion, tormented by his own ghosts, cannot follow her teaching. Hers is a simple message. "Life's all right," she tells Dion, "if you let it alone." To Brown, with exasperated pity, she cries, "Oh, why can't you ever learn to leave yourselves alone and leave me alone!" She means that men should find a way to rid themselves of the desire to win, to possess and even to see God. She says to Dion who complains that her luck at cards is better than his, "It knows you still want to win —a little bit—and it's wise all I care about is playing." Life is enough in itself. It is eternal, prolific and unimportant:

> You may be important but your life's not. There's millions of it born every second. Life can cost too much for even a sucker to afford it—like everything else. And it's not sacred—only the you inside is. The rest is earth. [286]

Men on earth are better off if, like the majority of sailors on the *Glencairn,* they live in unthinking relationship with the rhythm of life, accepting without question its continuity and its benevolence. In the context of *The Great God Brown,* and in the conflict of the visionary and the possessor, men cannot accept life as children do. They must perform acts of will, attempt to shape life and destroy themselves in the attempt. O'Neill's morality play, although its theological scheme cannot deny men salvation as they return to life in dying, damns them to suffering in their course on earth.

Significantly, neither Dion nor Brown finds any genuine human relationship to sustain him. Both men in the play love Margaret, but that love is little more than a subject for declamation. Margaret, consumed with her sons and her housework and her un-perceiving love for her husband, is perhaps intended as an example of one who lets life alone. In the prologue and epilogue she is linked with the moon and the sea and tidal pull of birth, yet her position as *Ewig Weibliche* is not dramatized with force. With neither Dion nor Brown does she achieve a relationship comparable even to that established between Rose and Tim in *The Web*. With Cybel, Dion has a communion, but again it is not such a profound human rela-tionship that it can redeem life's pain.

The absence of genuine character relationships is the first sign of O'Neill's departure from what had been an important conse-quence of his commitment to the realistic theatre. In depicting men and women he had known, in ransacking life as he had met it, he had been able to infuse most of his works with a sense of life that no one writing in the American theatre and few in Europe had been able to achieve. For all its appearance of expressionism, *The Emperor Jones* was rooted in a realistic conception of character, and even *The Hairy Ape* remained close to the kind of character depiction in the *Glencairn* plays. With *The Great God Brown*, however, O'Neill's art turned decisively away from what it had been in the past, away from man, toward God and toward the statement of a fully formed theology.

The aesthetics and the technical means of the Art Theatre, proved in practice by his five-year association with Macgowan and Jones, together with the freedom to experiment which that alliance per-mitted him, gave O'Neill a sense of mastery of the theatre not unlike a poet's security with words. Reticent about his ability with language, he was nothing but confident of his ability to make the stage work. *The Great God Brown* still generates an energy that in the theatre reduces its pretensions and its confusions to unimpor-tance. Almost alone among major dramatists in this country, O'Neill had the courage of the visionary in his concept of what the theatre could become. He saw—or thought he saw—the way to realize the dreams of the Cheneys and the Macgowans and hundreds of other prophets of new glory for the theatre. Rightly, he saw that nothing would emerge without themes worthy of the enterprise. In their quest, he wrote to Nathan a credo, wherein he stated that to do big work, a playwright must have a big theme—specifically, he must take as his subject man's search for God.[44] Big work meant religious themes and plays for a big theatre. In this spirit, he turned to his most ambitious enterprise, a play which undertook to set forth in strong, positive terms what *Marco Millions* and *The Great God Brown* had touched only by ironic negatives. *Lazarus Laughed*, "A Play for an Imaginative Theatre," is, in a sense, Dion Anthony's play, for it attempts to see God, to personate him ritualistically on the stage. Dion's attempt failed and so did O'Neill's, but O'Neill's failure, unlike Dion's, is not a failure of nerve, and, lacking the clear evidence which a major production of the work would provide, it is possible that the script may be less the author's failure than that of his theatrical associates and his audiences.

Lazarus Laughed is a work easily mocked. Its Biblical subject matter and its enormous masses of people cause the comparison with a Cecil B. de Mille film to rise easily to the lips. The scale of the work is vast, and there is ample space on its surface for critics to carve memorable initials. One of the first of these was George Jean Nathan, who felt the play had few virtues, and whose comments led to a quarrel unusual between the two. The play had been written rapidly. The scenario was finished in September, 1925, and the play itself written between February and May, 1926, although O'Neill continued to revise the work through 1927. Something of his sense of creative excitement can be gained from a letter he wrote to Macgowan on May 14, 1926.

> "Lazarus Laughed" was finished—first draft—the 11th, but there will be lots to do on it once Budgie gets it all typed. In the meantime, I am going to get started on the lady play "Strange Interlude," if I can—and my creative urge is all for going on.
>
> As for "Lazarus" what shall I say? It is so near to me yet that I feel as if it were pressed against my eyes and I couldn't see it. I wish you were around to "take a look" before I go over it. Certainly it contains the highest writing I have done. Certainly it *composes* in the theatre more than anything else I have done, even "Marco" (to the poetical parts of which it is akin although entirely different). Certainly it is more Elizabethan than anything before & yet entirely non-E. Certainly it uses masks as they have never been used before and with an intensely dramatic meaning that really should establish them as a sound and true medium in the modern theatre. Certainly, I know of no play like "Lazarus" at all, and I

know of no one who can play "Lazarus" at all—the lead, I mean. Who can we get to laugh as one would laugh who had completely lost, even from the depths of the unconscious, all traces of the Fear of Death? But never mind. I felt that about "Brown." In short, "Lazarus" is damned far from any category. It has no plot of any sort as one knows plot. And you had better read it and I had better stop getting more involved in explaining what I can't, for the present, explain to myself.*

O'Neill's response to his plays as he wrote them was always one of excitement. With *Lazarus Laughed,* however, there was something more. The repeated "certainly" in his letter to Macgowan protests too much and suggests that he had moved into a territory where he was anything but certain. In fact, he had outrun the possibilities of his theatre, and, with the history of the production difficulties of *The Fountain* and the as yet unproduced *Marco Millions* as warning, he must have known that *Lazarus Laughed* lay beyond the technical means of any theatre in the world. There were possible producers and possible actors. Reinhardt, who had achieved stunning effects with the mob scenes in Rolland's *Danton* and, in *The Miracle,* with religious pageant drama, was the name most often mentioned. As Lazarus, the famous opera *basso,* Boris Chaliapin, who perhaps could play the role in Russian, against the English of the rest of the cast, was suggested. Yet the project did not come close to realization, except in the designs by Norman Bel Geddes, who envisioned a stage that could accommodate all O'Neill had asked for.

What O'Neill requires is far less "fanciful" than what he had demanded in *Marco Millions.* The grand scale of *Lazarus Laughed* develops as a reality one of the principles of the Art Theatre aesthetics: it is a drama in which the crowd is a point of major focus. In *Continental Stagecraft,* Macgowan devotes a chapter to a Berlin production of Toller's *Masse-Mensch* and follows it with a detailed account of Reinhardt's pre-1914 productions in the Theatre of the Five Thousand. Essentially, this was a circus theatre, and writing of its technical demands, Macgowan emphasizes that "Only the

---

* In the paragraph following O'Neill continues to describe another play he has in mind, comparable to *The Emperor Jones* about the lynching of a white man: one which will focus on a masked mob transformed by lust and fear into brutes. Evidently, his experiment with the masked chorus in *Lazarus Laughed* was intended to be developed further.

biggest and severest forms could be used. . . . The player had to develop a simple and tremendous power. He had to dominate by intensity and by dignity, by the vital and the great. There had to be music in him, as there had to be music in the action itself."[45] He continues to discuss the way in which the spectators are involved in the action, becoming not peep-hole viewers, but participants, part of the crowd which is in its collective entity a major part of the work. As Macgowan set the idea forth in *The Theatre of Tomorrow,*

> One can conceive of a drama of group-beings in which great individuals, around whom these groups coalesce, could be fitly presented only under the impersonal and eternal aspect of the mask. [275]

Lazarus Laughed is evidently constructed to these requirements, and for the enlarged theatre which could accommodate the results.*

O'Neill was well aware of the first criterion for the success of such a play: simplicity. He understood that Macgowan's demand for power, intensity and dignity could be achieved only by broad and essentially simple strokes. None of the romantic elaborations of *The Fountain* or *Marco Millions* are present in *Lazarus Laughed.* Scenically, it is an easy play, requiring terraces, steps and a few set pieces, arches, columns and the like. What appears elaborate are the masks. Lazarus and the rest of the principal actors present no problem. Lazarus is unmasked, because, having overcome his fear of death, he is a whole person, with no need to hide. The supporting actors wear half-masks, in part because they must speak lines of some complexity and their lips must be free, their voices unmuffled, and in part because O'Neill wishes to suggest a difference between the *persona* which the mask represents, often grotesque or terrifying, and the simplicity of being, revealed in the mouth and lips. Thus Pompeia

> wears a half-mask on the upper part of her face, olive-colored with the red of blood smoldering through, with great, dark, cruel eyes—

---

* At one time, O'Neill contemplated a production of the play in which only the actor playing Lazarus would appear live. The rest of the play, including the crowds would be on film. [Cf. Gelb, 720] A variation of the project, anticipatory of present-day multi-media devices, might well prove possible.

a dissipated mask of intense evil beauty, of lust and perverted passion. Beneath the mask, her own complexion is pale, her gentle, girlish mouth is set in an expression of agonized self-loathing and weariness of spirit. [336]

The masks for the small chorus are over-size masks covering their full face. They were intended to contain megaphones. These and those of the crowd present substantial difficulties, but the plan, while elaborate, is not complex: O'Neill requires masks representing seven personality types, following a simplified Jungian scheme, for each of the traditional seven ages of man. He duplicates the scheme for women. Thus in the first scene, ninety-eight crowd masks, plus seven chorus masks are required. All of them are pronouncedly Semitic in character, and, as the play progresses from the Middle East through Greece to Rome, new masks are required, adhering to the same general scheme, but changing the racial characteristic of the face. It is a staggering technical requirement, not only in the building of the masks, but in the provision of the bodies to wear them. At the end of the second scene, for example, O'Neill calls for three crowds of forty-nine persons each, a chorus of seven, eight Roman soldiers, a Centurion, Lazarus, Miriam and a messenger—a total of 166 actors!*

The plan is elaborate and probably in any theatre impractical. Yet underlying the apparent complexity a simple and logical scheme is at work. That an audience might not follow the extrapolations of the plan is a little beside the point. Anyone familiar with the run-of-the-mill grand opera chorus will understand the importance and value of the masks. What the audience will *not* see is a tawdry group of badly made-up, middle-aged non-actors, bunched in the corners of the set, waving scarfs or fronds, each one trying with marked lack of success to develop some expression on his face appropriate to the death of Aida or the nuptials of the Princess Turandot. Grandiose though the scheme may be, O'Neill's masks are aimed at providing a true choric unity and at heightening the *character* of the "group-being." Commenting on the masks he had designed for the production of *The Ancient Mariner*, James Light said,

* See Appendix II. The Pasadena Playhouse production doubled 159 actors in 420 roles. Backstage in the small theatre, the crowd scenes must have been unique in theatrical history.

We are using masks in *The Ancient Mariner* for this reason: that
we wish to project certain dramatic motifs through that spiritual
atmosphere which the mask peculiarly gives. We do not use the
mask to imitate life, but to intensify the quality of the theme. The
mask cannot represent life. . . . But it can be used, as we are
trying to use it, to show the eyes of tragedy and the face of
exaltation.[46]

It is too easy to dismiss the chorus of *Lazarus Laughed* as an elaborate bore. To achieve the effect he wanted, which was far more
than an imitation of life, O'Neill was forced to mask the chorus. A
collection of individuals would not give him what he sought, a
choric drama of celebration, extraordinary in its dimension, compelling in its intensity.

The importance of the choruses and the crowds lie less in the
words they chant than in the sound pattern they create. Their
power is aural. They are like the drums and the grating clattering
sounds of Yank's boiler room. They seek to convince, not through
logic or poetic beauty, but through massed power. They provide
a vast orchestration for the action, to which the text is only a li-
bretto. On the page, the chorus lines appear to follow sequentially,
cue-to-cue. In the theatre, however, they overlap the speeches of
the protagonists, their sound and their words echoing what is said,
elaborating, emphasizing and augmenting the dialogue. For example in Act II, scene i, at the moment when Caligula finally faces
Lazarus and realizes his power, Lazarus mocks him gently, and begins to laugh. His laughter is echoed by the crowd and by Caligula himself. The crowd's laughter continues and grows as Caligula
asks why he loves to kill. Lazarus's answer rides on the tide of choric
laughter:

> Are you a speck of dust danced in the wind? Then laugh, dancing!
> Laugh yes to your insignificance! Thereby will be born your new
> greatness! . . . [A]s dust, you are eternal change and everlasting
> growth, and a high note of laughter soaring through chaos from
> the deep heart of God! . . .

The laughter continues under the dialogue for perhaps ninety seconds until Lazarus quiets it with a gesture. It is silent for three
lines, and then as Lazarus laughs again, the choric orchestration
softly enhances his description of what death was like:

He thought: "Men call this death"—for he had been dead only a little while and he still remembered. Then, of a sudden, a strange gay laughter trembled from his heart as though his life, so long repressed in him by fear, had found at last his voice and a song for singing. "Men call this death," it sang. "Men call life death and fear it. They hide from it in horror. Their lives are spent in hiding. Their fear becomes their living. They worship life as death!"

As he speaks, the choric laughter blends into words, interspersed with his phrases, and echoing and overlapping them:

Men call life death and fear it.
They hide from it in horror.
Their lives are spent in hiding.
Their fear becomes their living.
They worship life as death!

Lazarus's next words are a direct address to the crowd, which presumably will be heard in silence, but immediately following the short exhortation, the chorus of his followers and the chorus of Greeks burst forth joyfully, again in lines which sound contrapuntally, finally coming together in a full chorus:

Laugh! Laugh!
Fear is no more!
Death is dead!

Lazarus changes the direction, topping the chorus:

Out with you! Out into the woods! Upon the hills!

initiating a speech that concludes:

I am laughter, which is Life, which is the Child of God!

The words are picked up by the two choruses and the crowd, music is added, and Lazarus is drawn from the place in his chariot. [308-311] The choral sound is at its height.

The effect cannot be described, although a reading of the play with ears open may suggest something of its power.* Such a reading will also suggest two other matters of importance. The first is that O'Neill has continually played the choral climaxes against

---

* The one really difficult technical problem is the training of the chorus to speak in tempo and with the proper modulations of volume.

scenes of relative solitude and quiet, thus setting a rhythm of high and low, loud and soft, exultant and introspective, the most notable of the latter scenes being the long passage at the beginning of Act IV when the chorus is absent during the interview between Lazarus and Caligula, Tiberius and Pompeia. A sense of isolation surrounds the scene that has in it something of the reality of the fear of death. In part this is created by the silence, the absence of the chorus.

The second matter is that in writing the words for the chorus, O'Neill has been fully aware that he cannot write sentences of any complexity whatsoever. The choric lines are short—two to six words —relying on repetition and simple phrasing for their effect. Anything more, considering that they are most often spoken by a minimum group of forty-nine persons whose masks would have impeded articulation, would have reduced the words to the merest blur. Unison would have been impossible; syntactical complexity would have spelt ruin. The words are not the music, only the means to the music, and are, therefore, deliberately simplified.

In extending the choric element of the play to such unusual lengths, O'Neill was working characteristically toward enveloping and overpowering his audience. The ghosts in *Where the Cross Is Made,* which were staged live so the dramatist could discover how much an audience could bear, the empathetic call of the drums, and similar experiments devoted toward involving the audience in the psychological realities of the plays are the predecessors of the choruses of *Lazarus Laughed.* The most revealing comment O'Neill made about the work is recorded in a conversation with Paul Green.[47] Green stated that O'Neill spoke to him of his hopes for the new American theatre, "a theatre of the imagination unbounded and one in which the audience especially might participate more vitally and fully. . . . He hoped someday to write plays in which the audience could share as a congregation shares in the music and ritual of a church service." In terms reminiscent of Macgowan's analysis of Reinhardt's Theatre of the Five Thousand, he objected to the sharp division of most theatres between actors and audience, stage and auditorium, and hoped that the entire theatre can be unified and charged with emotion.

" 'This can only happen,' " Green quoted O'Neill's saying, " 'when the audience actively participates in what is being said,

seen and done. . . .' Then he told about his recent efforts somewhat in that direction, the play *Lazarus Laughed.* . . . 'What I
would like to see in the production of *Lazarus,*' he said, 'is for the
audience to be caught up enough to join in the responses—the
laughter and chorus statements even, much as Negroes do in one of
their revival meetings.' "

Such an expectation is shocking in its audacity, but it is the true
end of the choral scheme of the play. The choruses are to break
over the audience as a wave of sound, causing them to rise to Lazarus's state of exultation, causing them, in short, to believe.

What they are to believe is not complex. The seeds of the play
are to be found in *The Great God Brown.* Brown's face, at one
point, is compared to the portrait of a Roman emperor, and, ironically commenting on his own metamorphosis as Dion, Brown says,
"It's an age of miracles. The streets are full of Lazaruses." [315] The
message that Lazarus preaches is simplified Nietzschean doctrine
of the Ring of Being and the everlasting flow of life.

> O Zarathustra . . . to those who think like us, things all dance
> themselves: they come and hold out the hand and laugh and flee—
> and return. Everything goeth, everything returneth; eternally
> rolleth the wheel of existence. Everything dieth, everything blos-
> someth forth again; eternally runneth on the year of existence.[48]

The concepts with which O'Neill had demonstrated his familiarity
in *The Fountain* and *The Great God Brown* are here focused in
the preachment of a Zarathustra-like messiah. Lazarus, however, is
stripped of Zarathustra's scornful laughter, and the play does not
contain the darkly pessimistic core around which Nietzsche's apoca-
lyptic work is formed. Again, O'Neill has reduced the complexity,
in favor of a simple, fully positive expression of faith. The death of
God, because He has pitied men, is no part of Lazarus's doctrine.
Jesus wept and Lazarus laughed for the same reason: that God is
life, a force both psychic and physical. Death is dissolution into
life and God, the end of an interlude. Men, ruled inevitably by the
force of life, have no reason to fear a return to their elemental essence. O'Neill simplifies the Christian theology as much as he simplifies Nietzsche. To Lazarus, all faiths come to the same thing, a
view O'Neill had offered earlier in *The Fountain* and in *Marco
Millions.* In reality, what Lazarus preaches is what O'Neill sought

and what he hoped his audience would be sufficiently roused to accept: a faith for twentieth-century America, which because it lacks a formal theology men might accept.

Some of it is showmanship, Reinhardtian kitsch in the Jones-Macgowan manner. The essence of it, however, comes from the heart of belief. Macgowan had urged that America's theatre should seek in its own terms something of the exaltation of the ceremonial Greek theatre, and had called for theatre artists who had the vision that had sometime come to artists in other fields. In the theatre, such a visionary could speak not only to the perceptive and the educated as other artists did, but "to the uneducated and the dull, as well as to the receptive." The theatre, he said, is the art "nearest to life; its material is almost life itself. This physical identity which it has with our very existence is the thing that can enable the artist to visualize with amazing intensity a religious spirit of which he has sensed only the faintest indications in life. He can create a world which shines with exaltation and which seems—as it indeed is—a world of reality. He can give the spirit a pervading presence in the theater which it once had in the life of the Greeks and of the people of the Middle Ages. And when men and women see eternal spirit in such a form, who can say that they will not take it to them?"[49]

Lazarus Laughed is a play which answers in all particulars to this faith. It attempts to visualize with intensity a religious spirit that O'Neill had perceived dimly all his life. Lazarus, characterized early in the play as a man who in life was nothing but a bungling farmer, is reminiscent of Robert Mayo, but now transformed and exalted by his journey beyond the farthest horizon. Caligula, deformed, ape-like in his antics, is a distillation of other spiritually deformed characters with whom O'Neill has been concerned—the Hairy Ape, Marco, with his spiritual hump, the capering Billy Brown. Tiberius Caesar, Pompeia and Miriam also bring into sharp focus in a specifically religious context human characteristics in which, earlier, O'Neill has sensed a "faint indication" of spirit. For example, the closeness of Lazarus and Miriam to the earth, together with Miriam's strong maternal quality are reminiscent of the religious motifs in *Desire Under the Elms.* The list of parallels might be increased, but the point, essentially, is that O'Neill is here attempting to clarify his "doctrine," to translate experience by the alchemy of a strong, simple, positive assertion into faith, to give his truth "a pervading presence in the theater"—to turn theatre, in effect, into a church.

Annoyed by the positive assertion the play makes, some have said that O'Neill here demonstrates conclusively that he is not a "thinker." Yet one wonders. Sophocles' praise of man for his ability to till the fields in the *parabasis* of *Antigone* is startling and moving in its simplicity, but viewed as "thought" it is neither complex nor revealing. Hamlet's somewhat murky self-recriminations pass for thought, but there are not many who know what the soliloquy "To be or not to be . . ." is about, and certainly to the world-at-large the bromides of Polonius remain the major "thoughts" in the play. Shaw, perhaps the most intellectual of playwrights, was from the beginning almost universally damned for his thinking. In Brecht, a "Playwright as Thinker," the agit-prop drama comes into the realm of art, but again, although Brecht's thought is of the essence, it is not the thought that makes the best of Brecht great drama. The most recent movement in theatre, in America at least, has tended to veer away from the drama whose basis is intellect, from "alienation" effects, from forcing the spectator to be an analyst. It has moved instead, through games and improvisation and by such technical means as thrust stages and unconventional theatrical space in which, as Macgowan urged, the spectator and actors are one, toward a theatre of what has been called "Celebration"—a theatrical event, a happening, in which spectators are participants in the full sense. *Lazarus Laughed,* a play written by a man of the 1920's for the materialistic culture which sprang up in his society during the interregnum between two great wars, is a play of this modern kind. It does not achieve its end in the same way as the modern theatre seeks that end, but the ends are not very different. Nor, for that matter, are the themes which in the plays of the late 1960's and 1970's celebrate the essential simplicity of man, his closeness to the elements, his hatred of materialistic establishments, his need for a pervading sense of life.

Whatever judgment is finally made of *Lazarus Laughed,* that judgment must be based on an awareness of the theatrical conditions for which it was written. It is not in any true sense a Greek tragedy, although parallels may be drawn; nor is it, O'Neill to the contrary, "Elizabethan." O'Neill is more correct in claiming it as a unique work for the theatre, one which because of its demands will never receive a fully realized performance.*

The unique theatrical quality has perhaps obscured one aspect of the work which is also without parallel in O'Neill's writing, one indeed which may lie at the center of the extravagant development of this third "Wander Play." In his plays up to 1925, O'Neill had taken as his most characteristic protagonist a man with a touch of the poet who was doomed to frustration in attempting to recapture a remembered vision. Lazarus, however, has more than memory. He is not "touched" with poetry; he, in O'Neill's meaning of the word, *is* the poet, and has achieved the promise of his vision. For him no veil exists between life on earth and the secret at the heart of all life. In the presence of such a Poet-messiah, even the most inexorably visionless of creatures, the monstrous, the deformed, the pathological tyrants become touched with poetry. This is the dramatic relationship which gives power to the scenes in the Roman court and creates such strong acting roles for Tiberius, Miriam and especially Caligula. Unexpectedly for them, Lazarus draws back the veil and makes them see, draws them forth from their isolation in what Lazarus calls "a solitary cell whose walls are

---

* Nevertheless, it has proved capable on the stage. The reception of its only professional production by the Pasadena Community Playhouse in 1928 was favorable. More interesting, perhaps, and more revealing of the strength of the play, was a production by students at the University of California at Berkeley in 1950. The Berkeley production was staged in a large, open-air, Greco-Roman theatre. As O'Neill had stipulated in granting permission for the play's performance, the dialogue was not cut. However, the director, Fred Orin Harris, threw out all of O'Neill's choric scheme, and reduced the number to a chorus of no more than twenty men and women. No attempt was made to realize the massive choric punch of the script, and, interestingly, the only laughter that was heard in the production was the mocking laughter of the unbelievers. Lazarus's laughter was projected as a strong "action" of exultant joy in eloquent silence which fell gradually over the chorus. In the hush thus created, music was used to support and further project the sense of Lazarus's ecstasy. The effect, surprisingly, worked well, and although it fell far short of O'Neill's sense of what the chorus and the laughter could accomplish, the production was valid.

Framed by this simplicity there emerged a drama of genuine interest. Lazarus's story proved absorbing, and in performance, Pompeia, Caligula and notably Tiberius and Miriam emerged as some of the best character studies O'Neill has created. Miriam's continual silent presence by Lazarus's side proved to be exceptionally vital and, by her light, Lazarus's humanity became a reality. Tiberius's monologue in Act IV, scene i, which in this production occupied fifteen to twenty minutes' playing time, had a greatness of line, an elemental strength that ranked it close to Ephraim's monologue in *Desire Under the Elms*.

mirrors" [309] and causes them to yearn toward an ultimate unity with all life. Lazarus gone, the cell becomes again a reality, the mirrors which had been windows become clouded with fog and reflect only the ugliness of self. Lazarus and Caligula both know that "men forget" the power and truth of such vision. But they do not forget that it is there. He whom Lazarus leaves becomes touched with poetry.

Lazarus Laughed, whose time scheme, somewhat divorced from real geographical distance, runs from late twilight in the first scene until dawn in the last, is in essence a long journey through night.* In less impressive contexts, O'Neill has said that materialism will crush the soul of those touched with poetry. Now, scaling the action a notch higher, O'Neill says what may indeed be a truth: that men faced with a vision will crucify their messiahs, rather than accept their vision. Nevertheless, they cannot eradicate the memory of vision, nor the pain the memory causes.

* John Henry Raleigh compares the relationships in IV, i, with those of the Tyrone family in Act IV of *Long Day's Journey into Night.* Cf. Raleigh, *The Plays of Eugene O'Neill* (Carbondale, Ill., 1965), 47.

VIII
THE END
OF EXPERIMENT

1927—The "Triumvirate" disbanded and O'Neill signed with
the Theatre Guild in an association that lasted the rest of his life.
In Bermuda, the heat, the water-bound world seemed native elements,
and he found pleasure in his children who were often there.
But there was marital trouble. Returning to New York for rehearsals,
O'Neill saw much of Carlotta Monterey. He asked Agnes
to divorce him. She refused, and a long legal struggle began
that made Eugene and Carlotta "copy" and forced them
to spend much of their time dodging scandal-sniffing reporters.
They left the United States, vowing not to return
until they were married. A pursuing press followed them
chronicling "mysterious disappearances," private quarrels,
illness, and once, even reporting Eugene dead.
In 1929, the year *Strange Interlude* won his third Pulitzer Prize,
the year of his divorce and of his marriage to Carlotta,
he settled in France in a château near Tours,
where he began to live in the isolation of work
that was growing in scale, increasing in depth.
What he asked was that Carlotta create a home like a fortress
and that she undertake the guardianship of his creative life
and join him in his solitude. He asked for sacrifice;
she gave him her life.

THE Theatre Guild produced both *Marco Millions* and *Strange Interlude* in January, 1928, and thereafter, Eugene O'Neill sealed himself in an association that was to last for the rest of his active life in the theatre. The Guild in earlier times had not endeared itself to O'Neill. Five of his plays—*The Straw,* "*Anna Christie,*" *The First Man, The Fountain,* and *Welded*—had been rejected by the board of directors, and it was chiefly his desperation at finding a producer for *Marco Millions* that again led the playwright to consider signing with them. There was, however, a certain inevitability in the alliance. The Theatre Guild had begun as a Greenwich Village little theatre in rivalry with the Provincetown Players. For three years, between 1915 and 1918, the group, calling itself the Washington Square Players, had presented bills of one-act and full-length plays, including in October, 1917, the première of O'Neill's *In the Zone.* The repertory displayed an eclectic, intelligent selection of the best works of American authors and a significant number of plays by important foreigners. Suspending operations during the war, the organization reformed in December, 1918, as the Theatre Guild and began the series of productions that was to include virtually every important author of Europe and America. At least to mid-century, the Guild's offerings constituted the most important production record in the history of theatre in this country. No play was meretriciously commercial and none was shoddily produced. The Guild's subscription audiences extended from coast to coast, and, through its tours, the organization educated the nation in the important drama of the era.

Rapidly emerging from a tangle of success and failure as America's first dramatist, O'Neill turned to the Guild as an organization able to provide him with what even in the Provincetown days he had needed, a fully professional theatrical company which, at the same time as it adhered to the best production standards, did not represent the "Broadway Show Shop." With the failure of the Triumvirate to find a way of producing *Marco Millions*, O'Neill's disaffection with that organization became complete. *Strange Interlude* was offered to Katharine Cornell, who rejected it in favor of Somerset Maugham's *The Letter*. At this point, Lawrence Langner* visited O'Neill in Bermuda to discuss the possibility of producing *Marco Millions*. There he read *Strange Interlude,* and returned in high excitement to browbeat his co-directors into accepting both plays. Although *Marco Millions* suffered in production because of the Guild's necessary economies, *Strange Interlude* was felt to be by one critic** the best production any of his plays had received. O'Neill, although he occasionally uttered exasperated diatribes against the quality of his actors, seems to have been generally well satisfied with the Guild's results. In turn the Guild's loyalty to O'Neill was well repaid at the outset, for the relatively short run of *Marco Millions**** was amply offset by the commanding success of *Strange Interlude.*

For a play of such special character as *Strange Interlude* the popular reception was unexpected. With the curtain at 5:15 p.m., an hour's dinner intermission after Act V, and a final curtain after 11:00 p.m., the producers, however emboldened to the production of marathon plays by their presentation in 1922 of Shaw's *Back to*

---

* His principal associates on the Guild's Board of Directors were Lawrence Langner and Theresa Helburn. Langner, who had been schooled in the handling of temperamental playwrights by his acquaintance with Bernard Shaw, saw to it that the Guild in all its branches collaborated with O'Neill's demands. In return, O'Neill proved unusually cooperative with them. Langner's account of their work together in *The Magic Curtain* is an important record of O'Neill's whole-hearted collaboration with the producers during the rehearsal period of his plays.

** Joseph Wood Krutch, *The Nation*, February 15, 1928. In 1927, O'Neill had written to Krutch regarding the proposed production of *Strange Interlude* and inveighed against the American theatre, hoping only that the Guild would do no worse than the Provincetown Players and the Triumvirate had done for certain of his plays. He told Krutch that he had come to expect bad productions.

*** At this period, in order to build a permanent acting company, the Guild was attempting a repertory system. None of their plays were kept before the public for the full extent of their possible run. The incredible popularity of *Strange Interlude* put an end to any repertory ambitions the Guild had.

Methuselah, were understandably concerned that their audiences might prove incapable of such theatrical longevity. O'Neill's subject matter and its treatment, together with his implacable refusal to permit laugh lines, only increased their concern that an audience might refuse to put up with the experience. O'Neill, who in the past had repeatedly attempted to discover how much an audience could bear, found them able to stand up to all he offered, and *Strange Interlude* achieved a success no other American play had equaled. Such distinguished actresses as Pauline Lord and Judith Anderson headed touring companies, and a London production was organized. The published play became a national best seller—the first time a drama had attained that honor.* O'Neill received his third Pulitzer Prize for the work. It was filmed by Metro-Goldwyn-Mayer in 1932.** In all, according to Langner, O'Neill made about $300,000 from the production, and the Guild realized a similar sum.

To account for such a success at a remove of over forty years is difficult. O'Neill's story of the loves of Nina Leeds and her four men, Sam, her husband, Ned Darrell, her lover, Gordon, her son and her avuncular friend, Charlie Marsden, seems sprawling, over-

---

* O'Neill's relations with his publisher are discussed by Walker Gilmer in his biography *Horace Liveright* (New York, 1970), 175-84. *Strange Interlude's* success was the fulfillment of a long association between O'Neill and Liveright. From the publication of *Beyond the Horizon* in 1923, through that of *Dynamo* in 1929, the publisher had brought out thirteen volumes containing twenty-four of O'Neill's plays. Regular publication of his work was an important element in the development of his international reputation, as Gilmer points out. According to Gilmer, the association of O'Neill and Liveright was mutually satisfactory. Liveright unprotestingly had all of *Strange Interlude* reset because the author made so many changes on the galleys. Content with such special treatment, O'Neill worked in harmony with his publisher. For his part, Liveright could count on an immediate sale of ten thousand copies of any successful O'Neill play, a figure sufficient to classify the dramatist as one of the firm's most popular authors. Limited editions, expensively priced, sold out quickly, and *Strange Interlude* sold one hundred thousand copies, for which O'Neill is reputed to have received $250,000.

** The film was delayed by MGM's refusal to buy the play until settlement of a suit brought against O'Neill and the Guild by a woman who, under the pen name of Georges Lewys, had written a work entitled *The Temple of Pallas-Athenae.* Miss Lewys, in reality Gladys Lewis, author of *Call House Madam,* charged that her mildly erotic novel had provided the basis of O'Neill's plot. Judge John M. Woolsey, who shortly was to lift the ban against James Joyce's *Ulysses,* decided without difficulty in favor of O'Neill and the Guild and fined the plaintiff a substantial sum. The decision with its penalty against the plaintiff is said to have proved a deterrent to similar irresponsible actions.

explicit, coarse in texture. Such plot as there is—Nina's discovery, after she becomes pregnant, that her husband's family has a history of hereditary insanity, that she must have an abortion and, in order to have a child, must take a lover—seems now morbidly clinical. To some reviewers in 1928 it seemed the same—naïve in its use of psychological theory, overly long and unclear in its theme. To the bulk of its public, however, caught up in the headiness of the climactic boom year, 1928, *Strange Interlude* appeared as a work which dealt seriously with facets of human nature not yet fully explored. To readers of philosophers or psychoanalytic theorists, and to those who had had a chance to explore a smuggled copy of the French edition of Joyce's *Ulysses*, *Strange Interlude* offered nothing new. Yet Freud, Jung, Joyce were not the household words in 1928 that they later became. To a public relatively untutored in such matters, *Strange Interlude* unquestionably appeared as a revelation—a kind of primer of new thought, couched in language and action that opened new vistas in their understanding of human drives.

Yet there were other reasons for the success beside the subject matter. The length of the play was interesting. Going to dinner in medias res appealed to the chic as a thing to do of social importance.* As a dramatic technique, the asides and soliloquies offered something for easy discussion and for prediction concerning the future of the theatre. They brought Art Theatre experimentation before a substantial public for the first time, and the public responded eagerly.** Moreover, the play's narrative, which dealt so frankly, even clinically, with matters of abortion and adultery, gave the play a *succès de scandale* whose results, including a celebrated banning in Boston could be measured at the box office.***

* Otto Kahn, demonstrating typical panache, went home during the dinner intermission to change into evening clothes.
** Parody is some measure of success. The asides were endlessly a subject for amused burlesque, most importantly, perhaps, by Groucho Marx, whose dead-pan, eyes-to-camera delivery of irrelevant notes and comments on the farcical action may have been derived in part from the staging of the asides in the Guild production. At least in *Animal Crackers*, his second film, he directly parodied the O'Neill asides. For what it is worth, I remember a two-reel, slap-stick comedy about taxicabs entitled *Strange Innertube*. See also Erik Linklater, *Juan in America* (London, 1931), 81-84.
*** The production was taken to nearby Quincy for the benefit of the Guild's Boston subscription list. Langner notes that the profits from the sudden influx of patrons to a small Quincy restaurant during the dinner intermission was sufficient to enable its

Many such reasons could be adduced for the success. They are at best only ancillary to the heart of the matter, which is that in *Strange Interlude* the American public was given its first glimpse of the dramatist O'Neill was to become. Hints of the power that were now apparent could have been gathered from *Desire Under the Elms,* but that play in its first appearance commanded no such attention as *Strange Interlude.* The productions of the Triumvirate were always somewhat special, surrounded with pretensions to "Art" that no doubt put off many of the great central body of play-goers. About the Triumvirate was the sense, if not the fact, of the amateur. Despite their sincerity and their frequent excellence, their productions were a little out of the current—off-Broadway and therefore "unprofessional." It was not until the Guild placed *Strange Interlude* and its author squarely in the middle of the com-petition, definitely on-Broadway and thereby in the center of the theatre of the United States that O'Neill's full range as a dramatist became apparent.*

Although O'Neill in the beginning had conceived *Strange Inter-lude,* as he had *Marco Millions, Lazarus Laughed* and *Dynamo,* as a production for the Triumvirate, he himself, in working on the script, sensed a difference. Now he responded to a desire to achieve work of far greater complexity and scope than he or any other American dramatist had hitherto achieved. In early October, 1924, preparing copy for a collected edition of his plays, he wrote to Macgowan that he was becoming reacquainted with many of his plays that he had forgotten. In a letter to Macgowan dated Sep-tember 21, 1924, presumably commenting on the same task, he

---

owner Howard Johnson to begin his career as a national restaurateur. The banning put *Strange Interlude* into the category of censored works. One which Horace Live-right published and defended against censorship in 1925 was Maxwell Bodenheim's *Replenishing Jessica.* The book is a tawdry account of its heroine's "replenishment" at the rate of a love affair per chapter. Its opening paragraph conceivably could have influenced *Strange Interlude:* "Sometimes rooms are filled with all of the words that people do not say to each other. The unspoken words hang in the air, like an im-palpable contradiction, or else they hover in a richly unseen friendliness that strengthens the more faltering sounds from the lips of the speakers. The man and woman in the room feel this presence and often help it with their silences."

* O'Neill's previous "on-Broadway" successes included *Beyond the Horizon,* "*Anna Christie,*" *The Emperor Jones* and *The Hairy Ape.* All but "*Anna Christie*" had come to Broadway after "experimental" productions, including the special matinees of *Beyond the Horizon.*

noted that "I've made a discovery about myself in analyzing the work done, etc. in the past six winters which has led me to a resolve about what I must do in future. But it's too long to write about." What he did was to review his achievement from the time of the writing of *Beyond the Horizon,* and the implication is less that he found it wanting, as that he discovered a new direction.

What that direction was can be inferred from his comments on the writing of *Strange Interlude.* The play gave him trouble. He wrote Macgowan on August 7, 1926, that it could not be ready for the coming theatrical season. After a number of false starts, which he destroyed, he realized that the drama would require much more work than any earlier play and would need interminable revision before it was surely complete. "The point is," he wrote, "my stuff is much deeper and more complicated now and I'm also not so easily satisfied with what I've dashed off as I used to be." In June of the following year, in correspondence with Joseph Wood Krutch concerning the unrevised, but essentially final draft of the play, he agreed with Krutch about the "slightness" of most modern plays and commented, "To me they are all totally lacking in all true power and imagination—and to me the reason for it is too apparent in that they make no attempt at that poetic conception and inter-pretation of life without which drama is not an art form at all but simply tricky journalism arranged in dialogue." Of his two works-in-progress, he stated that "by using one or the other or both of the techniques employed in these two I feel that one can do anything one is big enough for in the drama, that there is no theme too com-prehensive or difficult to handle in the theatre. But 'techniques' is a word worn groggy and it only blurs what I'm trying to say. What I mean is freedom from all the modern formulas that restrict the scope of the theatre to the unreal real and the even more boring unreal unreal. Which sounds a bit scrambled. Well, I'm a bum explainer—and *Strange Interlude* is clearer about it than I am."[1]

By the "unreal real" O'Neill evidently meant the routine Be-lasco-style Broadway fare which imitated the surfaces of life with-out revealing any human truth. The "unreal unreal" apparently refers to the multitudes of shoddy productions in experimental styles that followed O'Neill's own experimentation, but which were experimental to little purpose beyond theatrical trickery. Filled with a new sincerity of purpose, O'Neill in *Strange Interlude* as well as in *Lazarus Laughed* moved to create a drama that would probe deeply, would be meditative in its themes, would have both scope and intensity, and would aim toward the highest tragic stature. *Strange Interlude* achieves none of these goals. That it approaches them suggests why audiences in 1928 were stirred by it to an unusual responsiveness. The opening of a new reach promised high excitement.

Strange Interlude was the first work of O'Neill's full maturity, and into it, O'Neill poured more of his developing self than he had earlier been able to do. The dominating figure of Nina Leeds is very different from any woman he had created before. She contains many of the qualities of the Strindbergian heroine which, Anna Christie excepted, had been his characteristic heroine. What is new, however, is the sympathy with which she is now viewed. The depiction of Nina develops in a direct line from the portraits of Eleanor Cape, Ella Harris, Abby Putnam and Cybel, but O'Neill, devoting more of his sympathy as well as his attention to her, discovers qualities in her possessiveness which Strindberg in his naturalistic plays did not admit. In *Welded,* the woman and man united could create a force like the God-force sought by his poet-heroes. In *Strange Interlude,* it is not a question of finding such a right relationship. It is enough to find the source of life and identity in the woman herself. O'Neill now posits that the woman *is* the God-force, and in finding her, the man can achieve a sense of belonging he can obtain nowhere else in life. Her possessive greed for his love provides his means of belonging. Significantly, perhaps, O'Neill's more positive attitude toward women developed at a time when he was falling in love with Carlotta Monterey and when his relationship with Agnes Boulton O'Neill had reached its end. A very different marriage was in prospect for him, and something of the wished-for harmony of that relationship is reflected in the attitude of each man in the play toward Nina. She is for them all the source of life, and well-being.

Nina, however, is not a portrait of Carlotta Monterey. As he took an increasingly subjective view of women, he was led not to portray any woman he married, but rather, in creating the figure of a woman who would be sufficiently desirable to hold a life-long sway over the men who were nearest to her, he turned to another source. The point rests on slim and circumstantial evidence, but it can be argued that Nina Leeds, so set about with ambiguous complexities of sympathy and alienation, is the first real portrait O'Neill attempted of his mother.

Some slight evidence is contained in the physical description of Nina and of Mary Tyrone, O'Neill's portrait of his mother in *Long Day's Journey Into Night*. Nina at the age of twenty is described as having a good figure with "slim strong hips." Mary at fifty-four has a "young, graceful figure . . . showing little evidence of middle-aged waist and hips." Nina's straw-blond hair frames her face, and Mary's "high forehead is framed by thick, pure white hair." Nina, too, has a high forehead and her face is "striking, rather than pretty, the bone structure prominent." Mary's face is thin, pale and like Nina's "with the bone structure prominent." The lips of Nina's "rather large mouth [are] clearly modelled above the firm jaw," while Mary's mouth is "wide with full, sensitive lips." Of Nina's blue eyes, O'Neill writes they are "beautiful and bewildering, extraordinarily large," while Mary's dark brown eyes are "unusually large and beautiful. . . ." O'Neill comments that Nina's "whole manner . . . is strained, nerve-racked, hectic, a terrible tension of will alone maintaining self-possession." Mary reveals from the outset a similar "extreme nervousness." Such resemblances might well be thought to be no more than coincidence, but in the action of the two plays confirmation can be found. For much of the later scenes in *Strange Interlude* the significant action centers on the concern of the men with Nina's well-being. Someone arrives; Nina is offstage. The question is asked as to her health and general state of mind. The reply is either negative or positive, and the response of the men is either contented or discontented, according to Nina's emotional and physical condition. In the same way, the happiness of the male members of the Tyrone family depends on Mary's health. Furthermore, both Mary and Nina move between well-being and fulfillment and an irritable, ill-concealed nervousness that racks them as much as it does the men. There is a legion of differences, but the unaware, trance-like timelessness in which Nina lives for much of the play bears at least an emotional resemblance to Mary's elegiac, drifting movement in her morphine-induced trance.

Such evidence is no more than suggestive, for *Strange Interlude* is not fully an autobiographical study. Like its immediate predecessors, it was written with Macgowan's dicta in mind. Indeed, Macgowan in *The Theatre of Tomorrow* predicts the return of the soliloquy and the aside:

> The soliloquy will return again as a natural and proper revelation of the mind of a character. Even the aside may redevelop as a deliberate piece of theatricalism. It will not be the slovenly device of a playwright for telling us something that he is too lazy or inexpert to impart in any other way, but a frank and open intercourse between the actor and his audience, a reaffirmation that this is a play which is being acted, a remarkable game between these two. [243]

A few pages farther along, discussing the content of the drama of the future, he notes that

> It will attempt to transfer to dramatic art the illumination of those deep and vigorous and eternal processes of the human soul which the psychology of Freud and Jung has given us through the study of the unconscious [248]

and he cites as promising examples Alice Gerstenberg's *Overtones,* Hervé Lauwick's *They* and H. L. Mencken's skit *The Artist,* each of which through the use of soliloquy and aside project the inner thoughts of the characters. *Strange Interlude,* however, is more than a product of theatrical theory. O'Neill's claim for its increased depth and complexity was surely valid and was a sign of his own maturation.

In the later courses of his life, O'Neill was to make one more wide-circling physical orbit before his explorations led him at last to his truth. By the end of 1926, he had settled in Bermuda, but was shortly to leave with Carlotta Monterey for a voyage that would take him around the world, and then would bring him to rest for a time in France, where, when his divorce from Agnes Boulton O'Neill became final, he would marry Miss Monterey. Although a reflexive restlessness was to lead him from France to Georgia, to California, and thence to New York and Boston before he died, the outer movement of his life, to a certain degree, became at last irrelevant. The significant turn under the shelter of his third marriage was inward, toward the center of self. Out of that self, O'Neill for thirteen years had spun fictions, some of which may have seemed to resolve problems or clarify complexities that beset his own life. In reviewing his works, he necessarily reviewed his life's problems and the remedies he had sought. Undoubtedly he found truth in what he had written, but it was, if the phrase is possible, a fictive truth—solutions to imagined situations, which did not resolve his own inner discordance. Insofar as it bore on the sexual and artistic competition in his marriage with Agnes O'Neill, the positive ending of *Welded*, for example, is no more than a passionately expressed hope, incapable of realization. Few such solutions are offered: the majority of his works, by so much as they related to his life, are expressions of pain and loss without genuine resolution attempted. That this should be so is understandable. The death of his father, mother and brother between 1920 and 1923, each under unusually painful circumstances, might well have shattered one who touched life less lightly and had less to know about himself than O'Neill. Whatever special combination of psychological and spiritual disorder with imaginative power that led O'Neill to a life as a playwright led him also in the end to an illumination that was truth without fiction.

By 1926, as he approached forty, with a new marriage before him, with the demands of the Triumvirate fading in importance, and with a mitigating space of time dulling the pain of the loss of his family, O'Neill's work began to change. Characteristically, he turned to search more deeply within himself. It is the personal "depth" rather more than the "complexity" of *Strange Interlude* which marks its importance.

The play is not without a limited complexity. As *Desire Under the Elms* was built on Nietzschean substructures, *Strange Interlude* was erected on foundations supplied in part by Freud and by Schopenhauer.* Back of the play lie Strindberg and Nietzsche as well,

* Miss Doris M. Alexander in *"Strange Interlude* and Schopenhauer," *American Literature*, XXV, May, 1953, has explored the relationship of the play to Schopenhauer's *The Metaphysic of the Love of the Sexes*. Stressing that Schopenhauer's concept of the *Will To Live*, a blind life force mastering the course of men's lives, would prove congenial to O'Neill, she demonstrates that the treatment of love in the play parallels in broad outline and in many specific details the view expressed by the philosopher: e.g., that the love affair between Nina and Darrell reflects Schopenhauer's opinion that men and women fall in love in order to serve the species and beget children, but that love is an illusion whose expectations cannot be satisfied and which leads to ultimate unhappiness and degeneration. In Miss Alexander's view, Sam, in his seemingly healthy materialism is a direct exemplification of the *Will To Live* in its rawest form, and, at the play's end, Nina and Charlie Marsden have successfully denied the life force, Marsden through his sexual chastity, Nina through having gone beyond sexual desire after the menopause. Miss Alexander's argument is essentially correct; O'Neill read Schopenhauer, along with Nietzsche and Freud, while he was writing the

and clearly O'Neill's own studies of marriage and of sexual relationships evolved in *Welded, Desire Under the Elms, All God's
Chillun Got Wings* and *The Great God Brown* proved formative
to the play. The soliloquy and the aside were a natural evolution
from the depiction of the repressed inner personalities in *The
Great God Brown* and had been anticipated earlier in the contrapuntal monologues in *Welded*. The continually evolving sense of
the woman as the consuming end of all man's desires—of the woman
as earth mother, of the discovery of God in marriage—had been
found earlier in the endings of *Welded* and *All God's Chillun Got
Wings*, in the relationship between Abby and Eben, and in the
portraits of Cybel and Margaret. Essentially, however, the play is
not more complex, despite its length, than many of its predecessors.
Again, its power lies in its sense of depth, in an almost obsessive
inner turn, corresponding to the turn O'Neill's own life took at the
time of the play's composition.

No claim can be made on behalf of the play's profundity of
character study. The men, to put the matter bluntly, are not interesting either as types or as more fully realized human characters.
O'Neill has divested them of any particle of the theatrical glamour
that had surrounded so many of his past heroes. Surprisingly, none
of them has a touch of the poet about him, unless Darrell's vague
leanings toward a career as a research scientist may be so catego-
rized. Sam Evans carries in him something of the qualities of
O'Neill's typical materialist, but he is not depicted as a visionless man
and treated as a figure of contempt as others were. Nina's speech
about her four men, Darrell, Sam, Marsden and her unborn child,
forming "one complete, whole male desire," suggests that the men
in *Strange Interlude* are really partial aspects of a whole male personality and that O'Neill has divided that being, as he later split

---

play in 1926. It may be suggested, however, that although he used him, he did not
entirely accept Schopenhauer's evaluation of sexual experience. If Marsden, for example, has denied the *Will To Live*, why is he a figure without wisdom, deservedly
held in contempt until the final moments of the play? Nor is it entirely clear that
love for Nina has ruined Darrell's life, as Miss Alexander claims. If so, the degeneration is as easily explained without reference to Schopenhauer. An audience trained by
plays and films in which the ruin of a man was effected by a fatal woman who
drained him of his will power would understand at once. O'Neill has evidently used
the philosopher, but the play's public knew more about Theda Bara and Gloria
Swanson than Schopenhauer.

a single personality, into two. Yet even "reassembled," it is difficult to see that a more than ordinary creature would result.

Nor is Nina much more profoundly developed. An audience is compelled to focus its attention on her through the obsessions which the men share as to her welfare. She is patterned after the Strindbergian destroyer, but O'Neill casts over her a veil of sympathy which removes the sharpness and the sting. There is no point in the play—even in the scene in which she wills her husband's death and attempts through an outrageous lie to break off her son's engagement—where a spectator is able to criticize her actions, except by divorcing himself entirely from the conditions under which the play operates. This is to say that as Nina's life is revealed, she reaches no point of development at which she must take a stand and in so doing offer herself to judgment. She makes no moral choice by which her character can be evaluated.* As a result, the only real development in Nina is physical, from youth to age. At the end, she is the character she was at the outset, and, while what that character amounts to has been told with novelistic detailing, it has not proved to be especially individuated. Nina is the precursor of a long line of neurotic heroines in the American theatre, but compared with many of her daughters, Blanche DuBois, for example, she is strangely faceless.

Therefore, not depth, but yet a *sense* of depth, a purely emotional, irrational theatrical effect, is what *Strange Interlude* offers. The play tells a narrative in time, and moves in the day-to-night, spring-to-fall cycles which O'Neill continually found suggestive, but unlike the earlier plays that developed cyclic progressions, this work is really without forward movement.** It is precisely titled: its days, its lifetime form an interlude.

The indications of time in the narrative are precise. The play begins three weeks before college opens on an afternoon in late August, 1919. Act II is set in the fall of 1920 and Act III in the "late spring" of 1921. Act IV is seven months later, and Act V in

* The exception is her decision to have a child by Darrell. However, since the moral choice is known to none but Darrell, no judgment of her action can occur, even from the audience. See below 309.
** As Timo Tiusanen notes, in the ground plan for the interior scenes, O'Neill requires that the furniture be placed in the same arrangement regardless of the location of the room. [*O'Neill's Scenic Images*, 218] The device, in a minor way, is intended to suggest that nothing changes from year to year or place to place.

April, 1922. Act VI is summer, 1923; Act VII, eleven years later, is laid presumably in the fall of 1934. Acts VIII and IX, ten years later still, are set in 1944. The play thus covers a span of twenty-five years. O'Neill, writing in 1926, projects the play eighteen years into the future, but the point passes without notice. No more revealing evidence is needed to demonstrate O'Neill's tendency to look at life without reference to a society, to tell his story only in terms of personality. Although some small account is taken of the immediate post-war world in the first two acts, thereafter, the play stalls in 1926, and reflects only the boom years immediately preceding the great stock-market crash, a point touched in a soliloquy of Marsden's, when he describes Sam as a "typical, terrible child of the age":

> . . . don't think of ends . . . the means are the end . . . keep moving! . . . It's in every headline of this daily newer testament . . . going . . . going . . . never mind the gone . . . we won't live to see it . . . and we'll be so rich, we can buy off the deluge anyway! . . . [122]

Nina, whose age in the play ranges from twenty to forty-five or forty-six, has gone through her change of life some time before the opening of Act VIII,* in which she appears as a very old lady, with completely white hair, her face old and "worn-out." In Act IX, O'Neill describes her as looking "much older." While Nina's unexpected aging might be medically possible, nothing in the play explains it unless it be her longing to "rot in peace." Her physical age overrides her chronological age as O'Neill moves at the end of play into a further future than he accounts for logically, a compression into a few moments of the rest of Nina's life. Time becomes a matter of emotional movement, independent of calendars and clocks, from everything, indeed, except the autumnal season.**

Within the time scheme of the narrative, of course, there are many events. There is a story to be told; the plot has a certain

---

* O'Neill suggests that Nina has gone through menopause at the age of forty. Cf. Nina's aside in Act VII, 138: "I'm thirty-five . . . five years more . . . at forty a woman has finished living . . . life passes by her . . . she rots away in peace!" Cf. also Sam's aside in Act IX, when Nina is forty-five: "I thought once her change of life was over she'd be ashamed of her crazy jealousy." [160]

** The effect is comparable to the aging of Miriam in *Lazarus Laughed*, who grows older as Lazarus grows younger. O'Neill calls for Darrell to look youthful in Act VII, but by Act VIII, his age is evident.

intricacy. Yet O'Neill appears to have heeded the complaints that the apostles of the Art Theatre made against plays that moved with efficient compression through a series of artificially induced tensions and resolutions to climactic moments at pre-determined points in the narrative structure. In *Strange Interlude* his refusal to compress or to provide stereotyped dénouements is notable. The narrative has no theatrical culmination unless it resides in the moment in Act IX when Nina almost involuntarily tells her son that Darrell is his father. Viewed as a climax, however, it is a minor happening. There has been no preparation for it, and since it occurs without Nina's willing it, it hardly provides a moment of fulfillment in the usual theatrical sense. Furthermore, the son does not understand what his mother has said. The moment slides away, and nothing that could cause crucial change has occurred. In a limited sense, *Strange Interlude* could be called "anti-drama," in that it avoids the normal narrative structure of the plays of its time. Certainly, it is a far cry from the sort of playwriting advocated by George Pierce Baker.

If, in the largest view, nothing happens, then the play's power must reside in another temporal and emotional continuum—in the realm of feeling expressed by the asides and soliloquies. Many have suggested the possibility of performing the play without the asides, relying on the actors to supply the emotional base for what is expressed in straight dialogue. His experience with *Welded* had taught O'Neill that actors would ride rough-shod over any pauses, "compress" their dialogue, and fighting silence, inject the adrenalin of their personalities into anything that they did not quickly understand.* In availing himself of a novelist's privilege of permitting his characters to express unspoken thoughts, he was ensuring that his actors would project more than a single facet of character.

But there was more to it than this. The director, Philip Moeller, staged the asides and soliloquies in a way that was precisely right. Having experimented with a variety of devices, such as designating an area on stage to which the characters would move to speak their thoughts, he settled for a simpler device, freezing the action while the aside was being spoken. The asides, therefore, blended smoothly

---

* O'Neill commented to Lawrence Langner during the rehearsals of *Strange Interlude* that "If the actors weren't so dumb, they wouldn't need asides; they'd be able to express the meaning without them. (Cf. *The Magic Curtain*, 236)

with the dialogue, yet emerged from another dimension of "physical quiet" as Moeller expressed it. The effect achieved was of eddying moments in time, small pools of feeling set out of the main current of narrative in an extraordinary counterpoint of movement and stasis, of time and timelessness, of sound and silence. *Strange Interlude* has two time "schemes," but it is the timeless emotional pattern which provides the sense of depth and which the play in its final moments enters, in defiance of temporal logic.

The quality of a still life created by the play's dual time patterns accounts for the real substance of the work. The nontemporal world lies out of time in simple being—a kind of eternity of feeling without motive or volition. The action of the characters on this plane is not unlike that of the sailors in *The Moon of the Caribbees.* In Nina and the men, despite their sophistication, there is something of the same drifting movement, through a series of shapeless, unfinished experiences. The inner plane of *Strange Interlude,* like the earlier one-act is in essence a plotless play, in that it relies on mood divorced from significant narrative development.

As in many of the earlier works, an act of will is seen as essentially destructive, leading often to a kind of madness. In *Strange Interlude,* all acts of will come to nothing, as Nina's revelation of her son's parentage has no consequences. The one important act of volition in the play—Darrell's decision to father Nina's child—is so strangely phrased as to make it appear as something far removed from the drives of either conscious or subconscious purpose. In the scene at the end of Act IV, when Nina confesses to Darrell that she has had an abortion and asks him to father her child, both characters seem will-less, as if they are moved by something outside themselves, and in such a way that neither can be held responsible for the decisions they are making. Nina begins by speaking sarcastically, refusing to admit any personal relationship with Darrell, calling him more often "Doctor" than "Ned." Her voice takes on a *"monotonous insistence,"* almost as if she were in a hypnotic trance. Under the pressure, Darrell, too, assumes *"a cold emotionless professional voice, his face like a mask of a doctor."* He stops calling her "Nina" and refers to her in the third person as "Sam's wife." As they speak, a sharp division of their personalities occurs, and each thinks of the other in terms of a role, "Sam's wife" and "Doctor," and each plays the roles assigned. It is as if the scene were played by four, rather than two actors:

> NINA   . . . This doctor is nothing to me but a healthy male . . . when he was Ned he once kissed me . . . but I cared nothing about him . . .

The same impersonal mode of address is reflected in her heard dialogue:

> This will have to be hidden from Sam so he can never know! Oh, Doctor, Sam's wife is afraid.

Darrell follows her in the indirect mode of address:

> Certainly Sam's wife must conceal her action! To let Sam know would be insanely cruel of her—and stupid, for then no one could be the happier for her act! [85-6]

A kind of scientific detachment overrides their problem. They are like strangers, speaking of mutual friends. Such drives of their wills as exist are buried in the unreal roles they play, and it is not until after Darrell has pointed out that the father must be someone who is not unattractive to Nina, that almost involuntarily Nina says that "Ned always attracted her." Her words which rise to the surface of their talk still maintain her role playing, but it is enough to bring the double image into single focus. Shortly Ned is able to think "he is Ned! . . . Ned is I! . . . I desire her! . . . I desire happiness! . . ." and to add gently, "But, Madame, I must confess the Ned you are speaking of is I, and I am Ned." To which she replies, "And I am Nina, who wants her baby." The role and the reality of both rejoin as the decision is made, but during the moments leading to decision the action of their wills is projected outside the two. It is as if they had made no deliberate choice affecting themselves.

In the sea plays, O'Neill has held that the sailors had no power of will, indeed no existence that was not in some way bound up with the life force moving in the sea. In *Strange Interlude,* the men hold a similar relationship to Nina. References to Charlie Marsden's mother, like those to Darrell's casual mistress and his research associate, suggest that the men have other points of contact, but none is strong or vitally dramatized. The men are defined only in relation to Nina, as if she, like the sea to the crew of the *Glencairn,* were the source of their being.* By the same token, Nina has no life beyond the men. Her relation to Sam's mother is contained in a single scene, one of the most moving in the play, expressed in terms of profound mutual suffering, but once its course is run, Nina moves on alone. Her relationship to her son's fiancée, Madeleine, produces an intense hatred, born of hysteria and jealousy. Yet, when Madeleine goes with Gordon, Nina is again left as she has always been, the sole central object of the devotion, now vestigially offered by Charlie Marsden, which her men have always paid her.

In the temporal narrative, the cause of that devotion is said to be sexual attraction. Her failure to give herself to her fiancé, the dead aviator, Gordon, brings her into conflict with her father who had counseled her against marrying him. In defiance of his dominance she gives herself to wounded men in the hospital where she is a nurse. Her marriage to Sam, her pregnancy, her abortion and her love affair with Darrell hold the action to specific sexual concerns, and when her son appears in the play as a young boy, his relationship to her is colored by sexual intuition: he catches her kissing Darrell and develops a hatred of him because he has taken Nina's love. In the final scenes, Nina's attempt to break the marriage of Gordon and Madeleine is again seen as a matter of sexual jealousy, and after Sam's death, her marriage to Marsden is specifically stated to be possible because it is sexless.

The concentration on Nina's sexual life might suggest that O'Neill saw her as a supreme "temptress," a femme fatale in the tradition of the mighty seductresses of stage and fiction. In fact, Nina has none of the traditional tricks of the vamp, nor is she especially beautiful or flirtatious. Such light conversation as she is permitted is arch but without vivacity or charm, and, while both she and Darrell speak and think with longing of the afternoons when they made love, little that is overtly sexual takes place between them. The reality of Nina's sexuality is revealed mainly by the desire of the men.

* Nina's son, Gordon, seen briefly as an adult in the last act is an exception. He is breaking from Nina to go with his fiancée. Sam's relation to his mother in Act III is limited to a brief, almost perfunctory scene of exposition, preparatory to the scene between Mrs. Evans and Nina.

There can be little question but that she feeds on the desire each of the men feel for her. Her own description of the process at the end of Act VI is explicit:

> My three men! . . . I feel their desires converge in me! . . . to form one complete beautiful male desire which I absorb . . . and am whole . . . they dissolve in me, their life is my life . . . I am pregnant with the three! . . . husband! . . . lover! . . . father! . . . and the fourth man! . . . little man! . . . little Gordon! . . . he is mine too! . . . that makes it perfect! . . . [135]

The predatory sexual need is recognized by the men. Marsden notes Nina's "strange devious intuitions that tap the hidden currents of life . . . dark intermingling currents that become the one stream of desire," [135] and he feels caught up with Sam and Darrell as one of her lovers, one of the fathers of her child. Darrell, on occasion fighting her, may hold that Nina has "used" his desire, yet he knows that he cannot escape her, that he has no will.* Thus, although he may try to make a life for himself away from Nina, her need is stronger than his, and he returns to fulfill his function of making Nina "happy," even though the active sexual phase of their life together is past.

Depending on whether or not she is receiving the devotion she finds essential, Nina is shown in one of two states of being. The first, the dominant mood she reveals in Acts I, II, IV, VII and VIII, is neurotic, tense, frustrated and vindictive. The second, the dominant phase of the other four acts, is contented, almost wholly at peace, as if she were moving deeply in the mainstream of life, filled with a current of vitality flowing in her like the power of nature itself. Notably, when she is in this mood, the men surrounding her are happy in her contentment. When she is in the other mood, they too are frustrated, and, in the case of Marsden and Darrell, attempt to break free from her power over them. Their well-being, in other words, is wholly bound up with hers. At the same time, it must be noted, that when she is completely fulfilled, Nina's life exists on the non-temporal plane of the play. Her satisfaction lies within her, is expressed in her thoughts, not her actions, and is described in terms of such recurrent forces as the tide and the seasons. On the other

* Cf. "her body is a trap! . . . I'm caught in it! . . . she touches my hand, her eyes get in mine, I lose my will! . . . [105]

hand, when she is not filled with such profound contentment, her neuroticism causes her to move in the temporal plane with actions that are essentially destructive of life, without belief or feeling, denying desire. Then she reveals a cruel and capricious willfullness, a power to hurt not only the men but herself. It is not that her need for the male desire is less, but that she is unable to receive it, as if she had been somehow made incapable of thirst, even though she is unsatisfied.

In this condition, lonely and afraid, she speaks most frequently of the ruling force of life as God the Father, a possessive deity, but one who is essentially indifferent. She says:

> I tried hard to pray to the modern science God. I thought of a million light years to a spiral nebula—one other universe among innumerable others. But how could that God care about our trifling misery of death-born-of-birth? I couldn't believe in Him, and I wouldn't if I could! I'd rather imitate His indifference and prove I had that one trait at least in common! [41]

Yet she is incapable of identification with such a God. She cries out to Marsden:

> The mistake began when God was created in a male image. Of course, women would see Him that way, but men should have been gentlemen enough, remembering their mothers, to make God a woman! But the God of Gods—the Boss—has always been a man. That makes life so perverted, and death so unnatural. We should have imagined life as created in the birth-pain of God the Mother. Then we would understand why we, Her children, have inherited pain, for we would know that our life's rhythm beats from Her great heart, torn with the agony of love and birth. And we would feel that death meant reunion with Her, a passing back into Her substance, blood of Her blood again, peace of Her peace! . . . Oh, God, Charlie, I want to believe in something! I want to believe so I can feel! [42]

As he had earlier in *Desire Under the Elms*, O'Neill here sees man's religious experience in terms of an opposition of God the Father and God the Mother. For Nina, when God the Mother rules, she can believe and feel; when God the Father takes command she can do neither. The indifference of God the Father leaves her empty but the life rhythms of God the Mother enable her to feel desire. For the men, when she is in the latter phase, Nina is more than a sexually desirable woman. She is, insofar as she can be so represented,

God the Mother in her own person. The point is made explicitly:

> Not Ned's child! . . . not Sam's child! . . . mine! . . . there!
> . . . again! . . . I feel my child live . . . moving in my life . . .
> my life moving in my child . . . breathing in the tide I dream
> and breathe my dream back into the tide . . . God is a
> Mother. . . . [109]

And again,

> There . . . again . . . his child! . . . my child moving in my life
> . . . my life moving in my child . . . the world is whole and per-
> fect . . . all things are each other's . . . life is . . . and this is
> beyond reason . . . questions die in the silence of this peace . . .
> I am living a dream within the great dream of the tide . . .
> breathing in the tide I dream and breathe back my dream into the
> tide . . . suspended in the movement of the tide, I feel life move
> in me, suspended in me . . . no whys matter . . . there is no why
> . . . I am a mother . . . God is a Mother . . . [91]

In *Lazarus Laughed*, O'Neill had shown God the Father as indifferent to human happiness, and as valuing man as he related to the
eternal process of life. By so much as Lazarus shares these qualities
he becomes God the Father incarnated on earth. In *Strange Interlude*, the other side of the pantheon is explored as Nina, in her
inner world, becomes God the Mother, at war with God the Father,
yet, in the end forced to accept the fact that her incarnation can
exist only in the strange dark interlude "in the electrical display of
God the Father." [199]

The dramatization of the quality of that interlude is dependent
on the double time pattern. To use O'Neill's term, in narrative
time, all the characters live in "unreal reality," moving meaning-
lessly toward their end. On the timeless plane, without reference to
motive and action, their existence takes on an aspect of eternity,
becomes in a measure an abstraction of relationships, both to one
another and to the essential force which determines their lives.
Nina's identity as the Mother God is dependent on her existence in
a world of feeling, on simple, almost vegetative being, on, in short,
her presence in the world defined and dramatized by the asides and
the soliloquies. In the last act, the asides occur much less frequently,
as Nina moves toward her end, and, in the autumnal garden, re-
laxes into a long peaceful twilight. Her sentient being comes to the

surface, the two time patterns combine, and the need for maintaining their duality lessens as the play's two realities merge and become identical. Time, at the end, no longer defines the external pattern. Life slips into an afternoon's sleep, and desire passes from the daughter of God the Mother.

The main contour of the drama, in its essential meaning, is similar to many less expansive works in O'Neill's past. Nina's attempt to discover and to belong to the force from which she takes her life, and the attempt of the men to belong to the God in her, is at heart O'Neill's primary theme. Its development in *Strange Interlude* is less poetically conceived than it had been in *The Emperor Jones* or *The Hairy Ape*, and O'Neill does not resolve it on the note of alienation and destruction that marks even the ending of *Desire Under the Elms*. Indeed, *Strange Interlude*, for all its novelty, is not obviously "theatrical." O'Neill has sought deliberately to control his tendency toward melodrama, to write in a more Chekhovian vein of a life pattern that does not end climactically, but simply wears away, decays in "smokeless burning." The play, of course, is not Chekhovian. O'Neill at this point in his career distrusted realism, and sought to give his play generality, symbolism and universality by direct expository means. He failed. Philip Moeller and Kenneth Macgowan spoke of the "new kind of dialogue" which the asides produced,* but the effect inevitably led toward a psychological case study, rather than toward important theological statements. O'Neill in his "Memoranda on Masks" spoke of the possibility of using masks to "express those profound hidden conflicts of the mind which the probings of psychology continue to disclose to us." At the same time, he spoke of masks as giving "a chance for eloquent presentation, a new form of drama projected from a fresh insight into the inner forces motivating the actions and reactions of men and women . . . a drama of souls . . ." and he described the value of masks as being "psychological, mystical and abstract."[2] In these

---

* Macgowan called the asides a device that "was more than soliloquy, and it did more than expose the thoughts of people. It was a living and exciting dialogue of a new kind. To the dramatic contrasts and conflicts of ordinary spoken dialogue O'Neill added the contrasts and conflicts of thought. There was the speech of Nina against the speech of Charlie, the thought of Nina against the speech of Nina, the thought of Nina against the thought of Charlie, and sometimes the speech of one against the thought of the other." Kenneth Macgowan, "The O'Neill Soliloquy," *The Theatre Guild Magazine*, February, 1929. [Reprinted in Cargill, 452.]

comments a tension is suggested between that which is purely "psy-chological" and that which is "mystical and abstract," a theologi-cally oriented "drama of souls." In a second article O'Neill said that *Strange Interlude* was "an attempt at the new masked psychological drama . . . without masks—a successful attempt, perhaps, in so far as it concerns only surfaces and their immediate subsurfaces, but not where, occasionally, it tries to probe deeper."[3] O'Neill's attempt to probe deeper led him inevitably toward theological, rather than psy-chological, considerations, and it is perhaps here as O'Neill suggests that *Strange Interlude* fails most signally. Although the essence of the theology is there, it is "masked" by the psychological intimations of the new dialogue. What is mystical and abstract in the work is obscured by the implication of purely psychological exploration. To write a religious drama, O'Neill needed to depart further from realism as he had done in *Lazarus Laughed,* and as he was to try twice again to do in *Dynamo* and *Days Without End.* Luckily, the failure of *Strange Interlude* to project its theology adequately did not mar, perhaps was the reason for, the play's success. Certainly, his two further attempts to write of man and God directly were failures, ones which led him to give over the attempt to find God and to take what amounted to a wholly new view of man.

Perhaps the most significant comment of the many O'Neill made about *Dynamo* was in a letter to Carlotta Monterey O'Neill, dated December 4, 1929,[4] in which he expresses concern that the play does not live up to the qualities he has found in his new marriage and so does not justify him in his wife's eyes. He describes the play as a backward step, and regrets the play is not truly a product of their marriage. In an unpublished letter to Joseph Wood Krutch, dated July 27, 1929, he again referred to the play as marking "a standing still, if not a backward move." He wrote that, having revised the work extensively for publication, he liked it better, but had decided that it should never have been written:

> It wasn't worth my writing and so it never called forth my best. But a good lesson for me. Henceforth unless I've got a theme that demands I step a rung higher to do it, I'm going to mark time and play the country gent until such a theme comes. It wasn't that I didn't have such themes when I wrote "D" but "D" was more de-veloped in my mind as a play and seemed an easy choice.

O'Neill correctly attributed much of the play's failure to the marital troubles which beset him during the time of its writing, and to his being unable to be in New York City during the rehearsal period. The play was completed in 1928 in France, where he and Carlotta Monterey had gone to wait out O'Neill's divorce from Agnes Boulton O'Neill. He did not return to the United States until 1931, when the Guild produced *Mourning Becomes Electra*. *Dynamo*, thus, is the only play O'Neill did not see through to production. Its significant failure is ample testimony to the importance of his presence in the theatre during pre-production periods.

In truth, however, *Dynamo* was an old idea by the time he wrote it, and it suffered something of the fate of *The First Man, Welded* and *The Fountain*, in each of which he had lost interest by the time of production. The play was conceived in 1924 while he was working on *Marco Millions* and *The Great God Brown*. He mentions it by title in a letter to Macgowan on August 19, 1924, and there calls the idea "queer and intriguing." It was intended for production by the Triumvirate, for on March 14, 1925, he wrote to Macgowan that the play should be produced in the Greenwich Village Theatre, not the Provincetown Playhouse where the ventilation was bad. "Imagine writing of the cosmic tides of Being when you're thinking of how nobody in the audience will be able to draw their own breath after Scene One!"

Work on *Dynamo* was stalled during 1926-27 while he wrote *Strange Interlude* and *Lazarus Laughed*. Not until August, 1927, did he have what he felt to be a completed scenario.[5] More delay followed, and he left for France after *Strange Interlude* opened with his notes for *Dynamo* in his pocket. The play was half-finished by April, 1928, and by September, shortly before he embarked on a world cruise, he sent Langner a script and elaborate production instructions concerning the sound effects and their meaning. He also announced that it was to form the first play of a trilogy on contemporary religious problems. Later he was to regret this announcement, of which the Guild and the newspapers made much. He wrote to Krutch, in a long postmortem, that the published text would throw light on his intention "which was psychological primarily in spite of the published quotes from my letters on the trilogy (I meant the word trilogy in the very loosest sense, three plays, entirely independent of each other but all written around the general spiritual futility of the substitute-God search) these quotes putting all the emphasis on the abstract scheme for the trilogy at the expense of the human drama in the foreground of our play, *Dynamo*. My fault again, I ought to know by this time that my letters are usually plays without any exposition and mislead or puzzle accordingly."[6]

The Guild accepted the play in October and produced it on February 11, 1929. It played for fifty performances, sufficient to satisfy the Guild's subscription audience and then closed. O'Neill continued to tinker, and, finally, rewrote it virtually in its entirety. The published script represents a radical reordering of scenes, the elimination of one character who appeared in the original production and much pruning and reshaping of the dialogue. None of these changes were tried out in the theatre, and it is therefore important to recognize that *Dynamo*, unlike any of O'Neill's other plays produced in his lifetime, is an unfinished work, one which never had its important final shaping for the theatrical machine.*

Furthermore, kept alive over a five-year period, *Dynamo* had evidently been blown by the changing winds of O'Neill's other plays, by shifts in his perspective and maturing attitudes. O'Neill was correct in saying that the play is a step backward, for the play belongs far more to the period of *The Hairy Ape* and *The Emperor Jones* than to the work of which he proved capable after *Strange Interlude*. As he wrote *Dynamo*, he was sketching the long autobiographical play to be called *Sea-Mother's Son*, and the first conception of *Mourning Becomes Electra* had already fired his imagination. *Dynamo* was written because it was there and could represent him in the theatre while the more massive works germinated.

In its structure, *Dynamo* is developed in a series of relatively brief scenes as were *The Emperor Jones* and *The Hairy Ape*, and much of the narrative material which expands the play beyond the length of its predecessors is not essential. Fife's baiting of Reuben with the lurid confession of a murder, for example, is an elaborate and unnecessary way of characterizing the older man as a freethinker. The fifteen-month gap between Acts I and II, which permits Reuben to turn from naïve idealist to cynical atheist offstage and allows time

---

* For example, the scene shift between Act II, scenes ii and iii, requires that the yard with its two practical houses be struck and replaced by the full powerhouse set. It is difficult to conceive how this could be accomplished in most theatres without an intermission. But an intermission clearly must follow scene iii, not ii.

for Reuben's mother to die, is also an expansion of little moment. The play feels like a shorter work and could easily have been more contained. Its central story, after all, is closely parallel to that of *The Hairy Ape*: the narrative of a man who turns from one God, because he has lost the sense of belonging, and comes in the end to another which destroys him. Without the picaresque elements of Yank's quest, Reuben's search has something of the same intensity and climaxes in the same sort of lurid destruction.

Although the final portrait is blurred, Reuben, whose name in the early scenarios was Benjamin,* is O'Neill's typical dreamer as the play begins. He has the sensitive face, and the weak mouth that characterizes the portraits of Robert Mayo and other quasi-autobiographical heroes. He is also developed in terms of his quest for a belief that will enable him to belong to an elemental life force, and, like many of the earlier heroes, he feels a special responsivity to the sea. In early scenarios for the play, O'Neill seems to have conceived of his destiny as similar to that of John Brown in *Bread and Butter*. The Reverend Light, considering his son's future, wants him to go to divinity school, but his wife wants the boy to have business training so that he may attain material success comparable to that of her daughters who have married successful business men. Although the daughters and sons-in-law were quickly eliminated, the image of the sensitive son torn between God and Mammon never disappeared entirely from the script.

From the incomplete first scenario, it is possible to see the outlines of the original conception of the play, the hero's turn from uncongenial materialistic success and from the life-denying Calvinist God of his father toward a substitute faith in the idea of electricity, which in the figure of the dynamo seemed a mysterious, feminine source of life. Although in the final version, O'Neill retained something of the mother's desire that Reuben should go into business and "marry a nice girl with money," the mother's materialism is not the

---

* The use of the names of the sons of Jacob has no clear meaning in the script. Reuben, as the first-born child of the loveless marriage between Jacob and Leah, was perhaps preferred to the name of Rachel's second son as being more appropriate to the domestic situation in the household of the Reverend Light. That Reuben slept with Jacob's concubine, Bilah, may have reflected in O'Neill's mind an appropriate parallel to Reuben Light's attempt to find mother substitutes in Ada Fife and her mother. On the other hand it may be simply that O'Neill's ear was more attracted to the trochee ending in "en" as it often was: Eben, Orin, Simon.

cause of her betrayal of Reuben. Rather, it is caused by her jealousy of her son's love for the neighbor girl, Ada. As O'Neill phrased the issue in an analysis to Benjamin de Casseres, "the boy's psychological struggle . . . begins when he is betrayed by his mother and casts her off along with his father's God; . . . he finally has to sacrifice the girl his mother hated to a maternal deity whom he loves sexually."[7] He noted that this story was three-fourths of the play and that it was a "human relationship" which counted.

Taken at this level, the play, although it is not to be entirely condoned, can at least be understood as the attempt of Reuben to recover his lost mother by immolating himself on the dynamo. In killing himself and Ada, he has gone through a ritual of self-purification, destroying the sources of his guilt and the vestiges of the Father God in himself so that he may be worthy of God the Mother. It is an ending not dissimilar to that renunciation and purification which marks Jim Harris's surrender of himself at the ending of *All God's Chillun Got Wings*.

Reuben's worship of the dynamo evolves from the conception that seems to have been the germ of the play, the essay by Henry Adams on "The Dynamo and the Virgin," that forms Chapter XXV of *The Education of Henry Adams*. There, Adams speaks of the dynamo as a moral force comparable to that which early Christians saw in the Cross. He writes of its humming as a warning to men to have respect for its power, and he adds, "One began to pray to it; inherited instinct taught the natural expression of man before silent and infinite force."[8] The dynamo's force, as Adams interpreted it, was a particularly American manifestation of the life force, seen in earlier times in Europe as the worship of Venus and the Virgin. "The Woman," he wrote, "had once been supreme," but in America, she had been covered with fig leaves by Puritans who knew that "sex was sin." Nevertheless, Adams noted, the Puritans knew that The Woman, in whatever representation she was made manifest, was not worshiped for her beauty: "She was goddess because of her force; she was the animated dynamo; she was reproduction—the greatest and most mysterious of all energies; all she needed was to be fecund."[9] The dynamo was, in short, an icon of God the Mother of whom O'Neill had written obliquely in *Desire Under the Elms* shortly before he began work on *Dynamo*, and who appeared in other forms in *The Great God Brown* and *Strange Interlude*, finished while *Dynamo* was still being written. In fact, the dynamo is the first, rather than the last, direct representation of the Mother God in O'Neill's theatre. That it proved somewhat obvious and clumsy for the Guild's audiences in 1929 is a token, perhaps, of how rapidly O'Neill's audiences were led toward sophistication, but taken in the period of its inception, it is no more clumsy or obvious than the crocodile god or the great ape in the zoo. Had the play in shortened form been produced in 1924 or 1925, it might well have succeeded as an exciting experiment.

In the interim between its conception and birth, O'Neill, reaching toward depth and complexity, hung more on the play than it could bear, and, as he acknowledged, he lost the essential psychological story.* He also, and without hope of restoration, destroyed his conception, derived from Henry Adams, of the dynamo as a real symbol of God. It is difficult to conceive of an interpretation that Reuben's death, arms spread as if crucified on the dynamo, is anything other than a triumphant return to the source of life. As he kills himself he cries "I don't want to know the truth! I only want you to hide me, Mother! Never let me go from you again! Please, Mother!" His is a plunge toward identity with the God-force. The sacrifice made, perhaps he belongs.

Unfortunately, the possibility of accepting the ending as it appears to have been intended is vitiated by the context in which Reuben moves—between the puritanical Calvinism of his father and the cracker-barrel atheism of Ada's father, Ramsay Fife. This conflict is a tedious one between, on the one side, Light's fundamentalist God whose vengeance is in the lightning, and whose exaction of the wages of sin is implacable and, on the other, Fife's belief that since the universe is Godless, the power of electricity is the sole source of life. It is a power which he jokingly equates with that of Lucifer. Fife and Light provide the intellectual polarities of the play, and, when he leaves his father, Reuben, by choosing the dynamo, chooses the atheism of Fife as his most profound religious perception. Since his final action reflects Fife's belief in electricity, Fife's atheism cuts across the meaning of the play's

---

* The chief aim of his revisions after the New York production was to reassert the psychological story, particularly the identity of Reuben's dead mother with the "Dynamo-Mother God." Evidently, in the production script, the conception was far from explicit. The matter is discussed in a letter to Krutch dated June 11, 1929.

last moments. The question is unanswered as to whether Reuben has committed an act of religious devotion or whether, out of madness and despair, he has followed Fife's atheistical teachings to their warped end. The situation is complicated by the presence in the person of Mrs. Fife of a Cybel-like goddess who dreams moonily throughout the play and whose feeling for the dynamo is like Reuben's. "I could sit forever and listen to them sing . . . they're always singing about everything in the world," she says, and hums to herself as the dynamo hums. Mrs. Fife sees the dynamo as essentially creative and intelligible while her husband denies it the power of a God except in jest. Thus with such conflicting opinions expressed as to the nature of the God which surround Reuben's story, his final act is unclear. No view, Reuben's or that of any other character, has supremacy at the play's end. The confusion was fatal and the play ends in an unresolved suspension: does Reuben find God? or does his death demonstrate "the general spiritual futility of the substitute-God search"?

The search for a substitute God was apparently to be the theme of the other parts of the trilogy whose titles were *Without Endings of Days* and *It Cannot Be Mad.* The third play was never written, and it is doubtful from O'Neill's description of the content of the trilogy whether the second play, which finally emerged as *Days Without End,* can be considered as thematically related to *Dynamo.* O'Neill wrote to de Casseres, "A general idea-title for the trilogy might be God Is Dead! Long Live—What? with science supplying an answer which to religion-starved primitive instinct is like feeding a puppy biscuit to a lion. Or something like that."[10] He discussed the matter more fully in letters to Langner and Nathan, to whom he wrote that *Dynamo*

> is a symbolical and factual biography of what is happening in a large section of the American (and not only American) soul right now. It is really the first play of a trilogy that will dig at the roots of the sickness of today as I feel it—the death of the old God and the failure of science and materialism to give any satisfying new one for the surviving primitive religious instinct to find a meaning for life in, and to comfort its fears of death with. It seems to me anyone trying to do big work nowadays must have this big subject behind all the little subjects of his plays or novels, or he is simply scribbling around on the surface of things and has no more real status than a parlor entertainer.

O'Neill's letter was published in the *American Mercury*, in January, 1929, and part of it was reprinted in the Guild's program for *Dynamo*. The credo, together with his instructions to Langner may well have guided critical and popular interpretations of the play, as he felt. Whatever the reason, *Dynamo* appeared to most to be concerned with the death of God, rather than with a man's attempt to find God the Mother in the dynamo's energy. The announced theme of the trilogy in effect canceled out the theme of the narrative, and the effect was—and to an extent still is—confusion confounded.

Dynamo, as its shape became more definite in O'Neill's mind, unquestionably had an effect on both *Strange Interlude* and *Lazarus Laughed*. The concept of electrical energy as being somehow equivalent to God is a recurrent image in both works, and Nina's presence as an incarnation of the Mother God in certain of the acts of *Strange Interlude* perhaps originated in the ideas behind *Dynamo*. By the same token, however, *Dynamo* was changed from its first conception by the two companion works. Clearly, the use of asides and soliloquies in *Dynamo*—O'Neill called them "Interludisms"—were not a property of the original design. It may well be that his partial failure to create in Nina a clear symbol of God the Mother caused him to try again and take up the *Dynamo* script in 1928 after it had lain fallow for several years. Certainly, *Dynamo* enabled him to explore the idea more concretely, more symbolically than he had been able to do with the psychological realism of *Strange Interlude*. In the final analysis, *Dynamo* is made up of sweepings from the O'Neill workshop, containing surprisingly flaccid writing, and an irrevocably ambiguous theme. He knew it. He stated flatly that " 'Dynamo' doesn't count," and swore that he had learned a lesson:

> Forty is the right age to learn! And I think my new work is going to show more poise, more patience with itself to reach at perfection, more critical analysis of itself and contemplation, more time given it for gestation and genuine birth, more pains. I've gone off half-cocked too many times, driven on to drive myself to write at any cost to the writing, then to finish and be done with it and start something new. It's time I achieved a more mature outlook as an artist—and now I know I have. Perhaps a complete upheaval, a total revaluing of all my old values was necessary to gain that attitude. Well, I've certainly been through that! Devil a doubt![11]

The new maturity was, in fact, at hand, but one more debt remained to be paid to the theory and practice of the Art Theatre. Not that *Days Without End* was written with Macgowan's principles in mind. By 1933, when he sent the script to Langner, he had already turned toward other subjects and was writing in a substantially different style, which, although it continued bold and direct, rooted out any obvious experimentation. Nevertheless, *Days Without End* is something of a throwback to the earlier experimental manner, and like the others, uses expressionistic techniques to explore the nature of man's quest for God. Although the question is important, it is impossible to determine whether O'Neill wrote his series of theological dramas because of some inner quest of his own, or whether he was led to these themes because the departure from realism showed him that they were there to be explored. Certainly all of his biographers make much of his being a renegade Catholic, and there can be little doubt that the Hound of Heaven pursued him at many times during his life. From the beginning, in his writing, there is revealed a sense of what George Herbert in *The Collar* termed "repining restlessness," in O'Neill's attempt to find for his heroes a point of faith in which they may rest. The faith rarely has significant ethical necessities. It is bred, rather, of the weariness of which Herbert spoke—the fatigue men feel far from their source, as they seek to return to what has created them. O'Neill's departure from the Catholic faith caused some of his personal restlessness, but he had left the Church early, as a boy, and thereafter, found in the sea something of the qualities he recognized as God. In *Dynamo*, Reuben speaks of the life in the sea, as he leans wearily against Mrs. Fife's shoulder:

> Did I tell you that our blood plasm is the same right now as the sea was when life came out of it? We've got the sea in our blood still! It's what makes our hearts live! And it's the sea rising up in clouds, falling on the earth in rain, made that river that drives the turbines that drive Dynamo! The sea makes her heart beat, too! [477]

The sea was no surrogate faith, and while he wrote of it, O'Neill's plays were simple and direct and lyric. With the new style, the presentation is no longer of men guarded in spite of themselves by the Sea-Mother. The techniques of expressionism demanded fuller awareness from his heroes; the plays of the experimental period show men roused to a greater consciousness of loss. The quest motif enters and with it emerges the agony of the search, the despair and the queer, torturous naming of a variety of manifestations of divinity to which the questers might belong. But the specifically religious themes come only as his theatrical style moves toward expressionism. For O'Neill, once he had gone "behind life," it was essential to find the life source.

Inevitably, the Catholic faith which he had known as a boy was one to be explored, but it is important to remember that shortly before he began serious work on *Days Without End*, he was sketching the autobiographical *Sea-Mother's Son*. Both the sea and Catholicism were, at the end of the 1920's, possible points of return. Both plays were filled with directly autobiographical material, and mark the first steps beyond the quasi-narcissism of the self-portraits toward direct autobiography. What perhaps conditioned his completion of *Days Without End* rather than *Sea-Mother's Son* was, first, that he had written *Dynamo*, to which *Days Without End* was an intended sequel, and second, that he had found Carlotta Monterey.

O'Neill's third marriage was for him a haven, embodying much of the relationship he had hoped for and tried to describe in so early a work as *Servitude* and more fully in *Welded*. The inscriptions of his plays, together with the letters to his wife that have been published in the volume *Inscriptions*, set forth this idealism fully. There, it is clear, that O'Neill tried many times to fulfill her request to write a poem. His inevitable theme was the perfection of their love and his own sense of fulfillment in it. Serena Royle, who played Elsa in the Guild production of *Days Without End*, felt that the play was O'Neill's poem to Carlotta.[12] Philip Moeller noted that both husband and wife acknowledged the play to be more hers than his, and that Carlotta hoped that someday O'Neill would return to the Catholic faith.[13] At the same time, however, as O'Neill's relationship with Carlotta deepened, he found it increasingly necessary to turn away from the world, toward himself and her for any real emotional and spiritual sustenance. The divorce from Agnes O'Neill was not a simple process, and O'Neill had become news. He fled with Carlotta and hid from the world until they could be married. He received his mail through intermediaries and refused to return to the United States. They set out on a world tour, which ended in a debacle in Shanghai when the press tracked him down and reported wild stories of his death. Not until July, 1929, when he finally was free to marry Carlotta, could he come safely from hiding, and even in the years thereafter he proved increasingly reclusive. At this stage in his life, as he moved into his forties, the tendency to introspection which he had always displayed dominated his behavior. All he now needed as a human being was his own life, peculiarly enclosed within the protective walls of his third marriage. He was not, at this juncture, far from autobiography. *Days Without End* takes an important autobiographical step at the same time as it attempts to hymn the marriage in which he found peace.*

It did not begin that way. In its earliest sketches, it was a close companion piece to *Dynamo*, duplicating in its narrative the action of a man for whom God is dead. O'Neill wrote,

> Mother worship, repressed and turned morbid, ends by becoming Death-love and longing—thus it is statue of Virgin and child, identification of mother and Elsa with Her, himself with child, longing for reunion with them through Mother Goddess than really drives him to suicide before statue of Virgin—while at the same time it is his old resentment against mother, against Elsa as mother substitute (infidelity) that keeps him from giving in to Catholicism—longing, confession. . . .[14]

Just as Reuben Light was alienated from his mother and sought in Ada and in Mrs. Fife substitutes which finally came to fulfillment in his self-sacrifice to the dynamo, so the hero of the sequel was to

* The recessive quality of the play and the marriage is suggested by O'Neill's use of a poem by Villiers de L'Isle-Adam, "A une enfant taciturne," which he copied as part of the dedication to Carlotta of the published copy of *Days Without End*. The poem reads,

> Since I have lost the words, the flower
> Of youth and the fresh April breeze—
> Give me thy lips; their perfumed dower
> Shall be the whisper of the trees.
> Since I have lost the deep sea's sadness,
> Her sobs, her restless surge, her graves—
> Breath but a word, its grief or gladness
> Shall be the murmur of the waves.
> Since in my soul a somber blossom
> Broods, and the suns of yore take flight—
> Oh, hide me in thy pallid bosom,
> And it shall be the calm of night!

The reference to the loss of the deep sea's sadness perhaps had for O'Neill a special relevance.

follow a similar course to his death, sacrificing himself to the Virgin in whom Mother and Wife become divinity. Henry Adams had taken the dynamo as a modern symbol paralleling the symbol of the Virgin in medieval life. Operating within the frame of reference that Adams provided, but shaping his action so that the new play's meaning would be closely related to that of *Dynamo*, it is probable that the hero's sacrifice would have provided a testimony similar to that provided by Reuben's death: to the death of God in modern society, but also more positively to the hero's reunion with God the Mother embodied in the statue of the Virgin. Probably, as was the case with *Dynamo*, *Days Without End* would have confounded itself between negative and positive implications.

The external forces operating on O'Neill's creation of the play perhaps made such an artificial, somewhat sterile conclusion impossible. The way to end the work remained a problem to the last. Through eight draft versions, the work was altered and no satisfactory conclusion reached. The heroine, Elsa, lived and died as did the hero, John Loving, who in the fifth draft of the play was split into two characters, John and his demonic alter ego, Loving. No other play O'Neill wrote proceeded with such uncertainty or remained in the final version so much a matter of trial and error. Even the title changed wildly from moment to moment, shifting from *Without Endings of Days* to *Without Ending of Days, Endings of Days, Ending of Days* and *On to Hercules* before O'Neill settled on *Days Without End*, calling to mind the phrase "World without End" from the Book of Common Prayer. The final title maintains an ambiguity in the pun: *"Without End"* means without ultimate spiritual goal, "endless" and "eternal." The alternative title, *On to Hercules*, was intended to suggest man as an eternal and heroic quester for a goal that was not to be found. *"Days Without End"* implies that a goal may exist, but the point is not made with conviction in the title nor in the play. Although O'Neill finally saves both John and Elsa and their marriage, and exorcises the doppelgänger, Loving, thus restoring John to his lost faith, the conclusion is without the force of truth.

That the ending remained unsatisfactory is perhaps because O'Neill did not function as a dramatist at all in the scenes leading to that point. The problem of how to end the play, of finding what meaning he really meant, obscured the fact that the ending arises from nothing and is not the climax of any significant development of character or narrative. Based on what precedes it, any conclusion would inevitably have been fully as arbitrary.

In developing the play, O'Neill transferred to his hero much of the artistic as well as the spiritual indecision which he felt at the time of its writing. No play of O'Neill's is so lacking in action, so wasteful in construction, so filled with needless changes of scene and undeveloped and uninteresting characters. The first act in John Loving's office and the second in his apartment do nothing but present straight exposition. The dialogue among John and Loving and the supernumerary partner, Eliot, and finally Father Baird is entirely devoted to what John has been in the past. The second act repeats the process for John's wife, Elsa, and her friend Lucy who has been John's mistress. The expository progression is carried on into the first scene of the third act, up to the point where Elsa belatedly realizes from John's description of the novel he is writing that the book is her husband's thinly disguised autobiography and that he has been unfaithful to her. When she walks from the house, the first—almost the play's only—significant action is taken. By Act III, scene ii, however, John is again discussing his spiritual struggle in the guise of telling the plot for his novel. In short, very nearly three-quarters of the play is consumed with a discussion of the spiritual condition of the hero and none of it is dramatized until John, in remorse that he has been the cause of his wife's crucial illness, turns to the Church and leaps toward faith. That it is not much of a leap is to be explained by the lack of life in the springboard.

John Mason Brown in reviewing the play in production noted that all the characters except John are "feeders," brought on stage to provide an opportunity[15] for some dialogue to occur, but having no dramatic function. Certainly the charge is just, as it relates to Eliot, the partner, Stillwell, the doctor, the maid, the nurse and John's inamorata, Lucy. Father Baird, John's uncle, has somewhat more to do as John's early Catholic mentor, but he plays no finally significant part in John's decision. The play's only action, setting aside a brief encounter between John and Elsa—who thereafter is *hors de combat* in a condition of delirium—comes at the end of Act III. In essence, the play is a four-act monologue by a man at a crisis of religious doubt. To make it possible for the theatre, O'Neill employs two tricks—splitting his character into a Jekyll and Hyde duality so that Faustian John and Mephistophelian Loving can debate the spiritual issue; and by having John write the autobiographical novel whose plot he narrates endlessly. If the contents of the novel sound a little like O'Neill's own rough notes for his plays, the point may be made that this is what they essentially are—character and situations for a play unwritten. O'Neill, dropping back to older theatrical times when the acts of plays were given titles, calls Acts I to III "Plot for a Novel," remembering perhaps the novelistic ambitions of *Strange Interlude*. Yet it seems clear that the real drama was O'Neill's attempt to write the play, a problem he transferred without much change or objectification to his hero.

The vapid dramaturgy is testimony that the play was written without real inspiration, and the details bear this out. The script is a compendium of ideas which derive from earlier plays. The questing hero, once again, is a modified self-portrait. The crude exposition of John's career [520] recalls a similar scene at the opening of *The First Man*. [554] Elsa in words clearly derived from Nina Leeds, describes John as her child, father, husband and lover, [518] and Nina is again recalled by Lucy's description of the overly deliberate way she seduced John which has some of the clinical tone of Nina's proposition to Darrell: "And I picked out this man—yes, deliberately! It was all deliberate and crazy! And I had to do all the seducing. . . ." [521] Elsa, although she has been married before, demands perfection of her marriage and particularly requires that her husband be faithful to her in words that recall Emma Crosby in *Diff'rent*: "I know he never had a single affair in his life before he met me. . . . I wouldn't have believed it of another man in the world, but with John I felt it was absolutely true to what I knew he was like inside him . . . It was what made me love him, more than anything else—the feeling that he would be mine, only mine, that I wouldn't have to share him even with the past." [522] Her ideal of marriage is virtually identical with that set forth in *Welded*:

> He said no matter if every other marriage on earth were rotten and
> a lie, our love could make ours into a true sacrament—sacrament
> was the word he used—a sacrament of faith in which each of us
> would find the completest self-expression in making our union a
> beautiful thing. . . . You see, all this was what I had longed to

> hear the man I loved say about the spiritual depth of his love for
> me . . . And I think we've lived up to that ideal ever since. I hope
> I have. I know he has. It was his creation, you see. [523]

Elsa's miraculous resurrection from the brink of death weakly echoes
the return of Miriam from the grave in *Lazarus Laughed*, just as
the duality of John and Loving brings to mind the opposition between Dion and Brown and the poet and nay-sayer who have occupied many of O'Neill's stages. Toward the end of the play, the concept of a controlling fate, reminiscent of the fate of the Mannons in
Mourning Becomes Electra emerges, [560] and the laughter of Lazarus is dragged in in such language as "Life laughs with God's love
again! Life laughs with love!" [567]—words that provide O'Neill
with a sufficient rhetorical thrust for his curtain line.

Days Without End, written without real craftsmanship or imagination, thematically arbitrary, if not confused, rephrasing old concepts and forcing them into the Catholic mold is the end of a line.
It is true that a sort of life moves occasionally in the play and, when
it does, the germ of new works can, in retrospect, be perceived. For
example, at one point, John describes a moment of conflict in his
novel in these words:

> That is, he saw clearly that this situation was the climax of a long
> death struggle between his wife and him. The woman with him
> counted only as a means. He saw that underneath all his hypocrit-
> ical pretense he really hated love. He wanted to deliver himself
> from its power and be free again. He wanted to kill it! [538]

It is a long journey from this to Hickey's monologue in *The Iceman
Cometh* and to the portrait of Con Melody in *A Touch of the Poet*,
but the idea is there, and it is new to O'Neill. Similarly, at the beginning of Act III, scene ii, as John talks about the Depression
period in America, he does so in words that anticipate the central
theme of the historical cycle, whose shape is even then coming to
mind: "[Americans] explain away their spiritual cowardice by whining that the time for individualism is past, when it is their courage
to possess their own souls which is dead—and stinking!" [542] But
such moments are few and the play remains without life. It was,
perhaps, O'Neill's most deserved failure,* and although it raised

---

* It should be noted that the play has been successfully performed in Europe, particularly in Ireland, where Yeats brought it to the Abbey Theatre.

critical controversy especially as to O'Neill's apparent embracement of Catholicism, the commentary amounted finally to little. It was not so much a question of spiritual salvation that mattered. The most profound question the play raises is one of the salvation of O'Neill's artistry which with this work seemed deeply in trouble.

IX
THE HISTORIAN

Mourning Becomes Electra (1929-31)
Ah, Wilderness! (1932)

1931—He returned at last to the United States.
At Sea Island, Georgia, he built "Casa Genotta," and settled in
to work on the long cycle of plays on American historical subjects.
There too, with the writing of *Ah, Wilderness!*, he began
the group of autobiographical plays that would crown his career.
Work continued with small interruptions through the 1930's,
but his health was failing and at times he was too ill to write.
He moved to California and in the hills near San Francisco
built Tao House, the last of his stately mansions.
In 1936, he won the Nobel Prize for Literature.
Eugene, Jr., now a meritorious classical scholar, married in 1931.
In 1943, Oona, who had been a well-publicized New York debutante,
married Charles Chaplin, a man of her father's age.
Despite his distinguished reputation, Eugene turned inward,
desperately trying to shut the world away,
battling sickness in his solitude, fighting the tremor
that concentrated in his hands and threatened to destroy
the one reality in his life, his writing.
The world darkened;
the war and his illness made his isolation intolerable,
but some light emerged: in 1945, Shane married,
and his son, born the next year, was named Eugene III.

DURING the period of its composition, O'Neill spoke less about *Mourning Becomes Electra* than he had about any other play he had composed up to that time, with the single exception of *Desire Under the Elms*. The pairing is perhaps a significant one, for the two plays have much in common—their use of Greek myths as a narrative base, their New England scene, the intense psychological focus of the subject matter, their historical perspective, their primary realism which avoids all the trappings of the Art Theatre and their inner conviction which in no little measure anticipates the mood of the late plays. Compared to the theological romances which surrounded them, the quality of these two plays is one of intense, even recessive concentration, bearing the quality of a private statement. O'Neill held them both close to his chest during their creation, as if he were unwilling to release them to the theatrical world until there was nothing more he was able to do with them.

O'Neill's mention of *Mourning Becomes Electra* in letters, even to his most intimate friends, is vague and general. To Joseph Wood Krutch on July 27, 1929, he wrote of the necessity for selecting a big subject for his art, and described his current project as one of the biggest ever attempted in modern drama, comparing it to plays by the Greeks and the Elizabethans in its possibilities. In the same letter he cried, "Oh for a language to write drama in! For a speech that is dramatic and not just conversation. I'm so strait jacketed by writing in terms of talk. I'm so fed up with the dodge-question of dialect. But where to find that language?" The cry presents the problem of matching the Greek theme with an appropriate dialogue—a problem which was to dog him after the production of the play. But nothing more is said of the nature of the work.

A similar statement to Benjamin de Casseres, to whom he wrote ordinarily with great candor, occurs in a letter dated April 20, 1930. He had, he said, finished the first draft of his new work, but he stated only that he worked on it harder than on any of his other plays. He had no idea when it would be ready for production. Not until August 23, 1930, did he reveal the subject matter in a letter to Manuel Komroff, and then his bare account—that it is a retelling of the Orestes story laid in New England at the close of the Civil War, that it is a "psychological drama of lust" and that it has more complicated relationships than any Greek treatment—was sent *"in strictest confidence."*

His secrecy and his refusal to predict a probable production season for the work suggests that he was conscientiously attempting to avoid the mistakes he made with *Dynamo,* which he let out of his hands before it was ready, and of which he talked too freely before its production. Now, living in France, under the shelter of his new marriage, he could seek to fulfill himself, taking all the time he needed, not going off, as he phrased it, "half-cocked," but struggling to achieve "a mature outlook as an artist." *Mourning Becomes Electra* was the first product of what he had termed "a complete upheaval, a total revaluing of all my old values."[1] The luxury of time for visions and revisions came about in part because O'Neill, after the success of *Strange Interlude* was in a good financial position, and in part because he was under no necessity of providing plays for a hungry theatre. The Theatre Guild could easily afford to wait and was as committed to O'Neill as he was to it. Thus the work proceeded slowly, arduously. Between November, 1929, and August, 1930, he told Komroff, he had spent 225 working days on the script, and it was then by no means completed. His plans for vacations in order to gain a perspective were frustrated by the intensity of his application to the task. Nothing, it seems true, existed in his life except the security of his marriage and his work.

Although he closed a circle of silence around the script, the composition of the play is better documented than most by a work diary he kept during the period of its creation. Published extracts from the diary date from spring, 1926, and continue through September, 1931, as he worked on the galley proofs shortly before the play was produced.

The first entry asks whether it is possible to get a "modern psychological approximation of Greek sense of fate" into a play intended to move an audience which no longer believes in supernatural retribution. Perhaps the Electra story or that of Medea would serve? A gap of two and a half years follows the original entry, and then in October, 1928, while on the Arabian Sea bound for China, he begins again on his "Greek tragedy plot idea," and appears to have settled on "Electra and family" as being "psychologically most interesting—most comprehensive intense basic human interrelationships." By November, the idea has taken firmer hold, and he notes that it will be important to give Electra a tragic ending worthy of her. With that he has found his area of contribution. "Why did the chain of fated crime and retribution ignore her mother's murderess?—a weakness in what remains to us of Greek tragedy that there is no play about Electra's life after the murder of Clytemnestra. Surely it possesses as imaginative tragic possibilities as any of their plots!" O'Neill's addition to the story, then, will be the punishment of Electra who "has too much tragic fate within her soul" to be allowed to slip from heroic legend into "undramatic married banality." With this definition of central narrative focus, he is ready to begin.

Other details followed slowly. By April, 1929, he had decided to set the story in an American historical setting, always provided that it remain a "modern psychological drama." The story needs time and distance, but the period is to be only a mask over the "drama of hidden life forces—fate—behind lives of characters." He recognizes that the Civil War with its heroic, even epic scale is the best possible period, permitting the desired modernity, yet also providing the time and distance essential to the tragic legend.

Quickly, thereafter, details of setting and time are sketched in: New England and the Puritan sense of retribution, the house that resembles with total architectural and thematic justification a Greek temple. He lists his departures from the Greek story at length in notes on the relationships of the characters to one another. At the end of the entry which conveys a sense of excited discovery, he is concerned to stress family resemblances, "as visible sign of the family fate," and he adds, "use masks (?)." By May the names of the characters are in order, developed on simple assonantal parallels with the Greek names, and he has found his title, using "Becomes" in the sense of "befits": "that is . . . it befits—it becomes Electra to mourn—it is her fate—also, in usual sense (made ironical here), mourning (black) is becoming to her—it is the only color that becomes her destiny." The play's structure is clear, a trilogy, and he has the titles of the first and third plays, *Homecoming* and *The Haunted*. He begins on the scenario in June, 1929, eight months after settling on the Electra story, and he has decided to write the first draft as "straight realism" in order to get the play into definitive form before worrying about the use of masks or soliloquies and asides.

The scenarios were finished by August, having raised a problem about which O'Neill was curiously bothered: how to arrange the murders so that no tedious police action would follow. The first draft was written between September, 1929, and February, 1930, and laid aside for a month. Rereading it in March, he found much of it "scrawny" but parts of it were "damned thrilling." What he had failed to provide was a "sense of fate hovering over the characters. . . . I get the feeling that more of my idea was left out of play than there is in it! In next version I must correct this at all costs—run the risk of going to other cluttered up extreme—use every means to gain added depth and scope." To get it, he determines to "use half masks and an 'Interlude' technique (combination 'Lazarus' and 'Interlude') and see what can be gotten out of that—think these will aid me to get just the right effect—must get more distance and perspective—more sense of fate—more sense of the unreal behind what we call reality which is the real reality!—the unrealistic truth wearing the mask of lying reality, that is the right feeling for this trilogy, if I can only catch it!" He writes an *aide-memoire* about the dialogue in which he reminds himself not to be too faithful to the speech of the historical period, and he discusses with himself the alternation of scenes, each play to begin and end with an exterior, and to create a rhythm between interior and exterior settings in the course of each play. One scene is to break this rhythm, that on Adam Brant's ship at the center of the second play: "(this, center of whole work) emphasizing sea background of family and symbolic motive of sea as a means of escape and release." The notes continue to discuss the chorus, the development of the South Sea Island motif, the desirable "characterlessness" of Peter and Hazel, the use of the chanty "Shenandoah" and the problem of controlling melodrama in the story. The entry ends with a reiteration of the diary's constant theme: "it must, before everything, remain modern psychological play—fate springing out of the family."

Between March and July, 1930, he wrote the second draft and records his fatigue on completing it. He promises himself a vacation, but within a week he is back at work, and on rereading the second draft, he finds its use of "Interludisms" cluttering. He writes himself a warning: "always hereafter regard with suspicion hangover inclination to use 'Interlude' technique regardless—that was what principally hurt 'Dynamo,' being forced into thought-asides method which was quite alien to essential psychological form of its characters—did not ring true—only clogged up play arbitrarily with author's mannerisms. . . . 'Interlude' aside technique is special expression for special type of modern neurotic, disintegrated soul—when dealing with simple direct folk or characters of strong will and intense passions, it is superfluous showshop 'business.' " A second rereading the next day convinced him that the masks introduced wrong connotations. The play's soliloquies were also troublesome. He sought to give them a stronger connection with the masks, and thought perhaps that by arranging soliloquies in a fixed structural pattern he could make both masks and soliloquies effective. He urges himself to "try for prose with simple forceful repeating accent and rhythm which will express driving insistent compulsion of passions engendered in family past, which constitute family fate." The next day, he began to rewrite the second draft and to cut it, a process he finished on September 16, 1930. The dialogue went well, and the omission of the asides was right. Now the play was to be laid aside to gain perspective.

Only four days elapsed. By the twentieth, he was back at work. The soliloquies and masks were bad because they introduced an "obvious duality-of-character symbolism quite outside my intent in these plays." They were dropped along with the asides, and by September 21, he knew that while the second draft had been profitable in that the "Interludisms" had given him new insights, it remained to rewrite the entire play "in straight dialogue—as simple and direct and dynamic as possible—with as few words—stop doing things to these characters—let them reveal themselves." The concept of the masks he decided to keep, but now he saw that make-up could achieve the effect he wanted—that of a death-mask "suddenly being torn open by passion." What the play needed, he felt, was a stronger structural rhythm: "Repetition of the same scene—in its essential spirit, sometimes even in its exact words, but between different characters—following plays as development of fate—theme demands this repetition." And he noted, "Mannon drama takes place on a plane where outer reality is mask of true fated reality—unreal realism."

The third complete draft was started two days later, on September 23, and finished by October 15. Finally, then, he took a vacation, returning to work in mid-November, expressing himself as "fairly well satisfied" with the last script, which he reworked until January 10, 1931. The script was typed, but by February 7, he found himself dissatisfied with the last revision, and began to prune back recent additions. The revision was finished on February 20, and he went to the Canary Islands, where on March 8 he read the typed script.

In type the script looked "damned good," although it was long and some sections needed rewriting, cutting, pointing up. This work was finished by March 26, and by April 9 new typed copies were prepared and the final script sent to the Theatre Guild. In August, 1931, he read the play in galley proof, and, after a lapse of nearly four months without reading the work, he found he was moved by it and that it had "power and drive and the strange quality of unreal reality I wanted—main purpose seems to me soundly achieved—there is a feeling of fate in it, or I am a fool—a psychological approximation of the fate in the Greek tragedies on this theme—attained without benefit of the supernatural." In addition he expressed himself as pleased with its structure as a trilogy. In August and September, he worked on the galley proofs. Some matters remained to be ironed out, but, as the Work Diary ends, he had little more to do that could not be accomplished during rehearsals. *Mourning Becomes Electra* was at last ready for the stage.[2]

The enormous consecutive creative effort was a staggering labor. Between May, 1929, when he wrote the scenarios, and February, 1931, when he finished the third draft, he was away from the script no more than two months and a few days. It was an expenditure of incredible strength that was to define, so far as the matter can be judged, the working habits of his mature years. The routines of ordinary life dropped away from him as he worked, and the result was very different from what had gone before.

Although the phrase "unreal realism" that runs through the diary suggests that some of the pretensions of the Art Theatre Show Shop still remained, the ruthless excision of the elements of technical exhibitionism for which he had become famous makes clear that the trilogy was truly the result of "a complete upheaval" of his old values, as he had claimed.

If further proof than that offered by the play were needed, a letter to Macgowan written on June 14, 1929, amounts to a renunciation of Art Theatre principles and of Macgowan's guidance:

> No more sets or theatrical devices as anything but unimportant background—except in the most imperatively exceptional case where organically they belong. To read *Dynamo* is to stumble continually over the sets. They're always in my way, writing and reading—and they are in the way of the dramatic action. Hereafter I write plays primarily as literature to be read—and the more simply they read, the better they will act, no matter what technique is used. *Interlude* is proof of this. I don't mean that I wouldn't use masks again in the writing if a *Lazarus* or *Brown* should demand it—but I do mean that my trend will be to regard anything depending on director or scenic designer for collaboration to bring out its full values as suspect. *Brown & Lazarus*, of course, don't. They will always convey more to a reader's imagination than any production can give. But I'm fed up with the show shop we call a theatre in the world today and I refuse to write any more which uses it. Constructivism and such stuff is all right for directors but it's only in an author's way. At least that's the way I feel now. Greater classical simplicity, austerity combined with the utmost freedom and flexibility, that's the stuff!

The new mood represented a deliberate retrenchment, a decisive and controlled return to a point of origin, a recession of art and spirit. It was an essential change if O'Neill was to continue to write for the theatre. He had built his reputation on the work he did for the theatre of the Triumvirate. He was famous for the furious breaking of theatrical icons as he plunged toward the goals the aestheticians descried with a literal, bold directness that shocked and excited his audiences. George Jean Nathan once said that audiences were more excited by the phenomenon of O'Neill than they were by his plays.[3] The comment is revealing and just. O'Neill was a "presence," and the première of one of his works was a national event, not quite in the category of other drama. Yet, as O'Neill disappeared into France, a new theatre, Depression-oriented and alive to social causes, emerged in the United States. It was not the kind of theatre in which O'Neill could take direct part, and it moved away from the tenets of theatrical art O'Neill had held. *Dynamo* failed and *Days Without End* would not write. Both plays were marred by failing power and a serious diminishment of genuine creative energy. Hence the need for a new direction.

Once before, O'Neill had come to such a pass after committing himself to the theories of George Pierce Baker and the 47 Workshop. Then after a period of doldrums, he gripped and forcefully changed direction. When he was young, it was an easy matter, much less difficult than the change after his commitment to Macgowan. Yet his process of return was the same in both instances. He recovered from Baker's doctrine by writing *Before Breakfast* in unrelenting imitation of Strindberg, with whom Baker was unconcerned. That play was a jumping-off spot for his first serious work.

As he had done before, he turned again from the false lights he had followed, selected a model he admired and in reworking older material found once more the sources of his creative life. This time, because the commitments of the past ten years were so strong, he could not do it easily. His own habits, his imagination, his involvement with brute size and with important themes, to say nothing of the expectations of his audiences, led him by no conscious route to the source of all tragedy, the *Oresteia* of Aeschylus, and to the later plays which spun off from it. From that primal fountain, he took new life.

The act, if such a subconscious thrust can be called an act, was, like all he did, daring and even presumptuous. Yet it can be seen in a historical perspective. *Mourning Becomes Electra* takes its place in the forefront of many modern dramas based on Greek themes and written by the greatest names in the modern theatre: Giraudoux, von Hoffmannsthal, Eliot, Sartre, Shaw among many others. It is part of the twentieth-century Greek revival; yet, for all this, the work emerged as the end product of private necessity. The irony presents itself: *Days Without End,* a story of salvation, meant damnation for its author; whereas his study of the damned brought his own salvation as an artist.

His modern parallels for the Electra story are appropriate and unforced. The Civil War and the New England Greek-style architecture provided a satisfactory time and place for his history.

The details of the relationships in the House of Atreus created the structure of the Mannon clan. The names, following the punning allusion to "Agamemnon" in Ezra Mannon, with its connotation of power and wealth, were developed by the alliterative scheme which at one time he tried to maintain in Lavinia by calling her "Elavinia." In the ancient servant of Electra he found Seth, just as Peter emerged from Pylades and Hazel from such innocents as Sophocles' Chrysothemis. In similar fashion, his chorus of gossips came naturally, if not entirely convincingly, from his source. Such details are obvious, but less so is O'Neill's remarkable fidelity to basic motifs of the myth: the presence of the sea in the Troy story finds congenial recapitulation in O'Neill's response to the sea and the islands of the South Pacific; the primitive need to honor the dishonored father, and the horrifying origin of the curse in the devouring of children is echoed in the fate of the Mannon heirs, Lavinia, Orin and Adam Brant; the sense of a haunted world, peopled with ghosts, and of men and women thrust into action by the dictates of a compulsive and destructive will and pursued by the furies of their own guilt are admirably brought into alignment with the legend. By the same token the trilogic structure parallels in its scope the cyclic evolution of the *Oresteia*.

In some thematic respects, *Mourning Becomes Electra* is closer to Euripides than to Aeschylus, owing to the Euripidean treatment, its psychological interest and the incorrigible self-justifications for acts of violence in which Euripides' Electra and Clytemnestra engage. The incest motif also has its strongest source in Euripides' *Orestes*. Nevertheless, O'Neill has worked freely with his Greek material, and, as he noted in his diary, in centering on Electra's destiny after the murder, he has added a fresh increment to the legend. Certainly, as the legend moves behind the work, pinning it to essentials, it makes the trilogy a larger play than it would otherwise have been. It is a greater achievement than *Strange Interlude*, and, compared with *Desire Under the Elms*, where similar legends, more deeply imbedded, heightened and generalized the story, the Electra plays seem more insistently impressive.

The mixture of ancient and modern, Aeschylus and Freud, has tended to obscure two important qualities of the trilogy. The first is that it is a history play, and an excellent one. Granted that the Civil War offered a luckily appropriate means of modernizing the post-Trojan-war period of the legend, O'Neill has been at pains to make his image of post-war New England faithful in spirit and fact to what it was. Without much apparent research and with stringently economic means he has created the past: a song, cannon shots celebrating the surrender, a few names from history, lilacs, almost inevitably associated through Walt Whitman's elegy with the death of Lincoln. In a letter to the Theatre Guild dated April 7, 1931, he noted that "the dialogue is colloquial of today. The house, the period costumes, the Civil War surface stuff, these are masks for what is really a modern psychological drama with no true connection with that period at all." His claim arises from the drive revealed in the work diary to find a substitute for elements of the legend and to make the play "modern," but in fact, those qualities of his imagination that were to make him turn for his last major works to America's historical past in order to explain its present were already operating to make the past a reality and to show therein an aspect of contemporary truth.

Thus, in his picture of the war, O'Neill creates unforgettable images that seem to have in them historical truth. Sometimes the treatment is elaborate as when Orin describes his falsely heroic charge in Act III of *The Homecoming*. The passage, which owes much to the anti-war literature of the late 1920's, also recalls Stephen Crane's description of similar heroics in *The Red Badge of Courage*. It is perhaps less a matter of what the war really was than what men felt it to be. Crane defined a point of view toward the past; O'Neill related it to his present. Past or present, the sequence has imaginative authority.

In less elaborate ways, his re-creation of the past proves unexpectedly strong. For example in describing his feeling of the safety of a military encampment at night, Ezra Mannon says,

> I can't get used to home yet. It's so lonely. I've got used to the feel of camps with thousands of men around me at night—a sense of protection, maybe! [53]

The words have no direct reference to the past, but they convey it vividly. The song "Tenting Tonight" sounds faintly in the mind, and the past awakes through the response of a character to his environment. As many who have lain awake in a barracks at night may recognize, the words are verifiable in present experience, and

again the passage seems true for both past and present. O'Neill's remark that the historical images are "surface stuff" is less than accurate. Even if his emphasis is on the present, at no point does the
play's modernity violate the image of the past. The two are con-
joined to convey truth.

A consequence of the play's being set firmly in historical time is
that the society in which the action moves is realized more fully than
in any of his mature works except *Desire Under the Elms*. Indeed, it
surpasses the story of the Cabots in its creation of the social community surrounding the central action. The presence of that community, like the historical past, is suggested by economical means. A
show curtain, painted to reveal the Mannon house surrounded by
woods, orchards, gardens, with a drive curving to its door past a
lawn, is in cinematic terms a long shot, giving a perspective on the
close-ups to follow. As the play begins, sounds from town drift on
the wind, keeping the presence of the community on the periphery
of awareness. The "chorus," small town civic types—carpenters,
sailors, clerks, doctors, gossips, visiting cousins, business men, min-
isters—convey something of the typicality of the chorus of *Lazarus
Laughed*, but they are not so diagrammatically conceived as to create a symbolic unit. They only sketch what O'Neill called "the human background for the drama of the Mannons." The background
is reinforced through the presence of Hazel and Peter, whose obligations to another kind of existence than that of the Mannons, is
always present; they have parents they respect and places to go other
than the central house. Finally, through Adam Brant, the world outside is brought into the play, and through him, the action is briefly
shifted from its focal center to his ship, *Flying Trades*, anchored in
the Boston harbor.

Both the historical frame and the full social context prevent the
play from becoming like *Strange Interlude*, a drama that exists only
in a limbo of purely personal emotions. The fact has important consequences. Lavinia's final act is strong in part because she lives in an
inhabited world. Unlike the Hairy Ape, she is not driven out by
faceless voices. Her needs are created by the society she inhabits, and
because her world has meaning, her self-inflicted punishment, a rejection of that world, gains significance, if not universality. Much
the same may be said of the initial isolation of the Mannons.

Legend, its parallel in history, and a fullness of social framework—each contributes new value to the play. To this list must be added the extensive use of Freudian psychology. O'Neill denied any obligation to Freud. He was irritated when critics saw Freudian patterns in *Desire Under the Elms,* and, after Barrett Clark had objected to what he felt was the too explicit Freudianism of the trilogy, he replied in aggrieved tones,

> . . . I find fault with critics [who] read too damn much Freud into stuff that could very well have been written exactly as is before psychoanalysis was ever heard of. . . . After all, every human complication of love and hate in my trilogy is as old as literature, and the interpretations I suggest are such as might have occurred to any author in any time with a deep curiosity about the underlying motives that actuate human interrelationships in the family. In short, I think I know enough about men and women to have written *Mourning Becomes Electra* almost exactly as it is if I had never heard of Freud, Jung or the others. . . . I am no deep student of psychoanalysis. As far as I can remember, of all the books written by Freud, Jung, etc., I have read only four, and Jung is the only one of the lot who interests me. Some of his suggestions I find extraordinarily illuminating in the light of my own experience with hidden human motives.[4]

Freud, however, had been part of his knowledge since at least the early days of the Provincetown Players, when Cook and his wife had written a satire on the pretensions of Freudian cultists, called *Suppressed Desires.* More importantly in 1926, he had taken part as a subject in Dr. G. V. Hamilton's research into marital problems, and at the conclusion had received a brief "psychoanalytic" counseling from Hamilton. The sessions, which lasted only six weeks, were conducted in the traditional manner of Freudian analysis, with the patient on a black leather couch. Although the principal matter of concern was to put an end to O'Neill's excessive drinking, O'Neill told Macgowan that he had learned he was suffering from an Oedipus complex.[5] The Freudian world was professionally opened to him through Hamilton.

Hamilton's survey, *A Research in Marriage,* was published in 1929, the year O'Neill began serious work on *Mourning Becomes Electra.* Perhaps more readily available to him, and certainly more readable, was a popular book derived from the same series of interviews and written, in collaboration with Hamilton, by Kenneth Macgowan, who like O'Neill had offered himself as a subject for the interviews. *What Is Wrong with Marriage*, also published in 1929, is essentially Macgowan's book. In a preface, Hamilton acknowledges that Macgowan had made himself a member of the research team, and that he had contributed greatly to the analysis of the materials for their human, rather than for their clinical value.*

Chapter IX of Macgowan's book is titled "Oedipus Rex"; Chapter X is "The Tragedy of Electra." Macgowan defines the Oedipus complex in these terms:

> You get a mother complex, in most cases, because your mother loved your father too little and loved you too much. It was as though she said at your birth: 'I don't love my husband, so I'm going to concentrate all my affection on this man-child of mine.' . . . The kind of mother who creates this complex—which Freud named for the Greek king Oedipus who unwittingly killed his father and married his mother—not only develops too great a love for her in her son. She goes on cultivating this abnormal fervor, and dominating his life . . . so tenaciously that often he cannot look on any other woman with longing—or at any rate with enough longing to make him break his chains.[6]

A little later, he speaks of the son's reaction to the taboo of incest as he feels sexual stirrings toward his mother, and of his attempt to find as a mate a woman who is either physically or temperamentally like his mother.

Somewhat less at ease in his analysis of the Electra complex, Macgowan recognizes that there is no term in English such as "father's girl" which carries connotations similar to "mother's boy." Without formally defining the complex, he notes that if a mother continually belittles her husband in the eyes of his daughter, thus destroying the child's image of her father, not only will the child be unable to marry happily, but "The consequences are likely to follow through a century." He narrates the story of a family whose great-great-grandmother ridiculed her husband before her daughter, and describes its consequences in similar patterns of behavior and similar unhappy marriages through several generations. "Here, indeed," he concludes, "were the sins of the mother visited upon the children even unto the fourth and fifth generations."[7]

While there is no evidence that O'Neill read Macgowan's book,

---

* For a detailed account of the influence of the study by Hamilton and Macgowan on the trilogy, consult Doris M. Alexander, "Psychological Fate in *Mourning Becomes Electra*," *PMLA*, LXVIII, December, 1953.

the probability is that his own participation in the research, the fact of his divorce and new marriage, together with his continuing friendship with Macgowan, led him to the work. The matter is of no great concern, for much of what was in the book undoubtedly was discussed at length.*

O'Neill at moments comes very close to Macgowan's simplifications, as when Mannon says to Lavinia, "I want you to remain my little girl—for a while longer at least," [51] or when he tells Christine, "I tried not to hate Orin. I turned to Vinnie, but a daughter's not a wife." [55] O'Neill is right in asserting that as a dramatist, and therefore presumably something of a student of human nature, he will necessarily see patterns that reflect Freudian truths. Yet this explanation, while it satisfies for Shakespeare and for Sophocles, does not quite relieve O'Neill of indebtedness to psychoanalytic theory, which loomed large in his life in the years immediately preceding the writing of the trilogy. Hamilton and Macgowan at least brought Freud well into his range of vision, and, perhaps unconsciously, he permitted a certain clinical definition of human relationships to creep into the play, as for example Christine's line to her daughter, "You've tried to become the wife of your father and the mother of Orin! You've always schemed to steal my place!" [33]

To write "a play containing a modern psychological approximation of the Greek sense of fate" caused O'Neill to substitute Freud for Apollo. The consequences to the trilogy were curious. O'Neill relentlessly analyzes the lives of five persons at the center of his drama. While Peter, Hazel and the townspeople are deliberately characterized by purely external means, and Seth is left on the edges of the action, Lavinia, Christine, Orin, Ezra and Adam are placed in a crucible. They are concerned with nothing but themselves, and even that concern is limited to the psycho-sexual problems which they all fatally share. The psychoanalytic approach makes such concentration possible, perhaps inevitable, and it is extraordinary that a play of this length, with so small a cast and so little variety of subject matter, can hold an audience for the length of such remorseless investigation. That it works is because, with the psychoanalytic lead, O'Neill provides an essentially *purgative* action. Whereas nothing happened to Nina Leeds, much happens to the Mannons. They dis-

* Cf. Gelb, 596: " 'In our circle,' Macgowan recalled, 'the interviews were the table topic of the day.' "

cover, they grow, and they change; and what happens to them is therapeutic as psychoanalysis is therapeutic.

For example, when Ezra Mannon returns from the war, he sits with Christine on the steps of the house. He tells her of his war experiences, of his longing for her, of his hope for a better marriage in a long quasi-soliloquy similar in situation and emotional content to that which Ephraim speaks to Abbie. As a scene it is among the most effective moments of the play, but what is perhaps most noteworthy about it is that Ezra, although he speaks to Christine as his wife, also asks of her the services a patient might ask of an analyst. He cannot look at her and asks her to shut her eyes so that she may hear him neutrally, dispassionately, as a psychiatrist might, and his words move in a free association around the pivots of loneliness and desire. It comes to nothing; she will not help him or try to understand. Even so, his attempt to purge himself by speaking his truth is a way of finding release from his interior torment.

Orin's long written confession, which relates the history of the Mannons' crimes, has something of the same motivation—the psychoanalysis of a family which may lead to purgation. He tells Lavinia, "I've tried to trace to its secret hiding place in the Mannon past the evil destiny behind our lives. I thought if I could see clearly in the past I might be able to foretell what fate is in store for us." [153] He has gone with Lavinia to the Islands that she might purge herself of her repressions and her sense of guilt, and he has come home to purge himself. Lavinia says, "You told me that if you could come home and face your ghosts, you knew you could rid yourself forever of your silly guilt about the past." [141] At the play's climax, when Orin attempts to force his sister to the inevitable act of incest, the scene takes on something of the quality of a classic recognition scene. Orin, the course of his self-discovery completed, loves his sister who is his mother, the ghost of the mother of Adam Brant, Marie Brantôme, and also "some stranger with the same beautiful hair—" [165] and, although his attempted seduction dies in its own disgust, it wrings from him the final plea for purgation: "Vinnie! For the love of God, let's go now and confess and pay the penalty for Mother's murder, and find peace together!" [165] A similar realization that peace can be obtained only through payment comes to Lavinia when, crying out to Peter to love her, she calls him by Brant's name, "Want me! Take me, Adam!" [177] As O'Neill insists, she is betrayed by her own subconscious, and recognizing its truth forswears love in her lifetime.

The course of purgative action, concentrated on the raising and recognition of submerged truths, while it can be paralleled in Greek and Elizabethan tragedy, is, if only by virtue of its concentrated and psychoanalytic phrasing, given a "modern" quality. Macgowan, in *What is Wrong with Marriage*, had said that men with Oedipal complexes seek to marry women like their mothers, and added that they will have a chance to be happy if the woman is physically like the mother. He does not hold out the same hope for women with "Electra complexes," although he recognizes that they will attempt to find happiness by marrying men like their fathers. O'Neill, translating the theories into a specifically incestuous context, sees in them a twisted thrusting for happiness and for a purge that at best kills desire.

In the course of the action his characters find no peace nor adjustment; the long analysis they undergo brings no satisfaction. That this is so is because O'Neill, while accepting modern psychoanalytic theory, still holds to the idea of crime and punishment that he inherited from the source in legend. In tragedy, human crime is punished by the Gods who control human destiny. A divinity shapes the end. O'Neill understands that psychoanalysis can mean an end to repression, and he causes all the Mannons to seek such an end, but he does not permit purgation to occur. Relying heavily on the Calvinistic traditions of the New England Puritan culture, his final view of the Mannons is as a dynasty bound as if by a divine edict to its destiny. "Bound" is the operative word in Seth's chanty "Shenandoah," and the repressions of Puritanism are constantly recalled through the presence of the spying townspeople, through the house and the ancestral portraits, and through the longings of all the Mannons for a different condition: for flowers, for the freedom of the sea, for the Blessed Islands. Yet they are bound as if they were in fact controlled by an angry God. The tangled web of love and lust in which they struggle is called an "evil destiny" that shapes their lives. Macgowan had spoken of a similar curse brought to families whose women had "Electra complexes," but O'Neill makes of the complex more than a psychological problem, by causing it to lead as the course of destiny in the *Oresteia* leads toward judgment, punishment, expiation of crime. O'Neill is careful to avoid significant reference to any deity as an agent of fate. Constantly the play is redirected from thoughts of God toward human responsibility. When Hazel speaks of God's forgiving Lavinia, Lavinia replies, "I'm not asking God or anybody for forgiveness. I forgive myself!" [174] In the same spirit, she judges, condemns and punishes herself. In this, however, she acts as her own "God," rather than as her own psychoanalyst. The promise of purgation offered by psychoanalysis is finally vitiated by the drive toward self-inflicted punishment. For all its Freudian modernity, the action is controlled by the dead decrees of Olympus.

The deliberate elimination of the Gods is perhaps the clearest sign of O'Neill's determination to make of his version of the Electra myth an uncharacteristic kind of play. In the context of his other plays written in the twenties, it is an altogether startling phenomenon. His theological plays for the Art Theatre had all been concerned with what O'Neill called the "Big Theme," the quest for God or a God substitute. Now the Gods are gone except for the atavistic traces they have left in the basic legend. What is more, no one seeks them: the motif of the questing dreamer is notable by its sudden absence. The religious concerns that emerge from the play are matters of historical place, a part of the background, but not a part of the play's thematic center. And no one in this study is touched with poetry. O'Neill has shucked off all his most characteristic thematic material as he turns toward a new kind of study. Except for *Days Without End,* he never returned to the old ways.

In place of former concerns new images arose and a new concept of human destiny emerged. In what O'Neill in his work diary called the "center of the whole work," the scene on Adam Brant's ship which comprises Act IV of the second play, *The Hunted,* certain elements of the new direction can be examined. Here, for a moment, O'Neill returns to the mood and manner of his early sea plays, but he created only a faded image. The scene reveals the afterdeck and, later, the cabin of Brant's clipper ship, *Flying Trades,* at anchor in Boston. Moonlight silhouettes the rigging, and from a neighboring ship the chanty "Shenandoah" drifts over the water. On the dock sits an old, drunken chantyman whom O'Neill describes in terms reminiscent of his former poet-hero: *"he has a weak mouth, his big round blue eyes are bloodshot, dreamy and drunken. But there is something romantic, a queer troubadour-of-the-sea quality about him.*" [102] Now, the poet, formerly O'Neill's constant hero, is old and useless, an insignificant figure on the edge of tragedy, as if Hamlet had become the Hell-Porter in *Macbeth*. He sings a chorus of "Shenandoah" and drunkenly laments the loss of his cash. Adam Brant, from the deck, orders him to keep quiet. They talk, the chantyman bragging of his ability to bring a crew into working order with his singing. He laments the coming of steam to ships and the death of the old days. With an unconscious word of prophecy, he says lugubriously, "Everything is dyin'! Abe Lincoln is dead. I used to ship on the Mannon packets an' I seed in the paper where Ezra Mannon was dead!" [105] He praises Adam's ship, and then drunkenly disappears singing the chanty, "Hanging Johnny": "They say I hanged my mother, / Oh, hang, boys, hang!" The exit of the chantyman is the last glimpse O'Neill was to give his audiences of the protected children of the sea. Thereafter, as *The Calms of Capricorn* was to attest, the sea was for drowning.

Next, Christine comes to Adam, and the scene gives way to frantic, melodramatic plotting. Christine is discovered as a murderess: "I'd planned it so carefully," she says, "but something made things happen!" The words echo Simeon Cabot's: "It's allus somethin'. That's the murderer," but here no sense of a directing life force is evident. Their own weaknesses, qualities Adam calls cowardice, have brought them to this desperate moment. Their loss is great. Adam must give up the ship he cares for more than the world. Earlier he has told Lavinia that to him ships are like women and that he loved them more than he had ever loved a woman. Now, he is aware that the sea is through with him. "The sea," he says, "hates a coward." What is left for them is to dream of happiness and safety on the "Blessed Isles" of the South Seas to which they plan to escape.

The image of the Blessed Isles is derived, in all probability, from the scene of the second book of *Thus Spake Zarathustra*. O'Neill, however, has made no further use of Nietzsche's philosophy, except to suggest that the islands, like the sea, like the longed-for mother, are all one, and that in them man can sink into rapture and forgetfulness. The description of the islands carry into the play some of the feeling of Dionysian ecstasy so pronounced in *Desire Under the Elms*. Ephraim had said to Abbie, "Sometimes ye air the farm an' sometimes the farm be yew," [236] and for both Orin and Adam, Christine is the embodiment of the beauty, security and peace of the earthly paradise. In *The Hunted*, Orin, telling his mother of Melville's *Typee*, speaks of a dream that came to him in a delirium. He was on Melville's islands, alone with his mother: "And yet I never saw you. . . . I only felt you all around me. The breaking of the waves was your voice. The sky was the same color as your eyes. The warm sand was like your skin. The whole island was you." [90] To all the Mannons, even Ezra, who proposes that he and Christine take ship to find such an island, the symbol of the Islands means the same hope. Yet in the tension of the moment, Adam, at least, appears to know that the Islands are an illusion. He speaks of them thirstily:

> I can see them now—so close—and a million miles away! The warm earth in the moonlight, the trade winds rustling the coco palms, the surf on the barrier reef singing a croon in your ears like a lullabye! Aye! There's peace, and forgetfulness for us there—if we can ever find those islands now! [112]

His last sentence denies their hope, and shortly Orin, who with Lavinia has been listening at the cabin skylight, torn with rage that Christine has shared the dream of the Islands with her lover, shoots him. Then hope stops. As he bends over the dead man, he is struck by the resemblance to his own face and anticipates his destiny: "He looks like me, too! Maybe I've committed suicide!" [115]

The scene awakens many echoes of earlier themes and images in O'Neill's plays. The Blessed Isles lie beyond the horizon, their intimacy with nature creating in the natives a freedom from sin and a closeness to a life source. Their essence is hope, as similar concepts gave "hopeless hope" to earlier questers. Now, however, hope is not even "hopeless." No one believes in the Islands. When Lavinia and Orin go there after Christine's death, their influence transforms Lavinia's personality, turning her from her martinet, military self to a woman who is startlingly like her mother but their effect is transitory. Within three days of her homecoming her repressions have returned. For Orin, there is no change whatever. The dream of the Blessed Isles is a sham, and since it is, conviction that the Islands, somehow, are set at the source of life, all feeling that the Islands are God—concepts that were urgently held in many earlier plays—are absent here. The Islands are only a refuge from a new and more urgent compulsion: to atone for guilt.

As the old dream ceases to have sustaining reality O'Neill shifts from theological and philosophical problems to ethical ones. In *Strange Interlude*, for all its emphasis on sexual behavior, nothing turned on an ethical dilemma. No blame attached to Nina for her early promiscuity; no questions beyond clinical speculation were raised with reference to her abortion or to her adultery. *Mourning Becomes Electra* is very different and very new. The only earlier hint of such concerns was in the ending of the trilogy's progenitor, *Desire Under the Elms*, when Abbie and Eben accepted the guilt of their crime and their punishment. At that point, the theological implications of the play lost their strength. The lovers became their own persons, not the creatures of the forces expressed through the earth. In the trilogy, hope being gone, what is left is damnation, an acknowledgment of guilt and acceptance of the consequence: human obligation. In the shipside scene, the love, which still perhaps contains an element of hope, of Lavinia and Christine for Adam, as well as the love of Orin for Christine, is perverted and turned into hate. Guilt follows in the course of the willful actions of the guilty. Now, for the first time in O'Neill's dramas, the will begins to play a significant role. His earlier studies of obsessed men, such as Captain Keeny in *Ile* or Captain Bartlett in *Where the Cross Is Made*, were studies of madness, men who forced themselves to move beyond their limits and to deny their destiny. What is perhaps most horrifying in *Mourning Becomes Electra* is that no one, not even Orin as he comes to the point of suicide, is insane. All the actions are deliberate, the product of desire energized by ruthless purpose.

The new commitment to will and its human consequences creates for O'Neill a new set of images, both poetic and theatrical. For one, there is the image of the desolate emptiness at the bottom of the sea, expressed in Orin's words to Hazel: "The only love I can know now is the love of guilt for guilt which breeds more guilt—until you get so deep at the bottom of hell there is no lower you can sink and you rest there in peace!" [160] The sea, which even so recently as *Dynamo*, had been thought of as a source of all life, is now hell itself.

Hell is reached through a dark doorway. When Lavinia Mannon moves to punish herself, throwing out from the house all the flowers, nailing up the shutters and turning her back on love, she marches through the door of the house that closes behind her. The image of the door, dividing life from death, sanity from madness, hope from despair, love from rejection, will become in the late plays one of O'Neill's principal images. The sound of its closing here sets the seal on Lavinia's punishment and fittingly climaxes this play of the damned.

Mourning Becomes Electra, perhaps O'Neill's most secular play, is also his least symbolic work to date. Such symbols as exist in the play, the house, for example, or the portraits, or the flowers, are all related to the human beings at the central focus. Now, none of the conflict between character and symbol that beset many of the minor works and even such major plays as *Strange Interlude* enters to plague this study of crime and retribution. There are no ambiguities; nothing is vague or suggested. The characters are drawn precisely, their story fully told, and they move toward a comprehensible and convincing destiny. Thus O'Neill returned to his point of origin, to the realistic theatre, from whence, with the single exception of *Days Without End*, he never again departed.* In this, perhaps, had he been alive to know of it, George Cram Cook might have felt a small triumph. Had he not said years earlier, in 1916, when the Provincetown Players produced *Thirst*, that O'Neill was a realist, not a writer for the Art Theatre?

The heart of an artist's mystery cannot be plucked out. Although external qualities of his imagination reveal themselves for analysis and evaluation, its generative powers hide its nature even from its possessor. It is a deep tidal current whose force and direction can be only dimly traced by the movement of surface waters. The exhausting labor of writing *Mourning Becomes Electra* was a disciplining of the imagination, a prolonged, painful contraction, a brutal reining-in of the self. For a decade, justified and encouraged by the belief of the partisans of the Art Theatre, O'Neill had written romances. His friends had pointed to the romantic drama as a way for the Art Theatre to move, and for O'Neill, starting from picaresque tales that asserted the life force of the sea as a God, the development toward the extravagant climax of *Lazarus Laughed* and the anticlimax of *Dynamo* was in the context of his time as inevitable as it was self-betraying. Yet O'Neill, despite a literary taste formed on Jack London and the turn-of-the-century British poets, was no romancer. Against the continuous expansion of his dramas

---

* An exception is the use of soliloquies in *More Stately Mansions*.

in length and narrative, there worked a desire to explore a small subject matter within clearly defined limits. The characteristics of his handwriting, tiny, chiseled, closed, bears symbolic testimony to the fact that his writing was really dedicated to exploring a private world, the life of a few people shut in a dark room out of time. To stretch the imagination and journey to Bethany, Xanadu, Spain or mysterious tropical forests was wrong. Whatever their numerical size, O'Neill's casts are essentially small family units. The new approach to characterization that had begun with *The Great God Brown* and *Strange Interlude* takes him inward and downward toward himself, and the plays become increasingly autobiographical. The limits narrow; the subject becomes what lies within himself. The artistic aim is no longer to find God but to know that subject completely. Thus, imagination contracted, and the discipline of *Mourning Becomes Electra* bore unexpected fruit.

There was first paralysis. *Days Without End* was a work which he forced to completion, but there is no freedom in it. The work, the last of the theological romances, the final tracing of man's quest for God, is lifeless, contrived; it is knotted, as if in some way the exhaustive work on the trilogy had produced a spasm of the imagination which left O'Neill powerless to continue.

Yet release came. Not for the play he fought to an end, but for another, one in which the imagination found a different outlet and moved easily forward to another country. In September, 1932, while he labored at the third draft of *Days Without End*, he awoke remembering the dream of a play. In a long day's work, he wrote out the scenario of *Ah, Wilderness!*, and within six weeks had completed the play.* "Only once before," O'Neill said, "has a plot idea [that of *Desire Under the Elms*] come to me so easily. I wrote it more easily than I have written any other of my works. . . ."[8] In the midst of the contorted, jammed creative work on *Days Without End*, the easy letting-go seemed almost miraculous, a matter for wonder that the imagination could slip its chain and work so spon-

* Gelb, 761. Langner, 282, says the writing required only four weeks. Clark, 137, quotes Burns Mantle as saying the first draft was completed "within a month" and that it was virtually the final form of the play. The script, together with that of *Days Without End*, was submitted to the Theatre Guild at the end of July, 1933, and was quickly put into rehearsal. It opened after a brief out-of-town try-out on October 2, 1933.

taneously. The play, however, was the first fruit of the self-discipline of *Mourning Becomes Electra*, and, while the ease was deceptive, the result was prophetic.

Ah, Wilderness! was not entirely the result of a sudden thawing of the imagination. In June, 1931, approximately a month after he and Carlotta O'Neill had returned from their long European exile, the two returned for a day to New London. O'Neill at first looked in vain for his former home, "Monte Cristo Cottage." When he found it, small and unimpressive, surrounded by new construction, he felt it a pitiful thing as the sources of memory revisited often seem. Mrs. O'Neill called the house "a quaint little birdcage," and quoted O'Neill as saying in some dismay that he should not have come.[9] What the sight stirred in him has no easy name. Regret and pain, to be sure, and perhaps more—a sense of debts unpaid and benefits forgot. His life, which in its exterior dimension had gone through a long succession of houses, each more stately than the last, was an encompassing circle around that house, the fixed foot of his movement through the world. Mrs. O'Neill rightly called it a cage, for it was so to O'Neill's spirit. There his needs had formed, his life-in-art begun. The physical return, after a long pilgrimage around the world, is symbolic of a more profound return to his source in anguish of the mind and spirit. He did not enter physically, but the house contained his truth, and he walked it in imagination almost—as the easy genesis of *Ah, Wilderness!* suggests— in spite of himself. Yet not quite. That summer, across the sound from New London, he sketched notes for a play he thought might be titled *Nostalgia*. Later, he wrote to Langner that *Ah, Wilderness!* represented "the paying of an old debt on my part—a gesture toward more comprehensive, unembittered understanding and inner freedom—the breaking away from an old formula I have enslaved myself with. . . ."* The old, dead world gave on a new creative life.

The sitting room of Nat Miller's house and the living room of the home of James Tyrone in *Long Day's Journey into Night* are in their plan substantially the same, as is the geography of the un-

---

* Langner, 284. O'Neill, thinking presumably of the autobiographical elements, and the need for self-understanding expressed in *Days Without End*, includes that play with *Ah, Wilderness!* as indicative of his new freedom.

seen house beyond it. There are two sets of double doors at the rear, those on the right opening onto a well-lighted front parlor and the stairs to the upper part of the house,* those at the left opening onto a dark back parlor, through which access is gained to the dining room and kitchen. An "inoffensive" rug covers both floors, and, although the number and kind of chairs, windows and books differ slightly, the only specific indication of difference is that the wallpaper of the Miller's house is "cheerful," a quality absent from the Tyrone household.**

In creating the Miller sitting-room, O'Neill made his first direct incursion on the autobiographical substructure of his life. He entered with joy, colored by nostalgia. With evident delight, he drew in detail the substance of his boyhood world—of the year 1906, when he, like his protagonist, Richard Miller, was seventeen*** and planning to go to a university in the fall. He created from the citizens he had known in New London, a series of pleasant portraits. The family of the postmaster John McGinley was large, a girl and seven boys, including an Arthur, a Tom, a Lawrence and a Winthrop. The Millers have one girl and five boys, including in addition to Richard an Arthur, a Tommy and two who do not appear, Lawrence and Wilbur. Arthur's close friend is named "Wint." Nat Miller, the editor of the local paper, is based on Fred Latimer, for whom O'Neill worked on the New London *Telegraph*. He recalled his affair with Maibelle Scott and invoked the shade of a girl friend from 1905, Marion Welch, to provide images of Richard's romance

* In *Ah, Wilderness!*, O'Neill calls for Richard to enter from upstairs "from the sitting-room." [269] In the play this is in error, since the scene is played in the sitting-room set and Mrs. Miller has gone through the front parlor to call her son from upstairs. O'Neill's slip may reflect the fact that the room in Monte Cristo Cottage which he used as a basis for both settings was in fact a kind of sun porch opening into both parlors. It was the kind of informal room that today would be called a "family room," and appears to have been a later addition to the house. It is possible that the name "sitting-room" was originally applied to the bright front parlor, and was later transferred by the family to the less formal accommodation. In any case, upstairs lies through the front parlor and it is from that direction that Mary Tyrone appears in the last act of *Long Day's Journey into Night*.

** In his interesting study entitled *O'Neill's Scenic Images*, 357, Timo Tiusanen has suggested that a version of the plan of this room recurs in ten settings in different plays—whenever O'Neill depicted a middle-class living room. He properly notes "an autobiographical origin of this scenic pattern." [357]

*** O'Neill, on July 4, 1906, was seventeen and a half; Richard is "going on seventeen."

with Muriel McComber. In other major and minor ways, he brought the New London citizenry to life.*

It is the Fourth of July. The town in the grip of an American folk ritual comes vividly to life: fireworks, lodge picnics, outings in the motor car, moonlit beaches, old songs, gardens and, underlying the pleasant manifestations, something of the actual economic and social structure of the "large small-town in Connecticut." Within the family, too, O'Neill has used actuality—as, for example, the blue fish "allergy" and the tale of the heroic swimming rescue which Nat Miller tells, and which were both drawn from the repertory of James O'Neill. Like *Mourning Becomes Electra*, the comedy is fixed in a historical perspective, and its evocation of the reality of the past is full and accurate.

That the comedy is also true is a point to be considered. Reading it with the hindsight provided by *Long Day's Journey into Night*, it seems a romantic falsehood, but 1906 was not 1912, the year in which the tragedy was set. By 1912, the books in the sitting-room cases had changed from "boys and girls books and best-selling novels of many past years" to a sterner collection including Nietzsche, Schopenhauer, Marx, Ibsen, Shaw, Strindberg, Swinburne, Rossetti, Wilde, Dowson. As Richard Miller matured to Edmund Tyrone, the books the boy hid on the shelf in his wardrobe were moved downstairs—a small sign of a darkening world closing around the family. O'Neill called the comedy "a dream walking," "a nostalgia for a youth I never had," and spoke of the play's having depicted "the way I would have *liked* my boyhood to have been."[10] At seventeen, however, O'Neill had yet to enter on his renegade and roving life, and there were moments when the sun shone and when laughter was heard in the dark rooms. Reviewers of the original production were reminded of Booth Tarkington's burlesques, of the pangs of adolescence, and pulled forth all the synonyms for "sentimental." At the same time they began to play an autobiographical game, reading "O'Neill" for "Richard Miller." Many of them suggested that at the heart of the matter there lay more than nostalgically glossed reminiscence.

O'Neill's life in 1906, as his biographers have depicted it, was not unhappy. He had learned of his mother's dope addiction when he was fifteen, but in the spring of 1906, she had returned from a sana-

* Cf. Gelb, 81-87; Sheaffer, *passim*.

torium in good spirits, and gave signs that she might yet overcome her addiction. She had also successfully passed through an operation for a breast tumor. James and she had gone abroad, and in New London, the two O'Neill boys were on their own. Richard Miller, evidently, is more innocent than Eugene was in that year. With Jamie, he made the rounds of bars and occasional brothels, living the life of a young rake with considerable enthusiasm. It was not, however, a dark world he experienced that summer. If he ever had it, the summer of 1906 was a time of freedom from pressure and pain.

Something of this is reflected in *Ah, Wilderness!* The experiences which he assembled to embody the story of a boy "in peg-top trousers [going] the pace that kills along the road to ruin" [181] are fragments of good times—a "dream walking," and like a dream shaping things that were into a thing that never was.

The play has a dream's truth, for under its surface a structure exists that is not easily seen in the play alone. The work contains many ironic echoes of past concerns. As Richard draws Muriel from the shadow into the moonlight on the beach, the movement of light and shadow on the pier when Dion seduces Margaret can be recalled. The poet's sensitiveness, characterized as "a restless, apprehensive, defiant, shy, dreamy, self-conscious intelligence," [193] that marks Richard as O'Neill's fictive self recalls many an earlier hero. So too, Richard, seeking a whore as a defiant gesture against the life he leads, may recall Eben and Dion and Michael Cape. The play's use of sound—the firecrackers, the sound of dance music in the distance, the sense of the turn of the seasons in an unending cycle of life, the use of chiaroscuro, defined by moonlight, are all spun from O'Neill's earlier technique and themes. The difference is that here all events, all "effects" project a sense of well-being and peace, and are not used to go aggressively, painfully "behind life." Yet behind the façade of well-being, as in the substructure of a dream, the truth exists.

However masked, *Ah, Wilderness!* is direct autobiography. In its fictions, he has combined what he has seen and admired outside his life into a disguised version of his own realities. The room, not fogbound but lighted to brightness by July sun and the moon, is the first clue. The family in the room is the second. Richard's father is wise, able, solicitous, friendly. In all respects, he is responsible and humanly successful. In the house, however, there is another man, Miller's brother-in-law, Sid Davis, merry, but shiftless, a habitué of the Sachem Club and the masculine world of the town. Sid is a failure, as lacking in responsibility as he is in malice. With the wisdom born of drunken experience, he cares for Richard when the boy comes staggering home from his first excursion to the town saloon, standing in loco parentis to the sick child. If Richard's two fathers be combined into one man there would be created the image of a man of talent and potential destroyed by a fatal lack of responsibility. In such a man, failure would emerge as a warping sense of guilt. Superimposed, the two characters suggest a figure not unlike that of O'Neill's father as he drew him in *Long Day's Journey into Night*. Divided, real guilt is dispersed.

Ella O'Neill, depicted as Mary Tyrone in the latter play, showed herself to have qualities of charm. She was, in the early part of the play, solicitous and capable of laughter and love. To the Tyrone men, she is what a mother should be. As the night moves on, these motherly characteristics dislimn, and she turns from her family, withdraws into herself, denies her womanliness and vanishes into the memory of her girlhood before sexual responsibility and its demanding devotions were forced on her. In the Miller household, as with the men, two women are in residence, Richard's mother, in all respects what a mother should be, and her sister-in-law, Lily Miller, a spinster, in love with Sid, yet refusing to accept him as he is and thus denying life by refusing responsibility for love. Their resemblance to Mary is not exact, for neither woman in the comedy is so tortured as the tragic heroine. Yet something of Mary's complex qualities are divided between the two.

The division makes it possible to treat both Sid and Lily gently because responsibility is removed from them as it could not be removed from Ella and James O'Neill. O'Neill, eliminating the crucially identifying details of his father's talent and his mother's addiction, creates the father's sister and the mother's brother. Their frustrated love for one another parallels and silently comments on the love of Nat Miller and his wife, and brings qualities to the whole that move it nearer to the truth without ruining the comedy. From the days of *Beyond the Horizon*, O'Neill had repeatedly brought forth upon his stage characters who stood in closely related opposition to one another: hero and alter ego, man and his double.

The comic tones hide the fact that he has done the same in this play, but it is important to recall that in the fifth draft of *Days Without End,* written shortly after *Ah, Wilderness!,* he split the central character into two roles. The division of his father and mother into two roles in *Ah, Wilderness!* alone makes possible their presentation in a comic context.

The freeing of the family members from guilt and responsibility continues. It is not Richard's older brother who introduced Richard to a life of "sin," but the brother's college friend who, ignorant of Richard's virginity, cannot be blamed for leading him astray. Thus Jamie's "stand-in" bears none of Jamie's responsibility for corrupting his younger brother. Significantly too, the family is filled out with another brother, Tommy, and the void left by the death of James O'Neill's second son is filmed over. Richard's own innocence obscures and mitigates Eugene's experience. Eugene, in 1906, has the experience to which Richard pretends. The difference was vast. Richard's introduction to sex is an adolescent fantasy: the "swift baby" from New Haven whom he meets in the night on the town and who tries in vain to coax him to take her upstairs bears no resemblance to the creature who initiated O'Neill into sexual life.[11] In the words of *The Iceman Cometh,* she is a "tart," not a "whore," and sex becomes a naïve posture of the will, not an ugly fact of experience.

The dark currents moving in the play are not to be suspected from the placid surface. The comedy denies them by perfecting imperfections and making pain impossible. Although Richard attempts to move out of the right current of his life, to perform a vindictive, self-destroying act of will, he by no means goes so far as Eugene was to go when he left New London for the bottom of the world. Richard's small excursion passes, and nothing essential is changed. He returns to life, and turns back into the slow cycling seasons. "There he is," his father says as Richard moves into the benevolent, gentle moonlight, which weaves a spell like that of the Caribbean moon: "There he is—like a statue of Love's Young Dream." To his wife Nat quotes *The Rubáiyát:*

> "Yet Ah, that Spring should vanish with the Rose!
> That Youth's sweet-scented manuscript should close!"

And he adds, "Well, Spring isn't everything, is it, Essie? There's a lot to be said for Autumn. That's got beauty, too. And Winter—if you're together." [298] Listeners can barely discern in the closing phrases Cybel's more urgent message to Dion, "Life is all right if you let it alone."

X

THE DOOR AND THE MIRROR

A Tale of Possessors, Self-dispossessed (1934—unfinished)
A Touch of the Poet (1935-42)
More Stately Mansions (1936—unfinished)
The Iceman Cometh (1939)
Hughie (1941)
Long Day's Journey into Night (1939-41)
A Moon for the Misbegotten (1941-43)

1946—The good years were gone. Eugene, Jr., was divorced, and Shane's baby, two months old, died in his crib. Two years earlier, Eugene had sold Tao House and returned to New York City. Now, his health comparatively stable, he busied himself with rehearsals of *The Iceman Cometh*. The tremor, however, persisted and writing was impossible. He canceled plans for a New York opening of *A Moon for the Misbegotten* and a production of *A Touch of the Poet*. In 1948, he was living in Marblehead, his health slightly improved. But Shane, that year, was picked up on a dope charge and from that time on was known as an incurable addict. As for his elder son, in 1950 he committed suicide, slashing his wrists, Roman-fashion. In 1951, Eugene quarreled seriously with Carlotta, but after a separation during which both were hospitalized, they were reconciled, and he gave her control of his literary trust. Although his literary reputation was at its lowest ebb, it was an important legacy, for shortly an O'Neill renaissance would win him his fourth Pulitzer Prize and place him among the three or four great dramatists of this century. But for O'Neill himself, nothing remained. The long journey ended in a Boston hotel room, November 27, 1953.

Harry Kemp

THE production of *Days Without End* in January, 1934, marked the end of O'Neill's active life in the theatre which had begun at Provincetown in 1916. Thereafter, he lived in an isolation unbroken except for a brief return to New York for the rehearsals of *The Iceman Cometh* and *A Moon for the Misbegotten* during the winter of 1946-47. In the eighteen-year period, New York City had seen première performances of thirty-four of his plays, and on all of them with the exception of *Dynamo*, he had worked closely in rehearsals, seeing them through to their final staged form. In 1934, he was forty-six years old; after an exhausting career, it was time for a change.

Around him, changes whose consequences were to reframe the world shook old truths, generated new attitudes and to all artists brought a sense of different obligation from what they had understood before. For the first time in its history, the United States developed a form of proletarian literature that was eagerly and widely read. The easy aestheticism of the 1920's was forgotten, and its preachers were ridiculed as *précieux*. The American artist tried now to describe and to understand the fact of the Depression and of a society impossibly careening toward a second world war. The social vacuum which had encapsuled *Strange Interlude* in 1926 was an impossibility in literature eight years later, as was the easy view of America's materialism that had characterized O'Neill's thinking from *Fog* to *The Great God Brown*. The Greenwich Village anarchists had passed unheeded into history, and the socio-economic attitudinizing which characterized the bulk of the proletarian art of the time gave onto a new kind of statement. The Roosevelt Administration made the Left respectable, and, in the theatre, writers proved rapidly responsive to the new direction. In 1935, the year before the Federal Theatre Project was established, the major dramatic successes were Maxwell Anderson's *Winterset,* Robert Sherwood's *Petrified Forest,* Odets's *Waiting for Lefty* and *Awake and Sing* and Sidney Kingsley's *Dead End.* The young playwrights were moving into a territory where O'Neill had never walked, and where he could not follow even had he chosen to do so, for he had no sense of social "cause" born from his embracing of political and economic theories. He could not cry out in such a line as the one John Howard Lawson put into the mouth of young Henry Fonda playing a Freedom Fighter in Spain: "Where's the conscience of the world?" It was simply not O'Neill's kind of question.

He had always been scornful of the Broadway Show Shop. His attitude was precisely defined by Con Melody's repeated quotation from Lord Byron which in his youth O'Neill himself quoted on many a drunken occasion: "I stood/Among them but not of them. . . ." For a time, indeed, he had led them, and in the longer reach of time, he would do so again. Now, however, the failure of *Days Without End*—which was significantly an artist's, not a producer's failure—marked the end of a major phase of his remarkable career. Although George Jean Nathan would from time to time grumble that the only thing that could save the current Broadway season was a new work by O'Neill, those he had stood among were content to forget him. He passed into that degrading limbo of lost dramatists: the academic reading list.

These were the outward signs. In fact, a change in his personal vision of experience as profound as the changes in society about him was occurring. In his own way, he began to explore, as were all serious dramatists, the sickness of his world; at the same time he explored himself, as if instinctively he knew that his answer to the larger social question was to be found only through unrelenting self-analysis. The two problems of society and the self had a single answer, for they were the same sickness. The war at its height bred in him—perhaps because he did not find satisfaction in a cause espoused—a profound depression of spirit that often made creative work impossible. He had always written in pencil in a microscopic hand, but now a growing tremor in his hands, the climax of a long period of serious illness, made sustained writing impossible. Unable to create on a typewriter or by dictation, he was often silenced.

Thus, the state of the world and of his own health induced in him that diffidence Thomas Hardy called "Unhope." Yet somehow the work went forward on two planes, the writing of a long cycle of plays on American history, *A Tale of Possessors, Self-dispossessed* and another series of autobiographical plays, which if it cannot in entire propriety be called a cycle, is one in effect. In the period between 1934 and the day in early 1953 when he and Mrs. O'Neill burned the uncompleted manuscripts of the historical cycle, he worked as steadily as he could to bring both great studies of man's life in the United States of America to completion. He failed, and the surviving texts of this period of his creative life are eloquent testimonies to the dimension of the loss. Had he completed his work, it might well have provided the only lasting crown of the theatre in the 1930's, indeed he might again have changed the course of American drama, as he had in the 1920's.

One matter was clear. In the work he undertook after 1934, he did not need the theatre. His brief emergence from isolation in 1946 came at a time when his health permitted him to travel, but when his energy for working on the cycle had all but gone. Returning to New York and re-entering the theatre brought some semblance of productivity, but the effort was exhausting and not really essential to his well-being. What he had to do needed silence, not theatrical testing. Lawrence Langner and Theresa Helburn, among many others, have commented on O'Neill's ability to ready a script for production in advance of rehearsals. In the many drafts, he worked the script, as it were, in a theatre in his mind. Except for minor cuts, no play of his needed the usual architectural revamping which out-of-town tours made possible for lesser craftsmen. With three exceptions, all the plays of O'Neill's mature years opened in New York City with no road-show preliminaries.* His final version was a theatre-worthy script.

Thus, his retirement from the theatrical world was not a retirement from the stage. He carried it with him and made few, if any, mistakes. Retreat was entirely for the sake of his creative health. First, at Sea Island, Georgia, then at Tao House in the ridge of hills

---

* The exceptions were *Days Without End, Ah, Wilderness!* and *A Moon for the Misbegotten.* The last two opened out-of-town in order that the actors could have adequate rehearsal time before live audiences so that laugh lines might be properly spaced.

east of San Francisco Bay, he worked under constant pressure on a project of solemn magnitude with the same unsparing dedication as he had in France while writing *Mourning Becomes Electra*. That he took joy in it is not clear. No other play evoked in him the simple delight that he had felt in *Ah, Wilderness!* Was there contentment in the freedom to do nothing but write? The plays contain too much pain of body and soul to suggest contentment. Pride? In reference to the late plays, he does not ordinarily comment on their being the most profound or the biggest or the best thing he has written—comments with which he was liberal in earlier times. In the end, as he approached silence, he does not appear even to have raced against time to complete the works. He knew their magnitude, and somewhat fatalistically faced the impossibility of the task, at first ruefully with small jokes to friends as a man sometimes mocks his own labors by clowning strain.* When jokes no longer helped, with no exterior manner of lament, he opened his hands and let the work go. What could not be completed was destroyed, the frayed ends cut clean. Mrs. O'Neill once said of her husband, "He was always a tidy man."

That Eugene O'Neill could not complete the historical cycle as it was designed is one of the greatest losses the drama in any time has sustained. Goethe's comment on Marlowe's *Dr. Faustus*, "How greatly it was planned," has more relevance to *A Tale of Possessors, Self-dispossessed*. It was a work of astonishing scope and scale. Theresa Helburn rightly called it a *comédie humaine*. Nothing in the drama, except Shakespeare's two cycles on British history, could have been set beside it. The two plays that have survived reveal something of the power of life that beat in it, but they show only vestiges of what its full plan realized would have provided: a prophetic epitome of the course of American destiny.

The agonies of the United States in the second half of the twentieth century are those described by O'Neill's title. Today it is no longer a question of "the conscience of the world." The world now sees the rebellion of the dispossessed as the consequence of the purchase of the world with the soul of a nation. Whatever O'Neill's emotions while writing the cycle, in the last analysis he wrote it because it was true. Like Zarathustra re-ascending the mountain,

---

* "Try a Cycle sometime . . . A lady bearing quintuplets is having a debonair, carefree time of it by comparison," he wrote to Langner on August 12, 1936.

O'Neill sought fuller wisdom in meditative isolation. But it *was* wisdom. The mature playwright had achieved that summit and could speak with truth and a note of prophecy.

With such assurance to end self-doubt, perhaps his life was somewhat eased. The total denial of ordinary good beyond that of his central creative life was an act of courage as much as it was a psychological and emotional necessity. To seek in life a mode of being where everything is deliberately wiped away except one reality—in O'Neill's instance, the pressure of a pencil on paper—one must be driven as most men are never moved toward the source of a single, fixed illumination in which life and death are merged and resolved in one another.

At Tao House, the view across the valley was of hills covered with long, golden-brown grasses spreading up the slopes of Mount Diablo against the eastern sky.* Below lay orchards of walnut and fruit trees, and the hot, dry summers passed quietly through the valley. Tao House commands this perspective, but the rooms in which O'Neill lived shut it away. The living-room windows were small and widely spaced. Such light as they admitted was broken by reflections in a large blue mirror on the opposite wall, so that the room had a sub-aqueous quality. In his small study, O'Neill again shut out light and separated himself from the domesticity of the house by three doors that isolated him in a soundless world. He had deliberately chosen the tragedian's cell Lazarus describes to Caligula: "Tragic is the plight of the tragedian whose only audience is himself! Life is for each man a solitary cell whose walls are mirrors." [309]

O'Neill had entered the cell of self before. As Dion Anthony, he had locked himself in it with Brown his mirrored image. The play was premonitory, and now in the mind, he moved in such a cell for the remainder of his time. Metaphorically, there were two cells. In the first, the outer cell, the mirrors gave on the past. In their perspective, he saw the history of his country spread out in the lives of the Harford family over many generations. Both world and time existed imaginatively in this room. Here, like Con Melody before the tavern mirror, he postured in costumes of the past and the past sprang to life in his image.

Behind the lighted room, there was another, closed, dark, hid-

* O'Neill called them "corduroy hills," and the subsequent purchasers of Tao House re-named it Corduroy Hills.

den—a room lighted by Orin Mannon's lamp, "burning out in a world of waiting shadows." In this room, the only mirror was the self, and all that could here be faced beside the self were the dead.

Between the two spaces of his isolation, the room of mirrors and the room of shadows, there stood a door he contemplated obsessively. From the outer room, it opened the way to peace and forgetfulness and the end of effort. Behind it, war did not exist, nor illness. What trouble could there be among the waiting shadows? From the inner room, the door was the only escape from a loneliness so intense it seemed like madness, from fantasies like Furies, from the hell he found inside himself. In his last years, he walked compulsively back and forth from outer to inner room, through the door which became in the end more than a metaphor.

In all but two of the last plays, the door is a central scenic element. It leads from the quiet depths of Harry Hope's saloon into the confusion of the New York streets. It is the door to Erie Smith's room to which he clutches the key and which he cannot bring himself to enter. It is the door through which Lavinia Mannon steps to face her dead, and the door that leads from tavern to bar in *A Touch of the Poet*. Most crucially it is the door to the summerhouse, the "temple of liberty" in the Harford garden, through which Deborah steps to self-imposed madness. In *Long Day's Journey into Night* and *A Moon for the Misbegotten,* there is no door. The inner room for these tales of old sorrow is sealed and there is no escape, but these excepted, in the last plays, the action centers on the movement of a central character through a door that connects a painful, hopeless world-in-time to a Nirvana of drifting illusion.

The source of *A Tale of Possessors, Self-dispossessed* lies deep in the torturous writing of *Dynamo* and *Days Without End.* Perhaps now it lies too deep for full analysis, for the two plays were intended as part of a projected trilogy whose unwritten third play became the point of departure for his cycle on American historical themes.

The third play, originally titled "It Cannot Be Mad" and later "On to Betelgeuse," was conceived along with *Days Without End* in 1927, shortly after O'Neill had completed *Lazarus Laughed.* What its original inception was is not known. O'Neill did not work on it for any consecutive period until October, 1928, when he and Carlotta Monterey were sailing to the Far East. By then, *Dynamo* had been completed, and the concept of a trilogy was in his mind. The working title, "Myths for the God-Forsaken," suggests that like *Lazarus Laughed* and *Dynamo*, the completed trilogy was to address the problems of belief in a modern, godless society.

He worked on "It Cannot Be Mad" and finished Act I and part of Act II in March, 1929. Then, the proofs of *Dynamo* arrived from his publisher. The failure of *Dynamo* on the New York stage led him to extensive re-writing of the proofs. At the same time, a very different trilogy, *Mourning Becomes Electra*, was taking shape in his imagination, and he set aside all other work for its sake. Not until it was completed and produced did he return to the unfinished trilogy, beginning the long sessions of work on the intractable *Days Without End* in 1932. By then, he had found a new title for the third play, "The Life of Bessie Bowen."* In 1933, unable to complete *Days Without End*, which was entering its fifth draft, he turned again to the Bessie Bowen story. At the same time, prophetically, he conceived the idea for a play called "Rolling River," which he subtitled "A play of generations."[1] In 1934, he reworked the Bowen scenario, but ultimately laid it aside for several years until he came at last to realize that with some modification he could use it as the final, summary play of the new "play of generations," the cycle, "A Tale of Possessors, Self-dispossessed," which was stretching out in O'Neill's imagination to almost unending length.

"The Life of Bessie Bowen" appears to have been based on the career of a woman industrialist from Rochester, New York, named Kate Gleason. Whether she was the source figure of O'Neill's heroine or whether her life provided a coincidental parallelism which O'Neill came to know at the time of her death in 1933 is uncertain. O'Neill's notes, however, contain an account of her remarkable career provided by Saxe Commins, a one-time resident of Rochester.** Born in 1865, she grew up a tom-boy in a family of brothers.

---

* The title and the heroine's name varied from time to time, "The Career of . . . Bessie Bolan" being the most definitive alternate. In her diary, Carlotta O'Neill noted that the re-spelling from "Bowen" was to distinguish O'Neill's heroine from "the other," by whom she presumably meant Elizabeth Bowen Jumel, known in girlhood as Betsy Bowen. The career of Mme. Jumel, whose ninety-year life spanned from 1775 to 1865, has many striking parallels to O'Neill's narrative, including her devotion to Napoleon and her alliance with Aaron Burr.

** Commins had been a dentist before he entered the publishing world. In 1921, O'Neill spent time in Rochester while Commins worked on his teeth. Kate Gleason

Interest in the machine tools her father manufactured caused her to enroll in Engineering Studies at Cornell University. Financial difficulties forced her to leave college and work in her father's business, where her drive and intelligence led her to enter the masculine-dominated world of the traveling salesman, with a success that helped pull the business out of its slump. Looking ahead at the competition in the manufacture of machine tools, she turned the business to a more sharply defined field, gears and gear planing machines. Shortly thereafter Bowen became the major supplier of gears and gear planers to the developing automobile industry.

By 1914 she was a highly respected citizen of Rochester. She was the first woman to be appointed a receiver by a bankruptcy court, taking charge of a machine tool shop with debts of $140,000. She managed in three years to show a profit of $1,000,000. She was the first woman to become president of a national bank, and in that capacity supervised the building of a model community of one hundred homes together with a golf course, club house, and apartment buildings. The project pioneered the use of concrete for domestic construction. Her charities were widespread and included the town of Septmont in France, where three thousand American soldiers had been killed in the attack on Soissons. Honors she received were extensive. She was the first woman member of the American Society of Mechanical Engineers, of the American Concrete Institute, and of the *Verein Deutsche Ingenieure.*

Although she was affable and outgoing in an Irish way, her personal life was never on display. She did not marry, and she maintained a masculine manner in all her associations. Only self-consciously did she put on the charming trappings of standard femininity and then only to gain her objectives in the man's world she worked in. At her mansion, her room was reached by a trap door and a retractable ladder that kept her privacy impregnable.[2]

The interest Kate Gleason's story generated in O'Neill's imagination no doubt rested partly on the remarkable achievement of an Irish woman, but her successful domination of the men with whom she came in contact and her somewhat ambiguous sexual orienta-

---

had recently built a spectacular home, modeled on the Alhambra in Granada, which she called "Clones" after her Irish mother's birthplace. It was a sight to see, and no doubt the swath its owner cut through conservative Rochester was a topic of interested conversation.

tion perhaps provided equal stimulus. As a "Myth for the God-Forsaken," her story could be brought into line with the frantic attempts of Reuben Light in *Dynamo* and John Loving in *Days Without End* to explore the dilemma of man in a godless civilization. Reuben and John Loving both need to belong to something larger, more encompassing, more maternal than they are. Being a woman, Bessie feels no such need. Her need is to rule men and to use them as rungs in a ladder to success. Success that brings increasing wealth is the only goal: greedy possession is the only motivation. In *Strange Interlude* and *Mourning Becomes Electra,* O'Neill had taken a view of woman as man's destroyer, but the weapon of destruction was her sexuality. Bessie Bowen attacked from a different angle, using her financial acumen rather than her sex to achieve her ends.

O'Neill's notes on the play show that he intended to begin his story in the last decade of the nineteenth century. At one time, he thought of telling her story in flashbacks beginning in Bessie's early childhood. In later notes he concentrated on her life from the moment she began to rise to power. The characters were to include Bessie's husband, Wade, a shy, unregarded man, who was, however, an inventor of genius; Bradford, a breezy salesman who becomes Bessie's lover for material advantages to himself; and Louise, Bradford's wife, the opposite of Bessie in sexual attractiveness. O'Neill conceived of Bessie as a squat, square-shouldered woman who, lacking physical beauty, sets out to make her way to the top of the business world by enslaving the men around her. Her husband's invention of a cooling system for the newly invented automobile gives her her start and she leaves her father's bicycle shop to become a force in the growing industry. The play was to end in 1934, when Wade, whom Bessie scorns, begins to work with rockets as the transportation of the future.

At some point in his imaginative transmutation of the life of Kate Gleason, he found the center for the cycle. Disregarding much of her career, O'Neill saw her as an emblem of all Americans who had put aside spiritual values in a greedy drive to possess material wealth. Greed was the motivation, and the theme, expressive of O'Neill's understanding of the causes that had led to depression-ridden America, was summarized by the passage from Mark 7:36: "What shall it profit a man if he shall gain the whole world and lose his own soul." In contrast to Bessie, Nina Leeds and the Mannon women were suffused in a romantic glow. Their destructive love affairs had only personal consequences. Bessie's power had important effects in a larger world of commerce. She moved out of the boarded-up rooms and the temporal vacuums inhabited by O'Neill's earlier female protagonists. The very nature of the industry she came to dominate—transportation—gave her tentacles that extended her reach through the country. No matter that her gain was personal loss, that she bought her lover, that her daughter was a lesbian, her son a narcotics addict. Bessie acted in accord with Kate Gleason's motto: *possum volo.*

Through a series of false starts and redactions, the Bessie Bowen play remained troublesome. After he had completed and seen through production *Ah, Wilderness!* and *Days Without End,* and after he had been subject to a variety of illnesses, O'Neill turned to a number of new play ideas. Some of these germinated during the autumn of 1934, but in December he returned to Bessie's story. His work diary records a series of outlines, rewritings, and false starts similar to those that had plagued *Days Without End,* its intended predecessor in the "God-Forsaken" trilogy. On New Year's Eve day, he recorded that he was "fed up on 'Bessie' for the moment," and, although he continued into January trying to force the play forward, by January 20, he noted "this damned play won't come right—not big enough opportunity to interest me—would be part of something, not itself." On the twenty-first he wrote "will chuck B.B. out of further present consideration."

The trouble with "The Life of Bessie Bowen" was twofold. First, it did not speak to O'Neill's ambitions as a playwright. The extraordinary reception of *Strange Interlude* and *Mourning Becomes Electra*—both "big" plays—led him to feel that he must write drama of greater scope than that of the average commercial playwright. No doubt there was an element of vanity in such a feeling, but he was surely right in sensing that his ambition had been in the past justified by the results. The domestic intimacy, of *Ah, Wilderness!* was a strange by-product, so uncharacteristic that he at one time considered having it produced under a nom-de-plume. Had *Days Without End* succeeded, had he been able to create the "God-Forsaken" trilogy, the three together might have proved a worthy successor to *Mourning Becomes Electra.* However, both *Dynamo* and *Days*

Without End had failed to impress their audiences, and when the projected third play showed signs of entering the same creative doldrums as had *Days Without End,* he surely felt the play to be small, uninteresting, and unworthy, and the proposed trilogy to be unworkable.

Another less personal concern perhaps underlay his sense that "The Life of Bessie Bowen" was too small a subject. He was increasingly alarmed at the condition of his country. He had returned from the years in France to a nation frozen by the Great Depression, and he heard the sounds of a second World War from Germany, Russia, and Spain. Like all thinking men, he was forced to ask the question: "What have we done wrong? How have we brought these things to pass?" Journalists, politicians, and many artists of lesser stature than he were facing up to a frightening world and speaking out. O'Neill's genius brought heavy responsibilities to try to understand the modern dilemma and to warn and to teach. Such an undertaking required the greatest force he could summon from his imagination and his energies in order to present to the world the most profound and far-reaching thoughts of which he was capable. Tracing the life of a single, eccentric woman was not enough. What must be found were representative lives of those who most clearly manifested the causal guilt. On December 4 and 5, 1934, as he worked on the Bowen play, he also made notes for a series he called "The Calms of Capricorn."

The idea produced new creative excitement, and on January 1, 1935, as the Bessie Bowen play entered its death struggles, he wrote of the new conception: "grand ideas for this Magnum Opus if can ever do it—wonderful characters!" By the month's end, all his efforts were consumed in the new project. He quickly outlined the first two plays, and shortly conceived in plan the third and fourth plays of the series, which, he noted on January 26, were to concern "4 sons." On the twenty-seventh, a pit opened, and he wrote "story of Harford and Sara before 1st play opens—this may develop into additional 1st play, making five in all." The next day, he wrote that he had outlined "the spiritual undertheme" of the work, and by early February, he had found a new title for the cycle, "A Touch of the Poet," transferring the original title to the play about a voyage on a clipper ship.

Through the rest of 1935 and until October, 1936, O'Neill worked without cessation on the cycle. Early in his work, on February 3, 1935, he decided that the new first play, then titled "A Hair of the Dog," was a genuine requisite. By April 25, as the theme became clearer, he conceived as a title for the cyle "A Threnody for Possessors Dispossessed." By June 9, he had in plan a sixth play, and by the end of August he felt a seventh to be essential to the scheme. This play was to be titled "Twilight of Possessors Self-dispossessed." On September 2, he recorded that the seventh play followed the main outline of the old Bessie Bowen story and needed no further work than the revised outline he had made a year earlier.

On July 3, 1935, he wrote to Robert Sisk at the Theatre Guild, detailing the plan as it lay open before him:

> As to the new project, I'll sketch it briefly for you. . . . It's a cycle of seven plays portraying the history of the interrelationships of a family over a period of approximately a century. The first play begins in 1829, the last ends in 1932. Five generations of this family appear in the cycle. Two of the plays take place in New England, one almost entirely on a clipper ship, one on the Coast, one around Washington principally, one in New York, one in the Middle West. As to titles, the "Electra" pattern will be followed—a general title for the cycle, and one for each play. Each play will be, as far as it is possible, complete in itself while at the same time an indispensable link in the whole. (A difficult technical problem, this, but I think I can solve it successfully.) There will, of course, be much less hang-over of immediate suspense from one play to another than in "Electra." Each play will be concentrated around the final fate of one member of the family but will also carry on the story of the family as a whole. In short, it is a broadening of the "Electra" idea—but, of course, not based on any classical theme. It will be less realistic than "Electra" in method, probably—more poetical in general, I hope—more of "Great God Brown" over and undertones, more symbolical and complicated (in that it will have to deal with more intermingling relationships)—and deeper probing. There is a general spiritual under-theme for the whole cycle and the separate plays make this manifest in different aspects.
>
> And so on. I won't give you more of that nature because prophecies on that score at this stage are subject to contradiction when actual writing comes. I'm only telling you from the way it shapes up in scenario. I've written detailed scenarios running to 25,000 words each of the first three plays, finished the outline but not the scenario of the fourth, and am now working on the outline of the fifth. I won't start actual dialogue on the first play until I've completed the scenarios of all—that means late next Fall at the rate so far.
>
> No religion to any of the plays except very incidentally as minor realistic details.

The family is half Irish, half New England in its beginning. But the New Englanders are a bit different from any I've tackled before—and so are the Irish.

How to produce? Nothing decided yet. The best scheme might be at the rate of two per season, keeping the past ones going, along with the new ones, in some sort of repertoire arrangement. A strictly no star company. The idea would be to build a repertoire company for this cycle. . . . I probably won't let the first play be produced until I've got three plays finished and a first draft written on the remaining four.

It was not to be so tidy a project. On September 7, a new play rose in his mind: "Playing around with the idea new first play to precede 'Hair of the Dog,' to go back to 1806 and show Abigail* as girl—marriage to Henry H[arford]—and their house & parents—Henry's father big character—title 'Greed of the Meek.' " He began at once, recording that the play was "forcing" itself on him. He fought against the expansion, writing on September 16 that he was "trying to put 'Greed of the Meek' out of mind—God knows don't want extra play tacked on this damned trilogy [sic] unless it absolutely must be written!" Possibly he should have fought harder, but the play had its will, and he wrote on.

The work continued into 1936 with minimal interruption. The title "A Hair of the Dog" was given to the eighth play and the title "A Touch of the Poet" fixed on for the play about the Melody family. The cycle now was to be called "A Legend of Possessors Self-dispossessed." By June 9, he had accepted the need of yet one more play, a new first play to be called "Give Me Death." The new ninth play was to be the story of the progenitors of the Harfords in the eighteenth century.

In October, he called a halt and went to Seattle, where he received the Nobel Prize. Shortly after, in Oakland, California, he fell ill. He did no consecutive writing until June, 1937, in California, when he began to re-think the entire nine-play scheme and to revise scenarios and outlines. On July 26, for example, he determined that Honey, the youngest son of Sara and Simon, would live to the saga's end and take his place in the old Bessie Bowen narrative, but he also realized that the final play would require the introduction of a new generation. Extensive revisions of the nine-play scheme followed, and by the year's end he had completed a draft of the first

---

* I.e., Deborah Harford.

play, which was, he noted in some dismay, longer than *Strange Interlude*. Leaving it for the moment, he turned to *More Stately Mansions* and then to the third draft of *A Touch of the Poet,* work which he finished in March, 1939. On June 5, his imagination revolted: "decide what I've done on 5th Play is n.g., so tear it up. Feel fed up and stale on Cycle after 4½ years of not thinking of any other work—will do me good to lay on shelf and forget it for a while—do a play which has nothing to do with it." The next day, he began work on *The Iceman Cometh*.

In January 1940, he returned to the cycle for a month, but by March *Long Day's Journey into Night* occupied his attention, and he finished its second draft in October. He returned almost at once to the cycle and was faced now with the inordinate length of many of the drafts. The first two plays presented special problems. As they were written, they could not be readily cut to an evening's length and, further, the plays were too complex and full of material he was not willing to lose. Either he must discard them and return to the seven-play scheme or break them up and make four plays out of two. By November 1, 1940, he had decided: the cycle was to be eleven plays long.

In 1942, after he had brought *Hughie* and *A Moon for the Misbegotten* to near completion, he returned for the last time to the cycle, deciding on February 16 to rewrite *A Touch of the Poet* in order "to get at least one play of Cycle definitely & finally finished." The work was completed by mid-November, and thereafter work on the cycle stopped. In 1952, with Carlotta's help, he burned the notes, outlines, and drafts that had occupied almost two decades of his mature lifetime.*

The surviving clutter of notes on the cycle raises many questions as to the design of the whole and to its ultimate value as a work of art. Judged from such indications of its narrative as can be garnered from the seven- and eleven-play outlines, the central narrative was over-full of political, financial, and psycho-sexual maneuverings of the most lurid nature, but no work of art is to be judged from such

---

* The destruction of the cycle was complete except for the finished *A Touch of the Poet,* a typed manuscript with holographic corrections of *More Stately Mansions,* and the scenario of *The Calms of Capricorn.* In addition some notes for the seven- and eleven-play cycles exist. From these unnumbered pages some concept of the direction of O'Neill's narrative and thematic plans can be derived. None of the notes is definitive, but they indicate the direction of O'Neill's explorations into the material.

sketchy preliminary imaginings. What is left shows O'Neill thinking
his way through an extraordinary story, throwing in every fantasy
and experimenting with various techniques, shifting concepts, working out relationships, introducing and then forgetting characters.
The notes provide a kind of barometer of his imagination as he
attempted to work out the mammoth plan. The plan, however, cannot be fully descried from what is left. No scenario can be developed
from the notes. Hunches and guesses are possible but many misgiv-
ings arise. What is certain and at the same time disturbing is the
extraordinary fullness of the scheme. The interweaving of character
relationships, the great number of events, the vast historical panorama that serves as referential background for the central story
create a great tangle.

From the notes, an approximate genealogical table of the principal characters can be drawn:

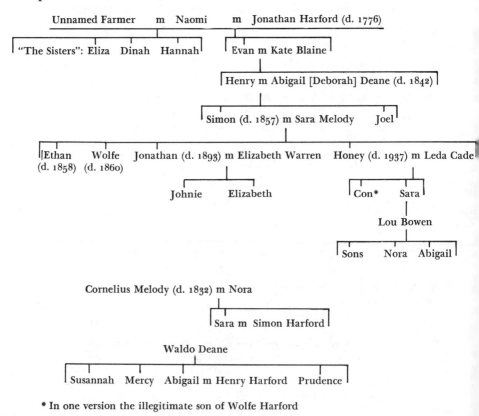

Unnamed Farmer   m   Naomi   m   Jonathan Harford (d. 1776)

"The Sisters": Eliza   Dinah   Hannah   Evan m Kate Blaine

Henry m Abigail [Deborah] Deane (d. 1842)

Simon (d. 1857) m Sara Melody   Joel

Ethan   Wolfe   Jonathan (d. 1893) m Elizabeth Warren   Honey (d. 1937) m Leda Cade
(d. 1858)   (d. 1860)

Johnie   Elizabeth   Con*   Sara

Lou Bowen

Sons   Nora   Abigail

Cornelius Melody (d. 1832) m Nora

Sara m Simon Harford

Waldo Deane

Susannah   Mercy   Abigail m Henry Harford   Prudence

* In one version the illegitimate son of Wolfe Harford

In organizing the whole, O'Neill thought of the first four plays as a thematic and narrative unit concerned with the three unmarried daughters of Naomi and an unnamed father. He referred to the unit as "The Blessed Sisters." The next two plays he subtitled "Sara and Abigail," and the next group of four, those plays dealing with the sons of Sara and Simon, as "The Four Brothers." The last play, "A Hair of the Dog," he conceived as an epilogue summarizing the cycle.

In the eleven-play plan, the first was titled "The Poor in Spirit," although he considered "The Pride of the Meek" and "Give Me Liberty" as alternatives. About 1775, Jonathan Harford, a Welsh renegade from Braddock's army, comes upon a farm owned by a widow, Naomi, the mother of three daughters: Eliza, Dinah, and Hannah. Naomi wants a man to help her on the farm and comfort her in bed. Jonathan is an idealist who has struck into the wilderness in search of a freedom as wild and primitive as that of the native American tribes who, in his view, roam the land without enslaving it and so never become its slaves. Despite his belief in a freedom without possession, he agrees to stay with Naomi, selling out to the woman, much as Robert Mayo gave up his dream in *Beyond the Horizon*.

Naomi is the first of the possessors. She mocks Jonathan's spiritual aesthestics as he talks of the beauty of the land, reminding him that a cow sees no beauty in the grass it chews. Her hope is to sell the farm and use the proceeds to enter the slave trade where profit is unlimited. As the play ends in 1757, Jonathan escapes to the wilderness, leaving his infant son, Ethan, in the care of the women.

The second play, "The Rebellion of the Humble" (alternatively titled "The Rights of Man" and "The Patience of the Meek") moved the story to 1775, at the time of Jonathan's return to the farm. Now he is fired by the idea of a revolution to drive the British out of the country. He adds an idealistic coda: when the British are gone, he will join with the Indians to drive out the Americans, and thereafter find a way to rid the land of all its human inhabitants, thus freeing it from any attempt to possess it. He goes to war and is killed at Bunker Hill. The play ends as the Sisters burn the farm and leave for the city.

The third play, "The Greed of the Meek," was to be laid in Newport or Providence, Rhode Island, between 1783 and 1794. The Sisters have profited at the slave trade. Evan, who in this plan has become the meekest of retiring Christians, distresses his half-sisters by his reticence. They arrange for him to be shanghaied by a friend of Jonathan's, a Captain Marlow, on a voyage whose hardships will make him more of a man. The experiment is a success, and on his return he seduces and later marries Kate Blaine.* Their excitement at the outbreak of the French Revolution with its promise of freedom takes the family to France, where Ethan is imprisoned as a devoted adherent of Robespierre. He is ultimately freed as an insignificant idealist whom the revolutionaries forget to guillotine. At home, he lives in solitude in his summer house, the "Temple of Liberty" described by Deborah, praising Aaron Burr and tending his plants. His wife falls in love with the local minister, Waldo Deane, whose daughter Abigail is a child of eight.**

The fourth play, "And Give Me Death" (or "Give Me Death"), was laid in 1806 and brought into sharp focus Deane's daughter, Abigail, whose day-dreaming of Napoleon and whose hope that her son Simon will become a poet are counterpointed by her attempt to control the Harford fortune—the motive that had led her into marriage with Henry Harford. The Sisters dread dispossession as they dread death itself, and a sordid series of intrigues follows with Abigail as the ultimate victor. The family appears to be so cursed by greed that it loses all moral restraints.

As a title for the subgroup, "The Blessed Sisters" is ironic. O'Neill saw Naomi's daughters as a fatal trio. He planned to introduce them in the act of spinning and conceived of them as weavers of destiny, as the malevolent fairies presiding over Ethan's birth, and as witches who cursed the family with greedy desires. In *A Touch of the Poet*, Deborah describes them as striving to possess her. They failed, she says, "because there was so little of me in the flesh that aged, greedy fingers could clutch." [83]. They do not fail in their possession of their half-brother or his son, and their fingers, extended by their control of transportation lines in steamships and coaches, spread through the land as they amass their fortune.

* The characterization of Ethan varies greatly from a piratical sea captain engaged in the slave and opium trades to the ineffectual character described by Deborah in Act II of *A Touch of the Poet*.
** In the third and fourth plays, O'Neill devoted much time to the Deane family. Late in his work, he commented that he had made a mistake trying to incorporate two families into the narrative. The complications they introduced were unnecessary.

The effects of the curse of greed are less clear in the central sub-group, "Sara and Abigail," than in the final group of four, "The Four Brothers," and in the epilogue, "A Hair of the Dog." In his letter to Robert Sisk, O'Neill stated that each of the plays would concern itself with "the final fate" of one member of the family. In the epilogue of *More Stately Mansions*, O'Neill sets this plan in train. Sara Harford speaks in soliloquy of her sons:

> Fine boys each of them! No woman on earth has finer sons! Strong in body and with brains, too! Each with a stubborn will of his own! Leave it to them to take what they want from life, once they're men! This little . . . farm won't hold them long! Ethan, now, he'll own his fleet of ships! And Wolfe will have his banks! And Johnny his railroads! And Honey will be in the White House before he stops, maybe! And each of them will have wealth and power and a grand estate— [279]

The speech sketches the course of the action to come. The surviving scenario of *The Calms of Capricorn*[3] traces the story of Ethan Harford and his attempt to master the sea with his clipper ship, *Dream of the West,* but the text offers only a confusing sense of what the play might have become. After a leisurely first act in two scenes concerning Simon Harford's "final fate," O'Neill concentrates on Ethan, Simon's eldest son, and his love-hate relationship with the sea. Casting far back in his career to develop the story—to the days of *S. S. Glencairn* and *Chris Christopherson*—O'Neill causes Ethan to reflect some of his own early love for the sea. Ethan readily admits to being possessed by it and to knowing the freedom from responsibilities such a possession can give—as he phrases it, "to let oneself be possessed in order to possess—to love and be free, to be freed by love. . . ." [11] Yet such a desirable spiritual condition cannot be easily gained. As a second mate, serving under hostile officers, he must take orders he hates and serve without pride in a kind of slavery that is the outer evidence of his enslavement by the sea. The sea is to blame, and Ethan feels he must find a way to conquer it. He cries out that to defeat the sea "is the only way I can achieve meaning in my own eyes, expiate myself, be able to forgive myself, to go on with pride. Right or wrong, it is my meaning." [11]

To live true to his "meaning," he must become the captain of a clipper ship and sail it around the Horn to the Golden Gate faster than any man has yet been able to do. It does not matter that in these years steamships are rapidly replacing sailing ships. To Ethan, such a race is a "last gesture of victory." If the ship is smashed to ruins it is of no moment: "I want this chance to accept the sea's challenge, that's all. If I win, I possess her and she cringes and I kick her away from me and turn my back forever. If I lose, I give myself to her as her conquest and she swallows and spews me out in death." [9]

Ethan's dream of defeating the sea by setting a speed record may have been suggested by O'Neill's own voyage into the Tropic of Capricorn to Buenos Aires in 1910. The captain of O'Neill's ship, the *Charles Racine,* was known for setting speed records with his sailing ships. He looked down on steamers and stated that he would sail "as long as the winds blow." Something too of the mystical nature of Ethan's feeling for the sea may have originated on that voyage where O'Neill responded to the power and beauty of the sea to the point where, as he would write in *Long Day's Journey into Night,* he lost himself—"actually lost my life. I was set free!" Louis Sheaffer quotes O'Neill as having felt on the voyage that "at such times I was in love with death."[4] The mystical relation between life, death, and the sea so crucial to Ethan's "meaning" was O'Neill's as well and underlies much of the thinking that produced *The Calms of Capricorn.*

Despite Ethan's acknowledgment of the power of the sea, the course he follows to gain his chance to accept its challenge is at best suspect. To become captain, he murders the first mate in a fist fight and later becomes an accomplice in the murder of the clipper's captain. Then, after a twenty-day idleness, becalmed in the Tropic of Capricorn, he rams the ship around the Horn to the threshold of the Golden Gate. At this point, Ethan and the sea finally come into direct confrontation. The wind dies, but Ethan, summoning all his strength of will, cries a command to the gods of the sea: "Send the wind, I say!" [54] The gods obey what appears to be his superior will but they are not beaten. The fog comes, and the ship is again becalmed off the San Francisco coast. Then, at last, Ethan acknowledges that the sea has won and goes to his death by drowning.

So long as the focus is on Ethan, the play's theme is clear. Ethan has been, as Sara says, touched with poetry:

> It's a hard fate for a woman to have been the daughter & wife & mother of men touched with the curse of the poet. For it's the

> moon you want and you hunt in the skies of the broad day when
> the rest of us don't see her there at all. [9]

Ethan's father sees the paradoxical nature of his son's goal. Simon
says,

> I think you will lose [the challenge], that if you win you will have
> lost most of all. But I also know that your losing will be your final
> victory and release . . . You are doing the only thing that a man,
> a lonely exile in the world of matter, can do—to choose his dream
> and then follow that dream to the end. [11]

As a "lonely exile in the world of matter," Ethan, like many of
O'Neill's protagonists, cannot face the nature of his Universe. Only
through adherence to a dream is life endurable. He does not much
resemble the inhabitants of Harry Hope's saloon, but his problem
and attempted solution have something of the same reliance on
achieving an impossible goal in a hostile, uncaring, existential world
of matter. His suicide when the sea defeats him and the dream dies
is the only resolution possible.

The thematic problem is that Ethan does not go to his death
alone. His suicide is developed as a *Liebestod*. Dying with him is
Nancy Payne, the wife of the captain, who is in love with Ethan and
has conspired with him to murder her husband so that Ethan may
have command of the ship. She has also helped Ethan conceal the
fact that he has killed the first mate. To complicate matters further,
Ethan does not return Nancy's whole-hearted love, and the relationship is beset by a double guilt—the murders and his false love-
making to the woman. When Nancy determines to take on herself
the burden of her husband's murder, Ethan must choose between
his own truth and her love for him. Bitterly and with some brutality, he tells her that he does not love her. That he has used her
carnally does not change her love for him. She is willing to let him
go without further claim. Her sacrifice breaks him, and he lies, telling her he does love her. The resolution to all the problems of
deceit and guilt and loss is for them to swim together out into the
fog, surrendering themselves to the sea.

The number of difficulties the love story introduces to the account
of Ethan's attempt to follow his dream are not really resolved by
the double suicide. Their deaths are expiation for two murders,
and, although the murders were caused by the necessities of Ethan's
dream, it is difficult to see how the love story relates thematically to

the story of the sea's challenge. Furthermore, in Ethan, O'Neill has come upon a protagonist who does not appear to make a claim on an audience's sympathy as, for example, Con Melody in his pursuit of a dream was able to do. The final scenes with Nancy and a scene between Ethan and Sara in which he makes his motives for the suicide explicit are only briefly sketched in the scenario, but after the extraordinary confrontation between Ethan and the sea in which he commands the winds to blow, the double suicide is an inadequate climax of what appeared at first to be the central story. Ethan admits a confusion O'Neill may have sensed with his story: "If it were only myself, I'd know what to do and do it this instant. I'd let the sea possess what it has won and beyond desire for possession, I might find peace at last." [61]

Around the story of Ethan and Nancy, O'Neill ranges a variety of characters who will dominate the action of the subsequent plays. The second son, Wolfe, is Ethan's opposite, a man indifferent to any challenge of fate or of man. Neither winning nor losing matter to him, a fact that makes him remote and cool to everything around him. Others see his indifference as a challenge, especially a whore, Leda Cade, who attempts to strike an amorous spark in him. Forced into a card game with Leda's lover, Graber, he wins continually, finally playing for and winning the woman. She means as little to him as any other of his winnings, and he tries unsuccessfully to give her back to the gambler.

The third brother, Jonathan, is ambitious to become a power in the financial world. He sees the possibilities in developing transportation lines, much as the Sisters had done earlier. On board is Theodore Warren, the owner of the ship, and his daughter Elizabeth. Elizabeth is self-contained and sexually somewhat frigid, but Jonathan seduces her so that she will marry him and give him the opening wedge through her father's wealth to the money and power he desires. Elizabeth, cognizant of his motives, accepts the fact that she is entering a marriage without love. Jonathan, she reasons, will make a good husband; if he does not, she is prepared to divorce him. At the play's end, they enter their coldly unloving arrangement.

The youngest son, Owen, nicknamed "Honey," is an amoral charmer. He is handsome, sings beautifully, and has a native ability to attract the admiration of strangers. Those who know him think of him as a born politician, and on the ship he uses his skills to extract information about gold strikes in the Sierra Nevada from a crew of miners on their way to the gold fields. In *The Calms of Capricorn* he has no clear narrative function, playing the clown with abandon.

Strangest of all the characters is Leda Cade. She is an apparent whore who maintains her professional status throughout the voyage, sleeping with most of the eligible males on the ship. She is a striking contrast both to the egomaniacal drives of Ethan and Jonathan and to the indifference of Wolfe. She treats the idea of love with contempt. When Nancy objects that her behavior makes love "nothing but—bodies," she replies,

> And what else is it? And why not? Bodies are all right, aren't they?—healthy and natural. Aren't we animals? Can you go to bed with a soul? Poetic drivel aside, love may start in heaven, but it goes on or it dies in bed. [32]

Mutual desire, she feels, wipes out ambition; nothing matters but to want and be wanted. That she is not wanted by Wolfe presents her with a challenge she has not won by the end of the voyage. The war between Leda and Wolfe will form the center of the following play.

Leda was conceived in relation to Sara Harford. In Leda, O'Neill saw something of the close alliance of sexuality and the life force that he had explored earlier in the figure of Cybel in *The Great God Brown,* but Leda is drawn more realistically than Cybel and is much tougher in behavior and appearance. She apparently was to stand in significant parallel to Sara. When the two women meet, Leda says, "I *am* glad to meet you. I'm sure we'll understand one another." In *More Stately Mansions,* Sara, like Leda, was willing to use sex to gain her ends, but *The Calms of Capricorn* takes this no farther. After the end of the first act, when Simon's death releases Sara from the problems of her marriage, O'Neill finds no significant function for her in the action. He allows her to comment on the characters of her children and to serve as their confidante, but she is relegated to the sidelines of the play. At the end she is beginning to drink to excess, taking on some of the characteristics of her father. Nothing is made of her potential likeness to Leda, and her dramatic function so far as O'Neill had developed it in the scenario appears to be only to provide a poetical Irish tone at some moments in the drama.

In his introduction to the published scenario of *The Calms of Capricorn,* Donald Gallup comments that it provides "the merest notes" for what O'Neill would have made of the narrative. This is evident truth, and no critical judgment on the material can reliably be made. In one particular, however, the innovative staging plan, O'Neill shows himself to have been working as boldly as in any play of his earlier "experimental" days. In 1930, in Paris, he began to read about the clipper ships, and later, in Georgia, he commissioned a model-maker, Donald Pace, to create models for him of well-known clippers. He supervised the accuracy of the models with care, sending some of them back to Pace for changes.[5] The ships were mounted on the walls of his study at Tao House and provided a continual point of reference for placing the scenes of *The Calms of Capricorn.* Acts III and IV demonstrate that O'Neill's genius for finding startlingly original solutions to difficult problems of staging had by no means diminished. He arranged for the ship's decks and cabins to be viewed from a variety of angles, with the interiors of the cabins and wheelhouse being on display as needed and the poop deck in its relation to the main deck providing a two-level stage. Over the set, the huge sails hang like the main drape in a theatre, and across the large stage with its manifold playing areas, the characters move as they would in reality on a ship, changing from place to place, seeking both public and private encounters. It is a complicated design, but an exciting one, approximating the reality of shipboard travel far more closely than any other plan could have accomplished.

The use to which O'Neill put the setting in planning the action is equally interesting and innovative. Faced with a large cast and with a great number of private alliances, O'Neill does not attempt group scenes after the second act, wherein the passengers are introduced. Rather he lets his characters range in a sequence of short scenes, dropping in on a conversation on the main deck, shifting in mid-speech to another being enacted in a cabin, building in fragmented glimpses a realistic rhythm of the action of the whole. On stage, the technique of narration was new. He had tried a similar use of his stage in *Desire Under the Elms,* but there, with a small cast and a single problem of concern, the multiplicity of action was not a problem. *The Calms of Capricorn* is innovatively cinematic in its structure and very different from anything O'Neill had attempted earlier.

The play's sound pattern is also imaginative. Basic to it is the off-stage chorus sung by a group of gold miners in the steerage. The singers do not appear, but Honey visits them often and keeps their presence alive in the audience's minds. Their song, which O'Neill calls "The Song of the Gold Seekers" and which is perhaps a ballad sung by Honey entitled "Sacramento," is heard continually during the time the ship is becalmed. It is punctuated by the rhythm of the ship's pump, which apparently was to tie the song to the action of the sea. In *The Moon of the Caribbees,* the native chant from the shore functions in the action in an identical way. The people on the motionless ship are troubled by it, curse it, come to hate it as it insistently underscores the greed of all the passengers. As the Caribbean chant does, it forces the characters to remember what they wish to ignore or forget. Occasionally, it moves into the action and is brought into combat with a sea chanty or a hymn sung to drown it out. At the end, as the ship is becalmed for a second time in the fog, it is overpowered by a chanty, and described as "beaten and exhausted" by the chanty's "desperate assertion."

The three remaining plays of the "Four Brothers" sub-group are much less fully sketched than is *The Calms of Capricorn.* Next in order was Wolfe's play, "The Earth Is the Limit," set in San Francisco in 1860, three years after the action of *The Calms of Capricorn.* Now Sara is in charge of a hotel, the Melody Inn, which she manages with a good business ability. Jonathan has developed his transportation holdings in partnership with Theodore Warren, and Honey takes his first steps toward a political career. Wolfe is the same passive ironist as in the preceding play. He wants nothing and holds no goal to be of benefit. Leda, who was the stake in the last card game aboard *The Dream of the West,* wants Wolfe as her husband. She reacts to his continued snubs by joining with Elizabeth in hostility to the Harford sons: "Who are they, that they dare deny us?" By the end of the play Elizabeth and Jonathan agree to marry, and Leda turns to Wolfe. Wolfe, however, will not be trapped by her predatoriness. To avoid any entanglement, to avoid being touched, he kills himself. In the play to follow, Sara will defend the suicide of her two older sons. Ethan's suicide was a payment for life, a demand of honor, but Wolfe's was differently motivated: "There was a high pride and scorn in him—a high dream in him you couldn't buy with gold or land—or touch with the love of a woman— he gave his life for it—there was the touch of a poet in him, a poet who couldn't sing and had to live his poem in silence and darkness." Wolfe in his freedom-seeking solitude perhaps was intended to re- semble the first Jonathan Harford, who left his family for the wil- derness in order to live in untrammeled freedom. In a more complex world, where the freedom of a wilderness can no longer be found, death becomes the only way to achieve the peace of total liberty.

Honey's rise to political power and Jonathan's pursuit of wealth and financial success form the twin centers of the ninth play, "Noth- ing Is Lost but Honor." The play opens in San Francisco at Wolfe's funeral and progresses into an unspecified time in the early 1870s. Honey, separating from any close alliance with his brother, becomes mayor of San Francisco and later a United States senator. He mar- ries Leda, and they have a strong, healthy child, Cornelius.* Jona- than is the son who lacks the touch of the poet and refuses to dream. "Facts are my dreams," he asserts and sets out with Elizabeth and her money to gain control of the transcontinental railroad. In a scene laid at Promontory Point, Utah, at the time of the driving of the golden spike, Jonathan's plan for domination is revealed. He has formed a crooked holding company and plans to create a finan- cial panic by forcing Honey to reveal on the Senate floor the names of those who have accepted bribes in the financial manipulations underwriting the railroad. When the stock prices drop, he plans to buy control. Bending Honey to his will, he succeeds in his plan, and at the play's end he has become a tycoon like Jay Gould. The com- ment is made that he will "mortgage America."

The play sketches a number of sexual encounters—between Honey and Elizabeth, Jonathan and Leda, and Leda and Elizabeth. The child of Jonathan and Elizabeth, Johnie, is sickly and unwanted. Sara has developed a lust for gold which she hopes will buy her "peace and contentment." She has also turned for solace to alcohol and, in a scene that is reminiscent of that between Mary Tyrone and

* At one time, O'Neill considered making the boy the illegitimate son of Wolfe, but the matter was not resolved.

Cathleen, spends time talking to her maid of an all-but-forgotten dream, the great Melody estate in Ireland.

The tenth play, "The Man on Iron Horseback," is set in Paris, New York, San Francisco, and Japan between 1876 and 1893. In the course of the play, both Sara and Elizabeth were to die, the latter a suicide. There are now two more children: Beth, Elizabeth's daughter, pretty, meek and calculating, and Sara, Leda's second child, a stolid, heavy, ugly girl. The play centers on Jonathan's financial manipulations, but perhaps its most startling development is his encounter with the Tao. In Japan, in a Buddhist temple, he senses the limits of his power. He considers for a moment matching his will against Eastern philosophy and religion by funding missionaries to convert the Buddhists. O'Neill debated having him kill himself in the temple, but instead caused him to suffer a stroke. He is returned from Japan on his death bed. Something of what O'Neill had in mind in bringing his Napoleonic materialist into contact with Oriental belief is hinted at in a note: "add general theme throughout—tragic battle of opposites—aspects expressed in Latin quote I remember—translated for this purpose—'I know the good way (Tao) and believe it is the Truth but I follow the bad way.'"

The final play, "Hair of the Dog," covered the period 1900-1932 and concerned Lou, the granddaughter of Leda and Honey. In the course of the play, she was to age from eighteen to fifty years and rise as Bessie Bowen had done to a position of great wealth. The play is barely sketched, but notes indicate that O'Neill was planning to show men and women as being lost in a wilderness to which their greed had led them. Faith and truth are dead, and the women are yearning for some ruthless possessor, some Napoleon (O'Neill jotted down the names of Christ, Hitler, Stalin, and Al Capone) to set them free from their own drives by enslaving them and freeing them from the guilt of their greed and the strictures of morality and religion.* The children offer no hope for the future. Lou's youngest son was to become a "hop head & anarchist idealist" who perhaps would come closer than the rest to the truth of modern life: his hope

---

* The idea of a dominant warrior figure ran through the cycle with Louis XIV, Robespierre, Napoleon, and Aaron Burr at various times serving as the emblem of dominant masculine strength. The concept may have had a bearing on the genesis of one of O'Neill's last unfinished plays, "The Last Conquest," a play about the coming of the anti-Christ.

is that the race may be destroyed so that the potential few survivors of the holocaust can be reminded by the ruins how badly men have lost their way. With this perspective, perhaps they may start again on the right path. His thought reflects that of the first Jonathan Harford who dreamed of ridding the country of all human inhabitants.

The final words of the cycle were to be spoken by Honey, who has stubbornly lived to be 100. In his last summing up, he equates greed with alcohol. Like alcohol, when greed controls you "there's a fever comes and a great thirst and a great drinking to kill it, and a grand drunk, and a terrible hangover and headache and remorse of conscience, and a sick empty stomach without greed or appetite. But take a hair of the dog and the sun will rise again for you—and appetite and thirst come back, and you can forget—and begin all over!" On this dark note, prophesying that nothing will change, the cycle was to end.

Enough is left of the plan of the whole to show that the plays of the cycle were to be strongly unified by repeated motifs, parallel actions and similar character traits reappearing through the generations. Each play was connected to the development of transportation, from Con Melody's mare to Wade's rockets. Lines of transportation moved throughout the land and across the sea like the fingers of the Sisters clutching power. Despite the great geographical range, the cycle returned to certain sites of basic meaning: Simon's cabin in the woods which formed his retreat in *A Touch of the Poet* is seen again in *More Stately Mansions* and *The Calms of Capricorn,* and it becomes the location of the great Harford mansion which in Sara's imagination resembles Melody castle, her father's estate in Ireland. Similarly, the "Temple of Liberty," the summer house in the Harford garden, is the place where Evan and Deborah escape into dreams. Their dreams are similar, Deborah's of an exotic life at the French court of Louis XIV or Napoleon, Evan's of becoming a power under Robespierre during the French Revolution. These in turn are paralleled by Con Melody's memories of his service under Wellington against Napoleon in Spain. Both Evan and Con force their dreams into a shadowy reality by wearing their old uniforms.

The plays repeat a central, basic theme: the corruption of an idealistic man by a domineering and grasping woman. In the stories of the Harfords, the destructive results of a dream denied would be reiterated in each generation, and as the stories of Jonathan, Evan, Simon, Ethan, and Con Melody were to show, the denial of the dream led to a kind of madness. That the loss of the dream was occasioned by the action of a possessive and greedy woman linked the actions to the point where each became a parable of sorts expressing O'Neill's dark view of his country's past and future, a world gained at the cost of the soul.

To know what the cycle would have been in its entirety is impossible. Its narrative appears to be filled with excess, reaching at times to melodramatic absurdity. Yet the plays were planned when O'Neill's genius was fully matured and when he was capable of writing *The Iceman Cometh* and *Long Day's Journey into Night*. That genius must be trusted in estimating what he might have accomplished with so large-scale and complex an account of eight generations of an American family. Perhaps the best testimony to what might have been are the two plays of the central section, "Sara and Abigail," or, since he changed "Abigail" to "Deborah," "Sara and Deborah." *A Touch of the Poet* is a completed work; *More Stately Mansions* exists in a long, semi-final draft version that did not receive its final honing and polishing. It escaped destruction only by accident. The difference in style between the two plays creates a number of problems. *A Touch of the Poet* is compact, tautly plotted and developed in the best traditions of the realistic theatre. *More Stately Mansions* is over-long and, although written predominantly in the realistic mode, contains scenes which go back to the soliloquies and asides of O'Neill's Art Theatre practices. During the writing of *Mourning Becomes Electra,* O'Neill had drafted a version of his trilogy using masks, asides, and soliloquies. Later, however, he eliminated all such vestiges of what he called "Interludisms," although he felt that having written them out he had gained new insights into his characters. Nevertheless he counseled himself to avoid the "thought-aside" method unless the characters clearly required such assistance to reveal their complexities.[6]

Discussing the techniques of characterization for the cycle as a whole, O'Neill wrote in a note dated May 18, 1937:

> Double characterization—2 planes of action
> Essential character in terms of compulsive thoughts—prejudiced hates, defiant rebellious self-assertions of the uncompromising

ego—going back to childhood—all this brought out in soliloquy. Then the planes shifting to realism all this becomes hidden, sly compromising, opportunist, calculating, etc.

Characters introduced in soliloquy first—each alone—relaxed as far as surroundings are concerned—outer calm permitting free expression of soul assertion

or on three planes as Curtain rises—darkness—unconscious assertion—the half-light—characters dimly perceived—solil[oquy] of conscious struggle living in part—then full light, realism. play begins in terms of surface life.

The note suggests that O'Neill was planning to write the cycle in a manner he had once called "super-naturalism,"[7] a style he had found praiseworthy in describing the "behind life" plays of Strindberg, and which he felt essential to the revelation of the complex drives of the sons of Sara and Simon Harford. Some scenes of the draft follow the method suggested by his note. Deborah, for example, is introduced in a long soliloquy which is her "soul's assertion." Other scenes of the play do not attempt the two planes of action, being satisfied to reveal the complexities of character in the same way that the complex nature of Con Melody is revealed, without altering the realistic mode of the play. In the end, the problems the stylistic differences create cannot be resolved, although it may be argued on the basis of his work with *Mourning Becomes Electra* that, when he got down to cutting the play to compassable length, causing it to conform to the realism of *A Touch of the Poet* might have proved a ready solution to many difficulties.

It is not surprising that O'Neill fixed on *A Touch of the Poet* as the play he could finish. It is the central play of the eleven-play scheme, standing in relation to the whole much as the scene on Adam Brant's ship stands at the center of *Mourning Becomes Electra*—isolated, a little apart, giving pause to the main action and providing a perspective on what had happened, at the same time as it replenishes the material for what is to come. The introduction of Sara and Simon provides a relief from the concentration on the fatal Sisters and the cursed family. Now there are new people to consider and, in the person of Nora Melody, a character drawn in profound contrast to any of the Harfords—a woman who simply and deeply loves. Furthermore, the action is complete in itself. The potential conflict between Deborah and Sara does not require a sequent play for its resolution. In the present action, the questions it has raised have been answered by Sara's love for Simon. The theme is completely stated.

Yet the play belongs in the whole. It sets forth the major motifs as in a microcosm. Deborah's two appearances in Act II re-tell in outline the history of the Harfords which has been enacted in the first four plays. Her account extracts from what has passed the major symbols and thematic essence and brings them to bear on the present action. And, although her view is of what has passed, what she says applies not only to the Melody family but to the Harford's sons who will soon be enveloped in the dark. As she phrases it: "The Harfords never give up their dreams, even though they deny them."

A Touch of the Poet unexpectedly recalls the Abbey Theatre play O'Neill saw in 1911, *Birthright* by T. C. Murray. The Irish folk drama which provided him with the root situation for *Beyond the Horizon* at the outset of his career and *Desire Under the Elms* at its mid-point served him yet one more time as he came to the end of his long life in the theatre. He remembered, perhaps without being fully aware of it, the situation in Murray's play when one of the family must shoot a mare in which he took particular pride. The scenes are not identical. In *Birthright,* the mare must be shot because she has been injured, but on the two stages the same kind of tension builds. *Birthright* also offers a parallel to the scene in which Nora waits for Con's return, working at her household chores until fear and exhaustion overcome her, and she sits numbly keeping watch. O'Neill's falling back on an earlier source of inspiration is of the same order of return to first commitments as is suggested by the play's title, which he took from a stage direction describing Robert Mayo in *Beyond the Horizon.** What such returns meant can only be surmised. Perhaps the tangles of the cycle's story caused him to turn back to a time in his creative life when the design of the whole was simpler and a play's action fell into a reasonable compass. Whatever the reason, it is possible to see in Cornelius Melody an older version of Robert Mayo, holding to dreams he cannot realize and who must therefore be ground to defeat by pervasive failure.

---

* "There is a touch of the poet about him expressed in his high forehead and his wide dark eyes." [81] In this connection O'Neill's return to Irish dialect comedy in *A Moon for the Misbegotten* may be mentioned.

Mayo, as O'Neill thought of him, was a man who renounced his dream for the sake of a trivial love affair. To some extent, Melody does the same. He has risen to the rank of major in Wellington's army, but he betrays himself by attempting to seduce a Spanish noblewoman and by killing her husband in a duel. What follows is a long road down. He sells his castle in Ireland, goes to America and invests in a once-prosperous tavern, formerly a coach stop on a now-abandoned post road into Boston. Like Mayo, he is a man who cannot cope with life beyond the dream. His illusion is his life.

Where he differs from Mayo is that his dream was once fulfilled. He had his moment of glory in his hand. Where Mayo merely reached for it, Melody, more grievously, lost it. Mayo must live in the expectation O'Neill came to call "hopeless hope." Melody lives with fragments of memory, constructing all he possesses from them. O'Neill significantly does not allow him to become pathetic. Melody is presumptuous, arrogant, overbearing, a domestic tyrant and, as Sara rightly calls him, "a drunken fool."[8] Perversely, by virtue of these qualities, he summons an audience's pity far more than the tubercular Robert Mayo can ever do. Mayo remains a literary construction; Melody moves as a man.

As the action turns, after his belligerent attack on the Harford mansion and his defeat by the household servants, the dream is shattered. Ex-Major Melody is not unlike those Homeric heroes whose armor "clattered about them" as they fell in battle. The dream was an armor, and as he falls, it too is destroyed. His decision to kill the mare and himself is right, as is his further understanding that having killed her, he has already killed himself. Melody is nothing without his dream. He has lived only in his chosen role.

The bar off the dining room of Melody's tavern is not Harry Hope's saloon. The Irish contingent who loaf there, sponging drinks off the proprietor, have nothing in common with Hope's roomers. Only Patch Riley, an old man whose "washed-out blue eyes have a wandering, half-witted expression," bears any resemblance to the drifters of *The Iceman Cometh*. When he is drunk, he sinks "deeper in dreams," where he is lost except when called upon to play a tune on his pipes. The rest, mortal peasants, are ordinary men, who come to get drunk and whose psychological need for the comfort of the bar has little in common with the need Hope's room-

ers have to float their dreams on a drink of nickel whiskey. Yet they
are dependent on Melody, as he, to a degree, depends on them. For
him, they and the barroom provide an escape. The bar is the one
place where he can strut in his dreams without fear of contradiction. There, refighting the Battle of Talavera, he is emperor of his
illusions; there he is free both of disturbing obligations, as to Nora,
and of criticism, as from Sara.

O'Neill keeps a watchful eye on the door to the bar. He knows
from moment to moment whether it is open, or closed, or locked. It
is locked, for example, during the crucial time in Act IV when
Melody returns from the donnybrook at the Harfords' and kills the
mare. No escape then must be open for him; he must stay and destroy the image by which he has lived. At other times, the bar is a
refuge. At the end of Act I, when Nora's concern for his welfare
becomes overwhelming, he retreats from his failure to respond to
her love, going through the door into the bar. He tries to do so
when Sara taxes him about the grocery bills that have gone unpaid
so the mare may be fed. Again, at the height of his vicious quarrel
with his daughter in Act III, he insults her, then breaks off and
heads compulsively for the bar. At the door he pauses, back to the
room, and squeezes out words asking her forgiveness. Sara, however,
has left in anger. The occasion is important. Sara's hatred, like
Nora's love, threatens the image of the hero of Talavera. As he
apologizes, Con seems for once to admit that he needs the reality
of love from his wife and daughter more than the dreams of the
Major. That he does not go into the bar suggests that he is ready
to accept the responsibilities accompanying love. His words are not
heard; he has removed his mask and no one has seen him. Truth
becomes one more empty gesture. He is not only tortured by the
role he has chosen, but he comes close to an admission that his life
is a lie without substance. O'Neill describes him: *"As he discovers
she is not there and has not heard him, for a second he crumbles,
his soldierly erectness sags and his face falls. He looks sad and hopeless and bitter and old, his eyes wandering dully."* [116]

At such a time, in such a moment of defeat, to enter the bar
would lead to destruction. Stripped of all illusion, Con has neither
love nor dreams to help him. To save some vestige of what he was,
he goes to the mirror and repeats the pantomime of arrogance that
he has created for the Major, forcing himself erect, reciting the

verses from Byron, pumping air into the deflated self. As he does so Gadsby, the Harford lawyer, enters, and the end begins. The sequence shows that in the rooms the family inhabits, the necessary, sustaining illusion can be maintained only with cruelty to those about him. The bar means freedom to exist in illusion and to escape. The glimpse of Con empty of pretense at the bar door is not in essence different from the revelation of what happens to the bums at Harry Hope's when Hickey takes their dreams from them. The action is, in vignette, the action of *The Iceman Cometh*.

After the shooting of the mare, when Melody emerges from his semi-comatose condition, the Major is dead. The loutish shebeen keeper has taken his place, and Con tells Sara that this role is true: "I'm not puttin' on the brogue to tormint you, me darlint. Nor play-actin', Sara. That was the Major's game." [168] He lies. The peasant is nothing but another role. He leers into the mirror and grotesquely mimics his antics as the Major, quoting Byron with a comedian's brogue: "I stood / Among thim, but not av thim . . . ," and breaks off, crying "Be God *I'm* alive and in the crowd they *can* deem me one av such! I'll be among thim and av thim, too—and make up for the lonely dog's life the Major led me." [177] With this he turns and moves toward the barroom door. Sara stops him and pleads with great passion for him to return, calling on his pride, begging his forgiveness. But he has turned the knob. She makes a last appeal and offers to give up Simon: "I'll even tell Simon—that after his father's insults to you—I'm too proud to marry a Yankee coward's son!"

As Melody hears her appeal, he crumbles *"until he appears to have no character left in which to hide and defend himself. He cries wildly and despairingly, as if he saw his last hope of escape suddenly cut off. 'Sara!* For the love of God, stop—let me go—!' " [178]

A moment more, and he is through the bar door, received with shouts of greeting. His final exit is his last escape, as he takes refuge in the role of shebeen-keeper and waits for the death that will follow within four years. To substitute the Irish shebeen-keeper for the role he had formerly played is meaningless. The new performance—*The Lower Depths* after *The Count of Monte Cristo*—is no nearer reality. He cannot rid himself of the need of a mask, for he has no substance without one. His need to clutch about him the ragged garment, the torn uniform in which he finally clothes himself, makes him a pathetic figure whom Sara can properly mourn. Yet she mourns an image, the dead Major. Such substance as he has is apparent only to his wife whose pride in her love survives all his failure and humiliation. Her love makes him something, if he exists at all. Without it, he is as lifeless as the men at the Bottom of the Sea Rathskeller in *The Iceman Cometh*.

If *A Touch of the Poet* was intended to provide an emblematic center in the cycle's structure, Melody's life becomes the epitome of the lives of all the major characters. Deborah in her talk with Sara describes the Harford men in words that apply equally to Con. She warns Sara that the Harford men "never part with their dreams even when they deny them."[9] Con's life shows that without the dream, man is nothing. The dream unfulfilled, mocked or destroyed, the man no longer has reason to live. Even denying his dream, by admitting its falsity, he must try to live by it. To do so is to live with frustrating illusion, and in retaliation Con—as do the Harford men—turns cruel and lives estranged from those who love him. "You can have no idea," Deborah tells Sara, "what revengeful hate the Harford pursuit of freedom imposed upon the women who shared their lives." [83] The life Sara and Deborah share with Simon in *More Stately Mansions* exemplifies the truth of what she says.

In *A Touch of the Poet*, Deborah is given two brief, strong scenes as she comes to the tavern to see her son who lies ill in an upstairs room. She appears cool, distant, fragile, elegantly aristocratic, almost a woman from the world of Melody's past. His crude attempts to seduce her fill her with disgust, but she also responds involuntarily to his sensuality. With Sara, she is aloof, mocking and "Cassandra-like," as she warns her of the danger in the Harford men. She appears to be a woman who has made her choices in the world and is prepared to live by them. Her son's book that "the pure freedom of Nature" is to inspire him to write amounts in her mind to only a "crude imitation of Lord Byron," [81] but she admits that her excursion to Simon's cabin has been strange to her. She tells Sara, with an echo of O'Neill's earlier awareness, of the power of Dionysian forces,

> I did find my walk alone in the woods a strangely overpowering experience. Frightening—but intoxicating, too. Such a wild feeling

of release and fresh enslavement. I have not ventured from my garden in many years. There, nature is tamed, constrained to obey and adorn. I had forgotten how compelling the brutal power of primitive, possessive nature can be—when suddenly one is attacked by it.

Her intention, however, is to return to her garden "and listen indifferently again while the footsteps of life pass and recede along the street beyond the high wall. I shall never venture forth again to do my duty." [86]

The implications of Deborah's return to her garden from the world of duty are not made wholly evident in *A Touch of the Poet.* In *More Stately Mansions,* it becomes clear that her reclusiveness is a retreat into dreams very like the illusions by which Melody has lived. In Deborah's walled garden nature is "meticulously tended and trimmed." The shrubs and trees are clipped into geometrical shapes, the sunlight falls in chiaroscuro patterns, and the effect *"is of nature distorted and humiliated by a deliberately mocking, petulant arrogance."* [95] In the center of the garden stands Deborah's little summerhouse, her father-in-law's "Temple of Liberty" built as a refuge in which he could act out his Jacobin dreams. There, wearing his old uniform, like Melody, he wasted his life, and there he died. To his daughter-in-law, the summerhouse is a similar refuge. It is a more elegant version of Melody's barroom. Inside, there is nothing but "darkness and dust and spider webs—and the silence of dead dreams." [112] But the Chinese red lacquer door, as crucial in *More Stately Mansions* as the barrom door in *A Touch of the Poet,* leads to forgetfulness and to the peace of the mad.

Deborah's fear of nature unmethodized, her retreat into the misshapen artifice of her garden are the outer signs of a division in her that is revealed, as are the oppositions of peasant and aristocrat in Melody, in her assumption of two very different roles. Unlike Melody's, Deborah's roles conceal more than emptiness. In the garden, she gives way to dreaming that she is the mistress of a man of supreme power, Louis XIV or Napoleon. Walking with her lover in the gardens at Versailles, she attracts all eyes and, triumphing over their jealousy, flaunts the fact of her power over the ruler by leading him to the summerhouse, in her imagination a "Temple of Love" he has built for her. There she permits him to make love to her. In her garden, she strolls up and down the paths daydreaming of romantic evil, and to those who come upon her she behaves as if she were indeed such a royal whore. The danger is clear, even to her. The dreams centering in the summerhouse have a fascination that can lead her away from normal life—tempt her to escape forever into dreams. She says,

> One has only to concentrate one's mind enough, and one's pride to choose of one's own free will, and one can cheat life, and death, of oneself. It would be so easy for me! Like pushing open a door in the mind and then passing through with the freedom of one's lifelong desire. I tell you . . . I saw that door, as real as the door I have just opened. . . . [28]

To pass through the "door in the mind," whose physical realization is the door to the summerhouse, is to pass through to madness, where Deborah knows she can "at least believe in a dream again." [102]

Opposed to the fear of being lost in dreams is her concern that life may be passing her by beyond the walls of her garden. Sometimes an aching loneliness possesses her, and she does not find, as Melody does in the mirror, a way of reaffirming illusions. Although she holds the Harfords in disdain, the possibility that she may choose madness terrifies her, and she forces herself to return to their world, to become an affectionate mother-in-law and grandmother to her four grandsons. She speaks passionately of an existence which is entirely simple, "the meaning of life so happily implicit, the feeling of living so deeply sure of itself, not needing thought, beyond all torturing doubt, the passive 'yes' welcoming the peaceful procession of demanding days." [171] In such an opposition, between the dreaming aristocrat and the simple, accepting woman, she finds her roles.

The roles, however, conceal a shadowy substance. Like Nina Leeds, Deborah cannot give over the attempt to "meddle in lives." Her son describes her as being "extremely greedy for others' lives," and he is right. Her eagerness to possess is so strong that even at her most giving (she speaks of longing for the "happy greedy laughter of children"), she seems to herself to be hypocritical. Having patched a peace with Sara, she jeers when alone, "At least old age has not impaired your talent for acting, Deborah!" A moment later she denies her insincerity: "No! You lie! You know you lie! I meant every word sincerely! I will make myself love her! She has given me life again!"[57] Her greed makes her doubt her own sincerity and her life swings between two illusions.

The metaphor of her desire to possess lies in a story she has told to her son when he was a child playing in her garden. It is the story of a young king, dispossessed of his inheritance by a "beautiful enchantress." The king must search for a door which he will know when he finds it to be the door leading to his lost kingdom. Deborah's story has no ending. As the king discovers the door and seeks to enter, he hears the voice of the witch behind it, warning him that she might have lied and caused him to follow a false hope: "If you dare to open the door you may discover this is no longer your old happy realm but a barren desert, where it is always night, haunted by terrible ghosts and ruled over by a hideous old witch, who wishes to destroy your claim to her realm." The king in fear remains by the door, unable to enter or to leave it. He becomes a beggar for alms from passers-by. [111]

The fairy tale of dispossession perhaps was intended as a central image for the entire cycle, as it is for the play in which it is told: like the king, Americans are condemned to wander the earth seeking to regain their "happy realm," the free land they have lost. For Deborah and her son its meaning is more personal. It expresses Deborah's own longing for entrance to a lost kingdom of her dreams. The king's door and the summerhouse door are the same. She, like the king, stands on the outside of the door in fear to enter. Yet in her other role, she becomes the dispossessor, the witch. She tells Sara that if she were in her place she would hate Simon and revenge herself on him: "I would make him pay for me until I had taken everything he possessed! And when he had no more to pay me, I would drive him out of my life to beg outside my door!" [133] In the last scene, she becomes what she has called the three spinsters who created the family fortune: a witch.

> *A great physical change is noticeable in her. Her small girlish figure has grown so terribly emaciated that she gives the impression of being bodiless, a little, skinny, witch-like, old woman, an evil godmother, conjured to life from the pages of a fairy tale.* [161]

To Simon, the story has remained a horror from his childhood. He yearns for a happy ending which Deborah denies him even to the last. When she determines to enter the summerhouse, to will herself to madness, he begs her to take him with her, to help him through the door into the happy kingdom, but she refuses and enters alone. When she returns she appears mad, but Sara cannot be sure, any more than she was sure of her father's deliberate choice of roles. Is Deborah mad or is she merely acting? The play does not resolve the issue, but leaves her in imperious possession of the only kingdom she could finally claim.

Simon's roles shift as he matures. In *A Touch of the Poet*, he is portrayed as a Mayo-esque dreamer, a poet-philosopher, writing in the tradition of Rousseau about the simple goodness in man. Sara, who calls him "a born dreamer with a raft of great dreams," somewhat breathlessly tells her mother that he has left his father's business in order to

> prove his independence by living alone in the wilds, and build his own cabin, and do all the work, and support himself simply, and feel one with Nature, and think great thoughts about what life means, and write a book about how the world can be changed so people won't be greedy to own money and land and get the best of each other but will be content with little and live in peace and freedom together, and it will be like heaven on earth. [29]

Early in *More Stately Mansions,* Simon describes the premise of his dream kingdom more exactly:

> In a free society there must be no private property to tempt men's greed into enslaving one another. We must protect man from his stupid possessive instincts until he can be educated to outgrow them spiritually. . . . I still believe with Rousseau, as firmly as ever, that at bottom human nature is good and unselfish. It is what we are pleased to call civilization that has corrupted it. We must return to Nature and simplicity and then we'll find that the People . . . are as genuinely noble and honorable as the false aristocracy of our present society pretends to be. [8]

Shortly, however, he renounces such an idealistic conception of man. "Rousseau," he says, "was simply hiding from himself in a superior, idealistic dream—as Mother has always done in a different way." He continues to consider the possibilities of another book,

> a frank study of the true nature of man as he really is and not as he pretends to himself to be . . . a daring assertion that what he is, no matter how it shocks our sentimental moral and religious delusions about him, is good because it is true, and should, in a

world of facts, become the foundation of a new morality which would destroy all our present hypocritical pretenses and virtuous lies about ourselves. [47]

Sara replies to this: "If it isn't just like you to start dreaming a new dream the moment after you've woke up from the old! It's the touch of the poet in you!" Simon denies it, and as idealism turns cynical, he plunges forward in the assurance that "Power is the only freedom." Late in the play he tells Sara and Deborah,

> What is evil is the stupid theory that man is naturally what we call virtuous and good—instead of being what he is, a hog. It is that idealistic fallacy which is responsible for all the confusion in our minds, the conflicts within the self, and for all the confusion in our relationships with one another, within the family particularly, for the blundering of our desires which are disciplined to covet what they don't want and be afraid to crave what they wish for in truth. In a nutshell, all one needs to remember is that good is evil, and evil, good. [172]

In Simon's character, role playing is somewhat less conscious than it is in Melody's or Deborah's. Nevertheless, neither idealism nor cynicism has significant reality for him. When he was a child, his mother instilled in him ideals of perfect freedom. Now that he is a man she has deserted him, leaving him nothing but a Napoleonic dream of achieving freedom through power. The two "dreams," as he calls them, "encourage a continual conflict in his mind, so that he lives split into opposites and divided against himself! All in the name of Freedom! As if at the end of every dream of liberty one did not find the slave, oneself, to whom oneself, the Master, is enslaved!" [49] Simon, to be sure, is Master, the head of the house of Harford, but at heart he is a crying child, clinging to his mother for protection. The child, far more than the man, threatens both women, who turn against him in what becomes a mortal struggle.

The pattern which has shown the Harfords and Melody attempting to hold to an idealistic dream and being forced to substitute its opposite in a greedy struggle for life is repeated in the person of Sara Melody. Sara's beauty is spoiled by her heavy ankles and stubby hands—peasant hands, her father calls them, knowing that the ambitious peasant will succeed, although with difficulty, in rooting out Simon's idealistic dreams. "He's set in his proud, noble ways," Melody says, "but she'll find the right trick! . . . She'll see the day when she'll wear fine silks and drive in a carriage wid a naygur coachman behind spankin' thoroughbreds, her nose in the air; and she'll live in a Yankee mansion, as big as a castle, on a grand estate av stately woodland and soft green meadows and a lake." [173]

At the end of *More Stately Mansions,* Sara blames herself for having caused Simon to desert his early dreams, saying that she has driven him to attempt to secure her father's aristocratic pretenses as her reality. The implication is that she has somehow forced him to trade his ideals for the greedy life of the Harford company. In fact, although the point is often made, in the published script, Sara is not shown to be responsible. Deborah and his brother ask his help when the company has come near failing upon his father's death. He agrees to aid them, and in this decision Sara plays no part. Later, Simon forces her to take charge of the Harford empire, deeding the control to her in bits, and teaching her how to assume his hated burden, but as to whether Sara's materialism is an essential of her nature, the plays remain ambiguous. Indeed, there is evidence in Act I, scene iii, that Sara has forced Simon to his study every night in order that he might either write or renounce his Rousseauistic book. By the same token, it is Deborah who asks Simon to take over the Harford Company, and thereafter uses him so that she may find her way back to a normal, less lonely life. Nevertheless, Sara clings with part of her desires to the idea of being a "grand lady," and in idle times in her husband's office, where she serves as his secretary and "mistress," she designs the stately mansion of her dreams.

The hunger for a new version of Melody Castle is part of the motive that causes her to accept Deborah's bargain. If she permits Deborah to live with them and to be with her grandchildren, Deborah will deed the mansion to Sara. Sara is won by the bribe, and thereafter becomes mistress of one of the finest houses in the community. At the same time, she is defensive of her peasant origins, and on occasion defiant in her use of the brogue, playing the peasant in a schizoid way, just as she had formerly done to mock her posturing father. What appears most true about her is that she is anxious at the end of *More Stately Mansions* to leave the world of false aristocrats and become a true peasant, a farm woman justifying her life by her labors. Only in such renunciation can she express truly her love for Simon. In any other existence than that of the peasant, her love is destroyed by greedy dreams.

What Sara tries to do is to love simply and wholly as her mother had done. Nora Melody is drawn with the most complete, uncomplex affection of any character in the O'Neill canon. She has found in her total acceptance of her husband a way to resolve all the conflicts of love and hate that beset O'Neill's characters, generally. She is without a mask, humble in her devotion. Like Miriam in *Lazarus Laughed* in her unabashed earthy simplicity, she finds her pride of life in her love. Others may speak of pride as governing their action. To live by pride is to live falsely. Nora lives by love, and pride comes because of it. She passes gently from the story, and although she appears in the unpublished first scene of *More Stately Mansions,* after Melody dies, she enters a convent and is forgotten.

Nora's legacy is inherited by Josie Hogan in *A Moon for the Misbegotten,* but a little of what she was remains alive in her daughter. Sara, at the end of *A Touch of the Poet,* speaks of the fullness of her love for Simon, to whom she has given herself. Simon has said that he can support her through his business knowledge gained from working briefly with his father's company, and has asked her if she will be satisfied with a simple life, so that he may write his book. She tells her mother "So I kissed him and said all I wanted in life was his love, and whatever meant happiness to him would be my only ambition. . . . And I meant it, Mother! With all my heart and soul! . . . Isn't that a joke on me, with all my crazy dreams of riches and a grand estate and me a haughty lady riding around in a carriage with coachman and footman! . . . Wasn't I the fool to think that had any meaning at all when you're in love? You were right, Mother. I knew nothing of love, or the pride a woman can take in giving everything—the pride in her own love!" [146] She speaks here as her mother had spoken. Her father, however, has another view of her:

> All I can see in you is a common, greedy, scheming, cunning peasant girl, whose only thought is money and who has shamelessly thrown herself at a young man's head because his family happens to possess a little wealth and position. . . . I cannot stand by and let him commit himself irrevocably to what could only bring him disgust and bitterness, and ruin to all his dreams. [113]

At the end of *A Touch of the Poet,* Sara stands poised between the two estimates, but in the plays to follow, Con's view of her triumphs, and her destiny, judging from the cycle notes, is to become a greedy alcoholic shut away in the mansion she built on the site of the woodland cabin where she first knew love.

The personalities of the Harfords and of all those with whom they associate* are divided between two antithetical roles—mother and wife, wife and whore, mother and whore, or child and master. The masks are used as the pieces in a game that the players enter with a savage delight. It is called "Bewilder with Opposites," and its point lies in the shock created by unexpected changes of the mask. Changing the masks terrifies and also permits continual shifting realignment of allegiances. It is as if the players, naked in their masks, were caught up in an intricately patterned charade and passed with grotesque and crippled stateliness before mirrors whose reflections mock the game of dispossession.

In the central figure of the game, Sara becomes Deborah's ally. The two women enter into a strange unspoken compact, almost as if they were coalescing the functions of Mother and Wife into a single whorish force. O'Neill writes of their behavior that *"They are like two mothers who, confident of their charm, take a possessive gratification in teasing a young, bashful son. But there is something more behind this—the calculating coquetry of two prostitutes trying to entice a man."* [128] Allied, they prove strong enough to resist Simon's greed for their love, and, like the witch in the fairy tale, they dispossess the son of his kingdom and reduce him to beggary. Then, when he is destroyed, and when the female power moves without check, they are able to make the substance of Deborah's fantasies and Sara's dreams real, and seduce, corrupt and command at will.

The coalition of the women leaves Simon alone. When he first senses it happening, he says,

> It has become dark in here and Mother and Sara have vanished—
> Mother took her hand and led her back—as if she opened a door
> into the past in whose darkness they vanished to reappear as one

---

* Nicholas Gadsby, the lawyer, masks with a conventional mercantile exterior a dreamer who allows himself to remember that Napoleon was such a short, fat man as he. Only Simon's brother Joel is without the mask, and he is viewed as a singularly lifeless creature.

woman—a woman recalling Mother but a strange woman—unreal, a ghost inhumanly removed from living, beautiful and coldly remote and proud—with a smile deliberately amused by its own indifference—because she no longer wants me—has taken all she needed—I have served my purpose—she has ruthlessly got rid of me—she is free—and I am left lost in myself, with nothing! [125]

Retaliating against rejection he attempts to divide the force that threatens him, so that when the women are separated he may possess both or at least choose between them. Deborah he confines to her garden, separating her from his children so that when he enters her world, he may be the only child of the adored and adoring mother. Sara too must be isolated and forced to play the role of Deborah's dreams, that of a powerful whore who controls a Napoleon of finance and whose power over both the man and his empire is unlimited. Deborah calls her fantasies "real life," [13] but Sara must go to her husband's office to live out Deborah's dream in fact, playing the role of her husband's "mistress," indulging him sexually on a garish couch under an ornate mirror, in return for control of the company.

The irony is that although Simon is fighting to survive, his actions reveal his desire both to submit to the women and to defeat them, by taking them as a single being, possessing one to possess them both. In making the sexual demands on Sara, Simon is enabled to live the life of one of his mother's fantasy lovers, but clearly his real need is to return to Deborah. "All we are is the past," he says, [73] and his past lies with his mother in an enchanted existence in the grotesque garden behind the wall, beyond the door in the mind. He pleads with Deborah to take him with her as she goes to lose herself in dreams. She rejects him, pushing him with unexpected force from the steps of the summerhouse. The thrust is like an act of emasculation. He falls, knocking himself unconscious. He awakes, cradled as a child by Sara, who becomes his mother now that Deborah has gone into the shadows.

Sara lovingly tells him that it was her father's "crazy dreams" that made her his enemy. Now she will try to restore to him the dreams that he had when she first loved him, when he was "the dreamer with a touch of the poet in his soul, and the heart of a boy!" [191] She says she will destroy the company and retire to the old Harford farm, and Simon can write poems and plan the book that will "save the world and free men from the curse of greed in them!"

[191] But Simon will not return. The final moments are reminiscent of the ending of Ibsen's *Ghosts*, the mad Oswald clinging to his mother:

> SIMON   *Dazedly—like a little boy.* I fell and hit my head, Mother. It hurts.
> SARA   I'll bathe it for you when we get in the house. Come along now. . . .
> SIMON   . . . Yes, Mother.
> SARA   *With a fierce, passionate, possessive tenderness.* Yes, I'll be your Mother, too, now, and your peace and happiness and all you'll ever need in life! Come! [194]

It is not a comforting conclusion, and Simon, like Melody who also reverted in his despair to a point of origin, will soon disappear from the history.

The destruction of Simon, like the death of Con Melody, is reminiscent of much that O'Neill had written earlier. It is not entirely an accident that the last words of *The Web*, spoken by the plainclothesman to Rose's deserted child—"Mama's gone. I'm your mama now"—are in substance identical with the last line of *More Stately Mansions*. O'Neill was from the first instinctively concerned with deserted children, orphans of God the Mother who yearned to return to the memory of old harmony. Such desire was the agony and the salvation of those touched with poetry. Men without visions, the materialistic descendants of Caligula, were in his first view the enemy, the possessors who denied the poet's attempt to be possessed. Later, however, the poets were corrupted by possessive drives from within, and they dispossessed themselves of the possibility of peace and harmony by their instinctive greed. In the cycle, they become the greedy meek, those who seek both liberty *and* death, who build stately mansions to shut themselves from heaven, whose limits are the earth and who, having gained, find nothing is lost save their honor. O'Neill's finely ironic titles all point in the same direction toward the depiction of man as an alienated, lost, vision-haunted denier of his dreams. The action of the cycle, although the theological implications of such a play as *Desire Under the Elms* are absent, recapitulates the major theme of O'Neill's earlier work. He had often written of possessors self-dispossessed and of men who have lost their souls.

Who has lost his soul has no reality. The center of his identity has diminished until what is left is an inarticulate cry of deep need. In place of the true center, man dons the masks of the game. Such assurance as the masks bring him is evanescent. Their reality is no more than that of an image caught in a mirror, Melody's mirror in the tavern before which he reassembles his life-lie, or that in Simon Harford's office, before which Sara constructs her image of the whore, or the soul's mirror of Deborah's fantasies, wherein she sees Death staring over her shoulder. [12] The images caught in them are arrogant; they distort nature as Deborah's garden does. They reflect the prisoner in his cell divided between roles assumed in pride and roles bred of dreams. They create nightmares, and they destroy the divided self by driving it to madness.

In telling his tales of the Harford family, O'Neill apparently intended to present their lives as emblematic of the history of the United States. Yet to conceive of the Harford dynasty as a metaphor for American destiny is to blur a subtle proportion. It is more true to say that American history is a symbolic extension of the Harford story, that the historical story is the secondary term of the vast image. Thus, Shakespeare used the story of national destinies in his tragedies to reflect and extend the internal division of his real point of focus, the tragic hero; thus O'Neill had used the story of a nation divided to reflect and to parallel the story of the divided Mannon household. The story of the nation as O'Neill tells it is in many respects less complex than the story of the Harfords. In the beginning, men lived in simple freedom. Simon's uncompleted book, written like *Walden* in rustic settings and in praise of minimal self-sufficiency, is intended to express the virtues of a world where men live without pride or greed. This is the perfect freedom sought by Jonathan Harford, determinedly rural, isolated, uncommitted to society. Hog-like man, however, finds simple harmony uncongenial. Instead of taking from the earth the small measure of his true need, he becomes an exploiter: "Power is Freedom." He will possess not only the earth but other men. His greed, born of his drive for liberty, makes him an enslaver. All the means to power, money, transportation, the slave trade itself, cause him to despoil his original heritage, transforming it to a materialistic wilderness, where enough is synonymous with too much, where Sara can say, "I am good because I am strong. You are evil because you are weak," [152] and where the enslaver is finally enslaved.

To a limited extent, the story traced in *A Touch of the Poet* and *More Stately Mansions* can be viewed as a microcosm of the national history. The growth of the Harford Company from the proprietorship of small mills to the possession of ships, banks, consumer outlets, arriving at last at the establishment of a self-sufficient trust epitomizes America's commitment to greedy expansion. O'Neill has clearly intended the personal stories to augment the national account. When, for example, Simon tells Sara "The Company is you. Your nature is its nature,"* or when he describes the "game" he plays at the office as "A fascinating game—resembling love," there is an obvious invitation to read the relationship between the two as somehow symbolizing forces at work in the national past.

Among the American dramatists of the thirties, quasi-allegorical narratives were a convenient way by which audiences could be induced to eat both cake and social message. S. N. Behrman's biographies of enchanting liberal ladies caught between lovers whose political stances were as important as their amatory prowess, Clifford Odets's studies of the corruption of golden boys, Robert E. Sherwood's melodramas that urged American intervention into the European war, not to mention lesser plays such as Sidney Kingsley's *Dead End* or Irwin Shaw's *The Gentle People,* all used the personal narrative to comment on the condition of the nation. Although elements in the two plays offer this possibility, in general O'Neill refused the allegorical gambit. The Melodys and the Harfords relate to American history in a more direct way. They represent nothing, but are what they are, men and women who have come from a background of European experience and who fight for their well-being in the New World.

Therefore, to attempt to read the cycle plays as allegories is to mistake the true emphasis. The main stress is on the personal account that details a Strindbergian pattern of female domination over the male, and that tells of a struggle that was to be repeated throughout the length of the work. The farmer's widow who causes the freedom-seeking deserter to give up his dream, the Sisters who rule over the life of Evan Harford and his family, Leda Cade and Elizabeth Harford, the female tycoon who was to dominate *A Hair of the Dog* all point to the same thematic center: the cycle was to show woman as the destroyer of ideals, dreams, and even life.

Woman's dream is of corruptive and spectacular power; man's

---

* [89] The lines echo with irony Ephraim's words to Abbie: "Sometimes ye air the farm an' sometimes the farm be yew," and Orin Mannon's association of the tropical islands with his mother's presence.

dream is of perfect, idealistic freedom. The cynical monarchial motivations of women conflict mortally with the democratic concepts that move men. Woman's power is achieved through control of man, and she sets herself to destroy his dreams that she may in owning him live free of his desire. His dreams destroyed, he becomes corrupt, but she survives in greedy health, feeding on his power. In revulsion at his own corruption, he seeks a purer condition of being, free of the complexities and disappointments women create for him. He turns for solace to the only hope he has, the memory of the woman he knew when he was a child, and he seeks in her one who will be both mother and mistress. Yet he is not a child, and he is further degraded by the sense that with both mistress and mother he is incestuously involved. For the same reason, the woman rejects him or emasculates him so that, reduced to impotence, he cannot harm her by stepping between her and her dreams. Should he fight her, she tricks, cajoles, seduces, but she does not give him his desires. She remains aloof or withdraws from him in pride and disdain, leaving him no protection. In the end what remains for him is to make babbling appeals for her charity or to escape into madness or death. The "final fate" of the Harford men held out no possibility of spiritual salvation. The picture O'Neill sketched of their destinies was of a desperate fall to a frightening end in a world that offered only vicious struggle as a way of life.

To this story, the history of an America corrupted by greed provides a large-scale metaphor, but the psychological relationships do not explain what happened to the country. "Possessors, Self-dispossessed" on its metaphorical and historical level means that those to whom the nation was given made themselves aliens to the land in seeking to possess it. On its psychological level, however, it must refer to the lost human beings, who are doomed to live in darkness haunted by the nightmares of a Godless world.

In other plays, on the other side of the door in the mind, O'Neill explored such lost men, men for the most part without women. In the cycle, the ability and the need to dream were the consequences of man's having in him a touch of the poet. As he wrote, however, O'Neill came to see the need to dream as a universal one, shared by all men, a human drive, possibly man's most basic urge. Any dream sustains, whether it gives hope or hopeless hope or acts like hope, a "dope-dream." The dream alone gives life. Nina Leeds

called life "a long drawn out lie with a sniffling sigh at the end,"
[40] and the pun has relevance to the lie of the pipe dreams to which
the derelicts in Harry Hope's saloon cling.

O'Neill wrote the first draft of *The Iceman Cometh* between June
8 and November 26, 1939. In this year, the world fell apart as Poland
was invaded and Britain and France declared war on Germany.
Throughout the end of the Depression, O'Neill had worked on the
cycle, finishing drafts of *And Give Me Death, The Greed of the
Meek* and *More Stately Mansions*. Work on *The Calms of Capricorn* had begun, but the world crisis made it impossible for him to
continue his account of the decline and fall of the United States. In
the midst of Armageddon, one does not bother to prophesy.
O'Neill's reaction to war was predictable. At Tao House, he re-
treated further into himself than he had ever gone before, as if the
only understanding that could come in a world gone mad was the
understanding of one's self. The following year he wrote *Hughie*
and the scenarios and some draft versions of its companion works
in the cycle of one-act plays called *By Way of Obit*. In 1941, he
wrote his last completed work, *A Moon for the Misbegotten*. Although he picked at the cycle, making revisions on *A Touch of the
Poet* as late as 1942, the work was at a stalemate. Whatever truths
it contained for O'Neill had finally to be explored in another past,
his own, and in another way than he had in the cycle. The last
four plays form a network of introspection whose effect is perhaps
best expressed in O'Neill's words about *The Iceman Cometh* contained in a letter to Lawrence Langner dated August 11, 1940:

> . . . there are moments in it that suddenly strip the secret soul of
> a man stark naked, not in cruelty or moral superiority, but with
> an understanding compassion which sees him as a victim of the
> ironies of life and of himself. Those moments are for me the
> depth of tragedy, with nothing more that can possibly be said.

Compassion produced by a full understanding of man's circumstances and man's essential nature, a compassion which beggars
analysis, is O'Neill's final achievement in theatre. The action of
each of the four last plays rests in a tale to be told, a tale that is
essentially a confession made in hope of absolution. Although the
confessional tale is often plotless, often nothing more than a dream,
it is a way of reaching out in the dark, of finding pity long denied to
old sorrow.

The introspective qualities of the last plays account for their essential lyricism. When *The Iceman Cometh* was first produced in 1946, under the somewhat ponderously reverential conditions that O'Neill's "return" to the New York theatre necessarily occasioned, it brought with it, from producers and reviewers, charges that O'Neill was indulging himself by refusing to cut the work. Langner tells of a time during rehearsals when he timidly reminded O'Neill that the same point had been made eighteen times. O'Neill told him "in a particularly quiet voice, 'I *intended* it to be repeated eighteen times!'"[10] Although it was obviously not a matter of calculated intention, O'Neill did not indulge in such repetition without full awareness of its theatrical consequences. Like many of his earlier efforts, the repetition not only in *The Iceman Cometh* but in *A Long Day's Journey into Night* is essential to the lyric mode of the work, for in these plays O'Neill became the poet he had earlier so often lamented he could not be.

Perhaps the nearest theatrical analogue to *The Iceman Cometh* is Dylan Thomas's *Under Milkwood*. Both are "plays for voices," and the voices are those of the dead, reiterating their stories endlessly in an eternity of silence. Under the circumstances of the play the period slang takes on the special qualities of lyric speech.* The movement is musical; the repetition of what is said, often almost without significant development, must be followed as if it were music, as patterned abstraction, implemented through contrapuntal repetitions. It is a kind of "sound effect," but here blended so completely with the action that it becomes the action. There are not many moments in theatre comparable to the canonical weaving of the narratives of betrayal, Hickey's and Parritt's, toward the end of the play. Hickey's long monologue is interspersed by short echoing comments from Parritt telling Larry Slade of his own act of betrayal. Parritt and Hickey do not, really, listen to the words that are said. That is to say they do not understand one another and from that understanding receive direction. Rather, they move toward the same end without conscious inter-awareness, impelled by purely verbal concatenations, each developing the theme of betrayal as a sound in the air. *The Iceman Cometh* does not need music, yet it should be heard as music is heard with an understanding that it progresses in patterns of sound, as much as in patterns of narrative action.

* O'Neill has taken care to make the speech of his characters accurate. Cf. for example, *Hugo of* The Iceman Cometh: *Realism and O'Neill,* Doris M. Alexander, *American Quarterly* V (winter, 1953), 357-66.

To argue that a play should not be justified by comparison to a musical form has validity. It is, after all, only an analogy, but O'Neill's predilection for Nietzsche would cause him to know that Nietzsche claimed tragedy to have been born from "The Spirit of Music." The lyric movement of the chorus in an Aeschylean or Sophoclean tragedy, *The Coephorii* or *Antigone*, for example, is the source of the play's energy, turning as a massive wheel at the center of the narrative, spinning off the tortured action, and giving it life and form. Similarly, *The Iceman Cometh* has a strong choric thrust, developed in lyric repetitions.

The Iceman Cometh is perhaps the most "Greek" of O'Neill's work, built around a central chorus, complete with *choregos* in Harry Hope, and the three principal actors, Hickey, Slade and Parritt. In creating his chorus, O'Neill turned to his memories of time spent in the saloons of lower New York—Jimmy the Priest's, The Golden Swan, nicknamed "The Hell-Hole"—and of their inhabitants. Most of the characters are modeled after acquaintances or friends he had observed and whom he placed on stage with special fidelity.* Yet, while he is concerned to specify their individuality with affectionate concern, he is also seeking, somewhat in the manner

---

* Arthur and Barbara Gelb and Louis Sheaffer have devoted extensive research to the identification of the real-life sources for O'Neill's characters. Of the cast only Rocky, Morello, the three women and, of course, Moran and Liebe, both extras, appear to have no actual counterparts, although even here the possibility is that they are formed from memory. The only significant exception appears to be Hickey. The Gelbs suggest [285] that he was based on a character named "Happy," a collector for a laundry chain whom O'Neill had known in The Hell Hole. An aspect of the portrait was derived from characteristics of Jamie, who, it will be remembered, had appeared in a supporting role in a play called *The Travelling Salesman*. Sheaffer points to a character named Adams in the unpublished *Chris Christophersen*. The play opens with a scene between Adams, Burns and "Johnny the Priest." Adams, like the inhabitants of Hope's saloon is asleep at a table. The action begins with Burns attempting to wake Adams. Johnny, the bartender-owner intervenes:

> JOHNNY   (*Frowning*) Leave him alone, Jack. He's been talking me deaf, dumb and blind all day. I'm sick o' listening to him. Let him sleep it off.
>
> BURNS   You? Huh! How about me? I'm going to make him buy 'nother drink, that's what—to pay me for listenin' to his bull, see? [2]

He wakes Adams, they argue about the purchase of a drink, and finally Burns dozes off while Adams sits "*staring at him with sodden stupidity.*" He comes to a short while later, becomes noisy and is sent protesting upstairs to bed. When he has gone, Johnny says of him, "Smart fellow, too—when he's sober. I've known him for twenty or thirty years. Used to be a clerk at a ship chandler's. Left that and became a travelling salesman. Good one, too, they say. Never stays long on one job, though. Booze

of the Elizabethan "Character" writers, to see in the individual a type. The word "type" occurs frequently in his descriptive stage directions of Hope's roomers: Hugo Kalmar bears "a strong resemblance to the type of Anarchist as portrayed . . . in newspaper cartoons"; Joe Mott's face is "mildly negroid in type"; Piet Wetjoen is "A Dutch farmer type." Where the word is not mentioned, the idea remains; James Cameron has "a quality about him of a prim, Victorian old maid." Cecil Lewis "is as obviously English as Yorkshire pudding and just as obviously the former army officer." McGloin has "the occupation of policeman stamped all over him." Ed Mosher "looks like an enlarged, elderly, bald edition of the village fat boy." [574-77] While the typicality of Willie Oban and of the bartender Rocky is not stressed (although Rocky is summarized as a "Neapolitan-American"), they are not essentially different from the other members of the chorus. The same is true of the three women: Pearl and Margie are called "typical dollar streetwalkers," [611] and Chuck Morello, the daytime bartender, like his nighttime counterpart, is seen as an "Italian-American." [615] Harry Hope, the chorus leader, is not viewed as typical in the same way. He maintains a certain individuality partly because it is through him that the liaison is made between the actions of the chorus and the principals. These—Larry Slade, Don Parritt and Theodore Hickman—are individuals, less by their appearance than by the complexity of their emotional problems.

The tableau thus formed, although externally static, has a powerful inner movement. The unity of the chorus is achieved by a remarkable theatrical tour de force. Each of the derelicts has, in the Stanislavskian sense, the same essential action: to foster himself in his dream. The actions create the unity of the microcosm O'Neill has woven. Against its fabric, the protagonists stand sharply drawn. Parritt, Slade and Hickey are seen, perhaps, as aspects of the same man. They overlap at least, in their acts of betrayal, their despair-

---

got a strangle hold on him. He's been fired again now. Good schoolin'—every chance, too. He's one of the kind ought to leave red eye alone. Always ending up his drunk here. Knows no one'll know him here 'cept me and he ain't shamed to go the limit. (*Philosophically*) Well, he's a good spender as long as he's got it. Don't be too rough with him." [6]

The detail of the portrait suggests that O'Neill drew it from a model, especially since Adams disappears from the script at this point. Here probably is the unnamed progenitor of Hickey.

ing desire to be rid of pity, their refusal to enter the world of the dreaming chorus. Yet, although they resemble one another, they stand opposed as antagonists as well, forming a hostile triangle against the unity of the background.

The physical picture awakens echoes of other works. O'Neill has evidently had his eye on Gorky's *The Lower Depths,* a play which he appreciated as "the great proletarian revolutionary play," saying that "it is really more wonderful propaganda for the submerged than any other play ever written, simply because it contains no propaganda, but simply shows humanity as it is—truth in terms of human life."[11] The relation between the two works bears analysis.[12] as does the relationship between O'Neill's play and Ibsen's *The Wild Duck,* which like *The Iceman Cometh* explores the fatal effects of the "life-lie." In configuration and *dramatis personae,* Harry Hope's birthday party bears a strong resemblance to the traditional images of "The Last Supper."* Such parallels are just and important and in part serve to explain why *The Iceman Cometh* now ranks among the most ambiguous of O'Neill's plays and has received the most extensive critical attention. In its original production, which marked the end of O'Neill's absence from the theatre, and in its 1956 revival in New York, a production that began the resurgence of interest in O'Neill's dramas, it has held a special position in the canon.

Yet viewed in its place in the progress of O'Neill's playwriting career it is not an ambiguous work. In part, it stands as an ironic

---

* Cf. Cyrus Day, "The Iceman and the Bridegroom," in *Modern Drama,* I, 1, May, 1958, pp. 3-9. Professor Day's article lists a number of resemblances between Hope's party and The Last Supper, including the twelve "disciples" of Hickey, the three women, the presence of Parritt as a suicidal Judas figure, the wine drinking, the midnight hour. Day is in error when he states that the stage grouping resembles Da Vinci's Last Supper. O'Neill throughout the play has been very specific as to where each person sits at the tables. At the party, Hickey and Hope face one another from opposite ends of the table, Larry and Parritt occupy the central positions facing the viewer where Da Vinci places Christ. The point is perhaps unimportant except that it raises the question as to who is the Christ figure at this "supper," Hickey or Harry Hope? Professor Day's view is that Hickey is a form of anti-Christ and that the play is blasphemously nihilistic ("Did [O'Neill] introduce concealed blasphemies into his play . . . ? And did he laugh in secret at critics who supposed he had written a compassionate play . . . ?"). The party is, after all, Hope's party, and it is Hope who rises from the death they suffer to bring life again to the bums. O'Neill's compassion in this play, while it may rest on ambiguities, and while it was born of despair, is not fraudulent.

comment on much that had preceded. Reverting to his earlier manner, spinning an all-but-plotless play filled with portraits of the down-and-out characters he has known as a young man, he recapitulates many of his early themes, particularly that of the "hopeless hope," but removes the romantic coloration with which he clothed the concept in *The Straw*, seeing it now as he was to show it again in *Hughie*, as the only lifeline man could find.

The title, drawn from the story of the wise and foolish virgins in Matthew 25:6, parodies, the description of the coming of the Savior: "But at midnight there was a cry made, Behold the bridegroom cometh." The savior who comes to Harry Hope's saloon is a strange messiah. The image of the iceman, suggestive of the chill of the morgue, and of a variety of off-color stories and songs featuring the iceman as a casual seducer,* is interpreted by Willie Oban as meaning death: "Would that Hickey or Death would come." [596] Hickey is a messiah of death, but his message, judged by its effect on its hearers, is closely parallel to that of O'Neill's other messiah, Lazarus of Bethany.

O'Neill's two choric dramas, both with titles derived from the New Testament, are at once remarkably alike and startlingly different from one another. In both *The Iceman Cometh* and *Lazarus Laughed*, a messianic figure appears preaching salvation to a world represented in microcosm by type characters. In each play, the recipients of the message prove resistant to it, and when it is forced upon them, prove incapable of acting in accord with it. In each, the messiah is set free to follow his own path to martyrdom by the murder of his wife. That path leads to burning—at the stake and in the electric chair. Such parallels are meaningless except as they relate to the central matter: the messages both messiahs preach, however different in effect and intention, are in essence the same. Of *Lazarus Laughed* O'Neill wrote "Death is the Father, Fear the Holy Spirit, Pain the Son."[13] To this trinity man pays his hom-

---

* Like the traveling salesman, the iceman gained a certain mythic dimension in American smoking-car jokes. Dudley Nichols recorded that O'Neill had wished to recall the Biblical quotation by his use of the archaic verb form, but that he also wanted to suggest the bawdy story of the husband who called upstairs to his wife, "Has the iceman come yet?" The answer: "No, but he's breathing hard." [Gelb. 831] The end of an era for the iceman as folk hero was marked by a song of minor popularity in vaudeville whose refrain went: "The Frigidaire can never replace the Iceman."

age. Lazarus's message to rid men of fear and pain is that they should see life as illusory, give over the dreams that haunt them like ghosts in the dark and acknowledge with clear eyes that they are part of life itself and can ask no higher good. Only then will they know the peace they instinctively seek. Lazarus's doctrine is a lonely one; he loves humanity, but has little room for tenderness and for individual love. Miriam must follow unnoticed behind him, yearning for the simplicity of her life in the hills of Bethany. Those who accept his paradox, that death is life, lose human contact and the powers of sympathy, hope, humility and belief in man. Caught in the Dionysian ecstasy of his laughter, they throw themselves on the swords of soldiers. It is a chill rendition of Matthew, 10:39: "He who loses his life for my sake will find it."

Hickey's remedy for the ills of the world, as that world is represented by the types in Harry Hope's back room, is equally cold, equally predicated on a belief that human life is an illusion. As Lazarus exhorts, so Hickey, by means of a series of long, brutal individual encounters in the rooms above the bar, forces the dreamers to give over their ultimate link with life, the sustaining pipe-dream of their worth as human beings. Their dreams hold at least an illusion of life's essence: movement in purposive action. Action, to be sure, will never be taken, but the dreams reveal a basic human truth: to foster life, man must preserve a minimal dream of movement. Hickey, whose promised peace is predicated on showing the dreamers that they will never take action and that their dream of doing so is a lie, brings the peace of death. Like much psychiatric theory, Hickey's Godless theology seeks "adjustment" to a meaningless reality, claiming that he who faces his life will find it. Yet if there is no life to be found, Hickey—not unlike Lazarus—becomes Death's priest.

The world which the dreamers inhabit has the fragile ecology of a tide pool. O'Neill calls the saloon "The Bottom of the Sea Rathskeller," and the imagery of drifting tidal life is pervasive.* It is a world that barely holds to the fringes of consciousness, moving hesitantly between sleeping and waking, fusing the two conditions into a continuous trance-like existence. The light that filters through the

---

*Interestingly, no one of the cast of characters has any connection with the sea, as if O'Neill were deliberately denying the source of his earlier poetic dreams.

dirty windows from the street is pale and insufficient to separate day from night. Time is meaningless. Voices are nearly unheard in the comatose silence. Existence at Harry Hope's is reduced to its lowest denominator, a hibernation of animals huddled together in dread of waking.

The dreamers have come to Hope's because, ostensibly, they are failures in the outside world, but their typicality makes it impossible to read their communal condition in terms of individual weakness. What lies outside is a world without value, a hostile society to which no man can possibly belong, and from which they must take refuge. At one point, Hickey mocks one of the men, saying, "You can't hang around all day looking as if you were scared the street outside would bite you!" [685] But the menace in the streets is real. The threatening automobile that Harry Hope conjures up to justify his failure to take the walk around the neighborhood is, however, imaginary, real. It is a symbol of a mechanized, animalistic, spiritless world, a world in which God is dead.

After the long, poetically oriented quest which he had conducted through the plays of the 1920's, seeking a God to which men could belong, O'Neill at last has come to agree with Nietzsche that men live in a Godless world. There is no longer the possibility of being possessed by Dionysian ecstasy. Men's dreams can have no fulfillment that is not in itself illusion; the mindless, unpoetic materialism of each of the dreams is sufficient testimony to the fact that in all the outer world there is nowhere to go, nothing worth having, nothing to which man may make offering as to a God. In the wake of Hickey's teaching, men are left as walking corpses wandering in an icy hell; all they can do is to wait for death. In *Waiting for Godot*, Samuel Beckett describes the same interminable course of life, as Gogo and Didi indulge in senseless repetitive discourse and vaudeville routines to pass time. The pipe-dreams of O'Neill's characters have the same function: they make life tolerable while the dreamers wait for Hickey or Death. As much as each of the dreamers permits himself to understand anything, he knows that the pipe-dreams, his own included, are a game, that they are not real. Each man mocks the dreams of the others as insubstantial and illusory, but the mockery is a defensive irony, an essential element of the self-identification the individual's dreams provide. What cannot be admitted is pity, for pity would acknowledge the truth each seeks to conceal from himself. Nietzsche said God died of such pity; in self-pity the lowest creature will come to despair.

For the dreamers, a deliberately fostered illusion is the sign of membership in the club. The subject of the pipe-dream is unimportant. Some dreams, like Hugo Kalmar's incoherent anarchist ravings, are little more than fragmented, formless memories, holding so little sense of life as to be meaningless. But whether or not the dream is coherent and contains a goal of action, its value lies less in its shape than in the fact that it forms part of the structure of illusion that "gives life to the whole misbegotten mad lot" [578] of dreamers. The saving possibility is the mutuality of the dreamers' condition, for the conjunction of the dreams, the body heat of sleeping animals, provides the warmth of the world. This fact too makes it possible for the dreamers to hope without desire.

The world in which they live exists beyond desire. Whiskey alone sustains physical life. Hunger for food is not expressed, and notably no movement of sexual desire disturbs the quiet. The three whores arouse no one to lust, nor do they try to become objects of desire among the dreamers. Even the proposed marriage of Chuck and Cora is based on other dreams than that of sexual gratification. Very different from the cycle plays, where sexual battles are fought to the death in an arena of passion, Hope's saloon is a world without women. Nevertheless, as in the cycle plays, the power of woman is felt, and here, too, it is a destructive power.

Hickey's wife, Evelyn, is dead. Rosa Parritt, Don Parritt's mother and Larry Slade's former mistress, has gone to the death of spirit her imprisonment will bring upon her. Yet the power of these women, carried into the dreamers' world by the men who have loved them, destroys for a time the structure of life fostered there. In the cycle plays, Deborah and Sara attempt to use Simon, to destroy his dreams and rid themselves of his desire. Rosa Parritt is pictured as an independent, fierce-willed woman who has held possessively onto her son at the same time as she has refused his love. His claim is that she has forced him into the radical movement, yet has permitted him no freedom of mature judgment. At the same time, he makes clear that he wants her to be his mother and resents her flaunting her lovers in the name of "Free Love." Her lover, Larry Slade, has left her in anger, calling her whore, for much the same reason, so that a bond between Larry and Parritt exists that is like, if it is not in fact, that between father and son,* and both feel guilty at having betrayed Rosa in order to be free of her rejection of their love. To love Rosa, a man must submit himself completely to her ambitions, but must make no demands in return. Betrayal is a defensive movement of their individuality.

On the other hand, Hickey's wife has made no ostensible demands on her husband. Hickey's description of her conveys the image of a gentle creature, the opposite of Rosa Parritt, but one who in a different way saps a man's individuality. She asks nothing, fears her husband's attention, yet her capacity for forgiveness, her confident faith in him proves to be as destructive as Rosa's independence. Like Margaret in *The Great God Brown*, Evelyn cannot see what is behind Hickey's face, even when he forces her brutally to look upon it. The blindness of her love makes Hickey live true to her dreams of him and fills him with guilt when he betrays her, just as Parritt and Slade are guilty in their compulsive betrayal of Rosa. O'Neill in the past, sensing that man must belong to some force that controls his being, had shown that those who ran from such possession were in the end caught and destroyed by it. In *The Iceman Cometh*, as in the cycle plays, the force, devoid of its theological implications and reduced to a sexual relationship, has the same effect. Parritt has betrayed his mother to the police, Hickey has murdered Evelyn, and Larry must send his "son" to his death to end his torment, resigning himself finally to the sort of living punishment that Lavinia Mannon accepts. Each seeks death as the only way of assuaging or atoning for the guilt the woman has thust upon him. Simon's final rejection by Deborah creates in him the same emptiness of spirit, and causes him to turn toward the death that comes in the second scene of *The Calms of Capricorn*.

The three betrayers are the only occupants of the saloon who need pity. They epitomize, perhaps, the men without dreams who live in the hostile streets beyond the barroom door. They come, at least, from such a world, and disturb the dreaming sea. Both Hickey and Parritt force pity into the waters, but it is pity without tenderness. Parritt demands that Slade take pity on him and punish him by commanding him to suicide. Hickey, who insists that Larry's in-

---

* Larry has stood in loco parentis to Parritt. Whether or not he is actually Parritt's father is deliberately left ambiguous. Slade denies it when Parritt suggests that he is, but with such vehemence as to raise the possibility.

stinctive sympathy for the dreamers is the wrong kind of pity, attempts to rip off their masks and free them of the torture of hope. The play charts his failure and notes as well the way returning illusion brings life again to the sterile waters. When he has gone, old currents move again at the bottom of the sea, and the men who have been wakened to a hideous and intolerable truth begin to dream again.

Hickey's therapy, through different means, is worked on Cornelius Melody. When his role as the romantic soldier is taken from him, he like the bums becomes a comatose, dying animal. He saves himself by assuming another role, as the bums reclothe themselves in illusions. Deborah Harford, too, enters a world like Hope's saloon when she enters the summer house at the end of *More Stately Mansions*, but she must live alone, in the isolation of insanity. Deborah's end is so dark as to be indiscernible.

The Iceman Cometh, however, is illuminated by "darkness visible," and it reflects the despair O'Neill himself felt in the year of its composition. On September 11, 1939, he wrote to Langner from Tao House,

> The whole business from 1918 to now has been so criminally, hoggishly stupid. That is what sticks in one's gorge, that man can never learn but must be always the same old God damned greedy, murderous, suicidal ass! I foresee a world in which any lover of liberty will continue to live with reluctance and be relieved to die.

That it would be a relief to die! The desire that surges to the surface of the lives of the three betrayers in the play was a common reaction in that year. O'Neill was not alone.

The death of the human spirit remained his theme. Shortly, he set to work on a play entitled *The Last Conquest*: "The World-Dictator fantasy of a possible future, and the attempted last campaign of Evil to stamp out even the unconscious memory of Good in Man's spirit. . . ."* But the play remained in scenario, and *The Iceman Cometh* was withheld from production because, as he told Langner, "A New York audience could neither see nor hear its meaning. The pity and tragedy of defensive pipe dreams would be

* O'Neill to Dudley Nichols, December 16, 1942. He had worked on the outline and scenario over the year prior to the bombing of Pearl Harbor.

deemed downright unpatriotic. . . . But after the war is over, I am afraid . . . that American audiences will understand a lot of *The Iceman Cometh* only too well."

Yet, as O'Neill had shown the fostering of illusion bred a certain comfort that was a protection from despair. As a kind of epilogue to *The Iceman Cometh,* the following year, he attempted to make what was positive there more explicit, to write with a charity that was beyond pity and more like love of those whose souls stir in shadows. The play was *Hughie,* the first of six contemplated one-act plays to be given the group title, *By Way of Obit.* Of the six only one other was written more fully than an outline. This play, possibly concerning an old Irish chambermaid, was destroyed,* together with the outlines and scenarios when the O'Neills left Tao House. But *Hughie* was left to reiterate with a difference the themes of *The Iceman Cometh.*

The fifty-minute play is an epitome of O'Neill's mature theatrical style and statement. A circle of light in a surrounding outer darkness that serves as a refuge in a hostile world whose presence is indicated by a consistent pattern of sounds; the passage of time so meaningless as to suggest an action outside of time; dialogue that is in essence two parallel almost uninterrupted monologues; characters who wear masks to conceal the agony of their inner lives; the image of life on the bottom of a sordid world where men's dreams provide the only warmth: what began so abortively in *A Wife for a Life* is here wrought into a perfect dramatic poem. The lyric mode of the play is abetted by the absence of any significant narrative plotting. The play depends on a purely emotional action evolved from the relationship established between Erie and Hughes, the Night Clerk. The dialogue, expressed in the rhythms and slang of Broadway argot of 1928, is used with the same awareness of its beauty and emotional power that Synge found in the dialect of the peasants of the Aran Islands. Like *The Iceman Cometh* and *A Moon for the Misbegotten* the action hinges on a tale to be told. Yet when it is set out, Erie's tale is no more than the vague account of lost affection, another expression of need, a lyric within a lyric.

---

* Cf. Langner, 403. "He had another one-act play which, together with [*Hughie*] might make a full evening in the theatre, but he did not give me this other play as it needed further revision." Gelb, 843, mentions the Irish chambermaid as subject.

The emotional center of the play perhaps evolves less from its words than from its silence. Such sounds as are heard in the hotel lobby—garbage cans, an El train, a fire engine and the like—accentuate the macabre stillness of a city in the early morning hours. The silence is a threatening force, an abnormal "spell" that *"presses suffocatingly upon the street, enters the deserted, dirty lobby."* [31] To the Clerk, the night seems like death, [30] and his mind "cowers" from it. Such hope as there is exists in the sounds that are the night's "obsequies": *"Only so many El trains pass in one night, and each one passing leaves one less to pass, so the night recedes, too, until at last it must die and join all the other long nights in Nirvana, the Big Night of Nights. And that's life."* [19] In the acted play, the Clerk's silence is to Erie like the silence of the city. The actor who plays Hughes must play but not speak the interior monologue. Only a few words rise to the surface; to Erie, he must seem another manifestation of death, like the threat outside, like Room 492 to which he cannot bear to return. Yet Hughes's silence is turning with a little life, born of vague hostilities, of physical pain in his feet, of boredom with overfriendly, anonymous hotel guests. Draped over the desk, he resembles a wax-works figure, but his mind pursues the sounds he hears in destructive fantasies of waking *"the whole damned city"* [17] with the garbage cans or of burning it down. It is only when an abnormally long pause of silence falls that he is forced out from the fantasies to hear the night sound nearest him, the voice of Erie Smith: *"His mind has been trying to fasten itself to some noise in the night, but a rare and threatening pause of silence has fallen on the city, and here he is, chained behind a hotel desk forever, awake when everyone else in the world is asleep, except Room 492, and he won't go to bed, he's still talking, and there is no escape."* [29]

Erie pours words into the silence, words that spatter and drain away unheard. They are a bragging, wise-cracking lament that centers on his loss of his dead friend, the former Night Clerk, Hughie. In the streets there lies a physical threat—of a beating from the men from whom he borrowed money to buy flowers for Hughie's funeral, and whom he cannot pay back. But the real threat is not physical: "I wouldn't never worry about owing guys, like I owe them guys. I'd always know I'd make a win that'd fix it. But now I got a lousy hunch when I lost Hughie I lost my luck—I mean, I've lost the old confidence. He used to give me confidence." [35]

For "confidence," read "life." Without Hughie, Erie falls in a void that is like death. He cannot bring himself to enter the cage of the elevator and ascend to Room 492. Instead he stands twirling his room key,* *"frantically as if it were a fetish which might set him free."*[28] To leave the light of the lobby, to go through the door for which he has the key is to die, much as Deborah, Con and the bums die by going through such a door. Erie clings to the key as if it were the substance of his life, as if life itself were somehow a key to death. Buying the hundred-dollar floral piece for Hughie's funeral to give him a "big-time send-off" has been the fulfilling act of his life. Accepting this, he also accepts that life holds nothing more for him, that he would be better off like Hughie, out of the racket his life has been. His mask has worn thin, and the darkness beneath shows through. At this point, he turns, defeated, and prepares to ascend to his room.

Yet his words have made contact, and in the play's final moments, the Night Clerk accepts the rules of Erie's game as Hughie had done. To Erie, the moment of realization that in the night he has touched another life is a *"saving revelation"*; [35] to Hughes it is even more: *"Beatific vision swoons on the empty pools of the Night Clerk's eyes. He resembles a holy saint, recently elected to Paradise."* [32] The vision of beatitude, a saint's vision, is no more than a pipe-dream, but it is enough. What is perhaps unclear in *The Iceman Cometh* is explicit here, that man's only sense of life comes through sharing a vision with another human being. The vision has no truth; it contains no hope. Yet it offers movement, and it is the focus of existence. It is a far remove from the dreams of Robert Mayo or of Juan Ponce de Leon, who saw, or sought to see, God in their visions. No such matter animates Erie and the Night Clerk or those living in Harry Hope's back room. The pipe-dream is only the way to sustain life; yet to dream is to endure.

The complex social imagery and the full psychological elabora-

---

* The use of the key is important stage business. It is the only non-verbal sound from within the lobby until the dice roll along the counter at the end of the play. O'Neill marks the turning point in the play, the moment when Erie hits the farthest ebb of his loneliness, with the stage direction *"For a while he is too defeated even to twirl his room key."* [30] The moment was underscored memorably in the Stockholm production when the actor, Bengt Eklund, dropped the key. In so bare a scene, the action, the loss of the fetish, assumed climactic proportions.

tion of the cycle held O'Neill's interest through the beginning of 1939. In that year, all solitudes were invaded, all walls broken. By June, the cycle was unofficially shelved, and O'Neill had turned to writing about the lives of the down-and-outs in *The Iceman Cometh* and *Hughie,* as if, by retreating into the debris of humanity, he might find shelter from names like Munich, Czechoslovakia and Poland. The dreams that in the cycle led a man toward action, out and into open warfare with his world, now changed, lost their power and became a form of memory as man turned weakly toward past illusions and huddled from the world. In bomb shelters, men do not behave very differently, perhaps, from the way they behave in *The Iceman Cometh.*

Mrs. O'Neill's diary for June 21, 1939, contains what is possibly the first recorded mention of another play he planned whose subject was his family and whose title was *Long Day's Journey into Night.* The play was begun shortly after the completion of *The Iceman Cometh* and, together with *Hughie,* was O'Neill's major creative effort of 1940. It was completed in September. Then, after a period of illness, he turned to its sequel, *A Moon for the Misbegotten.* He had written half of the first draft of that play when the Japanese bombed Pearl Harbor. O'Neill wrote to Dudley Nichols on December 16, 1941, that he had managed to finish the draft, but that the heart had gone out of its writing. Although he worked on it sporadically through 1943 and during the same period made revisions of *A Touch of the Poet* and developed the scenario of *The Last Conquest,* O'Neill's career as a playwright ended as the United States entered the war. By 1943, the tremor in his hand made sustained work impossible.

His illness and the war were real reasons for silence, but equally important was an underlying cause: having written the two plays about his family, O'Neill had no further place to go. *Long Day's Journey into Night* was the play he had been trying to write from the outset of his career; its achievement was his raison d'être as an artist. *A Moon for the Misbegotten* was an essential coda, an act of love, of charity and of contrition. Mrs. O'Neill recorded movingly what happened to O'Neill as he wrote. His work day was a long one, five hours in the morning and additional hours in the afternoon. As she described him, he was a man "being tortured every day by his own writing. He would come out of his study at the end of a day gaunt and sometimes weeping. His eyes would be all red and he looked ten years older than when he went in in the morning."[14] O'Neill said not without irony that he was writing plays he knew he could finish,[15] but the Tyrone plays were more than substitutes for the cycle. A lifetime's psychological and physical pressures had cornered him at last. It was a moment for truth and he told it.

When it was said, he was not entirely certain that it had emerged as truth. Edmund Tyrone, having told his father of all that has meaning for him, concludes his account of his quest by saying, "I couldn't touch what I tried to tell you just now. I just stammered. That's the best I'll ever do. . . . Well it will be faithful realism, at least. Stammering is the native eloquence of us fog-people." [154] He was wrong. *Long Day's Journey into Night* is not the work of a stammerer, but of a man who had become a master of his art, and whose native speech—not the words only, but the full acted drama —had the eloquence of a poet. The technical experimentation of the 1920's often caused him to beat frenetically against the limits of the stage. In the last four plays, the stage did all he asked of it without strain. The result is the highest achievement of the American realistic theatre.

What he asks is deceptively simple. Ironically, O'Neill's ultimate "experiment" was a return to four boards and a passion—to in other words, a confident reliance on his actors. He, who had gone to such elaborate lengths to ensure that his actors would fulfill his purposes, loading them with masks, asides, choral support and an infinity of pauses, now removed all exterior pressures. He was still generous with stage directions suggesting intonation and attitude, but he no longer tried to enforce a performance with the impedimenta of the Art Theatre. Everything, now, is in the role. An actor in these plays cannot hide behind personal mannerisms, clever business or habitual stage trickery. O'Neill has stripped all but the most minimal requirements from the stage, leaving the actors naked. They must play or perish.

Essentially, what is needed as setting for the four last plays are table surfaces and chairs. Properties are few, mostly bottles and glasses. Costume requirements are negligible. The most elaborate of the plays is *The Iceman Cometh,* which requires the bar structure and the essentials of the birthday feast, but even these are minimal in view of the play's length and the size of its cast.* What O'Neill makes from his simple materials is extraordinary. In the printed texts, he describes in elaborate detail each of the settings, listing titles of books on the shelves, giving the history of Hope's saloon and the hotel where Erie lives. It is information that he provides but does not insist on. An actor should know it, but an audience will perceive such details only through the filter of performance. It is said of Shakespeare that when he wishes the details of his setting to be specific, he makes it possible for the actor to show them. The same, despite the very different theatrical conventions, can be said of O'Neill in the last plays.

What an audience learns is surprisingly detailed, considering the limited means. The house of the Tyrones, its environment and the historical period are confidently set forth. Although the setting is bare, the audience knows that the house has four bedrooms and an attic and a cellar, that there is a big lawn ending in a hedge by the street, that the sea is near and that the town is a long streetcar ride away. The importance of the house to the action is evident, but it is through the action that the setting is fully evoked. So for the period. In creating the historical time for the two Tyrone plays, 1912 and 1923, O'Neill has relied on few specific historical details. The sinking of the *Titanic* or the arrival of Scott at the South Pole in 1912 might well have provided imagery for the desperately isolated Tyrones. The point, however, is that they *are* isolated, and no superficial references to period are needed to testify to the fact that they live in a society that is not very complex, in which they can find such privacy. By comparison, the world of *A Moon for the Misbegotten* is difficult, involved with new economic realities that Hogan resists as the post-war boom overruns his individualism. O'Neill has felt the difference, conveyed it in each line and attitude and has needed nothing more elaborate to evoke the period.

---

* Mention should be made of the use of the wagon stage in *The Iceman Cometh*. The setting, according to O'Neill's plan, was to be built twice as wide as the proscenium opening, and placed on a long wagon, extending into the wings. By shifting the wagon different sections of the bar and backroom could be exposed. It is an unassuming, efficient but unusual way of achieving some small variety in the setting. Virtually the only excess in the mounting of the last plays is the unnecessary change of scene from exterior to interior in the second act of *A Moon for the Misbegotten*. The change, accomplished by the removal of a wall of the house as in *Desire Under the Elms*, has no apparent purpose other than to lend variety to the scenic plan.

Like the details of setting and the historical period the time-scheme of *Long Day's Journey into Night* is simple and placed in the grain of the action without special technical elaboration. In many earlier plays, O'Neill pretended that the carefully designed, detailed planning of the progress of time had meaning. Occasionally, as with the sunset-to-dawn pattern of *Lazarus Laughed,* a somewhat gratuitous symbolism was achieved, but more often, the time structure was arbitrary and vague in its significance.

The arrangement of time in the autobiographical plays, however, is anything but arbitrary or extraneous. Around the time plan, O'Neill marshals such "effects" as he uses. Both plays begin in the full light of day to the sound of laughter. In *Long Day's Journey into Night,* as the Tyrones enter from the dining room, laughter sounds gently. Sun pours through the windows, the fog and the sound of the foghorn that has kept the family awake through the night have gone. The moment is poised and normal, but almost at once O'Neill denies its normalcy and starts the progression that had been a hallmark of his style from the first work he did for the theatre. The light dwindles, the fog returns, the foghorn sounds again. Gradually, the space diminishes to the area defined by a single light bulb over the central table in the room. The Tyrones' world is seen in its barest essentials. The proposition is clear, both to the actors and their characters: if life is to be created it must be evolved from the simple elements in this limited space. There are no extraneous symbols—isolating actors in follow-spots, diminishing the room by pulling in the walls of the set. Everything is in the action as the fog becomes the physical evidence of the isolation of the Tyrones.

The view of human nature set forth in the plays is of divided beings—the conception that earlier occasioned O'Neill's use of masks and other devices to suggest outer and inner lives. The Tyrones, however, need no masks. In their nearly mortal extremity, they have nothing to hide. Their pain fills their being so completely that their essential natures lie close to the surface. Thus Tyrone's charm, his friendliness and grace have worn thin under the erosion of despair. His actor's carriage and voice are ingrained in his demeanor, but as the night wears on and as the whiskey sickens him without making him drunk, the hidden man comes clearly into view. Jamie's cynical mask is dropped as the whiskey begins to talk, permitting the defenseless child in him to be seen. In the same way, as Mary descends farther into the doped state, the young girl alive within the pain-wracked woman comes forth to haunt them all. Whiskey and morphine effectively remove all disguise.

The words that come when the masks are off are in the form of soliloquies and monologues such as were from the first a characteristic of O'Neill's playwriting. Now, however, there is no breaking of the play's realistic limits. When, for example, Mary is left alone at the end of the scene with Cathleen in Act II, she speaks of her past in a long monologue that arises naturally from her addiction. As the morphine takes effect it causes her to babble, but she is still sufficiently aware not to be entirely dulled to her condition. Her words rise involuntarily out of her loneliness and guilt and speak of her longing for the life of the girl she was. It is as if she speaks to the girl in the past so as to assuage the loneliness of the present. Similarly, the long monologues of Edmund and his father in Act IV evoke the past as the only surcease from the doped present. Over their words there hangs no hint of Art Theatre Show Shop. O'Neill has enabled his actors to motivate the monologues and make them convincingly natural, psychologically real.

The two Tyrone plays hold firmly to the best realistic theatre practice. Yet for all their "faithful realism," it should be remarked that the dramas more readily than many earlier works approach the abstraction and symbolism so characteristic of the expressionist mode. The quality and force of that abstraction is difficult to define. O'Neill does not try to convince his audiences that the world of the Tyrones is a microcosm, as he suggested with the typified chorus of *The Iceman Cometh*. The Tyrones and the Hogans are particular people, moving in a specific time, facing highly individual problems. Like many other works of the realistic American theatre—*Come Back, Little Sheba* or *A Hatful of Rain,* for example—the plays are contained and domestic, well-told case histories. Yet to call *Long Day's Journey into Night* a "domestic tragedy" is to underestimate seriously its emotional effect. It is enlarged, not in the sense of Aristotelian "heightening," but more by its unremitting movement "behind life," in the phrase O'Neill once used to describe Strindberg's expressionist dramas. For a play to move "behind life" means that it expands inward, through the surfaces, and toward the core of life itself. The inner enlargement of the Tyrone plays enables an audience not only to scrutinize the motives

that produce the painful events but also to respond more fully
to the suffering these events create. No drama of modern times
contains more of pain's substance than *Long Day's Journey into
Night*, but in the final analysis, it is not the events, shocking though
they are, that grip the audience. The Tyrones suffer and the spectators are convinced that when suffering is the only reality, life is
truly as it is depicted in the play.

Verisimilitude does not necessarily lead to a universal statement.
However, when *Long Day's Journey into Night* is played, another
dimension opens. In the theatre, the suffering of the playwright is
more real, if that is possible, than that of his characters. The audience shares them both, and moves as in a dream that is both real
and more than real along the course of this "Wander Play." Pain
exists in a double layer, one that can seem a fiction, one that must
be a truth as the truth of suffering has seldom been stated. An emotion appropriate to an aesthetic experience and an emotion evoked
by reality join to create in the spectators a capacity for pity that
extends well beyond the boundaries of the theatre and rises to an acknowledgment of exceptional purity: that the universality of pain
makes pity and understanding and forgiveness the greatest of human needs.

At their climactic moments, both the Tyrone plays convey the
qualities of a dream. The fog or moonlight, the whiskey or dope
causes the characters to drift in slow emotional movements. Activity ceases, and each play becomes "a play for voices" that permits
the lyrics of lamentation and loss to be heard clearly. Physical objects are only the source of reverie. Edmund and his father play
cards. A bottle and glasses are on the table and above it an electric
chandelier. Only these have substance in the room. The two men sit
in near darkness and silence. A card is played or a drink is poured
or a light bulb is turned on. Something in the outer world is
touched, but it is a meaningless gesture. Then, as the object is
touched, the mind recoils, moving away from that physical contact
with the present into the past, wandering in a reverie that is as
formless and far-reaching as the night outside. The reverie ended,
the ballooning thought returns to the space where life is. Something else is touched; reverie begins again, in a movement that is
like a man's swimming, sinking and touching bottom in order to
rise up again into the currents of the water. In such scenes, time as

an adjunct of reality has stopped; forward motion has ended. The slow turning of memory is the play's only action. Life becomes a dream of pain.*

What the morphine brings to the surface in Mary Tyrone is awareness of the isolation that is both her need and her terror. As she appears in the first scene of the play, although small hints of what is to follow quickly become apparent, she seems a woman to whom her home and family are all, as they were to Essie Miller in *Ah, Wilderness!* The dependence of the men on her is marked, and not only in their concern for her health. She emerges in the few moments of normalcy as the source of life for them, the quiet hub around which they move, happy in her presence. The summer house seems to be truly a home, and the comforts it offers, though modest, are sufficient to their well-being. The illusion of the home is an essential image to establish at the outset, for it, of course, is not what it seems. The room is shabby, poorly furnished, a temporary residence at best. It is like the cheap hotels of Tyrone's road tours, where Mary has waited alone, unable to associate with theatre people, spending nights in idleness until her husband comes or is brought home from the theatre. Mary's life has taught her loneliness and provided her with the definition of a home as a place where "one is never lonely." [72] She remembers having had in her girlhood a "real" home, yet the memory is illusory. Idealizing her father, she has obliterated whatever faults existed in him. Tyrone tells Edmund her home was an ordinary one and her father a steady drinker. [137] His implied question is whether Mary's girlhood was indeed the happy time she remembers it to have been. O'Neill makes clear that her desire, even as a girl, was to escape into a lonely world—into the convent where she could be sustained by a vision and live a simple, virginal existence. That Mary loves her husband admits no question, yet in a larger sense, love has disturbed her spirit and violated her desire to retain her encapsuled purity. Love has led her into a world for which she was not and never could be

* The slow motion is very reminiscent of the rhythm of Strindberg's *A Dream Play*. The point is difficult of proof, the impression having arisen from seeing the two plays on successive evenings. Much more fragmented and "stylized" than O'Neill's work, *A Dream Play* also moves its action in the form of a reverie arising from the light touch of a "real" object. The sense of pervasive, universal suffering, together with the pity which the goddess Indra feels for man, is also in its emotional effect very like that created by O'Neill.

ready. She needs to be alone in a protected silence. She blames her failure vaguely on life, and she is right to do so. She says,

> None of us can help the things life has done to us. They're done before you realize it, and once they're done they make you do other things until at last everything comes between you and what you'd like to be, and you've lost your true self forever. [61]

In seeking her "true self," Mary is looking for a self that does not exist. Repeatedly she remarks that she cannot find her glasses and therefore cannot see to fix her hair. In other words, she cannot see what she is. She associates her Catholicism loosely with her need for morphine. Morphine is medicine to still the pain in her arthritic hands; the hands once played the piano; she studied music in the convent. "I had two dreams. To be a nun, that was the more beautiful one. To become a concert pianist, that was the other." [104] But the dreams of lost faith and spent talent are dreams of escape which affect her as the morphine does by pulling her from the present, from the house, from the irony of Tyrone's buying property without providing a home, and from her indifference that is like hatred of her family.

In the course of the play, Mary shifts repeatedly between a young girl and an embittered, self-contemptuous creature. Her guilt at failing to take care of her dead child, Eugene, is translated into insane hatred of her husband: "I know why he wants to send you to a sanatorium," she tells Edmund. "To take you away from me! He's always tried to do that. He's been jealous of every one of my babies! He kept finding ways to make me leave them. That's what caused Eugene's death. He's been jealous of you most of all. He knew I loved you best because—" [119] Frantically babying Edmund does not prevent her from blaming him for being born and starting her on the dope habit. Edmund is her scourge and should never have been born. Her hatred of Jamie is less ambiguous. Jamie's need for her is by no means reciprocated. She hates his cynicism, turns from him in fear that he will discover her need of the dope and silently accuses him of murdering the dead child. When the morphine talks in her, she treats her husband with a mixture of love and contempt, dwelling on his failures and yet maintaining the truth of her love for him. As Deborah Harford escaped in her dreams, Mary needs to turn from them all, to find a path that will take her deep into the fog, hating the loneliness, yet wanting to be rid of the obligations the men's love place upon her. Edmund describes the blank wall she builds around herself:

> It's . . . like a bank of fog in which she hides and loses herself. Deliberately, that's the hell of it! You know something in her does it deliberately—to get beyond our reach, to be rid of us, to forget we're alive! It's as if, in spite of loving us, she hated us! [139]

Mary's refusal of all her responsibilities has bred in her a guilt she is incapable of bearing. The morphine must be used to wipe out "the pain—*all* the pain—I mean in my hands." [103] In the morphine trance, she moves gently back in time, seeking to re-create the illusions of a happier world, before there was a past to make her what she has become. Her wedding dress, like Con Melody's red uniform, is a symbol of something that never was a substantial reality. Her quest is for a hope lost, a goalless search for salvation never to be attained.*

The men around Mary are condemned as she is to hopeless questing. Her husband like Con Melody is both poet and peasant. Under the graceful bearing of the aging actor, trained to eradicate the brogue, to gesture and speak with authority, there lies the fear of the poverty-stricken past. O'Neill has falsified to a degree the penny-pinching qualities in his father in drawing Tyrone,[16] yet the fear his father felt was undoubtedly a real one, as was the sense he expressed of having failed his potential as an actor. Like Mary, Tyrone is doomed to an endless life of regret for something lost in the past, holding to a hope that has no reality. "What the hell was it I wanted to buy?" he asks, and there is no answer unless it is protection and the quieting of irrational fears. His failure as an artist and as a husband had made him guilty beyond pardon. Like a lugged bear he stands as the target for all of his family's recriminations. Yet, perhaps more than any of the others, he shoulders the responsibilities of their lives. He has kindness in him, and a devo-

---

* At least as the play presents it. Mary speaks to Edmund of her plan to rid herself of the dope habit by entering a convent and praying for a restoration of the faith she had in the convent days. Then, "when the Blessed Virgin . . . sees no one in the world can believe in me even for a moment any more, then She will believe in me, and with Her help it will be so easy." [94] What is illusion in the play became a fact for Ella O'Neill, who cured her addiction by prayer.

tion to his wife that overrides all her animosity. For Edmund he demonstrates little close feeling. A generalized, somewhat distant affection is the most he reveals for his younger son. For Jamie, however, he has a strong feeling that is so positive it can turn easily into hostility. The two months during which Mary has returned to normal he describes to Jamie as "heaven," and he adds, "This home has been a home again. But I needn't tell you, Jamie." O'Neill amplifies the sense of understanding with a stage direction:

> *His son looks at him, for the first time with an understanding sympathy. It is as if suddenly a deep bond of common feeling existed between them in which their antagonisms could be forgotten.* [36]

It is Jamie's sobbing in the final moments of the play that breaks Tyrone, and Jamie who evokes in him his only shows of violence and perhaps also his most bitter expression of sorrow. As his son lies drunk and unconscious he says with sadness,

> A sweet spectacle for me! My first-born, who I hoped would bear my name in honor and dignity, who showed such brilliant promise! [167]

Tyrone, more than any other member of the family, honors the bonds of the home. He is capable of love but is often driven toward hatred. Even so, he never truly hates, but lives isolated within the frame of the bond, attempting to love in spite of everything. He turns from the pain of his life, to the local barroom; he buys bad real estate to purchase security he cannot find; he drinks to dope his mind to the point of forgetfulness. But he does not betray. He remains a simple man, free of cynicism, incapable of hatred. O'Neill's view of his father contains full charity.

O'Neill's picture of his younger self and of his brother Jamie is on the surface clear enough. Jamie, like his brother and father, is lost, embittered and cynical, wanting his mother whose rejection of him perhaps reaches farther back than the time when morphine forced her into drugged isolation. To compensate for her loss, he has sought to destroy himself with the profligate life of the Broadway rounder, and he has attempted to corrupt his brother, in the pretense of "putting him wise" to women and liquor. In Jamie, pain can have no anodyne. Liquor, far from dulling his loss, makes it unbearable, and, while Edmund is fussed over, even babied, no one tries to help Jamie. Nor is escape possible. Edmund can move into the fog—as he does in the third act—and find a kind of peace. The peace of belonging to a secret at the source of life, "the vision of beatitude" which he attempts to describe to his father, offers him a way out, just as Mary's dream of finding her girlhood faith and Tyrone's memory of Booth's praise have power to assuage the present. There is no vision of beatitude for Jamie in *Long Day's Journey into Night*. His need is always beside him, in Mary, but he cannot reach her. Like Tantalus, he has no refuge from desire. His is the howl of a soul lost in hell.

Edmund, as O'Neill presents him, is clearly drawn, and, as a dramatic character, offers adequate material to an actor, but there is perhaps less truth in his portrait than in the others. He is a strangely neutral figure, except in the scene with his father in Act IV. Even there he speaks out of a solitude that is unlike the isolation of the others. Although O'Neill has been at pains to show what the past has made his parents and brother, it is unclear what the past has made Edmund. O'Neill perhaps understandably suppresses the fact of his brief marriage and his child and omits the crucial event in 1912 of his divorce. He mentions that Edmund has been to sea, and almost perfunctorily adds that he has lived in the sewers of New York and Buenos Aires and has attempted suicide. None of these events, except insofar as his having been to sea conditions his vision of belonging, bear heavily on what he is. He seems to be the victim of the family, unwanted, betrayed, led astray by his brother and, now, with tuberculosis, suffering under his father's penuriousness. It is easy—perhaps too easy—to sympathize with Edmund. He is no more than an embittered adolescent, certainly a pale copy of what Eugene O'Neill was at that time.

How deliberate the suppression of personal qualities was is difficult to estimate. In *A Moon for the Misbegotten,* Jamie's brother is mentioned, but many descriptions of his reactions to Jamie's behavior were deleted in final revision. For example a speech of Jamie's in Act III, reads in the printed text, "Don't want to touch me now, eh? (*He shrugs his shoulders mechanically*) Sorry. I'm a damned fool. I shouldn't have told you." [151] In the typescript the speech contains a canceled reference to Jamie's brother:

> Don't want to touch me now? Well, I don't blame you. Except you promised. No, forget that. But you didn't know what you were

letting yourself in for. My fault. I shouldn't have told you. Too rotten and horrible. Never told anyone except my brother. He said "You dirty bastard"—then tried to excuse me because we'd always been such close pals—blamed it all on booze. He knows the booze game from his own experience—the mad things you do. All the same he couldn't forget. He loved her, too. He's never felt the same about me since. Tries to. He's a pal. But can't. Makes excuses to himself to keep away from me. For another reason, too. Can't keep me from seeing that he knows what I'm up against, and that there's only one answer. He knows it's hopeless. He can't help wishing I were dead, too—for my sake. (*Rousing himself, with a shrug of his shoulders—self-contemptuously*) Nuts! Why do I tell you about him. Nothing to do with you. (*Sneering*) A little more sob stuff. . . .

The responses of Jamie's brother in the second play are justifiably deleted. Whatever reticence O'Neill may have felt in describing his reactions to his brother's behavior, his views are irrelevant to the moment in the play. However, the elimination of detail about his own character in *Long Day's Journey into Night* is of another order. Edmund's somewhat poetic inclinations to lose himself in the fog and his desire to enter into a state of Dionysian ecstasy are recognizable characteristics of the young playwright as his early plays showed him to be. Such melancholy, mingled with narcissism, is little more than a normal stage of the developing adolescent ego. Yet, in this connection, one anecdote of the year 1912 is important.

It is an account by a nurse, Olive Evans, who cared for O'Neill shortly before he entered the sanatorium:

> Olive thought him vain because he was constantly studying himself in the bureau mirror and finally asked whether he would like the bureau moved to where he could see himself while in bed. "After I did it," she recalls, "I told him, 'Now you can see your madonna eyes,' and he looked shy and pleased. He had heavenly eyes, the most beautiful I've ever seen. So did Mrs. O'Neill—large, dark, dreamy eyes."[17]

How much may be read from the anecdote is uncertain, but the later remark to George Cram Cook, who had taxed him for continually looking in mirrors, should be remembered. When a man says he looks into mirrors to be sure he is there, the habit may indicate more than simple vanity. Con Melody's need to posture before the mirror to bolster his ego and his dreams is not much removed from O'Neill's need of the mirror to maintain his identity. *Long Day's Journey into Night* is a mirror, the last into which O'Neill looked, and it is of concern to explore what he found there when, for once, he committed himself to see himself unmasked and clear.

The characters most unambiguously drawn as self-portraits are the Poet in *Fog*, John Brown in *Bread and Butter*, Robert Mayo in *Beyond the Horizon*, Stephen Murray in *The Straw*, Michael Cape in *Welded*, Dion Anthony in *The Great God Brown*, Richard Miller in *Ah, Wilderness!* John in *Days Without End*, Simon Harford in *More Stately Mansions* and Edmund Tyrone in *Long Day's Journey into Night*. The physical portrait of each is that of a sensitive man, with big, wide-set dark eyes, a high forehead, dark hair brushed straight back, a dark, often sunburnt complexion, a narrow face with high cheekbones, a straight, thin nose and a full-lipped, sensitive mouth, suggesting weakness. His physique is tall, slender and wiry, and his demeanour is shy, restless, rebellious and a little delicate. All the details are not mentioned for all of the characters, and there are some variations in the color of eyes and hair. Yet in general, the image conforms—with the interesting exception of the frequently mentioned weak, sensual mouth—to photographs of O'Neill taken throughout his lifetime.

The reflection he saw in the stage mirror was a strangely softened portrait of the saturnine, hard, disciplined man he became in his maturity. The theatrical face reveals consistently a softer man, a somewhat sentimentalized dreamer. With the exceptions of Michael Cape and John Loving, the character is young, in his late adolescence or early twenties. He is artistic, a writer, painter or poet, and he holds himself apart from a world that he views as his enemy. He loathes its materialism and seeks to escape it by "belonging" to something beyond life. In this, he reveals a pervasive death-wish suggesting that he will try to avoid undergoing the process of struggle and maturation. Certain of the characters develop positively. John Loving, for instance, finds his faith, but by and large, the course the character charts through his life is a downward one, leading to the destruction of the bright, adolescent dreams.

Setting Simon Harford momentarily aside, no one of the characters finds a significant sexual fulfillment. Indeed, each one of them turns away from sexual experience. As Dion Anthony makes love to Margaret, he denies life, and he seeks out Cybel for reasons other than her sexuality. Michael Cape hopes for something beyond sexual love, that will prove "a faith in which to relax," [444] and he too refuses a sexual encounter with the prostitute. Richard Miller, who like Cape and Anthony turns away from the whore, is transfixed in innocence in a moment of pre-sexual puppy-love. Stephen Murray refuses Eileen Carmody's love so long as it offers sexual possibility. John Loving's casual adultery produces a convulsion of spirit that rocks his faith. John Brown and Robert Mayo emerge from their minimal sexual encounters filled with hostility toward the women who have caused them to betray their dreams. The self-portrait is oddly antiseptic. None of the characters O'Neill cast in his own image, Dion excepted, reveals his tendency toward dissipation, nor displays his knowledge of life in the lower depths.

Reasons for his imaging of himself as an innocent might be attributed to personal reticence, or to fastidiousness that rejected public confession. It is also true that each of the characters *is* an image, formed for a specific theatrical occasion, but like any reflection existing without past or future and empty of physical and psychological depth. With this possibility there can be no quarrel. Self-portraits or not, they are creatures of the imagination, and O'Neill cannot be denied the editorial rights and privileges of any author.

With the creation of Edmund Tyrone, however, the conditions change. Edmund is more than an imaginary figure. He is a figure from history and one upon whose truth-to-life an audience has a right to insist. Yet he is cut in the same pattern as the earlier self-portraits and emerges as a curiously two-dimensional reflection, whose past has been bowdlerized and whose negative characteristics are only lightly touched. It cannot be. If Mary and Tyrone and Jamie are "true," then Edmund should be equally so. If the characters in the play are "what the past has made them," then Edmund's past is of grave concern, as are the ambitions and desires that will move him on in the future. The past, however, is not there as it is with the others. The future is never suggested. He remains a participating observer, a little apart, an eavesdropping creature of the imagination. The truth, whatever it was, is at least distorted.

To seek for a reason why O'Neill drew such a suppressed self-portrait is to move toward areas of psychoanalysis that are not relevant here. Whatever the reason, it was not only simple reticence at public self-exposure or a lack of frankness in dealing with some aspects of his own nature in other guises. To counter charges of mere shyness, there is the figure of Simon Harford, whose face is very like that of Edmund Tyrone. Moreover, there are three others, very different characters from the dreaming poet, in whose general aspect something of the essence of O'Neill's theatrical image may be noted: Eben Cabot, Reuben Light and Orin Mannon.* Eben's physical characteristics are not described in detail. His hair is dark, he is tall and sinewy, and he has about him a "fierce repressed vitality." [203] Reuben is tall and thin, has the typical large, sensitive eyes and indecisive mouth, but his thick curly hair is red blond, and his jaw is "stubborn." [422] Orin Mannon, whose resemblance to his father and to Adam Brant is marked, is tall and thin and has the acquiline nose, dark complexion, black hair and sensitive mouth of the O'Neill portraits. Each of the four has in him the somewhat feminine weakness and the "touch of the poet" displayed in the routine self-portraits, but there is additionally represented a capacity for sensual experience, a maturity, a masculinity that the dreamers lack. Eben, closest to a dreamer of the four, has a harshness, an animal quality and an eagerness for sexual encounter that is manifested in his encounters with the prostitute, Min, and later with his stepmother. Reuben begins in a condition of adolescent weakness, but his nature hardens and in his seduction and murder of Ada, he too reveals his capability for passion. So with Orin and Simon, who emerge more fully, more in three dimensions and with greater strength and masculinity than do any of the easier, sympathetic self-portraits.

The lives of the four are similar, their desires astonishingly special. Each is oedipally in love with his mother. Each is embittered by her loss and feels either that she has betrayed him, or that by seeking to possess her, he has betrayed her. Yet without her he is lost and must in compensation seek a surrogate. Eben, Reuben and Orin, each in revulsion from the attempt to find the mother in another woman, call the surrogate a whore. Thus Eben, when he

* Eben, Reuben, Orin, Simon—the names are strikingly euphonious. They form an acronym of interest.

comes to believe that Abbie has seduced him in order that her child may possess the farm, tells her that he hates her and that she is "a damn trickin' whore!" [256] As he kills Ada, Reuben calls her "Harlot!" [488] and Orin, when Lavinia, who has blossomed and come to resemble her mother, confesses to kissing the Tahitian native, cries out "You—you whore! I'll kill you!" [155] Simon attempts to turn Sara into a whore, and at the same time to use her as a substitute for Deborah who has been lost in her dreams of being a royal whore.

The search for the surrogate mother turns each man toward a condition that is child-like. Reuben, Orin and Simon seek to become children again and to rejoin their mothers in death or in mad dreams. Eben, who in possessing Abbie has felt that he has also possessed his mother, moves toward a final position that is more resolute than the others. Yet midway in the play, the gratification of the child comes to him as well. To be sure, Dion's relations with Cybel have some of the characteristics of the search for the mother in the whore. The great difference between Dion and the others, however, is the degree of sexuality involved in the relationship. Between Dion and Cybel there is no sex, and furthermore there is between them no suggestion of incestuous desire as there is in the other plays.

The dissimilarity between these four characters and the other portraits of the poetic dreamer of which Edmund Tyrone is a culmination is vast. Importantly, the difference is not one of increased revelation, of plunging deeper into the dreamer to reveal more of the man. The difference is really in kind, and it evolves from a difference in subject. Although they wear a face that resembles that of Edmund Tyrone, they are in fact another character, one who conforms closely to the characterization O'Neill drew of his brother in both the Tyrone plays.

In *Long Day's Journey into Night*, Jamie's need for his mother is the central explanation for his despair. His revulsion against her and himself is extreme. It is he who calls Mary a "Hophead" and who marks her final entrance with the "self-defensively sardonic" cry: "The Mad Scene. Enter Ophelia!" [170] He confesses to hating Edmund because "it was your being born that started Mama on dope," [166] and he dates his own dereliction from the day he first "got wise" when he saw her injecting herself with morphine.

"Christ," he says, "I'd never dreamed before that any women but whores took dope." [163] What he feels to be his mother's whore-like behavior has left him with no belief. That Mary had appeared to be beating the habit "meant so much," he says. "I'd begun to hope, if she'd beaten the game, I could too." [162] When he realizes that she has defeated his hope, he heads for the local brothel and goes upstairs with the least attractive, and, it is to be assumed, the most maternal of the whores, Fat Violet, who drinks so much and is so overweight that the madam has determined to get rid of her. He summarizes the experience:

> By applying my natural God-given talents in their proper sphere, I shall attain the pinnacle of success! I'll be the lover of the fat woman in Barnum and Bailey's circus! . . . Pah! Imagine me sunk to the fat girl in a hick town hooker shop! . . . But you're right. To hell with repining! Fat Violet's a good kid. Glad I stayed with her. Christian act. Cured her of blues. Hell of a good time. You should have stuck with me, Kid. Taken your mind off your troubles. What's the use coming home to get the blues over what can't be helped. All over—finished now—not a hope! . . .
>
> "If I were hanged on the highest hill,
>   Mother o' mine, O mother o' mine!
>   I know whose love would follow me still . . ." [160]

The maternal whore and the mother whose addiction is a whore's addiction merge in Jamie's befuddled consciousness as the source of his self-disgust and his need.

The Fat Violet episode served in all probability as the basis for a romantic fantasy surrounding that need in *A Moon for the Misbegotten*. Jamie's account of his actions with the whore on the train while he was bringing his mother's body home suggests the same pattern of loss, the same despairing self-destruction as the earlier play did. Not having the mother, he must expend his spirit on the most repulsive facsimile he can find in an orgy of self-defilement. Later, he finds peace with Josie Hogan, the giant woman, who pretends to be a whore, but who is really a virgin, and who in the course of hearing Jamie's confession, holds him pièta-fashion through the long, calm night, as if she were a "virgin who bears a dead child in the night, and the dawn finds her still a virgin." [160] In his drunkenness, Jamie sometimes confuses Josie with the "blonde pig" on the train, but at other times she becomes much more than a substitute for his lost mother: she becomes a mother in truth. As she kisses him, *"There is passion in her kiss but it is a tender, protective maternal passion, which he responds to with an instant grateful yielding."* [141] Josie, finally, in her double role of mother and whore, can bring to Jamie his mother's forgiveness and blessing. As he sobs himself to sleep on her breast she tells him she forgives him as his mother forgives and loves and understands them both. [152] In his last play, it was fitting that O'Neill should create the woman who could be in reality for his brother what other of his characters—Eben, Reuben, Orin and Simon—had sought with such frenzy.

These four men, although they appear to have Eugene's face, are more nearly to be recognized as portraits of Jamie as the Tyrone plays depicted him. If this is so, three explanations for the transference may be considered. The first is that the oedipal tendencies were in truth Eugene's and that in presenting them on stage, he could not be sufficiently honest to expose himself, and, for this reason, when the character became expressly autobiographical in the Tyrone plays, disguised his need as Jamie's. Against this stands the biographical evidence, especially the story of Jamie's behavior after his mother's death as it is accurately recounted in *A Moon for the Misbegotten.* Clearly Jamie was possessed of an overt oedipal drive, and the portrait in the Tyrone plays rings true.

A second possibility is that both brothers reacted to the situation in identical ways. Some biographical evidence might support such a conclusion. O'Neill was well known in the brothels of New London and New York. *Strange Interlude* and *The Great God Brown* reveal that he was concerned imaginatively with the symbolism of the whore and the mother that could be found in ancient religious myths and particularly in those associated with Dionysus. Mrs. O'Neill said that on his deathbed her husband reached out and took her hand and said to her, "You are my mamma now." The phrase occurs in other wordings in the plays and could imply that the desire to find the mother in the wife underlay an oedipal necessity of long standing. Macgowan records that O'Neill told him after the interviews with Dr. Hamilton that he was suffering from an oedipus complex,[18] and Louis Sheaffer claims that in his nurse, Sarah Sandy, the young O'Neill found a surrogate mother.[19] Yet no biographer has presented an O'Neill so obsessed with the need for a mother as the four characters, if taken literally as self-portraits, might suggest he was. Sheaffer makes the point that O'Neill, feeling that the other members of his family blamed him for his mother's addiction, stood on the defensive with all three, and held himself alone, very much his own man. As Sheaffer relates it, O'Neill's sexual initiation, a hideously traumatic experience, might well mean that despite his youthful profligacy, there remained in him "a residue of puritanism, of regarding sex as immoral, a result to some extent of his Catholic indoctrination."[20] Sheaffer further suggests that the cult of the Virgin Mary, one that tended to foster "guilt feelings about the flesh," was something O'Neill carried with him from his early days in Catholic schools, and that it was kept alive if not increased in O'Neill by his mother's personality. He writes, "Ella, from all indications was sexually inhibited and lacking in sensuality; her drug addiction clearly signaled a retreat from the responsibilities and obligations of her position, including those as a sex partner."[21] Adequate resolution of the questions is impossible to achieve, but the biographical evidence points toward O'Neill's repression of any aggressive or overt sexual demonstrations toward his mother. On the other hand there is ample evidence that Jamie's life displayed an attraction for his mother openly and continually.

A third alternative may be suggested: that what O'Neill saw and explored at first in self-portraits—through the figures of Eben, Reuben, Orin and Simon—and later, in the Tyrone plays, through Jamie, was both himself *and* Jamie. Or, more specifically, he inspected that part of himself that was in effect Jamie's creation, that to which Jamie referred when he told Edmund, "Hell, you're more than my brother. I made you! You're my Frankenstein!" [164]

The implication of the Frankenstein image is that Jamie was both the creator and destroyer of his brother. Jamie reminds Edmund that it was he who first interested him in reading poetry and he who, because he wanted to write, gave his brother the idea of becoming a writer. By moulding Edmund's tastes and encouraging his talent, Jamie gave himself a kind of creative life. The negative aspect, however, appears as well, as Jamie brags how he introduced his brother to alcohol and to the whores with whom he found release. In the play, speaking in vino veritas, Jamie claims that he dragged Edmund down "to make a bum" of him, and that he did it in full consciousness:

> . . . Or part of me did. A big part. That part that's been dead so long. That hates life. My putting you wise so you'd learn from my mistakes. Believed that myself at times, but it's a fake. Made my mistakes look good. Made getting drunk romantic. Made whores fascinating vampires instead of poor, stupid, diseased slobs they really are. Made fun of work as sucker's game. Never wanted you succeed and make me look even worse by comparison. Wanted you to fail. Always jealous of you. Mama's baby, Papa's pet! [165]

Loving and hating his brother, Jamie has tried to create Edmund in his own image, possessing him in an almost demonic way. In the play, Edmund refuses to pay attention to Jamie's confession, but the Frankenstein image is nowhere denied.

The imagery implies that Jamie was responsible both for Edmund's positive qualities and also for their opposite, the negatives that led him to follow a course of self-destruction. To some extent these polarities exist in all of O'Neill self-portraits, starting with a simple opposition of a poetic man with a crassly materialistic society. Quickly, however, as O'Neill became capable of more complex conceptions of human nature, the creative and self-destructive forces were centered within the hero, as in Stephen Murray and Michael Cape. As yet, however, there was no radical division of personality, but this was to come and it was to be expressed in strange intermingling of personalities.

Between Dion Anthony and William Brown, a fraternal relationship exists. Yet it goes beyond this. Dion assumes Brown's rights when he takes Margaret, but later Brown reverses the relationship and absorbs Dion by wearing his mask. Speaking to the mask of the dead Dion, he talks of how he will assume Dion's role and says, "Then you—the I in you—I will live in Margaret." [307] Something of the same closeness may be sensed in Eben's relationship, not to his brothers, but to his father. The two are the "dead spit an' image" of one another, mirrored reflections, bound yet opposite. Again the conception of a man divided into very different, opposed but closely bound beings is in *Mourning Becomes Electra*, where Orin, Ezra and Adam have the same desires and the same face, and yet are locked in a death struggle. The most extreme example is, of course, John and Loving in *Days Without End,* where only by an act of exorcism can the negative force be eliminated from the divided soul.

The image shifts, dazzles, puzzles, but the provocative possibility is that O'Neill believed that his brother had done as he claimed, and that part of him *was* Jamie, and, therefore, that Jamie was more than his brother, was somehow an image of himself, an image that was a hostile double, bent on his destruction, a form of *doppelgänger.*

The myth of the demonic double is perhaps more a literary affectation than a reality in men's minds. Despite many early anticipations of the idea, the legend was given form in early nineteenth-century Gothic thrillers like *Frankenstein.* It persisted, however, in a not entirely literary form. In a brief, seminal treatise, *The Double,*[22] Otto Rank has shown that the legend can become an actuality in the neurotic fantasies of disturbed personalities. In legend, the double emerges from a mirror or shadow and detaches itself from the man who gave it form. Henceforth, the man is without reflection. Instead the double moves through life in a mysterious course parallel to his progenitor and at each crucial turn steps between the man and his achievement. The double accepts his triumphs, steals the love he has sought and in the end destroys him.

In anthropological investigation and in areas of psychoanalytic study the double, as Rank presents it, is a product of paranoid fantasy, involving fear of inexplicable and hostile pursuit. Yet Rank points out that in addition to paranoia another syndrome appears:

> We know that the person of the pursuer frequently represents the father or his substitute (brother, teacher, etc.), and we also find in our material that the double is often identified with the brother. It is clearest in Musset [in "December Night"] but also appears in Hoffman . . . , Poe, Dostoevsky, and others. The appearance for the most part is as a twin and reminds us of the legend of the womanish Narcissus, for Narcissus thinks that he sees in his image his sister, who resembles him in every respect. That those writers who preferred the theme of the double also had to contend with the male sibling complex follows from the not infrequent treatment of fraternal rivalry in their other works. [75]

Rank continues to discuss this fraternal rivalry toward the hated competitor in the love for the mother and ultimately the death wish of the subject. He adds, "The most prominent symptom of the forms which the double takes is a powerful consciousness of guilt which forces the hero no longer to accept the responsibility for certain actions of his ego, but to place it upon another ego, a double, who is either personified by the devil himself or is created by making a diabolical pact." [76] He also suggests that slaying of the double, "through which the hero seeks to protect himself permanently from the pursuits of his self, is really a suicidal act."* [79]

In O'Neill's plays, the double, divested of its Gothic horror, and therefore without the suggestions of paranoia, appears continually: in *Days Without End*, in the deep divisions of personality of many of the characters in *Strange Interlude* and the extant cycle plays, in *Ah, Wilderness!*, where the division of each member of O'Neill's family into two characters exorcises guilt, in Orin Mannon's sense that having killed Adam Brant he has killed himself—the list can be multiplied. What is of immediate interest, however, is that while the plays correspond with startling exactitude to much of Rank's analysis, O'Neill creates a significant variation on the pattern. The variation is suggested in *Beyond the Horizon*. Andrew has taken Robert's life and despoiled it, and in the context he may well be thought of as the double. But it is equally true that Robert has taken Ruth from Andrew and spoiled his brother's life. From another point of view, Robert might well be considered Andrew's double. In *The Great God Brown*, Billy steals Dion's talent and takes his wife by assuming his appearance. Clearly this is the way of the double, but so is Dion's macabre mockery of Billy and his theft of Margaret in the beginning of the play. As with Robert and Andrew, as with the doubles in the Mannon family, which is the

---

* The possible implications of Rank's study for an understanding of the complex personality of Eugene O'Neill are many. Rank points out, for example, that E. T. A. Hoffmann in whose *Tales* the double appears "was nervous, eccentric, and strongly dependent upon moods." When Hoffmann wrote stories of doubles, he actually saw doubles around him, and wakened his wife to show them to her. Rank continues "After one drinking bout, he wrote in his diary: 'Seized by thoughts of death: doubles'. . . . At the age of forty-seven he succumbed to a neurological illness, which [was] diagnosed as chorea [a condition characterized by a nervous twitching]. . . ." Rank adds that the disease "gives evidence of his neuropathic constitution, which he shared with most of his companions in adversity. . . ." [35]

self? Which the double? In O'Neill's plays it is not entirely evident that the self, in all instances a self-portrait, has sufficiently strong identity to make clear which of the "brothers" is the reflected image of the other.

A possible explanation lies in Jamie's image of Frankenstein. If it is true that O'Neill, however unconsciously, felt himself to be Jamie's creation and in particular viewed his own negative tendencies as implantations Jamie had made, it may be argued that he drew the self-portraits, both those presenting a corrupted, poetic innocent and those of the sensual, even destructive man, as a way of sorting out what lay within him. To understand Jamie was not difficult, as *Long Day's Journey into Night* attests, but to understand what Jamie had done to Eugene may have been nearly impossible. Was it that Jamie had stolen Eugene's life? Or was it that Jamie was Eugene's Loving? If Eugene was Jamie's Frankenstein, what was Eugene's truth? O'Neill's growing interest in the God-denying materialist, first seen in *Marco Millions* and continuing through the cycle, appears to reflect his growing need to analyze the uncreative qualities within himself. Searching in mirrors to discover whether anyone is there is to look for the double within. In the end it was the essence of Jamie in himself that became of concern and that may have led Eugene to draw Jamie as Eben, Reuben, Orin and Simon, as a way of looking at Jamie when Jamie became Eugene. It was an instinctive way of separating the elements within to discover what Eugene was and what it meant to be Jamie's Frankenstein.

This cannot be the truth of it. O'Neill was an artist, not a do-it-yourself psychoanalyst. Yet some implications of the suggestion may shed light on O'Neill's career as a playwright. After 1922, the year of his mother's death, with the single exception of his adaptation of *The Ancient Mariner,* all the extant plays reveal some direct autobiography. Far from inventing dramatic fictions to please and move his audiences, O'Neill's imagination turned to the creation of narrative masks for a central situation among four people he obsessively sought to understand. He did not dramatize the full situation all of the time, but aspects of it are to be found in the central focus of thirty-five of the plays. Edmund Tyrone, who stumbles in from the fog where he has walked as if he were "a ghost belonging to the fog," returns from the dead to tell his father of his vision of belonging to a life force. So Lazarus was resurrected to speak of the life force, and Hickey, coming from a murder, comatose, as if he were dead, returns to Hope's to preach a vision. The concern of Nina's three men for her welfare reflects the care of the three male Tyrones for Mary's health. The image of the poet destroyed by the materialist has multiple recurrences, and characters return: the mother who is a betrayer of her children and who resents being the object of their need; brothers bound in opposition; wives who persecute their husbands; fathers and children fixed in a pattern of love and hate; the maternal whore to whom men turn for surcease; men and women who feed on dreams. The list is long, but it evolves from a single, central source, the action of *Long Day's Journey into Night,* in which O'Neill's whole creative life centered. He had to write the play; literally, he lived to write it.

In the play's dedication, O'Neill thanks his wife for giving him "the faith in love that enabled me to face my dead at last and write this play—write it with deep pity and understanding and forgiveness for *all* the four haunted Tyrones." Pity, understanding and forgiveness surely are there for three of them, but for Edmund the understanding, the pity and perhaps the forgiveness is less pervasive. Edmund is only a slightly more mature version of the sentimental rebel O'Neill created in Richard Miller. Except in such episodes as his reaction to his father's attempt to put him into a cheap sanatorium, his responses to his family are not specifically defined. He repeatedly avoids conflict, refuses to face issues, remains neutral and a little passive. Partly the blandness may be because Jamie is now on stage in his own person, and much that O'Neill had previously explored of Jamie in himself is now, as it were, returned to its source. About Jamie, as about his mother and father, O'Neill, the playwright, is totally perceptive. Their relationships to one another as well as to Edmund are strongly and clearly defined. His to them are not. Perhaps, if *Long Day's Journey into Night* may be called a "dream play," an explanation might lie in the fact that Edmund is the dreamer's dream of himself. He moves like a dream's protagonist in wonder and dread, but is uncommitted to the dream's occurrences. Commitment, finally, belongs to the dreamer and not the dream. The play is O'Neill's last mirror, the last time he would look to see if he was "there." In itself, the image of the young, gentle, unhappy man he saw proved nothing, but having gone through the door in the mind to the fogbound room in the past, he perhaps understood himself as his figure was illuminated by the pain and concern of those about him. In the agony of the others, it is possible, the playwright's identity was at last to be found.

Long Day's Journey into Night ended his search for identity. Yet he remained concerned for the man who was so strangely a part of his being—for Jamie, who was condemned to live without love, and without any possibility of a sustaining vision of beatitude. *A Moon for the Misbegotten* is an act of love, supplying through its romantic fiction a blessing for a damned soul.

The play is set in September, 1923. At that time, Jamie O'Neill was in a sanatorium, where he had been carried in a strait jacket the previous May. After his mother's death the year before, Jamie had quite literally drunk himself to death. His hair had turned white, he had all but lost his eyesight, and when he died in the sanatorium on November 8, he achieved perhaps the only beatitude he ever knew.[23] In the play, Jamie is a dying man, but about his presence there is no suggestion of the physical horror that came to him in the end. O'Neill, while he did not mitigate the agonizing psychological causes of Jamie's behavior after his mother died, gave him in Josie Hogan a gentler fate. Josie, a metamorphosis of "Fat Violet," was perhaps inspired by a woman the brothers had known in their days in Greenwich Village, a free, lusty, great-bodied woman named Christine Ell. In her, O'Neill apparently found something of the paradoxes he later set forth in Josie—a shyness of spirit that conflicted with the grossness of her body and which she attempted to mask by rough whorish behavior.[24] However, although based lightly on fact, the play is at its core a fiction.

As a theatrical work, *A Moon for the Misbegotten* is one of O'Neill's most difficult plays, and its original production by the Theatre Guild in 1947 was not a lucky one. The casting of Josie according to O'Neill's literal specifications is a virtual impossibility in the professional theatre. Lawrence Langner, discussing the problem of finding the necessary "giantess," noted that the role calls for "exactly the kind of woman who, when she comes to see you and asks whether she should attempt a career in the theatre—you look embarrassed and reply, 'Well, I'm afraid you're rather a big girl—

how are we to find a man tall enough to play opposite you?' "[25] Yet, if it is true that Josie and Sara Melody were conceived as roles for the same actress, the physical characteristics become less important than the qualities of personality at the actress's command, a point O'Neill made in the original casting for the role.[26] The play is doomed to failure without superb acting. It is long, totally simplified and stripped of theatrical devices, a lyric drama, concentrated on character more than narrative.

The Theatre Guild opened the play out of town, in Columbus, Ohio, on February 20, 1947, and booked it for a short tour through Cleveland, Pittsburgh, Detroit and St. Louis. The circumstances, unusual for an O'Neill première, were, apparently, occasioned by O'Neill's mistrust of the actors which emerged after he had heard the first reading. O'Neill had some objections to James Dunn, the film actor who was playing Jamie, and theatrical gossip rumored that Rhys Williams was being groomed to replace J. M. Kerrigan as Hogan. Unexpectedly the play shocked the midwestern audiences. In Pittsburgh it was damned by the secretary of the local Chamber of Commerce, and in Detroit it was closed on the night of its second performance by a police censor who considered it an obscene slander on American motherhood, and demanded that the work be rewritten. When Armina Marshall, the Guild's producer, pointed out that O'Neill had won the Nobel Prize, the censor made a small contribution to the history of American letters by stating flatly, "Lady, I don't care what kind of prize he's won, he can't put on a dirty show in *my* town."* Although the play was allowed to continue after eight words were deleted, it closed in St. Louis. Langner attempted to persuade O'Neill to permit it to be reopened with a different cast, but O'Neill's illness and his disgust with the problems that beset the play on the tour caused him to refuse.[27]

His refusal may also have reflected an insecurity about the play itself. Mrs. O'Neill had never liked it and by 1952, the year before he died, he stated that he had come to loathe it.** How seriously the

---

* Miss Marshall's account is quoted in *The Magic Curtain*, 408. The charges of obscenity arose from such sensitivity as the discovery that the words "mother" and "prostitute" were used in the same sentence.

** Cf. *Inscriptions*, July 22, 1952, and Gelb, 849. The Gelbs quote Mrs. O'Neill as saying that the play was unnecessary after *Long Day's Journey into Night* and suggest that part of her distaste for it was to be attributed to the mood of savage despair O'Neill was in as he wrote it.

comment should be taken is difficult to determine. Something of the same attitude had developed over the years toward *"Anna Christie,"* another story of a woman in whom prostitution was more apparent than real, but in the later instance, O'Neill could not accuse himself as he did with the earlier play of writing a facile, well-made play. His loathing, perhaps, was born of his illness complicated by a series of substantial personal problems, including a serious marital crisis and his daughter's marriage to Charles Chaplin, followed by a sequence of tragedies—the suicide of his elder son, the death of his grandchild, and the realization that his younger son had become a dope addict. Quite possibly, when there was nothing left for him but to wait for death, and when the cycle of familial horror of which he had written began again, he came to loathe the attempt he had made to bring the story of his family to a concluding fulfillment. Nature's refusal to imitate art conceivably can on occasion silence an author with self-doubt.

There is no reason to deny the play's worth, despite its difficulties, for it is a carefully controlled, potentially rich work for the stage. The comedy of the first act, recapitulating the opening situation between Eben and his brothers in *Desire Under the Elms,* is developed in the purest tradition of the Abbey Theatre company,* but the characters are O'Neill's own. In Phil Hogan there exists more than a little reminder of Con Melody, quarreling with and yet loving his daughter, suggesting and yet not meaning that she trap her man with sex. Like Con, he is an actor, contemptuous of much in the world about him, yet caught by it, through his proprietorship of a worthless piece of real estate. At times, he approximates a bandy-legged parody of James Tyrone, Sr. Yet Hogan is held off-center. O'Neill is writing what is essentially a love story, a thing he has not done since *"Anna Christie,"* and Hogan, like old Chris, must move aside for the misbegotten lovers.

What O'Neill meant by "misbegotten" cannot be simply defined. The word is used by Larry Slade, who, speaking of the derelicts at Harry Hope's and perhaps of those in the world at large, says, "The lie of the pipe dream is what gives life to the whole misbegotten

---

* In casting, O'Neill had insisted that no one who was not of Irish blood could be cast in the play. His reason was that only Irish actors could achieve the quick changes of mood and temperament which the roles required. A similar problem of rapid transitions exists for the actors in *A Touch of the Poet.*

mad lot of us, drunk or sober." [578] His words suggest a kind of madness that the misbegotten share, together with a spiritual deformity—which in Josie Hogan's case is also a physical deformity. "Misbegotten" refers to the people at the bottom of society, Rose and Tim in *The Web*, the Hairy Ape, Erie—men who have no heritage and are outcasts from the world. O'Neill had earlier shown that even with nothing to sustain them it was possible for the misbegotten to belong, at least, to one another—to form, as it were, a society of the damned. The frame of that society was a vision, created from memory and hopeless desire. Such blessing as came to three of the haunted Tyrones grew from their memories that brought them "visions of beatitude"—visions that both caused and assuaged pain. Through their pipe-dreams Erie and Hughes communicate, and, in *The Iceman Cometh,* the community of dreams provides the only warmth. Earlier, O'Neill had written much of "belonging," of participating in ecstasy in the life force, the essence of the experience Edmund Tyrone relates to his father. Only by "belonging" could man be really at peace, but so long as he could hope to belong, he would not become alien in his world. But, when hope truly became hopeless, the misbegotten were born, those whose lives occupied O'Neill's last stage, and who, O'Neill sensed, might be taken as emblematic of the entire world.

In Jamie Tyrone, in Hickey and in Erie whose lives parallel Jamie's in many particulars, and in Con Melody at the end of *A Touch of the Poet,* O'Neill had shown that there was a depth lower than that the misbegotten inhabited—a world where man was entirely without the possibility of any sustaining illusion, where he must live in isolation, unable to reach and touch another human being, alone with his pain. However it is to be described, in O'Neill's imagery or otherwise, it was in fact the depth in which his brother lived, and it was from this that O'Neill attempted to redeem him.

A Moon for the Misbegotten is suffused with an elegiac tone, and like an elegy, the play attempts to mitigate the fact of death, both to assuage the sorrows of the living and to bless him who has died. Beyond that, as is proper with an elegy, the drama attests the value of the life that has been lived. Jamie had lived beyond the possibility of blessing and his life, in any absolute terms, considered as a perpetual source of pain for others as well as himself, could not be said to have had value. Certainly he was incapable of vision or gratifying memory. What remedy, then was possible, except to create the vision in the present? Or rather, to allow it to be created by his fictional brother and Josie Hogan, who is symbolic of all the women his brother slept with and also of the one woman he loved.

On Josie, the whore's mask sets convincingly. Her grotesque size, her unfeminine strength, her roughness of tongue are convincing reasons that she should play the slut. Equally convincing is the fact that no one has slept with her if for no other reason than that her power is more apparently masculine than feminine and that she has created about her a myth of unquenchable desire no man can satisfy. For a man to sleep casually with Josie would be to sacrifice his masculinity. But it is this fact—that a man must sacrifice himself to her—that makes possible Jamie's beatitude. He does not sleep with her, but in allowing her to possess him with her love, in opening himself until all that is hidden comes forth, in *responding* to her power by becoming her lover and her child, he discovers in her not only the woman, the whore, but the purity that is maternal and has the power to grant absolution. As he loves her and gives her himself, she becomes like a legendary Goddess, virgin, whore and mother, all women from Mary Tyrone to Fat Violet to the blonde pig on the train, and what is eternal in woman is called forth from her to absolve him before he dies.

It is vital to see that the Demeter-like creature she becomes is truly evoked. Josie is no arbitrary symbol. She too is misbegotten, and whatever there is of tribute in Jamie's love creates for her a solace not unlike that which she brings to him. The night is her salvation, as well as his. Together, the two lost ones find a way to belong, to become more than merely misbegotten. In their meeting (*pace* Rose and Tim), O'Neill shows them finding their way to a love purified of passion, losing themselves, as, earlier, he had sought to "belong" in Dionysian ecstasy to the life force. It is not very different, perhaps from what the Strindbergian couple in *Welded* had sought in marriage, and certainly it relates to the images of the God the Mother and her lovers in *Strange Interlude* and *The Great God Brown*. Yet there is a difference, and it is partly occasioned by the fact that Josie Hogan is not forced into a symbolic dimension, and that she too needs and finds blessing.

It is blessing, not ecstasy. What is "Dionysian" in it is more an illusion than a reality. The moonlight that bathes their scene casts an effective spell as in *The Moon of the Caribbees,* binding the lovers to one another, and, flatteringly, lending them grace. The dawn, so different from the ones Jamie remembered, gives a kind of promise. Both are illusory, and the lovers know it. In the moonlight, Jamie is at peace, but both know that with the coming of dawn, what they have found will fade. Beyond the night, nothing exists for them. Yet the long night's journey to dawn is enough. It has been a lifetime.

The love of Josie and Jamie has been fulfilled in the simplest terms. Like Nora's love for Con Melody, theirs is so humble, so purely selfless, that they can take pride in it, and accept it without pretense. As Jamie leaves, he attempts to betray it with Broadway talk in a scene reminiscent of that between Dion and Cybel in Act II, scene i of *The Great God Brown.* There as Dion leaves, Cybel bids him goodbye, knowing that he is to die. She sobs, gives him his mask, kisses him gently and says:

> CYBEL   . . . Don't get hurt. Remember, it's all a game, and after you're asleep I'll tuck you in.
>
> DION   (*in a choking, heart-broken cry*) Mother! (*Then he claps on his mask with a terrible effort of will—mockingly*) Go to the devil, you sentimental old pig! See you tomorrow! (*He goes, whistling, slamming the door.*) [288]

A similar motif appears in the scene at the end of *A Moon for the Misbegotten,* but Jamie is not permitted to make Dion's mocking exit. He has awakened and remembered what has passed between them in the night. The Broadway mask is clapped on, and he moves casually away from Josie, saying "See you later. . . ." Josie calls after him:

> JOSIE   (*Strickenly*) No! Don't, Jim! Don't go like that! You won't see me later. You'll never see me again now, and I know that's best for us both, but I can't bear to have you ashamed you wanted my love to comfort your sorrow—when I'm so proud I could give it. (*Pleadingly*) I hoped, for your sake, you wouldn't remember, but now you do, I want you to remember my love for you gave you peace for awhile.
>
> TYRONE   (*Stares at her, fighting with himself. He stammers defensively*) I don't know what you're talking about. I don't remember—

JOSIE   (*Sadly*) All right, Jim. Neither do I then. Good-bye and God bless
you. . . .

TYRONE   . . . Wait, Josie! . . . I'm a liar! I'm a louse! Forgive me, Josie, I
do remember! I'm glad I remember! I'll never forget your love
. . . I'll always love you, Josie. . . . Goodbye—and God bless you!
[173]

He leaves without looking back, taking with him the pride and
peace her love has brought him. Now, for Jamie, the beatitude
which sustained the other Tyrones exists in memory until he dies.

Death will be soon. Josie watches him moving away down the
road and speaks the play's curtain line. In it can be read O'Neill's
wish for all the Tyrones:

> May you have your wish and die in your sleep soon, Jim, darling.
> May you rest forever in forgiveness and peace. [177]

These were the last words O'Neill was to write for the stage and
they express what came in the end to be the consummation of his
tragedy. He had written them before in speaking of Ruth Mayo's
sinking *"into that spent calm beyond the further troubling of any
hope."* [169] Or of the Hairy Ape, who "perhaps" belonged in
death—for whom death was the only possible good. For Hickey, by
way of obit, all that it is possible to say are Larry's words, "May the
chair bring him peace at last, the poor tortured bastard!" [719]
Larry, indeed speaks an epitaph for all human animals when he
quotes the final couplet of Heine's poem to morphine:

> Lo, sleep is good; better is death; in sooth
> The best of all were never to be born. [591]

More gently, Jamie in *A Moon for the Misbegotten* has quoted
Keats:

> Now more than ever seems it rich to die,
> To cease upon the midnight with no pain
> In such an ecstasy. [104]

Man's last hope, the only hope that is not hopeless, is to die.

Long Day's Journey into Night and *A Moon for the Misbegotten*
are companion pieces in more than subject matter. The second
Tyrone play, a romantic fiction which provides an act of grace toward Jamie, is a necessary rounding off of the lives of all the Tyrones. Not that *Long Day's Journey into Night* is brutal. Its ending,

as Mary Tyrone steps softly through the dark room among the men frozen with pain, is gentle, erratic, rocking as a feather falling. It is distillation of sorrow, pure, beyond tears, but it is also agony. The play has cried loudly and convincingly that God is dead. In tragedy, God cannot be dead. Men must reach their fates for reasons that are comprehensible and, in the long contour of time, just. But not here. In no other play has God been so needed. His absence is so palpable that tragedy is created, but in such a way that pity itself becomes like terror. *Long Day's Journey into Night* needs the resolution *A Moon for the Misbegotten* brings as it offers, finally, a pervading relief in the knowledge that death is good, and that in welcoming it, man can find respite from terror, and in love, transcend pity.

It may be, too, that in writing finally only of Jamie, O'Neill in his last play found something of himself. Josie Hogan, like Nora Melody, in her simplicity of love testifies to the presence of a value in life that O'Neill earlier had ignored as he wrote of the distorted, suffering world of the misbegotten. Jamie's sacrificial confession is a commitment beyond suffering, and one which O'Neill through his fiction may have been making for himself as well as for his fictional brother. The consciousness of the playwright broods over both plays in much the same way as the awareness of Strindberg moves behind *A Dream Play*. Nathan, years before, had spoken of O'Neill's "presence" as being one of the most exciting qualities in his dramas. O'Neill, before the mirroring stage, was always his own audience. Perhaps in this lies the reason he shunned performances of his plays before the public, fearing an invasion of the privacy he as spectator required. Who can know? Who can know why he came to loathe *A Moon for the Misbegotten?* At first, it was an essential work. To speak of Jamie with charity and to invent the giant woman to comfort him was initially an act of pity and of love. It may have come to more than this. Bringing peace to Jamie meant by extension bringing peace to all the haunted Tyrones. The doubles were separated, his own image was suppressed but, even so, O'Neill, knowing that Jamie's agony was his own, found that Jamie's peace was also his. It was a necessary consummation.

But then the world broke in, the door in the mind shut and the light drained at last from the mirror.

BIBLIOGRAPHICAL NOTE

During O'Neill's lifetime and for a number of years after his death, research into his creative life was hampered by the strict security measures that guarded his privacy. There is no reason to quarrel with these restrictions since the conditions they imposed were essential to his work. In recent years, although access to basic materials is not entirely free, the situation has materially eased. Furthermore, in recent biographies and critical studies and in such helpful anthologies as *O'Neill and His Plays*, compiled by Oscar Cargill, N. Bryllion Fagin and William J. Fisher, much important commentary has been made generally available. Insofar as possible, I have worked with original materials, but if the passage quoted has been reprinted in a source that is easily accessible, I have provided reference to that work in my notes.

All substantive footnotes are in the text itself. Those signaled by superscript numerals are references only and may be found at the end of the volume. Page references to quotations from O'Neill's plays are given in square brackets at the end of the quotation. In quoting from the unpublished writing of O'Neill, in order to avoid the excrescent "sic," I have silently emended small errors of spelling and punctuation.

References in the text and footnotes to the published works of Eugene O'Neill are to the following volumes:

The Plays of Eugene O'Neill. New York, 1955. 3 vols.
> Contains all of the plays except those listed below.

Ten Lost Plays of Eugene O'Neill. New York, 1964.
> Contains *Abortion, Fog, The Movie Man, Recklessness, Servitude, The Sniper, Thirst, Warnings, The Web, A Wife for a Life.*

"The Rime of the Ancient Mariner." *Yale University Library Gazette*, XXV, 2
> (October, 1960).

Hughie. New Haven, Conn., 1959.

Inscriptions, Eugene O'Neill to Carlotta Monterey O'Neill. Privately printed,
> New Haven, Conn., 1960.

The Calms of Capricorn. Ed. Donald Gallup, New Haven, 1982.

Long Day's Journey into Night, New Haven, Conn., 1955.

A Moon for the Misbegotten, New York, 1952.

459

More Stately Mansions, New Haven, Conn., 1964.
Poems, 1912-1942. Ed. Donald Gallup, New Haven, 1979.
"Tomorrow." *The Seven Arts*, June, 1917.
A Touch of the Poet, New Haven, Conn., 1957.
Work Diary, 1924-1943. Ed. Donald Gallup, New Haven, 1981.

Copies of O'Neill's unpublished writings may be found in the following locations:

The Houghton Library, Harvard University, Cambridge, Mass.
> *Now I Ask You, The Personal Equation, The Reckoning, The Revelation of John the Divine, S.O.S.*

The Beinecke Rare Book and Manuscript Library, Yale University, New Haven, Conn.
> *Chris Christophersen.*

The Library of Congress, Washington, D.C.
> *Bread and Butter, Shell Shock.*

Additional bibliographical information may be found in

Ralph Sanborn and Barrett H. Clark, *A Bibliography of the Works of Eugene O'Neill*. New York, 1931.
Jordan Y. Miller, *Eugene O'Neill and the American Critic*. Archon Books, Hamden, Conn., 1962.
Oscar Cargill, N. Bryllion Fagin and William J. Fisher, *O'Neill and His Plays*. New York, 1961.
Timo Tiusanen, *O'Neill's Scenic Images*. Princeton, N.J., 1968.
Egil Törnqvist, *A Drama of Souls*. Uppsala, Sweden, 1968.

A NOTE ON THE REVISED EDITION

The principle revisions of the new edition of *Contour in Time* are to be found in the discussion of the cycle, *A Tale of Possessors, Self-dispossessed*. When I first wrote, in the 1960s, access to the cycle material was strictly limited. The full text of *More Stately Mansions* and the scenario of *The Calms of Capricorn* were unavailable, as were the surviving notes on the destroyed plays and scenarios. Since that time this material has been either published or made available at the Beinecke Library. I am deeply indebted to Dr. Donald Gallup and Dr. David Schoonover, former curators of the American Literature Collection of the library, for permitting me to write a fuller account than was earlier possible.

My first description of the cycle's content was necessarily a pastiche gathered from comments by a wide variety of writers. In one matter, I was led into serious error, the identification of O'Neill's Bessie Bowen with Mme. Stephen Jumel, née Bessie Bowen. The error was based on an unqualified assertion by Croswell Bowen in *The Curse of the Misbegotten*. The coincidence of the facts of Jumel's life with the material in the cycle is astonishing, and it is evident from some entries in Carlotta O'Neill's diaries that O'Neill knew of her. In many ways, her ninety-year lifespan with her love of Napoleon, her affection for fine coaches, her marriage to Aaron Burr, her building of the "stately mansion" that still stands beside the Harlem River predicted the account O'Neill was to develop of the Harford family. But she was not O'Neill's heroine. In this revision, in Jumel's place stands the true source figure, another remarkable American woman, Kate Gleason.

In recent years, many valuable critical studies of O'Neill and his work have appeared, and much of O'Neill's unpublished writing has been printed. For reasons which will be, I hope, self-evident, I have not revised my text or notes to include these books. However, the reader may find it easier to refer to these publications than to documents which in the 1960s were available only in libraries. Two volumes of O'Neill's letters have appeared: *"The Theatre We Worked For": The Letters of Eugene O'Neill to Kenneth Macgowan*, edited by Jackson R. Bryer, with introductory essays by Travis Bogard (New Haven. Conn., 1982), and *"Love, Admiration and Respect," The O'Neill-Commins Correspondence*, edited by Dorothy Commins (Durham, N.C., 1986). Additional sources arc: *The Unknown O'Neill*, an anthology edited by Travis Bogard (New Haven, Conn., 1987), and *The Complete Plays of Eugene O'Neill*, edited by Travis Bogard (New York, 1988).

461

NOTES

INTRODUCTION

1. Louis Sheaffer, *O'Neill, Son and Playwright* (Boston, Mass., 1968), 240. (Hereafter cited as "Sheaffer.")
2. Robert E. Brennan (ed.), *The Algonquin Wits* (New York, 1968), 15.
3. Kenneth Tynan, *The London Observer*, February 2, 1958.
4. Arthur and Barbara Gelb, *O'Neill* (New York, 1960, 1962), 885. (Hereafter cited as "Gelb.")

CHAPTER I

1. Sheaffer, 252.
2. Edward Barnes, *The Man Who Lived Twice* (New York, 1956), 53.
3. Sheaffer, 217.
4. Sheaffer, 311; Croswell Bowen, *The Curse of the Misbegotten* (New York, 1959), 57. (Hereafter cited as "Bowen.")
5. Quoted in Bowen, 60.
6. Sheaffer, 290.
7. Bowen, 59.
8. Gelb, 263.
9. Helen Deutsch and Stella Hannau, *The Provincetown: A Story of the Theatre* (New York, 1931), 15. (Hereafter cited as "Deutsch and Hannau.")
10. Sheaffer, 232.
11. Bowen, 30.
12. Joseph Conrad, *Youth and Two Other Stories*, in *The Works of Joseph Conrad* (London, 1923), XX, xi.
13. Joseph Conrad, *The Nigger of the Narcissus*, in *The Works of Joseph Conrad*, VII, 138.
14. Barrett H. Clark, *Eugene O'Neill: The Man and His Plays* (New York, 1947), 28. (Hereafter cited as "Clark.")

CHAPTER II

1. Cf. John V. A. Weaver, "I Knew Him When," *The New York World*, February 21, 1926. Reprinted in Oscar Cargill, N. Bryllion Fagin and William

Fisher, *O'Neill and His Plays* (New York, 1961), 27. (Hereafter cited as "Cargill.")

2. Wisner Payne Kinne, *George Pierce Baker and the American Theatre* (Cambridge, Mass., 1954). Reprinted in Cargill, 19.
3. "Professor G. P. Baker," *The New York Times*, January 13, 1935.
4. George Pierce Baker, *Dramatic Technique* (Boston, Mass., 1919), v. (Hereafter cited as "Baker.")
5. Baker, iii.
6. Baker, 41.
7. Baker, 308.
8. Baker, 407.
9. Baker, 107.
10. Baker, 509.

CHAPTER III

1. Susan Glaspell, *The Road to the Temple* (New York, 1927), 218. (Hereafter cited as "Glaspell.")
2. Glaspell, 252.
3. Glaspell, 245.
4. Glaspell, 264.
5. Edna Kenton, *"The Provincetown Players and the Playwright's Theatre, 1915-1922."* (Unpublished ms, n.d.), 3. (Hereafter cited as "Kenton.")
6. Glaspell, 216.
7. Kenton, 174; Glaspell, 307.
8. Kenton, 153; Glaspell, 287.
9. Glaspell, 309; Kenton, 197.
10. Quoted in Gelb, 234.
11. Kenton, 47.
12. Glaspell, 254.
13. Cf. Sheaffer, 383.
14. Clark, 56.
15. Sheaffer, 181.
16. Sheaffer, 395.
17. Clark, 58.
18. Clark, 60.
19. Agnes Boulton, *Part of a Long Story* (Garden City, N.Y., 1958), 319. (Hereafter cited as "Boulton.")
20. Gelb, 671.
21. Cf. Mary Heaton Vorse, *Time and the Town* (New York, 1942), 21.
22. Cf. Sheaffer, 203, 335.
23. Joseph Conrad, *Tomorrow*, in *The Works of Joseph Conrad* (London, 1923), VII, 262.

CHAPTER IV

1. Boulton, 162, 165.

2. Boulton, 252.

3. Boulton, 214.

4. Boulton, 254.

5. Glaspell, 255.

6. Quoted in Sheaffer, 421.

7. Gelb, 384.

8. Kenton, 105.

9. Cf. Gelb, 539; Sheaffer, 375.

10. Cf. Sheaffer, 374.

11. Cf. Sheaffer, 430.

12. Woollcott's review appeared on April 4, 1920.

13. Cf. Sheaffer, 209-14, for a summary of the several versions of the episode.

14. In an inscription to the fourth proof of *The Emperor Jones, Diff'rent* and *The Straw*, to Miss Mary A. Clarke. In the Beinecke Rare Book and Manuscript Library, Yale University, New Haven, Conn. (Hereafter cited as "Beinecke.")

15. The manuscript of *The Straw* is in the Princeton University Library.

16. Cf. Sheaffer, 254; Gelb, 236.

17. Quoted in Sheaffer, 464.

18. Unpublished letter, dated November 18, 1919, Stanford University Library, Stanford, Calif.

19. Unpublished letter, Dated March 23, 1920, Stanford University Library.

20. Alexander Woollcott, *The New York Times*, February 4, 1920.

21. Arthur Hornblow, "Mr. Hornblow Goes to the Play," *Theatre Magazine*, March, 1920.

22. Woollcott, *The New York Times*, February 4, 1920.

23. According to Gilbert Gabriel, *The New York American*, December 1, 1926.

24. Edward Barnes, *The Man Who Lived Twice*, 53.

25. Murray's influence is noted briefly by Sheaffer, 206.

26. T. C. Murray, *Birthright* (Dublin, 1911), 13.

27. *Birthright*, 25.

28. Cf. *The New York Times*, April 11, 1920.

29. Bowen, 88.

30. Edward Sheldon, *The High Road* (privately printed, 1912), 3.

31. *The High Road*, 16.

32. Robert Sherwood, *The Petrified Forest* (New York, 1936), 63.

33. Georges Bataille, *Death and Sensuality* (New York, 1969).

CHAPTER V

1. Deutsch and Hannau, 71.

2. Gelb, 202; 438.

3. *African Negro Sculpture*. Photographed by Charles Sheeler with a preface by Marius de Zayas. (Privately printed, n.d.).

4. Cf. *Peer Gynt*, V, vii.

5. Cf. *Peer Gynt*, V, v.

6. Cf. Moss Hart, *Act One* (New York, 1959), 96 ff.
7. Quoted in Gelb, 450.
8. James Forbes, *The Travelling Salesman* (New York, 1908), 47.
9. Quoted in Gelb, 437.
10. The manuscript is in the Princeton University Library.
11. O'Neill's account of the production of *Chris* is in his letters to George Jean Nathan reprinted in Isaac Goldberg, *The Theatre of George Jean Nathan* (New York, 1926), 146-56.
12. Cf. Louis Kalonyme, "O'Neill lifts Curtain on His Earlier Days," *The New York Times,* December 21, 1924.
13. Louis V. De Foe, in *The New York World*, November 3, 1921.
14. Cf. Arthur Hornblow, "Mr. Hornblow Goes to the Play," *Theatre Magazine,* January, 1922. Also an unsigned article, "Mr. O'Neill's New Play," *The New York Daily Mirror,* December 7, 1921.
15. Cf. O'Neill's letter in defense of *"Anna Christie"* in *The New York Times,* December 18, 1921.
16. *The Theatre of George Jean Nathan,* 154.
17. *The Theatre of George Jean Nathan,* 155.

CHAPTER VI

1. Sheldon Cheney, *The New Movement in Theatre* (New York, 1914-15), 15. (Hereafter cited as "Cheney.")
2. Cheney, 16.
3. Cheney, 16.
4. Cheney, 92.
5. Cheney, 213.
6. Cheney, 269.
7. Cheney, 123.
8. Cheney, 278.
9. Cheney, 102.
10. Kenneth Macgowan, *The Theatre of Tomorrow* (New York, 1921), 224. (Hereafter cited as "Macgowan.")
11. Macgowan, 248.
12. Macgowan, 265.
13. Macgowan, 218.
14. Macgowan, 228.
15. Kenneth Macgowan and Robert Edmond Jones, *Continental Stagecraft* New York, 1922), 5. (Hereafter cited as "Macgowan and Jones.")
16. Macgowan and Jones, 6.
17. Macgowan and Jones, 38.
18. Macgowan and Jones, 39.
19. Macgowan and Jones, 66.
20. O'Neill to Macgowan, August 9, 1921 (Beinecke).
21. O'Neill to Macgowan, March 29, 1921 (Beinecke).
22. O'Neill to Macgowan, n.d. Probably summer, 1923 (Beinecke).

23. O'Neill to Macgowan, n.d. Probably late summer, 1923 (Beinecke).

24. Macgowan and Jones, 221.

25. Quoted in Gelb, 520.

26. Quoted in Gelb, 545. See further, Egil Törnqvist, *A Drama of Souls*, Uppsala, Sweden, 1968, 182.

27. *The Provincetown Playbill*, January 3, 1924. Quoted in Deutsch and Hannau, 191.

28. Quoted in Gelb, 555. For the censorship furor, cf. Gelb, 548 ff.

29. Noted by Gelb, 10.

30. Eugene O'Neill, *Desire Under the Elms, The Fountain* (Wilderness Edition, New York, 1935), IX, xi. See also O'Neill's correspondence with Oliver Saylor, July 2, 1924 (Beinecke).

31. Gelb, 539.

32. Cf. *A Drama of Souls*, 261, note 37.

33. Sidney Howard to Barrett H. Clark, December 16, 1924. The Sidney Howard Papers are in the Bancroft Library of the University of California at Berkeley.

34. Gelb, 571.

35. Friedrich Nietzsche, *The Birth of Tragedy*, tr. William A. Haussmann (London, 1909), 26.

36. *The Birth of Tragedy*, 27.

37. *The Birth of Tragedy*, 121.

38. *The Birth of Tragedy*, 42.

39. *The Birth of Tragedy*, 41.

CHAPTER VII

1. Cf. Alexander Woollcott in *The New York Sun*, April 12, 1924.

2. *The Revelation of John the Divine*, 390A.

3. *The Revelation of John the Divine*, 413A.

4. *The New York Sun*, April 24, 1924.

5. *The New York Sun*, April 7, 1924.

6. George Jean Nathan, "The Rime of the Ancient Mariner," *The American Mercury*. June, 1924. Reprinted in Cargill, 166.

7. Macgowan, 262.

8. Macgowan, 238-43.

9. *The New York News*, December 11, 1925.

10. George Cram Cook, *The Spring* (New York, 1921), 52.

11. Macgowan, 245.

12. Quoted in Gelb, 470.

13. Cf. Stark Young's review in *The New Republic*, December 30, 1925. Quoted in Cargill, 172.

14. Gelb, 468.

15. Quoted in Gelb, 471.

16. Quoted in Gelb, 591.

17. Sheaffer, 389.

18. *The Saturday Evening Post*, September 14, 1918, 93-4.
19. Quoted in Clark, 85.
20. Macgowan, 257.
21. Macgowan, 261.
22. Macgowan, 263.
23. Lee Simonson, *The Stage Is Set* (New York, 1932), 38.
24. Lee Simonson, "Moving Marco," *The New York Times*, January 22, 1928.
25. Cf. Gelb, 352.
26. "A Letter from Eugene O'Neill," *The New York Times*, April 11, 1920.
27. A discussion of these plays may be found in an unpublished doctoral dissertation, "Strindberg's Wander Plays" by Jules L. Zentner, University of California, Berkeley, June, 1964.
28. O'Neill to Macgowan, September 2, 1925 (Beinecke).
29. Telegram, O'Neill to Macgowan, September 5, 1925 (Beinecke).
30. O'Neill to Macgowan, September 28, 1925 (Beinecke).
31. O'Neill to Macgowan, August 23, 1926 (Beinecke).
32. Unidentified clipping in the Provincetown Theatre Scrapbooks, The New York Public Library Theatre Collection.
33. Both reviews appeared on January 25, 1926.
34. "Memoranda on Masks," *The American Spectator*, November, 1932; "Second Thoughts," *The American Spectator*, December, 1932; "A Dramatist's Notebook," *The American Spectator*, January, 1933. Reprinted in Cargill, 116-22.
35. Cf. Cargill, 118.
36. Cf. Cargill, 118.
37. Cf. Cargill, 121.
38. O'Neill explained his scheme in a letter printed in *The New York Post*, February 13, 1926. Reprinted in Clark, 104.
39. Clark, 105.
40. Clark, 105.
41. *The Birth of Tragedy*, 86.
42. *The Birth of Tragedy*, 10.
43. *The Birth of Tragedy*, 30.
44. The credo is in a letter to George Jean Nathan, published in *The American Mercury*, XVI (January, 1929), 119. See below, 321.
45. Macgowan and Jones, 163.
46. *The Provincetown Playbill*, April, 1924. Quoted in Donald Gallup, "Eugene O'Neill's *The Ancient Mariner*," Yale University Library Gazette, XXV, 2 (October, 1960).
47. Quoted in Gelb, 602.
48. Friedrich Nietzsche, *Thus Spake Zarathustra*, tr. Thomas Common. In *The Complete Works of Friedrich Nietzsche*, ed. Dr. Oscar Levy (New York, 1916), 266.
49. Macgowan and Jones, 221.

CHAPTER VIII

1. O'Neill to Joseph Wood Krutch, June 10 and July 15, 1927 (Beinecke).
2. "Memoranda on Masks," *The American Spectator,* November, 1932. Reprinted in Cargill, 116.
3. "Second Thoughts," *The American Spectator,* December, 1932. Reprinted in Cargill, 119.
4. The letter is published in *Inscriptions: Eugene O'Neill to Carlotta Monterey O'Neill.*
5. Cf. Gelb, 638.
6. O'Neill to Krutch, June 11, 1929 (Beinecke).
7. O'Neill to Benjamin de Casseres, March 12, 1929 (Beinecke).
8. Henry Adams, *The Education of Henry Adams* (Boston and New York, 1918), 380.
9. *The Education of Henry Adams,* 384.
10. O'Neill to de Casseres, September 16, 1928 (Beinecke).
11. O'Neill to Eleanor Fitzgerald, May 13, 1929 (Beinecke).
12. Gelb, 783.
13. Moeller's notes are contained in an unpublished memorandum in the Stanford University Library. They are dated January 1, 1934, and were made during the Boston tryouts of *Days Without End.*
14. The scenarios are in Beinecke. They are quoted in Doris Falk's valuable study, *Eugene O'Neill and the Tragic Tension* (New Brunswick, N.J., 1958), 150.
15. In *The New York Post,* January 9, 1934. Reprinted in Jordan Y. Miller, *Playwright's Progress* (Chicago, Ill., 1965), 80.

CHAPTER IX

1. O'Neill to Eleanor Fitzgerald, May 13, 1929 (Beinecke).
2. "O'Neill's Own Story of 'Electra' in the Making," New York *Herald Tribune,* November 3, 1931. Reprinted in Barrett H. Clark, *European Theories of the Drama,* revised edition (New York, 1947).
3. George Jean Nathan, *The Intimate Notebooks of George Jean Nathan,* 195.
4. Clark, 136.
5. Gelb, 596.
6. Kenneth Macgowan, *What Is Wrong with Marriage?* (New York, 1929), 152.
7. *What Is Wrong with Marriage?,* 167.
8. Gelb, 762.
9. Gelb, 741.
10. Cf. in the order quoted, Clark, 137; Croswell Bowen, "The Black Irishman" (*PM,* November 3, 1946; reprinted in Cargill, 67); and Hamilton Basso, "The Tragic Sense" (*The New Yorker,* March 6, 1948).
11. Sheaffer, 101.

CHAPTER X

1. Eugene O'Neill, *Work Diary,* ed. Donald Gallup. 2 vols. (New Haven, Conn.: Yale University Library, 1981), entry for Jan. 11, 1933.

2. Helen Christine Bennett, "Kate Gleason's Adventures in a Man's Job," *The American Magazine* CVI (October, 1828), 4, and *Dictionary of American Biography,* vol. 21, supplement one (New York, 1944).

3. Eugene O'Neill, *The Calms of Capricorn,* ed. Donald Gallup (New Haven, Conn., 1982). Dr. Gallup developed the scenario into dramatic form and published it as a second volume to his edition.

4. Sheaffer, 165.

5. O'Neill's meticulous attention to the details of these models is documented in his correspondence with their maker. The original drafts of O'Neill's letters to Donald Pace, the model builder, are in the Beinecke Rare Book and Manuscript Collection, Yale University, New Haven.

6. See above p. 338.

7. In the Provincetown *Playbill* for *The Spook Sonata.* See above p. 187.

8. In *More Stately Mansions,* 21.

9. *A Touch of the Poet,* 84.

10. Lawrence Langner, *The Magic Curtain* (London, 1952), 405.

11. From an interview in the New York *Herald Tribune,* March 16, 1924. Reprinted in Cargill, 110.

12. Cf. Helen Muchnic, "Circe's Swine: Plays by Gorky and O'Neill," *Comparative Literature,* III (spring 1951), 119. Reprinted in Cargill, 431.

13. Unpublished notes for *Lazarus Laughed* (Beinecke).

14. Seymour Peck, "A Talk with Mrs. O'Neill, *The New York Times,* November 4, 1956. Reprinted in Cargill, 93.

15. Gelb, 6.

16. Cf. Sheaffer, 241.

17. Sheaffer, 240.

18. Gelb, 596.

19. Sheaffer, 85.

20. Sheaffer, 101.

21. Sheaffer, 102.

22. Otto Rank, *The Double, A Psychoanalytic Study.* Tr. and ed. by Harry Tucker, Jr. (Chapel Hill, N.C., 1971).

23. Gelb, 531.

24. Gelb, 362; Sheaffer, 435.

25. *The Magic Curtain,* 402.

26. Cf. Mary Welch, "Softer Tones for Mr. O'Neill's Portrait," *Theatre Arts,* May, 1957. Reprinted in Cargill, 85.

27. *The Magic Curtain,* 409.

APPENDIX I. The Staging of the Tao House Plays

In 1944, when O'Neill completed *A Touch of the Poet,* he sent it along with *The Iceman Cometh* and *A Moon for the Misbegotten* to Lawrence Langner at the Theatre Guild. Plans to produce the cycle play were set in motion. Casting discussions were begun with Spencer Tracy and Laurence Olivier mentioned for the role of Cornelius Melody. Robert Edmond Jones made preliminary drawings for the setting and the Guild management worked toward an opening in 1947, following that of *A Moon for the Misbegotten.* The difficulties with that play's out-of-town tryouts and with O'Neill's increasingly severe illness forced cancellation of the plans. The play was forced to wait a decade before it took its place on the stage.

Had the Theatre Guild received the entire, completed cycle, the organization would have been forced to depart radically from customary procedures of Broadway production. Indeed, to stage the plays would have required an acting organization unlike any that had been recorded in theatrical history. Assuming that the cycle was to be represented in its full eleven-play length, in all probability a minimum of five years would have been required to mount and play it. A company, supported by appropriate directorial and design echelons, devoted solely to the production of the plays of a single author would have been an indispensable requirement. The problem was clear to Theresa Helburn as early as 1936. She wrote O'Neill, when only seven plays were envisioned, "I realize . . . that the special problems and size of the task before us prob ably precludes any thought of a company not definitely focused on these productions, because working on your cycle will absorb all our surplus energy and more for the next two or three years. But we must continue this summer and next fall to organize our acting material so that we will have sifted through and tested out both its caliber and its spirit before our O'Neill season begins." Having been schooled in the problems of marathon plays not only by O'Neill but by Shaw's *Back to Methuselah,* which they had staged in 1922, the executives of the Guild quickly understood the true essence of the problem. O'Neill, however, called a halt to planning and refused to discuss the cycle or show any of his drafts. The project of forming a company was therefore shelved, although it was one to which O'Neill gave thought as his letter to Robert Sisk testifies. He wrote to Miss Helburn that when the cycle was finished, "Then we really could engage a repertoire company for the whole Cycle—show actors and actresses we [have] parts that would make it worth their while, out of pure self-interest, to tie up for several seasons under our conditions. No stars, of course, but show the young and ambitious their chance to become stars through this Cycle. No featured names, unless we ran into some with the right spirit of cooperation. Do this Cycle very much as if we were starting a new Guild or Provincetown Players, that's my idea. Keep it as far away from the amusement racket theatre and all Broadway connotations as we possibly can. Treat it as it should be treated from its very nature, as a special, unique thing. That's the only way to do it. It's not only the one right way to produce it, artistically speaking, but it's sound practical showmanship. I'm very obdurate on this point. In fact, to be blunt, I won't allow it to be done any other way."

O'Neill's belief that the cycle's opportunities would attract young actors was undoubtedly correct. He recognized that the cycle would play in a long rotation with new plays being fed in as they were readied over a two- or three-year period, until at last the whole work was on view. To hold actors for so long a time meant, of course that he had to consider their reappearance in a variety of roles, assuming new ones after their initial characters had disappeared from the stage.*

---

* According to Ronald D. Scofield, in the *Santa Barbara News-Press,* September 17, 1967, O'Neill approached Ingrid Bergman after her performance as Anna Christie in a 1941 West Coast production with an invitation "to commit herself for six years to star in the great cycle of plays he was then engaged in creating." Mrs. O'Neill had responded favorably to Miss Bergman's performance when she saw her play in San Francisco. The actress was invited to Tao House where she met O'Neill. It was at about this time that Langner gave thought to forming an acting company in San Francisco so that O'Neill at Tao House could be at hand to supervise rehearsals. [Cf. *The Magic Curtain,* 400]

There is some evidence that O'Neill, in writing the plays, concerned himself with the problem of retaining his actors over the long stretch of production the cycle would have required. He kept the casts of the plays small—ten in *A Touch of the Poet,* somewhat more in *More Stately Mansions*—and he appears to have made it possible for actors to play more than one role. In *Mourning Becomes Electra,* O'Neill had stressed the importance of the resemblance of characters in the various branches of the Mannon family. In a similar way, it is probable that the physical types of the major characters of the earlier plays would have been perpetuated in the generations that appear later in the cycle, and that the physical requirements—age, general physique and cast of features—of minor characters would be serviceable for roles in several plays. The fact that the two surviving plays are adjacent to one another in the plan, and thus provide only for a continuity of the same actor in the same role, makes final determination of this matter impossible, but it would have been uncharacteristically extravagant for O'Neill to have done anything else.

What is an obvious theatrical economy, however, may well have taken a far from obvious turn in O'Neill's thinking toward an end that would have staggered even the indomitable board of directors of the Guild. On the evidence only of physical type with specific points of characterization set aside, it can be suggested that O'Neill thought of the company as playing not only the cycle, but the autobiographical plays as well, including *Hughie* and *The Iceman Cometh.*

The essential features of Deborah Harford are that she is about five feet tall, slender, with masses of white hair,* a pale complexion, with large brown eyes that appear black against her skin, a dainty, aquiline nose, high forehead, a full mouth and thin tapering hands. Mary Tyrone is of medium height, has a young graceful figure, masses of white hair, a pale complexion, very large brown eyes which appear black, a long straight nose, a high forehead, a full, wide mouth and long tapering fingers. Cornelius Melody is tall, with broad shoulders and a deep chest, iron-grey hair and a finely chiseled nose, and he gives the appearance of ravaged handsomeness. James Tyrone, Sr., is 5′8″, but seems taller by reason of his military carriage, has grey hair, a good profile and a handsome face

---

* It is red-brown in *A Touch of the Poet.*

that is beginning to break down. The only difference is in color of eyes, Tyrone's being light brown, Melody's being grey. Simon Harford is tall, loose-jointed and wiry, with thick brown hair, light brown eyes set wide in his face, a big straight nose, a "fine" forehead, a wide "sensitive mouth" and a long, Yankee face with "Indian" characteristics. Edmund Tyrone is 5'11", with a thin, wiry frame, dark brown eyes which dominate his face, a handsome profile, high forehead, a sensitive mouth and a long narrow face with "Irish" characteristics. Sara Melody has a strong, full-breasted body, black hair, fair skin, deep blue eyes, a thick, sensual mouth, heavy jaw and big stubby hands. Nothing is said of her height. Josie Hogan, the peasant heroine of *A Moon for the Misbegotten,* is 5'11" and broad-shouldered, and has a wide waist and strong hips, deep-chested with large firm breasts, a fair complexion, dark blue eyes, a long upper lip and heavy jaw. The chief difference, height aside,* is the nose, Sara's being straight and fine, Josie's being "small." Finally, there is a marked similarity in physical type between Phil Hogan, Erie Smith and Theodore Hickman, whose ages range from the late forties to fifty-five. Phil is 5'6", somewhat fat, with thin sandy hair, small blue eyes, a snub nose and a round head. Erie Smith is of medium height,** fat, with sandy hair going bald, blue eyes, a snub nose and a big round head. Hickman is of medium height, stout, balding with a fringe of hair of unspecified color, blue eyes, a "button" nose and a round head. Erie and Hickey are alike in having a small pursed mouth, while Phil's is big with a long upper lip. An actor, however, could accommodate such a difference.

There are, of course, other aspects of the appearances of all the characters here mentioned. The point is this: that where the same physical trait is described, the conformity is remarkable, and while the evidence is far from decisive, it is suggestive that O'Neill was considering not only a company to play the cycle in repertory but also the non-cycle plays. The idea of a "Eugene O'Neill Repertory Company" had arisen before, in conversation with Macgowan and Jones during the twenties, and it recurred periodically during

---

* Given a relatively tall, big-bodied actress, the height could be adjusted by shoe lifts. In neither of the cycle plays does Sara give the impression of any delicacy. Her peasant qualities are stressed by her father, and she is evidently intended to contrast strongly with the slight figure of Deborah whom she must lift and carry.
** O'Neill calls Jamie Tyrone (5'9") "tall."

O'Neill's association with the Guild. At times, perhaps even the Provincetown Players had seemed to approximate such a group. Now, however, the need was full and clear, insofar as the cycle was concerned. The other plays were perhaps to be fed into the same proposed theatrical hopper.

Whether or not the writing of the late plays were to have such unusual and potentially revolutionary theatrical consequences, the overlapping of the character-types suggests that all of the late plays were formed with an inner unity, whose significance lies as much in their composite whole as it does in the individual work. Sara and Josie are the same woman. Josie lives in a "shebeen" like that from which Sara's family have come, and both are deeply aware of the handicap and the strength of this peasant heritage. It is at once burden and badge of honor, but it is not easy to live with. Sara, who can speak without the brogue if she chooses, uses it as Josie does as a weapon to taunt, to score points and to degrade herself. The Irish in her comes to be her strength, the only power that enables her to live amidst the Harford's elegant jealousies. Although she was born in a castle in Ireland, she was not born to this Yankee mansion, and her desire to return to the old farm of the Harfords bespeaks the peasant heritage whose visible signs are her thick ankles and heavy hands. When she elects to play the peasant, her performance is part role, part reality. Josie assumes a similar part, a rough, whorish, animal creature. It is a role her strength and size permit her, but beneath it she is a woman—a sensitive, even fragile, girl, whose desires are simple and whose need is that she be seen for what she is. Both women set out to trap the men they love by forcing them to marriage after they have slept with them. Sara succeeds in *A Touch of the Poet*, but the marriage that ensues is founded in anything but love. To keep her man, Sara must play the whore, as Josie did. Josie, on the other hand, does not succeed in seducing Jamie Tyrone, and nothing follows from their meeting. The meeting, however, blessed by a fine-drawn tenderness, is sufficient to itself. For a moment, Josie can become what she truly is, and the moment is the sum of her happiness. In countering motion around the same orbit, the two characters move to the same immediate end, the achievement of their love.

Between Mary Tyrone and Deborah Harford, similar parallels exist. In their patrician fragility—the quality they both possess of seeming to be even as old women very young and well-brought-up girls—in their ambiguous attitude of love and hate for their sons, in their denial of sexuality, in their dependence and their refusal to be touched, in their need for social status and their hatred of the community and most important in their power to retreat deliberately into a swirl of dreams, they appear as identicals. There is little distance between Deborah's willful, self-induced madness by means of her fantasies of life at the courts of France and Mary Tyrone's flight into a morphine trance. Mary's need of morphine is an escape of the same order as Deborah's, from a world and its conflicts that she cannot face. Her isolation in the summerhouse in New London, surrounded by a straggly hedge and a negligible garden, is of the same order as Deborah's escape into her summerhouse, set in a walled garden where nature's forms are fantastically trimmed and distorted. Life goes by beyond the hedge and outside the walls. Deborah's fear of isolation and her struggle against it is not essentially different from Mary's attempt to overcome the morphine; nor is Mary's vision of her life in the convent with which *Long Day's Journey into Night* concludes a less pernicious fantasy than Deborah's dreams. Neither woman can walk in the world, and the fact corrupts the lives of those who love them.

Cornelius Melody and James Tyrone, Sr., are in the same way double exposures. Melody lives with the memory of a great honor, Wellington's praise after Talavera, just as Tyrone recalls Booth's praise of his acting. Both have a touch of the peasant as well as the poet in them, revealed in their deep-rooted fear of the horrifying poverty of old-country Ireland. Both make unprofitable real-estate deals. They reject modernity: Melody's hatred of Jacksonian democracy is of the same intensity as Tyrone's dislike of modern authors. Both love but are alienated by their wives and children. Both make a pretense of the grand manner, born in the one case of chivalric derring-do and in the other of an actor's manner acquired in a romantic melodrama, and in each instance, the period is the same—the era of Napoleonic heroics. Both men are actors in their quoting, their strutting and in the use of their roles as a mask to hide their pain. Even their military bearing is the same, lending them the appearance of stature and grace when they are at their most graceless.

Such differences as exist between the pairs is more a result of the context in which they move than a matter of basic character. Both the autobiographical plays and the cycle involve a historical perspective, yet the former, despite their involvement with the past, are not in any meaningful sense "period plays." Even *The Iceman Cometh*, with minimal changes, could be played in any period—a low tavern by Hogarth, a Gorkian Lower Depths, or a mid-twentieth-century skid-row flophouse. Like *Hughie*, *A Long Day's Journey into Night* and *A Moon for the Misbegotten*, the play has its being out of time, in a world so dark and silent that only conjured illusion gives it substance. The cycle plays are predicated on the opposite. When Melody leaves his world of chivalric illusion, as when Deborah enters hers, there must be a sense of difference from the former reality. Both enter a timeless shadowy world, in spirit if not in fact. What surrounds them—the particular places, particular times, and a panorama of romantic history that can feed their dreams—must have destructive reality. The two sets of plays are negative and positive prints of the same view of life, the one dark and evanescent, the other distinct and highly colored. Their difference is to be explained by understanding on which side of the "door in the mind" O'Neill stood when he provided roles for his last cast of actors.

APPENDIX II. The Casts of O'Neill's Plays

Cast lists of the first production and of significant revivals of O'Neill's plays are arranged chronologically according to the date of the opening. Cross references to major revivals are provided.

Bound East for Cardiff (See also November 3, 1916)

The Wharf Theatre, Provincetown, Mass., July 28, 1916
Produced by The Provincetown Players
Directed by Eugene O'Neill and E. J. Ballantine

YANK	George Cram Cook
DRISCOLL	Frederic Burt (?)
COCKY	E. J. Ballantine
DAVIS	Harry Kemp
THE CAPTAIN	David Carb
THE SECOND MATE	Eugene G. O'Neill

Also in the cast: John Reed, Wilbur Daniel Steele.

The cast for this, the first production of an O'Neill play, cannot be entirely reconstructed. The Provincetown Players in the beginning allowed the author to direct his own work. Design credits appear infrequently in the early days.

Thirst

The Wharf Theatre, Provincetown, Mass., August, 1916
Produced by The Provincetown Players
Directed by George Cram Cook
Designed by William Zorach

THE GENTLEMAN	George Cram Cook
THE DANCER	Louise Bryant
THE MULATTO SAILOR	Eugene G. O'Neill

479

Bound East for Cardiff (See also July 28, 1916)

The Playwright's Theatre, New York, N.Y., November 3, 1916
Produced by The Provincetown Players

YANK	George Cram Cook
DRISCOLL	William Stewart
COCKY	E. J. Ballantine
DAVIS	Harry Kemp
SCOTTY	Frank Shay
OLSON	Bion Norfeldt
A NORWEGIAN	Donald Corley
SMITTY	Lew Parrish
IVAN	Francis Buzzell
THE CAPTAIN	Henry Marion Hall
THE SECOND MATE	Eugene G. O'Neill

Before Breakfast

The Playwright's Theatre, New York, N.Y., December 1, 1916
Produced by The Provincetown Players
Directed by Eugene G. O'Neill assisted by James O'Neill

MRS. ROWLAND	Mary Pyne
ALFRED	Eugene G. O'Neill

Fog

The Playwright's Theatre, New York, N.Y., January 5, 1917
Produced by The Provincetown Players
Designed by Margaret Swain and B. J. O. Norfeldt

THE POET	John Held
THE BUSINESS MAN	Hutchinson Collins
THE WOMAN	Margaret Swain
THE THIRD OFFICER	Karl Karstens

The Sniper

The Playwright's Theatre, New York, N.Y., February 16, 1917
Produced by The Provincetown Players
Directed by Nina Moise

ROUGON	George Cram Cook
THE VILLAGE PRIEST	Donald Corley
A CAPTAIN OF THE GERMAN INFANTRY	Theron M. Bamberger
A PRIVATE OF THE REGIMENT	Morton Stafford
ANOTHER PRIVATE	Robert Montcarr
JEAN, A PEASANT BOY	Ida Rauh

In the Zone

The Comedy Theatre, New York, N.Y., October 31, 1917
Produced by The Washington Square Players

SMITTY	Frederick Roland
DAVIS	Robert Strange
YANK	Jay Strong
OLSON	Abram Gillette
SCOTTY	Eugene Lincoln
IVAN	Edward Balzerit
DRISCOLL	Arthur Hohl
COCKY	Rienzi de Cordova

The Long Voyage Home

The Playwright's Theatre, New York, N.Y., November 2, 1917
Produced by The Provincetown Players

BARTENDER	George Cram Cook
OLSON	Ira Remsen
DRISCOLL	Hutchinson Collins
COCKY	O. K. Liveright
FIRST GIRL	Ida Rauh
SECOND GIRL	Alice MacDougal

'Ile

The Playwright's Theatre, New York, N.Y., November 30, 1917
Produced by The Provincetown Players
Directed by Nina Moise
Setting by Louis B. Ell

BEN	Harold Conley
THE STEWARD	Robert Edwards
CAPTAIN KEENEY	Hutchinson Collins
MR. SLOCUM	Ira Remsen
MRS. KEENEY	Clara Savage
JOE	Louis B. Ell

The Rope

The Playwright's Theatre, New York, N.Y., April 26, 1918
Produced by The Provincetown Players
Directed by Nina Moise

ABRAHAM BENTLEY	O. K. Liveright
ANNIE	Dorothy Upjohn
PAT SWEENEY	H. B. Tisdale
MARY	Edna Smith
LUKE BENTLEY	Charles Ellis

Where the Cross Is Made

The Provincetown Playhouse, New York, N.Y., November 22, 1918
Produced by The Provincetown Players
Directed by Ida Rauh

NAT BARTLETT	James Light
DR. HIGGINS	O. K. Liveright
SUE BARTLETT	Ida Rauh
CAPT. ISAIAH BARTLETT	Hutchinson Collins
HORNE	Louis B. Ell
CATES	Foster Damon
JIMMY KANAKA	F. Ward Roege

The Moon of the Caribbees

The Provincetown Playhouse, New York, N.Y., December 20, 1918
Produced by The Provincetown Players
Directed by Thomas Mitchell

YANK	Harry Winston
DRISCOLL	Hutchinson Collins
OLSON	William Forster Batterham
DAVIS	W. Clay Hill
COCKY	O. K. Liveright
SMITTY	Charles Ellis
PAUL	Percy Winner
LAMPS, THE LAMPLIGHTER	Phil Lyons
CHIPS, THE CARPENTER	Fred Booth
OLD TOM, THE DONKEYMAN	William Stuart
BIG FRANK	Howard Scott
MAX	Jimmy Spike
PADDY	Charles Garland Kemper
THE FIRST MATE	Louis B. Ell
BELLA	Jean Robb
SUSIE	Bernice Abbott
PEARL	Ruth Collins Allen
VIOLET	Unknown

The Dreamy Kid

The Provincetown Playhouse, New York, N.Y., October 31, 1919
Produced by The Provincetown Players
Directed by Ida Rauh
Designed by Glenn Coleman

MAMMY SAUNDERS	Ruth Anderson
CEELY ANN	Leathe Colvert
IRENE	Margaret Rhodes
ABE	Harold Simmelkjaer

Beyond the Horizon

Morosco Theatre, New York, N.Y., February 3, 1920
Produced by John D. Williams
Directed and designed by Homer Saint-Gaudens

ROBERT MAYO	Richard Bennett
ANDREW MAYO	Edward Arnold
RUTH ATKINS	Helen MacKellar
CAPTAIN DICK SCOTT	Max Mitzel
MRS. KATE MAYO	Mary Jeffrey
JAMES MAYO	Erville Alderson
MRS. ATKINS	Louise Closser Hale
MARY	Elfin Finn
BEN	George Hadden
DR. FAWCETT	George Riddell

Chris Christopherson

Apollo Theatre, Atlantic City, N.J., March 9, 1920
Produced by George C. Tyler
Directed by Frederick Stanhope

JACK BURNS	Claude Gourand
ADAMS	Max L. Schrade
LONGSHOREMAN	Frank Devlin
JOHNNY THE PRIEST	James C. Mack
LARRY, A BARTENDER	William E. Hallman
A POSTMAN	Harry MacFayden
CHRIS CHRISTOPHERSON	Emmett Corrigan
MICKEY	Dan Moyles
DEVLIN	George A. Lawrence
MARTHY	Mary Hampton
ANNA CHRISTOPHERSON	Lynn Fontanne
CAPTAIN JESSUP	Roy Cochrane
THE STEWARD	George Spelvin
PAUL ANDERSEN	Arthur Ashley
EDWARDS	William Smith
JONESY	John Rogers
GLASS	Gerald Rogers

Exorcism

The Provincetown Playhouse, New York, N.Y., March 26, 1920
Produced by The Provincetown Players
Directed by Edward Goodman

NED MALLOY	Jasper Deeter
JIMMY	M. A. MacAteer
MAJOR ANDREWS	William Dunbar
MR. MALLOY	Remo Bufano
NORDSTROM	Lawrence Vail

The Emperor Jones

The Provincetown Playhouse, New York, N.Y., November 1, 1920
Produced by The Provincetown Players
Directed by George Cram Cook
Settings by Cleon Throckmorton

BRUTUS JONES	Charles S. Gilpin
HARRY SMITHERS	Jasper Deeter
OLD NATIVE WOMAN	Christine Ell
LEM	Charles Ellis
SOLDIERS	S. I. Thompson, Lawrence Vail, Leo Richman, James Martin, Owen White
THE LITTLE FORMLESS FEARS	S. I. Thompson
JEFF	S. I. Thompson
THE NEGRO CONVICTS	Leo Richman, Lawrence Vail, S. I. Thompson, Owen White
THE PRISON GUARD	James Martin
THE PLANTERS	Frank Schwartz, C. I. Martin, W. D. Slager
THE SPECTATORS	Jeannie Begg, Charlotte Grauert
THE AUCTIONEER	Frederick Ward Roege
THE SLAVES	James Martin, S. I. Thompson, Leo Richman, Owen White, Lawrence Vail
CONGO WITCH DOCTOR	S. I. Thompson

Diff'rent

The Provincetown Playhouse, New York, N.Y., December 27, 1920
Produced by The Provincetown Players
Directed by Charles O'Brien Kennedy
Designed by Cleon Throckmorton

EMMA CROSBY	Mary Blair
CAPTAIN JOHN CROSBY	H. B. Tisdale
MRS. CROSBY	Alice Rostetter
JACK CROSBY	Eugene Lincoln
CALEB WILLIAMS	James Light
HARRIET WILLIAMS	Elizabeth Brown
ALFRED ROGERS	Iden Thompson
BENNY ROGERS	Charles Ellis

Gold

Frazee Theatre, New York, N.Y., June 1, 1921
Produced by John D. Williams
Directed by Homer Saint-Gaudens

ABEL	Ashley Buck
BUTLER	George Marion
CAPT. ISAIAH BARTLETT	Willard Mack
SILAS HORNE	J. Fred Hollaway
BEN CATES	Charles D. Brown
JIMMY KANAKA	T. Tamamoto
MRS. BARTLETT	Katherine Grey
SUE BARTLETT	Geraldine O'Brien
DANNY DREW	Charles Francis
NAT BARTLETT	E. J. Ballantine
DR. BERRY	Scott Cooper

"Anna Christie"

The Vanderbilt Theatre, New York, N.Y., November 2, 1921
Produced and directed by Arthur Hopkins
Designed by Robert Edmond Jones

JOHNNY THE PRIEST	James C. Mack
FIRST LONGSHOREMAN	G. O. Taylor
SECOND LONGSHOREMAN	John Hanley
A POSTMAN	William Augustin
CHRIS CHRISTOPHERSON	George Marion
MARTHY OWEN	Eugenie Blair
ANNA CHRISTOPHERSON	Pauline Lord
MAT BURKE	Frank Shannon
JOHNSON	Ole Anderson
LARRY	Unknown
THREE SAILORS	Messers Reilly, Hansen and Kennedy

The Straw

Greenwich Village Theatre, New York, N.Y., November 10, 1921
Produced by George C. Tyler
Directed by John Westley

BILL CARMODY	Harry Harwood
NORA	Viola Cecil Ormonde
TOM	Richard Ross
BILLY	Norris Millington
DR. GAYNOR	George Woodward
FRED NICHOLLS	Robert Strange
EILEEN CARMODY	Margalo Gillmore
STEPHEN MURRAY	Otto Kruger

MISS GILPIN	Katherine Grey
MR. SLOAN	Unknown
MISS HOWARD	Dothea Fisher
DR. SIMMS	Unknown
MRS. ABNER	Nora O'Brien
MISS BAILEY	Alice Haynes
MRS. TURNER	Grace Henderson
DR. STANTON	George Farren
MRS. BRENNAN	Jennie Lamont

The First Man

The Neighborhood Playhouse, New York, N.Y., March 4, 1922
Produced and directed by Augustin Duncan

CURTIS JAYSON	Augustin Duncan
MARTHA	Margaret Mower
JOHN JAYSON	Harry Andrews
JOHN JR.	Gordon Burby
RICHARD	Alan Bunce
ESTHER	Margherita Sargent
LILY	Marjorie Vonnegut
MRS. DAVIDSON	Marie L. Day
MARK SHEFFIELD	Eugene Powers
EMILY	Eva Carder
EDWARD BIGELOW	Frederic Burt
A MAID	I. Hill
A TRAINED NURSE	Isabel Stuart

The Hairy Ape

The Provincetown Playhouse, New York, N.Y., March 9, 1922
Produced by The Provincetown Players
Directed by James Light with the assistance of Arthur Hopkins
Designed by Cleon Throckmorton with the assistance of Robert Edmond Jones

ROBERT SMITH	Louis Wolheim
PADDY	Henry O'Neill
LONG	Harold West
MILDRED DOUGLAS	Mary Blair
HER AUNT	Eleanor Hutchison
SECOND ENGINEER	Jack Gude
A GUARD	Harry Gottlieb
A SECRETARY	Harold McGee
LADIES, GENTLEMEN, STOKERS	Josephine Hutchinson, Greta Hoving, Esther Pinch, Lucy Shreve, Jack Gude, Clement O'Loughlen, Anterio Argondona, Em Jo, Allen Delano, Patrick Barnum, Harold McGee, Harry Gottlieb, Alexander Boije, George Tobias

Welded

Thirty-ninth Street Theatre, New York, N.Y., March 17, 1924
Produced by Macgowan, Jones and O'Neill in association with Edgar Selwyn
Directed by Stark Young
Designed by Robert Edmond Jones

ELEANOR CAPE	Doris Keane
MICHAEL CAPE	Jacob Ben-Ami
JOHN DARNTON	Curtis Cooksey
A WOMAN	Catherine Collins

The Ancient Mariner

The Provincetown Playhouse, New York, N.Y., April 6, 1924
Produced by Macgowan, Jones and O'Neill
Directed by James Light and Robert Edmond Jones
Designed by Robert Edmond Jones

THE ANCIENT MARINER	E. J. Ballantine
FIRST WEDDING GUEST	James Shute
SECOND WEDDING GUEST	H. L. Rothschild
THIRD WEDDING GUEST	Charles Ellis
CHORUS	Clement Wilenchick, William Stahl, Harold McGee, Benjamin Keiley, Robert Forsyth, John Taylor
HELMSMAN	James Meighan
BRIDE	Rosalind Fuller
BRIDEGROOM	Gerald Stopp
LIFE-IN-DEATH	Rita Matthias
FIRST SPIRIT	Henry O'Neill
SECOND SPIRIT	Gerald Stopp
PILOT	Rupert Caplan
PILOT'S BOY	John Brewster
HERMIT	Henry O'Neill

All God's Chillun Got Wings

The Provincetown Playhouse, New York, N.Y., May 15, 1924
Produced by MacGowan, Jones and O'Neill
Directed by James Light
Designed by Cleon Throckmorton

Scene 1:

JIM HARRIS	William Davis
ELLA DOWNEY	Virginia Wilson
SHORTY	George Finley
JOE	Malvin Myrck
MICKEY	James Ward
LITTLE GIRLS	Grace Burns, Alice Nelson, Evelyn Wynn

The Remaining Scenes:

JIM HARRIS	Paul Robeson
MRS. HARRIS	Lillian Greene
HATTIE	Dora Cole
ELLA DOWNEY	Mary Blair
MICKEY	James Martin
SHORTY	John Taylor
JOE	Frank Wilson
ORGAN GRINDER	James Meighan
SALVATIONISTS	Barbara Benedict, Clement O'Loughlen, William Stahl
MEN AND WOMEN	Kirk Ames, Eloise Anderson, Harold Bryant, Polly Craig, Hume Derr, Oscar Flanner, Lila Hawkins, Paul Jones, Spurgon Lampert, Sadie Reynolds, Kathleen Roarke

Desire Under the Elms

The Greenwich Village Theatre, New York, N.Y., November 11, 1924
Produced by MacGowan, Jones and O'Neill
Directed and designed by Robert Edmond Jones

SIMEON CABOT	Allen Nagle
PETER CABOT	Perry Ivins
EBEN CABOT	Charles Ellis
EPHRAIM CABOT	Walter Huston
ABBIE PUTNAM	Mary Morris
A YOUNG GIRL	Eloise Pendleton
FARMERS	Romeyn Benjamin, Arthur Mack, William Stahl, Jim Taylor
THE FIDDLER	Macklin Marrow
A SHERIFF	Walter Abel
AN OLD WOMAN	Norma Millay
DEPUTIES	Arthur Mack, William Stahl
OTHER FOLKS FROM SURROUNDING FARMS	Albert Brush, Hume Derr, Donald Oenslager, Alma O'Neill, Lucy Shreve, Mary Ture, Ruza Wenclawska

The Fountain

The Greenwich Village Theatre, New York, N.Y., December 10, 1925
Produced by Macgowan, Jones and O'Neill
in association with A. L. Jones and Morris Green
Directed and designed by Robert Edmond Jones

IBNU ASWAD	Stanley Berry
JUAN PONCE DE LEON	Walter Huston
PEDRO	William Stahl
MARIA DE CORDOVA	Pauline Moore
LUIS DE ALVAREDO	Egon Brecher
YUSEF	John Taylor

DIEGO MENENDEZ	Crane Wilbur
VINCENTE DE CORDOVA	Edgar Stehli
ALONZO DE OLVIEDO	Perry Ivins
MANUEL DE CASTILLO	Morris Ankrum
CRISTOVAL DE MENDOZA	Ralph Benzies
CHRISTOPHER COLUMBUS	Henry O'Neill
HELMSMAN	Philip Jones
FRIAR QUESEDA	Edgar Stehli
NANO	Curtis Cooksey
BEATRICE DE CORDOVA	Rosalind Fuller
DUENNA	Liza Dallet
A SOLDIER	William Stahl
AN INDIAN CHIEF	Ray Corning
A MEDICINE MAN	John Taylor
FATHER SUPERIOR	Henry O'Neill
JUAN	John Taylor
HIS SERVANT	Philip Jones

The Great God Brown

The Greenwich Village Theatre, New York, N.Y., January 23, 1926
Produced by Macgowan, Jones and O'Neill
Directed and designed by Robert Edmond Jones

WILLIAM A. BROWN	William Harrigan
HIS FATHER	Milano Tilden
HIS MOTHER	Clifford Sellers
DION ANTHONY	Robert Keith
HIS FATHER	Hugh Kidder
HIS MOTHER	Eleanor Wesselhoeft
MARGARET	Leona Hogarth
CYBEL	Anne Shoemaker
MARGARET'S SONS	Starr Jones, Paul Jones, Teddy Jones
TWO DRAUGHTSMEN	Frederick C. Packard, Jr., John Mahin
CLIENT	Seth Kendall
THREE COMMITTEEMEN	Stanley Barry, Adrian Marsh, William Stahl
POLICE CAPTAIN	Ellsworth Jones
MARGARET'S SONS (4 YEARS LATER)	Tupper Jones, Starr Jones, Paul Jones

Marco Millions

The Guild Theatre, New York, N.Y., January 9, 1928
Produced by The Theatre Guild
Directed by Rouben Mamoulian
Settings by Lee Simonson

CHRISTIAN TRAVELER	Philip Leigh
MAGIAN TRAVELER	Mark Schweid
BUDDHIST TRAVELER	Charles Romano
A MAHOMETAN	Robert Barrata
A CORPORAL	Albert Van Dekker
KUKACHIN	Margalo Gillmore
MARCO POLO	Alfred Lunt
DONATA	Natalie Browning
TEDALDO	Morris Carnovsky
NICOLO	Henry Travers
MAFFEO	Ernest Cossart
A DOMINICAN MONK	Albert Van Dekker
A KNIGHT CRUSADER	George Cotton
A PAPAL COURIER	Sanford Meisner
ONE ALI BROTHER	Mark Schweid
OLDER ALI BROTHER	H. H. McCollum
THE PROSTITUTE	Mary Blair
A DERVISH	John Henry
AN INDIAN SNAKE CHARMER	John Henry
A MONGOL PRIEST	Philip Leigh
A TARTAR MINSTREL	William Edmonson
EMISSARY FROM KUBLAI	Albert Van Dekker
KUBLAI	Baliol Holloway
CHU-YIN	Dudley Digges
BOATSWAIN	H. H. McCollum
GHAZAN	Morris Carnovsky
GENERAL BAYAN	Robert Barrata
MESSENGER FROM PERSIA	Charles Romano
PAULO LOREDANO	Philip Leigh
A CONFUCIAN PRIEST	Mark Schweid
A MOSLEM PRIEST	H. H. McCollum
A BUDDHIST PRIEST	Charles Romano
A TARTAR CHRONICLER	Philip Leigh
TAOIST PRIEST	Unknown

Strange Interlude

John Golden Theatre, New York, N.Y., January 30, 1928
Produced by The Theatre Guild
Directed by Philip Moeller
Designed by Jo Mielziner

CHARLES MARSDEN	Tom Powers
PROFESSOR LEEDS	Philip Leigh
NINA LEEDS	Lynn Fontanne
SAM EVANS	Earle Larimore
EDMUND DARRELL	Glenn Anders

MRS. AMOS EVANS	Helen Westley
GORDON EVANS AS A BOY	Charles Walters
MADELEINE ARNOLD	Ethel Westley
GORDON EVANS AS A MAN	John J. Burns

Lazarus Laughed

Pasadena Community Playhouse, Pasadena, Cal., April 9, 1928
Produced by The Pasadena Community Players
Directed by Gilmor Brown
Designed by James Hyde
Music by Arthur Alexander
Director of Movement, Katharane Edson

LAZARUS	Irving Pichel
HIS FATHER	Maurice Wells
HIS MOTHER	Esther M. Cogswell
MARTHA AND MARY (HIS SISTERS)	Margaret Morrow, Dorothy Warren
MIRIAM (HIS WIFE)	Lenore Shanewise
AN ORTHODOX PRIEST	William Earle
MESSENGERS	Ralph Urmy, Charles Bruins
AN AGED ORTHODOX JEW	Jerome Coray
A CENTURION	Richard Menefee
GAIUS CALIGULA	Victor Jory
CNEIUS CRASSUS	Max Turner
FLAVIUS	Richard Menefee
MARCELLUS	Maurice Wells
TIBERIUS CAESAR	Gilmor Brown
POMPEIA	Dore Wilson
A SOLDIER	Jerome Coray

The cast also included 159 players doubling in approximately 420 roles, as Lazarus's Guests, Chorus of Old Men, Roman Soldiers, Orthodox Jews, Nazarenes, Followers of Lazarus, Greeks, Roman Senators, Chorus of Youths and Girls, Chorus of Senile Old Men. Their names, in alphabetical order, were John Altschul, Don Anderson, Robert Armstrong, Rupert Bagley, Dale Baldwin, Vance Beach, Ellida Bentley, Helen Besse, Helen Biddle, James Brady, Robert Brahm, Charlotte Brandenburg, George Brandt, Charles Bruins, Normand Buoy, Imelda Burns, Alice Butchart, Aldan Cameron, Frances Cardell, Frederick Carlson, Emmet Carlton, Edward Casso, William Chaney, Helen Chisum, Edyth Clark, H. F. Clarke, Mary Cole, Albert Conrad, Francis Cooper, Jerome Coray, Edwin Corle, Norma Cunningham, Raymond Davis, Charles de la Platte, Fred Dennis, George Dickinson, Norman Elliott, Armand Ferguson, Elizabeth Flint, John Floyd, Paul Floyd, Donna Foster, Harold Franklin, Emily Fricke, Anson Frohman, Aubrey Gay, Gilbert Gause, Robert George, Alice Gertmenian, Fred Groch, William Handen, Olive Hanson, Jack Harling, Frances Hayes, Margaret Hayes, Ieda Hegna, Harry Hellegas, Miriam Henderson, Robert Hendricks, Helen Henry, Frederick Herf, Frank Hewson, Thomas A. Hogan, Don Honrath, Robert Hudson, Walter Hughes, Irving Ingram, Henry Ives, Araxie Jamgochian, Gertrude Jensen, Frederick Johnson, James Johnstone, Everett Kadel, Curtis Karpe, Walter Kenney, Stewart Kent, Muriel Kibbe, Bernard King, Claude King, Leila Knox, Albert La Salle, Frank Laidlaw, Robert Lawson, Mathilda Levin, Linwood Libby, Dorothy Lockwood, Jane Loufbourrow, Helen Mahoney, Olive Manson, Virginia Mathews, Helen March, Paul Maxey, Donald McBurney, William McCann, Eleanor McCarthy, Thomas McEachern, Larry McManus, Haven Miller, Elizabeth Mines, Frederika Monten, Frederick Moore, Maxine Morgan, Robert Morris, Alice Forsyth Mosher, Laura Mosher, John Moss, Lulu Nelson, Wesley Nightingale, Jack Noble, Jadwiga Noskowiak, Fred Olmstead, Barbara Pearce, Eugene Peet, Grace Perry, Edith Peterson, Minna Philips, Fred Phleger, Jean Poirer, Dick Pollard, John Posey, Elaine Rabinowitz, Therese Reader, Ellsworth Replogle, Gretchen Reudiger, Cornelia Richardson, Percy Riker, Bess Rivkin, Philip Robinson, Charles Rogers, Louise Rose, Eric St. Clair, Joseph Sauers, Richard Salisian, Edna Schrooer, Frank Simon, O. H. Sipple, Boyd Smith, Herbert Sollars, Doris Sparks, Graydon Spalding, Gordon Spaulding, John Spoon, Clement Squires, John Stewart, Mildred Stockwell, Fredrick Swigert, William Temple, Walter Thomas, Ross Thompson, Vera Todd, Pauline Turner, Catherine Turney, Elizabeth B. Turney, Ralph Urmy, Leon Vinci, Elizabeth Wheeler, Joseph Wheeler, Ruth Wilson, Robert Young.

Dynamo

Martin Beck Theatre, New York, N.Y., February 11, 1929
Produced by The Theatre Guild
Directed by Philip Moeller
Designed by Lee Simonson

REVEREND LIGHT	George Gaul
MRS. LIGHT	Helen Westley
REUBEN LIGHT	Glenn Anders
RAMSAY FIFE	Dudley Digges
MAY FIFE	Catherine Calhoun Doucet
ADA FIFE	Claudette Colbert
JENNINGS	Hugh Forrester
ROCCO	Edgar Kent

Mourning Becomes Electra

The Guild Theatre, New York, N.Y., October 26, 1931
Produced by The Theatre Guild
Directed by Philip Moeller
Designed by Robert Edmond Jones

Homecoming

SETH BECKWITH	Arthur Hughes
AMOS AMES	Jack Byrnes
LOUISA	Bernice Elliott
MINNIE	Emily Lorraine
CHRISTINE	Alla Nazimova
LAVINIA MANNON	Alice Brady
CAPTAIN PETER NILES	Philip Foster
HAZEL NILES	Mary Arbenz
CAPTAIN ADAM BRANT	Thomas Chalmers
BRIGADIER GENERAL EZRA MANNON	Lee Baker

The Hunted

MRS. JOSIAH BORDEN	Augusta Durgeon
MRS. EVERETT HILLS	Janet Young
DR. JOSEPH BLAKE	Erskine Sanford
JOSIAH BORDEN	James Bosnell
EVERETT HILLS	Oliver Putnam
CHRISTINE	Alla Nazimova
HAZEL NILES	Mary Arbenz
PETER NILES	Philip Foster
LAVINIA	Alice Brady
ORIN MANNON	Earle Larimore
A CHANTYMAN	John Hendricks
ADAM BRANT	Thomas Chalmers

The Haunted

ABNER SMALL	Erskine Sanford
IRA MACKEL	Oliver Putnam
JOE SILVA	Grant Gordon
AMOS AMES	Jack Byrnes
SETH BECKWITH	Arthur Hughes
PETER NILES	Philip Foster
HAZEL NILES	Mary Arbenz
LAVINIA	Alice Brady
ORIN	Earle Larimore

Ah, Wilderness!

The Guild Theatre, New York, N.Y., October 2, 1933
Produced by The Theatre Guild
Directed by Philip Moeller
Designed by Robert Edmond Jones

NAT MILLER	George M. Cohan
RICHARD	Elisha Cook, Jr.
SID DAVIS	Gene Lockhart

ESSIE	Marjorie Marquis
ARTHUR	William Post, Jr.
MILDRED	Adelaide Bean
TOMMY	Walter Vonnegut, Jr.
LILY MILLER	Edna Heinemann
DAVID MCCOMBER	Richard Sterling
MURIEL MCCOMBER	Ruth Gilbert
WINT SELBY	John Wynne
BELLE	Ruth Holden
NORA	Ruth Chorpenning
BARTENDER	Donald McClelland
SALESMAN	John Butler

Days Without End

The Henry Miller Theatre, New York, N.Y., January 8, 1934
Produced by The Theatre Guild
Directed by Philip Moeller
Designed by Lee Simonson

JOHN	Earle Larimore
LOVING	Stanley Ridges
WILLIAM ELIOT	Richard Barbee
FATHER MATHEW BAIRD	Richard Loraine
ELSA	Selena Royle
MARGARET	Caroline Newcombe
LUCY HILLMAN	Ilka Chase
HERBERT STILLWELL	Frederick Forrester
NURSE	Margaret Swope

The Iceman Cometh (See also May 8, 1956, September 29, 1985)

The Martin Beck Theatre, New York, N.Y., October 9, 1946
Produced by The Theatre Guild
Directed by Eddie Dowling
Designed by Robert Edmond Jones

HARRY HOPE	Dudley Digges
ED MOSHER	Morton L. Stevens
PAT MCGLOIN	Al McGranery
WILLIE OBAN	E. G. Marshall
JOE MOTT	John Marriott
PIET WETJOEN	Frank Tweddell
CECIL LEWIS	Nicholas Joy
JAMES CAMERON	Russell Collins
HUGO KALMAR	Leo Chalzel
LARRY SLADE	Carl Benton Reid
ROCKY PIOGGI	Tom Pedi

DON PARRITT	Paul Crabtree
PEARL	Ruth Gilbert
MARGIE	Jeanne Cagney
CORA	Marcella Markham
CHUCK MORELLO	Joe Marr
THEODORE HICKMAN	James E. Barton
MORAN	Michael Wyler
LIEB	Charles Hart

A Moon for the Misbegotten (See also May 2, 1957)

Hartman Theater, Columbus, Ohio, February 20, 1947
Produced by The Theatre Guild
Directed by Arthur Shields
Designed by Robert Edmond Jones

JOSIE HOGAN	Mary Welch
MIKE HOGAN	J. Joseph Donnally
PHIL HOGAN	J. M. Kerrigan
JAMES TYRONE	James Dunn
T. STEDMAN HARDER	Lex Lindsay

Long Day's Journey into Night (See also November 7, 1956, January 28, 1976)

Kungl. Dramatiska Teatern, Stockholm, Sweden, February 10, 1956
Produced by Dramaten
Directed by Bengt Ekerot
Designed by Georg Magnusson

JAMES TYRONE	Lars Hanson
MARY TYRONE	Inga Tidblad
JAMES TYRONE, JR.	Ulf Palme
EDMUND TYRONE	Jarl Kulle
CATHLEEN	Caterine Westerlund

The Iceman Cometh (See also October 9, 1946, September 29, 1985)

Circle in the Square Theatre, New York, N.Y., May 8, 1956
Produced by Leigh Connell, Theodore Mann, José Quintero
Directed by José Quintero
Settings by David Hays; costumes by Deirdre Cartier

HARRY HOPE	Farrell Pelly
ED MOSHER	Phil Pheffer
PAT MCGLOIN	Albert Lewis
WILLIE OBAN	Addison Powell
JOE MOTT	William Edmonson

PIET WETJOEN	Richard Abbott
CECIL LEWIS	Richard Bowler
JAMES CAMERON	James Greene
HUGO KALMAR	Paul Andor
LARRY SLADE	Conrad Bain
ROCKY PIOGGI	Peter Falk
DON PARRITT	Larry Robinson
PEARL	Patricia Brooks
MARGIE	Gloria Scott Backe
CORA	Dolly Jonah
CHUCK MORELLO	Joe Marr
THEODORE HICKMAN	Jason Robards Jr.
MORAN	Mal Throne
LIEB	Charles Hamilton

Long Day's Journey into Night (See also February 10, 1956, January 28, 1976)

Helen Hayes Theatre, New York, N.Y., November 7, 1956
Produced by José Quintero, Leigh Connell, Theodore Mann
Directed by José Quintero
Setting by David Hays; costumes by Motley

JAMES TYRONE	Frederic March
MARY TYRONE	Florence Eldridge
JAMES TYRONE, JR.	Jason Robards, Jr.
EDMUND TYRONE	Bradford Dillman
CATHLEEN	Katherine Ross

A Touch of the Poet (See also October 2, 1958, December 28, 1977)

Kungl. Dramatiska Teatern, Stockholm, Sweden, March 29, 1957
Produced by Dramaten
Directed by Olof Molander
Designed by Sven Fahlstedt

MICKEY MALOY	Björn Güstafson
JAMIE CREGAN	Bengt Eklund
SARA MELODY	Eva Dahlbeck
NORA MELODY	Sif Ruud
CORNELIUS MELODY	Lars Hanson
DEBORAH HARFORD	Inga Tidblad
DAN ROCHE	Arthur Cederborgh
PADDY O'DOWD	Olle Hilding
PATCH RILEY	John Norrman
NICHOLAS GADSBY	Rune Carlsten

A Moon for the Misbegotten (See also February 20, 1947)

Bijou Theatre, New York, N.Y., May 2, 1957
Produced by Carmen Capalbo and Stanley Chase
Directed by Carmen Capalbo
Designed by William Pitkin

JOSIE HOGAN	Wendy Hiller
MIKE HOGAN	Glenn Cannon
PHIL HOGAN	Cyril Cusack
JAMES TYRONE	Franchot Tone
T. STEDMAN HARDER	William Woodson

Hughie (See also December 22, 1964)

Kungl. Dramatiska Teatern, Stockholm, Sweden, September 18, 1958
Produced by Dramaten
Directed by Bengt Ekerot
Settings by Marik Vos; costumes by Gunnar Gelbort

"ERIE" SMITH	Bengt Eklund
CHARLIE HUGHES	Allan Edwall

A Touch of the Poet (See also March 29, 1957, December 28, 1977)

Helen Hayes Theatre, New York, N.Y., October 2, 1958
Produced by Robert Whitehead Productions
Directed by Harold Clurman
Designed by Ben Edwards

MICKEY MALOY	Tom Clancy
JAMIE CREGAN	Curt Conway
SARA MELODY	Kim Stanley
NORA MELODY	Helen Hayes
CORNELIUS MELODY	Eric Portman
DEBORAH HARFORD	Betty Field
DAN ROCHE	John Call
PADDY O'DOWD	Art Smith
PATCH RILEY	Farrell Pelly
NICHOLAS GADSBY	Luis Van Rooten

More Stately Mansions (See also September 12, 1967)

Kungl. Dramatiska Teatern, Stockholm, Sweden, September 11, 1962
Produced by Dramaten
Directed by Stig Torsslow
Settings by Sven Fahlstedt; costumes by Agneta Pauli

DEBORAH HARFORD	Inga Tidblad
SIMON HARFORD	Jarl Kulle

SARA HARFORD   Gunnel Broström
JOEL HARFORD   Henrik Schildt
BENJAMIN TENARD   Olof Sandborg
NICHOLAS GADSBY   Tord Stål

Hughie (See also September 18, 1958)

Royale Theatre, New York, N.Y., December 22, 1964
Produced by Theodore Mann and Joseph Levine
in association with Katzka-Berne
Directed by José Quintero
Settings by David Hays; costumes by Noel Taylor

"ERIE" SMITH   Jason Robards, Jr.
CHARLIE HUGHES   Jack Dodson

More Stately Mansions (See also September 11, 1962)

Ahmanson Theatre, Los Angeles, Cal., September 12, 1967
Produced by Elliot Martin
Directed by José Quintero
Settings by Ben Edwards; costumes by Jane Greenwood

JAMIE CREGAN   Barry Macollum
MICKEY MALOY   Vincent Dowling
NORA MELODY   Helen Craig
SARA   Colleen Dewhurst
SIMON HARFORD   Arthur Hill
CATO   John Marriott
DEBORAH   Ingrid Bergman
NICHOLAS GADSBY   Fred Stewart
JOEL HARFORD   Lawrence Linville
BENJAMIN TENARD   Kermit Murdock

A Moon for the Misbegotten (See also February 2, 1947, May 2, 1957)

Morosco Theatre, New York, N.Y.. December 29, 1973
Produced by Lester Osterman and Richard Horner
Directed by José Quintero
Scenery and lighting by Ben Edwards
Costumes by Jane Greenwood

JOSIE HOGAN   Colleen Dewhurst
MIKE HOGAN   Edwin J. McDonough
PHIL HOGAN   Ed Flanders
JAMES TYRONE   Jason Robards
T. STEDMAN HARDER   John O'Leary

Long Day's Journey into Night (See also February 10, 1956, November 7, 1956)

Brooklyn Academy of Music, Brooklyn, N.Y., January 28, 1976
Produced by Kennedy Center for the American Bicentennial Theatre Series
Directed by Jason Robards
Set design by Ben Edwards
Lighting by Ken Billington
Costumes by Jane Greenwood

JAMES TYRONE	Jason Robards
MARY TYRONE	Zoe Caldwell
JAMES TYRONE, JR.	Kevin Conway
EDMUND TYRONE	Michael Moriarty
CATHLEEN	Lindsay Crouse

A Touch of the Poet (See also March 29, 1957, October 2, 1958)

Helen Hayes Theatre, New York, N.Y., December 28, 1977
Produced by Elliot Martin
Directed by José Quintero
Scenery and lighting by Ben Edwards
Costumes by Jane Greenwood

MICKEY MALOY	Barry Snider
JAMIE CREGAN	Milo O'Shea
SARA MELODY	Kathryn Walker
NORA MELODY	Geraldine Fitzgerald
CORNELIUS MELODY	Jason Robards
DAN ROCHE	Walter Flanagan
PADDY O'DOWD	Dermot McNamara
PATCH RILEY	Richard Hamilton
DEBORAH	Betty Miller
NICHOLAS GADSBY	George Ede

The Iceman Cometh (See also October 9, 1946, May 8, 1956)

Lunt-Fontanne Theatre, New York, N.Y., September 29, 1985
Produced by Lewis Allen, James Nederlander, Stephen Graham,
    and Ben Edwards
Directed by José Quintero
Scenery by Ben Edwards
Lighting by Thomas R. Skelton
Costumes by Jane Greenwood

ROCKY PIOGGI	John Pankow
LARRY SLADE	Donald Moffat
HUGO KALMAR	Leonardo Cimino
WILLIE OBAN	John Christopher Jones
HARRY HOPE	Barnard Hughes
JOE MOTT	Roger Robinson
DON PARRITT	Paul McCrane
CECIL LEWIS	Bill Moor
PIET WETJOEN	Frederick Neumann
JAMES CAMERON	James Greene
PAT MCGLOIN	Pat McNamara
ED MOSHER	Allen Swift
MARGIE	Natalia Nogulich
PEARL	Kristine Nielsen
CORA	Caroline Aaron
CHUCK MORELLO	Harris Laskawy
THEODORE HICKMAN	Jason Robards
MORAN	Paul Austin
LIEB	Walter Flanagan

INDEX OF PROPER NAMES*

*Excluding place names and names of fictional characters. Major discussions are indicated by *italic* type.